Yours faithfully
James Sprunt

James Sprunt's

Chronicles
of the
Cape Fear River
1660 - 1916

Second Edition

originally published by
Edwards & Broughton Printing Co.
Raleigh
1916

This edition published by

Books
A JEF Publications Company

First Printing 2005

Published in the United States of America by Dram Tree Books, a JEF Publications company.

Publisher's Cataloging-in-Publication Data
(Provided by Quality Books, Inc.)

Sprunt, James, 1846-1924
    Chronicles of the Cape Fear River. 1660-1916 / James Sprunt - 2nd ed.
        p.cm
        Includes index.
        ISBN 0-9723240-5-4

        1. Cape Fear River Valley (N.C.) -- History.
        2. Wilmington (N.C.) -- History. 3. United States -- History -- Civil War, 1861-1865--Blockades   I. Title

    F262.C2S68 2005   975.6'2
                                 QBI05-200014

10 9 8 7 6 5 4 3 2

Dram Tree Books
2801 Lyndon Avenue
Wilmington, N.C. 28405-3045
(910) 538-4076
dramtreebooks@ec.rr.com

*Discounts available
for educators.
Call or e-mail for terms.*

To

SAMUEL A'COURT ASHE

A LOYAL AND DEVOTED
SON OF THE CAPE FEAR
IN RECOGNITION OF HIS EMINENT SERVICE TO OUR COMMON-
WEALTH AND TO LITERATURE IN HIS ADMIRABLE HISTORY
OF NORTH CAROLINA A WORK OF SUCH PARTICU-
LAR MERIT AS TO BRING CREDIT TO HIS
BIRTHPLACE AND TO ADD TO THE
HIGH FAME OF
THE CAPE FEAR PEOPLE

Preface

The reception of the *Cape Fear Chronicles,* not only by friends of the author but by the general reader, and in particular by historical scholars, has been most unusual. The general expression of gratification at its publication and the generous recognition of its value are emphatic assurances that Mr. Sprunt's endeavor to preserve the memories of the Cape Fear has been appreciated beyond his expectations. Numerous and insistent have been the requests for a second edition, to which he has finally yielded, and in doing so he has embodied much additional matter of interest and importance equal to that contained in the first edition. The incorporation of this new matter has necessitated some changes in the old, most of which have been merely verbal, but in a few instances more important changes have been made to secure greater uniformity and conform to more recent information concerning certain local traditions and memories. No trouble has been spared in either edition to secure the greatest exactitude in details, and especially has this been true of the edition now presented.

Mr. Sprunt has long been interested in historical literature, and through his liberality many publications of interest and value have in recent years been made. The fund he placed at the disposal of the University of North Carolina has enabled that institution to publish a series of historical monographs of peculiar interest, the one published in 1903 being of particular importance to Wilmington and the Cape Fear people. And in addition to being a liberal promotor of the writings of others, his personal output in the field of historical literature has been a distinctive and valuable contribution. His research has been extensive and remarkably successful; especially has he been indefatigable in rescuing from oblivion the history of the Cape Fear and clothing in his own inimitable style the romantic tales and stirring deeds that belong to the development of that section of North Carolina.

In recognition of his service to the State in constructive citizenship and in his writings and in appreciation of his personal excellence and merit, the University of North Carolina last year conferred upon Mr. Sprunt the degree of doctor of laws. And more recently the old historic College of William and

Mary, in Virginia, chartered in 1693, unanimously elected him a member, *causa honoris,* of the Alpha Chapter of the Phi Beta Kappa Society of that college. This is the honor literary society of America, organized at William and Mary in 1776, and in the selection of those invited to become members the greatest care is exercised, membership being equivalent to an honorary degree conferred by any of our colleges and giving the recipient special distinction.   S. A. ASHE.

November 10, 1916.

Contents

Foreword

From early youth I have loved the Cape Fear River, the ships and the sailors which it bears upon its bosom. As a boy I delighted to wander along the wharves where the sailing ships were moored with their graceful spars and rigging in relief against the sky-line, with men aloft whose uncouth cries and unknown tongues inspired me with a longing for the sea, which I afterwards followed, and for the far-away countries whence they had come.

In later years, I heard the stories of the old-time Cape Fear gentlemen, whose memories I revere, and I treasured those annals of our brave and generous people; I knew all the pilots of the Cape Fear, whose record of brave deeds and unswerving loyalty to the Confederacy, under great trial and temptation, and whose steadfast industry in their dangerous calling are worthy of all praise; and now, actuated by an earnest desire to render a public service after many years' contact with its men and affairs, I have essayed to write in the following pages a concise narrative of the sources and tributary streams of the Cape Fear River, the origin of its name, the development of its commerce, and the artificial aids to its navigation, with a few historic incidents of its tidewater region.

The limited scope of this undertaking does not reach beyond the mere outlines of its romantic, dramatic history, of which much has been ably written by George Davis, Alfred Moore Waddell, Samuel A'Court Ashe, and other historians of the Cape Fear.

I have often looked from my window upon the historic river and seen the white sails glistening in the morning light, and when the evening shadows deepened I have gazed upon the wide expanse resplendent with the glory of the stars and have heard the sailors in the bay singing "Larboard watch, ahoy!" while the anchor lights of half a hundred ships were twinkling at their moorings, and it was something to remember in after years.

Memory lingers with a certain endearment upon the daily activities in the harbor in that far-gone day, when the course of life was more attuned to the placid flow of the river than in this rushing, jarring time. No more is heard the long-drawn cry of the stevedore, "Go ahead, horse" and "Back down lively." No more do we hear the song of the chanty man rise shrill and clear to the accompaniment of chuckling blocks and creaking yards, nor the hearty, deep tones of the chorus as the old-time sailor men tramped round the windlass from wharf to wharf, singing:

"Oh, blow, ye winds, I long to hear you,
    Blow, bullies, blow!
Oh, blow today and blow tomorrow,
    Blow, my bully boys, blow!

"Oh, blow today and blow tomorrow,
    Blow, bullies, blow!
Oh, blow away all care and sorrow,
    Blow, my bully boys, blow!"

"A tremulous echo is all that is left of these old-time refrains," but some of our older citizens will recall these plaintive though senseless ditties, also the John Kooner songs, which have enlivened many a dull hour in the old seaport of the Cape Fear.

Many years ago, when the arched courthouse stood at the foot of Market Street, a party of prominent citizens were discussing under its roof the events of the day in the soft light of a beautiful full moon, and while they talked they heard the tramp of twenty sailor men from a near-by French ship moored at Market Dock; and then in clear and exquisite tones the sailors sang with all the enthusiasm it inspired the Marseillaise battle hymn. Colonel Burr, who heard them, told me many years after that it was one of the most delightful memories of a lifetime.

But now the distracting hammering against rusting steel plates, the clanking of chains against the steamship's sides, and the raucous racket of the steam donkey betoken a new era in the harbor of Wilmington; yet the silent river flows on with the silent years as when Vassall sent the first settlers, or as when Flora Macdonald sailed past the town to the restful haven of Cross Creek; and the Dram Tree still stands to warn the outgoing mariner that his voyage has begun and to welcome the incoming storm-tossed sailor to the quiet harbor beyond.

I have obtained the data of the commercial development of the river largely from official sources or reliable records, and I have copied verbatim, in some technical detail, the generous responses to my inquiries by Maj. H. W. Stickle, Corps of Engineers, U. S. A.; Capt. C. S. Ridley, assistant engineer, U.

S. A.; Mr. R. C. Merritt, assistant engineer; Mr. Joseph Hyde Pratt, State geologist; Dr. Joseph A. Holmes, director Bureau of Mines; Capt. G. L. Carden, commanding U. S. revenue cutter *Seminole*; Mr. H. D. King, inspector lights and lighthouses, Sixth District, and Hon. S. I. Kimball, general superintendent of the Life Saving Service, now embraced in the Coast Guard, to each of whom I make this grateful acknowledgment.

This book is intimately associated with two good friends, Capt. Samuel A'Court Ashe and Miss Rosa Pendleton Chiles, to whom I am especially indebted for their invaluable aid, and sympathy, and advice; for without their generous assistance this work might not have been accomplished.

Exploration and Settlement

ORIGIN OF THE NAME CAPE FEAR.

By George Davis.

The origin of the name Cape Fear and its confusion in some of our early maps with Cape Fair led, many years ago, to a discussion by the Historical and Scientific Society of Wilmington, of which this writer was the secretary. A prominent Wilmingtonian of his day, Mr. Henry Nutt, to whose indefatigable, intelligent efforts and public spirit the closure of New Inlet was largely due, stoutly maintained in a forceful address before that body that the name was originally Fair and not Fear.

Mr. George Davis subsequently took the opposite view in his valuable contribution entitled *An Episode in Cape Fear History*, published in the *South Atlantic Magazine*, January, 1879, which I here reprint under the above title.

Is it Cape Fair? Or Cape Fear? Adjective or noun? "Under which king, Bezonian?" This old familiar name under which our noble river rolls its waters to the sea, is it the true prince of the ancient line, or a base pretender, usurping the seat of the rightful heir, and, after the fashion of usurpers, giving us terror for beauty, storm for sunshine?

There are some among our most intelligent citizens who maintain that the true name was, and ought to be now, Cape Fair; and that it was originally so given because the first adventurers, seeing with the eye of enthusiasm, found everything here to be fair, attractive, and charming. And it has even been said very lately that it was never called by its present name until after 1750, and never officially until 1780. (Address of H. Nutt before H. and S. Society.) Unfortunately, in the mists which envelop some portions of our early history, it is sometimes very difficult to guard against being betrayed into erroneous conjectures by what appear to be very plausible reasons; and the materials for accurate investigation are not of easy access. It is not surprising, therefore, that this opinion should have existed for some time, not generally, but to a limited extent. Beyond all doubt it is erroneous, and the proofs are conclusive that our people have been right in finally rejecting the Beautiful theory, and accepting the Fearful. I know of no authority for this opinion except the occasional spelling of the word. The strength of the argument seems to be this: Captain

1

Hilton was sent in 1663 for the purpose of examining the country; he did examine it, reported in glowing terms as to its beauty and attractiveness, and throughout his report spelled the name Fair. I answer, Very true. But three years later, in 1666, Robert Horne published his *Brief Description of Carolina*, under the eye, and no doubt by the procurement, of the Proprietors; he describes the country in much more glowing terms of praise than Hilton did, but spells the name, throughout, Fear. And where are we then? And later still, in 1711, a high authority, Christopher Gale, chief justice of North Carolina, like a prudent politician who has not made up his mind which party to join, spells it neither Fair nor Fear, but Fare. (2 Hawks, 391.) That the name in early times was not infrequently spelt Fair is unquestionable. Besides Hilton's report, it is so given in the Letter of the English Adventurers to the Proprietors, 1663; in the Instructions of the Proprietors to Governor Yeamans, 1665; in Lawson's history and map, 1709; and on Wimble's map, 1738. And perhaps other instances may be found.

But all these, if they stood alone and unopposed, could hardly form the basis of any solid argument. For all who are accustomed to examine historical documents will know too well how widely independent of all law, if there was any law, our ancestors were in their spelling, especially of proper names. Pen in hand, they were accustomed to dare every vagary, and no amount of heroic spelling ever appalled them.

Some examples will be instructive in our present investigation. Take the great name of him who was "wholly gentleman, wholly soldier," who, falling under the displeasure of a scoundrel King and languishing for twelve long years under sentence of ignominious death, sent forth through his prison bars such melodious notes that the very King's son cried out, "No monarch in Christendom but my father would keep such a bird in a cage"; who, inexhaustible in ideas as in exploits, after having brought a new world to light, wrote the history of the old in a prison, and then died, because God had made him too great for his fellows—that name which to North Carolina ears rings down through the ages like a glorious chime of bells—the name of our great Sir Walter. We know that it was spelt three different ways, Raleigh, Ralegh, and Rawlegh.

And Sir Walter's heroic kinsman, that grand old sea-king who fought his single ship for fifteen straight hours against fifteen Spaniards, one after another, muzzle to muzzle, and then yielded up his soul to God in that cheerful temper wherewith men go to a banquet: "Here die I, Richard Greenville, and with a joyful and quiet mind, having ended my life like a true soldier that has fought for his country, Queen, religion, and honor." He was indifferently Greenville, Grenville, and Granville.

And take another of these sea-kings of old who sailed to America in the early days—that brilliant, restless, daring spirit who crowded into a few brief years enough of wild adventure and excitement to season a long life, and then died little more than a boy—he was indifferently Cavendish and Candish.

Who, without assistance, could recognize Bermuda in the "still vexed Bermoothes" of Shakespeare? And Horne's pamphlets, of which I have spoken, could only improve it into Barmoodoes.

Coming down to the very time of which we are speaking, one of the first acts of the Lords Proprietors after receiving their magnificent grant was to publish the important document to which I have alluded, the *Declaration and Proposals to all who will plant in Carolina*. It is signed by some of the most famous names in English history—George, Duke of Albemarle, the prime mover in bringing about the restoration of the King; Edward, Earl of Clarendon, Lord High Chancellor, and grandfather of two English queens, but far more famous as the author of that wonderful book, the *History of the Great Rebellion;* Anthony, Earl of Shaftesbury, Lord High Chancellor and one of the greatest parliamentary leaders that England ever produced, but far greater as the author of that second charter of Anglo-Saxon liberties, the Habeas Corpus Act. This very gifted and very famous Earl of Shaftesbury, who, I am sorry to say, was more distinguished for brilliant talents than for virtuous principles, besides being one of the Proprietors had an additional claim to our remembrance which has not been generally known. At a meeting of the Proprietors held at the Cockpit the 21st of October, 1669 (Rivers, 346), he was elected the first chief justice of Carolina. As he never visited America I presume his office was in a great degree purely honorary. But he certainly executed its functions to the extent at least of its official patronage. For the record has been preserved which shows that on the 10th of June, 1675, by virtue of that office, he appointed Andrew Percival to be register of Berkeley Precinct.

He had not then been raised to the peerage, but was only Sir Anthony Ashley Cooper. He gave his two family names to the rivers at Charleston, and then took himself the title of Shaftesbury.

Such were some of the signers of this pamphlet. Surely these men knew. Surely they would give us some unimpeachable English. Well, we have an exact copy of the pamphlet and I give you my word that, according to our notions, the spelling of it is enough to put the whole school of lexicographers in a madhouse. Instance the following: "Clarending," "Northine," "plantacon," "proposealls," "grannte," "ingaige," "groathe," etc., etc. These examples, which might be indefinitely multiplied, are sufficient to show that he is a bold speculator who will venture to build an opinion on the spelling of a name.

But the opposing proofs are quite conclusive, and I do not scruple to promise that for every authentic map or document, prior to the year 1700, in which the name is written Fair, I will point out at least two in which it is written as at present. An examination of some of the most important of them will remove all doubt from the subject.

In DeBry's map of Lane's expedition, 1585, no name is given to the cape, but we find it distinctly laid down, and indicated by two Latin words which are very significant, *promontorium tremendum*. And in the narrative of Sir Richard Greenville's first expedition, in the same year, we find the very first recorded mention of the name, which ought to be sufficient of itself to fix its certainty for all time. For we read there, for the month of June, 1585, this entry: "The 23d we were in great danger of a wreck on a breach called the Cape of Fear."

And two years later, in the narrative of the first voyage under White, we are told in July, 1587, that "had not Captain Stafford been more careful in looking out than our Simon Fernando, we had been all cast away upon the breach called the Cape of Fear."

And here we have another orthographic problem to solve. Both of these old worthies speak of the Cape of Fear as being not a *beach,* but a *breach;* and, on the strength of that, possibly some severe precisian may hereafter start the theory, and prove it too, that the cape was no cape at all, but only a breach or channel through the Frying Pan Shoals.

Coming down near a hundred years to the time of the first settlements, we find the original spelling preserved in the Letter of the Proprietors to Sir William Berkeley, 1663; in the Proposals of the Proprietors already mentioned, 1663; in Horne's *Brief Description of Carolina* and on the accompanying map, 1666; in the map styled *A New Description of Carolina,* 1671; in the Instructions of the Proprietors to the Governor and Council of Carolina, 1683, and in a great many others.

These proofs would seem to leave nothing wanting to a clear demonstration of the real name. But there is something yet to be added. They show that during the same period of time the name was spelt both ways indifferently, not only by different persons, but the same persons, who had peculiar means of knowing the truth. It is clear, therefore, that the two modes were not expressive of two different ideas, but only different forms of expressing the same idea. What then was the true idea of the name—its *raison d'être?*

In pursuing that inquiry our attention must be directed to the cape alone, and not to the river. For, as we have seen, the cape bore its name for near a hundred years during which the river was nameless, if not unknown. And, when brought into notice afterwards, the river bore at first a different name, and only after some time glided into the name of the cape. Thus, in the Letter of the Proprietors to Sir William Berkeley, 8th of September, 1663, after directing him to procure a small vessel to explore the sounds, they say, "And whilst they are aboard they may look into Charles River a very little to the Southward of Cape Fear." And so in the Proposals of the Proprietors, 15th of August, 1663, "If the first colony will settle on Charles River, near Cape Fear," etc., etc., and in Horne's map, 1666, the name is Charles River.

Looking then to the cape for the idea and reason of its name, we find that it is the southernmost point of Smith's Island—a naked, bleak elbow of sand, jutting far out into the ocean. Immediately in its front are the Frying Pan Shoals, pushing out still farther, twenty miles, to sea. Together they stand for warning and for woe; and together they catch the long majestic roll of the Atlantic as it sweeps through a thousand miles of grandeur and power from the Arctic towards the Gulf. It is the playground of billows and tempests, the kingdom of silence and awe, disturbed by no sound save the sea gull's shriek and the breakers' roar. Its whole aspect is suggestive, not of repose and beauty, but of desolation and terror. Imagination can not adorn it. Romance can not hallow it. Local pride can not soften it.

There it stands today, bleak, and threatening, and pitiless, as it stood three hundred years ago, when Greenville and White came nigh unto death upon its sands. And there it will stand, bleak, and threatening, and pitiless, until the earth and the sea shall give up their dead. And, as its nature, so its name, is now, always has been, and always will be, the Cape of Fear.

THE CAPE FEAR RIVER AND ITS TRIBUTARIES.

The Cape Fear River, said to have been known to the Indian aborigines as "Sapona," later to the explorers and to the promoters in England as the Charles River, and the Clarendon River, is formed by the junction of the Haw and the Deep Rivers, in Chatham County, North Carolina. From their confluence, which is about 173 miles by river above Wilmington, it flows in a southeasterly direction through Harnett, Cumberland, and Bladen Counties, and between Brunswick and New Hanover to the sea. The Haw River rises in Rockingham and Guilford Counties and flows in a southeasterly direction through Alamance, Orange, and Chatham Counties to its junction with the Deep River, a distance of about 80 miles, measured along its general course. The Deep River is of about the same length as the Haw. It rises in Guilford County and flows through Randolph and Moore Counties, and joins the Haw in Chatham.

The Deep River drains about 1,400 square miles. Its tributaries are only small creeks, the most important being Rocky River. The Haw River drains about 1,800 square miles, and its tributaries are also small, but are larger than those of the Deep River. The principal ones, descending from the headwaters, are Reedy Fork, Alamance Creek, Cane Creek, and New Hope River.

Between the junction of the Deep and the Haw Rivers and Fayetteville, a distance of about 58 miles, the most important tributaries which join the Cape Fear are Upper Little River, from the west, 32 miles long; and Lower Little River, from the west, 45 miles long. There are other small creeks, the most important being Carver's Creek and Blount's Creek.

Between Wilmington and Fayetteville the most important tributary is Black River, which enters from the east about 15 miles above Wilmington and has a drainage basin of about 1,430 square miles. There are several creeks which enter below Fayetteville, the principal one being Rockfish Creek, which enters 10 miles below Fayetteville.

The entire drainage basin above Fayetteville covers an area of 4,493 square miles, and the total drainage area of the Cape Fear and all its tributaries is about 8,400 square miles.

At Wilmington the Cape Fear River proper is joined by the Northeast Cape Fear River. Their combined average discharge at Wilmington for the year is about 14,000 feet a second. Floods in their tributaries have but little effect on the water level at Wilmington. The lower river is tidal, and the effects of tidal variations are felt about 40 miles above the city on both branches.

The city of Wilmington is on the east side of the river, opposite the junction of the two branches, and nearly all wharves, mills, and terminals are situated on the same side. The width of the river at Wilmington is 500 to 1,000 feet. Four miles below, it becomes 1½ miles wide, and is of the nature of a tidal estuary, varying in width as it flows to the sea from 1 to 3 miles. The distance from Wilmington to the ocean is 30 miles.

IMPROVEMENTS BELOW WILMINGTON.

The improvement of the river was begun by the State of North Carolina between Wilmington and Big Island by embankments, jetties, and dredging in 1822, and continued until 1829, when the Federal Government undertook the work of improvement and continued it to 1839. Work was resumed in 1847 and continued up to the War between the States. It was again resumed in 1870 and has been carried on continuously since that date.

A report of the Committee on Bar and River Improvements to the Chamber of Commerce, January 15, 1872, contains the following interesting information:

"The earliest reliable information we have of the Cape Fear River, its entrance and harbor, is to be found in a map by Edward Moseley, in 1733, and another by James Wimble, in 1738. Both of these maps, although apparently imperfect, nevertheless represent the harbor as capacious, of good anchorage, well landlocked, easy of access, and with four fathoms water upon the bar (supposed at mean low tide). About this draught of water was carried by a bold and direct channel on the west side of Big Island[1] to the town of Wilmington.

---

[1] The river channel was at that time on the west side of Big Island. Since then it has been artificially diverted to the east side of Big Island.

"The next we hear of the Cape Fear River is through Wheeler's *History of North Carolina* (extracted from the *London Magazine*), giving an account of the most violent equinoctial storm which had ever occurred along the coast, forcing open an entrance into the river at a point known as the 'Haul-over,' now known as the New Inlet. This storm commenced on the 20th of September, 1761, and lasted four days.

"This inlet, from long neglect, has become formidable, detracting a large portion of the river water from its legitimate outlet, to the great detriment of the river and lower harbor.

"In 1775, a map of the Cape Fear River, more accurate in its details than the two first alluded to, was published in London, which laid down the New Inlet, but did not materially vary the harbor, outlet, or draught of water upon the bar, or the channel of the river up to the town of Wilmington.

"At a meeting of the Safety Committee of Wilmington, held on the 20th of November, 1775, John Ancrum presiding, the following preamble and resolutions were passed:

" 'The committee, taking into consideration the damage with which the inhabitants of the Cape Fear River are threatened by the King's ships now in the harbor, and the open and avowed contempt and violation of justice in the conduct of Governor Martin, who, with the assistance of said ships, is endeavoring to carry off the artillery, the property of this province, and the gift of his late Majesty of blessed memory, for our protection from foreign invasion, have

" 'Resolved, That Messrs. John Forster, William Wilkinson, and John Slingsby, or any one of them, be empowered to procure necessary vessels, boats, and chains, to sink in such part of the channel as they or any of them may think proper, to agree for the purchase of such boats and other materials as may be wanted, and to have them valued, that the owners may be reimbursed by the public. And it is further ordered, that the said John Forster & Co. do consult the committee of Brunswick on this measure and request their concurrence.'

"A knowledge of the men of that period, with the boisterous circumstances which surrounded them, is sufficient evidence that this order was implicitly obeyed and effectually executed, no report of their action being required or expected.

"Tradition assures us that these obstacles were placed across the channel at Big Island. We therefore feel justified in saying that the channel, as laid down by all previous maps, was, at that time and place, obstructed agreeably to the order, as subsequent events would seem to imply. From time to time, logs, stumps, and other drift matter brought down by freshets lodged against the obstructions, backing up nearly to the narrows and forming what is known as the flats or shoal of logs, which, as it increased, gradually forced the water through an opening on the west side of Big Island, and in course of time scoured out a channel sufficient to accommodate the commerce of the port, and so remained until the year 1826.

"In the year 1797-8, a survey and map of the Cape Fear River, its harbors and outlets, was made by Joshua Potts. At this time, thirty-seven years after the breaking out of New Inlet, we find very little alteration in the harbor or outlet—the bar representing 20 feet of water (supposed at mean low tide), while the channels of the river up to Wilmington had undergone material change, and very much depreciated."

A report of the same committee, made four years earlier than the one just quoted, refers to the Potts survey, and says:

"Older charts than this exhibit a greater draught of water, particulars of which, however, are not accurately remembered by your committee. Many old citizens now living remember to have seen at our wharves vessels drawing 15 to 18 feet of water. But about the year 1820, as the depth of water increased on New Inlet, in like proportion it diminished on the Main Bar, maintaining upon both the aggregate of about 25 feet. The late Capt. Thomas N. Gautier, who was a merchant of this place during the period of time included between the years 1790 and 1810, told one of your committee that during that period, among many others, he had loaded one ship to 30 feet draught, which proceeded down the river to sea, on her voyage to London, without difficulty or interruption. These facts in the history of the past are conclusive evidence, in the minds of your committee, that the true and real cause of the present alarming condition of the navigation of our bars and river is to be found in the existence of the New Inlet, and that alone."

A report of Alexander Strauss to the mayor and aldermen of Wilmington, under date of March 6, 1870, says:

"The bar in the Old Ship Channel has shoaled 2½ feet in the last five years, and therefore any procrastination in the work will be injurious to our commerce, as I believe it can be shown that year by year since 1840 the obstruction has increased, and unless speedy action is taken it will result in the total destruction of our harbor. I base my opinion on data gained from different surveys made from the year 1733 to

1869. On the survey of 1733, a depth of 21 feet is shown in the Old Ship Channel at mean low water, and in 1869 only 5½ can be found in the same channel."

The condition of the river prior to the opening of New Inlet (which occurred during an equinoctial storm in 1761) is rather uncertain, but old maps indicate that there was a low-water depth of 14 feet across the bar at the mouth, the least depth between Wilmington and the mouth being 7½ feet. There is also some uncertainty as to the conditions in 1829, when the improvement was undertaken by the United States, but the most reliable information is that there was then about 7 to 7½ feet at low water in the river, about 9 feet in Bald Head Channel, 9 feet in Rip Channel, and 10 feet at New Inlet. Work on the bar was begun in 1853, at which time the bar depths at low water were 7½ feet in Bald Head Channel, 7 feet in Rip Channel, and 8 feet at New Inlet, the governing low-water depth in the river having been increased to 9 feet.

The original project of 1827 was to deepen by jetties the channel through the shoals in the 8 miles next below Wilmington. This project resulted in a gain of 2 feet available depth. The project of 1853 was to straighten and deepen the bar channel by dredging, jettying, diverting the flow from the New Inlet, and closing breaches in Zeke's Island. This project was incomplete when the War between the States began. Up to that time, $363,228.92 had been spent on the improvement. The work done during this period was measurably successful. The report of the commission of 1858 referring to it says:

"The works recommended by the board of 1853 were, in the opinion of the commission, entirely efficient, so far as they were carried out, having, as is shown by the Coast-Survey maps, caused an increase in the depth of Oak Island Channel of between one and two feet."

After the war the first project was that of 1870, to deepen the bar channel by closing breaches between Smith's and Zeke's Islands, with the ultimate closure of New Inlet in view. The project of 1873 included that of 1870 and in addition the dredging of the bar channel and the closing of New Inlet. This work was in charge of Gen. J. H. Simpson, U. S. A., who was succeeded in the management of it by Col. William P. Craighill. The main construction was under Maj. Walter Griswold, assistant engineer, whose services were able and highly acceptable. Mention should be made also of Henry Nutt, Esq., chairman of the Committee on Bar and River Improvements of the Chamber of Commerce, whose activities greatly advanced the work. The *Wilmington Journal* of March 20, 1872, contains the following acknowledgment of his services:

"We are unwilling to give expression to the bright hopes of the future we anticipate for our goodly old town. But whether that success be attained in full or scant measure, the name of Henry Nutt will, and ought to be, held in grateful remembrance by all our people to the last generation, as the earnest, persistent, and enthusiastic friend of this great work."

The project of 1874 was to obtain by dredging a channel 100 feet wide and 12 feet deep at low water up to Wilmington. The project of 1881 was to obtain by dredging a channel 270 feet wide and 16 feet deep at low water up to Wilmington. These projects had been practically completed in 1889. At that time the expenditure since the war amounted to $2,102,271.93.

The project adopted September 19, 1890, was to obtain a mean low-water depth of 20 feet and a width of 270 feet from Wilmington to the ocean. This project has been modified several times.

For the five years ending June 30, 1915, there was expended for river improvements $1,440,844.02, and the commerce on the Cape Fear River at and below Wilmington averaged 929,-336 tons, with an average valuation of $50,978,671.06 for the five calendar years. At the close of the year ending June 30, 1915, there had been a total expenditure of $5,974,868.48. The project below Wilmington under execution was adopted in the River and Harbor Act approved July 25, 1912, and provides for a channel depth of 26 feet at mean low water, with a width of 300 feet, increasing at the entrance and curves in the river and widening to 400 feet across the bar. The project is eighty per cent completed, the depth having been secured throughout the entire distance, additional work being required only to widen the channel where the width is deficient. On June 30, 1915, a mean low-water channel 26 feet deep and from 280 to 400 feet wide existed on the ocean bar and 26 feet deep and 300 feet wide in the river channels, excepting at Snow's Marsh Channel, where the 26-foot channel was from 150 to 270 feet wide.

The various projects adopted by the Federal Government involved the closing of New Inlet and the construction of a defensive dike from Zeke's Island, on the south side of New

Inlet, to Smith's Island. The dam closing New Inlet was constructed between 1875 and 1881 and is 5,300 feet long. It is built of stone, its first cost being $540,237.11. It was badly damaged by a storm in 1906, and the cost of its restoration and of other minor repairs made since its completion was $103,-044.75, making its total cost to date $643,281.86. Swash Defense Dam, south of New Inlet, was constructed between 1883 and 1889 and is 12,800 feet long. It is also built of stone, the first cost being $225,965. The cost of restoring this dam after the storm of 1906, including other repairs made since its completion, was $170,109.53, making the total cost to date $396,-074.53. With the exception of the construction of these two dams, the results have been accomplished almost wholly by dredging.

It is interesting to note in this connection that the total expenditures of the Federal Government upon Charleston Harbor to June 30, 1915, amounted to $5,084,771.90, and the total expenditures on Cape Fear River at and below Wilmington to the same date was $5,985,990.01.

NORTHEAST CAPE FEAR RIVER.

Northeast Cape Fear River has a total length of 130 miles (70 miles in a straight line) and has been under improvement since 1890, the project including the clearing of the natural channel for small steamers to Hallsville, 88 miles above its mouth, and for pole boats to Kornegay's Bridge, 103 miles above its mouth.

The work has consisted in removing snags and other incidental obstructions from the channel and leaning trees from the banks. For several years past, work has been for the purpose of maintenance only. To June 30, 1913, there had been spent on this stream for improvement and maintenance $33,738.86. At present 8 feet can be carried to Rocky Point Landing, 35 miles from the mouth, 5 feet to Smith's Bridge, 52 miles up, and 3 feet to Croom's Bridge, 8 miles further, at all stages. Above that point it is only navigable during freshets.

BLACK RIVER.

This stream has been under improvement since 1887. The original project of 1885 included clearing the natural channel and banks to Lisbon and cutting off a few points at bends, modified in 1893, and omitting the part above Clear Run, 66 miles above the mouth. This was completed in 1895. Since that time it has been under maintenance. The total amount expended to June 30, 1913, for improvement and maintenance was $32,877.26. The work has consisted in removing obstructions from the channel and leaning trees from the banks, and in a small amount of dredging.

At present a depth of 5 feet can be carried to Point Caswell at low stages, above which point there is but little navigation excepting during freshet stages.

Town Creek.

Town Creek is a tributary to Cape Fear River, entering it from the west about 7½ miles below Wilmington. It is not now under improvement, but was placed under improvement in 1881, the project being to obtain 4-foot navigation at low water by removing obstructions from the mouth to Saw-Pit Landing, 20 miles above. After spending $1,000, this project was abandoned. An appropriation of $8,500 was made in 1899 to be expended in obtaining a mean low-water channel 5 feet deep and 40 feet wide to Russell's Landing, 19¾ miles above the mouth, and to clear the creek to Rock's Landing, about 4 miles farther up. The 5-foot channel was obtained to Russell's Landing by dredging, and snags were removed from the channel for the next mile above, when the funds were exhausted, and no further appropriation has been made.

Brunswick River.

About four miles above Wilmington, the Cape Fear River divides, the western branch forming Brunswick River. It flows in a southerly direction and again enters the Cape Fear River about four miles below Wilmington.

This river has never been under improvement, but the River and Harbor Act of June 13, 1902, provides for an expenditure not exceeding $1,000 of the money appropriated for the improvement of Cape Fear River, at and below Wilmington, in removing obstructions at the lower mouth of Brunswick River. Obstructions were removed from a width of 100 feet during 1903 at a cost of $519, securing a channel at its mouth 100 feet wide and 7 feet deep.[1]

---

[1] The foregoing technical information is from the reports of the U. S. Corps of Engineers, by the courtesy of Major Stickle.

According to the recitals in the oldest deeds for lands on Eagles' Island and in its vicinity on either side, the Northeast and the Northwest branches of the Cape Fear River come together at the southern point of that island. What is now called Brunswick River, on the west side of the island, was then the main River; and Wilmington was on the Northeast branch, and not on the main stream of the Cape Fear. That portion of the river which runs from the Northeast branch by Point Peter, or Negrohead Point, as it is called, to the Northwest branch at the head of Eagles' Island, is called in the old deeds and statutes of the State the "Thoroughfare," and sometimes the "Cut-through" from one branch to the other; and the land granted to John Maultsby, on which a part of Wilmington is situated, is described as lying opposite to the mouth of the "Thoroughfare." At another time, what is now known as Brunswick River was called Clarendon River.

THE CAPE FEAR INDIANS.

The tribal identity of the Cape Fear Indians has never been clearly established. We find Indian mounds, or tumuli, along the river and coast and in the midland counties, and we are told that the head waters of the Cape Fear River were known to our aborigines as "Sapona," a tribal name also known farther north, and that "King" Roger Moore exterminated these Indians at Big Sugar Loaf after they had raided Orton; but there is nothing in the mounds, where hundreds of skeletons are found, nor in the pottery and rude implements discovered therein, to identify the tribe or prove the comparatively unsupported statements which we have hitherto accepted as facts. Capt. S. A. Ashe says: "The Cape Fear Indians along the coast were Southern. The Saponas who resided higher up were probably Northern. They were not exterminated by 'King' Roger; in fact, in 1790 there were still some in Granville, and a considerable number joined the Tuscaroras on the Tuscarora Reservation on the Roanoke. They were both Northern, probably, otherwise the Saponas would not have been welcome."

There is reason to believe the tradition, generally known to our older inhabitants, that the Indians from the back country came regularly in the early springtime to the coast of the Cape Fear for the seawater fish and oysters which were abundant, and that their preparation for these feasts included the copious drinking of a strong decoction of yopon leaves, which produced free vomiting and purgation, before they gorged themselves to repletion with the fish and oysters.

The beautiful evergreen leaf and brilliant red berries of the yopon still abound along the river banks near the remains of the Indian camps. The leaves were extensively used as a substitute for tea, which was unobtainable during our four years' war, and the tea made from them was refreshing and tonic in its effects.

Dr. Francis P. Venable says: "It belongs to the *Ilex,* or holly genus. My first analysis was on a small sample from New Bern and showed 0.32 per cent caffeine. Securing a larger sample from near Wilmington, I found 0.27 per cent. The maté, or Paraguay tea, is also gotten from an *Ilex* and contains 0.63 per cent. The percentage of tannin in the yopon is rather high and I suppose has something to do with the medicinal effect."

Dr. Curtis, an eminent botanist of North Carolina, says: "*Yopon I. Cassine,* Linn. An elegant shrub ten to fifteen feet high, but sometimes rising to twenty or twenty-five feet. Its native place is near the water (salt) from Virginia southward, but never far in the interior. Its dark green leaves and bright red berries make it very ornamental in yards and shrubberies. The leaves are small, one-half to one inch long, very smooth and evenly scalloped on the edges, with small rounded teeth. In some sections of the lower district, especially in the region of the Dismal Swamp, these are annually dried and used for tea, which is, however, oppressively soporific—at least for one not accustomed to it."

Our yopon (the above) is the article from which the famous Black Drink of the Southern Indians was made. At a certain time of the year they came down in droves from a distance of several hundred miles to the coast for the leaves of this tree. They made a fire on the ground, and putting a great kettle of water on it, they threw in a large quantity of these leaves, and sitting around the fire, from a bowl holding about a pint, they began drinking large draughts, which in a short time caused them to vomit easily and freely. Thus they continued drinking and vomiting for a space of two or three days, until they had sufficiently cleansed themselves, and then, every one taking a bundle of the leaves, they all retired to their habitations.

NOTES ON THE ARCHAEOLOGY OF NEW HANOVER COUNTY.

BY DAVID I. BUSHNELL, JR.

It is with no small satisfaction that I have obtained by the courtesy of such eminent authority as that of Mr. David I. Bushnell, jr., of the Bureau of American Ethnology, who is now in Wilmington for investigations on the vanishing race, the following paper; and Mr. Bushnell has quoted from Mr. W. B. McKoy's valuable contributions on the same subject. I also include Dr. Joseph A. Holmes's report upon his personal investigations of the mounds in Duplin County, and a paper by Capt. S. A. Ashe on the Indians of the Lower Cape Fear.

In reference to the Woccon, Saxapahaw, Cape Fear, and Warrennuncock Indians, we find it stated: "Of the North Carolina tribes bearing the foregoing names almost nothing is known, and of the last two even the proper names have not been recorded. The Woccon were Siouan; the Saxapahaw and Cape Fear Indians presumably were Siouan, as indicated from their associations and alliance with known Siouan tribes; while the Warrennuncock were probably some people better known under another name, although they cannot be identified."[1] Unfortunately the identity of the Cape Fear Indians has not been revealed, and it may ever remain a mystery. The name was first bestowed, by the early colonists, upon the Indians whom they found occupying the lands about the mouth of the Cape Fear River, and more especially the peninsula now forming the southern part of New Hanover County. It is also possible the term "Cape Fear Indians" was applied to any Indians found in the vicinity, regardless of their tribal connections, and, as will be shown later, the area was frequented by numbers of different tribes. Although the native people were often mentioned in early writings, it is doubtful whether the Indian population of the peninsula ever exceeded a few hundred.

Evidently Indians continued to occupy the lower part of the peninsula until about the year 1725, at which time, according to a well-substantiated tradition, they were driven from the section. "Roger Moore, because of his wealth and large number of slaves, was called 'King' Roger. There is a tradition on the Cape Fear that he and his slaves had a battle with the Indians at Sugar Loaf, nearly opposite the town of Brunswick. Governor Tryon, forty years later, mentions that the last battle with

---

[1] Mooney, James. *The Siouan Tribes of the East.* Bulletin Bureau of Ethnology, Washington, 1894, p. 65.

the Indians was when driving them from the Cape Fear in 1725. The tradition would seem to be well founded."[1]

At the present time, nearly two centuries after the expulsion of the last Indian inhabitants from the peninsula, we find many traces of their early occupancy of the area. Oysters and other mollusks served as important articles of food, and vast quantities of shells, intermingled with numerous fragments of pottery of Indian make, are encountered along the mainland, facing the sounds. These masses of shells do not necessarily indicate the sites of villages, or of permanent settlements, but rather of places visited at different times by various families or persons for the purpose of gathering oysters, clams, etc. The majority of these were probably consumed on the spot, while others, following the custom of the more northern tribes, may have been dried in the smoke of the wigwam and thus preserved for future use.

The many small pieces of pottery found, mingled with the shells, are pieces of vessels, probably cooking utensils, of the Indians. Many pieces bear on their outer or convex surfaces the imprint of twisted cords; other fragments show the impressions of basketry. In a paper read before the Historical and Scientific Society, June 3, 1878, Mr. W. B. McKoy described this stage of pottery-making, after the clay had been properly prepared: "The mortar is then pressed by the hand on the inside of a hastily constructed basket of wickerwork and allowed to dry for a while; the basket is then inverted over a large fire of pitch pine and the pot is gradually hardened and blackened by the smoke, having the appearance of a thick iron pot. By constant use afterwards the particles of carbon that have entered the pores of the clay are burnt out and then the pot has a red appearance."[2] Fragments occur upon which the designs are characteristic of pottery from the interior and farther south; other pieces are undoubtedly the work of the southern Algonquin tribes. Within a radius of about one hundred miles were tribes of the Algonquin, Siouan, and Iroquoian stocks. Small parties of the different tribes were ever moving from place to place, and it is within reason to suppose that members of the various tribes, from time to time, visited the Cape Fear peninsula; thus explaining the presence of the variety of pottery discovered among the shell-heaps on the shore of the sound.

---

[1]Ashe, S. A. *History of North Carolina*. Greensboro, 1908. Vol. 1, p. 213.
[2]Published in the *Daily Review*, Wilmington, July 6, 1878.

2

The most interesting village site yet examined is located about one and one-half miles south of Myrtle Sound, three miles north of the ruins of Fort Fisher, and less than one hundred yards from the sea beach. Three small shell-mounds are standing near the center of the area. The largest is about thirty inches in height and twenty feet in diameter. Quantities of pottery are scattered about on the surface, and a few pieces of stone are to be found. Sugar Loaf is less than one mile from this site in a northwesterly direction. Here, in the vicinity of the three shell-mounds, was probably the last Indian settlement on the peninsula.

A level area of several acres at the end of Myrtle Sound was likewise occupied by a settlement, and fragments of pottery are very plentiful, these being intermingled with quantities of oyster and clamshells scattered over the surface. Many pieces of the earthenware from this site are unusually heavy and are probably parts of large cooking vessels.

Northward along the sound are other places of equal interest, some having the appearance of having been occupied during comparatively recent years. This may be judged from the condition of the shells and the weathering of the pottery. Other remains may date from a much earlier period; but all represent the work of the one people, the Indians, who had occupied the country for centuries before the coming of the Europeans.

On both sides of Hewlet's Creek, near its mouth, are numerous signs of Indian occupancy. On the north side, in the rear of the old McKoy house, are traces of an extensive camp, and many objects of Indian origin are said to have been found here during past years. On the opposite side of the creek is a large shell-heap in which fragments of pottery occur. Several miles northward, on the left bank of Barren Inlet Creek, about one-half mile from the sound, are signs of a large settlement. Here an area of four or five acres is strewn with pottery. This was probably the site of a permanent village as distinguished from the more temporary camps met with on the shore of the sound.

A careful examination of various sites existing on the peninsula would be of the greatest interest. The burial places of the ancient inhabitants of the country would undoubtedly be discovered, and this would assist in the identification of the people who bore the name "Cape Fear Indians," all traces of whom are so rapidly disappearing.

INDIAN MOUNDS OF THE CAPE FEAR.

BY PROF. J. A. HOLMES.

(Wilmington, N. C., Weekly Star, October 26, 1883. Reprinted Journal Elisha
Mitchell Scientific Society 1883-4, pages 73 to 79.)

So far as is known to me, no account of the Indian burial
mounds which are to be found in portions of eastern North
Carolina, has, as yet, been published. This fact is considered a
sufficient reason for the publication of the following notes concerning a few of these mounds which have been examined in
Duplin and some other counties in the region under consideration.

It is expected that the examination of other mounds will be
carried on during the present year, and it is considered advisable
to postpone generalized statements concerning them until these
additional examinations have been completed. It may be stated,
however, of the mounds that have been examined already, that
they are quite different from those of Caldwell and other counties of the western section of the State, and of much less interest
so far as contents are concerned. As will be seen from the
following notes, they are usually low, rarely rising to more than
three feet above the surrounding surface, with circular bases,
varying in diameter from 15 to 40 feet: and they contain little
more than the bones of human (presumably Indian) skeletons,
arranged in no special order. They have been generally built
on somewhat elevated, dry, sandy places, out of a soil similar to
that by which they are surrounded. No evidence of an excavation below the general surface has as yet been observed. In the
process of burial, the bones or bodies seem to have been laid on
the surface, or above, and covered up with soil taken from the
vicinity of the mound. In every case that has come under my
own observation charcoal has been found at the bottom of the
mound.

Mound No. 1.—Duplin County, located at Kenansville, about
one-half mile southwest from the courthouse, on a somewhat
elevated, dry, sandy ridge. In form, its base is nearly circular,
35 feet in diameter; height 3 feet. The soil of the mound is
like that which surrounds it, with no evidence of stratification.
The excavation was made by beginning on one side of the mound
and cutting a trench 35 feet long, and to a depth nearly 2 feet
below the general surface of the soil (5 feet below top of mound),
and removing all the soil of the mound by cutting new trenches

and filling up the old ones. In this way all the soil of the mound, and for two feet below its base, was carefully examined. The soil below the base of the mound did not appear to have been disturbed at the time the mound was built. The contents of the mound included fragments of charcoal, a few small fragments of pottery, a handful of small shells, and parts of sixty human skeletons. No implements of any kind were found. Small pieces of charcoal were scattered about in different portions of the mound, but the larger portion of the charcoal was found at one place, 3 or 4 feet square, near one side of the mound. At this place the soil was colored dark and seemed to be mixed with ashes. There were here, with the charcoal, fragments of bones, some of which were dark colored, and may have been burned; but they were so nearly decomposed that I was unable to satisfy myself as to this point. I could detect no evidence of burning, in case of the bones, in other portions of the mound. Fragments of pottery were few in number, small in size, and scattered about in different parts of the mound. They were generally scratched and cross-scratched on one side, but no definite figures could be made out. The shell "beads" were small in size—10 to 12 mm. in length. They are the *Marginella roscida* of Redfield, a small gasteropod, which is said to be now living along the coasts of this State. The specimens, about 75 in number, were all found together, lying in a bunch near the skull and breastbones of a skeleton. The apex of each one had been ground off obliquely so as to leave an opening passing through the shell from the apex to the anterior canal—probably for the purpose of stringing them.

The skeletons of this mound were generally much softened from decay—many of the harder bones falling to pieces on being handled, while many of the smaller and softer bones were beyond recognition. They were distributed through nearly every portion of the mound, from side to side, and from the base to the top surface, without, so far as was discovered, any definite order as to their arrangement. None were found below the level of the surface of the soil outside the mound. In a few cases the skeletons occurred singly, with no others within several feet; while in other cases, several were found in actual contact with one another; and in one portion of the mound, near the outer edge, as many as twenty-one skeletons were found placed within the space of six feet square. Here, in the case last mentioned, several of the skeletons lay side by side, others on top of these, parallel to them, while still others lay on top of and across the first. When one skeleton was located above another, in some cases, the two were in actual contact; in other cases, they were separated by a foot or more of soil.

As to the position of the parts of the individual skeletons, this could not be fully settled in the present case on account of the decayed condition of many of the bones. The following arrangement of the parts, however, was found to be true of nearly every skeleton exhumed. The bones lay in a horizontal position, or nearly so. Those of the lower limbs were bent upon themselves at the knee, so that the thigh bone (femur) and the bones of the leg (tibia and fibula) lay parallel to one another, the bones of the foot and ankle being found with or near the hip bones. The knee cap, or patella, generally lying at its proper place, indicated that there must have been very little disturbance of the majority of the skeletons after their burial. The bones of the upper limbs also were seemingly bent upon themselves at the elbow; those of the forearm (humerus) generally lying quite or nearly side by side with the bones of the thigh and leg; the elbow joint pointing toward the hip bones, while the bones of the two arms below the elbow joint (radius and ulna) were in many cases crossed, as it were, in front of the body. The ribs and vertebræ lay along by the side of, on top of, and between the bones of the upper and lower limbs, generally too far decayed to indicate their proper order or position. The skulls generally lay directly above or near the hip bones, in a variety of positions; in some cases the side, right or left, while in other cases the top of the skull, the base, or the front, was downward.

But two of the crania (A and B of the following table) obtained from this mound were sufficiently well preserved for measurement; and both of these, as shown by the teeth, are skulls of adults. C of this table is the skull of an adult taken from Mound No. 2, below.

Crania.	Length.	Breadth.	Height.	Index of Breadth.	Index of Height.	Facial Angle.
A	193 mm.	151 mm.	144 mm.	.746	.746	74°
B	172 mm.	133 mm.	136 mm.	.772	.790	66°
C	180 mm.	137 mm.	147 mm.	.761	.816	63°

The skeletons were too much decomposed to permit the distinguishing of the sexes of the individuals to whom they belonged; but the size of the crania (adults) and other bones seem to indicate that a portion of the skeletons were those of women. One small cranium found was evidently that of a child—the second and third pairs of incisor teeth appearing beyond the gums.

Mound No. 2.—Located 1¾ miles east of Hallsville, Duplin County, on a somewhat elevated, dry, sandy region. Base of mound nearly circular, 22 feet in diameter; height, 3 feet, surface rounded over the top. Soil similar to that which surrounds the mound—light sandy. Excavations of one-half of the mound exposed portions of eight skeletons, fragments of charcoal and pottery, arranged in much the same way as described above in case of Mound No. 1. The bones being badly decomposed, and the mound being thoroughly penetrated by the roots of trees growing over it, the excavation was stopped. No implements or weapons of any kind were found. There was no evidence of any excavation having been made below the general surface, in the building of the mound, but rather evidence to the contrary. The third cranium (C) of the above table was taken from this mound.

Mound No. 3.—Located in a dry, sandy, and rather elevated place about one-third of a mile east of Hallsville, Duplin County. In size and shape this mound resembles those already mentioned: Base circular, 31 feet in diameter; height 2½ feet. No excavation was made other than what was sufficient to ascertain that the mound contained bones of human skeletons.

Mound No. 4.—Duplin County, located in a rather level sandy region, about one mile from Sarecta post office, on the property of Branch Williams. Base of mound circular, 35 feet in diameter; height 2½ feet. Soil sandy, like that which surrounds it. Around the mound, extending out for a distance varying from 5 to 10 yards, there was a depression, which, in addition to the similarity of soils mentioned above, affords ground for the conjecture that here, as in a number of other cases, it is probable the mound was built by the throwing on of soil from its immediate vicinity. Only a partial excavation was made, with the result of finding human bones, and a few small fragments of charcoal and pottery.

Since the above mounds were visited, I have obtained information as to the localities of mounds, similar to those described in the eastern, southern, and western portions of Duplin County; and I can hardly doubt but that a closer examination of this region will prove them to be more numerous than they are now generally supposed to be.

In Sampson County, the localities of several mounds have been noted; only one of these, however, so far as I am informed, has been examined with care. This one (Mound No. 5), examined by Messrs. Phillips and Murphy of the Clinton School, is located about 2½ miles west of Clinton (Sampson County), on the eastern exposure of a small hill. In general character it resembles the mounds already described. Base circular, 40 feet in diameter; height 3½ feet; soil sandy loam, resembling that surrounding the mound. Contents consisted of small fragments of charcoal, two bunches of small shell "beads," and parts of 16 human skeletons. These skeletons were not distributed uniformly throughout the portion of the mound examined. At one place there were 9, at another 6, and at a third 5 skeletons, lying close to, and in some cases on top of, one another. In this point as in the position of the parts of the skeletons ("doubled-up") this mound resembles those described above. The bones were generally soft from decay. The small shells were found in bunches under two skulls; they are of the same kind (*Marginella roscida,* Redfield) as those from Mound No. 1, and their ends were ground off in the same way. No bones were found below the surface level, and there was no evidence of excavations having been made below this point. No stone implements of any kind were found in the mound. One-half of this mound was examined.

In Robeson and Cumberland Counties several mounds have been examined; and for information concerning these, I am indebted to Mr. Hamilton McMillan.

Five mounds are reported as having been examined in Robeson County, averaging 60 feet in circumference, and 2 feet high, all located on elevated, dry ridges, near swamps or watercourses; and all contained bones of human skeletons. One of these mounds, located about two miles east of Red Springs, examined by Mr. McMillan in 1882, contained about 50 skeletons. Many of these bones near the surface of the mound, in Mr. McMillan's opinion, had been partly burned—those nearer the bottom were in a better state of preservation. There was an "entire absence of skulls and teeth" from this mound—a somewhat remarkable fact. A broken stone "celt" was found among the remains; but with this one unimportant exception, no mention has been made of implements having been found.

In addition to the above, Mr. D. Sinclair, of Plain View, Robeson County, has informed me that he has seen four mounds in the southern portion of this county—two near Brooklyn post office, and two between Leesville and Fair Bluff, about five miles from the latter place.

In Cumberland County, two mounds are reported by Mr. McMillan as having been examined. One of these, located about ten miles south of Fayetteville, was found to contain the crumbled bones of a single person, lying in an east and west direction. There was also found in this mound a fragment of rock rich in silver ore. The other mound, located ten miles southwest from Fayetteville, near Rockfish Creek, was examined by Mr. McMillan in 1860, and found to contain a large number of skeletons, * * * bones were well preserved and, without exception, those of adults. The mound was located on a high, sandy ridge, its base about 20 feet in diameter; height 2½ feet.

In Wake County one mound has been reported as being located on the northeast and several on the southwest side of the Neuse River, about seven miles east from Raleigh; and from the former it is stated that a large number of stone implements have been removed. But I have been unable to examine these or to obtain any definite information concerning them. One mound in this county, examined in 1882 by Mr. W. S. Primrose, of Raleigh, is worthy of mention in this connection, as it resembles in general character the mounds of Duplin County. This mound is located about ten miles south of Raleigh, on a small plateau covered with an original growth of pines. Base of mound circular, about 14 feet in diameter; height 2 feet. The contents of the mound consisted of small fragments of charcoal, and the bones of 10 or 12 human skeletons, much decayed, and arranged, so far as could be determined, without any reference to order or regularity. No weapons or implements of any kind were found.

INDIANS OF THE LOWER CAPE FEAR.

BY S. A. ASHE.

The Indians along the Pamlico and Albemarle were of Northern origin; those on the Cape Fear were of Southern origin. The Yamassees, who originally lived along the coast east of Savannah, were driven back into Georgia soon after the settlement. The Indians dwelling on the Santee, the Pee Dee, and their branches, seem to have been different from the Yamassees, and offshoots from one tribe or nation—the Old Cheraws. There was an Indian tradition that before the coming of the Englishmen the principal body of that tribe, called Cheraw- (or Chero-) kees, after a long fight with the Catawbas, removed to the mountains; but the minor offshoots, along the rivers of South Carolina, were not disturbed.

When the Cape Fear Indians were at war with the settlers at Old Town, the Indians along the southern Carolina coast knew of it, but did not take up arms against the English, and were very friendly with those who, along with Sandford, visited them in 1665. The Indians on the lower Cape Fear are said to have been Congarees, a branch of the Old Cheraws. Soon after the settlement, they were driven away. In 1731, Dr. Brickell, who made an extended journey to the western part of North Carolina in an embassy to the Indians in the mountains, in his *Natural History of North Carolina,* said: "The Saponas live on the west branch of the Cape Fear River; the Toteras are neighbors to them; the Keyawees live on a branch that lies to the northwest."

Two or three years later, Governor Burrington mentioned that the small tribes that had resided near the settlements had entirely disappeared; and in 1733, he also mentioned the fact that "some South Carolina grants had been located on the north side of the Waccamaw River, on lands formerly occupied by the Congarees."

The ending "ee" signifies, perhaps, "river." It is surmised that the true name of Lumber River was Lumbee. Another termination was "aw"—Waxhaw, Saxapahaw, Cheraw, Burghaw. The Burghaw Indians occupied what we call Burgaw.

REPORT OF COMMISSIONERS SENT FROM BARBA-DOES IN 1663 TO EXPLORE THE COAST.

(Lawson's History of North Carolina, page 113.)

From Tuesday, the 29th of September, to Friday, the 2d of October, we ranged along the shore from lat. 32 deg. 20 min. to lat. 33 deg. 11 min., but could discern no entrance for our ship after we had passed to the northward of 32 deg. 40 min. On Saturday, October 3, a violent storm overtook us, the wind being north and east; which easterly winds and foul weather continued till Monday, the 12th; by reason of which storms and foul weather we were forced to get off to sea, to secure ourselves and ship, and were driven by the rapidity of a strong current to Cape Hatteras, in lat. 35 deg. 30 min. On Monday, the 12th, aforesaid, we came to an anchor in seven fathoms at Cape Fair Road, and took the meridian altitude of the sun, and were in lat. 33 deg. 43 min., the wind still continuing easterly, and foul weather till Thursday, the 15th; and on Friday, the 16th, the wind being N.W., we weighed and sailed up Cape Fair River some four or five leagues, and came to an anchor in six or seven fathom, at which time several Indians came on board and brought us great store of fresh fish, large mullets, young bass, shads, and several other sorts of very good, well-tasted fish. On Saturday, the 17th, we went down to the Cape to see the English cattle, but could not find them, though we rounded the Cape, and having an Indian guide with us. Here we rode till October 24th. The wind being against us, we could not go up the river with our ship; but went on shore and viewed the land of those quarters.

On Saturday we weighed and sailed up the river some four leagues or thereabouts.

Sunday, the 25th, we weighed again and rowed up the river, it being calm, and got up some fourteen leagues from the harbor's mouth, where we moored our ship.

On Monday, October 26th, we went down with the yawl to Necoes, an Indian plantation, and viewed the land there.

On Tuesday, the 27th, we rowed up the main river with our longboat and twelve men, some ten leagues or thereabouts.

On Wednesday, the 28th, we rowed up about eight or ten leagues more.

Thursday, the 29th, was foul weather, with much rain and wind, which forced us to make huts and lie still.

Friday, the 30th, we proceeded up the main river seven or eight leagues.

Saturday, the 31st, we got up three or four leagues more, and came to a tree that lay across the river; but because our provisions were almost spent, we proceeded no further, but returned downward before night; and on Monday, the 2d of November, we came aboard our ship.

Tuesday, the 3d, we lay still to refresh ourselves.

On Wednesday, the 4th, we went five or six leagues up the river to search a branch that run out of the main river toward the northwest. In which we went up five or six leagues; but not liking the land, returned on board that night about midnight, and called that place Swampy Branch.

Thursday, November 5th, we stayed aboard.

On Friday, the 6th, we went up Green's River, the mouth of it being against the place at which rode our ship.

On Saturday, the 7th, we proceeded up the said river, some fourteen or fifteen leagues in all, and found it ended in several small branches. The land, for the most part, being marshy and swamps, we returned towards our ship, and got aboard it in the night.

Sunday, November the 8th, we lay still; and on Monday the 9th, went again up the main river, being well stocked with provisions and all things necessary, and proceeded upward till Thursday noon, the 12th, at which time we came to a place where were two islands in the middle of the river; and by reason of the crookedness of the river at that place, several trees lay across both branches, which stopped the passage of each branch, so that we could proceed no further with our boat; but went up the river by land some three or four miles, and found the river wider and wider. So we returned, leaving it as far as we could see up, a long reach running N.E., we judging ourselves near fifty leagues north from the river's mouth.

* * * * * * *

We saw mulberry trees, multitudes of grapevines, and some grapes, which we eat of. We found a very large and good tract of land on the N.W. side of the river, thin of timber, except here and there a very great oak, and full of grass, commonly as high as a man's middle and in many places to his shoulders, where we saw many deer and turkeys; one deer having very large horns and great body, therefore called it Stag Park.

It being a very pleasant and delightful place, we traveled in it several miles, but saw no end thereof. So we returned to our boat and proceeded down the river and came to another place, some twenty-five leagues from the river's mouth on the same side, where we found a place no less delightful than the former; and, as far as we could judge, both tracts came into one. This lower place we called Rocky Point, because we found many rocks and stones of several sizes upon the land, which is not common. We sent our boat down the river before us, ourselves traveling by land many miles. Indeed we were so much taken with the pleasantness of the country, that we traveled into the woods too far to recover our boat and company that night.

The next day, being Sunday, we got to our boat; and on Monday, the 16th of November, proceeded down to a place on the east side of the river, some twenty-three leagues from the harbour's mouth, which we called Turkey Quarters, because we killed several turkeys thereabouts. We viewed the land there and found some tracts of good ground, and high, facing upon the river about one mile inward; but backward, some two miles, all pine land, but good pasture ground.

We returned to our boat and proceeded down some two or three leagues, where we had formerly viewed, and found it a tract of as good land as any we have seen, and had as good timber on it. The banks of the river being high, therefore we called it High Land Point.

Having viewed that, we proceeded down the river, going on shore in several places on both sides, it being generally large marshes, and many of them dry, that they may more fitly be called meadows. The woodland against them is, for the most part, pine, and in some places as barren as ever we saw land, but in other places good pasture ground.

On Tuesday, November the 17th, we got aboard our ship, riding against the mouth of Green's River, where our men were providing wood, and fitting the ship for sea. In the interim we took a view of the country on both sides of the river there, finding some good land, but more bad, and the best not comparable to that above.

Friday, the 20th, was foul weather; yet in the afternoon we weighed, went down the river about two leagues, and came to an anchor against the mouth of Hilton's River, and took a view of the land there on both sides, which appeared to us much like that at Green's River.

Monday, the 23d, we went with our longboat, well victualed

and manned, up Hilton's River; and when we came three leagues or thereabouts up the same, we found this and Green's River to come into one, and so continued for four or five leagues, which makes a great island betwixt them. We proceeded still up the river till they parted again; keeping up Hilton's River, on the larboard side, and followed the said river five or six leagues further, where we found another large branch of Green's River to come into Hilton's, which makes another great island. On the starboard side going up, we proceeded still up the river, some four leagues, and returned, taking a view of the land on both sides, and then judged ourselves to be from our ship some eighteen leagues W. by N.

*   *   *   *   *   *   *

Proceeding down the river two or three leagues further, we came to a place where there were nine or ten canoes all together. We went ashore there and found several Indians, but most of them were the same which had made peace with us before. We stayed very little at that place but went directly down the river, and came to our ship before day.

Thursday, the 26th of November, the wind being at south, we could not go down to the river's mouth; but on Friday the 27th we weighed at the mouth of Hilton's River, and got down a league towards the harbor's mouth.

On Sunday, the 29th, we got down to Crane Island, which is four leagues, or thereabouts, above the entrance of the harbor's mouth. On Tuesday, the 1st of December, we made a purchase of the river and land of Cape Fair of Wat Coosa, and such other Indians as appeared to us to be the chief of those parts. They brought us store of fresh fish aboard, as mullets, shads, and other sorts, very good.

There was a writing left in a post, at the point of Cape Fair River, by those New England men that left cattle with the Indians there, the contents whereof tended not only to the disparagement of the land about the said river, but also to the great discouragement of all such as should hereafter come into those parts to settle. In answer to that scandalous writing, we, whose names are underwritten, do affirm, that we have seen, facing both sides of the river and branches of Cape Fair aforesaid, as good land and as well timbered as any we have seen in any other part of the world, sufficient to accommodate thousands of our English nation, and lying commodiously by the said river's side. On Friday, the 4th of December, the wind being fair, we put to sea, bound for Barbadoes; and on the 6th of February, 1663-4, came to an anchor in Carlisle Bay—it having pleased God, after several apparent dangers both by sea and land, to bring us all in safety to our long-wished-for and much-desired port, to render an account of our discovery, the verity of which we do assert.

ANTHONY LONG.

WILLIAM HILTON.

PETER FABIAN.

CHARLESTOWN—THE FIRST ATTEMPTED SETTLEMENT ON THE CAPE FEAR.

The first trading on the Cape Fear River of which we have any record was by a party of adventurers from Massachusetts in the year 1660.

The historian Bryant says: "There were probably few bays or rivers along the coast, from the Bay of Fundy to Florida, unexplored by the New Englanders, where there was any promise of profitable trade with the Indians. The colonist followed the trader wherever unclaimed lands were open to occupation. These energetic pioneers explored the sounds and rivers south of Virginia in pursuit of Indian traffic, and contrasted the salubrity of the climate and the fertility of the soil with that region of rocks where they made their homes, and where winter reigns for more than half the year. In 1660 or 1661, a company of these men purchased of the natives and settled upon a tract of land at the mouth of the Cape Fear River. Their first purpose was apparently the raising of stock, as the country seemed peculiarly fitted to grazing, and they brought a number of neat cattle and swine to be allowed to feed at large under the care of herdsmen. But they aimed at something more than this nomadic occupation, and a company was formed in which a number of adventurers in London were enlisted, to found a permanent colony."

The most authentic account of the first settlement on the river states that about the time the New Englanders explored that region, John Vassall and others at Barbadoes, purposing to make a settlement on the coast of Virginia, sent out Capt. William Hilton in his ship, the *Adventurer,* to explore the coast; and he made a favorable report of the Cape Fear. Soon afterwards, the New England colonists arrived, but, learning of Hilton's visit, thought it best not to make a settlement at that time; so they turned loose their cattle on the island and left a paper in a box stating that it was a bad place for a settlement. Vassall now again sent Hilton and with him Anthony Long and Peter Fabian to make a more thorough examination.

On Monday, October 12, 1663, the *Adventurer* came to anchor a second time in what they called "The Cape Fair Roads," and then the explorers proceeded to examine the lands along the river. Their "main river" was our Northeast. They called the Northwest branch, the Hilton, and the "Cut-off," the Green. They ascended both branches about seventy-five miles and were much pleased. Along the main river, they named Turkey Quarter, Rocky Point, and Stag Park, names that have been perpetuated to this day.

While these explorations were being made, the King granted the whole country south of Virginia to the Lords Proprietors, and the promoters of the proposed colony, both in New England and in Barbadoes, applied to the Lords Proprietors for terms of settlement. These gentlemen sought to foster the enterprise, and in compliment to the King named the river, the Charles, and the town to be built, Charlestown, and the region they called Clarendon County. Eventually, the New England Association, John Vassall and his friends at Barbadoes, and Henry Vassall and the other London merchants who were to supply the colony, were all brought into a common enterprise; and on May 24, 1664, the first settlers disembarked at the junction of the river and Town Creek, about twenty miles from the bar. These were followed by accessions from New England and Barbadoes until the number of colonists reached six hundred. John Vassall was appointed the surveyor and was the chief man in the colony, being the leading promoter of the enterprise, while Henry Vassall managed affairs at London. The Proprietors, however, selected as governor the man they thought of greatest influence at Barbadoes, Col. John Yeamans; and the King, to show his favor to the colony, conferred on Yeamans the honor of knighthood. He also made a gift to the colony of cannon and munitions for defense. In November, 1665, Sir John reached the colony, and shortly thereafter the first assembly on the Cape Fear was held. There was already a war with the Indians, arising, according to some accounts, from the bad faith of the Massachusetts men who had sold into slavery some Indian children, as well as the adult Indians they were able to take prisoners. There was also dissatisfaction with the regulations of the Proprietors, and especially because the colonists were not allowed to elect their own governor, as the people of Massachusetts did. Sir John soon 'left the colony and returned to Barbadoes; and as some of the Proprietors had died, and, England being at war with Holland, the others were too busy to attend to the affairs of the infant colony, for more than a year Vassall's appeals to the Proprietors received no answer. The settlers becoming disheartened, Vassall did all he could to satisfy them, but they felt cut off and abandoned. After they had found a way to reach Albemarle and Virginia by land, he could no longer hold them. On October 6, 1667, Vassall wrote from Nansemond, Virginia, a touching account of the failure of the colony.

After the departure of the colonists from Charlestown in 1667, Clarendon County again became a solitude. A few years later a new Charlestown was begun farther south, and in the management of this new settlement Sir John Yeamans proved himself a wise and efficient governor and a meritorious and beneficent administrator. After his death the settlement was removed to the junction of the Ashley and Cooper Rivers, where it flourished and endured.

SANDFORD'S ACCOUNT OF CONDITIONS ON CHARLES RIVER.

(Colonial Records, Vol. I, page 119.)

The Right Honoble the Lords Proprietors of the Province of Carolina in prosecucion of his sacred Ma^{tles} pious intencons of planting and civillizing there his domin^s and people of Northerne America, wch Neighbour Southward on Virginia (by some called Florida (found out and discovered by Sr Sebastian Cabott in the year 1497 at the charges of H: 7: King of England co) Constituted S^r. John Yeamans Baronet their Lt Generall with ample powers for placing a Colony in some of the Rivers to the Southward and Westward of Cape St Romania who departing from the Island Barbadoes in Octob: 1665 in a Fly boate of about 150 Tonns accompanyed by a small Friggatt of his owne and a Sloope purchased by a Comon purse for the service of the Colonyes after they had been separated by a great storme att Sea (wherein the Friggatt lost all her Mast and himselfe had like to have foundred and were all brought together againe in the beginning of November to an Anchor before the mouth of Charles River neere Cape Feare in the County of Clarendon, part of the same Province newly begunn to be peopled and within the Lt Gen^{lls} Commission. They were after blowne from their Anchors by a suddaine violent Gust, the Fly boate Sr John was in narrowly escapeing the dangerous shoales of the Cape. But this proved but a short difference in their Fate, for returning with a favorable winde to a second viewe of the entrance into Charles River but destituted of all pilates (save their owne eyes (which the flattering Gale that conducted them did alsoe delude by covering the rough visage of their objected dangers with a thicke vaile of smoth waters) they stranded their vessell on the middle ground of the harbours mouth to the Westward of the Channell where the Ebbe presently left her and the wind with its owne multeplyed forces and the auxiliaryes of the tide of flood beate her to peeces. The persons were all saved by the neighborhood of the shore but the greatest part of their provision of victualls clothes, &c: and of the Magazine of Armes powder and other Military furniture shipped by the Lords Proprietors for the defence of the designed settlement perished in the waters the Lt Gen^{ll} purposed at first imediately to repaire his Friggatt (which together with the Sloop gate safely into the River when the Fly boate was driven off) and to send her back to Barbados for recruity whilst himself in person attended the issue of that discovery which I and some other Gentlemen offered to make Southwards in the Sloope, But when the great and growing necessityes of the English Colony in Charles River (heightened by this disaster) begann clamorously to crave the use of the Sloope in a voyage to Virginia for their speedy reliefe, Sr John altered that his first resolution and permitting the sloope to goe to Virginia returned himself to Barbadoes in his Friggatt. Yett that the designe of the Southern Settlement might not wholy fall, Hee considered with the freighters of the sloope that in case she miscarryed in her Virginia voyage they should hire Captain Edward Stanyons vessell (then in there harbour but bound for Barbados) to performe the Discovery and left a commission with mee for the effecting it upon the returne of the Sloope or Stanion which should first happen.

The sloope in her comeing home from Virginia loaded with victualls being ready by reason of her extreme rottenness in her timbers to Sinke was driven on shoare by a storme in the night on Cape looke out (the next head land to the north and Eastward of Cape Feare and about 20 Le: distant her men all saved except two and with many difficulties brought by their boate through the great Sound into Albemarle River neare the Island Roanoke (within this same province of Carolina, to the English Plantation there—

Captain Stanyon in returning from Barbados weakly maned and without any second to himselfe driven to and agen on the seas for many weekes by contrary winds and conquered with care, vexation and watching lost his reason, and after many wild extravagances leapt over board in a frenzye, leaveing his small Company and vessell to the much more quiet and constant though but little knowing and prudent conduct of a child, who yett assisted by a miraculous providence after many wanderings brought her safe to Charles River in Clarendon her desired port and haven. * * *

[Then Sandford gives an account of his voyage along the coast of southern Carolina, the following extract being of interest.]

Indeed all along I observed a kind of emulation amongst the three principall Indians of the Country (vizt:) those of Keywaha Eddistowe and Port Royall concerning us and our Friendshipp each contending to assure it to themselves and jealous of the other though all be allyed and this notwithstanding that they knew wee were in actuall warre with the natives att Clarendon and had killed and sent away many of them For they frequently discoursed with us concerning the warre, told us that the Natives were noughts, the land sandy and barren, their Country sickly, but if wee would come amongst them wee should finde the contrary to all their evills, and never any occasion of dischargeing our gunns but in merryment and for pastime.

   *   *   *   *   *   *   *

ROBT: SANDFORD.

MASSACHUSETTS SENDS SOME RELIEF.

(Hutchinson's History of Massachusetts, page 238.)

In 1667, the people at Cape Fear being under distressing circumstances, a general contribution by order of court was made throughout the colony for their relief. Although this was a colony subject to the Proprietary Government of Lord Clarendon and others, yet the foundation was laid about the time of the Restoration by adventurers from New England, who supposed they had a right to the soil as first occupants and purchasers from the natives, and, issuing from Massachusetts, to the same civil privileges; but they were disappointed as to both.

THE END OF THE SETTLEMENT ON CHARLES RIVER—THE FIRST CHARLESTOWN.

JOHN VASSALL TO SIR JOHN COLLETON.

(B. P. R. O., Shaftesbury Papers, Bdle. 48, No. 8.)

NANCYMOND IN VIRGINNY 6th October 1667.

Honnorable Sir,

I presume you have heard of the unhapy Loss of our Plantation on Charles River the reason of which I could never soe well have understood had I not com hither to heare; how that all that came from us made it their business soe to exclaime against the Country as they had rendered it unfitt for a Christian habitation; which hindered the coming of the people & supplys to us soe as the rude Rable of our Inhabitants ware dayly redy to mutany against mee for keeping them there soe long; insomuch that after they had found a way to com hither by land all the arguments and authority I could use wold noe longer prevail which inforced mee to stop the first ship that came till I could send for more shipping to carry us all away togeather espetially such weak persons as ware not able to goe by land the charge and trouble whereof and the loss of my Estate there having soe ruened mee as I am not well able to settle myself heare or in any other place to live comfortably. But had it pleased God to bring my Cauzen Vassall safe hither wee had bin yett in a flourishing condition. I sent one Whiticar last November on purpose at my owne charge to give the Lords an account of our condition but hee was taken by the way soe as I have not heard a word from any of you since I receaved my Commissions by Mr. Sandford and indeed we ware as a poore Company of deserted people little regarded by any others and noe way able to supply ourselves with clothing and necessaries nor any number considerable to defend ourselves from the Indians all which was occationed by the hard termes of your Consetions which made our friends that sett us out from Barbadoes to forsake us, soe as they would neither suply us with necessaries nor find shipping to fetch us away, yet had wee had but 200£ sent us in

Clothing wee had made a comfortable shift for annother yeare, and I offered to stay there if but twenty men would stay with mee till wee had heard from your Lordships, for wee had corne enough for two yeares for a farr greater number and tho' the Indians had killed our Cattle yett wee might have defended our-selves but I could not find 6. men that wold be true to me to stay: soe was constrained to leave it to my greate loss & ruin, and I fear you will not have a much better account of your plantation at Roanoke unless a better course be taken to incorage their stay for they are not without greate cause of complaints.

This with my very humble servis presented is all at present
From   Your honnors humble servant
                              JOHN VASSALL
To the Honorable Sir John Coliton
     Knight and Barronett at Nerehald
          These present
               In Essex.

SAMUEL MAVERICKE TO SEC. Lᵈ ARLINGTON.

(B. P. R. O., Shaftesbury Papers, Vol. XXI, 134.)

The plantations at Cape Feare are deserted, the inhabitants have since come hither, some to Virginia.
                         Yoʳ most obliged
                              humble Servant
     Boston   SAMUELL MAVERICKE
          Oct. 16, 1667.

CAPE FEAR PIRATES OF 1719.

There was a wide breadth of wilderness between the settle-ments in North and South Carolina, and before 1725 it was not determined to which province the Cape Fear River belonged. About 1692 Landgrave Smith located a grant of 48,000 acres on that river, and other South Carolina grants were located near the confluence of its two branches; but there was no permanent settlement made. One Lockwood, from Barbadoes, however, made a settlement farther to the south, which the Indians de-stroyed, and hence the name to this day of "Lockwood's Folly."

The solitude remained unbroken until in 1719, when Steed Bonnet, an infamous pirate, established himself within the harbor and made such depredations on the commerce of Charleston that Colonel Rhett organized an expedition against him. A notable battle took place near where Southport now stands, ending in the destruction of Bonnet's vessel and the capture of many of the pirates. Two days later other pirate vessels were taken at sea, and more than a hundred pirates were hanged at one time on the wharves of Charleston. It is supposed that some of Bonnet's men escaped and made their way up the river, eventually amalgamating with a small tribe of Indians on the Lumber River, where, soon after the permanent settlement of the Cape Fear, in 1725, a considerable number of English-speaking people were found.

Permanent Settlement

THE TOWN OF BRUNSWICK.

On the 24th of January, 1712, was commissioned the first governor of the province of North Carolina, separate and distinct from the province of South Carolina.

In the year 1711 a horrible massacre of the colonists in Albemarle occurred, which was characterized by such fiendish cruelty on the part of the Indians, led principally by Tuscaroras, that the colony on the Neuse and Pamlico was blighted for years and well-nigh destroyed. One hundred and thirty persons were butchered in two hours under the most appalling circumstances. Women were laid upon the house floors and great stakes driven through their bodies; other atrocities were committed too frightful to think of, and more than eighty unbaptized infants were dashed to pieces against trees. Although it appears that there were occasional difficulties with the Indians during the early settlements, this seems to have been the first general uprising in the province. It led to the Tuscarora War, which would probably have exterminated the white people in North Carolina but for the timely and generous assistance of South Carolina, which voted £4,000 sterling, and dispatched troops immediately to Albemarle without so much as asking for security or promise to pay. It is this war which leads us to the introduction of Col. James Moore, son of Gov. James Moore, of South Carolina, who came from South Carolina with a second force of troops to the help of our colonists, and by his active and efficient campaign made short work of the Tuscaroras and restored peace to our sorely troubled people.

Meanwhile, a third army had come from South Carolina under Maj. Maurice Moore, a younger brother of Col. James Moore, who after peace remained in Albemarle. The next year the people of South Carolina were themselves in danger of extermination because of a most terrible Indian war, and Maj. Maurice Moore was dispatched with a force to their relief. He marched along the coast, crossing the Cape Fear near Sugar Loaf, and was so well pleased with the river lands that he conceived the idea of settling them. The Lords Proprietors, however, had prohibited the making of any settlement within twenty miles of that river, and it was some time before he could carry out his plan. Finally, in 1725, he and his kindred and friends in Albemarle and South Carolina joined in settling the Cape Fear country. His brother, Roger Moore, came with his hundreds of slaves and built Orton, while Maurice Moore selected a most admirable site on a bluff near Orton, fifteen miles below the present city of Wilmington, and laid out a town which he called Brunswick, in honor of the reigning family. Brunswick quickly prospered, for a steady stream of population flowed in, and the trade of the river grew rapidly. In 1731 Dr. Brickell wrote in his *Natural History of North Carolina,* "Brunswick has a great trade, a number of merchants and rich planters." At that early period forty-two vessels, carrying valuable cargoes, sailed from the port in one year.

I have before me the original book of entries and clearances of His Britannic Majesty's custom house at the port of Brunswick, in the province of North Carolina, beginning with A. D. 1773, in the reign of George III., and running for three years. It is strongly bound in leather, somewhat injured by abuse for other purposes during Revolutionary times, but it contains in fine, legible handwriting, wonderfully well preserved, a record of over three hundred vessels, with the particulars of their cargoes and crews. Among the names of the trading vessels, some of which are remarkable, are the brig *Orton,* the brig *Wilmington,* and the schooner *Rake's Delight.*

Some of the cargoes are significant; 20 negroes, 50 hogsheads of rum, 1,000 bags of salt, etc. The outward cargoes to ports in the provinces, to the West Indies, and to London, Bristol, and other distant destinations, were mostly lumber, staves, tar, indigo, rice, corn, wheat, and tobacco.

The full-rigged ship *Ulysses,* Captain Wilson, brought from Glasgow, Scotland, October 18, 1773, to Brunswick, furniture, leather, saddles, earthenware, shoes, linen, hats, gunpowder, silks, glass, iron, lead, and "shott," also port wine, rugs, toys, and household articles.

Other Scotch brigs, notably the *Baliol,* brought many settlers to the Cape Fear, most of whom went farther up to Cross Creek, now Fayetteville. Among these was the distinguished lady, Flora Macdonald.

There are no available records of trade and commerce pertaining to Brunswick or to the new settlement at Wilmington. It appears, however, that many of the plantations established sawmills, from which lumber, along with the products of the farms, was shipped in plantation brigs and schooners to distant ports. At Orton a large sawmill was run by water power, and vessels were loaded in the river opposite the mill with lumber, rice, and indigo.

In its early years Brunswick was in Carteret Precinct, for when Carteret Precinct, as the counties were formerly called, was established in 1722, it ran down the coast to the unknown confines of North Carolina, and back into the wilderness without limitation.

So the settlement at Brunswick, in 1725, was in Carteret, until New Hanover Precinct was established; and then it was in New Hanover, which at first embraced the territory now in Duplin, Sampson, Bladen, and Brunswick Counties. It was not until shortly before the Revolution that Brunswick was cut off from New Hanover.

As the Cape Fear region was originally in Carteret Precinct, some of the early grants and deeds for lands in New Hanover and Brunswick were registered at Beaufort, the county seat of Carteret.

A VISIT TO THE CAPE FEAR IN 1734.

(Georgia Historical Papers, Vol. II, page 54.)

I intend after my return to Charleston to take a journey, by land, to Cape Fear in North Carolina, which I have heard so much talk of. * * *

I set out from Charleston on the 10th of June, on my travels to Cape Fear, in North Carolina, in company with thirteen more, and the first night reached Mr. More's, in Goose Creek. * * *

The next morning, just as we were setting out from thence, our tired horses came in, when we ordered them to be left there till further orders; we left the boys behind to come after us as well as they could. We reached Little Charlotta by dinner time, which is about fifteen miles from Ash's, or Little River; we dined there, and in the afternoon crossed the ferry, where we intended to sleep that night. We reached there about eight the same night, after having crossed the ferry.

It [Lockwood's Folly] is so named after one Lockwood, a Barbadian, who attempted to settle it some time ago; but, by his cruel behavior to the Indians, they drove him from thence, and it has not been settled above ten years. We left Lockwood's Folly about eight the next morning, and by two reached the town of Brunswick, which is the chief town in Cape Fear; but with no more than two of the same horses which came with us out of South Carolina. We dined there that afternoon. Mr. Roger More hearing we were come, was so kind as to send fresh horses for us to come up to his house, which we did, and were kindly received by him; he being the chief gentleman in all Cape Fear. His house is built of brick, and exceedingly pleasantly situated about two miles from the town, and about half a mile from the river; though there is a creek comes close up to the door, between two beautiful meadows, about three miles length. He has a prospect of the town of Brunswick, and of another beautiful brick house, a building about half a mile from him, belonging to Eleazar Allen, Esq., late speaker to the Commons House of Assembly, in the province of South Carolina. There were several vessels lying about the town of Brunswick, but I shall forbear giving a description of that place; yet on the 20th of June we left Mr. Roger More's, accompanied by his brother, Nathaniel More, Esq., to a plantation of his, up the Northwest branch of Cape Fear River. The river is wonderfully pleasant, being, next to the Savannah, the finest on all the continent.

We reached The Forks, as they call it, that same night, where the river divides into two very beautiful branches, called the Northeast and the Northwest, passing by several pretty plantations on both sides. We lodged that night at one Mr. Jehu Davis', and the next morning, proceeded up the Northwest branch; when we got about two miles from thence, we came to a beautiful plantation, belonging to Captain Gabriel, who is a great merchant there, where were two ships, two sloops, and a brigantine, loaded with lumber for the West Indies: it is about twenty-two miles from the bar; when we came about four miles higher up, we saw an opening on the northeast side of us, which is called Black River, on which there is a great deal of good meadow land, but there is not any one settled on it.

The next night we came to another plantation belonging to Mr. Roger More, called the Blue Banks, where he is a-going to build another very large brick house. This bluff is at least a hundred feet high, and has a beautiful prospect over a fine large meadow, on the opposite side of the river; the houses are all built on the southwest side of the river, it being for the most

part high champaign land: the other side is very much subject
to overflow, but I cannot learn they have lost but one crop. I
am credibly informed they have very commonly fourscore bushels of corn on an acre of their overflowed land. It very rarely
overflows but in the wintertime, when their crop is off. I must
confess I saw the finest corn growing there that I ever saw in
my life, as likewise wheat and hemp. We lodged there that
night at one Captain Gibbs', adjoining to Mr. More's plantation,
where we met with very good entertainment. The next morning
we left his house, and proceeded up the said river to a plantation
belonging to Mr. John Davis, where we dined. The plantations
on this river are very much alike as to the situation; but there
are many more improvements on some than on others; this house
is built after the Dutch fashion, and made to front both ways—
on the river, and on the land. He has a beautiful avenue cut
through the woods for above two miles, which is a great addition
to the house. We left his house about two in the afternoon, and
the same evening reached Mr. Nathaniel More's plantation,
which is reckoned forty miles from Brunswick. It is likewise
a very pleasant place on a bluff upwards of sixty feet high. I
forbore mentioning any thing either as to the goodness or the
badness of the land in my passage from South Carolina, it being, in short, nothing but a sandy bank from Winneaw ferry to
Brunswick; and, indeed, the town itself is not much better at
present: it is that which has given this place such a bad name on
account of the land, it being the only road to South Carolina
from the northern part of the continent, and as there are a great
many travellers from New York, New England, &c., who go to
Charleston, having been asked what sort of land they have in
Cape Fear, have not stuck out to say that it is all a mere sand
bank; but let those gentlemen take a view of the rivers, and they
will soon be convinced to the contrary, as well as myself, who,
must confess, till then was of their opinion, but now am convinced by ocular demonstration, for I have not so much as seen
one foot of bad land since my leaving Brunswick. About three
days after my arrival at Mr. More's, there came a sloop of one
hundred tons, and upwards, from South Carolina, to be laden
with corn, which is sixty miles at least from the bar. I never
yet heard of any man who was ever at the head of that river, but
they tell me the higher you go up the better the land, and the
river grows wider and wider. There are people settled at least
forty miles higher up, but indeed the tide does not flow, at the

most, above twenty miles higher. Two days after, I was taken very ill of an ague and fever, which continued on me for near a month, in which time my companions left me, and returned to South Carolina. When I began to recover my health a little, I mentioned to Mr. More the great desire I had to see Wacca-maw Lake, as I had heard so much talk of it, and been myself a great way up the river; that I was sure by the course of the country I could not be above twenty miles from thence. He told me he had a negro fellow, who he thought could carry me to it, and that he would accompany me himself, with some others of his acquaintance. On the 18th of July we set out from his house on horseback, with every one his gun, and took the negro with us. We rode about four miles on a direct course through an open pine barren, when we came to a large cane swamp, about half a mile through, which we crossed in about an hour's time, but I was astonished to see the innumerable sight of musquetoes, and the largest that I ever saw in my life, for they made nothing to fetch blood of us through our buckskin gloves, coats, and jackets. As soon as we got through that swamp, we came to another open pine barren, where we saw a great herd of deer, the largest and fattest that ever I saw in those parts: we made shift to kill a brace of them, which we made a hearty dinner on. We rode about two miles farther, when we came to another cane swamp, where we shot a large she-bear and two cubs. It was so large that it was with great difficulty we got through it. When we got on the other side, it began to rain very hard, or otherwise, as far as I know, we might have shot ten brace of deer, for they were almost as thick as in the parks in England, and did not seem to be in the least afraid of us, for I question much whether they had ever seen a man in their lives before, for they seemed to look on us as amazed. We made shift as well as we could to reach the lake the same night, but had but little pleasure; it continued to rain very hard, we made a large fire of lightwood, and slept as well as we could that night. The next morning we took a particular view of it, and I think it is the pleasantest place that ever I saw in my life. It is at least eighteen miles round, surrounded with exceedingly good land, as oak of all sorts, hickory, and fine cypress swamps. There is an old Indian field to be seen, which shows it was for-merly inhabited by them, but I believe not within these fifty years, for there is scarce one of the Cape Fear Indians, or the Waccamaws, that can give any account of it. There is plenty of deer, wild turkeys, geese, and ducks, and fish in abundance; we shot sufficient to serve forty men, though there were but six of us. We went almost round it, but there is on the northeast side a small cypress swamp, so deep that we could not go through it; we returned back again on a direct line, being resolved to find how far it was on a straight course from the Northwest branch of Cape Fear River, which we found did not exceed ten miles.

We returned back to Mr. More's that same night, having satisfied our curiosity, and the next morning set out with an intent to take a view of the Northeast branch, on which there is a great deal of good land, but not in my opinion, for the generality, so good as on the Northwest, but I think the river is much more beautiful. We lay that first night at Newton, in a small hut, and the next day reached Rocky Point, which is the finest place in all Cape Fear. There are several very worthy gentlemen settled there, particularly Col. Maurice More, Captain Herne, John Swan, Esq., and several others. We stayed there one night, and the next morning set out on horseback to take a view of the land backward, imagining that there might be only a skirt of good land on the river, but I am sure I rode for about twenty miles back, through nothing but black walnut, oak, and hickory; we returned the same night to Rocky Point, and the next morning set out for a plantation belonging to Mr. John Davis, within six miles of Brunswick, where I was a second time taken ill, so that I thought I should have died; but by the providence of God, and the care of good Mrs. Davis, I recovered in a fortnight's time, so that I was able to set out on my journey to South Carolina. I took leave of that worthy family on the 10th of August, when she was so kind as to force me to take a bottle of shrub, and several other things with me. I reached Mr. Roger More's the same night, where I was again handsomely received, but being resolved to set out on my journey the next morning, he generously offered me a horse to carry me to the house where I was obliged to leave mine on the road, as likewise a servant to attend me, which I refused. I left his house the next morning, being the 11th of August, at half an hour after seven, and reached Brunswick by eight. I set out from thence about nine, and about four miles from thence met my landlord of Lockwood's Folly, who was in hopes I would stay at his house all night.

     *   *   *   *   *   *   *

When I was about halfway over the bay, I intended to stop

at the next spring and take a tiff of punch; but by some unfortunate accident, I know not how, when I came within sight of the spring, my bottle unluckily broke, and I lost every drop of my shrub; but examining my bags, I accidentally found a bottle of cherry brandy, with some ginger-bread and cheese, which I believe good Mrs. More ordered to be put up unknown to me. I drank two drams of that, not being willing it should all be lost in case it should break, and mounting my horse, took some ginger-bread and cheese in my hand and pursued my journey.

*   *   *   *   *   *   *

I reached Witton's by noon, and had my possum dressed for dinner. * * * I arrived at Charleston on the 7th [17th] day of August, where I remained till the 23d of November, when I set sail for England and arrived safe in London on the 3d of January, 1734-5.

ERECTION OF WILMINGTON—DECAY OF BRUNSWICK.

In the cove near Governor Tryon's residence, still known as Governor's Cove, were anchored in colonial times His Majesty's sloops of war *Viper, Diligence, Scorpion,* and *Cruizer;* and the frigate *Rose,* a prison ship, was anchored in the stream. This roadstead proved to be unsafe in stormy weather, and because of that fact and of the growth of a village fifteen miles farther up the river called New Liverpool, afterwards Newton, and lastly Wilmington, which absorbed the trade of the two branches of the river near that point and prospered, a gradual exodus from Brunswick began and continued; so that while Wilmington flourished and became the capital of the province, Brunswick dwindled and during the Revolutionary War was wholly abandoned.

In 1731 John Maultsby took out a warrant for 640 acres of land opposite the "Thoroughfare," and John Watson located a similar warrant adjoining and below that. In 1732 a few enterprising men settled on Maultsby's grant for trade, and called the place New Liverpool. The next spring Michael Higgins, Joshua Grainger, James Wimble, and John Watson joined in laying off a town on Watson's entry, which they called Newton.

Gov. Gabriel Johnston arrived in November, 1734, and he at once espoused the cause of Newton as against Brunswick, the older town. He bought land near Newton and led his friends to do so. Determined to give it importance, he ordered that the Council should meet there, and also that the courts should be held there instead of at Brunswick; and, indeed, as a sort of advertisement, he made May 13, 1735, a gala day for the village. On that day he had the land office opened there, also the Court of Exchequer to meet there, as well as the New Hanover Court, and, likewise, the Council. Then he sought to have the village incorporated under the name of Wilmington. For a brief time the influence of Brunswick prevailed against him, but he finally succeeded.

The Act of Incorporation,[1] passed in 1739 by the Assembly, is as follows:

An Act, for erecting the village called Newton, in New Hanover County, into a town and township, by the name of Wilmington; and regulating and ascertaining the bounds thereof.

SECTION 1. Whereas, several merchants, tradesmen, artificers, and other persons of good substance, have settled themselves at a village called Newton lying on the east branch of Cape Fear; and whereas, the said village by reason of its convenient situation at the meeting of the two great branches of Cape Fear River, and likewise, by reason of the depth of water, capable of receiving vessels of considerable burthen, safety of its roads beyond any other part of the river, and the secure and easy access from all parts of the different branches of the said river, is, upon all those and many other accounts, more proper for being erected into a town or township, than any other part of the said river.

SEC. 2. Be it therefore enacted by His Excellency Gabriel Johnston, Esq., Governor, by and with the advice and consent of His Majesty's Council and General Assembly of this province, and it is hereby enacted, by the authority of the same, that the village heretofore called Newton, lying on the east side of the northeast branch of Cape Fear River, in New Hanover County, shall, from and after the passage of this Act, be a town and township, and the said village is hereby established a town and township by the name of Wilmington, the bounds whereof shall be and are circumscribed in manner following: That is to say, to the northeast, by the lands of His Excellency Gabriel Johnston, Esq.; upwards and below, by the lands of Michael Dyer; to the westward by the northeast branch of Cape Fear River; and to the eastward, by a line drawn between the

---

[1]Swann's *Collection Public Acts*, North Carolina, 1739, Chapter IV., p. 99.

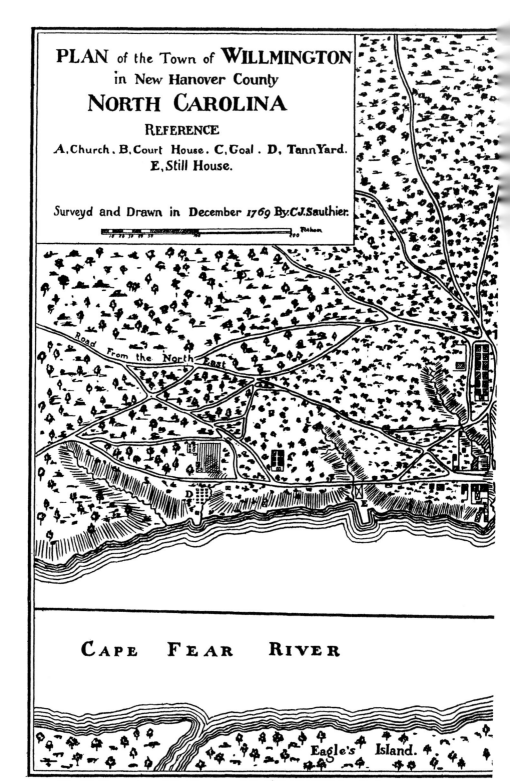

PLAN of the Town of **WILLMINGTON**
in New Hanover County
NORTH CAROLINA
REFERENCE
A, Church. B, Court House. C, Goal. D, Tann Yard.
E, Still House.

Surveyd and Drawn in December *1769* By C.J. Sauthier.

Road From the North East

CAPE FEAR RIVER

Eagle's Island.

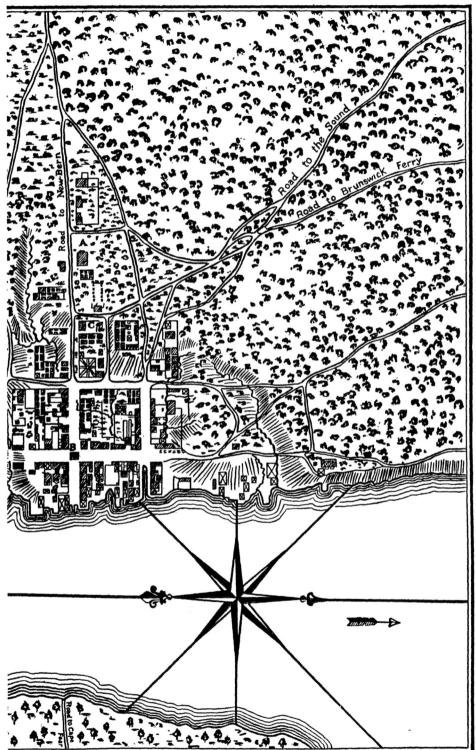

Road to New-Bern

Road to the Sound

Road to Brunswick Ferry

Road to Cape Fear

said lands of His Excellency Gabriel Johnston, Esq., and Michael Dyer, one hundred and twenty poles distant from the river.

SEC. 3. And be it further enacted, by the authority aforesaid, that forever, after passing of this Act, the inhabitants of and near the said town, qualified as hereinafter mentioned, shall have the privilege of choosing one Representative for the said town, to sit and vote in General Assembly.

SEC. 4. And for ascertaining the method of choosing the said Representative, be it further enacted, by the authority aforesaid, that every tenant of any brick, stone, or framed inhabitable house, of the length of twenty feet, and sixteen feet wide, within the bounds of the said town, who, at the day of election, and for three months next before, inhabited such house, shall be entitled to vote in the election for the Representative of the said town, to be sent to the General Assembly; and in case there shall be no tenant of such house in the said town on the day of election, qualified to vote as aforesaid, that then, and in such case, the person seized of such house, either in fee-simple, or fee-tail, or for term of life, shall be entitled to vote for the Representative aforesaid.

SEC. 5. And be it further enacted, by the authority aforesaid, that every person who, on the day of election, and for three months next before, shall be in actual possession or an inhabitant of a brick house, of the length of thirty feet, and sixteen feet wide, between the bounds of the said town upwards, and Smith's Creek, and within one hundred and twenty poles of the Northeast branch of Cape Fear River, shall be entitled to, and have a vote in the election of a Representative for the said town (unless such person be a servant), and shall, as long as he continues an inhabitant of such house, within the said bounds, enjoy all the rights, privileges, and immunities, to which any inhabitant within the said town shall be entitled, by virtue of said Act.

SEC. 6. And be it further enacted, by the authority aforesaid, that no person shall be deemed qualified to be a Representative for the said town, to sit in the General Assembly, unless, on the day of election, he be, and for three months next before, was seized, in fee-simple, or for the term of life, of a brick, stone, or framed house of the dimensions aforesaid, with one or more brick chimney or chimnies.

SEC. 7. And be it further enacted, by the authority aforesaid, that forever, after the passing of this Act, the Court of the County of New Hanover, and the election of the Representatives to be sent to the General Assembly, and the election of Vestrymen, and all other public elections, of what kind or nature soever, for the said county and town, shall be held and made in the town of Wilmington, and at no other place whatsoever, any law, statute, usage, or custom, to the contrary, notwithstanding.

Sec. 8. And be it further enacted, by the authority aforesaid, that from and after the passing of this Act, the Collector and Naval Officers of the port of Brunswick (of which port the said town of Wilmington is the most central and convenient place, both for exportation and importation, by reason of its navigation and situation), shall constantly reside in the said town, and there keep their respective offices, until His Majesty shall be pleased to give his directions to the contrary. And likewise, the Clerk of the Court of the County of New Hanover, and the Register of the said county, shall constantly hold and execute their respective offices in the said town of Wilmington; and that if either of the said officers neglect or refuse so to do, he so neglecting or refusing, shall, for every month he shall be a delinquent, forfeit and pay the sum of five pounds proclamation money; to be sued for and recovered, by him who shall sue for the same, in the general court of this province, or in the County Court of New Hanover, by action of debt, bill, plaint, or information, wherein no essoin, protection, injunction, or wager of law shall be allowed, and one-half of such forfeiture shall be for the use of the person who sues for the same, and the other half shall be paid to the commissioners, for the time being, appointed for regulating the said town.

Sec. 9. And for the due regulating the said town, be it further enacted, by the authority aforesaid, that Robert Halton, James Murray, Samuel Woodard, William Farris, Richard Eagles, John Porter and Robert Walker, Esquires, are hereby established and appointed commissioners for the said town; and the said commissioners, or a majority of them, and their successors shall have, and be invested with all powers and authorities within the bounds of the said town of Wilmington, in as full and ample manner as the commissioners for the town of Edenton have or possess, by virtue of any law heretofore passed.

Sec. 10. And whereas the justices of the County Court of New Hanover, at the court held at Brunswick, on Tuesday the eleventh day of December last, have imposed a tax of five shillings per poll, to be levied on the tithable inhabitants of the said county, between the first day of January and the first day of March, one thousand seven hundred and thirty-nine; and afterwards, one other tax of five shillings per poll, to be levied on the said inhabitants, between the first day of January and the first day of March, one thousand seven hundred and forty, towards building a courthouse and gaol in the town of Brunswick, for the said county.

Sec. 11. Be it enacted, by the authority aforesaid, that the justices of the said County Court shall, and are hereby directed to apply the said levy or tax towards finishing and completing the courthouse already erected in the said town of Wilmington, and towards building a gaol in the said town.

Sec. 12. And be it further enacted, by the authority aforesaid, that if any one or more of the said commissioners shall die, or remove out of the county, that then and in such case, the surviving or remaining commissioners shall, within six months after the death or removal of such commissioner, present to His Excellency the Governor, or Commander-in-Chief for the time being, three persons, one of which the said Governor or Commander-in-Chief is hereby empowered to nominate and appoint; and the commissioners so appointed shall be invested with the same powers and authorities as any commissioner nominated by this Act.

GABRIEL JOHNSTON, ESQ., *Governor.*
WILLIAM SMITH, *President.*
JOHN HODGSON, *Speaker.*

THE SPANISH INVASION, 1747.

On November 20, 1740, a considerable force, enlisted on the Cape Fear, left Wilmington under the command of Capt. James Innes to fight the Spaniards at Cartagena; they were carried off by disease and but few returned. The next year the Spaniards in retaliation seized Ocracoke Inlet and committed tremendous depredations. And again, in 1744, they scoured the coast. Three years later, they made another foray. In July, 1747, they entered the Cape Fear, but the militia were prompt in meeting them, and held them in check, taking some prisoners. From there they went north, entered Beaufort Harbor, and, on August 26, after several days' fighting, gained possession of the town. Emboldened by this victory, they returned to the Cape

4

Fear, and, on September 4, 1747, began to ascend the river. New Hanover County then included what has since become Brunswick, and the people from Duplin to Lockwood's Folly sprang to their horses and hurried to Brunswick. Eleazar Allen, Roger Moore, Edward Moseley, and William Forbes were appointed commissioners to take measures for defense; while Maj. John Swann was invested with the immediate command of the troops. The companies of Capt. William Dry, Capt. John Ashe, and Capt. John Sampson, from the upper part of the county, alone numbered 300 men; so the defenders doubtless were about a thousand. On the 6th, the Spaniards possessed themselves of Brunswick, and for four days the battle raged. At length, on September 10, one of the Spanish vessels was blown up and the others were driven off. All that day Colonel Dry was burying dead Spaniards, for a considerable number of them perished, and twenty-nine were taken alive. It was from the destroyed vessel that the painting in the vestry room of St. James's Church in Wilmington, "Ecce Homo," was taken. The spoils from the wreck were appropriated for the use of the churches in Brunswick and Wilmington.

Because of these incursions, a fort was built the next year to guard the river—Fort Johnston. It was garrisoned by companies raised in the vicinity, and some of the young officers trained to arms there afterwards became distinguished in the French and Indian War and in the Revolution, among them Gen. James Moore and Gen. Robert Howe.

THE WAR OF JENKINS' EAR.

Catherine Albertson, in her very interesting book entitled *In Ancient Albemarle,* says, with reference to this interesting episode:

The real cause of this war in 1740 was the constant violation on the part of the English of the commercial laws which Spain had made to exclude foreign nations from the trade of her American colonies. But the event which precipitated matters and gave to the conflict which followed the name of "The War of Jenkins' Ear" was as follows:

The Spaniards captured an English merchant vessel, whose master they accused of violating the trade laws of Spain. In order to wring a confession from the master, Captain Jenkins, his captors hung him up to a yardarm of his ship until he was nearly dead, and then let him down, thinking he would confess.

But on his stoutly denying that he had been engaged in any nefarious dealings, and since no proof could be found against him, the captain of the Spanish ship cut off one of the English captain's ears, and insolently told him to show it to his countrymen as a warning of what Englishmen might expect who were caught trading with Spain's colonies in America.

Captain Jenkins put the ear in his pocket, sailed home as fast as wind and wave would carry him, and was taken straight to the Houses of Parliament with his story. Such was the indignation of both Lords and Commons at this insult to one of their nation, and so loud was the clamor for vengeance, that even Walpole, who for years had managed to hold the English dogs of war in leash, was now compelled to yield to the will of the people, and Parliament declared war on Spain.

Immediately upon this declaration, King George called upon his "trusty and well-beloved subjects in Carolina" and the other twelve colonies, to raise troops to help the mother country in her struggle with arrogant Spain. Carolina responded nobly to the call for troops, as the following extract from a letter from Gov. Gabriel Johnston to the Duke of Newcastle will testify: "I can now assure Your Grace that we have raised 400 men in this province who are just going to put to sea. In those northern parts of the colony adjoining to Virginia, we have got 100 men each, though some few deserted since they began to send them on board the transports at Cape Fear. I have good reason to believe we could have raised 200 more if it had been possible to negotiate the bills of exchange in this part of the continent; but as that was impossible we were obliged to rest satisfied with four companies. I must, in justice to the Assembly of the province, inform Your Grace that they were very zealous and unanimous in promoting this service. They have raised a subsidy of 1,200 pounds, as it is reckoned hereby, on which the men have subsisted ever since August, and all the transports are victualed."

No record has been kept of the names of the privates who enlisted from Carolina in this war. Nor do we know how many of those who at the King's call left home and country to fight in a foreign land ever returned to their native shores; but we do know that these Carolina troops took part in the disastrous engagements of Cartagena and Boca-Chica; and that King George's troops saw fulfilled Walpole's prophecy, made at the time of the rejoicing over the news that Parliament had declared war on Spain: "You are ringing the joy bells now," said the great prime minister, "but before this war is over you will all be wringing your hands."

After the two crushing defeats of Cartagena and Boca-Chica, the troops from the colonies who still survived embarked upon their ships to return home; but while homeward bound a malignant fever broke out among the soldiers, which destroyed nine out of every ten men on the ships. But few of those from Carolina lived to see their native home again. That they bore themselves bravely on the field of battle, none who know the war record of North Carolina will dare deny, though, as regards her private soldiers in this war, history is silent.

One of the officers from Carolina, Captain Innes, of Wilmington, made such a record for gallantry during the two engagements mentioned, that in the French and Indian War, in which fourteen years later not only the Thirteen Colonies, but most of the countries of Europe as well, were embroiled, he was made commander-in-chief of all the American forces [in Virginia], George Washington himself gladly serving under this distinguished Carolinian.

THE SITE OF FORT JOHNSTON.

(Extracts from an address delivered by Dr. J. G. DeRoulhac Hamilton, alumnus professor of history, University of North Carolina, before the North Carolina Society of Colonial Dames at Southport, N. C.)

Fort Johnston dates from the War of the Austrian Succession, or, as it was known in the colonies, King George's War. In this contest, in which the mother country was engaged with both France and Spain, many of the colonies took an active part. The Southern colonies were all in an exposed condition and seemed in imminent danger of attack, particularly from Spain. Then it was, in 1745, that the Assembly of North Carolina, after reciting that

"Whereas, from the present War with France and Spain, There is great Reason to fear that such Parts of this Province which are situated most commodious for Shipping to enter may be invaded by the Enemy; and whereas, The Entrance of Cape Fear River, from its known depth of water and other Conveniences for Navigation, may tempt them to such an enterprise, while it remains in so naked and defenceless a Condition as it now is, * * * for the better securing of the Inhabitants of the River from Insult and Invasion," appointed a board of commissioners, consisting of Gov. Gabriel Johnston, for whom the fort was to be named, Nathaniel Rice, Robert Halton, Eleazar Allen, Matthew Rowan, Edward Moseley, Roger Moore, William Forbes, James Innes, William Farris, John Swann and George Moore, who were charged with the duty of erecting a fort large enough to contain twenty cannon, and provided for the payment of the expenses of construction by appropriating therefor the powder money exacted from vessels entering the port. In 1748 two thousand pounds were appropriated for the work, and at various times later the amount was increased. The fort was completed in 1764, by William Dry, and very poorly built it was, too, for the tapia, or "tabby work," as it was called, contained such a large proportion of sand that every time a gun was fired part of the parapet fell down. Governor Tryon said that it was a disgrace to the ordnance in it, but he described its situation as admirable in every respect, and Josiah Quincy, who visited it in 1773, said it was delightful.

The first commander of the fort was Capt. John Dalrymple. Of this officer, the least said, the better. General Braddock, in order to get rid of him, gave him the appointment and sent him to Governor Dobbs. This is not an unfair example of the English method of making colonial appointments at that time. Dalrymple went to England, and upon his return was arrested by Governor Dobbs and thrown into prison, but upon appeal to the Board of Trade, he was restored to command and held it until his death at the fort in 1766. Governor Tryon at once recommended Robert Howe for the vacancy and placed him in command, but Abraham Collett received the commission and under Governor Martin took command of the fort. The position was retained by him until the downfall of the royal government.

Twice before 1776 was the wisdom of the colonial leaders in not strengthening the fort justified. When those patriots of the Cape Fear, under the lead of Harnett, Ashe, and Waddell, defied the Governor and the armed power of England and thereby prevented the execution of the Stamp Act, placing themselves high in our roll of honor, Governor Tryon had the mortification of seeing the guns of the fort spiked by Captain Dalrymple, lest they be turned by Waddell and his force against the English war vessels that lay in the harbor. The garrison of the fort, consisting of Captain Dalrymple and two men, then took refuge elsewhere.

In July, 1775, Governor Martin, considering that only about a dozen men composed the garrison, decided that the best policy was to dismount the cannon and place them under the protection of the guns of the *Cruizer,* then lying at anchor in the harbor. He wrote Halifax:

"Fort Johnston, my lord, is a most contemptible thing, fit neither for a place of arms nor an asylum for the friends of the government. On account of the weakness and smallness of it, it is of little consequence, and the King's artillery, which is all that is good about it, will be as well secured under cover of the *Cruizer's* guns, at less charge, as upon the walls of that little wretched place."

The general correctness of this statement is one of the most fortunate circumstances of North Carolina Revolutionary history.

The Wilmington Committee of Safety, already influenced by the deep anger of the people against Captain Collett, whose conduct even Governor Martin considered indefensible, had, in the meantime, decided upon the capture of the fort, and on July 18, the Governor received from John Ashe a notice, signed "The People," which announced the intention of the committee to take possession. That night he took refuge on the *Cruizer,* and the patriots, occupying the fort, set fire to the buildings, and the next day what remained of them was destroyed. With this departure of Martin, royal government in North Carolina ceased. One of the purest and most gifted sons of the Cape Fear has said of this:

"Thus nobly upon the Cape Fear closed the first act of the drama. And when the curtain rose again George by the grace of God, King, was King no longer; but the Constitution reigned, and the free people of North Carolina governed themselves."

After the capture of the fort, it was occupied by patriot troops under Robert Howe. Later in the war, five British regiments encamped on the site, but it played no important part during the Revolution, and the remainder of its history can be briefly told. At the close of the Revolution, the only people living near the fort were a few pilots. The healthfulness of the situation, however, interested a number of residents of Wilmington, and steps were taken for laying off a town. One, situated on the lands of Maj. John Walker, was incorporated, but disappeared simultaneously with its incorporation. But in 1792, an act of the Assembly set up the town of Smithville, naming it in honor of that patriot and philanthropist, Benjamin Smith, who afterwards became governor of North Carolina. And Smithville it remained, a good North Carolina name, preserving in our nomenclature the memory of that public benefactor, until a few years since, when this monument of the past was destroyed and the name of Southport substituted. I trust that I may live to see the day when Smithville shall be restored to North Carolina.

The site of the fort remained the property of North Carolina until 1794, when it was ceded to the United States on condition that a fort should be erected there. The condition was not fulfilled until 1809. Then the Legislature receded the site to the United States.

In 1825 the construction of Fort Caswell was begun, and after its completion Fort Johnston was of less importance. In 1836 the garrison was withdrawn.

Its importance during the War between the States was obscured by the glory of its neighbor, Fort Fisher, and since the war Fort Johnston has been entirely abandoned for Fort Caswell.

It remains, then, a relic of the past. It was the scene of a calm and brave defiance, flung in the teeth of England's power, and it is well to mark the spot and at the same time to dedicate here a monument which shall forever commemorate the valor and patriotism of the men of the Cape Fear.

COLONIAL PLANTATIONS ON THE CAPE FEAR.

In his admirable *History of New Hanover County,* a labor of love for which the accomplished author never received the smallest compensation, the late Col. Alfred Moore Waddell describes sixty-six prominent plantations and their proprietors on the Lower Cape Fear in colonial times. Of the manner of life of these planters, he says in *A Colonial Officer and His Times:*

"In the southern end of the province, at Brunswick and Wilmington, and along the Cape Fear, there were an equally refined and cultivated society and some very remarkable men. No better society existed in America, and it is but simple truth to say that for classical learning, wit, oratory, and varied accomplishments, no generation of their successors has equaled them.

"Their hospitality was boundless and proverbial, and of the manner in which it was enjoyed there can be no counterpart in the present age. Some of them had town residences, but most of them lived on their plantations, and they were not the thriftless characters that by some means it became fashionable to assume all Southern planters were. There was much gaiety and festivity among them, and some of them rode hard to hounds, but as a general rule they looked after their estates, and kept themselves as well informed in regard to what was going on in the world as the limited means of communication allowed. There was little display, but in almost every house could be found valuable plate, and, in some, excellent libraries. The usual mode of travel was on horseback, and in 'gigs,' or 'chairs,' which were vehicles without springs but hung on heavy straps, and to which one horse, and sometimes by young beaux, two horses, tandem, were driven; a mounted servant rode behind, or, if the gig was occupied by ladies, beside the horse. The family coach was mounted by three steps, and had great carved leather springs, with baggage rack behind, and a high, narrow driver's seat and box in front. The gentlemen wore clubbed and powdered queues and knee-breeches, with buckled low-quartered shoes, and many carried gold or silver snuffboxes which, being first tapped, were handed with grave courtesy to their acquaintances when passing the compliments of the day. There are persons still living who remember seeing these things in their early youth. The writer of these lines himself remembers seeing in his childhood the decaying remains of old 'chairs,' and family coaches, and knew at that time several old negroes who had been body servants in their youth to the proprietors of these ancient vehicles. It is no wonder they sometimes drove the coaches four-in-hand. It was not only grand style, but the weight of the vehicle and the character of the roads made it necessary.

"During the period embraced in these pages, four-wheeled pleasure vehicles were rare, and even two-wheeled ones were not common, except among the town nabobs and well-to-do planters. The coaches, or chariots, as a certain class of vehicles was called, were all imported from England, and the possession of such a means of locomotion was evidence of high social position. It was less than twenty years before the period named, that the first stage wagon in the colonies, in 1738, was run from Trenton to New Brunswick, in New Jersey, twice a week, and the advertisement of it assured the public that it would be fitted up with benches and covered over 'so that passengers may sit easy and dry.' "

Some of the prominent Lower Cape Fear men of colonial and Revolutionary days were, Governor Burrington, of Governor's Point; Gen. Robert Howe, of Howe's Point; Nathaniel Moore, of York; Gov. Arthur Dobbs, of Russellboro—all below Orton. "King" Roger Moore, of Orton; James Smith, of Kendal; Eleazar Allen, of Lilliput; John Moore, of Pleasant Oaks; Nathaniel Rice, of Old Town Creek; John Baptista Ashe, of Spring Garden, afterwards called Grovely; Chief Justice Hasell, of Belgrange; Schencking Moore, of Hullfields; John Davis, of Davis Plantation; John Dalrymple (who commanded Fort Johnston), of Dalrymple Place; John Ancrum, of Old Town; Marsden Campbell, of Clarendon; Richard Eagles, of The Forks; Judge Alfred Moore, of Buchoi; John Waddell, of Belville; Gov. Benjamin Smith, of Belvidere. These were all below Wilmington. Many others equally important resided on their plantations above Wilmington. All are recorded in Colonel Waddell's *History of New Hanover County,* but these are mentioned here in support of the statement that the Cape Fear planters of olden time were men of mark.

COLONIAL ORTON.

Many of the old homesteads described by Colonel Waddell have fallen into decay and some of the residences have entirely disappeared, but Orton, on the lower Cape Fear River, still stands as it did in colonial days, when it was the home of "King" Roger Moore, of Gov. Benjamin Smith, of Richard Quince, and in later years of Dr. Fred J. Hill and Col. Kenneth McKenzie Murchison.

It is a majestic domain of more than ten thousand acres, and the house is still regarded by competent critics as one of the finest examples of pure colonial architecture in America.

The lordly residence of Chief Justice Eleazar Allen, upon the adjacent plantation of Lilliput, which was distinguished in his day for a large and liberal hospitality, has long since disappeared, but the grand old oaks which lifted their majestic branches to the soft south breezes in colonial times still sing their murmured requiem above a "boundless contiguity of shade."

Here, upon the banks of our historic river, which stretches two miles to the eastern shore, is heard the booming of the broad Atlantic as it sweeps in its might and majesty from Greenland to the Gulf. Along the shining beach, from Fort Fisher to Fort Caswell, its foaming breakers run and roar, the racing steeds of Neptune, with their white-crested manes, charging and reforming for the never-ending fray.

The adjacent plantation of Kendal, originally owned by "King" Roger Moore, from whom it passed to his descendants, was later the property of James Smith, a brother of Gov. Benjamin Smith, and it was here, near the banks of Orton Creek, which divides this estate from the splendid domain of Orton, that the quarrel between the Smith brothers ended by the departure of James to South Carolina (where, in 1834, his six sons assumed their grandmother's name, Rhett, and became the founders of the famous Rhett family), leaving his intolerant and choleric brother, Benjamin, to a succession of misfortunes, disappointments, and distresses, which brought him at last to a pauper's grave.

Behind Kendal is McKenzie's milldam, the scene of a battle between the British troops and the minute men from Brunswick and Wilmington, when, in 1775, the British fleet lay in the river.

We linger at Orton, the most attractive of all the old colonial estates on the Cape Fear. For a hundred and eighty-nine years it has survived the vicissitudes of war, pestilence, and famine, and it still maintains its reputation of colonial days for a refined and generous hospitality. Here, in the exhilaration of the hunter, the restful seclusion of the angler, the quiet quest of the naturalist, the peaceful contemplation of the student, is found surcease from the vanities and vexations of urban life. For nearly two centuries it has been a haven of rest and recreation to its favored guests.

> "Here, like the hush of evening calm on hearts opprest,
> In silence falls the healing balm of quiet rest,
>   And softly from the shadows deep
>   The grand oaks sing the soul to sleep
> On Nature's breast."

The house, or Hall, built by "King" Roger Moore in 1725, with its stately white pillars gleaming in the sunshine through the surrounding forest, is a most pleasing vista to the passing mariner. The river view, stretching for ten miles southward and eastward, includes "Big Sugar Loaf," Fort Anderson, Fort Buchanan, and Fort Fisher.

We love its traditions and its memories, for no sorrow came

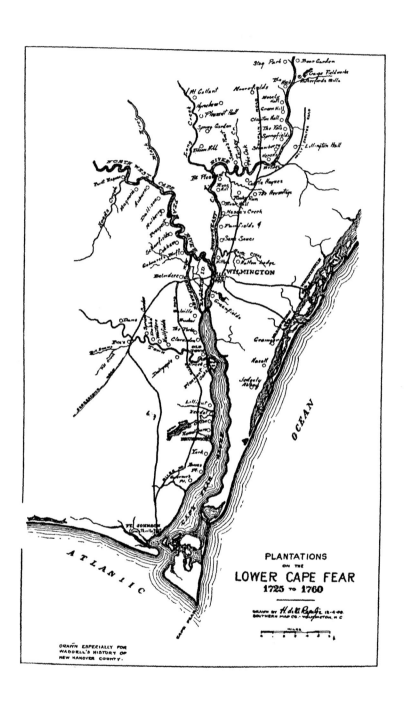

PLANTATIONS
ON THE
LOWER CAPE FEAR
1725 TO 1760

DRAWN BY H. dI M. Rapalje 12-4-09
SOUTHERN MAP CO. WILMINGTON, N.C.

MILES

DRAWN ESPECIALLY FOR
WADDELL'S HISTORY OF
NEW HANOVER COUNTY.

to us there. The primeval forest with its dense undergrowth of dogwood blossoms, which shine with the brightness of the falling snow; the thickets of Cherokee roses, which surpass the most beautiful of other regions; the brilliant carpet of wild azaleas, the golden splendor of the yellow jessamine, the modest *Drosera,* the marvelous *Dionæa muscipula,* and the trumpet *Sarracenia;* the river drive to the white beach, from which are seen the distant breakers; the secluded spot in the wilderness commanding a wide view of an exquisite landscape, where, safe from intrusion, we sat upon a sheltered seat beneath the giant pines and heard the faint "Yo ho" of the sailor, outward bound; a place apart for holy contemplation when the day is far spent, where the overhanging branches cast the shadow of a cross, and where, later, through the interlacing foliage, the star of hope is shining; the joyful reception at the big house, the spacious hall with its ample hearth and blazing oak logs; around it, after the bountiful evening meal, the old songs sung and the old tales told, and fun and frolic to keep dull care beyond the threshold.

Through the quiet lanes of Orton to the ruins of Governor Tryon's palace is half a mile. Here is the cradle of American independence; for upon this spot, until recently hidden by a dense undergrowth of timber, occurred, between six and seven o'clock on the evening of the 19th of February, 1766, the first open resistance to the British Stamp Act in the American colonies, by 450 armed men, who surrounded the palace and demanded the surrender of the custodian of the obnoxious symbols of the King's authority.

Ten minutes' walk farther down brings us to the ruins of the colonial church of St. Philip, the scene of many notable incidents and the resting place of early pioneers. It was built by the citizens of Brunswick, and, principally, by the landed gentry, about 1740. In 1751, Mr. Lewis Henry DeRosset, a member of Gov. Gabriel Johnston's council, and subsequently an expatriated Royalist, introduced a bill appropriating to St. Philip's Church at Brunswick and to St. James's Church at Wilmington, equally, a fund that was realized by the capture and destruction of a pirate vessel, which, in a squadron of Spanish buccaneers, had entered the river and plundered the plantations.

The walls of St. Philip's Church are nearly three feet thick, and are solid and almost intact still, while the roof and floor have disappeared. It must have possessed much architectural beauty and massive grandeur, with its high-pitched roof, its lofty doors, and its beautiful chancel windows.

A little to the west, surrounded by a forest of pines, lies Liberty Pond, a beautiful lake of clear spring water, once stained with the blood of friend and foe in a deadly conflict—hence its traditional name. It is now a most restful, tranquil spot, with its profound stillness, the beach of snow white sand, the unbroken surface of the lake reflecting the foliage and the changing sky-line.

Turning to the southeast, we leave the woodland and reach a bluff upon the river bank, still known as Howe's Point, where the Revolutionary patriot and soldier, Gen. Robert Howe, was born and reared. His residence, long since a ruin, was a large frame building on a stone or brick foundation, still remembered as such by several aged citizens of Brunswick.

A short distance from the Howe place, the writer found some years ago, in the woods and upon a commanding site near the river, under many layers of pine straw, the clearly defined ruins of an ancient fort, which was undoubtedly of colonial origin. Mr. Reynolds, who lived at his place near by, said that his great grandfather informed him forty years ago that long before the War of the Revolution this fort was erected by the colonial government for the protection of the colonists against buccaneers.

Hence to the staid old county seat is a journey of an hour; it was originally known as Fort Johnston. The adjacent hamlet was subsequently called Smithville. In the old courthouse, which is its principal building, may be seen the evidence that on the death, January 17, 1749, of Mr. Allen, aged 57 years, the plantation Lilliput, where he was buried, became the property (and, it is said, the residence for a brief period) of the great grandson of Oliver Cromwell, Sir Thomas Frankland, commanding the frigate *Rose,* who was subsequently Admiral of the White in the British Navy.

In connection with the inscription on Chief Justice Allen's tomb—that he died in January, 1749—it is to be noted that in December, 1749, he was acting as chief justice. At that period the calendar year began and ended in March, so that January, 1749, followed December of that year. The alteration in the calendar was made by act of Parliament in 1751.

ORTON.

A stately mansion girt by God's great woods,
Each clod of earth a friend to me and mine.
Each room a home within the one vast home,
Where naught of all its perfect pomp
Can mar the sweet simplicity and ease of entertainment.
There dwells the warmth of generous hospitality
That counts no act a favor and no gift a sacrifice.
There sordid things and anxious cares come not.
No strangers' words or presence there intrude.
There love of life—clean, wholesome, healthful life—prevails.
And there the peace of God pervades
Each hour of perfect day and night.
One day within its woods,
One night beneath its roof,
To tired body gives a newborn vigor,
To wearied mind a keen creative power,
To the soul a sense of clean, sweet peace,
And to the hour of regretful leaving
A loving and lasting benediction.

Rev. Richard W. Hogue.

CRANE NECK HERON COLONY ON ORTON PLANTATION.

By Rosa Pendleton Chiles.

Stretching for miles through the vast domain of Orton Plantation is a great pond, and in an elected spot above its still waters nests the only colony of egrets remaining in North Carolina today.

For centuries the heron has made its home in the primeval solitude of saltmarsh, untrodden swamp, or silent waters of some hidden pond, where the cypress springs like a sentinel from the deep and spreads its limbs for nesting ground. Bold must be the hunter, though tempted by the glimmer of gold, who, braving mosquitoes and reptiles, threads his way over the trackless morass, paddles his boat along the tortuous meanderings of the smaller water courses, or plunges through the dense growth fringing their banks, following the heron to its nest in pine or cypress. Yet we know only too well some who are fearless enough to make the effort, and the story of their success is written in the tragedy of millions of bird lives and the deeper tragedy of some human lives. Notwithstanding the caution of this noble bird in seeking a home in the well-nigh impenetrable

waste of marsh or cypress-grown water, it has escaped extermination only through the aid of its human friends.

There are twenty heron colonies along the Atlantic coast, but
only three are protected by individuals; the rest are cared for
by the National Association of Audubon Societies. One of these
is the Crane Neck colony, belonging to Mr. James Sprunt, the
present owner of Orton Plantation, and wholly preserved by
him. He who notes the sparrow's fall put into the heart of
Mr. Sprunt a great love for wild creatures, and it is a joy and
satisfaction to him to afford the heron wise enough to seek
refuge at Crane Neck complete protection from the mercenary
and merciless plume-hunter. Here the snowy egret, American
egret, great blue, little blue, black-crowned night, Louisiana,
and green herons nest and chatter of the brooding time in as
great security as others of their kind, peopling, perchance, the
same pond, and mingling their familiar "quock, quock" with
the rippling waters as the first ship sailed up the Cape Fear,
enjoyed more than two hundred and fifty years ago. No doubt
the adventurous explorers, Hilton, Fabian, and Long, witnessed,
as those fortunate enough today may witness, the heron flight
high in the rare air of the purpling dawn, woven into its ravish-
ing cloud-films and vanishing with them.

> "They near, they pass, set sharp against the sky;
>   Grotesques some Orient artist might have drawn
>   Blue on a golden dawn;
> They pass, are gone like leaves blown cloud-high,—
> And oh, my heart is mad to follow where they fly!"

Such may have been the sentiment of the early adventurous
spirit, dreaming of conquest; such seems now the sentiment of
certain heirs of that conquest, dreaming of greed. But the
heron of Crane Neck flies in peace.

This colony was brought to the attention of the ornithological
world in 1898 by Mr. T. Gilbert Pearson, secretary of the
National Association of Audubon Societies, himself a North
Carolinian, and the association, of which Mr. Sprunt is a member, feels unusual satisfaction in the preservation by its owner
of this single egret colony in the State. According to the report
of Mr. Pearson at this time, "the colony contains probably 800
pairs of little blue herons, about the same number of Louisiana
herons, 125 pairs of great blue herons, 40 pairs of American
egrets, 25 pairs of snowy egrets, and probably 20 pairs of black-

crowned night herons, also a few green herons, and now and then a few anhingas."

The curator of the State Museum, Mr. H. H. Brimley, visited the colony in 1913, and reported a somewhat smaller number than Mr. Pearson now estimates, but both have stated that the colony holds its own. Mr. Brimley makes the encouraging statement that "the American egrets have increased in number during the past few years, and that the snowy egrets have at least held their own," and adds, "No evidence of any kind was noted of the plume herons having been 'shot up.'" Concluding, Mr. Brimley says: "The pride taken in this interesting heron colony by its owner, Mr. James Sprunt, of Wilmington, and his interest in the conservation of all wild life, is responsible for its immunity from being 'shot up.' It is widely known, locally, and the means of reaching it are known even to some of the old-time plume-hunters, and to the efforts of Mr. Sprunt in preserving these birds all praise is due." The feeling expressed by Mr. Brimley is the feeling entertained by all bird-lovers, who rejoice that the heron has this safe retreat.

PLANTATIONS ON THE NORTHEAST RIVER.

By Dr. John Hampden Hill.

About forty-one years ago Dr. John Hampden Hill,[1] a prominent Cape Fear planter of Lilliput, a gentleman of culture and refinement, generally respected and admired, wrote some interesting reminiscences of the Lower Cape Fear, and for personal reasons instructed his friend, Mr. DuBrutz Cutlar, to reserve them from publication until after the author's death. Upon my earnest solicitation, however, he permitted me to copy these papers in the year 1892 and to use them in a series of newspaper articles entitled *A Colonial Plantation.* I reproduce them here as worthy of more permanent record.

After this section began to be visited, and settlements made by emigrants from Europe and from the other provinces, amongst the earliest places that attracted attention was Stag Park. It was first located and patented by George Burrington, then governor of the province of North Carolina. This Governor Burrington was a very worthless and profligate character, so much so, that on one occasion being at Edenton, he was pre-

[1]Dr. Hill was born April 28, 1807, at Hyrneham, and died February 19, 1893, at Goldsboro, full of years and the consolations of an honorable Christian life.

sented by the grand jury of Chowan County for riotous and disorderly conduct on the streets, with a party of rowdy companions. Of such material as this did our English rulers make governors for the guardianship of the lives and fortunes of their loyal subjects in these provinces.

Burrington returned to England, and there contracted a debt to a Mr. Strudwick, for which he mortgaged the Stag Park estate of ten thousand acres, and a large body of land which he owned in what was known as The Hawfields, in Orange County. Mr. Strudwick sent his son, Edmund, to look after his property, thus acquired in this country.

The tradition was that this gentleman had fallen into disfavor with his friends on account of having married an actress in the city of London, which was the cause of his coming to settle in America. His residence was divided between Stag Park and The Hawfields. He left a son whom the writer has only heard mentioned as Major Strudwick and as quite an influential citizen of Orange County, where he chiefly resided. He married a Miss Shepperd, of Orange, by which marriage there were several sons and daughters, of whom the late Mr. Samuel Strudwick, of Alabama, was the eldest. This gentleman was a successful planter and acquired a large estate. He was of high intelligence, and remarkable for his fine conversational talent.

Dr. Edmund Strudwick, of Hillsboro, is well known as one of the ablest physicians of the State, and is especially eminent as a surgeon. Betsy, the eldest daughter, married Mr. Paoli Ashe, and was the mother of the Hon. Thomas S. Ashe, one of the associate justices of the Supreme Court of North Carolina, and a gentleman distinguished alike for professional ability and great worth and purity of character.

Stag Park was sold about the year 1817 for division among the heirs, and was purchased by Ezekiel Lane, Esq., for $10,000. This gentleman we will have occasion to mention further on.

The next place, descending the Northeast, is The Neck, the residence of Gov. Samuel Ashe, who, together with his brother, Gen. John Ashe, was amongst the most prominent and influential characters in the Cape Fear region, both before and after the Revolutionary War. Governor Ashe held with distinction the office of judge up to the time he was elected governor. His eldest son, John Baptista Ashe, was also elected governor, but died before he could be inducted into office. There were two other sons of Governor Ashe, Samuel and Thomas. The latter was the grandfather of the present Judge Ashe, already spoken of, and the former will be mentioned further on. There was still another son named Cincinnatus, who, with some other youths of the Cape Fear gentry, volunteered as midshipman on board a privateer, fitted out at Wilmington, and commanded by a Captain Allen, an Englishman. The vessel went to sea, and was supposed to have been sunk by a British ship, or foundered in some other way, as she was never more heard of. The writer remembers when he was a child an old lady, a Mrs. Allen, entirely blind, the widow of the English captain, who lived with the families of the Northeast, first one and then another, with whom she was always a welcome guest, and treated with much respect and consideration.

Below The Neck, and within the precinct known as Rocky Point, was Green Hill, the residence of Gen. John Ashe. This gentleman did more, probably, than any other man in the province towards arousing the spirit of resistance against what was called British oppression. He was the prime mover and leader of the party which resisted the Governor in his attempt to enforce the Stamp Act. And when the War of the Revolution did break out, he raised a regiment at his own expense, so ardently were his feelings enlisted in the cause.

The history of General Ashe's services is, or ought to be, known to the people of the Cape Fear. But it may not be known that he died in obscurity, and the place of his interment can not be pointed out. The story is that on a visit to his family at Green Hill when in feeble health, he was betrayed by a faithless servant to a party of soldiers, sent out from the garrison at Wilmington for his capture. Taken to Wilmington, he was confined in Craig's "bull-pen," as it was called. Here his health became so feeble that he was released on parole, and attempted to get to his family at Hillsboro. But he reached no farther than Sampson Hall, the residence of Col. John Sampson, in the county of that name. Here he died and was buried, and there is neither stone nor mound to mark the spot.

General Ashe left a son who also served in the War of the Revolution—Maj. Samuel Ashe. He was an active politician of the Democrat-Republican party, and represented for many years the county of New Hanover in the Legislature. Of the three daughters of General Ashe, one married Colonel Alston, of South Carolina. Gov. Joseph Alston of South Carolina was her son. Another married Mr. Davis; and the third, Mr. Wil-

5

liam H. Hill. The last was the mother of Mr. Joseph Alston Hill, the most talented man of the family, with the most brilliant promise of distinction when he died at the age of thirty-six. This Green Hill property is now owned by the estate of the late Maj. John Walker.

The Ashe family in early times after the Revolution differed in politics with the generality of the Cape Fear gentry. The Governor and his sons, with the exception of Col. Samuel Ashe, were leaders of the Republican or Jeffersonian faction, whereas the large majority of the gentry and educated class were Federalists of the Hamilton school. After the adoption of the Federal Constitution and a republican form of government was established, there is no doubt but that a good deal of feeling and prejudice existed against what was called too much liberty and equality, and the practice of some of the old Republicans was not always consistent with their professed principles.

The next place of note, and adjoining Green Hill to the north, was Moseley Hall, the residence of the Moseley family, one of prominence in colonial times. One of them, Sampson Moseley, Esq., was a member of the King's council and surveyor-general of the province, but the writer does not know that any of the male members of the family survived the Revolution, or that any of their descendants whatever are left. They were nearly allied by blood to the Lillingtons. One of the daughters of the family married a Mr. Carlton Walker, and left one son, John Moseley Walker, who died soon after coming of age, and the estate passed to his half-brothers and sisters. This was a large and quite valuable place and was said to have been handsomely improved, but all that the writer remembers seeing were the remains of what were said to have been fine old avenues.

Crossing Clayton Creek, we come to the next place below, known in olden times as Clayton Hall, the residence of a Mr. Clayton, a Scotch gentleman, who died leaving no descendants, though I believe the Restons of Wilmington were his nearest kin. This property, which was at one time regarded as the best plantation in New Hanover County, was purchased by Col. Samuel Ashe. Colonel Ashe, when I knew him, was about the only survivor of the olden times on the Northeast River. He had been a soldier in the War of the Revolution, had entered the army when he was but seventeen years old and served through the last three years of the war, was at the siege of Charleston, and was there made prisoner. Colonel Ashe was a gentleman of commanding appearance, tall and erect, with prominent features, deep-sunken, but piercing eyes, of fine manners and bearing, of remarkable colloquial powers, and manner and style of narration most engaging. Especially was his fund of anecdotes and incidents relating to the olden times most interesting, and seemed almost inexhaustible. Of him Mr. George Davis, in his address at Chapel Hill in 1855, spoke as follows: "In my early youth I remember an old man, bowed by age and infirmities, but of noble front and most commanding presence. Old and young gathered around him in love and veneration to listen to his stories of the olden times. And as he spoke of his country's trials, and of the deeds and sufferings of her sons, his eyes flashed with the ardor of youth, and his voice rang like the battle charge of a bugle. He was the soul of truth and honor, with the ripe wisdom of a man and the guileless simplicity of a child. He won strangers to him with a look, and those who knew him loved him with a most filial affection. None ever lived more honored and revered. None ever died leaving a purer or more cherished memory. This was Col. Samuel Ashe, 'the last of all the Romans.' "

The old Clayton Hall mansion, left for a long time untenanted, went to decay, and there was nothing left of it when the writer can remember but the foundation. He can remember an old vault, which stood to the north of the creek, in which it is said the remains of Mr. Clayton rested. After Colonel Ashe came in possession of the place, he built immediately on the bank of the creek, so that you could stand on one end of his piazza and fish. The spring out of which they got their drinking water flowed from the base of a rock, which formed the bank of the creek, and when the tide was up, the spring was overflowed.

It was a great treat to visit the old colonel and hear him talk of olden times. His memory was remarkable and his style of narration uncommonly good.

He seemed familiar with the genealogy of every family that had ever lived on the Cape Fear, and their traditions. It is much to be regretted that some one who had the capacity could not have chronicled his narratives as they were related by himself.

Colonel Ashe removed from Rocky Point when he was well advanced in years to a place which he owned on the Cape Fear, in the neighborhood of Fayetteville, where he lived several years. His only male descendant of the name in the State, I believe, is Capt. Samuel A. Ashe, of Raleigh.

Colonel Ashe, on his removal, sold the Clayton Hall estate to Dr. James F. McRee, who retired from the practice of medicine in Wilmington and made his residence here, where he carried on planting operations with fair success. He abandoned the old settlement, and built on what was known as the Sand Ridge, and renamed the place, calling it Ashe-Moore, in compliment to the two families so long known and distinguished in the Cape Fear region. Dr. McRee had acquired a higher reputation than any other physician of his day in the Lower Cape Fear, or even in the whole State. The writer enjoyed the privilege of being his pupil, and of his long friendship, and to speak of him in such terms as he esteemed him, as a noble gentleman and physician, might seem like extravagant eulogy.

The next place on the river is The Vats. Here the river changes its course, making a sharp, sudden bend, and a prominent point of rocks jutting into the stream gives the name of Rocky Point to all that portion of country lying west, as far as the Wilmington & Weldon Railroad. This place was first located by Maj. Maurice Moore, one of the earliest pioneers of the Cape Fear section. It is related that Major Moore and Governor Burrington, both of them exploring in search of rich lands, happened to reach this point about the same time. As they stepped on shore from their boats, both claimed possession by right of prior location and occupation. But the colonel stoutly resisted His Excellency's pretensions, and by dint of strong will held the property. The arbitrary disposition exhibited on this occasion rather strikingly illustrates what is said to have been characteristic of the Moore family, especially that branch of it. The lands of this place were very rich, and it continued in the Moore family for several generations. It was finally sold by Judge Alfred Moore to Mr. Ezekiel Lane, a most worthy gentleman, who here laid the foundation of quite a large estate, acquired by farming alone. Commencing with small means, he became the largest landowner in the county of New Hanover, his estate being mostly composed of those Rocky Point lands.

The next two places, adjoining and to the south of The Vats, were Spring Field and Strawberry, owned by Mr. Levin Lane, a son of Mr. E. Lane, a planter like his father, and a most worthy and highly respectable gentleman. Mr. Lane resided at Strawberry.

Let us return to The Vats and cross the river by the ferry

there. Traveling eastward by the New Bern Road about four miles, we come to Lillington Hall, the residence of Gen. Alexander Lillington.[1] It would seem like a singular selection for a gentleman to make for a residence, just on the border of the Great Holly Shelter pocosin or dismal, and quite remote from the other gentry settlements. But in those days stock raising was much attended to, and here immense tracts of unoccupied lands furnished rich pasturage and fine range.

General Lillington was nearly allied to the Moseleys, of Moseley Hall, and came to reside on the Cape Fear about the same time with them. He was an ardent Whig and patriot, and taking up arms early in the Revolution, he soon distinguished himself as a bold and sagacious leader. On the attempt of the Scotch settlers about Cross Creek to move on Wilmington for the purpose of coöperating with the British force intended to invade and subjugate North Carolina, General Lillington speedily organized the militia of New Hanover and Duplin Counties and marched rapidly in the direction from which the enemy approached. Selecting a position at Moore's Creek where it was crossed by a ridge, he threw up intrenchments and awaited the approach of the Scots. On the arrival of General Caswell, the superior in command, he approved of Lillington's plans and arrangements for meeting the enemy. The result of the battle which ensued is well known to history, and its success was, by his contemporaries, mainly attributed to Lillington's prompt movement and skillful arrangements.

The Lillington Hall mansion was a quaint old structure of ante-Revolutionary date, and standing alone; there was no house that approached it in size or appearance in that wild region. When the writer visited there while a youth there was quite a library of rare old English books which would be highly prized at this day. At that time it was owned and occupied by Mr. Samuel Black, a highly respectable and worthy gentleman, who had married the widow of Mr. George Lillington, the youngest son of the colonel. This place, like all the residences of the early gentry, has gone out of the family and into stranger hands.

As there is no other place of note on the east side of the river, we will recross the ferry at The Vats, and following the road

---

[1]General Lillington married a daughter of Mr. William Watters, one of the most esteemed planters of Brunswick. The Watters family in every generation has been most highly regarded for its worth and excellence. Mrs. Lillington is said to have been on the field with her husband at the Battle of Moore's Creek.

leading west to where it crosses the main county road, come to Moore Fields. This was the residence of George Moore, Esq., one of the most prominent gentlemen of his day, both before and after the Revolution. I remember the old mansion as it stood, but much dilapidated. Not a vestige of it is left now. There had been raised near the house two mounds for rabbit-warrens, and near by was a fishpond. Mr. Moore was the father of a numerous progeny. He was twice married. His first wife was a Miss Mary Ashe, a sister, I believe, of Governor Ashe; the second was a Miss Jones. There is extant an old copy of the Church of England Prayer-book in the possession of one of his descendants (Dr. William H. Moore) in which are recorded the births and names of his children by these marriages, and there were twenty-seven. From these or the survivors, for many of them must have died during infancy, have sprung many of the families of the Cape Fear region, some of whose descendants are still living there, among whom can be mentioned the Hon. George Davis, who has no superior, if any equal, here or in any other part of the State. Also, the Hon. Thomas S. Ashe is one of the lineal descendants of this old stock. There was one of the granddaughters, Miss Sallie Moore, who was reputed to be the greatest beauty of her day. Her father, William Moore, removed to the State of Tennessee, where she was heard of still living a few years since.

George Moore of Moore Fields, as he was familiarly called, was remarkable for his great energy and good management; a man of considerable wealth, owning many slaves. He had a summer residence on the sound, to reach which he crossed the Northeast River at The Vats ferry; and from a mile or two to the east of it, he had made a perfectly straight road, ditched on each side, twenty miles in length. This road, though no longer used, can still be traced. It is related that when corn was wanted at the summer place, one hundred negro fellows would be started, each with a bushel bag on his head. There is quite a deep ditch leading from some large bay swamps lying to the west of the county road. It used to be called the Devil's Ditch, and there was some mystery and idle tradition as to why and how the ditch was cut there. It was doubtless made to drain the water from those bays, to flood some lands cultivated in rice which were too low to be drained for corn.

We will now pass down the old Swann Point Avenue to the county road, and, traveling west, soon reach and cross Turkey

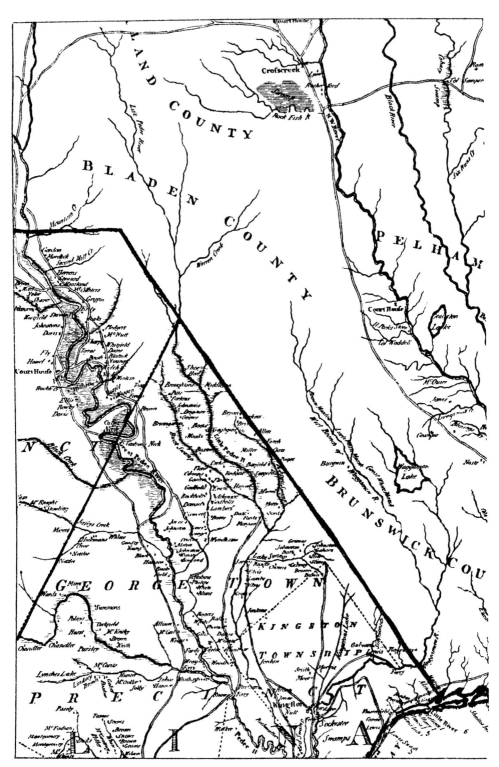

THIS MAP IS INACCURATE IN SOME RESPECTS.   PELHAM WAS ONCE PROPOSED
AS THE NAME OF A NEW COUNTY, BUT EVENTUALLY WHEN THE
COUNTY WAS CREATED IT WAS CALLED SAMPSON

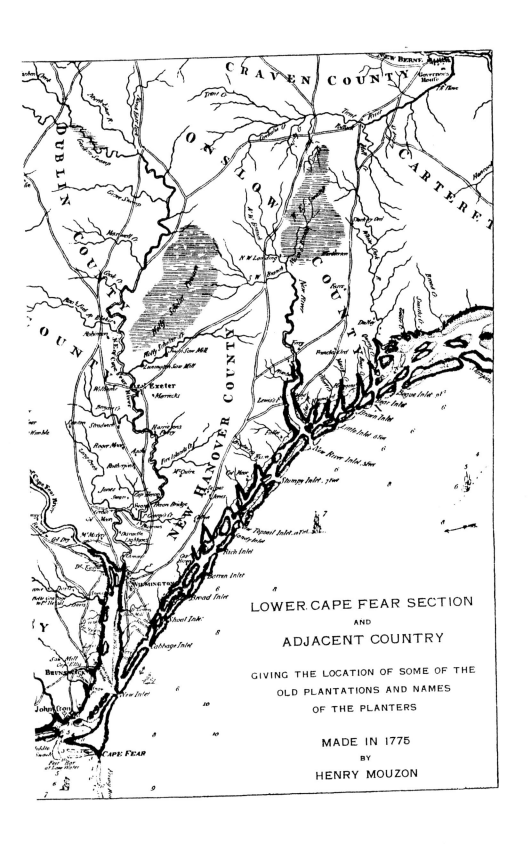

LOWER CAPE FEAR SECTION

AND

ADJACENT COUNTRY

GIVING THE LOCATION OF SOME OF THE
OLD PLANTATIONS AND NAMES
OF THE PLANTERS

MADE IN 1775

BY

HENRY MOUZON

Creek, and come to that famous old plantation, Spring Garden, the residence of Frederick Jones, Esq., noted in his day as being the most industrious and successful farmer in all the country round. Mr. Jones was a Virginian, induced to settle on the Cape Fear by Mr. Swann, whose niece he had married. Besides the son, who assumed the name of Swann, there were five daughters, one of whom married Mr. John Hill, of Fair Fields. She was the mother of the late Dr. Frederick J. and John Hill. Another married Michael Sampson, Esq., of Sampson Hall. The remaining three daughters married three brothers, Scotch gentlemen, by the name of Cutlar. Only one of these left children, Dr. Roger Cutlar, who was the father of the late Dr. Frederick J. Cutlar, of Wilmington, eminent in his profession and beloved for his purity of character. From this good old Spring Garden stock, comes also the writer's best esteemed and most worthy friend, DuBrutz Cutlar, Esq.[1]

We will now retrace our steps across Turkey Creek. Passing over the river at The Oaks and going through what was called Legare's Neck, we come to Castle Haynes. Legare's, a deep neck formed by the river on one side and Prince George's Creek on the other, was widely known as a favorite resort for deer and a famous hunting ground. Castle Haynes was the residence of a Mr. Haynes, of whose history the writer has heard but little, except that he was the ancestor of the Waddell family, among whom I have heard related the tradition of his sad death by drowning. It is said that he was ill of a fever and, while in delirium, he rose from his bed and rushed to the creek, which was near by, plunged in, and was drowned before assistance could reach him.

This Mr. Haynes married a daughter of Rev. Richard Marsden, who prior to 1736 served long as a minister on the Cape Fear, and left two daughters: Margaret, who married Mr.

---

[1]Besides the plantations here mentioned in this paper, near the lower Ferry were Mulberry and The Oaks, the latter being the residence of Mr. Swann. Mulberry was the headquarters of General Lillington while hemming in the British forces that occupied Wilmington. And where the railroad crosses the county road, one mile south of Rocky Point station, was Hyrneham, built by Colonel Hyrne, and famous in the early days of the settlement. Later, it was the birthplace of Dr. Hill. Hyrneham, like The Oaks, was built of brick, the walls nearly three feet thick. They were commodious and handsome residences. Farther west were Mt. Gallant, the home of Col. John Pugh Williams; Pleasant Hall, William Davis' residence, and Swann Point, where the old councilor John Swann lived. The river was crossed by Heron Bridge, and on the south side was Mt. Blake, the residence of the McKenzies. Being occupied by Major Craig, it was burned by General Lillington in 1781.

George Burgwyn, and Mary, who became the wife of Col. Hugh Waddell, from which union sprang the Waddell family, so long and honorably known on the Cape Fear.

Turning east from Castle Haynes and crossing the county road, we come to The Hermitage, the residence of the Burgwyn family. The founder of this family was Mr. John Burgwyn, an English gentleman, in olden times an opulent merchant, who carried on an extensive commerce between Wilmington and Bristol in England. He must have had fine taste, as displayed by the manner in which the grounds around The Hermitage were laid off and improved. Its fine avenues and handsomely arranged pleasure-grounds surpassed everything in the whole country round. Mr. George Burgwyn, who occupied The Hermitage after his father's death, was also a gentleman of good taste, and devoted much attention to the decoration of the place, keeping it in handsome condition.

Mr. George Burgwyn reared a numerous and highly respectable family. His oldest son, Capt. John Burgwyn, of the United States Army, was killed in battle in the Mexican War, and his grandson, Gen. George B. Anderson, died of a wound received at the Battle of Antietam.

We will turn now westward and, crossing the county road at a short distance, come to Rocky Run, where lived Dr. Nathaniel Hill. In earlier times this place was the residence of Mr. Maurice Jones, whose daughter Dr. Hill married. Of the history of this gentleman, Mr. Jones, the writer never heard much. But a tradition worth relating will illustrate his firmness and remarkable self-possession and presence of mind. He was a great woodsman, and in the habit of still-hunting. On one occasion he was creeping to shoot a deer, which was feeding at a dog-wood tree. When, feeling that something was dragging at one of his legs, he turned his head and saw that it was a large rattle-snake, which had struck and fastened its fangs in the buckskin leggings that all huntsmen wore at that day, he deliberately crawled on, dragging the snake as he went. Getting within proper range, he fired and killed the deer, then, turning, killed the snake.

Dr. Nathaniel Hill was sent to Scotland when he was quite young, where he was placed with an apothecary. Having completed a full term at this business, he entered the medical college at Edinburgh, where he remained until he had completed his medical course. Returning home before he was quite of age, he entered actively upon the practice of his profession at Wilmington. Full of energy and earnestness, with remarkable sagacity and decision, he very soon acquired the confidence of the community. His reputation was established and not surpassed in the whole Cape Fear region.

After a laborious and lucrative practice of twenty-five years, Dr. Hill retired with an independent estate to Rocky Run, where he had built a comfortable and commodious house. Here, before the prime of his life was over and in the full vigor of manhood, he took up his abode and for many years dispensed a liberal hospitality to a large circle of friends and relatives.

On the first day of January of each year, that being Dr. Hill's birthday, a numerous party of friends and relatives always assembled at Rocky Run to celebrate the event with feasting and good cheer. Then it was that those fine deer hunts came off, which were so skillfully conducted that they were invariably successful. The standers were judiciously placed, and the bringing down of the game depended on their skill as marksmen. In the management of these hunts, the guests, whether old or young, were invariably placed at the best stands, the doctor taking the chances as they might arrive for himself. He always carried a long flint-and-steel single-barrel silver-mounted gun, and it was not often that he failed to bring down the deer coming fairly by him within one hundred yards. Many a day of sport has the writer enjoyed with this noble old gentleman at his fine old seat. Most systematic and punctual in his habits, invariably as we rose from the breakfast table (8 o'clock in winter) the driver was waiting with horses and dogs, eager for the drive, and as punctually we returned by 2 o'clock, the dinner hour, as the family were never kept waiting.

The old Rocky Run mansion was destroyed by fire many years since, and the place has shared the fate of all others on the Northeast and fallen into stranger hands.

The next two places below on the river were Rose Hill, the residence of the Quince family, and Rock Hill, of the Davises, two rather inconsiderable and inferior rice plantations. The Quinces were among the earliest of the gentry settlers on the Cape Fear. I have heard an old story related about a Mr. Parker Quince, somewhat characteristic, I presume, of himself and his times. It seems that he was a merchant and quite a trafficker. In sending an order for goods on one occasion to London (from whence most all importations were made) a dozen cheeses were included and several gross of black tacks. Instead of the cheeses, they sent a dozen English chaises, and for the tacks there was sent an immense number of black jacks, as they were called, a kind of japanned-tin drinking mug; his correspondent apologizing for not completing the order as to the cups, as he had bought up all that could be found in the shops of London. Mr. Quince either spelled badly or wrote illegibly, probably a little of both.

There was one of the Quinces, who, for some family reason or other, adopted the name of Hasell—William Soranzo Hasell.[1] He was much esteemed and the intimate friend of many of the gentlemen of his day. When party politics ran high between the old Federalists and Republicans he edited a paper called *The Minerva,* advocating the principles of the Federal party, and was well sustained and caressed by his friends. He must have been a man of fine literary taste, judging from the number of old volumes of the best English literature with his name and coat of arms inscribed on them, which I have come across in the old libraries.

Rock Hill was handsomely located on a bluff commanding a fine view of the river. It was in olden times the residence of Mr. Jehu Davis, and more lately of Mr. Thomas J. Davis, his son. The name of Davis, both in early and later times on the Cape Fear, has always been associated with all that was highly respectable and honorable, and it has been most eminently sustained in the person of Hon. George Davis, of Wilmington, and the late Bishop Davis, of South Carolina.

Proceeding farther down, but not immediately on the river, was once a place known as Nesces Creek, on a creek of that name, which before the Revolution was the residence of Arthur Mabson, Esq., a gentleman noted for his great energy and industry, by which he had accumulated a considerable estate, but he died the first year of the war, at the early age of forty. This place was long ago abandoned, and I do not suppose there is a vestige of its improvements left.

Crossing Nesces Creek and going a mile or so farther on, we come to where once stood Fair Fields, also gone totally to ruin. Here lived Mr. John Hill, a gentleman of note in his day, frequently representing the county in the Legislature. He had been a soldier in the Revolution, entered the army while quite

---

[1] He took the name of his mother, who was Susannah Hasell, a granddaughter of Chief Justice Hasell.

young, and served with General Greene in his southern campaigns.

Passing on, we come to Sans Souci. Of the early history of this place the writer knows nothing. For many years past it has been the residence of the late Mr. Arthur J. Hill.

Crossing Smith's Creek, we come to Hilton. This was the residence of Cornelius Harnett, Esq., and the old mansion was erected by him. It is not surprising that this point should have attracted the admiration of those who first selected it and built upon it. A fine bluff, near the junction of Smith's Creek with the river, it has a commanding and extensive view up and down the stream. Although much out of repair and the grounds mutilated by the deep cut of a railroad passing through them, it is still the most attractive spot near the city of Wilmington.

Cornelius Harnett was about the most noted and conspicuous personage of his day in the whole Cape Fear region. No man more entirely commanded the confidence and admiration of the community in which he lived.

Either on account of feeble health or advanced life, Mr. Harnett was not an active participant as a soldier in the War of the Revolution; both heart and means were nevertheless enlisted in the cause, and after Wilmington was occupied by the British, he was wrested from a sick bed and confined in their prison, where he died in consequence of their harsh and brutal treatment.

Mr. Harnett, I believe, left no descendants, and in after times Hilton became the property and the residence of William H. Hill, Esq. This gentleman was said to have possessed fine qualities of both head and heart. Genial of temper and fond of conviviality, he attracted many friends around him, and was always the life of his company. He was a leading spirit among the gentlemen of the Federal party, when politics ran high, and represented the Wilmington district in Congress during the administration of the elder Adams.

SOCIAL CONDITIONS.

In McRee's valuable *Life and Correspondence of James Ire-dell,* that gifted Wilmingtonian says:

"Mr. Hooper was nine year Mr. Iredell's senior, and already a man of mark at the bar and in the Assembly. To estimate at its full value his deference to Iredell, these facts must be borne in mind. Mr. Hooper was a native of Boston, and a graduate of Cambridge, Mass. After studying law with James Otis, he removed to North Carolina, in 1764. He became a citizen of Wilmington. That town and its vicinity was noted for its un-bounded hospitality and the elegance of its society. Men of rare talents, fortune, and attainment, united to render it the home of politeness, and ease, and enjoyment. Though the foot-print of the Indian had, as yet, scarcely been effaced, the higher civilization of the Old World had been transplanted there, and had taken vigorous root. There were Col. John Ashe (subse-quently General Ashe), the great popular leader, whose address was consummate, and whose quickness of apprehension seemed intuition, the very Rupert of debate; Samuel Ashe, of stalwart frame, endowed with practical good sense, a profound knowl-edge of human nature, and an energy that eventually raised him to the bench and the post of governor; Harnett, afterwards president of the Provincial Council, 'who could boast a genius for music and a taste for letters,' the representative man of the Cape Fear; Dr. John Eustace, the correspondent of Sterne, 'who united wit, and genius, and learning, and science'; Col. Thomas Boyd 'gifted with talents, and adorned with classical literature'; Howe (afterwards General Howe), 'whose imagination fasci-nated, whose repartee overpowered, and whose conversation was enlivened by strains of exquisite raillery'; Dr. John Fergus, of stately presence, with velvet coat, cocked hat, and gold-headed cane, a graduate of Edinburgh, and an excellent Latin and Greek scholar; William Pennington, comptroller of the customs and afterwards master of the ceremonies at Bath, 'an elegant writer, admired for his wit, and his highly polished urbanity'; Judge Maurice Moore, of 'versatile talents, and possessed of extensive information, as a wit, always prompt in reply; as an orator, always daring the mercy of chance'; Maclaine, irascible, but intellectual, who trod the path of honor early *pari passu* with Iredell, Hooper, and Johnston, and 'whose criticisms on

Shakespeare would, if they were published, give him fame and rank in the republic of letters'; William Hill, 'a most sensible, polite gentleman, and though a Crown officer, replete with sentiments of general liberty, and warmly attached to the cause of American freedom'; Lillington, destined soon at Moore's Creek to render his name historic; James Moore, subsequently appointed a brigadier general, whose promises of a brilliant career were soon to be terminated by a premature death; Lewis Henry DeRosset, member of the Council, a cultivated and elegant gentleman; Adam Boyd, editor of the *Cape Fear Mercury* (subsequently chaplain to the Continental Line), 'who, without pretensions to wit or humor, possessed the rare art of telling a story with spirit and grace, and whose elegiac numbers afforded a striking contrast to the vivid brilliancy of the scenes in which he figured'; Alfred Moore, subsequently an associate justice of the Supreme Court of the United States; Timothy Bloodworth, stigmatized by his enemies as an impracticable radical, 'everything by turns,' but withal a true exponent of the instincts and prejudices, the finest feelings and the noblest impulses of the masses. These were no ordinary men. They were of the remarkable class that seem ever to be the product of crises in human affairs. Though inferior to many of them in the influence that attends years, opulence, and extensive connections, yet in scholarship and genius, Mr. Hooper was preëminent. I use the word genius in contradistinction to talent. He had much nervous irritability, was imaginative and susceptible. With a well-disciplined mind, and of studious habits, he shone with lustre whenever he pleased to exert himself.''

To the above we add the name of Lieut. Thomas Godfrey, who, having served in the war against the French at the North in the Pennsylvania forces, moved from Philadelphia and settled in Wilmington. He possessed the creative faculty in an eminent degree and many of his poems have remarkable beauty. The writer has been fortunate enough to secure a copy of his poetical works, prefaced by some account of the author and his writings. This volume was published in Philadelphia in 1765 and contains about two hundred and fifty pages. Its publication could only be made by subscription, and of the two hundred and sixty subscribers it is gratifying to observe that twenty-four were North Carolinians. Their names are given as follows: William Bartram, jr., James Bailey, William Campbell, Alexander Chapman, Robert Cochran, William

Davis, Col. Caleb Grainger, Benjamin Heron, Alexander Duncan, Walter DuBois, Cornelius Harnett, Obediah Holt, Robert Johnson, Col. James Moore, Archibald Maclaine, Archibald McDuffie, Alexander Martin, Mrs. Anne Nissfield, William Purviance, John Robeson, Robert Schaw, Patrick Stewart, James Stewart, and William Watkins. Nearly all of these names are familiar to us, and it is apparent that the poet was appreciated during his life in Wilmington and numbered among his friends men of the first consequence in our community, doubtless having congenial associations with Harnett, Maclaine, Moore, and others of like distinction.

The rare old volume, yellowed by age and procured only after years of search, says: "Mr. Thomas Godfrey, the Author of the following Poems, was born in Philadelphia, in the year 1736. His Father, who was of the same name, was a Glazier by trade, and likewise a Citizen of Philadelphia—a person whose great natural capacity for Mathematics has occasioned his name to be known in the learned world, being (as has been heretofore shown by undeniable evidences) the original and real inventor of the very useful and famous Sea-Quadrant, which has been called Hadley's. He died when his son was very young and left him to the care of his Relations, by whom he was placed to an English school, and there received 'a common education in his mother tongue'; and without any other advantage than that, a natural genius, and an attentive perusal of the works of our English Poets, he soon exhibited to the world the strongest proofs of poetical capacity."

Besides his talent for poetry, he is said to have possessed a fine ear for music and a strong inclination towards painting, desiring to have lessons in the latter; but his relatives had other plans, and his biographer, continuing, says: "He was put to a watch-maker in this city, but still the muses and graces, poetry and painting stole his attention. He devoted therefore all his private hours to the cultivation of his parts, and towards the expiration of his time he composed those performances that were published with so much favorable notice."

At length he quitted the business of watch-making and got himself recommended for a lieutenant's commission in the Pennsylvania forces, raised in the year 1758, for the expedition against Fort DuQuesne, in which station he continued until the campaign was over and the provincial troops disbanded.

The succeeding spring he had an offer made him of settling as a factor in North Carolina, and, being unemployed, he accepted the proposal and presently embarked for Wilmington, where he lived more than three years. In Wilmington he completed the dramatic poem the *Prince of Parthia,* as appears by a letter dated November 17, 1759. "By the last vessel from this place," says Godfrey in this letter, "I sent you the copy of a Tragedy I finished here, and desired your interest in bringing it on the stage. I have not yet heard of the vessel's arrival, and believe, if she is safe, it will be too late for the Company now at Philadelphia." He was but twenty-two years of age when this drama was completed.

On the death of his employer, Godfrey left North Carolina and returned to Philadelphia; but finding no advantageous opening there he determined to make another voyage abroad, and procuring some small commissions went as a supercargo to the island of New Providence, where he was for some months. From New Providence, led as it were by some sad fatality, he sailed once more to Wilmington, North Carolina, "where, a few weeks after his arrival," says his biographer, "he was unexpectedly summoned to pay the debt of nature, and death put a stop to his earthly wanderings by hurrying him off this shadowy state into boundless eternity. He happened one very hot day to take a ride into the country, and not being accustomed to this exercise and of a corpulent habit of body, it is imagined that the heat overcame him, for the night following he was seized with a violent vomiting and malignant fever, which continued seven or eight days, and at 10 o'clock a. m., on the third of August, 1763, put a period to his life in the twenty-seventh year of his age.

"Thus hastily was snatched off in the prime of manhood this promising genius, beloved and lamented by all who knew him. His sweet, amiable disposition, his integrity of heart, his engaging modesty and diffidence of manners, his fervent and disinterested love for his friends endeared him to all those who shared his acquaintance. and have stamped the image of him in indelible characters on the hearts of his more intimate friends." He was interred in the burial ground attached to St. James's Church in Wilmington and a tombstone marks the spot.

McRee, referring to him in his *Imperfect Sketch of the History of the Town of Wilmington,* published in the *Wilmington Chronicle* of September 16, 1846, says: "He wrote several

pieces descriptive of the vicinity where he dwelt.   One was on
Masonboro Sound, and possessed great beauty, being remarkable
for its felicity of diction and thought and its graphic excellence.
"The verses of this poet," he adds, "were once greatly in vogue
in the neighborhood in which he selected a home and found
friends warm and steady; and there were but few gentlemen
who could not repeat from memory some passages from his pen."

His works were first published by the *American Magazine,*
and later some were copied in the English magazines.   His
American publishers gave the highest praise to his efforts and
were also much interested in proclaiming his father's genius.
"Nature," say they, "seems not to have designed the father for
a greater mathematician than the son for a poet."   In publishing his *Court of Fancy* in 1762, they say: "What shall place
him high in the lists of poets is a poem of considerable length
called the *Court of Fancy,* in managing which he shines in all
the spirit of true creative poetry."

His last publication, *The Victory,* which is designated as a
"nervous and noble song of triumph," appeared in the *Pennsylvania Gazette* in 1763.   The *Prince of Parthia* is regarded as
the first attempt in America at dramatic composition, and is
spoken of as "no inconsiderable effort towards one of the sublimest species of poetry, and no mean instance of the author's
strong inherited genius."   Of his published writings his biographer says: "Upon the whole, I persuade myself that the
severest critic, looking over smaller matters, will allow these
writings of Mr. Godfrey to be aptly characterized in the following lines from the *Court of Fancy:*

> 'Bold Fancy's hand th' amazing pile uprears,
> In every part stupendous skill appears;
> In beautiful disorder, yet complete,
> The structure shines irregularly great.' "

LIBRARIES ON THE CAPE FEAR.

It is to be much regretted that so few memorials of the social
and intellectual life of the old Cape Fear people have been preserved.   They enjoyed the elegance that attends wealth and
they possessed libraries that bespeak culture.

When Edward Moseley was passing through Charleston in
1703, he was employed to make a catalogue of the library books
there; and, on locating in Albemarle, he at once began the col-

lection of a library. Later, he presented a library to the town of Edenton. When, about 1735, he removed to Rocky Point and built Moseley Hall, he brought his library with him.

But perhaps superior to Moseley's was the library of Eleazar Allen, at Lilliput. The inventory of this collection of books has been preserved. Made at his death, about 1749, it shows over three hundred volumes in English and Latin, including the standard works of that era—the classics, poetry, history, works of fiction, as well as works of a religious nature; and, besides, some fifty in French, not only histories, travels, poetry, and fiction, but also French translations of the most celebrated Latin authors. One finds in that atmosphere a culture unsurpassed elsewhere in America.

The Hasells likewise had a good library; also Judge Maurice Moore; and Gen. John Ashe had one he prized so highly that he made special efforts to preserve it, but unfortunately it was destroyed during the last year of the Revolutionary War.

While there were libraries at the homes of the gentlemen in the country, at Wilmington there was the Cape Fear Library, one volume of which, at least, has been preserved—a volume of Shakespeare, with notes made by Archibald Maclaine, of Wilmington, a nephew of the historian Mosher, which are of unusual merit. Many of the Rocky Point books appear to have been collected at Lillington Hall, and others have been preserved in the Hasell collection. A part of the Hasell collection, embracing books of Moseley printed before 1700, of Alexander Lillington, and of others, has been placed in the State Library at Raleigh.

COLONIAL GOVERNORS OF NORTH CAROLINA.

(Extracts from an address delivered by Mr. John Jay Blair before the North Carolina Society of Colonial Dames at Brunswick, N. C.)

I have selected for my subject the governors who resided here on the Cape Fear, with a view to the formulating of a connected story of their respective administrations, together with a reference to events in the province which are of sufficient importance to have any bearing upon its life.

On the 25th of February, 1731, Burrington, who had just arrived in the colony, took the oath of office before the Council, assembled at Edenton.

Probably the fairest estimate of Burrington is that given by

William Saunders in his prefatory notes to the third volume of the *Colonial Records:* "Historians have fallen into grave errors in regard to Governor Burrington. They go on to state, but upon what evidence is not known, that he ended his life after rioting in his usual manner all night in the Bird Cage Walk in the corner of St. James's Park in London; and the impression is created that his disgraceful death occurred soon after his return to London. The statement is certainly untrue in several material points. Precisely when he returned to England does not appear, but from an entry in the journal of the Board of Trade it is shown that he was there on the 10th of June, 1735. Other entries and communications show that he was in frequent communication from that time until December, 1736, after which no reference is made to him."

That he was a man of violent temper, of a contentious disposition, overbearing and domineering towards his subordinates is sustained without question by the historical records of the times. It is known that he was ordered to appear before the court and that three distinct warrants for his arrest were issued. The papers, however, were never served, an entry having been made on the court record that the indictment was quashed. It is said that he escaped from the colony on a pretext of visiting South Carolina, but sailed for England immediately upon reaching Charleston.

What, then, in view of all the conflicting statements, is the real character of Burrington?

1. Previously he had been governor of the province under the Lords Proprietors, his reappointment serving as undoubted evidence of his ability.

2. His official papers are well written and show an intimate knowledge of the country and of measures best adapted to promote its development.

3. He is known to have been a scientist of considerable ability, having made a study of the animal and vegetable life of the Cape Fear.

4. Considerable attention was given by him to making soundings and surveying rivers and harbors in the interest of navigation.

At this point an extract from some of his letters can be introduced with propriety: "North Carolina was little known or mentioned before I was governor for the Proprietors (1725). When I first came I found the inhabitants few and poor. I took all methods I thought would induce people from other countries to settle themselves in this. Perfecting a settlement on the Cape Fear River cost me a great sum of money and infinite trouble. I endured, the first winter I spent there, all the hardships that could happen to a man destitute of a house to live in; that was above a hundred miles from a neighbor in a pathless country and was obliged to have all provisions brought by sea at a great expense to support the number of men I carried there, paid, and maintained at my sole expense.

"It can hardly be imagined what pains I took sounding the inlets, bars, and rivers of this province, which I performed no less than four times. I discovered and made known the channels of the Cape Fear River and Port Beaufort and Topsail Inlet, before unused and unknown. In attempting these and other discoveries by land and water, I often ran the hazard of drowning and starving; and never retained any other reward or gratification but the thanks of two assemblies in this country for all the pains I took and the money I expended in carrying on and completing these enterprises."

In the light of history, Burrington, then, must stand out as a man of ability, but possessing grievous faults of such a nature as to disqualify him for the position which he occupied. One writer says he was a wiser ruler than his predecessor, Everard, and possessing no more faults; he was, too, to say the least, as wise as his successor, Gabriel Johnston, and no more arbitrary.

Events of Burrington's administration:

1. Marking the boundary line between North Carolina and Virginia.

2. Laying out roads, building bridges, and establishing ferries. From Edenton to Wilmington a road was run nearly two hundred miles, with three long ferries to cross.

The next administration, that of Gabriel Johnston, beginning in 1734 and extending over a period of nearly twenty years, was marked by many incidents and events which had important and vital bearing upon the future destiny of the colony.

The fact that Gabriel Johnston had resided upon the Cape Fear is not generally recognized. His immediate place of residence and incidents connected with his life have both been obscured and subordained by matters of graver importance.

He has come down to us with the reputation of having done more to promote the prosperity of the colony than all the other colonial governors put together. One historian says he deserves the gratitude of every citizen of the State; another lauds him as a benefactor, a paragon of learning and of education; another states that he was the ablest of all the colonial governors. As a mark of honor a noted fort and a county in the State have borne his name.

An incident in his administration which can properly be introduced here, is a record of events which led to the removal of the county seat from Brunswick to Wilmington. The legislative records show that the discussion extended over a long period of time, but was finally accomplished during his administration, the name Wilmington being given to the new seat of government in honor of his patron, Spencer Compton, Earl of Wilmington and Viscount Pevensey. The records show his course in this matter to have been harsh and arbitrary.

In one of his letters to the Board of Trade, he discloses some interest in the country's industrial progress. He condemns the method of manufacturing tar, encourages the raising of hemp, refers to the colonists planting mulberries for the raising of raw silks and cultivating the vine for the production of wines. He refers to the making of oil from the olive and from nuts and seeds which grow spontaneously here, and says the collector's books show that forty-two ships were loaded from the Cape Fear within twelve months. A letter from the Board of Trade in reply to this says: "When you mentioned forty-two ships that went from the Cape Fear River, you ought to have sent us a more particular account thereof, as likewise what the said ships were loaded with. It is with pleasure we read the account you have given us of the people settled on the Cape Fear River."

Events of Johnston's administration:

1. A fort built as a protection against the Spaniards on the south bank of the Cape Fear, and called in honor of the Governor, Fort Johnston.

2. A printing press was imported into the province from Virginia by James Davis.

3. In 1749 emigrants from Scotland flocked to the Cape Fear.

4. In 1752, September 2 was reckoned the 14th, omitting eleven days.

5. In 1738, the division of the province into three counties, Albemarle, Bath, and Clarendon, was abolished, the precincts now being called counties, with a sheriff appointed for each.

6. In 1740, England having declared war against Spain, 400 men were raised in the colony.

7. The population of North Carolina at the beginning of Johnston's administration was nearly 50,000 in all, and at the close about 90,000.

8. Records show that emigrants followed the streams in forming their settlements, searching for "bottom lands."

The next governor appointed by the Crown was Arthur Dobbs, who arrived in New Bern in the fall of 1754 and assumed control of the government.

His term of office is known to have been marked by considerable contention and discord, frequently on matters which were frivolous and unimportant.

For the greater part of his life he resided at Brunswick and in the Old Town Creek settlement. Numerous allusions were made in his letters to the building of churches in Brunswick and Wilmington.

Without some extended reference to St. Philip's Church and the related ecclesiastical status of the colony during Burrington's and Dobbs's administrations this record would be incomplete.

In a letter to the bishop of London, April 23, 1734, John LaPierre writes from "New Hanover, alias Cape Fear," "I was the first minister of the Church of England that came to these places to preach, which I did during three years and a half."

In a letter of July 7, 1735, Richard Marsden wrote to the bishop of London: "I have been at Cape Fear near seven years, and can truly say that I have from my heart and soul done my utmost to promote the glory of God."

On April 7, 1760, during Dobbs's term of office, the church wardens and vestry "begged to recommend Rev. John McDowell as a good minister of the Church of England, who has been in this province since 1754, and officiated in our neighboring parish of St. James until May, 1757, and the next year in Brunswick and Wilmington, and from that time our minister in this parish.

"We are building a very large brick church, which is near done, and hope soon to have a glebe, but at present we are a poor parish, very heavily taxed on occasion of the present war with the French and Indians, therefore can't afford to give a competency so as to maintain him and his young family in a decent manner."

An extract from a letter of the Rev. John McDowell in 1760, to the bishop of London, gives the following information: "Nothing can give me greater pleasure than to hear that my conduct is approved. I have been south as far as the borders of South Carolina assembling a great number of people from both provinces, and we were obliged to assemble under the shady trees. I baptized one day on that visit thirty-two children and adults, among them five free mulattoes.

"It is impossible for me to live here where my salary is so small and everything so dear. I could not have continued so long had I not had some fortune with my wife, which, if I continue here much longer, must go. I was obliged to sell a slave last year to help us to subsist, though no persons ever lived in a more frugal manner."

April 15, 1760, Governor Dobbs recommended McDowell fixed in this parish: "I therefore join with them in these applications, as it is the parish I reside in, and propose when the church is finished, which is now roofing, to be His Majesty's chapel in this government, to which he has been pleased to give the communion plate, surplice, and furniture for the communion table and pulpit, Bible and Common Prayer-books, to have the service performed with decency. This church will be the largest and most complete in this province, and may be an exemplar for building other churches."

April 17, 1760, McDowell writes: "It is with great pleasure that I can acquaint society that my parishioners of Brunswick have a fine large church, by far the largest in the province, in great forwardness—the brickwork is done and a great part of the roof up. We hope to have the church covered and fit for the purpose of divine service this ensuing summer, and a parsonage house to be actually built and a glebe purchased for me.

"His Excellency, Governor Dobbs, will put up a pew for himself, a chancel-rail, a pulpit, and a reading desk; and will give a carpet for the communion table, plate and linen for the communion service, and a surplice for the minister." This was his seventh year of service.

April 16, 1761, McDowell writes: "The roof of the new church at Brunswick is all fallen down again. It was struck with lightning last July, and afterwards a prodigious and immoderate amount of rain falling on it made it all tumble down; and there it lies just as it fell; the chapel is a most miserable old house, only 24 by 12, and every shower or blast of wind blows through it."

The principal event of Dobbs's administration was the accession, in 1761, of George III. to the throne.

Mr. Haywood, in the preface of his book on Governor Tryon, makes the following suggestive observation: "Ever since I have learned to rely more upon documentary evidence than upon the individual opinions of writers, I have been convinced that history has dealt too harshly with the memory of Governor Tryon."

Governor Tryon was born in the handsome family residence in Surrey in the year 1729. He arrived in the province at Cape Fear on Wednesday, October 10, 1764, and next day waited on Governor Dobbs, who had already been apprised of his coming. Dobbs refused to relinquish the office at once, which was a bitter disappointment to Tryon, who wanted to put into immediate effect the policies which he had outlined.

The Governor's mansion being still in possession of the incumbent in office, Tryon experienced great inconvenience in securing accommodations for himself and his family, who accompanied him.

The venerable Governor Dobbs was destined never to leave North Carolina, for, on the 28th of March following, death brought relief to the aged ruler, and when his remains were laid to rest on the Town Creek Plantation, there being not a clergyman within a hundred miles of Brunswick, the burial service had to be conducted by a justice of the peace.

One of the first official acts of Governor Tryon was to arrange for the establishment of a seat of government at New Bern, with the result that the town began to prosper.

The third session of the Legislature having met on the 3d of May, after a short encomium on his predecessor's administration, he advised the houses to improve the hour of tranquillity in promoting the internal polity of the province, making the following recommendations: "The establishment of a clergyman in each parish, whose salary should be paid out of the public treasury. That they reflect upon the present state of the Church that it might no longer suffer from so great neglect; that provision be made to enable the postmaster general to establish a line of post roads through the province of North Carolina, also a committee appointed to contract for conveying the mail from Suffolk, Va., to South Carolina.

The most noteworthy event of this decade was the passage by Parliament of the notorious Stamp Act. An attempt on the part of the Governor was made to pacify the people of Wilmington, but their opposition to the Stamp Act was persistent, and on the 26th of June, the mayor, recorder, and aldermen of Wilmington presented an address to Governor Tryon congratulating him on its repeal and on the happy prospect of the union and harmony thereby established between the colony and the mother country.

"In 1767, on the rise of the Legislature," says Martin, "Governor Tryon lost no time in carrying into effect his darling scheme of building a palace, having exerted all his influence to obtain the passage of the bill for its erection. This measure was thought by many to have laid the foundation of the series of disorders and commotions which terminated in the Battle of Alamance. However, it afforded him an opportunity of leaving behind an elegant monument of his taste in building and giving the ministry an instance of his great influence. For the plan of a governor's house was substituted that of a palace worthy of the residence of a prince of the blood. The purchase of the ground and the erection of the foundation absorbed the sum which the Legislature had been pleased to bestow, which was an ample appropriation for the completion of the building."

The last years of colonial rule, under Gov. Josiah Martin, were filled with incidents of thrilling and dramatic interest. A dark cloud of uncertainty and doubt seemed to hang over the destinies of our country. This period can not be passed over without reference to an event of such momentous import and immortal significance as to deserve forever a place upon the banner of our Commonwealth. I refer to the date, April 12, 1776, and the accompanying resolution:

"Resolved, That the delegates of this colony in the Continental Congress be empowered to concur with the delegates of the other colonies in declaring independence."

After a period of nearly two hundred years the flag which had been planted on the coast of North Carolina began to wane, the unfitness of England to govern her colonies had become more and more obvious, and amid the commotions and excitement of an indignant nation an American independence was at last asserted by the people of Mecklenburg. So this dramatic chapter can be closed with a sentence from Jones's *Memorials of North Carolina:* "It is curious to observe that the annals of a single State should contribute the two great events in the history of the present age—the alpha and omega of the dominion of England over her old North American colonies."

COLONIAL MEMBERS OF THE GENERAL ASSEMBLY.

(Compiled by the North Carolina Historical Commission.)

BOROUGH MEMBERS FROM WILMINGTON.

1739 (40)-1740	William Farris
1742-1743	William Farris
1744-1745	William Farris
1746	Thomas Clark
1746 (47)-1754	Lewis DeRosset
	Cornelius Harnett
1754-1760	Cornelius Harnett
1760	Cornelius Harnett
1761	Cornelius Harnett
1762 (April)	Cornelius Harnett
1762 (November)	Cornelius Harnett
1764-1765	Cornelius Harnett
1766-1768	Cornelius Harnett
1769	Cornelius Harnett
1770-1771	Cornelius Harnett
1773 (January)	Cornelius Harnett
1773-1774	Cornelius Harnett
1775	Cornelius Harnett

NEW HANOVER COUNTY MEMBERS.

1734	John Swann
	Job Howe
	Maurice Moore
1736	Maurice Moore
	John Swann
1738-1739	Nathaniel Moore
	John Swann
1739-1740	John Swann
	Maurice Moore
1744-1745	John Swann
	George Moore
1746	Samuel Swann
	Rufus Marsden
	John Swann
1746-1754	Rufus Marsden
	John Swann
	John Ashe
1754-1760	George Moore
	John Ashe
1760	George Moore
	John Ashe

1761	George Moore
	John Ashe
1762 (April)	George Moore
	John Ashe
1762 (November)	John Ashe
	Alexander Lillington
1764-1765	John Ashe
	James Moore
1766-1768	John Ashe
	James Moore
1769	John Ashe
	James Moore
1770-1771	John Ashe
	James Moore
1773 (January)	John Ashe
	James Moore
1773-1774	John Ashe
	William Hooper
1775	John Ashe
	William Hooper

PROVINCIAL CONGRESSES.

BOROUGH MEMBERS FROM WILMINGTON.

Aug. 1774	Francis Clayton
April 1775	Cornelius Harnett
Aug. 1775	Cornelius Harnett
	Archibald Maclaine
April 1776	Cornelius Harnett
Nov. 1776	William Hooper

NEW HANOVER COUNTY MEMBERS.

Aug. 1774	John Hooper
	William Hooper
April 1775	William Hooper
	John Ashe
Aug. 1775	George Moore
	Alexander Lillington
	Samuel Ashe
	William Hooper
	James Moore
	John Ashe
April 1776	John Ashe
	John Devane
	Samuel Ashe
	Sampson Moseley
	John Hollingsworth
Nov. 1776	John Ashe
	Samuel Ashe
	John Devane
	Sampson Moseley
	John Hollingsworth

Resistance Before the Revolution

THE STAMP ACT ON THE CAPE FEAR.

(Extracts from an address delivered by Capt. S. A. Ashe before the North Carolina
Society of Colonial Dames at Old Brunswick, N. C.)

When the next year [1765] a bill was introduced to carry the resolution into effect, it met with considerable opposition in the House of Commons, for the protests of the colonists were not unheeded. Still, the ministry, under Lord Bute, persisted, and the measure was carried. All America was at once stirred. Bold and courageous action was taken in every colony, but in none was a more resolute spirit manifested than here upon the Cape Fear. The governor was Tryon, who had but lately succeeded to that office. He was an officer of the army, a gentleman by birth and education, a man calculated by his accomplishments and social qualities to shine in any community. He sought the speaker of the House, and asked him what would be the action of the people. "Resistance to the death," was the prompt reply. That was a warning that was full of meaning. It pledged the speaker to revolution and war in defense of the people's rights.

The Assembly was to meet in May, 1765. But Tryon astutely postponed the meeting until November, and then dissolved the Assembly. He did not wish the members to meet, confer, consult, and arrange a plan of opposition. He hoped by dealing with gentlemen, not in an official capacity, to disarm their antagonism and persuade them to a milder course. Vain delusion! The people had been too long trained to rely with confidence on their leaders to abandon them now, even though Parliament demanded their obedience.

The first movement was not long delayed. Within two months after the news had come that the odious act had been passed, the people of North Carolina discarded from their use all clothes of British manufacture and set up looms for weaving their own clothes. Since Great Britain was to oppress them, they would give the world an assurance of the spirit of independence that would sustain them in the struggle. In October information was received that Dr. Houston, of Duplin County, had been selected in England as stamp master. At once proceedings were taken to nullify the appointment. At that time Wilmington had less than 500 white inhabitants, but her citizens were very patriotic and very resolute.

Rocky Point, fifteen miles to the northward, had been the residence of Maurice Moore, Speaker Moseley, Speaker Swann, Speaker Ashe, Alexander Lillington, John Swann, George Moore, John Porter, Colonel Jones, Colonel Merrick, and other gentlemen of influence. It was the center from which had radiated the influences that directed popular movements. Nearer to Onslow, Duplin, and Bladen than Wilmington was, and the residence of the speaker and other active leaders, it was doubtless there that plans were considered, and proceedings agreed upon that involved the united action of all the neighboring counties. At Wilmington and in its vicinity were Harnett, DeRosset, Toomer, Walker, Clayton, Gregg, Purviance, Eustace, Maclaine, and DuBois, while near by were Howe, Smith, Davis, Grange, Ancrum, and a score of others of the loftiest patriotism. All were in full accord with the speaker of the Assembly; all were nerved by the same spirit; all resolved to carry resistance, if need be, to the point of blood and death.

We fortunately have a contemporaneous record of some of their proceedings. The *North Carolina Gazette,* published at Wilmington, in its issue of November 20, 1765, says:

On Saturday, the 19th of last month, about 7 o'clock in the evening, near five hundred people assembled together in this town and exhibited the effigy of a certain honorable gentleman; and after letting it hang by the neck for some time, near the courthouse they made a large bonfire with a number of tar barrels, etc., and committed it to the flames. The reason assigned for the people's dislike to that gentleman was from being informed of his having several times expressed himself much in favor of the stamp duty. After the effigy was consumed, they went to every house in town and brought all the gentlemen to the bonfire, and insisted on their drinking "Liberty, Property, and No Stamp Duty," and "Confusion to Lord Bute and All His Adherents," giving three huzzahs at the conclusion of each toast. They continued together until 12 of the clock, and then dispersed without doing any mischief.

Doubtless it was a very orderly crowd, since the editor says so. A very orderly, harmless, inoffensive gathering; patriotic, and given to hurrahing; but we are assured that they dispersed without any mischief.

And continues the same paper:

On Thursday, the 31st of the same month, in the evening, a great number of people assembled again, and produced an effigy of Liberty, which they put in a coffin and marched in solemn procession with it to the churchyard, a drum in mourning beating before them, and the town bell, muffled, ringing a doleful knell at the same time; but before they committed the body to the ground, they thought it advisable to feel its pulse, and, finding some remains of life, they returned back to a bonfire ready prepared, placed the effigy before it in a large two-armed chair, and concluded the evening with great rejoicings on finding that Liberty had still an existence in the colonies.

Not the least injury was offered to any person.

The editor of that paper, Mr. Stewart, was apparently anxious to let his readers know that the people engaged in these proceedings were the very soul of order and the essence of moderation. So far they had done no mischief and offered no injury to any one. But still they had teeth, and they could show them. The next item reads:

Saturday, the 16th of this instant, that is November: William Houston, Esq., distributor of stamps for this province, came to this town; upon which three or four hundred people immediately gathered together, with drums beating and colors flying, and repaired to the house the said stamp master put up at, and insisted upon knowing "Whether he intended to execute his said office or not." He told them, "He should be very sorry to execute any office disagreeable to the people of this province." ¹But they, not content with such declaration, carried him into the courthouse, where he signed a resignation satisfactory to the whole. They then placed the stamp master in an armchair, carried him around the courthouse, giving at every corner three loud huzzahs, and finally set him down at the door of his lodging, formed a circle around him, and gave three cheers. They then escorted him into the house, where were prepared the best liquors, and treated him very genteelly. In the evening a large bonfire was made and no person appeared on the streets without having "Liberty" in large letters on his hat. They had a table near the bonfire well furnished with several sorts of liquors, where they drank, in great form, all the favorite American toasts, giving three cheers at the conclusion of each.

"The whole was conducted," says the editor, "with great decorum, and not the least insult offered to any person."

This enforced resignation of the stamp master was done under

---

¹It is not to be inferred from Dr. Houston's action in this matter, in 1765, that he was in favor of taxation of the colonies by Great Britain. Benjamin Franklin, then the agent of several of the colonies in London, assumed, as a matter of course, that the Stamp Act would be operative, and he recommended some of his friends to accept the office of stamp master. Dr. Houston did not apply for the appointment, and when the people arrayed themselves against it, he did not oppose them. Also, when, ten years later, the Revolution began, he was in full sympathy with other patriots in North Carolina and was a friend of independence and separation.

the direction of Alderman DeRosset, who received from Houston his commission and other papers, and necessarily it was a very orderly performance. The ringing huzzas, the patriotic toasts, the loud acclaim, echoing from the courthouse square, reverberated through the streets of the town, but Mr. Stewart is quite sure that no mischief was done, and not the least insult was offered to any person. These and other similar proceedings led the Governor to send out a circular letter to the principal inhabitants of the Cape Fear region, requesting their presence at a dinner at his residence at Brunswick on Tuesday, the 19th of November, three days after Dr. Houston resigned; and after the dinner, he conferred with these gentlemen about the Stamp Act. He found them fully determined to annul the act and prevent its going into effect. He sought to persuade them, and begged them to let it be observed at least in part. He pleaded that if they would let the act go into partial operation in the respects he mentioned, he himself would pay for all the stamps necessary. It seems that he liked the people, and they liked and admired him, and difficult indeed was his position. He was charged with the execution of a law which he knew could not be executed, for there was not enough specie in the province to buy the necessary stamps, even if the law could be enforced; but, then, the people were resolved against recognizing it in any degree. The authority of the King and of the Parliament was defied, and he, the representative of the British Government, was powerless in the face of this resolute defiance. While still maintaining dignity in his intercourse with the people, the Governor wrote to his superiors in London strongly urging the repeal of the law. A week later the stamps arrived in the sloop of war *Diligence*. They remained on the sloop and were not landed at that time.

Now was there a lull; but the quietude was not to remain unbroken. In January two merchant vessels arrived in the harbor, the *Patience* and the *Dobbs*. Their clearance papers were not stamped as the act required. The vessels were seized and detained while the lawfulness of their detention was referred to Attorney General Robert Jones, then absent at his home on the Roanoke. But the leaders of the people were determined not to submit to an adverse decision. They held meetings and agreed on a plan of action.

In view of the crisis, on January 20, the mayor of the town retired to give place to Moses John DeRosset, who had been the foremost leader in the action previously taken by the town.

One whose spirit never quailed was now to stand forth as the head of the Corporation.

On the 5th of February, Captain Lobb, in command of the *Viper*, had made a requisition for an additional supply of provisions, and Mr. Dry, the contractor, sent his boat to Wilmington to obtain them. The inhabitants, led by the mayor, at once seized the boat, threw the crew into the jail, and, in a wild tumult of excitement, placed the boat on a wagon and hauled it through the streets with great demonstration of fervid patriotism. The British forces on the river were to receive no supplies from Wilmington; their provisions were cut off, and they were treated as enemies—not friends—so long as they supported the odious law of Parliament. Ten days later came the opinion of Attorney General Jones to the effect that the detained merchantmen were properly seized and were liable to be confiscated under the law. This was the signal for action. The news was spread throughout the counties, and the whole country was astir. Every patriot "was on his legs." There was no halt in carrying into effect the plan agreed upon. Immediately the people began to assemble, and detachments, under chosen leaders, took up their march from Onslow, Bladen, and Duplin. On the 18th of February, the inhabitants of the Cape Fear counties, being then assembled at Wilmington, entered into an association, which they signed, declaring they preferred death to slavery; and mutually and solemnly they plighted their faith and honor that they would at any risk whatever, and whenever called upon, unite, and truly and faithfully assist each other, to the best of their power, in preventing entirely the operation of the Stamp Act.

The crisis had now arrived. The hand of destiny had struck with a bold stroke the resounding bell. The people, nobly responding, had seized their arms. At all times, when some patriot is to throw himself to the front and bid defiance to the established authority of government, there is a Rubicon to be crossed, and he who unsheathes his sword to resist the law must win success or meet a traitor's doom. But the leaders on the Cape Fear did not hesitate at the thought of personal peril. At their call, the people, being armed and assembled at Wilmington, chose the men who were to guide, govern, and direct them. They called to the helm John Ashe, the trusted speaker of the Assembly, and associated with him Alexander Lillington and Col. Thomas Lloyd, as a Directory to manage their affairs

at this momentous crisis. Their movement was not that of an
irresponsible mob. It was an orderly proceeding, pursuant to a
determined plan of action, under the direction of the highest
officer of the province, who was charged with maintaining the
liberties of the people. In effect, it was the institution and
ordaining of a temporary government.

It was resolved to organize an armed force and march to
Brunswick, and Col. Hugh Waddell was invested with the command of the military. Let us pause a moment and take a view
of the situation at that critical juncture. Close to Brunswick,
in his mansion, was Governor Tryon, the representative of the
King; no coward he, but resolute, a military man of experience
and courage. In the town itself were the residences and offices
of Colonel Dry, the collector of the port, and of other officers
of the Crown. Off in the river lay the detained merchant vessels and the two sloops of war, the *Viper,* commanded by Cap-
tian Lobb, and the *Diligence,* commanded by Captain Phipps,
whose bristling guns, 26 in number, securely kept them; while
Fort Johnston, some miles away, well armed with artillery, was
held by a small garrison. At every point flew the meteor flag
of Great Britain. Every point was protected by the ægis of His
Sacred Majesty. For a subject to lift his hand in a hostile
manner against any of these was treason and rebellion. Yes,
treason and rebellion, with the fearful punishment of attainder
and death—of being hanged and quartered.

Well might the eloquent Davis exclaim, "Beware, John Ashe!
Hugh Waddell, take heed!"

Their lives, their fortunes were at hazard and the dishonored
grave was open to receive their dismembered bodies! But
patriots as they were, they did take care—not for themselves,
but for the liberties of their country. At high noon, on the 19th
day of February, the three directors, the mayor and other officers of Wilmington, the embodied soldiery, and the prominent
citizens, moved forward, crossed the river, passed like Cæsar
the fateful Rubicon, and courageously marched to the scene of
possible conflict. It was not only the Governor with whom they
had to deal, but the ships of war with their formidable batteries
that held possession of the detained vessels. It was not merely
the penalties of the law that threatened them, but they courted
death at the cannon's mouth, in conflict with the heavily armed
sloops of war, from whose power they had come to wrest the
merchantmen. But there was neither halt nor hesitation.

As they crossed the river, a chasm yawned deep and wide, separating them from their loyal past. Behind them they left their allegiance as loyal British subjects; before them was rebellion—open, flagrant war, leading to revolution. Who could tell what the ending might be of the anticipated conflict!

There all the gentlemen of the Cape Fear were gathered, in their cocked hats, their long queues, their knee-breeches, and shining shoe buckles. Mounted on their well-groomed horses, they made a famous cavalcade as they wound their way through the somber pine forests that hedged in the highway to old Brunswick. Among them was DeRosset, the mayor, in the prime of manhood, of French descent, with keen eye, fine culture, and high intelligence, who had been a soldier with Innes at the North; bold and resolved was he as he rode, surrounded by Cornelius Harnett, Frederick Gregg, John Sampson, and the other aldermen and officers of the town.

At the head of a thousand armed men, arranged in companies and marching in order, was the experienced soldier, Hugh Waddell, not yet thirty-three years of age, but already renowned for his capacity and courage. He had won more distinction and honors in the late wars at the North and West than any other Southern soldier, save only George Washington; and now in command of his companies, officered by men who had been trained in discipline in the war, he was confident of the issue. Of Irish descent, and coming of a fighting stock, his blood was up, and his heroic soul was aflame for the fray.

Surrounded by a bevy of his kinsmen, the venerable Sam and John Swann; his brothers-in-law, James, George, and Maurice Moore; his brother, Sam Ashe, and Alexander Lillington, whose burly forms towered high above the others; by Howe, Davis, Colonel Lloyd, and other gallant spirits, was the speaker, John Ashe, now just forty-five years of age, on whom the responsibility of giving directions chiefly lay. Of medium stature, well knit, with olive complexion and a lustrous hazel eye, he was full of nervous energy—an orator of surpassing power, of elegant carriage and commanding presence. Of him Mr. Strudwick has said: "That there were not four men in London his intellectual superior," and that at a time when Pitt, Fox, Burke, and others of that splendid galaxy of British orators and statesmen gave lustre to British annals.

How, on this momentous occasion, the spirits of these men and of their kinsmen and friends who gathered around, must

7

have soared as they pressed on, resolved to maintain the chartered rights of their country! Animated by the noble impulses of a lofty patriotism, with their souls elevated by the inspiring emotions of a perilous struggle for their liberties, they moved forward with a resolute purpose to sacrifice their lives rather than tamely submit to the oppressive and odious enactments of the British Parliament.

It was nightfall before they reached the vicinity of Brunswick, and George Moore and Cornelius Harnett, riding in advance, presented to Governor Tryon a letter from the governing Directory, notifying him of their purpose. In a few minutes the Governor's residence was surrounded, and Captain Lobb was inquired for, but he was not there. A party was then dispatched towards Fort Johnston, and thereupon Tryon notified the British naval commanders and requested them to protect the fort, repelling force with force. In the meantime, a party of gentlemen called on the collector, Mr. Dry, who had the papers of the ship *Patience;* and in his presence broke open his desk and took them away. This gave an earnest of the resolute purpose of the people. They purposed to use all violence that was necessary to carry out their designs. Realizing the full import of the situation, the following noon a conference of the King's officers was held on the *Viper,* and Captain Lobb, confident of his strength, declared to the Governor that he would hold the ship *Patience* and insist on the return of her papers. If the people were resolved, so were the officers of the government. The sovereignty of Great Britain was to be enforced. There was to be no temporizing with the rebels. The honor of the government demanded that the British flag should not droop in 'the face of this hostile array. But two short hours later a party of the insurgents came aboard and requested to see Captain Lobb. They entered the cabin, and there, under the royal flag, surrounded by the King's forces, they demanded that all efforts to enforce the Stamp Act cease. They would allow no opposition. In the presence of Ashe, Waddell, DeRosset, Harnett, Moore, Howe, and Lillington, the spirit of Captain Lobb quailed. The people won. In the evening the British commander, much to the Governor's disgust, reported to that functionary that "all was settled." Yes. All had been settled. The vessels were released; the grievances were redressed. The restrictions on the commerce of the Cape Fear were removed. The attempt to enforce the Stamp Act had failed before the prompt, vigorous, and courageous action of the inhabitants. After that, vessels could come and go as if there had been no act of Parliament. The people had been victorious over the King's ships; with arms in their hands, they had won the victory.

But the work was not all finished. There, on the *Diligence,* were obnoxious stamps, and by chance some loyal officer of the government might use them. To guard against that, the officers were to be forced to swear not to obey the act of Parliament, but to observe the will of the people. Mr. Pennington was His Majesty's controller, and, understanding that the people sought him, he took refuge in the Governor's mansion and was given a bed and made easy, but early the next morning Col. James Moore called to get him. The Governor interfered to prevent; and immediately the mansion was surrounded by the insurgent troops, and the Directory notified the Governor, in writing, that they requested His Excellency to let Mr. Pennington appear, otherwise it would not be "in the power of the directors appointed to prevent the ill consequences that would attend a refusal." In plain language, said John Ashe, "Persist in your refusal, and we will come and take him." The Governor declined to comply. In a few moments he observed a body of nearly five hundred men move towards his house. A detachment of sixty entered his avenue. Cornelius Harnett accompanied them and sent word that he wished to speak with Mr. Pennington. The Governor replied that Mr. Pennington was protected by his house. Harnett thereupon notified the Governor that the people would come in and take him out of the house, if longer detained. Now the point was reached. The people were ready; the Governor was firm. But Pennington wisely suggested that he would resign, and immediately wrote his resignation and delivered it to the Governor—and then he went out with Harnett and was brought here to Brunswick, and required to take an oath never to issue any stamped paper in North Carolina; so was Mr. Dry, the collector; and so all the clerks of the County Courts, and other public officers. Every officer in all that region, except alone the Governor, was forced to obey the will of the people and swear not to obey the act of Parliament.

On the third day after the first assemblage at Wilmington, on the 18th, the directors, having completed their work at Brunswick, took up the line of march to return. With what rejoicing they turned their backs on the scene of their bloodless triumph. It had been a time of intense excitement. It had been no easy task to hold more than a thousand hot and zealous patriots well in hand, and to accomplish their purposes without bloodshed. Wisdom and courage by the directors, and prudence, foresight, and sagacity on the part of the military officers were alike essential to the consummation of their design. They now returned in triumph, their purposes accomplished. The odious law was annulled in North Carolina. After that, merchant vessels passed freely in and out of port, without interference. The stamps remained boxed on shipboard, and no further effort was made to enforce a law which the people had rejected.

Two months after these events on the Cape Fear, Parliament repealed the law, and the news was hurried across the Atlantic in the fleetest vessels. The victory of the people was complete. They had annulled an act of Parliament, crushed their enemies, and preserved their liberties. Thus once more were the courageous leaders of the Cape Fear, in their measures of opposition to encroachments on the rights of the people, sustained by the result. On former occasions they had triumphed over their governors: now, in coöperation with other provinces, they had triumphed over the British Ministry and the Parliament of Great Britain.

While in every other province the people resolutely opposed the Stamp Act, nowhere else in America was there a proceeding similar to that which was taken at Wilmington. Nowhere else was the standard of Liberty committed to the care of a governing board, even though its creation was for a temporary purpose; nowhere else was there an army organized, under officers appointed, and led to a field where a battle might have ensued. Had not His Majesty's forces yielded to the will of the insurgents, the American Revolution would probably have begun then—and here—on the soil of Old Brunswick.

WILLIAM HOUSTON, THE STAMP AGENT— ANOTHER VIEWPOINT.

(Extracts from an address delivered by Mr. J. O. Carr before the North Carolina Society of Colonial Dames of America, at Old Brunswick, May 5, 1915.)

One hundred and fifty years have elapsed since the Houston episode, and it is not too early to begin to do justice to the victim; nor will it detract from the heroism of the patriots of 1765, who were inspired by a righteous indignation against every form of oppression.

By a careful, discriminating reading of all the subject-matter at our command, it will be easily seen that the indignation of the people of 1765 was not directed against Houston, nor against any conduct of his, but against the principle of the British stamp tax.

In order to get a comprehensive view of Houston as a man it is necessary to consider him before 1765 and after 1765.

HOUSTON BEFORE 1765.

William Houston did not live in Wilmington nor in Brunswick, but resided in Duplin County on the Northeast River, about sixty miles north of Wilmington, in a direct line. He was an associate of Henry McCulloch in his attempt to colonize North Carolina, and was one of the original settlers who came to this community some time between 1737 and 1748. This locality was then a part of the county of New Hanover.

Houston was a man of unusual ability and was known as an "honorable gentleman." By profession he was a surgeon and apothecary. A tradition, too well founded in the community in which he lived to be seriously disputed, at least forms the basis for a well-established belief that royal blood flowed in his veins. The General Assembly of 1749 and 1750 established the county of Duplin and St. Gabriel's parish, and William Houston was named as a member of the vestry of that parish. From 1751 to 1761, inclusive, he was a member of the General Assembly from Duplin County, and following that date was a justice of the peace, along with other leading citizens of his county; and in those days the office of justice of the peace was a position of considerable importance.

When he was appointed stamp agent for the port of Brunswick, he was residing on his farm in Duplin County, on a high elevation on the Northeast River, at a place known as "Soracte"—so called, no doubt, from the mountain by that name in Italy on which was built the ancient Temple of Apollo.

On the 19th of October, 1765, after he had been appointed stamp agent and notice of such appointment had reached Brunswick direct from England, Houston was hanged in effigy in the town of Wilmington, the only reason given for such action being that the several hundred citizens who participated were "informed of his having several times expressed himself much in favor of the stamp duty"—and it is possible that he honestly favored such a tax, but there is no evidence that he favored it without the people's consent.

Again, on the 31st of October, 1765, a large number of people met in Wilmington and placed an effigy in a coffin and moved under the beat of drums to the churchyard—no doubt St. James's Church—where the interment was to take place; but after feeling its pulse, decided that Liberty still survived, and no burial took place. Also, Dr. Houston was hanged in effigy at New Bern and at Fayetteville about the same time.

During all of these exhibitions of patriotism, Dr. Houston was pursuing his duties as surgeon and apothecary at "Soracte," now known as "Sarecta," and he afterwards protested that he had not solicited and did not even know of his appointment as stamp agent at the time of such demonstrations. It was not until Saturday, the 16th day of November, nearly a month after his first hanging and demise, that Dr. Houston came to town, where three hundred people, with drums beating and flags flying, proceeded to his lodging-place and inquired whether he intended to execute the office of stamp agent. Without hesitation he informed them that he "should be sorry to execute any office disagreeable to the people of the province"; and as an exhibition of good faith voluntarily signed the famous promise, which was done of his own free will and accord; and he was not even required to take an oath, as has been generally believed. If this promise had been signed under force or duress, he would hardly have been given an ovation; but after he had indicated his sentiments on this matter there was a love feast and he was put in an armchair and carried around the courthouse and around one of the chief squares of the city of Wilmington and finally put down at his lodging-place.

A careful and discriminating reading of the entire story must convince the thinking man that instead of a riot and a lynching in the city when Dr. Houston came to town, there was something in the nature of a banquet in his honor, on the discovery by the people that the sentiments of the man selected by the Crown to sell stamps were in harmony with theirs; and no doubt Dr. Houston enjoyed the eats and drinks as much as any one, though the drought in those days around "Soracte" was doubtless not as marked as it is today.

HOUSTON AFTER 1765.

The episode in Wilmington did not in any way affect the standing of Dr. Houston in his own county, where he was highly honored and respected by his fellow-citizens. In 1768 he was appointed a justice of the peace in Duplin County, and likewise again in 1771. In 1777 he was chairman of the "Court Martial" in Duplin County, whose duties were to hunt down Tories and deserters and to bring to justice Americans who were not faithful to our cause; and together with James Kenan and Joseph Dickson, whose names were synonymous with patriotism in that community, he acted in this capacity, and as chairman of the commission. He continued to serve his county in public positions, and as late as 1784 was appointed a justice of the peace by Alexander Martin, in which capacity he served for some time thereafter. The time of his death or the place of his burial can not be stated with certainty, but it is thought that he was buried in the community in which he lived.[1] His descendants to this day have exhibited the same elements of brilliancy and patriotism seen in Dr. Houston.

RUSSELLBOROUGH—SCENE OF FIRST ARMED RESISTANCE.

About half a mile to the south of Orton House, and within the boundary of the plantation, are the ruins of Governor Tryon's residence, memorable in the history of the United States as the spot upon which the first overt act of violence occurred in the War of American Independence, nearly eight years before the Boston Tea Party, of which so much has been made in Northern history, while this colonial ruin, the veritable cradle of American liberty, is probably unknown to nine-tenths of the people of the Cape Fear at the present day.

This place, which has been eloquently referred to by two of the most distinguished sons of the Cape Fear, both direct de-

---

[1]Since the preparation of the above paper, I have found the following memorandum among my historical data: "William Houston in after life moved from Duplin County to Tennessee and then, it is said, to Texas. He had a number of sons, the youngest of whom was Samuel Houston, who spent his life in Duplin County and was the father of the late Capt. William J. Houston, Mrs. George W. Carroll, Mrs. J. N. Stallings, and Mrs. Oates." This information was furnished me by the family of Mrs. George W. Carroll.   J. O. CARR.

scendants of Sir John Yeamans, the late Hon. George Davis and the late Hon. A. M. Waddell, and which was known as Russellborough, was bought from William Moore, son and successor of "King" Roger, by Capt. John Russell, commander of His Britannic Majesty's sloop of war *Scorpion,* who gave the tract of about fifty-five acres his own name.   It subsequently passed into the possession of his widow, who made a deed of trust, and the property ultimately again became a part of Orton Plantation. It was sold March 31, 1758, by the executors of the estate of William Moore to the British governor and commander-in-chief, Arthur Dobbs, who occupied it and who sold it or gave it to his son, Edward Bryce Dobbs, captain of His Majesty's Seventh Regiment of Foot or Royal Fusileers, who conveyed it by deed, dated February 12, 1767, to His Excellency, William Tryon, governor, etc.   It appears, however, that Governor Tryon occupied this residence prior to the date of this deed, as is shown by the following official correspondence in 1766 with reference to the uprising of the Cape Fear people in opposition to the Stamp Act:

BRUNSWICK, 19 February, 1766,

Eleven at Night.

SIR:—Between the hours of six and seven o'clock this evening, Mr. Geo. Moore and Mr. Cornelius Harnett waited on me at my house, and delivered me a letter signed by three gentlemen. The inclosed is a copy of the original. I told Mr. Moore and Mr. Harnett that I had no fears or apprehensions for my person or property, I wanted no guard, therefore desired the gentlemen might not come to give their protection where it was not necessary or required, and that I would send the gentlemen an answer in writing tomorrow morning. Mr. Moore and Mr. Harnett might stay about five or six minutes in my house. Instantly after their leaving me, I found my house surrounded with armed men to the number, I estimate, at one hundred and fifty. I had some altercation with some of the gentlemen, who informed me their business was to see Captain Lobb, whom they were informed was at my house; Captain Paine then desired me to give my word and honor whether Captain Lobb was in my house or not. I positively refused to make any such declaration, but as they had force in their hands I said they might break open my locks and force my doors. This, they declared, they had no intention of doing; just after this and other discourse, they got intelligence that Captain Lobb was not in my house. The majority of the men in arms then went to the town of Brunswick, and left a number of men to watch the avenues of my house, therefore think it doubtful if I can get this letter safely conveyed. I esteem it my duty, sir, to inform you, as Fort Johnston has but one officer and five men in garrison, the fort will stand in need of all the assistance the *Viper* and *Diligence* sloops can give the commanding officer there, should any insult be offered to His Majesty's fort or stores, in which case it is my duty to request of you to repel force with force, and take on board His Majesty's sloops so much of His Majesty's ordnance stores and ammunition out of the said fort as you shall think necessary for the benefit of the service.

I am, your most humble servant, WM. TRYON.

To the Commanding Officer, either of the *Viper* or *Diligence* sloops of war.

The writer, who has made his home at Orton, had often inquired for the precise location of the ruins of Governor Tryon's Russellborough residence without success; but about fifteen years ago, acting upon Colonel Waddell's reference to its site on the north of Old Brunswick, the service of an aged negro who had lived continuously on the plantation for over seventy years was engaged. He, being questioned, could not remember ever having heard the name Russellborough, nor of Governor Dobbs, nor of Governor Tryon, nor of an avenue of trees in the locality described. He said he remembered, however, hearing when he was a boy about a man named "Governor Palace," who lived in a great house between Orton and Old Brunswick.

We proceeded at once to the spot, which is approached through an old field, still known as "Old Palace Field," on the other side of which, on a bluff facing the east and affording a fine view of the river, we found hidden in a dense undergrowth of timber the foundation walls of Tryon's residence. The aged guide showed us the well-worn carriage road of the Governor, and also his private path through the old garden to the river landing, a short distance below, on the south of which is a beautiful cove of white and shining sand, known, he said, in olden times, as the Governor's Cove. The stone foundation walls of the house are about two feet above the surface of the ground. Some sixty years ago the walls stood from twelve to fifteen feet high, but the material was unfortunately used by one of the proprietors for building purposes.

The old servant pointed out a large pine tree near by, upon which he said had been carved in colonial times the names of two distinguished persons buried beneath it, and which in his youthful days was regarded with much curiosity by visitors. The rude inscription has unhappily become almost obliterated by several growths of bark, and the strange mysterious record is forever hidden by the hand of time.

A careful excavation of this ruin would doubtless reveal some interesting and possibly valuable relics of Governor Tryon's household. Near the surface was found, while these lines were being written, some fragments of blue Dutch tiling, doubtless a part of the interior decorations; also a number of peculiarly shaped bottles for the favorite sack of those days, which Falstaff called sherris sack, of Xeres vintage, now known as dry sherry.

In recent years the site of Governor Tryon's palace upon this spot has been marked by a substantial monument built of bricks and stones taken from the foundation of the building and suitably inscribed by the North Carolina Society of Colonial Dames of America.

SONS OF LIBERTY IN NORTH CAROLINA.[1]

South Carolina Gazette, July 5, 1770.

We hear that in consequence of a letter lately addressed to the Sons of Liberty in North Carolina, under cover to Col. James Moore, a meeting had been appointed, and held on the 2d of last month, where a number of gentlemen from the several southern counties in that province were chosen as a committee to meet at Wilmington on this day, to consult upon such measures as may appear most eligible for evincing their patriotism and loyalty in the present critical situation of affairs; which committee are, Col. James Lloyd, Cornelius Harnett, Frederick Gregg, William Campbell, Esq., Messrs. John Robeson and William Wilkinson, for the town of Wilmington; George Moore, Frederick Jones, Esq., Col. James Moore, Messrs. Samuel Ashe and James Moran, for New Hanover County; Richard Quince, sr., Richard Quince, jr., Esqrs., and Mr. John Wilkinson, for the town of Brunswick; John and William Davis, Esqrs., Messrs Samuel Watters, Thomas Davis, and Samuel Neale, for Brunswick County; Messrs. John and George Gibbs, and John Grange, jr., for Bladen County; Col. James Sampson and Felix Kenan, Esq., for Duplin County; William Cray, Henry Roads, and Richard Ward, Esqrs., for Onslow County; and Walter Gibson, Farquhar Campbell, and Robert Rowan, Esqrs., for Cumberland County.

---

[1] The Sons of Liberty were originally formed in the fall of 1765.

South Carolina Gazette, July 26, 1770.

We are informed that on the 22d of last month the Virginians extended their Economical Plan and Non-Importation Agreement, agreeable to those of this province, and that some General Resolutions were to be framed last week by the inhabitants of North Carolina, to manifest their unanimity with the rest of the colonies.

South Carolina Gazette, August 9, 1770.

(WILMINGTON, CAPE FEAR), July 11.

At a meeting of the General Committee of the Sons of Liberty upon Cape Fear, in Wilmington, the 5th day of July, Cornelius Harnett, Esq., was chosen chairman, and the following resolution unanimously agreed on, viz.:

I. Resolved, That the following answer to the letter received from the Sons of Liberty in South Carolina, of the 25th of April last, be signed by the chairman and sent by the first conveyance.

To the Sons of Liberty in South Carolina:—

Gentlemen:—

Your favour of the 25th of April last was laid before the Sons of Liberty upon the Cape Fear, at a general meeting in this town, on the second of last month, and received with the highest satisfaction.

We have the pleasure to inform you that many of the principal inhabitants of six large and populous counties attended, when it was unanimously agreed to keep strictly to the Non-Importation Agreement entered into last fall, and to coöperate with our sister colonies in every legal measure for obtaining ample redress of the grievance so justly complained of.

Happy should we have thought ourselves if our merchants in general would have followed the disinterested and patriotic example of their brethren in the other colonies; we hope, however, their own interest will convince them of the necessity of importing such articles, *and such only*, as the planters will purchase.

We should have done ourselves the pleasure of answering your letter much sooner, but the gentlemen of the committee living at such a distance from each other prevented it.

We beg to assure you that the inhabitants of those six counties, and we doubt not of every county in this colony, are convinced of the necessity of adhering strictly to their former resolution, and you may depend they are as tenacious of their just rights as any of their brethren on the continent and firmly resolved to stand or fall with them in support of the common cause of American liberty.

Worthless men, as you very justly observe, are the production of every country, and we are also so unhappy as to have a few among us "who have not virtue enough to resist the allurement of present gain."

Yet we can venture to assert, that the people in general of this colony will be spirited and steady in their support of their rights as English subjects, and will not tamely submit to the yoke of oppression—"But, if by the iron hand of power," they are at last crushed, it is their fixed resolution either to fall with the same dignity and spirit you so justly mention or transmit to their posterity, entire, the inestimable blessing of our free constitution.

The disinterested and public-spirited behaviour of the merchants and other inhabitants of your colony justly merits the applause of every lover of liberty on the continent. The people of any colony who have not virtue enough to follow so glorious examples must be lost to every sense of freedom and consequently deserve to be slaves. We are,

> With great truth, gentlemen,
> > Your affectionate countrymen,
> > > CORNELIUS HARNETT, *Chairman.*

Signed by order of the General Committee.

WILMINGTON, CAPE FEAR, July 5, 1770.

II. Resolved, That we will strictly and inviolably adhere to the Non-Importation Agreement entered into on the 30th day of September last until the grievances therein mentioned are redressed.

III. Resolved, That we will not on any pretense whatever, have any dealings or connexion with the inhabitants of the colony of Rhode Island, who contrary to their solemn and voluntary contract have violated their faith pledged to the other colonies and thereby shamefully deserted the common cause of American liberty; and if any of their vessels or merchants shall arrive in Cape Fear River with intention to trade, we will to the utmost of our power, by all legal ways and means, prevent any person buying from, or selling to them, any goods or commodities whatever, unless they give full satisfaction to the colonies for their base and unworthy conduct.

IV. Resolved, That the merchants of Newport, Rhode Island, and all others on the continent of North America, who will not comply with the Non-Importation Agreement, are declared enemies to their country, and ought to be treated in the most contemptuous manner.

V. Resolved, That we will not purchase any kind of goods or merchandise whatever, from any merchants or other person who shall import or purchase goods for sale contrary to the spirit and intention of the said Agreement, unless such goods be immediately re-shipped to the place they were imported from or stored under the inspection and direction of the committee.

VI. Resolved, That the members of the committee for the several counties in the Wilmington district, and particularly those for the towns of Wilmington and Brunswick, do carefully inspect all importations of goods, and if any shall be imported contrary to the true intent and meaning of the said Non-Importation Agreement, that they give public notice thereof in the *Cape Fear Mercury*, with the names of such importers or purchasers.

VII. Resolved, That copies of these resolutions be immediately transmitted to all the trading towns in this colony. The Committee of the

Sons of Liberty upon Cape Fear, appointed for the town of Wilmington to inspect into all goods imported, take this opportunity to inform the public that Mr. Arthur Benning, of Duplin County, hath imported in the sloop *Lancashire Witch* from Virginia a small assortment of goods, several articles of which are not allowed by the Non-Importation Agreement. But it appears at the same time to the committee those goods were expected to arrive before the 1st. of January last, having been ordered by Mr. Benning some time in July last. His correspondent sent them to Virginia, where they have lain a considerable time since.

We have the pleasure to inform the public, that Richard Quince, Esq., a member of the General Committee and who may with great propriety be deemed a principal merchant, hath joined heartily in the Non-Importation Agreement. It will, no doubt, be looked upon as a very great misfortune to this country that some merchants and others seem resolved not to follow so disinterested an example, but, on the contrary, are daily purchasing wines and many other articles contrary to the said Agreement. Should those gentlemen still persist in a practice so destructive in its tendencies to the liberties of the people of this colony, they must not be surprised if hereafter the names of the importers and purchasers should be published in the *Cape Fear Mercury*. This is intended to serve as a friendly admonition, and, it is hoped, will be received as such and have its due effect.

The Revolution

THE INSTITUTION OF THE REVOLUTIONARY GOVERNMENT.

On July 21, 1774, there was an important meeting of the inhabitants of the Wilmington district held at Wilmington.

It being understood that the Governor had determined that the Legislature should not meet, this meeting was called to take steps for the election of delegates to a Revolutionary Convention.

William Hooper presided; and Col. James Moore, John Ancrum, Fred Jones, Samuel Ashe, Robert Howe, Robert Hogg, Francis Clayton, and Archibald Maclaine were appointed a committee to prepare a circular letter to the several counties of the province, requesting them to elect delegates to represent them in the convention.

This was the first movement to provide for a Revolutionary Government, and the delegates elected were the first elected by the people in any province in right of the sovereignty of the people. It was at this same meeting that the cry, "The Cause of Boston is the Cause of All," arose. Money and a shipload of provisions were at once subscribed for the suffering people of Boston, and Parker Quince offered his vessel to carry the provisions and himself went to deliver them.

In response to the letter sent out by the committee, delegates were chosen in every county except five. The convention met at New Bern on August 25, 1774, and a Revolutionary Government was instituted.

PROCEEDINGS OF THE COMMITTEE OF SAFETY.

(Extracts from the Proceedings of the Committee of Safety of New Hanover County.)

WILMINGTON, November 23, 1774.

At a meeting of the Freeholders in the courthouse at Wilmington for the purpose of choosing a Committee of said town to carry more effectually into execution the resolves of the late Congress held at Philadelphia, the following names were proposed and universally assented:

Cornelius Harnett, John Quince, Francis Clayton, William Hooper, Robert Hogg, Archibald Maclaine, John Robinson, James Walker.

Wednesday, January 4, 1775.

The Committee met at the courthouse. Present, Cornelius Harnett, Archibald Maclaine, John Ancrum, William Hooper, and John Robinson.

At the same time the Freeholders of New Hanover County assembled to choose a committee for the county to join and co-operate with the committee of the town, which the members present agreed to. Then the Freeholders present, having Cornelius Harnett in the chair, unanimously chose George Moore, John Ashe, Samuel Ashe, James Moore, Frederick Jones, Alexander Lillington, Sampson Moseley, Samuel Swann, George Merrick, Esquires, and Messrs. John Hollingsworth, Samuel Collier, Samuel Marshall, William Jones, Thomas Bloodworth, James Wright, John Larkins, Joel Parrish, John Devane, Timothy Bloodworth, Thomas Devane, John Marshall, John Calvin, Bishop Dudley, and William Robeson, Esquires, a committee to join the committee of Wilmington.

Monday, March 6, 1775.

The Committee met according to adjournment.

The following Association was agreed on by the Committee and annexed to the resolves of the General Congress, to be handed to every person in this county and recommended to the Committees of the adjacent counties, that those who acceded to the said resolves, may subscribe their names thereto.

We, the subscribers, in testimony of our sincere approbation of the proceedings of the late Continental Congress, to the annexed have hereto set our hands, and we do most solemnly engage by the most sacred ties of honor, virtue, and love of our country, that we will ourselves strictly observe every part of the Association recommended by the Continental Congress.

Mr. James Kenan, chairman of the Duplin Committee, pursuant to a letter from this committee at its last meeting attended.

Resolved, That all the members of the committee now present go in a body and wait on all housekeepers in town with the Association before mentioned and request their signing it, or declare their reasons for refusing, that such enemies to their country may be set forth to public view and treated with the contempt they merit.

Resolved, That it is the opinion of this committee that all dances, private as well as public, are contrary to the spirit of the eighth article in the Association of the Continental Congress, and as such they ought to be discouraged, and that all persons concerned in any dances for the future should be properly stigmatized.

Mr. Harnett desired the opinion of the Committee respecting a negro fellow he bought in Rhode Island (a native of that place) in the month of October last, whom he designed to have brought with him to this province, but the said negro ran away at the time of his sailing from Rhode Island. The question was put whether Mr. Harnett may import said negro from Rhode Island.

Resolved unanimously, That Mr. Harnett may import the said negro from Rhode Island.

Tuesday, March 7, 1775.

Resolved, That three members of this committee attend the meeting of the Committee at Duplin on the 18th instant. Mr. Samuel Ashe, Mr. Sampson Moseley, and Mr. Timothy Bloodworth were accordingly nominated to attend the said Committee.

WHIGS AND TORIES.

On the last day of May, 1775, Josiah Martin, the royal governor of North Carolina, locked his palace at New Bern and fled to Fort Johnston, arriving there on June 2. Two weeks later he issued his proclamation warning the people to desist from their revolutionary proceedings. As if in answer, on June 19, the inhabitants of New Hanover, having assembled, united in an association "to sacrifice our lives and fortunes to secure the freedom and safety of our country." The next day, June 20, the committeemen of Duplin, Bladen, Onslow, Brunswick, and New Hanover met at Wilmington and adopted the New Hanover Association, which was also signed, later, in Cumberland. Three weeks elapsed, and then the people of the Lower Cape Fear, having determined to dislodge the garrison of the fort, on the 18th of July seized and burnt the fort, the Governor and his soldiers taking refuge on the vessels.

Knowing that there was a large number of loyal adherents in the interior, Governor Martin devised a plan by which a strong

British force was to be sent from England to the Cape Fear, where they would be joined by the Loyalists from the upper counties and the province would be subjugated. Accordingly, when the time approached for the British fleet to arrive, the Loyalists began to embody, the first movement being on February 5, with instructions to concentrate at Campbellton. As quickly as this action was known, the news was hurried to Wilmington and other points throughout the province. The messengers reached Wilmington on the 9th with the startling intelligence, and the greatest excitement prevailed.

For eighty hours, night and day, there was severe, unremitting service, making preparation for defense. Companies of troops rushed in from Onslow, Duplin, and Brunswick, the whole country being aroused. Colonel Moore with his Continentals, Colonel Lillington with his corps of minute men, Colonel Ashe with his Independents, hurried to the vicinity of Campbellton to arrest the progress of the Loyalists, while Colonel Purviance, in command of the New Hanover Militia, remained at Wilmington, throwing up breastworks, mounting swivels, and constructing fire-rafts to drive off the British vessels should they attempt to seize the town. The sloop of war *Cruizer* did ascend the river, but, avoiding Wilmington, tried to pass up the Clarendon, or Brunswick, River. She was, however, driven back by riflemen who lined the banks.

The Battle of Moore's Creek[1] followed on February 27, and the plan of the Governor was defeated. All during March and April British vessels came into the harbor, but the grand fleet bearing the troops from England, being detained by storms, did not arrive until the end of April, when there were more than a hundred ships in the river. The plan of the Governor having failed, towards the end of May the fleet sailed, expecting to take possession of Charleston, leaving only a few ships in the river. Later, these likewise were withdrawn, and for nearly five years the people of Wilmington were left undisturbed.

---

[1] A monument commemorating this well-known battle was erected by the citizens of Wilmington and its vicinity in 1857. Falling into decay, in 1907 it was repaired by the Moore's Creek Monument Association, aided by an appropriation of the United States Congress secured by Representative Charles R. Thomas, then representing the Third Congressional District of North Carolina.

At the same time and at the same place a monument was erected to the brave women of the Revolution, on one side of which appears the name of Mary Slocumb, who, it is said, rode sixty-five miles alone at night to care for her husband and other patriot soldiers engaged in the Battle of Moore's Creek.

8

At length, South Carolina being subjugated, Lord Cornwallis proposed to enter North Carolina, and as a part of his operations, on the 28th of January, 1781, Maj. James H. Craig took possession of Wilmington. His force consisted of eighteen vessels, carrying a full supply of provisions and munitions, and 400 regular troops, artillery, and dragoons. At that time Brunswick was entirely deserted, and Wilmington contained but 200 houses and only 1,000 inhabitants. The entire Cape Fear region was defenseless. The losses of the Cape Fear counties at Camden and in other battles at the South had been heavy, while many of the militia and the whole Continental Line had been surrendered by Lincoln at Charleston. Thus the Whig strength had been greatly weakened, while there were in the country but few guns and no powder and lead. On the other hand, the Loyalists had been strengthened by accessions from those who wearied of the war.

Major Craig at once dispatched detachments to scour the country, seize prominent Whigs, collect forage, and arouse the Loyalists, who in some counties largely outnumbered the Whigs. After the Battle of Guilford Courthouse, Cornwallis retreated to Wilmington, his army arriving there on the 7th of April. In the closing days of April, when he had repaired his damage as well as he could, he marched through the eastern counties to Virginia, leaving the subjugation of North Carolina to Major Craig.

Large bodies of Loyalists, well supplied by the British with arms and ammunition and too strong to be successfully resisted, now marched at will throughout the Upper Cape Fear, suppressing the Whigs and taking many prisoners, confining them in prison ships or in Craig's "bull-pen" on shore.

After Cornwallis had passed on to Virginia, General Lillington returned to his former position at Heron Bridge, over the Northeast; but in June he was forced to retire into Onslow County, and Craig established an outpost at Rutherford Mills, on Ashe's Creek, seven miles east of Burgaw, where he constructed a bastion fort. In the meantime Craig had been active in organizing the Loyalists, and issued a proclamation notifying the inhabitants that they were all British subjects and must enroll themselves as Loyalist Militia, and those who did not do so by the first day of August were to be harried, their property seized and sold, and themselves destroyed. On the last day of grace Craig began a march through the eastern counties, his loyal lieutenants being very vigorous in the counties on the Northwest and the Haw and the Deep Rivers. When he reached Rock Creek, two miles east of Wallace, he found Colonel Kenan with some 500 militia ready to contest his passage, but Kenan's ammunition was soon exhausted and the British successfully crossed and dispersed the militia. For ten days Craig remained in Duplin and harried the Whigs, and then, after being joined by 300 Loyalists, he moved towards New Bern. Lillington was at Limestone Bridge, but hurried on the road to the Trent to keep in Craig's front. He had about 600 men, but only three rounds of ammunition, and had been directed not to hazard a battle. On the 17th of August General Caswell reported to the Governor: "General Lillington is between New Bern and the enemy, and I am fearful will risk an action. I have done everything I can to prevent it, and have let him have a sight of Your Excellency's letter, wherein you mention that no general action must take place." Craig entered New Bern, and then marched towards Kinston, but turned south and went to Richlands, and, after obtaining a supply of forage, returned to Wilmington. At the east, the Whigs now rallied everywhere, those in Duplin, having suffered greatly, being thoroughly exasperated. They surprised a body of Tories, "cut many of them to pieces, took several and put them to instant death." The retaliation on each side was fierce and ferocious, until at length the Tories subsided. But in Bladen and higher up the Tory detachments, each numbering several hundred, held the country and drove the Whigs out. However, on August 28, Colonel Brown, with about 150 Bladen men, won a complete victory at Elizabethtown and broke the Tory power in Bladen. But a fortnight later, Fanning, whose force numbered 1,000 men, took Hillsboro, captured the Governor, and fought the Battle of Cane Creek.

It was not until October that General Rutherford was able to collect enough men to march to the relief of Wilmington. Early in November he reached the Northeast, ten miles above the town, and established himself there, hemming Craig in. But now momentous events happening at Yorktown had their effect on the Cape Fear. On the 17th of November, Light-Horse Harry Lee (the father of Gen. Robert E. Lee) arrived at Rutherford's camp, bringing the glad news of the surrender of Cornwallis. Immediately the whole camp united in a *feu de joie,* and then Rutherford crossed the river and took post at Schaw's, four miles from the town. On the following morning, November 18, Major Craig and his troops boarded his ships and took their departure, and although the Tory bands continued to wage a relentless and murderous warfare on the Haw and the Deep, Wilmington thereafter enjoyed quiet and repose.

THE BATTLE OF ELIZABETHTOWN.

(The Wilmington Weekly Chronicle, February, 1844.)

One of the most daring and successful onsets upon Tories by the Whigs during the Revolutionary War was at Elizabethtown, in the county of Bladen, of this State. No notice of the battle was found in any history of that period. We understood that there was an imperfect relation of it published in a Federal paper twenty-five or thirty years ago. That a memorial to so gallant an act might be revived and placed within reach of some future historian, we addressed a letter to a distinguished gentleman of Bladen, desiring such information in regard to the affair as he should possess or be able to collect. The annexed letter from him furnishes a very satisfactory account of the information sought for, and will doubtless be perused by every North Carolinian with much interest. Our respected correspondent, probably through inadvertence, omitted to put down the date of the battle. It was 1781, and, as near as we can ascertain, in the month of July.

BLADEN COUNTY, Feb. 21st, 1844.

A. A. BROWN, ESQ.,
    Editor of the Wilmington Weekly Chronicle.

DEAR SIR:—Yours of the 3d inst. was received, soliciting such information as I possess or may be able to collect respecting the battle fought at Elizabethtown during our Revolutionary struggle between the Whigs and Tories. I have often regretted that the actions and skirmishes which occurred in this and New Hanover County should have been overlooked by historians. The Battle of Elizabethtown deserves a place in history and ought to be recollected by every true-hearted North Carolinian with pride and pleasure. Here sixty men, driven from their homes, their estates ravaged and houses plundered, who had taken refuge with the Whigs of Duplin, without funds and bare of clothing, resolved to return, fight, conquer, or die. After collecting all the ammunition they could, they embodied and selected Col. Thomas Brown in command. They marched fifty miles through almost a wilderness country before they reached the river, subsisting on jerked beef and a scanty supply of bread. The Tories had assembled, 300 or more, at Elizabeth-town, and were commanded by Slingsby and Godden. The former was a talented man and well fitted for his station; the latter, bold, daring, and reckless, ready to risk everything to put down the Whigs. Every precautionary measure was adopted to prevent surprise and to render this the stronghold of Toryism. Nobody was suffered to remain on the east side of the river. Guards and sentries were regularly detached and posted. When the little band of Whig heroes after nightfall reached the river not a boat was to be found. But it must be crossed, and that speedily. Its depth was ascertained by some who were tall and expert swimmers. They, to a man, cried out, "It is fordable; we can, we will cross it." Not a murmur was heard, and with-out a moment's delay they all undressed, tied their clothing and ammunition on their heads (baggage they had none), each man, grasping the barrel of his gun, raised the bridge so as to keep the lock above water, descended the banks, and entered the river. The taller men found less difficulty; those of lower stature were scarcely able to keep their mouths and noses above water; but all safely reached the opposite shore, resumed their dresses, fixed their arms for action, made their way through the low ground then thickly settled with men, ascended the hills, which were high and precipitous, crossed King's Road leading through the town, and took a position in its rear. Here they formed, and, in about two hours after crossing a mile below, commenced a furious attack, driving in the Tory sentries and guards. They continued rapidly to advance, keeping up a brisk and well-directed fire, and were soon in the midst of the foe, mostly Highland Scotchmen, as brave, as high-minded as any of His Majesty's subjects. So sudden and violent an onset for the moment produced disorder; but they were rallied by their gallant leader and made for a while the most determined resistance. Slingsby fell mortally wounded and Godden was killed, with most of the officers of inferior grade. They retreated, some taking refuge in houses, the others, the larger portion, leaping pell-mell into a deep ravine, since called the Tory Hole. As the Tories had unlimited sway from the river to the Little Pee Dee, the Whigs recrossed, taking with them their wounded. Such was the general panic produced by this action that the Tories became dispirited and never after were so troublesome. The

Whigs returned to their homes in safety. In the death of Slingsby the Tories were deprived of an officer whose place it was difficult to fill; but few were equal to Godden in partisan warfare. This battle was mostly fought by river planters, men who had sacrificed much for their country. To judge it correctly it should not be forgotten that the country from Little Pee Dee to the Caharas was overrun by the Tories. Wilmington was in possession of the British and Cross Creek of the Tories. Thus situated, the attack made on them at Elizabethtown assumed much of the character of a forlorn hope. Had the Whigs not succeeded they must have been cut off to a man. If they had fled southward the Tories would have risen to destroy them. If eastward, the Tories in that case, flushed with victory, would have pursued them, and they would have sought in vain their former asylum. This action produced in this part of North Carolina as sudden and happy results as the Battles of Trenton and Princeton in New Jersey. The contest was unequal, but valor supplied the place of numbers.

It is due to Colonel Brown, who, when a youth, marched with General Waddell from Bladen and fought under Governor Tryon at the Battle of Alamance and was afterwards wounded at the Big Bridge, to say he fully realized the expectations of his friends and the wishes of those who selected him to command; and when the history of our State shall be written this action alone, apart from his chivalric conduct at the Big Bridge, will place him by the side of his compatriots Horry, Marion, and Sumter of the South. It must, it will, form an interesting page in our history on which the young men of North Carolina will delight to dwell. It is an achievement which bespeaks not only the most determined bravery, but great military skill. Most of these men, like the Ten Thousand Greeks, were fitted to command. Owen had fought at Camden, Morehead commanded the nine months' men sent to the South, Robeson and Ervine were the Percys of the Whigs and might justly be called the Hotspurs of the Cape Fear.

The foregoing narrative was detailed to me by two of the respective combatants, who now sleep with their fathers; the substance of which I have endeavored to preserve with all the accuracy a memory not very retentive will permit. A respectable resident of Elizabethtown has recently informed me that he was a small boy at the time of the battle and lived with his mother in one of the houses to which the Tories repaired for safety;

that he has a distinct recollection of the fire of the Whigs, which appeared like one continuous stream. Documentary evidence I have none.   With great respect,

. . . .

The Battle of Elizabethtown took place August 29, 1781. The consequences of that victory were far-reaching. Colonel Slingsby had at Elizabethtown a great number of Whigs held as prisoners, who were restored to liberty and augmented the Whig strength in Bladen. The guns, ammunition, provisions, and other spoils taken supplied the Whigs, who were in the extremest need. Not only were the Loyalists broken up and dispersed, but the Whigs were so strengthened that afterwards the Tories, who had been masters of Bladen, made no opposition to them. Still the condition of the Whigs in Bladen, as in all the other Cape Fear country, remained deplorable.

OLD-TIME CAPE FEAR HEROES.

Col. James Innes, who appears to have had some military training before he came to the Cape Fear, about 1735, so distinguished himself in the war against the Spaniards, in 1740, that when the French and Indian War came on Governor Dinwiddie of Virginia appointed him to the command of all the forces in Virginia.

Col. Hugh Waddell, a young Irishman who came to Wilmington, won a great reputation during the French and Indian War; but Innes and Waddell both died before the Revolution, as also did Moses John DeRosset, likewise an officer in the former war.

Among others who served in the French and Indian War were Col. Caleb Grainger, Capt. Thomas McManus, James Moore, Robert Howe, and John Ashe. Howe had been in command of Fort Johnston, and Ashe, colonel of militia, was for a time on Innes' staff.

When the Provincial Congress began to raise troops, in 1775, James Moore was elected colonel of the First Continentals, and at the outset he remained to defend the Cape Fear. He was soon appointed brigadier general in the Continental Army, and for a while in 1776 was in command of the forces in South Carolina. He died on the Cape Fear, while leading his brigade to the North. He was an officer of great ability.

Robert Howe was colonel of the Second Continentals, which he shortly led to Norfolk, where for a time he was in command. Like Moore, he was appointed brigadier general in the Continental Army, and he succeeded Moore in command of the forces in South Carolina, but later joined Washington and had a distinguished career. After the war he died in Bladen and was buried on his plantation, The Grange.

Alexander Lillington was colonel of the minute men of the Cape Fear district. He became colonel of the Sixth Continentals and later general of militia. He led his command to the aid of Lincoln at Charleston, but on the expiration of the term of duty he and his men retired from the city before it was too late. The next year he was in command resisting the British on the Cape Fear. He survived the war, but died a few years later.

Gen. John Ashe was the first brigadier general of the militia of the Cape Fear district. As major general, in 1779 he led a detachment to Georgia, but was defeated by British regulars. In 1781 he was taken prisoner, and he died the same year at Colonel Sampson's, Sampson Hall.

After the surrender of the North Carolina Continentals at Charleston, two new battalions were organized, Col. John Baptista Ashe, who had served at the North, being lieutenant colonel of one and winning fame at Eutaw Springs.

Lieut. Sam Ashe (the younger) was captured at Charleston, and after exchange served with Greene till the end of the war.

For three years Maj. Sam Ashe, a son of Gen. John Ashe, had a cavalry company at the North.

Col. Thomas Clark, a native of the Cape Fear, was colonel of the Continentals, and served so well that the General Assembly urged Congress to appoint him brigadier general. With nearly all the North Carolina Continentals he was made prisoner when General Lincoln surrendered at Charleston.

Samuel Purviance was colonel of the New Hanover Militia.

In the First Regiment were Captains William Davis, Alfred Moore, John Walker, and Caleb Grainger; Lieutenants John Lillington, William Hill, Thomas Callender, and Samuel Watters, and Ensign Maurice Moore, jr. On the staff were Richard Bradley, William Lord, and Adam Boyd, while James Tate was chaplain.

In the Fourth Regiment were Captains Roger Moore, John Ashe, jr., and John Maclaine.

Dr. James Fergus was surgeon of the Sixth Regiment.

Capt. John Hill won laurels at the bloody Battle of Eutaw Springs.

Griffith John McRee was the commanding officer of the North Carolina Continentals with Greene at the end of the war and was a most efficient and distinguished officer.

Major McRee left three sons, one, Capt. William McRee, of the United States Engineers, planned the Lundy Lane campaign; another, Gen. Sam McRee, distinguished himself in the Mexican War; and the other, Dr. James Fergus McRee, was perhaps the most learned North Carolinian of his time.

One of the most picturesque characters of this period was Maj. Jack Walker. He was born near Alnwick Castle, under the shadow of the Grampian Hills, and in 1761, while yet a youth of twenty, he landed at Old Brunswick. In stature he stood six feet four, and he possessed enormous strength. There were no lions for him to conquer, but once when a mad bull raged through the streets of Wilmington, Samson-like, he seized the infuriated animal by the horns, threw him to the ground and held him. As major of the North Carolina Continentals, he fought valiantly at the North. Ever a warm patriot, he was violent against those who sympathized with the Tories. The people loved him, affectionately calling him "Major Jack," and he wielded great power among them. Although he amassed a considerable fortune, he never married, his large estate descending to a favorite nephew, Maj. John Walker, who was the father of Hon. Thomas D. Walker, Alvis Walker, John Walker, Capt. George Walker, Dr. Joshua C. Walker, Henry Walker, Calhoun Walker, and of the wives of Gen. W. H. C. Whiting, Maj. James H. Hill, Capt. C. P. Bolles, Capt. John Cowan, and Mr. Frederick Fosgate.

The above record is by no means complete, as during the troublous time of the Revolution every patriot family on the Cape Fear contributed its utmost to the cause of independence.

CORNELIUS HARNETT'S WILL.

In the sacred name of God, Amen.

The twenty-eighth day of April, one thousand seven hundred and eighty-one, I, Cornelius Harnett of New Hanover County, in North Carolina, Esquire, tho weak in body, but of perfect mind and memory, do make & ordain this to be my last will and testament in manner & form following, viz:

Imprimus. I give, devise, and bequeath to my beloved wife, Mary, all my estate, real, personal, & mixed, of what nature or kind soever, to her, her heirs & assigns forever.

Item. I do hereby nominate and appoint my said wife, Mary, Executrix, and Samuel Ashe & William Hill, Executors, to this my last will and testament, hereby revoking and dis- annulling all former wills by me heretofore made. Ratifying and confirming this & no other to be my last will & testament.

In witness whereof I have hereunto set my hand and seal the day and year above written.

CORNL. HARNETT   (Seal)

Signed, sealed, published, pronounced, and declared by the said Cornelius Har- nett as & for his last Will & Testament in presence of

ANNE HOOPER.
THO. MACLAINE.
JNO. JUSKE.

I, Cornelius Harnett having executed the within written will, think it not improper to add that as I have ever considered expensive funerals as ostentatious folly, it is my earnest request (and from my present circumstances now doubly necessary) that I may be buried with the utmost frugality.

CORNL. HARNETT.

NEW HANOVER COUNTY.
JANUARY TERM, 1782.

The within last will & Testament of Cornelius Harnett, Esquire, was exhibited in Court and proved by the oath of Thomas Maclaine, a subscribing witness thereto, who swore that he saw the testator sign, seal, publish, and declare the same to be and contain his last will and testament. Also, that he was of sound and disposing mind and memory. Ordered, that letters testamentary do issue to Mary Harnett, Executrix to the said will. At same time Mrs. Harnett qualified agreeable to law.   THO. MACLAINE, *Clk.*

This will was filed in my office by H. H. Robinson, clerk of Bladen County, this 20th January, 1846.

L. H. MARSTELLER,
Clk N. Hanover Cty Ct.

FLORA MACDONALD.

By David Macrae.

Shortly after the four years' war, a distinguished Scottish traveler and lecturer, David Macrae, visited Wilmington, and was entertained for several weeks by my father, the late Alexander Sprunt, who sent him with credentials to the "Scotch Country," where he was cordially received and honored. Mr. Macrae delivered in Wilmington several lectures, which were largely attended, and he generously devoted the proceeds to the benefit of local charities.

He subsequently wrote the following account of Highlanders in North Carolina, with particular reference to Flora Macdonald, whose romantic life on the Cape Fear is worthy of a more enduring memorial.

Visit to the Highland Settlement.

In the month of February, one clear, sharp morning, I left Wilmington on my way up the Cape Fear River to follow the old track of the Highland emigrants, and see their settlement.

The steamers on that river, as indeed on most of the long rivers in America, are stern-wheelers—large, slim, white, and deck-cabined, with only one paddle, but that of stupendous size, standing out like a mill-wheel from the stern and making one think, on seeing the steamer in motion, of a gigantic wheel-barrow drawn swiftly backwards. The advantage of the stern wheel for shallow and winding rivers is that it allows of a narrower beam than two paddles, and takes sufficient hold to propel a steamer in water too shallow for the screw. Our steamer that morning (flat-bottomed, of course, as all American river steamers are) drew only eighteen inches of water, and went at great speed.

We had not been steaming long up the broad pale earthy-brown river, through the flat expanse, with its rice plantations, its forest land, and its clearings, with the black stumps still standing like chessmen on a board, when I was struck with the extraordinary appearance of the leafless woods, which looked as if a deluge had just subsided, leaving the trees covered with masses of sea-weed.

I gazed on this phenomenon with much wonder, till it suddenly occurred to me that this must be the famous Carolina moss (*Tillandsia*) of which I had often heard, but which I had not yet seen in any quantity. I satisfied myself by asking a tall, shaggy man, in leather leggings and a tattered cloak of Confederate gray, who was standing near me.

"Don't it grow whar you come from?" asked the man, with the usual inquisitiveness of thinly peopled regions. On learning that I was a stranger from the old country, he became exceedingly courteous, and told me that the moss I had inquired about was very common in that State, and was much used by the people for stuffing seats and cushions and bedding, being first boiled to kill it. He said it seemed to feed upon the air. You could take a handful and fling it over the branch of another tree, and it would grow all the same.

After a sail of some hours we reached a point from which a railway runs in a southwesterly direction, traversing part of the "Scotch Country." Here we got into "cars," and were soon bowling through the lonely forest on the narrow iron bed, sometimes over tracks that were irregularly covered for miles with still water, in which the trees and bushes that rose from it stood reflected as on the bosom of a lake. Now and then, at long intervals, we stopped at some little wayside station in the forest, with its cheerful signs of human life, its casks of turpentine and its piles of corded wood, around which the pines were being hewn down and cut, some of them into bars, others into cheese-like sections, for splitting into the shingles that are used for roofing instead of slates or tiles. Occasionally the train stopped in places where there was no station at all, to let some one out at the part of the forest nearest to his home. The conductor, who was continually passing up and down through the cars, stopped the train, whenever necessary, by pulling the cord that is slung along the roof of all American trains and communicates with the engine.

We now began to get up into the higher country, amongst forests of giant pines, where the ground was rough, and where the sandy soil, looking in some places like patches of snow, seemed, for the most part, untouched by the hand of man. It was into these vast solitudes, of which we had as yet but touched the skirt, that the Highlanders, driven from their native land during the religious and political troubles of the last century, had come to find a home.

North Carolina was long a favorite field for Highland emigration. More than a hundred and forty years ago, when Alexander Clark, of Jura, went out to North Carolina and made his way up the Cape Fear River to Cross Creek, he found already there one Hector McNeill, (known as "Bluff" Hector, from his occupying the bluffs over the river,) who told him of many others settled farther back, most of them exiles from Scotland, consequent on the troubles that followed the downfall of the Stuarts, some of them Macdonalds who had been fugitives from the massacre of Glencoe. The numbers were largely increased by the failure of the Jacobite Rebellion in 1745. The persecution to which the Highlanders were subjected after the scattering of the clans at Culloden made many of them eager to escape from the country; and when the government, after the execution of many captured rebels, granted pardon to the rest on condition of their taking the oath of allegiance and emigrating to the plantations of America, great numbers availed themselves of the opportunity. They were followed gradually by many of their kith and kin, till the vast plains and forest lands in the heart of North Carolina were sprinkled with a Gaelic-speaking population.

In 1775, the Scotch colony received a memorable accession in the person of Flora Macdonald, who, with her husband and children, had left Scotland in poverty to seek a home with their friends in the American forests. The heroine was received at Wilmington[1] and at various points along her route with Highland honors; and the martial airs of her native land greeted her as she approached Cross Creek, the little capital of the Highland settlement. She arrived, however, at an unhappy time. The troubles between Great Britain and the colonies were coming to a head, and in a few months hostilities began.

It is somewhat singular that many of these Highland colonists, the very men who had fought against the Hanoverian dynasty at home, were now forward to array themselves on its side. But they had been Jacobites and Conservatives in Scotland, and conservatism in America meant loyalty to the King. Many of them, however, espoused the cause of independence, and the declaration prepared in the county of Cumberland, immediately after the famous declaration of the neighboring county of Mecklenburg, has many Highland names attached. The crafty Governor, fearing the spread of anti-British sentiment, and knowing the influence of Flora Macdonald amongst the Scottish settlers, commissioned one of her kinsfolk, Donald Macdonald, who had been an officer in the Prince's army in

---

[1] At Wilmington a public ball was given in her honor.

1745, to raise a Highland regiment for the King, and gave the
rank of captain to Flora's husband. This identified the heroine
with the Royalist party, and had the effect of securing the ad-
hesion of hundreds of gallant men who would otherwise have
held back or joined the other side. When the royal standard
was raised at Cross Creek, 1,500 Highlanders assembled in
arms. Flora, it is said, accompanied her husband, and inspired
the men with her own enthusiasm. She slept the first night in
the camp, and did not return to her home till she saw the troops
begin their march. The fate that awaited this gallant little
force is known to all readers of history. It had got down the
river as far as Moore's Creek, on its way to join Governor
Martin, when, finding further advance checked by a force of
Revolutionists under Lillington and Caswell, while another
under Colonel Moore was hurrying up in pursuit, it was driven
to attack the enemy in front on ground of his own choosing.
In the first onslaught its officers fell, confusion ensued, and
after a severe struggle the Highlanders were routed.[1] Flora's
husband was taken prisoner and thrown into Halifax jail.

Many of those who escaped are said to have joined another
Highland regiment which was raised for the King under the
title of the North Carolina Highlanders and fought the Revolutionists till the close of the war. So deeply had they identified themselves with the royal cause that when the war was
ended most of them, including Flora Macdonald and her husband, left America and returned to Scotland. Those who remained in the settlement, divided by the war, were soon reunited
by peace, became, as in duty bound, good citizens, and resumed
the task of taming the savage wilderness in which they had cast
their lot.

When the troubles between North and South were gathering
to a head in 1860, the Highlanders, with their conservative
instincts, were almost to a man opposed to secession. But,
taught to believe that their allegiance was due primarily, not to

---

[1]J. A. McAllister, of Lumberton, N. C., says:

"In connection with the Battle of Moore's Creek, it may interest a
good many to know that the capture of Gen. Donald McDonald was
effected by William Whitfield and his brother-in-law, Williams. This
fact I learn from the genealogical record of the Whitfield-Bryan families. It is stated in the record that William and his brother, Needham
Whitfield, both took part in the battle. William belonged to the light
horse. He and Needham were sons of William Whitfield and his wife,
Anne Bryan, and there are but few families in North Carolina more
numerous or more highly respected."

the Federal Government but to the State, no sooner did North Carolina go out, than they, with Highland loyalty, followed; and no men crowded to the front more eagerly, or fought more valiantly or more desperately to the bitter end.

Almost every man of those I met had served in the Confederate Army, and had left dead brothers or sons on the battle-field. Others, following the example of those who had left Scotland after the downfall of the Stuarts, and America after the triumph of the Revolution, had left the States altogether, and gone off to Mexico.

Amongst those I found at Wilmington was one who was a fine specimen of the material that the Highlands have given to Carolina, a spare, dark-visaged, soldierly fellow—Gen. William MacRae—whose personal valour and splendid handling of his troops in battle had caused him to be repeatedly complimented by Lee in general orders.

He seemed to belong to a fighting family. His eight brothers had all been either in the army or the navy. Their father, Gen. Alexander MacRae, had fought in the war with England in 1812, and, on the outbreak of the War between the States, though then a man of seventy years of age, again took the field, and commanded what was known as MacRae's battalion. He died not many weeks after I parted from him at Wilmington. He was the grandson of the Rev. Alexander MacRae, minister of Kintail, two of whose sons fell fighting for the Pretender at Culloden. The others emigrated to North Carolina, and one of them, Philip, who had also served in the Prince's army, cherished so deadly a hate of the English in consequence of the atrocities of Cumberland, that he would never learn the English language, but spoke Gaelic to the day of his death. The family settled in Moore County, which is part of what is still called the "Scotch Country."

The Life of Flora Macdonald was published by her granddaughter in the form of an autobiography, said to be based on family records. The following is the passage in which the Scottish heroine is made to describe the episode in her life connected with America:

"In 1775 my husband put in practice a plan he and I often talked over—that of joining the emigrants who were leaving their native hills to better their fortunes on the other side of the Atlantic. We were induced to favour this scheme more particularly as a succession of failures of the crops and unforeseen family expenses rather cramped our small income. So, after making various domestic arrangements, one of which was to settle our dear boy Johnnie under the care of a kind friend, Sir Alexander McKenzie, of Devlin, near Dunkeld, until he was of age for an India appointment, we took ship for North America. The others went with us, my youngest girl excepted, whom I left with friends; she was only nine years old. Ann was a fine young woman, and my sons as promising fellows as ever a mother could desire. Believe me, dear Maggie, in packing the things, the Prince's sheet was put up in lavender, so determined was I to be laid in it whenever it might please my Heavenly Father to command the end of my days. On reaching North Carolina, Allan soon purchased and settled upon an estate; but our tranquillity was ere long broken up by the disturbed state of the country, and my husband took an active part in that dreadful War of Independence. The Highlanders were now as forward in evincing attachment to the British Government as they had furiously opposed it in former years. My poor husband, being loyally disposed, was treated harshly by the opposite party, and was confined for some time in jail at Halifax. After being liberated, he was officered in a royal corps—the North Carolina Highlanders; and although America suited me and the young people, yet my husband thought it advisable to quit a country that had involved us in anxiety and trouble almost from the first month of our landing on its shores. So, at a favorable season for departure, we sailed for our native country, all of us, excepting our sons, Charles and Ronald, who were in New York expecting appointments, which they soon after obtained; Alexander was already, dear boy, at sea. Thus our family was reduced in number. On the voyage home all went well until the vessel encountered a French ship of war, and we were alarmed on finding that an action was likely to take place. The captain gave orders for the ladies to remain below, safe from the skirmish; but I could not rest quiet, knowing my husband's spirit and energy would carry him into the thick of the fighting; therefore I rushed up the companion-ladder—I think it was so called—and I insisted on remaining on deck to share my husband's fate, whatever that might be. Well, dear Maggie, thinking the sailors were not as active as they ought to have been—and they appeared crest-fallen, as if they expected a defeat—I took courage and urged them on by asserting their rights and the certainty of the victory. Alas! for my weak endeavors to be of service; I was badly rewarded, being thrown down in the noise and confusion on deck. I was fain to go below, suffering excrutiating agony in my arm, which the doctor, who was fortunately on board, pronounced to be broken. It was well set, yet from that time to this it has been considerably weaker than the other. So you see I have periled my life for both the houses of Stuart and Brunswick, and gained nothing from either side!"

Early Years

ALYRE RAFFENEAU DELILE.

Vice-consul dans la Caroline du Nord, professeur de botanique à la Faculté de Médecine de Montpellier, membre de l'Institut d'Egypte, correspondant de l'Institut de France, chevalier de la Légion d'honneur, etc.

In 1802, when First Consul of France, Napoleon honored the town of Wilmington by sending to this port as vice-consul the gifted young scientist Raffeneau Delile, whose scientific work, although he was at that time but twenty-four years old, had won for him the grateful recognition of France. *"Quoi qu'il arrive il faut que je sois regretté, si j'ai eu quelque valeur; c'est à l'oeuvre que l'on connaît l'ouvrier: 'A fructibus eorum cognoscetis eos,' a dit l'Evangile."* (Whatever happens, I must be regretted if I have had worth; it is by the work that we know the workman: 'By their fruits you shall know them,' saith the Gospel.) Thus wrote Delile in affectionate confidence to his son five years before his death, and his distinguished contemporary, M. Joly, in an historic eulogy, quotes the scientist's own words in his estimate of the man whose work won for him an imperishable name.

Alyre Raffeneau Delile was born in Versailles in 1778. His ancestors had held positions at court from the time of Francis I., and he inherited the post held by his father, but his larger heritage was the principles of honor and strict integrity. His early boyhood was passed under the shadow of the impending Revolution, but though his father was attached to the court during that critical period, he encouraged Delile in forming independent opinions, leaving him free to espouse actively either the cause of the King or of the people. With no predilection for public affairs, however, he gave himself to the study of botany and anatomy, and when an interne in the Hospital of Versailles, learned Greek and some Latin from one of the Prussian soldiers who then filled its wards. Later, he entered a medical school in Paris which Bonaparte, then professing interest in chemistry, sometimes visited; but for Bonaparte abstract study could not shut out the call to the great arena of military activity and conquest. At that time the mysteries of Egypt beckoned with even greater persuasiveness than had the laurels of Italy, and the African expedition was made ready. To the credit of Napoleon be it ever remembered that he desired to conquer more than lands and peoples, and to accompany him on that memorable journey to Egypt to solve its mysteries and add distinction to French culture he chose fifteen of the greatest savants of France, among them René Louiche Desfontaine, the noted botanist, who had already visited Egypt, bringing back probably the largest single collection of foreign plants then in existence. But Desfontaine declined the honor of going and requested it for Raffeneau Delile, then but twenty years old. Realizing that his youth and inexperience might embarrass him in such a company, Delile refused to go unless there should be conferred upon him the title of a superior officer. His request was granted, and he went forth with "those soldiers of letters, the new Argonauts." In Egypt his knowledge of Greek was of great value to him in deciphering inscriptions on obelisks and temples and in tombs. It was Boussard, an officer of this expedition, who found the Rosetta stone, and it is possible that Delile was one of the first to read some of the Greek inscription[1] upon that. These scientists formed themselves into the Institute of Egypt, planned after the *Institut National,* and Delile was made director of the Botanical Gardens of Cairo, which he enriched by specimens gathered in the valley of the Nile, on the borders of the Red Sea, and in the desert. He thoroughly explored the world of plants, wrote extensively, and read before the Institute of Egypt memorials that carried his name across the Mediterranean. But misfortune came, and on August 31, 1801, Alexandria capitulated to the English, leaving to the mercy of the conquerors the marvelous collections of Bonaparte's scientific expedition. It was when these were claimed that the illustrious naturalist Geoffroy Saint-Hilaire, in the names of his colleagues, Delile and Savigny, made to the haughty English general the heroic response: "We will not yield. Your army will enter this place in two days. Ah, well, between now and then the sacrifice will be consummated. We will ourselves burn our treasures; you will afterwards dispose of our persons as seems good to you." It is needless to say that the collection was saved to the French.

Scarcely had Delile returned to France, when Bonaparte sent him to Wilmington as under-commissioner of commercial rela-

---

[1]To Champollion belongs the honor of deciphering the hieroglyphic and using it as a key to the decipherment of the monuments of Egypt.

tions, with the title of vice-consul. The position was not in harmony with his tastes, but he applied himself to his tasks with intelligence and zeal, and his rectitude and pleasing personality won for him the esteem and affection of all. While here he became the friend of Thomas Jefferson, then President of the United States, and other distinguished Americans.

The rich vegetation of North Carolina, with its variety and abundance of new and interesting specimens, furnished relief from the more uncongenial task of observing the current price of commodities at the port and counting the revenues that passed through his hands. Dr. M. A. Curtis, the noted botanist of North Carolina, in the *Boston Journal of Natural History,* 1834, said: "It is confidently believed that no section of the Union of equal extent contains such a rich and extensive variety of plants as is to be found about Wilmington," and he mentioned the fact that in little more than two seasons, at intervals from other engagements, he had found more than a thousand specimens, with much ground still unexamined. It is easy to imagine how a man like Delile reveled in these new-found gardens, and all the more because his august patroness, soon to be the Empress Josephine, particularly requested him to collect in America all the plants which might be of interest in France; and the director of the establishment of Malmaison, M. de Mirbel, engaged him to respond as soon as possible to the commission of the future empress. Bonaparte, also, took the liveliest interest in the plan of Josephine to naturalize foreign flora in France, and, becoming emperor, it was his desire to bring under one sceptre plants grown in every corner of the globe, and to acclimatize them in the greenhouses of Malmaison. "Here," M. Joly tells us, "flourished the violet of Parma, the rose of Damascus, the lily of the Nile," and—shall we say the marvelous *Dionæa muscipula, Drosera,* and *Sarracenia* of Carolina? Delile is said to have established in Wilmington an herbarium in connection with his collection for Josephine, and his specimens of American grains he sent to the distinguished botanist Palisot de Beauvois, who published a classification of them in general with other specimens in his *Agrostographie.* The writer of this sketch had the good fortune to come upon a copy of the *Agrostographie* corrected by Palisot himself, in which he makes acknowledgment to those who aided in his work, and among them Delile. It is regretted that no book of Delile's giving an account of the plants of Carolina is at hand. He wrote *Memoire sur quelques espèces de graminees propres à la Caroline du Nord,* also, *Centurie des plantes de l'Amerique du Nord,* but these are not available to the writer. At the time of his death he was writing on the *Flora d'Amerique,* which he expected to publish soon.

Leaving Wilmington abruptly in 1806, Delile went to New York and obtained a degree in medicine, after which he first thought of practicing that profession in New Orleans, and then of becoming an American planter. His mother combatted the latter intention, however, and, reminding him of the friendship of the Empress Josephine, emphasized the fact that it was not necessary to be exiled from a country in which he had such good and powerful friends. Shortly after this he was recalled to France by a decree of the consuls to join a commission charged with erecting a monument to science.

In 1819 he came to the chair of botany and *materia medica* in the faculty of Montpellier, already made illustrious by half a dozen of the most distinguished men of France. As director of *le jardin des plantes de Montpellier,* he added lustre to his name and to that of the establishment. The botanical gardens of Montpellier, created in 1596 by Henry IV., were the first established in France, and to an already bountiful collection Delile added treasures of the vegetable world found in Egypt and in North Carolina and other parts of the eastern section of the United States. His gardens seem in a measure to have been converted by him into a department of agriculture, in which he studied vegetation with practical intent, both for domestic economy and for industrial development.

In the reign of Louis XVIII., he held at court the position his father and grandfather had held—that of *porte-malle*—but he soon renounced it, writing Voltaire: "It is from the court that one ought to flee; it is in the country that one ought to live."

In 1806 he sent from New York to a friend in France a catalogue of the botanical gardens established in 1801 at Elgin, New York, by the celebrated Dr. Hosack, and in doing so discussed briefly American trees, remarking that it would be very easy to naturalize them in France, especially the cypress of North Carolina, the white oak, the swamp oak, the green oak of Virginia, and the yellow oak, the last valuable to art on account of the beautiful color extracted from its bark, and the rest for decorating parks. He called attention in particular to the fact that our trees are able to stand more cold in winter and heat in summer than those of France.

Delile was a man of wonderful sweetness of character. When he came to live in Wilmington, it was as if France had sent a part of her better self—not a money-changer at the port, but a bit of fragrance wafted across the seas to unite us by bonds closer than those made by the exchange of merchandise.

He numbered among his friends the most illustrious men of France, England, Germany, and India. He wrote more than sixty treatises, chiefly upon botanical subjects, but a number upon medical subjects. Among his best known works are his *Flore d'Egypte, Memoires sur l'Egypte, Flore du Mont Sinai, Voyage horticole et botanique en Belgique et en Hollande, These sur la phthisie pulmonaire,* and *Avis sur les dangers de l'usage des champignons sauvages dans la cuisine.*

Rosa Pendleton Chiles.

Note.—On account of Raffeneau Delile's four years' sojourn in Wilmington and the interesting fact of his introducing North Carolina plants into France, the author has felt justified in requesting the preparation of the foregoing sketch from French sources, there being, as far as can be ascertained, no adequate account in English, although Delile's work is recognized by American botanists at the present day. The source from which Miss Chiles has drawn chiefly is M. Joly's *Éloge historique d'Alyre Raffeneau Delile,* of which her sketch is in part a translation.

BEGINNING OF FEDERAL FORTIFICATIONS ON THE CAPE FEAR.

(Extracts from the Memoirs of Gen. Joseph Gardner Swift, U. S. A., first graduate and afterwards commandant of the Military Academy of West Point.)

Proceeding by the right bank of the Cape Fear River to Negro Head Point ferry, opposite Wilmington, I arrived at Mrs. Meeks' boarding-house in that town on June 17, 1805, the anniversary of the Battle of Bunker Hill, and on that day reported myself by letter to my chief, Major Wadsworth, at West Point, using the day and 1775 as the figurative date of my letter by way of friendly memento. After presenting my letter of introduction, I took the packet for Fort Johnston and there paid my respects to the commandant of the post, Lieut. John Fergus, an uncle of Cadet McRee, and commenced a happy acquaintance with the surgeon of the post, John Lightfoot Griffin, with whom I established quarters at Mrs. Ann McDonald's. Here I also met Gen. Benjamin Smith, and to the last of the month had conferences with him as to the best mode of executing his contract with the War Department in the construction of a battery on the site of old Fort Johnston, Smithville.

Early in July I employed Mr. Wilson Davis, one of the most intelligent of the pilots, and with his aid I sounded the entrance over Main Bar, which is shifting sand, into the harbor of Cape Fear, and also the entrance at New Inlet, and then viewed the capacity of the anchorage within, together with the relative position of the several points of land near the entrances, of which I made a plot, and upon which I based my report of the 26th of July to the Secretary of War. The substance of this report was that the main objects to be secured were those that had been set forth by my late chief, Colonel Williams, to wit: to cover an anchorage in the harbor and to command its entrance by a small enclosed work on Oak Island, and an enclosed battery at Federal Point, at New Inlet, and also to complete the battery of tapia at the site of old Fort Johnston, the last being contracted for by Gen. Benjamin Smith. Pending the decision of the War Department upon this report, much of the summer was a leisure among agreeable families from Wilmington, that passed the warm season in slight frame houses at "The Fort," as the village of Smithville is called. Among these was the family of Capt. James Walker, to whose daughter Louisa and her cousin Eliza Younger I was introduced at a dinner given to Dr. Griffin and myself by Captain Walker. There were the families of Mr. John Lord and of the founder of the place, Mr. Joshua Potts, and of Gen. Benjamin Smith, who was to construct the public work under contract, and of Captain Callender, the surveyor of the port, who had been an officer of the army in the War of the Revolution, etc. General Smith became the governor of the State. He owned a large extent of property on Cape Fear River, and was of the family of Landgrave Thomas Smith, the colonial governor of South Carolina in the preceding century. He had become security for the collector of the port of Wilmington, who was a defaulter to the government, and it was to discharge this liability that General Smith had contracted to build the tapia work at the fort. His lady, Mrs. Sarah Dry Smith, was highly accomplished and was an hospitable friend to Dr. Griffin and myself, and one of the finest characters in the country. She was the daughter and heiress of Col. William Dry, the former collector in the colonial time, and also of the King's council. This lady was also a direct descendant from Cromwell's admiral, Robert Blake. There was also residing at the fort the family of Benjamin Blaney. A native he was of Roxbury, near Boston. He had migrated to Carolina as a carpenter, and had by industry acquired a competence to enable him to dispense aid to the sick and needy and other charities, in the performance of which he was an example of usefulness, charity, and unostentation. Most of the families at the fort were Federalists, and, though all deplored the event, they were the more sensibly impressed with the news of the death of Alexander Hamilton, who in this month of July had been slain in a duel with Colonel Burr, the account of which had been written to me by Colonel Williams. The whole Union was in a measure moved to grief by this sad event. Colonel Hamilton occupied a large space in the public mind. He had been the able leader of Federalism—of a class of men who may in truth be said to have been actuated by far higher motives than those of mere party.

My advices from West Point were that Major Wadsworth, Capt. W. A. Barron and Mr. DeMasson formed the academic corps; that Lieutenant Wilson was on duty at Fort Mifflin, Lieutenant Macomb in South Carolina, and Lieutenant Armistead in New York.

In my excursions on the water of Cape Fear I was aided by Captain Walker, Dr. Griffin, and Mr. Blaney, who as sportsmen were familiar with the numerous shoals and channels and anchorages thereof, so that the returns were not only in game but also in giving me knowledge of the capacity of this harbor, situate as it is on one of the most shallow and troublesome coasts to navigators. The anchorage, covered from the ocean by Bald Head, or Smith's Island, extending from the Main Bar to the New Inlet, and upon which island there is a growth of live oak and palmetto, and abounding with fallow deer.

Intimacy with Mr. Walker furnished me with many items of the war in Carolina, with which he was familiar, although not taking part in the battles, for he had been a moderate Tory, averse to taking arms against the mother country, in which his friend and brother-in-law, Louis DeRosset, had influenced him. Mr. DeRosset was of the King's council. Mr. Walker had been the executor of Gen. James Moore, the planner and director of the American force at the Battle of Moore's Creek, fought by Lillington and Caswell. From the papers of that officer he had gathered many an anecdote of the march of Cornwallis. Mr. Walker had been in the Regulators' War of 1770 and then commanded a company in the Battle of Alamance, in the western part of the State. He was cured of much of his Toryism by the tyrannical conduct of Maj. J. H. Craig, the British governor at Wilmington, afterwards governor-general of Canada. The conduct of this man had been oppressive and needlessly cruel to the people of Wilmington, and Captain Walker had been able to influence some relief for those who were in arrest, etc. He and his brother-in-law, John DuBois, had been appointed commissioners to arrange the cartel of prisoners, and to negotiate for the families who were to leave Wilmington when Cornwallis marched to Virginia, thus showing the confidence that both Whig and Tory had reposed in those gentlemen. Mr. Walker's family were of the settlers called "Retainers," coming from Ireland under the auspices of Colonel Sampson and of his father, Robert Walker. Among the families of "Retainers" were those of the Holmeses, Owens, Kenans, etc., now become independent planters and distinguished citizens. The father of Captain Walker, the above Robert, was of the same family with that of the Protestant hero, the Rev. George Walker, of Londonderry. The mother of Captain Walker was Ann, of the family of Montgomery, of Mount Alexander in Ireland, who had made a runaway match with Robert Walker. Capt. James Walker married Magdalen M. DuBois, the daughter of John DuBois and Gabriella DeRosset, his wife.

In the month of September, in reply to my report of the 26th of July, I received orders from the War Department to proceed with as much of the work therein contemplated as was embraced in General Smith's contract upon the tapia work at the site of old Fort Johnston, that had been there constructed in 1748 by His Excellency Gabriel Johnston, then colonial governor. In clearing away the sand I found much of the old tapia walls far superior to our contemplated plan for the battery of tapia.

Soon after this the slaves of General Smith commenced the burning of lime in pens, called kilns, made of sapling pines formed in squares containing from one thousand to one thousand two hundred bushels of oyster shells (alive) collected in scows from the shoals in the harbor—there abundant. These pens were filled with alternate layers of shells and "lightwood" from pitch pine, and thus were burned in about one day—very much to the annoyance of the neighborhood by the smoke and vapor of burning shellfish, when the wind was strong enough to spread the fumes of the kilns. In the succeeding month of November I commenced the battery by constructing boxes of the dimensions of the parapet, six feet high by seven in thickness, into which boxes were poured the tapia composition, consisting of equal parts of lime, raw shells, and sand and water sufficient to form a species of paste, or batter, as the negroes term it.

At the close of this month of November a large Spanish ship called the *Bilboa* was cast away on Cape Fear in a storm. It was alleged by the crew, who were brought by Pilot Davis to my quarters, that the ship was laden with sugar, and that there was much specie in the run; that the captain and mate had died at sea, and that having no navigator on board they had put the ship before the wind and run her on shore near the cape. There were twenty-one in this crew, a villainous looking set of rascals, that I had no doubt they were. Lieutenant Fergus detained them in the block-house at the fort until the collector sent inspectors to conduct the crew to Charleston, where the ship was known to some merchant. These men all had more or less of dollars in their red woolen sashes tied around their waists. On their arrival in Charleston they were detained some time, but no proof could be found against them and they went free. The pilots and others were for some time after this exploring the remains of the wreck, but nothing was found among the drift save spars and rigging.

FIRST STEAMBOAT ON CAPE FEAR RIVER.

Let us contrast the swift steamer *Wilmington* with the primitive example of former days—let us turn back for three-quarters of a century, when the town of Wilmington contained only a tenth of its present population, and recall an incident, related to the writer by the late Col. J. G. Burr, which created the greatest excitement at the time, and which was the occasion of the wildest exuberance of feeling among the usually staid inhabitants of the town—the arrival of the first steamboat in the Cape Fear River. A joint stock company had been formed for the purpose of having a steamer built to ply between Wilmington and Smithville or Wilmington and Fayetteville. Capt. Otway Burns, of privateer *Snap-Dragon* fame during the War of 1812, was the contractor. The boat was built at Beaufort, where he resided. When the company was informed that the steamer was finished and ready for delivery, they dispatched an experienced sea captain to take command and bring her to her destined port. Expectations were on tiptoe after the departure of the captain; a feverish excitement existed in the community, which daily increased, as nothing was heard from him for a time, owing to the irregularity of the mails; but early one morning this anxiety broke into the wildest enthusiasm when it was announced that the *Prometheus* was in the river and had turned the Dram Tree. Bells were rung, cannon fired, and the entire population, without regard to age, sex, or color, thronged the wharves to welcome her arrival. The tide was at the ebb, and the struggle between the advancing steamer and the fierce current was a desperate one; for she panted fearfully, as though wind-blown and exhausted. She could be seen in the distance, enveloped in smoke, and the scream of her high-pressure engine reverberated through the woods, while she slowly but surely crept along. As she neared Market Dock, where the steamer *Wilmington* is at present moored, the captain called through his speaking-trumpet to the engineer below: "Give it to her, Snyder"; and while Snyder gave her all the steam she could bear, the laboring *Prometheus* snorted by, amid the cheers of the excited multitude. In those days the river traffic was sustained by sailing sloops and small schooners, with limited passenger accommodations and less comfort. The schedule time to Smithville, was four hours, wind and weather permitting, and the fare was one dollar each way.

NOTE.—Steamboats were used on the Cape Fear very soon after their introduction. On October 16, 1818, the *Henrietta* began to run regularly between Wilmington and Fayetteville, and in April, 1819, President Monroe was carried on the *Prometheus* from Wilmington to Smithville. The *Prometheus* was probably on the river long before 1819.

THE DISASTROUS YEAR OF 1819.

The growth of Wilmington was naturally slow, notwithstanding the energy of the inhabitants. Indeed, because of the constant exodus of North Carolinians to the new country at the West and South, the population of the State hardly increased at all during the early years of the last century. The population of New Hanover County in 1810 was 11,465, and in 1820 it had fallen off to 10,866. In 1820 the population of Wilmington was, whites, 1,098, slaves, 1,433, free negroes, 102—a total of 2,633.

Especially, because of the absence of good roads and facilities for transportation—save by the river to Fayetteville—there was but little opportunity for extending the trade of the town.

Further, the trouble with England, the embargo, the interruption of commerce by the War of 1812, with the attendant financial embarrassments, brought loss and ruin in their train.

Superadded was the scourge of yellow fever during the summer of 1819, the disease in that season being more prevalent throughout the Southern and Middle Atlantic States than had at any other time been known. Baltimore, as well as the more southern ports, was entirely paralyzed. As in 1862, many families fled from Wilmington into the interior.

Hardly had the desolation subsided and commerce revived, when Wilmington was visited by the most disastrous conflagration recorded in its history. The total loss, as stated by some standard authorities, was about one million dollars, but the *Cape Fear Recorder* estimated it at between six and seven hundred thousand dollars—an almost total obliteration of the wealth of the town.

We quote from the *Raleigh Register and North Carolina State Gazette* of Friday, November 12, 1819:

It is our painful duty to register a very extensive and calamitous fire which took place at Wilmington in our State; and we do it with those strong feelings of sympathy and regret which such events naturally inspire. We cannot portray the circumstances in which the town was placed more feelingly than it is depicted by the Editor of the *Cape Fear Recorder;* "who feels them most can paint them best."

FIRE! Wilmington (says the *Recorder*) has experienced more awful calamities by fire than any other place in the Union. Thrice, within twenty years, has the devouring element laid in ashes the abodes of her inhabitants. Enterprise, industry, and the assistance of her neighbors, gave her, measurably, resuscitation, until the recent pressure of the times bended her down almost to the sinking point. Embarrassments in pecuniary matters had reached that state which appeared to baffle relief. Sickness and death followed in the melancholy train. Despair had almost concluded that she could not sink beyond this. Hope, the bright luminary by which man's path in this world of care is heightened and cheered, brought consolation, and pointed to better days. Disease had ceased—the periodical work of death completed—the late deserted abodes of her inhabitants filling—vessels arriving daily in her port—the appearance of business reviving. On Thursday morning, the 4th inst., about three o'clock, the cry of fire was given, and the delusion vanished. Her bright hopes were destroyed.

The frightful picture is before us and it is our duty to present it to our distant readers. The fire originated back of a small building occupied by Mr. Samuel Adkins as a grocery store, situated on the wharf, near Dock Street, and adjoining the large brick warehouse lately occupied as the '76 Coffee-house, in part of which was the office and counting house of Gabriel Holmes, Esq.

From the best calculation we can make, the whole number of houses destroyed was about three hundred, of every description, including the Presbyterian Church, lately erected; and the total loss of property between six and seven hundred thousand dollars.

The following persons are those who have lost by the destruction of buildings:

Col. Archibald F. McNeill, John London, Col. Thomas Cowan, John Swann, jr., William McKay, Estate of Thomas Jennings, Seth Hoard, Joseph Kellogg, Estate of J. London, Mrs. McRee, Jacob Levy, Richard Bradley, Edward B. Dudley, William J. Love, S. Springs, James Dickson, Hanson Kelly, David Smith, Henry Urquhart, John Walker, George Jennings, Robert Rankin, State Bank, Estate of Nehemiah Harris, Estate of James Allen, M. Blake, Estate of M. Murphy, James Usher, Mrs. Hoskins, Mrs. Toomer, William Harris, James Marshall, Estate of P. Harris, Louis Paggett, Estate of Hilliary Moore, Reuben Loring, William C. Lord, Gilbert Geer. This list is no doubt incomplete.

Among those who suffered by the destruction of other property the principal in amount are, Isaac Arnold, Edmund Bridge, jr., Eleazar Tilden, Dudley and Van Cleff, Dudley and Dickinson, Miles Blake, Seth Hoard, Richard Lloyd, J. Angomar, George Lloyd, H. Wooster, Patrick Murphy, B. C. Gillett, W. C. Radcliffe, Stewart Robson.

It is almost impossible to ascertain the amount of individual losses. Every person within the bounds of the fire, and all those without it who removed their property, lost more or less. But the extent of a loss, as it regards merely its amount, is not the criterion of its injury— it is he that has lost his all, the unprotected, the friendless, and the helpless, that ought to excite our pity and compassion, and calls for our assistance.

Only one life was lost—Capt. Farquhar McRae, after the fire had almost subsided, who ventured within a building for the purpose of saving property not his own. The walls fell, he was crushed to atoms. He was a useful citizen in his sphere of life and would have been regretted even had he died on the couch of disease.

To the sufferings of others Wilmington has never remained indifferent—limited as were her means, to know them was all that was necessary for her to contribute her mite. She is now in distress— hundreds of her inhabitants are suffering. The knowledge of her situation will, we are certain, confer relief.

And all this is the work of an incendiary. Suspicion has been afloat, but we suspect it has not been directed toward the right person. Higher views than those of plunder must have been the object, for we have heard of not much success and of very few attempts.

(Raleigh Register and North Carolina State Gazette, Friday, December 3, 1819.)

WILMINGTON FIRE—We have pleasure in stating that a subscription has been opened for the relief of the sufferers by this disastrous event, not only among the citizens of Raleigh, but among the members of both houses of the Legislature. The precise amount is not at present ascertained; but we trust it will be such as will show the liberality of the subscribers, considering the hardness of the times.

OTHER EARLY FIRES.

In the preface to his *History of New Hanover County,* published in 1909, Col. Alfred Moore Waddell said:

"What is called the Lower Cape Fear region of North Carolina has long been recognized by the writers of our history as the most interesting and, as one of them designated it, 'the most romantic' section of our State. Yet, up to this time, although partial sketches, historical and biographical, have appeared, no attempt at a regular history of it has been published, and now such a history cannot be written because of the destruction, by fire and other agencies, of a large part of the material requisite for the purpose. There was, perhaps, no part of the country where so many planters' residences with all their contents were lost by fire as on the Cape Fear and its tributaries, and it is well known among the descendants of those planters, some of whom were members of the learned professions, that by these fires many manuscripts, family records, and documents of various kinds that would have been invaluable as material for the preparation of a local history, were lost. Besides these fires on the plantations, the town of Wilmington was, at an early period, as well as several times afterwards, nearly destroyed in the same way, with the same results.

"None of the ancient official records of the town of Brunswick were preserved, and a considerable part of the county records was destroyed by Northern soldiers when the town of Smithville was captured by them in 1865. Some of the town records of Wilmington of an early period have also disappeared."

Many years ago, I searched in vain the ruins of the first settlement of Charlestown, at Town Creek, for records of that date, but my search was rewarded later by the discovery in the ruins of a house, said to have been the residence of Nathaniel Rice, of the book of entries and clearances of the port of Brunswick in a partly mutilated condition. I also searched at Lilliput among the ruins of Eleazar Allen's residence, without result; also, the ruins of Governor Tryon's Castle Tryon, or palace, at Orton, which revealed a piece of pottery stamped "W. Dry,

Cape Fear, 1765," and a large bunch of housekeeper's keys upon an iron ring and hook which fitted into a leather belt with a spring by which a key could be withdrawn and replaced. Other relics of less importance were discovered, but no papers. All of these ruins, as well as the ruins of St. Philip's Church, showed the devastation of fire in charred woodwork and melted colored glass.

As early as 1771, Wilmington suffered from a terrible conflagration, and an act of Assembly was passed to regulate the affairs of the town, in view of possible fires. In the account just given of the destruction wrought in 1819, it is mentioned that, in the previous twenty years, there had been several destructive conflagrations.

Mr. J. T. James says: "Wilmington, in common with many other of her sister towns and cities, has suffered often and seriously from the terrible scourge of fire; so much so, indeed, that these visitations have, from time to time, seriously retarded its growth. Scarcely would the citizens recover from the effects of one blow, ere they would be called upon to suffer again. The old chronicles tell us that in November, 1798, a most destructive fire occurred. On July 22, 1810, three stores and five houses, situated near what is now the corner of Market and Second Streets, but then known as Mud Market, were consumed by fire caused by lightning. In 1819, there was a most terrible conflagration, and the four squares bounded by Water, Princess, Second, and Dock Streets were destroyed. In 1827, the square south of the site of the present market house was again burned. In 1840 the square north of the market was consumed for the second time, together with the courthouse, which then stood at the intersection of Front and Market Streets. In 1843 occurred one of the most serious conflagrations of any ever experienced. On April 30 of that year a fire originated in the alley just north of the Cape Fear Bank building and swept with rapid strides to the north. All exertions to check it were in vain, and it was not until everything west of Front Street and north of the bank alley and portions of every square east of the same street and bordering upon it and north of Chestnut were consumed, that its fiery course could be stopped. This fire also destroyed the workshops and buildings of the Wilmington and Weldon Railroad Company, and the Methodist Episcopal Church, then situated, as now, upon the corner of Front and Walnut Streets. Three years afterwards, in 1846, the square next south of the market house was again and for the third time destroyed by fire."

Reference was made to two of these fires by Sir Charles Lyell, the famous geologist, who was in Wilmington in December, 1841, and again in January, 1842, and still again in December, 1845. In a letter written by him from Wilmington in December, 1845, he said: "The streets which had just been laid in ashes when we were here four years ago are now rebuilt; but there has been another fire this year, imputed very generally to incendiarism, because it broke out in many places at once. There has been a deficiency of firemen, owing to the State having discontinued the immunity from militia duty, formerly conceded to those who served the fire engines." Some mention of the fire of 1843 is also made in the article on Governor Dudley.

FIRST CAPE FEAR IMPROVEMENTS.

I find in the annual report of William P. Craighill, then major of Engineers, and brevet lieutenant colonel, United States Army, for the year 1873, a brief history of old surveys and maps and charts made of the Cape Fear River between its mouth and the port of Wilmington, which is a record of some value to us. I have also found in the records of the War Department of 1828, a lengthy report by Capt. Hartman Bache, of the Engineer Corps, transmitted by Maj. Gen. Alexander MacComb, chief engineer, to Hon. James Barbour, Secretary of War, who in turn transmitted it to Congress, which had called for it by resolution dated the 20th of December, 1827. This report is not only interesting but valuable, as it indicates the initial measures recommended and subsequently carried out by the Federal Government for the removal of obstructions to navigation between the bar and the port of Wilmington, the navigation of the river being greatly hampered by shoal water, which afforded, under the most favorable conditions, a channel of less than nine feet.

It also appears from this report and from other data, that the State work under Mr. Hamilton Fulton, State engineer in 1823, was unsuccessful and was condemned in its most important features by Captain Bache and by those who were directly interested in the commerce of the Cape Fear River.

About the year 1819 the State authorized Mr. Peter Brown, an eminent lawyer residing at Raleigh, then intending to visit

Great Britain, to employ an engineer for the purpose of improving our rivers and water transportation; and Mr. Brown engaged Hamilton Fulton, at a salary of $5,000.

The work of putting in the jetties below Wilmington seems to have been under Mr. Fulton's direction; but it is said that the engineer in charge was Mr. Hinton James,[1] who had been the first student to enter the State University. Afterwards, Mr. James, it is said, was mayor of Wilmington; and he lived in the town to a ripe old age. Mr. Fulton's work may have been founded on correct principles, but his plans, not only for the Cape Fear River, but for other improvements, were beyond the financial resources of the State, and after some years they were abandoned.

Steamboat Line to Charleston.

The progress of river improvement by the Federal Government during a period of ten years, from 1829 to 1839, was very slow, and it resulted in a gain of only two feet depth below Wilmington; but, after an hiatus of eight years, in 1847 it began to be pushed forward with great diligence and success from Wilmington to the sea, resulting in a safer channel of thirteen feet at high water and nine feet at low water. It is notable that in 1853 some of the citizens of Wilmington, enterprising men that they were, impatient at the slowness with which river and harbor bills were passed by Congress and anxious to continue the work without interruption, subscribed $60,000 (a large sum in those days for a small community) in furtherance of the improvement of the river and bar under the direction of an officer of the United States Engineer Corps. This was officially approved June 9, 1853, by Hon. Jefferson Davis, Secretary of War. The officer in charge of the work was General Woodbury, who married a daughter of General Childs. Meanwhile, there was much enterprise shown by the merchants of Wilmington in shipbuilding, in a large and increasing turpentine and lumber trade, in the establishment of packet lines to Baltimore, Philadelphia, and New York, and in a daily mail steamboat line to Charleston, consisting of the steamers *Vanderbilt, North Carolina, Gladiator,* and *Dudley.*

---

[1] His tombstone was recently discovered by Rev. Andrew J. Howell, of Wilmington, in the graveyard of the old Hopewell Presbyterian Church in the northern part of Pender County, formerly a part of New Hanover County. The inscription on the plain marble slab states that Mr. James was born September 20, 1776, and died August 22, 1847.

10

The following remarkable official statement was made by the United States engineers in 1853:

"The Cape Fear River is the natural and actual outlet of the products of 28 or more counties in North Carolina and of several counties in South Carolina. In one item of future exports other Southern States are interested and the whole country must be so in time of war: Coal in large quantities and of an excellent quality has been found upon the waters of the Cape Fear, about 120 miles from its mouth, and at no distant day, it is supposed, will become a regular article of export. We may, therefore, have—what must be regarded as a national benefit at all times, and in time of war as of very great importance—a depot of coal upon the Cape Fear, independent of supply from the North, and beyond the reach of the enemy. But this depot will, in great measure, be lost to the country unless the Cape Fear shall be improved so as to admit our ships of war."

Unfortunately, the mining of this coal a few years later did not prove a success.

CONGRESSIONAL AID TO RIVER IMPROVEMENT.

It was not until 1826 that Congress began to make appropriations for river and harbor improvements, and three years later the Cape Fear River was included in the list. For ten years an annual appropriation of $20,000 was regularly made, and then because of a change in public policy such appropriations ceased. The Democratic party was opposed to internal improvements at the expense of the government. From 1838 to 1866 only a few river and harbor bills were passed. Mr. William S. Ashe, the representative from the Cape Fear district in 1854, differed with his party on the subject of internal improvements and succeeded in getting through a bill carrying $140,000 for the Cape Fear River, the particular object being to close New Inlet, forcing all the water of the stream over the Main Bar. In order to accomplish his purpose he had to persuade many of his Democratic associates to withdraw from the chamber, and so many withdrew that, although his bill received a large affirmative vote, there was no quorum, and he had to call in others to make a quorum. On the final vote the bill passed, but there were still more than eighty Democrats absent. That was the beginning of the effort to close New Inlet, which was nearly accomplished when the war stopped operations, but when blockade running began, every one rejoiced that the inlet was still open.

In after years Senator Ransom exerted himself with success for the improvement of the river, but the greatest improvement has been accomplished under the influence of Senator Simmons, at the time acting chairman of the Committee on Commerce, having such matters in charge. He has secured a 26-foot channel, increasing immensely the commercial facilities of Wilmington, which her business men have quickly developed. Senator Simmons has likewise secured the adoption of a project to canalize the river from Wilmington to Fayetteville, and has been a strenuous advocate of the Coastal Canal, now about to be constructed. He has long appreciated the value of inland waterways and was a member of the Commission on Waterways sent to Europe by Congress a few years ago. In 1909 he was a prime factor in securing the adoption of the proposition to have a survey made for an intercoastal waterway from Boston to the Rio Grande. In 1912 he secured the adoption of the Norfolk and Beaufort section of that great undertaking and the purchase by the government of the Albemarle and Chesapeake Canal. He also secured the deepening of that waterway to twelve feet.

The River and Harbor Bill now pending carries a provision for a survey to increase the depth of water from Wilmington to thirty-five feet.

RAILROADS—THE FIRST PROJECT.

In March, 1833, the commissioners of the city of Fayetteville were instructed to negotiate a loan of $200,000 to be invested in the Cape Fear and Yadkin Valley Railroad, which, with individual subscriptions, would be more than enough for the organization of the company, and work could be begun in the spring of 1834.

On May 1, 1833, the *People's Press* advertised that the subscribers to the stock of the Cape Fear and Yadkin Valley Railroad, by applying to Dr. William P. Hort, would be refunded the amount of money paid by them on their shares, after deducting 12 per cent for disbursements. It was further stated that the project was abandoned because of lack of support by the inhabitants of the western section, who would not contribute one cent to the enterprise of establishing a railroad from the seaboard to the mountains.

THE FIRST DECLARATION OF STATE POLICY.

On July 4, 1833, the Internal Improvement Convention assembled in Raleigh with one hundred and twenty delegates, representing twenty-one counties in the eastern and northern sections. It seems to have been the first concerted effort towards organized action looking to the establishment of a railroad. Governor Swain presided and Gen. Samuel F. Patterson and Mr. Charles Manly were appointed secretaries. The personnel of the convention must have been remarkable, as the record says "So many distinguished and talented men are said never before to have assembled in the State."

In this convention Governor Graham, then in the prime of his rare powers, urged as the internal-improvement policy of the State, three north-and-south lines of railroad. He was antagonized by Joseph Alston Hill, of Wilmington, one of the most gifted orators of that period, who advocated east-and-west lines, marketing the products of the State through North Carolina ports. It was a battle of giants, and Hill won the victory.

The convention adopted resolutions to the effect that the General Assembly ought to raise by loan such sums as will "afford substantial assistance in the prosecution of the public works; *that no work should be encouraged for conveying produce to a primary market out of the State;* that the Legislature be asked to take two-fifths of the stock of companies; that a Corresponding Committee of twenty be appointed in each county, and that a second convention be held on the fourth Monday in November."

The delegates from Wake, Johnston, Lenoir, Wayne, Sampson, Craven, and New Hanover resolved that "means be devised for carrying into effect the scheme of a railroad from Raleigh to Waynesboro (Goldsboro), and thence to Wilmington."

The committee for the town of Wilmington was composed of Edward B. Dudley, William B. Meares, William P. Hort, Joseph A. Hill, and Alexander MacRae. Circulars were issued to the citizens of Wake, Johnston, Wayne, Sampson, Duplin, New Hanover, and Brunswick to ascertain what amount of aid they would contribute, and stating that $113,000 had been subscribed by the citizens of Wilmington, and that a total of $150,000 would be raised.

In July, 1833, the citizens of Wilmington formulated a proposition to make application to the Legislature to incorporate the town of Wilmington, the object being to raise funds on which immediate action could be taken in the construction of railroads; but in January, 1834, the bill "to incorporate the city of Wilmington and extend the limits thereof" was rejected.

The Origin of the Railroad Project.

Communication from Wilmington to the North was by means of an occasional packet ship and two lines of stages, one by way of New Bern and the other through Fayetteville and Raleigh.

The commerce of the town had but slowly increased and the future prospect was gloomy. A railroad or two, very short lines, had been constructed elsewhere, and this new method of travel was being talked about; but as yet it had not been proven a success.[1] Such was the situation when Mr. P. K. Dickinson, a young Northern man who had located in the town, went one summer to New England and saw there a little railroad in operation. It had only wooden stringers, with narrow, thin, flat iron on top, and the carriages were of light construction. Mr. Dickinson was greatly impressed with its capabilities. Convinced of its success, he became enthusiastic, and hurried back to Wilmington with the news that he had found what was needed to assure the future welfare of the town—a railroad. He was so enthusiastic, so insistent and persistent, that his idea took shape, and the people determined to have a railroad. With Wilmington to resolve is to act, and the Wilmington and Raleigh Road was chartered; but Raleigh would not subscribe, while the Edgecombe people would, so, although the line from Wilmington to Goshen pointed to Raleigh, the construction was northward to Weldon. Mr. Dickinson was one of the chief promoters and remained through life the leading director. He was one of the most useful, most esteemed and valued citizens of the town, and his large lumber plant, located north of the railroad terminal, was one of the great industries of Wilmington.

---

[1]The first American-built locomotive was put on the South Carolina Railroad, November 2, 1830. The first roads were operated by horsepower.

THE WILMINGTON AND WELDON RAILROAD.

In January, 1834, the bill to incorporate the Wilmington and Raleigh Railroad became a law; but the terms of the charter were so restricted that an amended charter was obtained in December, 1835, conferring larger privileges and changing the course of the proposed road. At the time of granting the first charter it was the intention to construct a railroad merely to connect the principal seaport with the seat of the government; but, as the project was more thoroughly considered, the advantages of building to some point on the Roanoke to connect with the Virginia lines, thereby completing one of the important links in the line of iron rail that was to extend from Maine to Florida, was realized, and in the amended charter the new corporation was given the privilege of changing its destination.

The first meeting of the stockholders was held on March 14, 1836, in the Wilmington Courthouse, and organized by electing Edward B. Dudley president (at a salary of $2,000), and the following directors: Andrew Joyner, W. D. Moseley, James S. Battle, Aaron Lazarus, Alexander Anderson, William B. Meares, James Owen, P. K. Dickinson, R. H. Cowan, and Thomas H. Wright. Gen. Alexander MacRae was elected superintendent, and James S. Green, secretary and treasurer. After passing several resolutions and agreeing to start the building of the road at both Halifax and Wilmington at the same time, the meeting adjourned to meet again on the first Monday in November and thereafter annually on the first Monday in May. After Mr. Dudley was elected governor, he was succeeded in the presidency by Gen. James Owen.

The building of the road was commenced in October, 1836, although little was done until January, 1837, and on March 7, 1840, the last spike was driven. Its actual length was 161½ miles, and at the time of its completion it had the following equipment: Twelve locomotives, which were named, *Nash, Wayne* (built by R. Stephenson & Co., Newcastle-on-Tyne, England), *New Hanover, Edgecombe, Brunswick, Duplin,* and *Bladen* (built by William Norris, Philadelphia, Pa.), *Greene, Halifax,* and *Sampson* (built by Burr & Sampson, Richmond, Va.), etc. There were also in use eight 8-wheel passenger coaches, 4 post-office cars, 50 freight cars, and 4 steamers, viz.:

the *North Carolina, Wilmington, Governor Dudley,* and *Cornelius Vanderbilt.*

The entire road was constructed under the following supervision: Walter Gwyn, chief engineer; Alexander MacRae, superintendent; Matthew T. Goldsborough, principal assistant engineer of the Southern Division, and Francis N. Barbarin, principal assistant engineer of the Northern Division. The road was first laid with plate iron 2 inches by $\frac{5}{8}$ inch on wooden stringers.

On April 5, 1840, the celebration of the completion of the railroad was held in Wilmington. The report says:

"A large number of gentlemen assembled in the town from various parts of the State and from Virginia and South Carolina at an early hour in the morning. The bells gave out sonorous peals and the shipping in the harbor came up, their flags waving. Cannon were fired every fifteen minutes throughout the day, with a national salute at meridian. At 2 p. m. a procession, composed of invited guests and citizens, including the president, directors, and officers of other roads, the Board of Internal Improvement, the Literary Board, the president, directors, engineers, agents and others in the employ of the Wilmington and Raleigh Railroad, was formed on Front Street, under the direction of Gen. Alexander MacRae, marshal of the day, assisted by Maj. R. F. Brown, and marched thence to the dinner table, escorted by the Wilmington Volunteers with their fine band of music.

"The dinner was set out at the depot under sheds temporarily prepared for the purpose. About five hundred and fifty were at the tables, which were amply prepared for hungry men.

"Gen. James Owen, the president of the company, presided, assisted by the directors, acting as vice presidents. Good feeling ruled the hour and good cheer gave quick wings to the nurslings of wit.

"Then followed a number of toasts—fifty-seven toasts and eleven letters with toasts."

Other reports are as follows:

Nov. 8, 1841.—"Annual meeting of the stockholders of the Wilmington and Raleigh Railroad Co. Gen. James Owen declined further service as president. Edward B. Dudley was elected in his stead and the following gentlemen were elected directors: P. K. Dickinson, Alexander Anderson, Thomas H. Wright, Robert H. Cowan, of Wilmington, Samuel Potter, of Smithville, and B. F. Moore, of Halifax."

Nov. 1842.—"Annual meeting of the stockholders of the Wilmington and Raleigh Railroad Co. Edward B. Dudley was reëlected president. Directors: Alexander Anderson, P. K. Dickinson, Samuel Potter, James S. Battle, A. J. DeRosset, and James T. Miller."

Nov. 12, 1847.—"The annual meeting of the stockholders of the Wilmington and Raleigh Railroad was held here. Gen. Alexander MacRae was elected president and E. B. Dudley, P. K. Dickinson, Gilbert Potter, James T. Miller, O. G. Parsley, and William A. Wright, directors. (The same as last year except William A. Wright in the place of Dr. John Hill, deceased.)"

At this last meeting it was resolved, "That the stockholders of the Wilmington and Raleigh Railroad Co., in general meeting assembled, do hereby pledge to the Wilmington and Manchester Railroad Co. a subscription of $100,000, to be paid on the completion of the said Manchester Railroad from the proceeds of the sale of steamboat and other property, which will at that time become unnecessary for the purpose of this company: Provided that our Legislature take such action as may authorize said subscription."

Nov. 10, 1848.—"Annual meeting of the stockholders of the Wilmington and Raleigh Railroad Co. No change made in the president or Board of Directors, except four directors on the part of the State were to be appointed by the Internal Improvement Board."

In December, 1848, a bill was introduced in the Legislature authorizing the Wilmington and Raleigh Railroad Company to mortgage the road and its appurtenances for about $600,000 for the purpose of purchasing iron to relay its tracks, and in January, 1849, $620,000 was authorized and an extension of ten years granted for the repayment to the State of $300,000 for money borrowed. Dr. A. J. DeRosset was sent to England, where he purchased 8,000 tons of iron, to be paid for by the bonds of the company secured by mortgage on the road.

The rail commenced to arrive in October, 1849, and in January, 1850, Congress passed an act for the relief of the Wilmington and Raleigh Railroad, providing for the paying of import duties on the rail by deducting annually the amounts due from the Post Office Department for carrying the mails. It was then the T-rail was introduced, which superseded the flat iron.

In August, 1850, Dr. John D. Bellamy, of Wilmington, was

elected to succeed Col. James T. Miller as a director, and in November of the same year, at the regular meeting of the Board of Directors, Gen. Alexander MacRae and the entire Board of Directors were reëlected. A surplus of $45,000 was directed to be applied to the extinguishment of the debts of the company.

It was about this time that the Wilmington and Manchester Railroad was completed, giving a through rail connection to the South, and thus making still more important the Wilmington and Weldon Railroad, as the Wilmington and Raleigh Railroad came to be called, its name being changed by the Legislature in 1855.

It is interesting to note, with reference to the far-seeing qualities of the men of 1835 and 1836, that a few years ago the chairman of the board discovered a letter written in the fine Spencerian hand of Governor Dudley, the first president, outlining the policy for the Wilmington and Raleigh Railroad, in view of his resignation in order to enter Congress. The extraordinary character of this proposed policy revealed the fact that the policy of the Coast Line under its new administration has been following precisely the line of action indicated by Governor Dudley at the beginning of its existence.

THE LONGEST RAILROAD IN THE WORLD.

Probably the most momentous, the most dramatic incident in the commercial history of Wilmington occurred in the fall of 1835 in the south wing of Gov. Edward B. Dudley's residence at the southwest corner of Front and Nun Streets, where a number of prominent Wilmington citizens had assembled to subscribe their names to the stock of an extraordinary adventure— the building of a railroad from Wilmington to Raleigh, to be called the Wilmington and Raleigh Railroad.

The town contained at that time a population of about three thousand souls, a majority of whom were negro slaves, and here an assembly of about twenty courageous men of the little corporation actually subscribed a larger sum than the entire taxables of Wilmington amounted to in that year to build the longest railroad in the world. It is well to remember, in our boasted age of progress, the splendid example of the fathers of 1835, whose foresight and self-sacrifice laid the foundations of our success. Perhaps the largest subscription was that of Governor Dudley— $25,000.

During the years that followed, the most important topic of local concern was the railroad, which so overtaxed the means of its promoters that even with the added endorsement of the directors its official order for a hundred dozen shovels was rejected.

The late Robert B. Wood, one of the railroad contractors of 1836 and later, informed me many years ago, that this incident led to a proposal by the railroad directors and contractors that Mr. John Dawson, then a prosperous dry-goods merchant on Market Street and a stockholder in the railroad, should add to his business a hardware department, comprising tools and implements needed for railroad work, assuring him of their undivided patronage. This was agreed to, and the well-known extensive hardware establishment of John Dawson, which led that business until Mr. Dawson died, had its origin and advancement in that way.

Mr. Wood also informed me that the method of advertising the meetings of stockholders and directors, which were often held, was unique. He owned a docile gray mare which was frequently borrowed by the officials on urgent business, and also used to make known the meetings by a large placard hung on either side of the saddle, in which a negro slave rode constantly ringing a large brass hand-bell, and parading the principal streets, proclaiming "Railroad meeting tonight."

Some of the newspaper illustrations of the "cars," as the train was termed in its early days, show a vehicle closely resembling the old stagecoach, with a greater number of passengers on top than are shown inside.

Timid apprehensions of danger were allayed by the official assurance upon the time-table that under no circumstances will the cars be run after dark.

The time of the departure of the northern train depended upon the arrival of the Charleston mail and passenger boats, which ran daily to connect with the cars at Wilmington. This elastic schedule, affected by the tides and wind and weather, sometimes varied as much as an hour from day to day, and the Wilmington passengers for the North usually pursued their regular avocations until the warning bell of the approaching steamer was heard all along the wharf, when a hurried departure was made for the train at the foot of Red Cross Street.

A prominent chemist of Wilmington told me that upon one occasion when he was delayed the train had reached Boney Bridge before the accommodating conductor saw his frantic signal to stop, but, true to the spirit of the times, the engineer immediately reversed the train and ran back two blocks in order to take him on board.

Upon the arrival at Wilmington of the train from the North, it was the custom of the general staff, on occasions, to meet the passengers with welcome speeches and with a gracious bow to present to every lady a bouquet of choice flowers. Conspicuous in this fine courtesy was the secretary and treasurer, Mr. James S. Green, who was sometimes so laden with floral offerings that his arms embraced quite a respectable flower garden. His affability was proverbial, and I well remember as a youth the sweet and gentle salutations of his later years. Well might Jenny Lind, the distinguished recipient of his gracious courtesies, have said to him upon her arrival in Wilmington, as Oliver Wendell Holmes said to some one else, "If your garden is as full of roses as your heart is of kindliness, there is no room for the sidewalks." Such delicate attentions were a part of the hospitality of the Cape Fear people of the olden times. The cultivated citizens of Wilmington unconsciously exhibited towards all respectable strangers in the streets and in the hotels such marked deference in their salutations and welcome that the impressions of intelligent travelers on business or pleasure were most favorable. Our esteemed octogenarian, Mr. Walker Meares, tells me that it was the custom of prominent citizens to make formal calls upon the strangers who came here in the forties, and to welcome them with stately dignity and courtly expressions to the thriving town of Wilmington.

DEVELOPMENT OF THE RAILROAD.

When President Dudley retired from the presidency in 1847, he was succeeded by Gen. Alexander MacRae.

In those early days there were numerous difficulties in operation, but General MacRae proved himself to be a most capable and efficient manager. The Board of Directors was composed of some of the most competent business men of Wilmington—men unsurpassed for capability, energy, and integrity. They placed the bonds of the road in London on advantageous terms, and the construction was cheap and without unnecessary expenditure.

In 1854 William S. Ashe became president. General conditions were now changing. The South was emerging from infantile weakness, and industries were developing and multiplying.

On the completion of the North Carolina Railroad, Colonel Fisher and Mr. Ashe arranged for western products to come to Wilmington through Goldsboro, and a line of steamers was put on from Wilmington to New York, carrying North Carolina's products to the markets of the world from a North Carolina port—the consummation of Mr. Ashe's purpose when he drew the charter of the North Carolina Railroad.

But passenger traffic was of equal importance to the road, and Mr. Ashe sought to build up a great through passenger business. He sought to eliminate as far as practicable all breaks at terminals, and to relieve travel of its inconvenience and tedium, and in conjunction with Senator David L. Yulee, the president of the Florida Railroad, he developed Florida travel until it reached large proportions and became a highly remunerative business.

Recognized throughout the South as a dominant influence in railroad matters and a most successful manager, in 1861, at the request of President Davis, Mr. Ashe took supervision of all Confederate transportation east of the Mississippi River, but he still remained president of the Wilmington and Weldon Railroad until his death, in September, 1862.

THE COMMERCE OF WILMINGTON.

From the beginning among the merchants of Wilmington were some men of enterprise, who owned their own ships, which were engaged in trade with Great Britain as well as with our Northern ports and the islands of the Caribbean Sea.

Forest products at first furnished a considerable part of the exports, while the imports were such as a newly settled country needed. But as the population of the interior thickened and products became diversified, Wilmington became the center of a varied and extensive commerce and its importance as a commercial *entrepôt* increased, while many of its merchants became men of importance who deserved to rank as eminent in the world of trade. The following quotations indicate the commercial importance of Wilmington between 1830 and 1840.

The *Boston Courier* of July 23, 1830, says: "One hundred and fifty-one more vessels have entered the port of Wilmington this year than last, including in the number 1 ship, 2 barks, 181 brigs, the rest (410) schooners. These tar-and-shingle skippers, which carry large topsails, everywhere besprinkle our coast. Now Wilmington is the grand railroad and steamboat thoroughfare. She is taking the position that belongs to her and recalling the proud days of her prosperity before the American Revolution."

The *Richmond Compiler* says: "One hundred and fifty-one more vessels have entered the port of Wilmington this year than last. This shows great advance in trade. We have been surprised to hear that the tonnage of Wilmington exceeds that of Richmond, although the town has not one-fourth of our population. It must be a place of great enterprise, if we judge from what has been done within the last few years. We feel admiration for such a people and take pleasure in expressing it."

A memorial of the Internal Improvement Convention to the General Assembly of North Carolina at the session of 1838, embodying the following tables, shows what the foreign trade was at that time:

"The tables annexed show the tonnage employed in the foreign trade, entered and cleared at Wilmington from October, 1836, to October, 1837; also the tonnage employed in the foreign trade of the ports of Norfolk, Petersburg, and Richmond for the same time, as taken from the report of the Secretary of the Treasury.

"From these tables it appears that in the year 1837 the tonnage entered and cleared in the foreign trade from Wilmington exceeded that of Norfolk 6,384 tons, and exceeded both the ports of Richmond and Petersburg together 17,694 tons. We are informed on high authority that the coast trade of Wilmington employs a greater tonnage than her foreign trade. We have not the means of ascertaining its actual amount, as it is not reported. If this be true, and we believe it to be so, not only on the high authority from which we received it, but because we know the maritime trade of North Carolina is principally a coasting-trade, it would follow that the tonnage employed in the trade of the port of Wilmington is greater than the three great ports of Virginia—Norfolk, Richmond, and Petersburg."

COMPARISON OF FOREIGN TRADE OF WILMINGTON WITH THAT
OF NORFOLK, PETERSBURG, AND RICHMOND IN 1838.

WILMINGTON TONNAGE ENTERED AND CLEARED.

American vessels 12,378
Foreign vessels 3,827

                                      16,205   Entered.....16,205

American vessels 25,600
Foreign vessels 3,929

                                      29,529   Cleared......29,529

VIRGINIA TONNAGE ENTERED.

Petersburg, American vessels 3,693
Richmond, American vessels 2,822
           Foreign vessels.............. 1,197

                                   7,712   7,712

Norfolk,   American vessels 4,357
           Foreign vessels 10,000

                                  14,357   14,357

VIRGINIA TONNAGE CLEARED.

Petersburg, American vessels 2,748
Richmond,   American vessels 13,240
            Foreign vessels 4,340

                                  20,328   20,328

Norfolk,   American vessels 12,771
            Foreign vessels 12,222

                                  24,993   24,993

WILMINGTON IN THE FORTIES.

JOHN MACLAURIN, a prominent merchant and a Presbyterian elder, who died in the year 1907, was one of the most remarkable men of our community in his day and generation. Proud of his Scottish lineage, he possessed those sterling traits of heart and mind which likewise adorned the lives of many of his fellow-countrymen in the Cape Fear region—"absolute dependableness in all thinking and in all dealing, a lively sense of justice, a cultivated taste, critical judgment, with a splendid capacity for moral indignation." He was an honor to his city and Commonwealth.

He was a friend and admirer of Colonel Burr, who was some twelve years his senior, and he wrote for the local newspapers some charming reminiscences of Wilmington in the forties over the pen name "Senex, Jr.," parts of which I have selected for more permanent record.

I.

After little observation, one will note in the topography of Wilmington that Fifth Street, running parallel to the Cape Fear River, is the backbone of a ridge upon which the city is built. The plateau which lies upon the summit of this ridge is variable in width, including oftentimes Fourth and even Third Streets on the one side and Sixth and Seventh Streets on the other, in somes cases with the level ground almost overhanging the river, as between Ann and Church Streets. We speak of the natural lay of the land as the topography—before the many changes that within the past fifty years have been made by grading and filling the streets. The average height of the ridge is fifty feet above tidewater, and the highest point, supposed to be at or near the intersection of Seventh and Red Cross Streets, perhaps ten feet higher. The descent towards the river is seamed by several branches, or runs, taking their rise sometimes as far back as Third Street and emptying into the river a few hundred yards apart. Within the limits of "Wilmington of the Olden Time" these were the streams rising between Third and Fourth Streets and emptying at the foot of Mulberry: Jacob's Run, rising at Fourth Street near Princess and pursuing a southwest course until the river receives its waters at Dock Street; and Tanyard Branch, rising at Third Street between Orange and Ann Streets and running nearly due west, emptying into the Cape Fear River at a point between the same streets. Boiling Springs

Branch does not come strictly within our limits, but so near by that it is given its place here. Rising about Fifth Street and Wooster, it runs west with an inclination slightly south and empties near the foot of Dawson Street.

The river front as we see it now gives little idea of the water line even fifty years ago. The business of that time was done between Orange and Mulberry Streets, most largely perhaps north of Dock. After the building of the Wilmington and Weldon Railroad, the trend of business was constantly toward the depot. The wharves south of Orange Street were used for the storage of staves, river lumber, and tar. The distillation of turpentine was then in its infancy and a slight factor in business operations. Above Mulberry Street the water of the river came up to Nutt Street in all places where the land had been made, as it was called, by filling in the water lots with ballast or sand. When steamers were first placed in line between Wilmington and Charleston, a bridgeway was constructed to reach the boats and transfer passengers and baggage from the railroad landing place. Above Campbell Street on the river front, fifty years ago, were woods, or rather swamp. Above Bladen, a sheer bluff rose from the foot of the swamp, and just beyond Harnett Street on the summit of the bluff stood "Paradise," then owned by Mr. Robert H. Cowan. The locality in general was less euphoniously styled "Hogg's Folly"—precisely why no one seems to know, but certainly because some one of the name had begun an enterprise of some kind or other which proved an impracticability on his hands.

Before entering upon any report of people and places it may be well to note how the natural features have been changed within the past half century. We will follow the courses of some of the streams we have referred to, confining ourselves to the limits embraced in the original plan of the town; viz.: Between the Cape Fear River and Fifth Street, long known as "Old Boundary," and between Campbell Street and what was afterwards known as Wooster. Sometime, doubtless near the completion of the Wilmington and Raleigh (now Wilmington and Weldon) Railroad, it became desirable to level Front Street across Mulberry. This seems to have been done without the precaution of making a drain to carry off the water, which was thus backed up Mulberry Street and formed a pond extending as far as Second Street, and which must have been several feet deep. This body of water was known as the "Horse Pond," and remained a source of discomfort and a menace to health until sometime in the forties. It was quite deep and fish were sometimes caught from its waters.

Nowhere have changes been more or greater than on the line of Jacob's Run. Fifty years ago the lots between Third and Fourth Streets, now occupied by the courthouse and the jail of the county, were a quagmire. Princess Street, between the streets named, was a slope from the point now occupied by the City Hall (the top of the hill was then several feet higher than now) down to the stream below. Third Street, at and near Princess, is several feet higher than it was in 1840, and the same is to be said of Second Street at the intersection of Market. At this point the mud in times long since past was so prevalent that the locality, being then occupied by a market house and town hall, was known as "Mud Market." Improvement of a like character was made, at an earlier date probably, at or near the intersection of Dock and Front Streets. There is a tradition that small canoes or batteaux came up Jacob's Run from the river at high tide to Mud Market. This occurred before the memory of any one now living, but it is founded on the testimony of perfectly truthful gentlemen. As late as 1840 the sidewalk on the south side of Market, near Second, was some feet higher than the street itself, and several steps were the means of ascent or descent. Willow Spring Branch was overlooked in what has gone before. It took its rise above Second Street, near the line of Third, and thence to the river. The lots on the west side of Second Street, between Dock and Orange Streets, show how much the land just here was raised on the line of Second Street. Where the dwelling on the east side of Second Street, Judge Russell's residence, and the dwelling on McLean's Alley now stand was a depression, and the street has been raised some eight or ten feet at least. Apparently to protect the Willow Spring from the caving-in of earth, a wall of cypress logs was run on the line of the street and on the alley. From near the middle of Third Street between Orange and Ann, at a point some fifteen or twenty feet from the eastern line, the hill sloped abruptly until about the western line it was arrested by a brick wall. This depression made Third Street impassable in this immediate locality except on the margin indicated. The wall referred to protected a spring at its foot, and thence the stream flowed on to form a tanyard near Second Street, established in 1826 by Isaac Northrop and John M. VanCleff and afterwards owned

11

by Mr. Northrop and John T. Hewitt. Second Street was then much lower than now. But nowhere within the city limits have there been such changes as on the line of Front Street, between Orange and Ann. Third Street at this point was then as low as the coal yard of W. G. Fowler, at its eastern limit, now is. From this point rose a steep hill, upon the summit of which stood the Baptist Church. The dwelling into which the church was transformed marks the elevation. In those days, of course, Front Street could only be traveled in wheeled conveyances with difficulty, and to reach Front Street from the river by the line of Ann or Nun Streets was impracticable.

Before entering upon the main subject, however, it may be well to discuss in a general way the prevalent customs or habits of the people of a half century or more ago, and their modes of business, and to note any other matters concerning the times that may be interesting or instructive. There were very few residences east of Fifth Street (at that time in the eastern boundary). The present residence of the bishop of East Carolina was then owned and occupied by Mr. James S. Green, and was the only house on the entire block on which it was situated. A few houses were on the eastern side of Fifth Street, but none farther out, so that in this part of town all east of Sixth Street may be said to have been in the woods. On Market Street there was little, if any, extension of habitation. In fact, between Seventh and Eighth, near Market, was the public hanging ground, and chinquapin hill, where that fruit could be gathered in season, then comprehending in general the ground anywhere on or about Market and Eighth Streets. Around the northern and especially the southern boundary, settlement was sparser still. Dry Pond, bounteously full of water in the wet season and guiltless of a semblance of moisture in the dry, then sat placidly on the snow-white sand amid the scrubby oaks and prickly pears and wire grass without a habitation about it.

In 1840 the population of Wilmington was 4,268, and the limits were circumscribed as we have heretofore stated them.

At the time of which we are now writing not even gas lighting had been dreamed of. Kerosene was then, and even for twenty years after, totally unknown. Camphine, a refined preparation of spirits turpentine, was a recent and most decided improvement on the lamp oil or tallow-dipped candles. This article, camphine, came into almost universal use, having very high illuminative power, though exceedingly inflammable, and so extremely dangerous. Its cheapness was a great recommendation, and its only rival, if it was a rival, for illuminating purposes, was sperm candles, which were beyond the reach of those in moderate circumstances. Somewhat later on adamantine candles, because of good lighting power with little accompanying hazard, in a great measure displaced camphine. The candle then became the most universal house and office illuminator, and the candlesticks and snuffers were indispensable household articles. The streets were lighted with big lamps filled with whale oil and placed at the intersection of the streets. The lighting, as may be readily conceived, served to do little more than make the darkness visible.

Matches were not known a hundred years ago. In fact, the first properly called friction matches were invented in England in 1827, and greatly improved in 1838, but still they were neither quick nor sure, easily lighted nor safe; not safe because of being tipped with phosphorus, a substance fatally poisonous to many of those engaged in the manufacture, and even to some who used the matches. In 1855 were invented the safety matches, which have since been evolved into those in use at present. Before the days of matches, flint and steel had to be resorted to for the making of fire, and because of the cost of matches these primitive and uncertain means were the only resources of the poor for many years after matches were introduced. For the reason just given it was of the utmost importance to keep up fire day in and day out, and in many families it was true that for years upon years fire in the house was never suffered to go out. A common thing it was in summertime to place a paper bearing the merest glimmer of light afloat in a cup of oil at bedtime and so keep up the fire until morning.

Fuel comes naturally to be considered now. It was generally simply the forest growth, or the refuse of sawmill operations. Coal was not unknown, of course, in 1840, or its value as fuel underrated, but until the days of railroad communication the cost of the carriage of coal, even to get it to navigable water, made it generally unavailable as fuel.

Allusion has been made to the street lighting. Hardly had "Old Matt" set his feeble lamps alight, when the sound of night watchmen, very few and wide apart, were to be heard crying the hours of night. "Ten o'clock and all's well!" was a cry that will be recalled by some who may read these lines. But this served too well to announce the whereabouts of the watch to nightly depredators and was discontinued on that account. Besides these watchmen, occasionally, when diabolism was specially prevalent, and always on Saturday night, perhaps, citizen patrolmen walked the streets until a late hour, sometimes during the entire night. The town bell rang at nine o'clock p. m. as a signal when the negroes were to be out of the street, unless by special and definite permission of their owners. The same bell regulated the hours for breakfast and dinner, and one hour after the call to these in each case, the "turn out bell" gave the call from refreshment to labor.

Every doctor compounded his own prescriptions in those days, and physicians' offices were simply drug stores, minus the patent medicines and perfumery and fancy articles which druggists keep in stock. The doctor usually charged for his service to a family a round sum by the year, and made his visits on horseback, with his saddlebags containing medicine and invariable accompaniments; and his lancet, let us not forget, for phlebotomy was the universal practice.   SENEX, JR.

II.

An esteemed friend, fully and accurately informed, suggests correction of the writer's surmise that the "Horse Pond," corner of Front and Mulberry Streets, was artificially formed, as was suggested in the former article, and says that it existed previous to 1812; and further that boys of seventy or eighty years ago were wont to swim in its waters.

A buggy was hardly known a few decades ago. The rich traveled in closed carriages, very much lighter, but in appearance very similar to stages. They were costly, and those in moderate circumstances contented themselves with horseback riding. This was the mode of travel generally for both sexes on journeys or in church attendance, but two-wheeled vehicles, drawn by one horse, were sometimes called into requisition; the gig for two persons and the sulky for one.

How changed school discipline and training of the schools within the past sixty years or so! Even good old "Miss" (Mrs.) "Coxetter" used the birchen rod, and Miss Maggie McLeod, who lingered with us almost until now, and Miss Laura Rankin knew well its virtue and spared not to apply. In the Old Academy days, before our time, the older citizens hesitated not to tell, almost with clenched teeth, how "Old Mitchell" wielded the rod in a way that would not have disgraced a Comanche. But Jesse Mulock was bad enough. "Old Mulock"—for to schoolboys teachers are all old—was a man of powerful grip, and when he kept over the Hewlett bar, on Front Street, where Craft's furniture store now stands, or later in the room over French's shoe store, where Sol. Bear's store is now located—in either place he had a room above that in which the idea was taught to shoot, a room to which unruly youth were transported to undergo the horrors of the hickory. We hear little now of chinquapin or birch or hickory. "The fair, delightful plans of peace" prevail in the schoolrooms of today and do perhaps as well. But this must be allowed: if the youths of olden time learned less they learned it thoroughly. They lost in extent and variety, but did they not gain in solidity? In 1840 one went to school eleven months of the year, barring Saturday and Fourth of July and Christmas, perhaps, and with Mr. Mulock even Saturday was liable to be appropriated to map-inspection, or a lecture on astronomy—a sort of dessert to the intellectual feasts of the other five days.

Daguerre discovered the art of retaining impressions upon chemically prepared plates in 1839, and of course daguerreotyping was not practically known in Wilmington in 1840. On the mantelpieces of almost every home were silhouettes; that is, profiles cut out of paper or cardboard with more or less neatness and laid on a black surface. These silhouettes were usually very accurate likenesses, so far as a side view could be such. The portraits painted for those who could afford them were sometimes far otherwise. In the early days of the forties traveling on land was mostly by private conveyance. The four-horse stage-coach carried mails and passengers on special routes where not superseded by the few railroads then in existence. The stage carried one from place to place at a cost of, say 10 cents a mile, at the rate of six miles an hour, without extra charge for the bumpings and thumpings experienced. In 1845 one might go from Wilmington to New York in seventy hours, stopping at each railroad terminus to change cars and recheck (or remark) baggage. Postages previous to 1845 were $12\frac{1}{2}$ cents for a single sheet of paper and 25 cents for a double sheet. All papers were folded and sealed with wafers or sealing wax. Postpaid envelopes were in use in Paris in the seventeenth century and the Sardinian States used them in 1818. Stamps were introduced

into the United States in 1840; the government did not adopt
their use, however, until 1847, although tentatively they were
used in New York in 1845, and an adhesive stamp was used in
St. Louis in the same year. It will readily be understood that
few letters were written when 25 cents was the rate of postage,
and that, as payment was required on receipt of the letter, the
published list of uncalled-for letters was of extraordinary length.
What were known as ship letters sometimes came by vessels into
the port of Wilmington. They were required to be deposited in
the post office, the conveyancer receiving part of the postage.

The mails early in this century were conveyed from place to
place in express transmission, or on more important routes by
post boys, with relays of horses at short distances. The stage-
coach, perhaps at the same time, certainly a little later and until
the advent of railroads, was used as the mail conveyancer. The
route south from Wilmington was across the ferry at foot of
Market Street and the causeway, via Georgetown, S. C., and
Charleston. East, the route then and now—but not so well
now—was and is known as the New Bern Road. North, the
way seems to have been over Little Bridge, via Waynesboro
(now Goldsboro), and so on. The blowing of the horn announcing the coming stage was a source of infinite delight to the small
boys of the period, black and white alike.

The change in the character of business transactions in Wilmington between 1830 and 1850, though not nearly so great as
that between 1870 and 1890, is nevertheless worthy of note.
The exports in the early thirties were mainly, almost exclusively, lumber, shingles, and staves to the West Indies, and rice,
naval stores, and cotton to the North; the importations, principally sugar, molasses, and rum, especially rum. One looking
over the advertisements of those days can hardly fail to be
struck with the amount of Jamaica rum and New England rum
offered for sale. The Washingtonian temperance movement in
the late twenties and throughout the thirties had undoubtedly a
great effect in changing the habits of the people and so in diminishing the demand for liquors. In course of time the channel
of West Indian trade became in a great measure diverted from
Wilmington. The trade in the forties was not what it had been
in the decade previous.

The means and manner of conducting business in 1840 were
essentially different from what they became a decade or two
later. In every countinghouse of any pretensions there was a

tall desk with slopes on all four sides and a plane surface on top
to hold the necessary implements or articles for the transaction
of business. Every desk had one or more boxes of wafers and a
stamp for ordinary letter sealing, and sealing wax with the
candle hard by for extraordinary cases. The pen used was
usually the quill, for though the steel pen had been invented
some time before, it had not come into general use; in fact, in
1840 was quite a rarity. Joseph Gillette patented his improvement in 1831, but it was slow work to supersede the goosequills
which every school-teacher had to mend for his pupils, generally,
and every boy had in time to learn to make and mend for himself. The box of sand to dry the manuscript—a most annoying
device it was—took the place of blotting paper, which then had
not come into use. Safes there were, of course, pretentiously
dubbed "patent asbestos" and "salazuander," but they were in-
finitely inferior to the chilled-iron fireproof safes now in use.

A word or two now as to the way traffic, that is the ordinary buying and selling of merchandise, was conducted previous
to 1840, and indeed through the forties and perhaps later. It
must be recollected that most men of means owned slaves; especially did farmers and planters own many of them. Then, as
now, planters had regular accounts with the dealers—dealers
rather than factors—and these dealers furnished the planters
with every article, large or small, that they needed. On the
first of January of each year the account of the planter was
made up and presented. He paid it if he chose or such part as
he chose, and a note bearing interest at 6 per cent was given for
the balance. The next year the same process was gone through.
At intervals the entire debt was liquidated, if the debtor chose,
or if the creditor compelled. In general, however, dealers of
means kept their notes as an investment. Occasionally a note
was transferred in the purchase of property, or the notes were
"shaved" to enable a holder to raise cash under stress, but in
many cases new notes with interest added (and thus compounded) were taken from time to time, usually every year,
and no settlement was made. The death of the maker of the
obligation, however, made a settlement imperative. When he
who owed was found to be getting "shaky," the note was put
in suit in order to collect, and some property had to be sold, a
negro or two, not improbably, to satisfy the judgment.

The planter upon whose estate debt was thus accumulating
was providing against the evil day by using his money to buy

negroes or add a few acres here or there to his landed possessions, the natural increase of negroes being of itself a very considerable means of acquiring wealth. The course that was pursued between merchant and planter was based on property, very
much the same as that between the merchant and all persons of
fair credit, who preferred to give their notes to paying their
debts in cash. Annual arrangements were the rule. The banks
discounted good paper to run ninety days; at the end of the time
they required interest paid and then renewed the paper, and so
on indefinitely. They were happy in thus running credits to
planters for years and compounding the interest every ninety
days. Of course they paid out their own notes (promises to
pay), and, as in fact a very large part of these notes never came
back for redemption, they made a prosperous business.

Senex, Jr.

III.

Why may we not before getting into matters of more consequence refer to the *"morus multicaulis* craze"? The *multicaulis*
is a variety of the white mulberry, and its leaves were, in days
that are gone, presumably are now, especially esteemed as food
for the silkworm. The enthusiasm of its culture did not raise
the hopes nor its collapse produce the dire consequences of the
"tulip craze," the "South Sea Bubble," and others that have
come down to us through the corridors of time, and in the early
days of 1840 it had nearly run its rather brief course. At that
time the numerous advertisements offering and belauding it had
about ceased to appear, and those who were to realize fortunes
from the manufacture of silk had well-nigh ceased to mourn
over their departed hopes. Still, the *morus multicaulis* was to
be found, probably, in some of the lots around town, and it had
hardly disappeared from the upland field connected with the
rice farm of Mr. James S. Green, near Kidder's mill, in which
a few acres had been devoted to its cultivation.

One of the most important of our industries is truck farming.
Many persons engage in it of course solely with a view to disposing of their product in this city, but others raise vegetables and
small fruits almost exclusively, if not entirely, for early shipment to Northern markets. Among the latter are Chinese truck-
men, who raise vegetables hardly considered edible with us, and
ship them directly to factors of their own race, doubtless in

Philadelphia or New York. But in or about 1840 it was not so. Very many persons had around their residences sufficient ground for patches of vegetables, green peas, cucumbers, roasting-ears, and the like, and so many a town lot was really a half-acre farm. In the nature of things, as the town grew, or rather as the town had grown, fresh vegetables became a felt want. When the time and the necessity came into conjunction Mr. John Barnes appeared on the scene. At the old London corner, where Solomon now has his store, in market hours Mr. Barnes could always be found with vegetables in their season, always the best, too, of their kind. His farm was located quite beyond the limits, even beyond "Dry Pond," though it would be reckoned in that precinct. It comprised what now is the square bounded by Queen and Seventh and Wooster and Eighth Streets, about five acres. On this little plot of bald sand-hill land, by indefatigable industry and practical skill, Mr. Barnes managed to support himself and family, not forgetting to give them at least a good solid English education. Here were raised the first cabbages ever produced on soil hereabout. In fact, until Mr. Barnes introduced them it was not supposed that they could be headed around here. And watermelons—there is no adjective available to describe them. They were always to be expected on the Fourth of July, and Barnes's watermelons and the *Gladiator* or the *Wilmington* or whatever line boat went on the annual excursion were part and parcel of the celebration of the day. At the time of which we write Mr. Martindale raised watermelons also and furnished buttermilk, and it was a time of delight to the average boy on a hot summer day when the old white-covered cart, drawn by the clay-bank mare, the whole directed by old Aunt Sally Martindale, would be seen coming around old Jack Green's corner townward. Mr. Barnes died of yellow fever on November 14, 1862, aged sixty. To meet increasing demand, the truck gardening in and around Wilmington was developed, of course. Dr. James F. McRee, having retired from practice, found at Hilton both pleasure and profit in this kind of farming. F. B. Agnostini afterwards went into it on the Little Bridge Road near San Souci Plantation. Mr. Christopher A. Dudley engaged in it at Summerville, below Greenfield, and John Gafford a mile or two beyond Jump-and-Run Branch. And we must not forget old Dr. J. Tognio, who leased a part of Love Grove Plantation, on Smith's Creek, a Frenchman of some attainments, we believe, in a literary way, but hardly a success in truck farming. When or whither he retired is not known to us.

"Say something about schools," says a friend, and we are disposed to comply. What follows must be largely reminiscent. We would like to speak of some schools, Miss Maggie McLeod's, for instance, but could say nothing of personal knowledge. This much is known, however, that this good old lady, who, well on in the eighties of her life, left us only a year or two since for her heavenly home, laid the educational foundation deep and strong for many of the best citizens of today. The same ought to be said of the teaching of Miss Laura Rankin, now Mrs. Rothwell, whose temperance societies and strict moral training otherwise implanted principles which will tell throughout eternity. Rev. A. P. Repiton, Rev. Mr. Shepherd, and Rev. W. W. Eells taught schools that were well patronized, but for the reason given above we can do no more than note them.

The forties were the birchen time in schooling. Methods were drastic—if that is the word. They had moderated from the days of Mitchell in the Old Academy, for then the methods might, without a strain upon language, be called sanguinary. But there were exceptions. Good old Mrs. Easter Coxetter— did she whip? Well, we do not recall it, but the goggles made out of the "Jack of hearts"—was it? (we are not up on that nomenclature), we do remember, and a friend whose recollection is vivid says the three-legged stool and the dunce's cap were used. That was not all, however. The dear old lady had us on Friday evening to recite the Apostles' Creed, and maybe the Ten Commandments and the Lord's Prayer. And here we took our first lessons in the Episcopal catechism—and our last. Yes, she was a dear old lady, a dear old saint, now over half a century in heaven. In a former article Mr. Jesse Mulock was referred to, and we only note here that Wilmington has had few, if any, better teachers than he.

Cape Fear Lodge, No. 2, I. O. O. F., was organized on the 13th of January, 1842—the place, a room over the grain store of B. F. Mitchell & Son. The charter members were Gen. Alexander MacRae, W. S. G. Andrews, Willie A. Walker, and Valentine Hodgson from Weldon Lodge, No. 1. Thomas H. Howey and Levi A. Hart were initiated the same night. The lodge soon moved its quarters to an upper room of a building on the corner of the alley next south of the Purcell House. This is only preliminary to saying that in 1842 a committee consisting of Col. John MacRae, Rev. B. L. Hoskins, and Owen Fennell, Esq., was appointed to report on the propriety of establishing a school. On June 10, 1843, we quote from the *Wilmington Chronicle*, "Trustees of Wilmington Academy resolved to lease the eastern end of their property to Cape Fear Lodge, No. 2, I. O. O. F., for twenty-five years for the erection of a school-house, at an annual rental of a peppercorn."

The Odd Fellows' School was established, and a benevolent work was thus done for Wilmington which ought to be remembered with profoundest gratitude by all who were recipients of the benefits conferred by the institution. With all books and stationery furnished, the tuition fee was only $3 a quarter—and it was a quarter, or well-nigh so—for a scholastic year was then eleven months. The school was opened in October, 1843, with Mr. Robert McLauchlin, of Baltimore, principal. Mrs. McLauchlin had charge of the female department. Mr. McLauchlin was tall, strongly built, and well proportioned, without a pound of superfluous flesh. His hair, which was exceeding scant, was of a reddish color, and his beard the same. The boys regarded him as a veritable Samson. He did not use, too well we remember—he did not use the ruler as the instrument of correction. You know there was a firm belief prevalent that a ruler could be broken by crossing eyelashes in your hand and moistening them with spittle. Somehow or other the process always failed, but that was because the lashes did not lie right, of course. But Mr. McLauchlin would jerk a boy up on tiptoe with his left hand and thrash him with his right. By way of variation he sometimes threw out his cork leg, drew a boy over it, and then—but it is not necessary to be precise on what is really very much a matter of feeling. Some readers know just how it was. The writer does.

But there came a day, Monday, the 21st of April, 1845, when we had gathered at school and were dismissed because our teacher was too indisposed to be present. We made the welkin ring with shouts of delight that we were to have a holiday. A few of us went with Henry and Robert and Billy, the MacRae boys, into the woods to enjoy our Indian play, or whatever it might be, and in a few hours returned to learn that Mr. McLauchlin was dead. We mourned for him, because we loved him. He was strict and maybe severe, but never unjust and never cruel, and we loved him with a love both strong and true. He was buried on the lot, northwest corner of Fourth and Dock

Streets, and the Odd Fellows erected a marble shaft to his memory. His remains and the stone that marked their resting place were afterwards removed to Oakdale Cemetery.

Mr. Levin Meginney[1] succeeded Mr. McLauchlin in charge of the school, with Mrs. Richardson at the head of the girls' department. Mr. Meginney continued in charge until the school was given up by the Odd Fellows, long after 1850, and then, buying the property he converted the school building in part into a dwelling, which he occupied with his family. The schoolhouse still stands, and the school is continued under the charge of Prof. Washington Catlett.

In 1846 a classical department was added to the school, in charge of Mr. Robert Lindsay, a Scotchman and graduate of St. Andrew's University, Scotland. He was a thorough classical scholar, and if proficiency of his pupils is a test—and who will deny it?—a good teacher, but as a disciplinarian he was a sad failure. He had not found his place in school teaching, and about 1850, having tried it here and elsewhere until that time, he removed farther South. There he studied law and went into politics and became governor of Alabama. While in the Alabama Legislature, in connection with the Internal Improvement Board, of which he was chairman, we think, he was largely instrumental in building the Mobile and Ohio Railroad, and as governor he raised the bonds of Alabama above those of any other Southern State at the time.

We now close with naming the first class of the Odd Fellows' School, about the time of Mr. McLauchlin's death: Henry MacRae, Robert B. MacRae, Robert C. Green, Irving C. Ballard, John D. Taylor, Owen Fennell, Sidney G. Law, Joseph H. Flanner, William H. Hall, John J. Poisson, Washington C. Fergus, and John McLaurin. Irving Ballard and Henry MacRae afterwards taught in the school.

In the classical department under Mr. Lindsay were Sidney G. Law, Robert B. MacRae, Owen Fennell, Nicholas W. Schenck, Hardy L. Fennell, Washington Fergus, Alvis Walker, William H. Bettencourt, John L. Hill, Robert C. Green, Henry M. Drane, James A. Wright, Daniel Newton, John William Kelly, Arthur J. Hill, and John McLaurin.

The good work done by the school has been referred to. It was in its aim and purpose and in its results very like to that

---

[1]Mr. Meginney's school is mentioned at greater length elsewhere in the *Chronicles.*

done by Mrs. Hemenway, under the management, direction, and control of Miss Amy M. Bradley, something like a quarter of a century afterwards. Wilmington ought never to cease to hold both the one and the other everlastingly in grateful remembrance.   SENEX, JR.

IV.

Before proceeding to weightier matters let us gather up the loose-lying threads of memorial thought. Our friend aforesaid reminds us, on the subject of trucking, that the vegetables brought into table supply in 1840 were very limited. Lettuce was brought from Charleston, cabbages, as has been said, were not raised around here, and tomatoes were "love apples," pretty to look upon but not regarded as edible. Strawberries, now to be had in the height of the season at five cents per quart, were then 25 cents a saucer, and there were few in a saucer—cream, however, was thrown in. Hopkins, a little more than two miles east of the city and a stone's throw north of the New Bern Road, was the resort of courting couples for strawberries and cream, which suggests that courting was expensive in those days, at least to the financial partner of the concern.

And on the subject of the militia: how wondrously they were equipped—with long guns and short guns and rifles and shot-guns and muskets—all flint and steel, for though percussion caps were invented as far back as 1818, and had become pretty well known by 1830—Colt using them on his repeating pistols invented in 1836—yet the United States Government did not use them before about 1842, and although the army might easily have been furnished with percussion muskets in the Mexican War, 1846, General Scott preferred the flint-lock gun, "considering it dangerous to campaign in an enemy's country with an untried weapon."

Oh, how those flint and steel locks did try the temper and the patience of the average youth of the days of 1840. See the lark, well away to be sure, but mounted on a hillock, and his bright yellow breast exposed invitingly! Snap goes the flint upon the steel; he winks his eye and whisks his tail and soars away. That chance is gone, for the day perhaps. And how tantalizing it must have been in war, in the very heat of the battle, to have the flint fail to strike fire or the powder to flash in the pan.

This accounts for the constant use of bayonets and throws the needed light upon pictures of the olden time where the musket is so often seen used as a club.

What became of the court when the courthouse was burned in 1840? Well, for a while the sessions of court were held in Society Hall, as it was called, a building in the rear of St. James's Church, but quite promptly the county magistrates had the courthouse building erected on Princess Street, the same building which only about a year or so ago was vacated that the present elegant and commodious quarters might be occupied. The jail of 1840 was the building still standing on the northeast corner of Second and Princess Streets, and now used as a wagon-making shop.

Judges were elected by the Legislature in 1840 and for over twenty years thereafter. The office was held for life or during good behavior unless sooner voluntarily vacated by the occupant. Commissioners of navigation were appointed by the commissioners of the town of Wilmington. Later in the forties they were elected by the citizens of Wilmington and so continued to be for a score or so of years.

The commissioners of the town in 1840 had been elected in 1839. They were named in a previous article. They held office for two years. So did those elected in 1841, viz.: James F. McRee, magistrate of police; Armand J. DeRosset, jr., Thomas W. Brown, Charles D. Ellis, and John MacRae. In the Legislature of 1842-1843 a bill was passed "For the better regulation of the town of Wilmington," which provided for annual elections of commissioners and increased the number to be elected to seven. Why this should be decidedly objectionable does not appear, but it was. The publication of intention for thirty days, required in such cases, was made in a Raleigh paper, and it was announced when the bill became a law that not more than a dozen citizens of Wilmington knew what was doing, which, compared with some things since, confirms Solomon's statement that "there is no new thing under the sun." A digression may be pardoned here. The same Legislature passed an act establishing common schools in North Carolina and apportioning two districts (of 35 in the county) to Wilmington. The commissioners selected in January, 1843, under the new law, were John MacRae, C. D. Ellis, T. W. Brown, Alexander Anderson, Thomas J. Armstrong, William A. Wright, and Oscar G. Parsley.

State elections in 1840 were held on different days in the various counties. The first was held on July 23 and the last on August 13 (*Wilmington Chronicle,* May 13, 1840). Hyde, Pitt, Washington, Wayne, and others had voted July 30, 1840 —this was noted in the *Chronicle* of August 5, 1840. On August 12 the paper contained the election news from these counties, or some of them. New Hanover voted on August 13 and the result was given in the *Chronicle* of August 19, 1840. Elections for State officers and members of Congress from that time to the present have been held on the same day throughout the State, formerly on the first Thursday in August, latterly contemporaneously with the presidential election when occurring in the same year.

John M. Morehead was elected governor in 1840 over Romulus M. Saunders by some 5,000 votes, perhaps more, but the Legislature was Democratic in both branches.

But 1840 was a grand presidential year. The Whig party, from a mere coterie having its origin in a New York City charter election in 1834, had in six years grown to immense proportions. It had all the enthusiasm of phenomenal growth. The Democratic party—the party of Andrew Jackson and Martin Van Buren—had dominated for twelve years past, and had all the power and prestige pertaining to that fact. Not a great while before this at a Tammany meeting in New York City two factions, whom it will suit to call "Regulars" and "Reformers," were in high dispute. The "Reformers," finding themselves losing ground, turned off the gas, but the "Regulars," prepared for the occasion, instantly whipped out a hundred candles from as many pockets and with the scratch of as many "Loco Foco" matches the hall was again alight and the business proceeded. There were no matches other than "Loco Foco" in those days, and this incident, with little good reason seemingly, gave a name of derision to the Jacksonian or regular Democratic party.

William Henry Harrison and John Tyler were the Whig nominees for the Presidency. Martin Van Buren, then occupying the presidential chair, and Richard M. Johnson were the nominees of the Democratic party. Van Buren was a man of wealth; Harrison, if not poor was at least not wealthy, and had lived in his early days—his friends did not let the people forget it—in a log cabin. It is said that a Democratic editor, if not building better than he knew, at least building otherwise than he intended, said: "Give Harrison a log cabin and a barrel of hard cider and he will not leave Ohio." The Whig party caught it up and used it for all it was worth, and it was worth hundreds of thousands of votes. Log cabins sprang up everywhere as the meeting places for Tippecanoe and Tyler clubs, with the hard cider always on tap. The first name referred, of course, to the war record of General Harrison, and "Tippecanoe and Tyler, too"—"Tip and Ty," for short—was the slogan of the party. It was all very taking. The boys even enjoyed it hugely and the ladies wore the brass medal with the log cabin and the cider barrel represented upon it. The writer was a future voter at the time, and on the off-road prospectively. He became possessed of a Harrison medal, and it must be confessed was quite proud of it. A horror-stricken relative soon bought him out, however, and he never afterwards deflected from his ancestral principles. But this is too personal, perhaps.

One incident arises very vividly to mind and calls for notice. A ship full-rigged and beautiful to look upon was built at the shipyard (now that of Capt. S. W. Skinner), to be taken to Raleigh to the grand Whig convention rally of the party in North Carolina on October 5. *Constitution* was the name of the ship. James Cassiday was on deck as captain, and the crew were Don MacRae, John Hedrick, John Marshall, Eli Hall, John Walker, and Mike Cronly—then youths of fifteen to eighteen years. The last named is the only survivor.

A large delegation of citizens went up from Wilmington to the convention. Dr. John Hill, from the residence of General James Owen, then standing where now stands the Carolina Central Railroad office, addressed the crew of the ship and the enthusiastic throng assembled there, and the boat then proceeded on her trip. By rail she was taken to Goldsboro and thence by wagon, for lack of rail, to Raleigh. The ship was left in Raleigh to be given to the county represented in the convention which in the presidential election should give the largest increase in the Whig vote over the Governor's poll, in proportion to population. Surry County got the ship.

Another incident: The Log Cabin in Wilmington stood just where George Honnet's jewelry store now is. The fire of January previous had destroyed the buildings then standing there and they had not been rebuilt. Many an enthusiastic meeting had been held in the cabin and many thrilling speeches delivered; many rousing songs had been sung, or shouted, and many a barrel of cider doubtless had been drunk before the eventful night of November 5, 1840. On that night, or rather early next morning, the town was aroused by an explosion. The Log Cabin had been blown up. There was indignation, righteous indignation, of course, and plenty of it, and Alexander Anderson, magistrate of police, offered a reward of $400 for proof sufficient to convict the perpetrator of the deed.

The perpetrator was not caught. Indeed, as the election came off a very few days thereafter and Harrison and Tyler went in with a hurrah, receiving 234 electoral votes to Van Buren's 60, the matter was, as usual in such cases, suffered to pass into oblivion, to be resurrected at the hands of an exploring semi-antiquarian, who may be allowed to subscribe himself,

SENEX, JR.

V.

About 1810 or 1811 the *Wilmington Gazette*[1] was published by a Mr. Hasell. The *Cape Fear Recorder* was established in the spring of 1818. Later, for several years, it was edited by Archibald McLean Hooper. Contemporaneously with the *Recorder* for a short time the *Wilmington Herald,* a Universalist paper, was published by Rev. Jacob Frieze, assisted, perhaps, by others. In the *Recorder* of February 6, 1828, appears a very suggestive advertisement announcing that the *Herald* was necessarily discontinued. On January 9, 1833, appeared the first number of the *People's Press,* edited by P. W. Fanning and Thomas Loring. The *Wilmington Advertiser,* edited by H. S. Ellenwood, was published at this time; how long before this is not known. On April 2 of this year Mr. Ellenwood died. His reputation as that of a gentleman of scholarly tastes and aptitudes survives until the present. Mr. Fanning soon learned, as so many who essay newspaper publication do, that the editorial chair is far from being a post of luxurious ease, and on May 1, 1833, he laid down the pen after an article in which with the honesty and frankness characteristic of him he explained his disgust with the profession, or rather with his experience of the journalistic life. The *People's Press* then combined with the *Advertiser,* having as sole editor, Mr. Thomas Loring. On

---

[1]This account of Wilmington newspapers is published, notwithstanding a fuller account elsewhere in the *Chronicles,* because of much intimate information here given which is supplementary to the longer article on this subject.

12

January 8, 1836, the name *People's Press* was dropped and
the paper appeared as number one, volume one, of the *Wilmington Advertiser*. The *Press* and the *Press and Advertiser*
had been known as ultra-Jacksonian papers. The *Advertiser*
as successor had become exceedingly moderate, if not independent in its tone, and on the 27th of May Mr. Loring retired.
Here is a gap in our history; Mr. Loring sold out and presumably the *Advertiser* was continued. Trace of it is found in
1839 and 1840, and the valedictory of Mr. Frederick C. Hill,
under whose editorial management it was published during
these last years, appeared in the issue of May 27, 1841. The
paper ceased to exist from that date. Mr. Hill was highly educated, a gentleman of refined manners and scholarly tastes and
reputed to have wielded the pen in a telling way. It is to be
regretted that the files of the *Advertiser* are lost; not even a
single number of the paper is within reach. This paper was
intensely, not necessarily violently, Whig in politics.

The *Wilmington Chronicle* was established by Asa A. Brown
March 12, 1839. Mr. Brown had for many years been a merchant in Wilmington and presumably was a novice in journalism, but from the first the *Chronicle* was ably edited, and during the dozen or more years of its existence it did yeoman service in advocating and defending the principles of the Whig
party. Of the *Wilmington Messenger,* edited by Dr. William
J. Price in advocacy of Democratic principles, nothing accurate
can be learned. That it was published in May, 1843, is known,
and reference to it in the *Chronicle* of April 3, 1844, shows that
it was in existence at that time. In the same way it is known
that the *Wilmington Journal,* its successor, was published in
November of the same year. The *Messenger,* material and good
will, it is understood, between the dates last named and probably
after the presidential election of 1840, passed into the hands of
Messrs. David Fulton and Alfred L. Price. These gentlemen
published the *Journal* until the death of the former, when his
brother, James. Fulton, took editorial charge. The *Journal*
(weekly) has continued to this day, and is now owned and
edited by Joshua T. James, Esq. The *Daily Journal* under
Messrs. Fulton and Price did not appear until sometime in the
early fifties and does not come within our scope. Of Dr. Price's
management and success we can not speak knowingly, but doubt
not the paper was altogether satisfactory to the Democratic
party, whose principles it championed. The Fultons were ex-

ceptionally able in their profession, Irishmen, native born, if we mistake not, and their paper wielded great influence throughout the Cape Fear section and beyond.

Mr. Loring, formerly editor of the *Advertiser,* published the *Independent* in Raleigh for a while from early in July, 1843; but in February, 1846, he returned to Wilmington and with Mr. William Stringer published the *Tri-Weekly Commercial Review.* They claimed that their paper was Whig in politics, but independently so. It was published well into the fifties, whither we do not follow it.

Other papers may have been published, but if such is the case no information concerning them is now available. Perhaps these articles may bring to light something essential to a complete history of these matters. It will be gladly welcomed. Whether or not the *Wilmington Christian Herald,* to be published by Samuel Chandler, ever materialized does not appear. The prospectus was published in 1839.

It is usual to decry the avidity with which the papers of the nineties gather up the most trivial matters of local happening, but one who gleans from the papers of "auld lang syne" can not but wish they had possessed the disposition complained of. Very many matters that would go far to throw light upon the people or the times of those days apparently were too well known to need be chronicled, and so many an important link to history is wanting. The local editor and the ubiquitous reporter were not known in those days.

And now let us get more definitely and distinctly into the forties, leaving any digressions to come in incidentally. Time, Wednesday, January 1, 1840. Place, intersection of Front and Market Streets. Occasion, annual hiring of negroes. Various colors were there, black perhaps predominating. It was a time of times, a busy time, for in a few hours all the domestic arrangements depending on servitude were to be unsettled and for twelve months rearranged. Many a housewife had been looking to the first of the year in the hope of a change that would give her more of ease and less perhaps of labor than she had enjoyed or suffered during the year just past, and many a servant had been bearing with more or less of patience, longingly looking to a change of master or of mistress. Some were to be bettered, some to be worsted, but the star of hope was over all, and though there would be rain—was there ever a first without rain?—and though it had passed into a proverb that the heavens wept on hiring day for the deeds of darkness done, still it was hardly to be reckoned a day of sadness or of gloom. Uncertainty there was, and with uncertainty a doubt akin to fear, yet over all and above all the star of hope arose. There were some tears, but there were many smiles. There was some gloom as one went to a master always reckoned hard, and there was also gladness as another went to his or her chosen place of servitude. Owners in general heard the complaints of their slaves, and in tenderness and sympathy as well as from self-interest provided for them; they saw that they were fed and clothed or they would know the reason why.

But, whether bright or dark, those days are gone, and who would bring them back? And yet it is easier to call them wrong than to prove them so.

In 1840, as has been said, Wilmington contained 4,268 souls. Of these 1,004 were white males and 916 white females. Of free colored people there were 356, of slaves 1,992. Mr. Alexander Anderson was magistrate of police. At that date every little town or village did not aspire to be governed by a mayor, and despite the title of the chief officer, guardsmen were simply town guards and not policemen or police. Mr. Anderson had resided in Wilmington just forty years; he arrived here from the North January 1, 1800. He was at the time president of the Branch Bank of the State, and was occupying or had occupied every office of honor or trust the citizens could confer upon him. He rises before our memory as very like his son, Dr. Edwin A. Anderson, who was taken from us but a year or two ago. Quite as venerable he was in appearance; indeed, for years before his death he was known as "Old Mr. Sandy Anderson." He died November 15, 1844, at the age of sixty.

James F. McRee, Armand J. DeRosset, sr., E. P. Hall, and W. J. Harriss had been elected town commissioners in 1839 and, save Dr. Harriss, who died in the spring of 1839, were still in office.   SENEX, JR.

VI.

It might properly have been mentioned in connection with the history of newspapers published in Wilmington, that the *Chronicle* in the opening days of 1840 was printed in a building standing where the shoe store of Peterson & Rulfs now stands, on the west side of Front Street, a very few yards above Market. The building was destroyed by fire in January of that year, and discontinuance of the paper was enforced for eight or ten weeks. When revived the printing and publishing quarters were in a warehouse in the alley north of the Cape Fear Bank building until June, 1840, when the office was reëstablished in a building which had been erected on the old site. Here it continued through the forties, and until it ceased to appear.

The *Wilmington Journal,* in the fall of 1844, was published in the Bettencourt Building, corner Front and Princess Streets, now occupied by I. H. Weil. The Journal Building, on Princess Street, was built for it when it launched out into publication of the daily edition, and there it remained for probably a quarter of a century or more.

The *Tri-Weekly Commercial* was published by Stringer & Whitaker—not Loring & Stringer as we stated—on the southwest corner of Front and Market in what was long afterwards known as the Commercial Building, and which is now occupied by the confectionery establishment of Mrs. E. Warren & Son. The offices and pressroom were in an upper story, the lower being occupied as a dry-goods store by Kahnweiler Brothers. For the convenience of the public, the arrivals of the mails then being exceedingly irregular, there stood upon the roof of the Commercial Building a flagstaff from which a flag floated at the proper times, with the word "Steamboat" in white letters upon a blue ground, or "Cars" in white upon a red ground, thus announcing that the mails had arrived and soon would be at the disposal of the public.

Some information has come to hand relative to Mr. William Soranzo Hasell, who edited the *Wilmington Gazette:* He was born in Wilmington and here lived and died. Graduated from Yale College in 1799, being then only eighteen years of age, he studied for the profession of law, but soon abandoned it and for a time kept a bookstore and circulating library, afterwards along with this occupation editing the *Gazette* until 1815, when he died, aged thirty-four. In 1840 there stood on the southwest corner of Third and Ann Streets—set well back from either street and fronting on Ann—a house showing decided marks of the ravages of time, but still a building of massive proportions, pink-stuccoed, and bearing indications otherwise, especially taken along with the surroundings, of having been the residence of people of wealth. It was known at the period of which we write as the "Williams Castle," but was understood to have been formerly the property of a Mr. Hasell, almost certainly of the gentleman of whom we have been writing or his parents.

Of the physicians of Wilmington in 1840 Dr. John D. Bellamy alone survives. Mentally his bow still abides in strength, and the chances and changes of well-nigh fourscore years have not otherwise in the main dealt unkindly with him. He came to Wilmington late in the thirties, studied with Dr. William J. Harriss, and at the death of Dr. Harriss, in 1839, succeeded to his extensive and laborious practice. In May, 1846, Dr. William W. Harriss was taken into copartnership, and in the course of three or four years Dr. Bellamy retired and devoted himself to other business, principally farming. He owned large estates, the work of superintending and managing which was quite as lucrative as medical practice, and far less toilsome.

The loss of a physician in large practice for obvious reasons causes deeper sorrow, and sorrow more extensive in its reach, than that of any other member of a community, not even faithful pastors being excepted, and this affection, which entwines around the hearts of those who receive the doctor's services, doubtless is the great compensation for the privations and trials and strains upon the sympathetic nature which inevitably attend medical practice. Especially must this be so in villages and smaller towns, where physicians come into closer social relations than in the larger cities. These observations apply with special force to the loss sustained in the death of Dr. Harriss, who has been referred to, and of others who are yet to be mentioned.

Dr. Armand J. DeRosset, sr., in 1840 was seventy-three years of age, and still in vigorous practice. He had been for a quarter of a century in charge of the Seamen's Hospital and continued in service until late in the fifties, practicing on horseback when ninety years of age. He died in 1859, aged ninety-two.

Dr. James F. McRee, sr., was, like Dr. DeRosset, not only a skillful and beloved physician, but one of the most influential citizens of his day. It has been noted that both these gentlemen were commissioners of the town in 1840. In 1840, and possibly for years thereafter, Dr. McRee was magistrate of police, the chief officer of the place. On April 26, 1843, he took into copartnership his son, Dr. J. F. McRee, jr., and not a great while after retired to enjoy abundant and well-earned rest, while engaging in the scientific studies to which he was naturally disposed and in which he greatly delighted.

Before settling in Wilmington Dr. William A. Berry had been in the medical service of the United States. He retired from practice in the later fifties with ample means. He succeeded Dr. DeRosset as hospital physician in 1845, and died in 1875.

The profession did not hold Dr. Edwin A. Anderson continuously in its practice. In 1840 and for a year or two thereafter he followed it, and then went into sawmilling and afterwards into merchandizing and turpentine distilling. Subsequently he resumed practice and was engaged in it up to, or nearly up to, his death, about a year ago.

The recollections of the writer as concerns the doctors of fifty-five years ago are more vivid regarding Dr. Louis J. Poisson, perhaps, than any other. He comes before the mind, not very distinctly, it is true, as of medium height, spare in figure, with an intellectual cast of countenance and features rather sharp, though not unpleasantly so. A gentleman of affable manners without the least suspicion of lack of frankness, one whose gentleness would win a boy of eight or ten, even in spite of the dread which must needs accompany his ministrations. For a while before the death of Dr. Poisson he was quite infirm in health. In 1842 or 1843 he took into copartnership Dr. James H. Dickson, who had returned from New York City, and October 26, 1843, he died at the early age of thirty-four.

It has been said that fifty or sixty years ago physicians compounded their own prescriptions and practiced on horseback. The diseases they had to meet were not those which are now encountered, nor the medicines they used the same as now. The old-fashioned bilious fever was a terror in those days. We now never hear it mentioned. Those were the days of bloodletting and of cataplasms. Salts and senna and calomel and jalap were household articles, and the children in the spring were regularly called up to receive the matutinal dose of aloes. Quinine was hardly known and Peruvian bark had to do its work, along with dogwood bitters and other things which now will hardly be found in the pharmacopœia.

No profit was to be had certainly in taking medical care of the poor of the county and furnishing the medicines for them at $50 a year, yet that was all allowed for the service. The slaves, however, who were over half the population, were provided for by their masters.

What has been written has referred only to the regular allopathic practice. Homeopathy, though Hahnemann had done and suffered in behalf of his principle of *similia* for thirty years or more, was not known here. The Thompsonian Botanic practice, in which number six figured conspicuously, was represented by Dr. W. H. Buffaloe, who held forth on Second Street, near what is now called Meginney's corner, as the successor of one Dr. Foy who had engaged in similar practice about this time.

The county poorhouse throughout the forties stood on the square bounded by Fourth, Walnut, Fifth, and Red Cross Streets. It was located near the center of the square and was the only house within the area. But the "Poorhouse Square," as it was called, was not the only one upon which a single building stood on guard, as it were, to all the space around. The "Thunder-and-Lightning House" occupied in 1840 a similar position on the square bounded by Fourth, Orange, Fifth, and Dock Streets. The peculiar name attached to the building, it has always been supposed, was because of its having several times received the bolts of the elements. On the square upon which the First Presbyterian Church now stands there was in 1840 but one house occupied by white people. That was the building, pulled down a few years ago, which stood immediately in the rear of the church and which was purchased, with the land upon which the house of worship stands, from the late A. H. VanBokkelen. The house now owned and occupied by Capt. John F. Divine, was owned by Mr. Aaron Lazarus in 1840 and was the only dwelling on that square. The greater part of the square, all owned by Mr. Lazarus and known as the Lazarus lot, was a delightful grove, where, by the kind permission of the owners, Queen of May celebrations were held. Possibly other localities might be cited like to these, but it is unnecessary. The town was not compactly built and some not yet in their seventies remember picking chinquapins where the synagogue now stands, gathering persimmons in the "Old '76" lot on Ann between Front and Second, or picking low-bush huckleberries on Church near Fourth. Here and there all over the present city are dwelling-houses that were built many years before 1840. On Market the present residence of Dr. A. J. DeRosset is one of them—in 1840 and long before occupied by Dr. A. J. DeRosset, sr. Opposite, on the southwest corner of Market and Third,

still stands the house which was the headquarters of Lord Cornwallis in 1781. The building on the northeast corner also dates
back a hundred years or so—so the building adjoining on the
east and others in the same locality. The present residence of
Mr. M. Cronly and some others on that square go back many
decades; indeed, one might count a full half score between
Orange and Ann, Fifth Street and the river. So on the west
side of Second Street between Market and Dock are houses that
carry us back to the days of yore. In 1840 Mr. Murdock
McKay lived in one, a Mrs. Bishop in another. Around the
corner on Dock going towards the river are two residences of
the kind we are speaking of. It is not necessary to mention
others; they can, when built of wood, easily be distinguished.
Whenever the sides are built of common three-inch cypress or
juniper shingles they go back almost certainly well on to a century in age—sometimes over. The brick store on the southwest
corner of Front and Princess, occupied by I. H. Weil, and the
wooden buildings on the southwest corner of Market and Second
Streets along the southern line of Market, known as the Bettencourt property, might be termed fire repellers. The flames have
surged around them time and again but have never left even the
smell of fire upon them.

The buildings mentioned, and others, have been more or less
modernized from time to time, sometimes to the extent of entire
transformation. But the dwelling-house on the southwest corner
of Fifth and Orange Streets, now owned and occupied by Rev.
Daniel Morrelle, in 1840 the residence of Gen. Alexander
MacRae, and years before that of Mr. Davis, the father of Hon.
George Davis, is very likely more nearly now what it was one
hundred years ago than any other residence in the city.

Before we leave this subject let us call attention to the fact
that on the organization of St. John's Lodge of Masons, say
one hundred years ago, they occupied the old Brown building
on the south side of Orange between Front and Second Streets.
The lodge was afterwards removed to the corner of Front and
Chestnut Streets—southwest corner—and again to Front near
Red Cross, where early in 1841 the building was sold and converted into a hotel kept by David Jones—not the proprietor of
that dread place so well known to seamen as "Davy Jones's
locker." In the same year, 1841, the lodge found rest from its
wanderings in its present location on Market Street.

One of the most noted buildings of "auld lang syne," which

was razed to the ground only a few years since to give place to the dwellings on the east side of Front Street, between Orange and Ann, was the "Old '76." It was a large two-story brick building, stuccoed white, with wide piazzas above and below running all the way around. It sat right upon the run of Tan Yard Branch, and its first floor was several feet lower than the present level of Front Street. It was a sailor boarding house, but was utilized by the politicians of the early days as a rallying place for their forces on the eve of exciting elections.

SENEX, JR.

VII.

Attention has been called to the fact that in enumerating buildings of great age or of peculiar construction the residence of the late John Walker, Esq., is worthy of being considered. This building stood near the center of the square bounded by Front, Princess, Second, and Chestnut Streets, fronting on Princess. Set back well from the street, it had a very spacious yard in front. The house was built of brick, had a double piazza —such is the recollection of the writer—and was covered with Dutch tiles in corrugated form. There is reason to believe it was built in 1781. It had been tenantless for a long time previous to its destruction, which was several years ago.

It may as well be confessed here that the list of boys in the classical school of Mr. Robert Lindsay—which list was given recently—was sadly defective in omitting the names of Oscar G. Parsley and David S. Cowan, those truly good boys.

In the early forties the judges of the Superior Courts were Dick, Manly, Settle, Battle, Bailey, Nash, and Pearson. Some of these afterwards attained eminence in the Supreme Court. The Court of Pleas and Quarter Sessions, commonly known as the County Court, had a session each spring, summer, fall, and winter. Attorneys were licensed first to practice here, and later, very soon after ordinarily, received license to practice in the Superior Courts. The last County Court held in New Hanover in the name of the King was held on January 2, 1776, and the next court was on January 7, 1777. The justices present were George Moore, William Purviance, John Robinson, Timothy Bloodworth, Sampson Moseley, John Lillington, Samuel Swann, John Ancrum, William Wilkinson, William Jones, and John DuBois. They were commissioned by the Governor, and after duly organizing they elected two inspectors for Wilmington and a sheriff for the county. Jonathan Dunbibin was elected register in place of Adam Boyd, who held the position under the old regime. We digress here to say that this Adam Boyd formerly edited the *Cape Fear Mercury,* which appeared in Wilmington October 13, 1769, and was discontinued in 1775.

The county justices seem to have undergone little or no change throughout their entire existence of nearly a century. In ordinary trial sessions, one magistrate presided, having on the bench with him two or three other magistrates. The position of chairman, or chief magistrate, required considerable legal knowledge and invested one with a good deal of power. Col. James T. Miller and Mr. William A. Wright held the post and performed the duties admirably for years.

Not one of the resident lawyers of 1840 is now living. Mr. M. London, who died quite recently, had been engaged in merchandizing for several years before he entered upon the practice of law. He was licensed to practice about January 1, 1840, and was one of the ablest lawyers who ever practiced at the bar in New Hanover County. Owen Holmes died suddenly in June, 1840. Messrs. William A. Wright, Joshua G. Wright, T. C. Miller and Daniel B. Baker lived and practiced throughout the forties. Mr. George Davis was admitted to practice very early in 1841; afterwards John London, who died soon after licensure; and Griffith J. McRee still later; Thomas D. Meares, James A. Peden, John A. Lillington, T. Burr, jr., Hill Burgwyn, Thomas D. Walker, David Fulton, William Hill, John L. Holmes, and others whose names are not at hand. Mr. William B. Meares, one of the strongest members of the bar, had retired before 1840 to give attention to other interests. He died October 11, 1842. Messrs. David Reid and Hardy Lucian Holmes came to Wilmington from other counties. They stood high on the roll of attorneys.

In those days the whipping post was an instrument or an institution or a means for punishment of offenders—a most efficient one, too. It savored of barbarity undoubtedly and was terribly degrading, still there are crimes for which the whipping post is and ever will be the only befitting punishment. As to barbarity, it does not approach in that respect the public strangling to death of human beings. This was universal in those days, and even now is tolerated in North Carolina where the county commissioners find a public demand for it. Happily the

day is past when any such heathenism can be exhibited in New
Hanover County.

Many now living will remember that Charles, a slave of
P. K. Dickinson, was publicly hanged between Seventh and
Eighth Streets about midway and a few yards back of the southern line of the street. A few years later Thomas Broughton
was hanged on the square to the north and just opposite for the
murder of a Portuguese named De Silva. A curious incident is
connected with the trial and execution of Broughton. For quite
a while no clue could be found leading to the detection of the
assassin of De Silva. But Broughton, why so impelled is not
known, went before the grand jury and attempted to criminate
another man. His examination brought suspicion upon himself
and led to further investigation. Articles that had belonged to
De Silva were found in his possession and other criminating circumstances were brought to light. He was tried and on purely
circumstantial evidence was convicted. An appeal was taken to
the Supreme Court on the ground of inadmissibility of the testimony of the foreman of the grand jury above referred to, which
testimony was given on the trial. This was the grand jury before the one that indicted Broughton. The higher court over-
ruled the objection and Broughton was hanged. He protested
his innocence on the gallows. Nevertheless, the impression was
well-nigh universal that he was guilty of the crime for which he
suffered.

The courthouse on the first of January, 1840, stood at the
intersection of Front and Market Streets, say about 50 feet
across Front and about 75 or 80 feet across Market. The brick
pavement, answering to the lower floor of a residence, was about
one foot, possibly a little more, above the level of the street. A
broad arch gave entrance at either end on Front Street. On the
sides running across Market a small arch in the center served
as entrance, and on each side of this arch and on both sides of
the building were similar arches across which were benches,
rather shelves, serving as seats. The boys of that day found
delight in playing in and around this part of the courthouse,
and the older ones met there in the hot summer afternoons to
discuss politics and save the country.

The court room proper and such other rooms as were necessary
were in the upper story and were reached by a stairway located
in the southwest corner. The building was constructed of brick
and was painted bright yellow on the outside, trimmed with

white and painted white on the inside. By an act of the Legislature of 1756, the courthouses of the State were to be used for all public purposes. Somewhere about 1843 or 1844 the County Court, overlooking this or in ignorance of it, prohibited political meetings in the courthouse, but they were very soon set back on the matter.

The town hall in 1840 stood at the intersection of Market and Second Streets, and was in structure very much like the courthouse, though not provided with seats, we think, for the comfort of loungers. It was open below and paved, and may at one time have been used as a market house in the lower part. The locality went by the name of "Mud Market." The market house of the writer's day was a most unsightly structure which stood on Market Street between Front Street and the river, about 150 feet from Front Street and running back some fifty or sixty feet. It was built of brick. The pavement serving for the floor was reached by mounting a large piece of ton timber which served for a step. The entrance was a wide arch, and the entire roof was supported by pillars forming the upright sides of arches. At the farther end, because of elevation in consequence of slope of the streets, were a platform and stairs as means of entrance and exit. Under this end of the market house was a room which at one time served as a guardhouse. This building gave place in the spring of 1848 to a market house on the same site; a very great improvement in appearance and in suitableness for its purpose. It was 25 feet wide and about 100 to 125 feet long, with a roof of galvanized iron resting on light iron pillars. In turn this gave place some twenty years later to the present one on Front Street.

William Henry Harrison was nominated on December 4, 1839, as the Whig candidate for President. A meeting to ratify the nomination was held in the courthouse on the night of January 16, 1840, and was addressed by delegates who had returned from the nominating convention. On the morning of the 18th the courthouse was in ashes. About midnight, or a little before, of the 17th a fire broke out in the store of John Dawson on the northeast corner of Front and Market Streets and rapidly swept into ruin all the houses on the entire square except the building (which is still there) on the southeast corner of Front and Princess and the dwelling-house of Mr. J. P. Calhorda immediately in the rear. The flames crossed Front Street and were arrested at the Bank of Cape Fear building in their progress north. But they swept off everything between the corner of Front Street and the river and destroyed every building on the river front. On the square where the fire originated the Clarendon Hotel stood on the present site of the Purcell House, and the post office was a room on the alley. Wilkings' stables, as they were called, though Winslow S. Wilkings had died in October, 1837, stood where Fennell's stables are now. The northern side of Market Street was then as now occupied by grocery and dry-goods and other stores; and on the alleys were dwellings, as well as on Front, Market, and Princess Streets. In many cases those dwellings were rooms above the stores.

On the other square, at the corner just across from Dawson's, stood the shop (office it would now be called) of Dr. Armand J. DeRosset, sr. This was consumed with the *Chronicle* office just north of it and the dry-goods and general sales stores of Wright and Savage, John Wooster, Samuel Shuter, C. B. Miller, Daniel Dickson, Kelly & McCaleb, and others on the line of Market Street, the custom house, then standing on the same site as now, the store and warehouses of Aaron Lazarus, and the business houses of many others on Water Street, north of Market.

The shop of Dr. DeRosset was entered by a row of steps cornering on Market and Front Streets, and running up some six or eight feet from the street. The custom house is not remembered by the present writer, to whom the river front at that time was forbidden ground. The customs were collected and the business appertaining thereto transacted for a while after the fire in a room just where is now the office of A. S. Heide, Esq., Danish vice consul. At this time Gen. Louis H. Marsteller was collector of customs. Afterwards the custom house was on North Water Street between Princess and Chestnut Streets. Mr. W. C. Lord was collector here under appointment of President Tyler, but in a few months, the President having changed his political status, Mr. Lord was superseded by Mr. Murphy V. Jones. The present custom house became ready for occupancy during Mr. Jones's incumbency of the collectorship, or possibly a very little while before he entered upon its duties, say in the latter part of 1842 or early in 1843.

One incident connected with this fire every one then in his teens or older very vividly remembers—the blowing up of Philip Bassadier. In those days when water had to be pumped into and thrown from fire engines by the hardest kind of physical labor, it might seem unnecessary to say that other means than throwing water had to be resorted to to stay the progress of the flames. The most efficient means then known was the blowing up of buildings by gunpowder—no dynamite then. This work was, if not in 1840, certainly afterwards, confided to persons of discretion who received their authority direct from the town commissioners. It became necessary to resort to the means referred to in the Dawson fire, and in blowing up some buildings about the center of the square, where the fire originated, Philip Bassadier went up. He was taken off terribly bloody and very seriously wounded, it was supposed at the time mortally wounded. But Philip, who, by the way, was one of the politest of men, albeit not of the Caucasian race, lived to be the admiration of the small boys of the period, and to furnish music for pleasure-loving youths for many years. But of this we may come to speak at another time. SENEX, JR.

(Since writing the above a letter has been received from one unusually informed and accurate on local matters of the olden time, and who, but for the disrespect seemingly attached, and the utter incongruity of association, might be called "Old Nick." It will receive due attention hereafter.)

VIII.

The friend referred to in the last article furnishes some corrections or additions from very accurate remembrance, and place is gladly given them. He was a pupil of Miss Laura Rankin (since Mrs. Rothwell) when she taught in what was and is known as Northrop's Alley, running through from Front to Second Street between Dock and Orange. Other boys were George Harriss, Mike Cronly, Eli Hall, Henry Law, and of a younger set, Nehemiah Harriss, John Morris, Dick Savage, Nick Schenck, and so on. Girls in the same school were Sarah Peck, Augusta Law, Emily Howard, Fanny Lippitt, Caroline VanViel, Caroline and Clarissa Northrop, Mag and Kate McLaurin, Aletta Jane Schenck, Sarah and May Savage, Harriet and Caroline Brown, and others. Mr. Walsh, later a Presbyterian minister, afterwards taught in the same place.

We are reminded, too, that Mr. Jesse Mulock, who came from Orange, N. Y., first taught in a house on the site now occupied by Burr and Bailey, and afterwards where mentioned in a former article. His school became very prosperous and he brought out his brother Charles (was it not John?), but was driven from the field by the Odd Fellows' School. He then went into the shipping commission business, having for his clerk Anthony D. Cazaux. Afterwards, he engaged in turpentine distilling, and finally returned North, where he died in a good old age.

Mr. Mulock's principle in teaching was thoroughness. There were no heads nor tails to his classes. Boys came up to the front bench to recite and standing erect were questioned, or went to the blackboard to do the "sums," as the problems in mathematics were called. Smith's grammar was used and Walker's dictionary. A part of speech was named and parsed, with the reason why for everything. A word was spelled and defined, and a sentence constructed with the word properly used therein. There was no precise verbal memorizing required, and there could be no dodging nor evasion. The chinquapin was always ready for use and was in frequent demand. Boys were detained sometimes until long after nightfall, as "Nick" puts it, "staying in until perfect, even to the bringing of your candle for night study." Being a very small boy, the writer was excused from night service. Day's algebra, we thought, was the hardest algebra to be sure. It most certainly tried one's intellectual calibre more than Davies', which was used in the Odd Fellows' School. But we are reminded that Mr. Mulock was patient with all boys and helpful to all, even while he required good conduct and exacted perfect lessons.

As to Madame Clement's and Miss Verina Moore's schools, about which we are asked, they came on after the forties—that is our recollection. Miss Verina afterwards married Dr. R. H. Chapman, a Presbyterian minister, taught school in Goldsboro, perhaps also in Asheville, and died at the latter place a few years since.

Our last article closed with the blowing up of Philip Bassadier. He was, as has been said, of mixed blood and appears to have come to Wilmington from one of the West Indian Islands long before the days of the forties. At that time he was recognized as a character. He was exceedingly Frenchy in his politeness and doubtless the only tonsorial artist in the town. At least the following advertisement, which appeared in the *Chronicle* of November 1, 1843, would indicate that then for the first time Walsh Revells or some one else was making his opposition felt. Here is Philip's ad., after an announcement of his readiness to serve the public: "He has carried on this business in Wilmington for upwards of forty years, which he thinks some evidence of merit in the use of razors and scissors, and as giving him some claim to public patronage." There seems to be force in the claim. Philip, with his grey-white kinky hair, brown complexion, and knee breeches—well, maybe not—looms up before us now. His shop stood at the corner of the alley next north of Boatwright's store, on the precise site of that store in fact, a small one-story wooden building with the inevitable striped pole in front, and there he was to be found presumably for forty years before 1843. The shop was destroyed by fire on the early morning of November 26, 1846. Perhaps too much time and space are given to Philip Bassadier, but he can not be dismissed without reference to his musical ability, displayed as violinist on festive occasions of all kinds, at the theatres, etc., and especially of his services as bugle man to the Clarendon Horse Guards about 1845 and later. The Horse Guards, under command of Dr. James F. McRee, jr., and later of Capt. William C. Howard, to the small boys of the period stood as representative of military pomp and prowess, but the company itself did not call forth more admiration than Philip Bassadier as, early in the morning on the day of the "turn out," he blew his bugle at one street corner, then in a gallop rushed to another, reined up, and again awakened the echoes with his blast. We see him now in his cocked hat and red flannel coat and note the beaming pride on his countenance, and we almost hear the shouts of delight of the urchins enjoying it all.

The Wilmington Volunteers on April 30, 1840, celebrated their ninth anniversary. They were then in command of Junius D. Gardner. Afterwards Capt. O. G. Parsley was chief in command, and previously, probably, Capt. John MacRae. This company was the pride of our town in those days, and on the anniversaries it always had target practice at Hogg's Folly, and thereafter marched through the streets, the well-torn target in the rear and the best marksman, usually Billy Burch, or Mr. Jimmy, his brother, conspicuous in the ranks by reason of the yellow plume which decorated his cap and proclaimed his skill. The New Hanover Rifle Corps paraded the first time November 3, 1841, with R. F. Brown as captain, R. G. Rankin, first lieutenant, J. B. Cumming, second lieutenant, and Louis H. Pierce, third. In 1846, about June, the Wilmington Guards were formed, with James Anderson, captain, Alexander MacRae, jr., first lieutenant, Henry Nutt, second lieutenant, and

13

James Burch, orderly sergeant. These companies might come and they might go, but it was the militia ununiformed—not necessarily uninformed—that rolled on forever. The Thirtieth Regiment of North Carolina Militia, under command of Col. John MacRae, and afterwards of others, was a great institution. The upper division paraded at Long Creek and the lower division assembled annually at Wilmington in the fall of the year. On this review Brigadier General Marstellar came out with his staff and sometimes Maj. Gen. Alexander MacRae with his. Colonel Andrews, Col. James T. Miller, Col. John MacRae, Maj. W. N. Peden, and maybe others graced these occasions. It was a time of times for the boys. The Wilmington Militia, with Dr. Billy Ware as orderly sergeant in front, stretching his abbreviated limbs to keep the regulation step, was a conspicuous part. The parade took place in what was then called "Oregon." It was about the time that the Oregon boundary question was up, and the politicians shouted for "phifty-four phorty or phight," and afterwards fell back to "phorty-nine." In "Oregon"—that is about where the Chestnut Street Presbyterian Church now stands, or a little north of it.

The Wilmington and Raleigh Railroad Company was chartered by the Legislature early in 1834. On January 1, 1836, announcement was made that $200,000 had been subscribed to the capital stock, and when $300,000 should be subscribed the company would be organized and work commenced. Work was commenced in October of the same year, and after struggling against difficulties such as are not known in these latter days, and at an immense sacrifice to those who put their financial means into the work and to those who gave their business time and energies to it, the last spike was driven March 7, 1840. The road was chartered in the expectation of running from Wilmington to the State capital, but it was soon found that the funds for completion could not be obtained in that direction and the present route was located. The name was not changed to Wilmington and Weldon until comparatively recently. None of the equipment was what we are accustomed to now. The engines could not pull even a light train up a slight incline, and so the passengers and baggage had to be run up the hill as at present, and while the passengers descended a long flight of steps and walked to the boat landing, one or two hundred yards away, the baggage was shot down an incline to a hand-car and rolled away to the steamers in waiting. Happily, baggage smashers had not arrived at the perfection to which they have since attained and Saratoga trunks were then unknown. It was the day of bandboxes and bundles to try the patience of husbands or other male attendants. Checks for baggage were unknown. They soon came into vogue, but for special railroad lines only. Engines in those days were doll babies or sandfiddlers to the giants in size and weight and power of the present time. A train of eight or ten cars each with carrying capacity not one-fourth probably of the present was a sight to see, and the coaches were not coaches as we know them at all, but cars made somewhat like unto the stagecoaches they superseded. Think of the time advertised between New York and Philadelphia, 100 miles, being eight hours.

Capt. James Owen was president of the road at its completion, Gen. Alexander MacRae, superintendent, and Walter Gwyn, who had been in charge throughout the building, was still chief engineer of construction. The four steamers owned by the company and forming a line to Charleston—the *Vanderbilt, Governor Dudley, North Carolina,* and *Wilmington*—were not comparable in size or in convenience to the palaces of the present day in similar service elsewhere, but they were nevertheless very comfortable, very staunch and strong, and commanded by experienced, careful, and fearless seamen—such men as Captains Davis, Marshall, Ivy, Smith, Bates, Sterrett, Wade, and others. One or two accidents occurred, however, but without loss of life. On or about January 7, 1839, the *North Carolina* and the *Vanderbilt* collided off Georgetown Light, and both had to go into Charleston for repairs. On Sunday, July 26, 1840, at 1 a. m., thirty miles northeast of Georgetown, the *Governor Dudley* and the *North Carolina* came into collision, and in a very few minutes the latter vessel went down beneath the waves. All the passengers were saved, but some, all probably, without befitting clothes. Some members of Congress were aboard, among them Hon. Dixon H. Lewis, the 500-pounder of Alabama. In his disrobed state he was a curiosity as well as an object of sympathy when he arrived in Wilmington. The *Governor Dudley* was not hurt by the collision and came on to port. She was seriously delayed, of course. The *North Carolina* had not been long in the service since her former accident. The steamer *Huntress* was put on the line temporarily in place of the sunken steamer, and the *Gladiator* afterwards came in permanently. When the boats were first put on the line between Wilmington and Charleston, say in 1839, possibly a little before, the Cape Fear River had to be lighted at the expense of the railroad company, as navigation at night was a necessity, but Congress in 1840 appropriated $5,000 a year for this service and lighting the river has since been a charge of the General Government.

Perhaps nothing more strongly marks the difference in railroads between 1842 and 1895 than the fact that between Monday noon, July 11, 1842, and Thursday night, July 14, 1842, three heavy trains were lost between Wilmington and Weldon. No one could tell what had become of them. A deluging rain had submerged the country between the Roanoke and the Tar Rivers, causing three breaches in the road-bed. One or more trains got between the rivers and lost all communication with the outer world, and one or two others had been thrown from the track, in a like situation, by fallen trees.

Nothing has been said about perils of travel in those days of snakeheads and slow brakes, but time and space are up.

SENEX, JR.

THE PUBLIC SPIRIT OF WILMINGTON.

(The Fayetteville Observer of January, 1850.)

The public spirit of the citizens of our sister town is really amazing; it seems to have no limit when any scheme is presented which is regarded as essential to the prosperity or honor of the place. And the resources of the community seem to be as abundant as the spirit with which they are employed is liberal.

Some twelve or fourteen years ago, when the population was but three or four thousand, she undertook to make a railroad 161 miles long (the longest in the world), and a steamboat line of equal length. For this purpose she subscribed more than half a million dollars, we believe.

This accomplished with almost the total loss of the half million, so far as the stock was concerned, however profitable in other respects, one might have expected a pause at least if not a total cessation in the march of improvements, and so it would have been with almost any other people. But soon the Wilmington and Manchester Railroad was projected, and Wilmington subscribed to it $180,000. Then came the Deep River and Navigation Company, and she gave $30,000 to $40,000, we believe, to that. Next the Central Railroad, and she subscribed about $50,000, and finally, it being found necessary to raise an additional sum for the Manchester Road, she held a meeting on the 5th inst., at which $50,000 more, making $230,000 in all, was subscribed to that work. (This was increased to $100,000 by the 10th, making $280,000.)

Thus this community, even now not containing more than eight or nine thousand inhabitants, of whom probably not more than two-thirds are white, has contributed to public works eight or nine hundred thousand dollars—nearly as much as is required from the State to secure the Central Railroad.

With all this prodigious expenditure, who hears of any pressure of bankruptcy—any interruption of her onward course of prosperity? Truly, "There is that scattereth and yet increaseth."

It is not for the purpose of honoring Wilmington merely that we make this statement, but it is to encourage the friends of internal improvement throughout the State, and, if possible, to remove the objections of those who doubt the policy or profitableness of the system.

ACTIVITIES ON THE RIVER, 1850-1860.

In the fifties there were frequently as many as ninety vessels in the port of Wilmington loading or unloading, or waiting for berths at anchor in the stream. The wharves were lined two vessels deep, and those waiting for orders were moored nearly as far down the river as the Dram Tree. It was a season of great activity.

Also, a large coastwise business in corn in bulk was carried on with Hyde County, and for this trade a fleet of small schooners called "Corn Crackers" was employed. It was most exhilarating on a fine day to see this tiny fleet, twenty to thirty white wings, rounding the Dram Tree, led by the *We're Here, I'm Coming,* and *So Am I,* with every stitch of canvas spread to the favoring breeze on the last stretch to the Custom-house Wharf.

Direct importations of coffee from Rio de Janeiro, of sugar and molasses from Cuba, Jamaica, and Demerara, of hoop-iron and cotton ties from England, of salt from Turks Island and Liverpool employed many square-rigged foreign vessels; and three times as many beautifully lined American schooners added miscellaneous cargoes from the North to the overladen wharves of Wilmington.

The following table illustrates the business of Wilmington from December 1, 1851, to December 1, 1852:

COASTWISE EXPORTS FROM WILMINGTON FROM DECEMBER 1, 1851, TO DECEMBER 1, 1852.

Sawed timber, 17,135,889 feet	$272,585.77
Pitch-pine timber, 1,025,202 feet	12,815.01
Spirits turpentine, 96,277 barrels	1,707,999.75
Rosin, 320,219 barrels	560,383.26
Tar, 17,522 barrels	35,044.00
Pitch, 6,660 barrels	9,157.00
Turpentine, raw, 63,071 barrels	220,748.50
Cotton, 12,988 bales	454,580.00
Rice, clean, 2,300 casks	37,375.00
Rice, rough, 64,842 bushels	58,357.80
Peanuts, 93,255 bushels	93,255.00
Corn, Indian, 5,663 bushels	3,009.64
Staves, 27,000	105.00
Cotton yarn, 2,434 bales	97,360.00
Sheetings, 1,702 bales	102,120.00
Flax seed, 165 casks	6,052.25
Flax seed, 1,253 bags	
Sundries	320,613.86
Coastwise total	$3,991,561.84
Foreign exports	549,107.74
Total coastwise and foreign	$4,540,669.58

A FEW OF THE PRINCIPAL FOREIGN EXPORTS ARE SUBJOINED.

Lumber, feet	15,201,000
Timber, feet	2,383,814
Turpentine, barrels	33,596

The class of merchants and professional men of those days was highly respectable and respected; nearly all were men of education and refinement, and they were always keenly interested in public affairs. I note from memory some of the more important business men and firms of importers, commission merchants, and shipbrokers, physicians, bankers, and lawyers who were established between Orange Street and Red Cross Street on the river front, along Water Street and Nutt Street, and uptown:

T. C. & B. G. Worth	James H. Chadbourn & Co.
N. G. Daniel	Kidder & Martin
Pierce & Dudley	Joseph H. Neff

C. W. Styron
James D. Cumming
W. H. McKoy & Co.
Houston & West
J. R. Blossom & Co.
A. H. VanBokkelen
J. E. Lippitt
H. B. Eilers
J. L. Hathaway & Utley
A. W. Coville
DeRosset & Brown
Murray & Murchison
James T. Petteway & Co.
Ellis & Mitchell
Hall & Armstrong
W. H. McRary & Co.
M. McInnis
Avon E. Hall
Harriss & Howell
J. & D. MacRae & Co.
B. G. & W. J. Monroe
Clark & Turlington
Henry Nutt
C. H. Robinson & Co.
A. D. Cazaux
Alexander Oldham
Smith & McLaurin
O. G. Parsley & Co.
Joseph H. Flanner
W. B. Flanner
James I. Metts, sr.
G. O. VanAmringe
H. P. Russell & Co.
P. K. Dickinson
Thomas D. Walker, president
    Wilmington & Manchester
    Railroad.
William S. Ashe, president Wil-
    mington & Weldon Railroad.
John Dawson
P. W. Fanning
John S. James
W. C. Bettencourt
Zebulon Latimer
Adam Empie
Thomas C. Miller
Thomas H. Wright, banker
Joshua G. Wright
Gilbert Potter
James S. Green
William A. Williams

Rankin & Martin
Anderson & Savage
O. P. Meares
W. B. Meares
George Davis
W. A. Wright
Robert Strange
Duncan K. MacRae
Samuel J. Person
DuBrutz Cutlar
Griffith J. McRee
Alexander Anderson
Dr. E. A. Anderson
Stephen Jewett
Timothy Savage
H. R. Savage
L. A. Hart
George Myers
Charles D. Myers
J. S. Robinson
Hedrick & Ryan
J. S. Williams
James Dawson
Richard J. Jones
Dr. J. Fergus McRee
Dr. J. F. McRee, jr.
Dr. James H. Dickson
Dr. F. J. Cutlar
Dr. William J. Harriss
Dr. John D. Bellamy
Dr. William George Thomas
Dr. F. J. Hill
Dr. John Hill
Dr. W. A. Berry
Dr. J. C. Walker
John Wood
Dr. F. W. Potter
Dr. John Hampden Hill
Louis Erambert
Col. James G. Burr
Alfred Alderman
James S. Alderman
Edward B. Dudley
James Owen
Alexander MacRae
Asa A. Brown
E. P. Hall
Joseph H. Watters
Rev. Father Murphy
Rev. John L. Pritchard
S. D. Wallace

John Cowan
John Wooster
A. M. Waddell
William C. Lord
R. W. Brown
George W. Davis
J. W. K. Dix
John C. Latta
Isaac Northrop
Zeno H. Green
Jacob Lyon
James Wilson
S. P. Watters
Walker Meares
Talcott Burr, Jr.
James T. Miller
Alexander Sprunt
Rt. Rev. Bishop Atkinson
Cyrus S. Van Amringe
H. R. Savage
Daniel B. Baker
N. N. Nixon
Daniel L. Russell
R. H. Cowan
John A. Taylor
Rev. Dr. R. B. Drane
Dougald McMillan
Samuel Davis
W. S. Anderson
Eli W. Hall
William MacRae
W. L. Smith
Thomas L. Colville
John C. Bailey
James M. Stevenson
James Dawson
Robert B. Wood
George R. French

A. L. Price
John L. Holmes
M. London
John C. Heyer
E. A. Keith
F. J. Lord
T. D. Love
Rev. M. B. Grier
Rev. Charles F. Deems, D.D.
Joseph Price
G. H. Kelly
Henry Flanner
W. P. Elliott
M. M. Kattz
L. B. Huggins
William G. Fowler
L. Vollers
Edward Savage
A. H. Cutts
G. A. Peck
Hugh Waddell
James A. Willard
W. H. Lippitt
Junius D. Gardner
John Judge
James Fulton
Thomas Loring
William B. Giles
Richard A. Bradley
William N. Peden
Gaston Meares
Joseph S. Murphy
William Reston
John Reston
John Colville
William Watters
A. A. Willard

And last, but not least, mine host, Jack Bishop, who kept the Pilot House on the wharf and furnished the best table fare in Wilmington to a large number of merchants, master mariners, and pilots at very moderate prices—he whose breadth of beam and suggestive sign combined to make him known as "Paunchous Pilot"—and his genial neighbor at the foot of Dock Street, Jimmie Baxter, who always wore a battered beaver hat, regardless of corresponding conventionalities of dress, and with his brother Barney supplied the ships with pantry stores.

Some of us still remember Jimmie Baxter's kindly salutation with its warning for the day: "And if ye meet the Divil in the way, don't shtop to shake hands wid him."

FORGOTTEN AIDS TO THE NAVIGATION OF THE CAPE FEAR.

In June, 1851, the topsail schooner *Gallatin,* of the United States Coast Survey, appeared off the Main Bar and sailed into the quiet harbor of Smithville, the base of operations.

She was commanded by Lieutenant Commanding John Newland Maffitt, United States Navy, and the six lieutenants under him included several who rose to the rank of commander, and one to the distinction of admiral in the United States Navy. Three of them were subsequently distinguished in the annals of the Cape Fear: Maffitt, the daring commander of the Confederate States Corvette *Florida;* J. Pembroke Jones, commander of the Confederate States Ram *Raleigh,* and subsequently commander of other vessels of war, and, finally, a prominent officer in the naval service of the Argentine Republic; and Lieut. Charles P. Bolles, a master in the art of triangulation and topography, whose name with that of Maffitt appears upon all the old charts of the Cape Fear.

Professor Bache, the eminent superintendent of the Coast Survey at Washington, in his official reports to Secretary Corwin, makes frequent reference to the valuable services of Lieutenant Commanding Maffitt; who had charge of the hydrography in this section of the Atlantic coast. In one report he says: "Lieutenant Commanding J. N. Maffitt, United States Navy, assistant in the Coast Survey, in command of the schooner *Gallatin,* has executed the soundings of the bar of the Cape Fear River, commencing at the most southern point of Cape Fear, extending at a distance of from two and a half to three and a half miles from shore to the northward and westward, including the Main Bar, middle ground, and Western Bar, the river up to New Inlet, that bar, and Sheep's Head Ledge."

In the execution of this work 25,688 soundings were made, 18,010 angles measured, and 389 miles of soundings run; thirty-five specimens of bottoms were preserved, and fifteen observations of currents made. After this work was completed, Lieutenant Maffitt proceeded to make a hydrographic reconnaissance of the New River bars and of the river above the obstructions. In making this reconnaissance, 5,870 soundings were made, 481 angles measured, and fifty miles of soundings run.

With reference to the social life of these gentlemen, Mrs. Maffitt says: "When Lieutenant Maffitt visited Smithville its citizens were composed of the best people in the Cape Fear region. Its residences, generally deserted in the winter months, were filled during the summer and early fall with the élite of Wilmington society, then in its zenith of culture, refinement, and that open and profuse hospitality for which it has from early colonial times been distinguished. The officers of the Coast Survey and their families were domiciled at the barracks in the garrison grounds. The residents opened their hearts and homes to them and vied with each other in rendering their stay a pleasant one.

"Like most small communities having few interests outside of themselves, there was at times a tendency to indulge in unpleasant gossip, and in order to quell this by giving a new source of interest, Lieutenant Maffitt proposed organizing a dramatic company; and, to insure the actors against unkind criticism of amateurs, he made it a condition of entrance to the plays that all who desired to witness the performance should sign their names as members of the company before receiving their tickets. And this proved a perfect success."

Dr. W. G. Curtis says: "The old residents of Smithville, before the season was over, gave this troupe the credit of driving out the gossips or closing their lips. In a word, the whole society became a mutual admiration society. Harmony prevailed everywhere. Sermons were preached every Sunday at the chapel and the services were well attended; but the members of the church often said that the good feeling of all the attendants, brought about by our troupe, put them in a better frame of mind to listen to the teachings from the pulpit."

Of Captain Maffitt of the Confederacy much has been written. Of this intrepid commander, it was said by a distinguished visitor in 1868: "Amongst the many interesting men I met at Wilmington was the well known Captain Maffitt, whose adventurous career upon the high seas, as commander of the *Florida,* excited so much attention at the time.

"I found the captain a cultivated and gentlemanly man, small-sized and spare in figure, but with a finely-cast head, a dark, keen eye, a strong tuft of black whiskers on his chin, and a firm little mouth that seemed to express the energy and determination of his character. I remember very well his dignified appearance as he stepped about in his short military cloak, with his keen and somewhat stern look. He was in reduced circumstances, having staked his whole fortune and position upon the Lost Cause; but, like so many of his old military and naval associates, he was trying his hand at business and striving to reconcile himself to the new order of things."

In *The Life and Services* of this remarkable man of the Cape Fear, his gifted widow, Mrs. Emma Martin Maffitt, has contributed to our history a volume of intensely interesting and instructive literature.

Well may we say of him, as was said of the gallant Ney, "He was the bravest of the brave."

CAPE FEAR COAL.

I am informed by Mr. Joseph Hyde Pratt, State geologist, that coal was found in two sections of our State, one in Chatham and Moore Counties, the other in Stokes County.

Mining was done on the deposits of Chatham and Moore Counties, and for many years a small amount of coal was gotten out; but the industry was not profitable because the coal basin is not extensive. The seams are thin; and the few wider ones are cut up with slate, and so mixed with sulphur that the quality has always been bad.

The use of this North Carolina coal during the War between the States led to the capture of several fine blockade-running steamers, whose supply of Welsh coal had been seized by the Confederate officials and "Egypt" coal substituted. This was so worthless that it was impossible to raise and keep steam, and consequently these unfortunate and valuable ships fell an easy prey to the Federal cruisers.

With reference to my further inquiries on this subject, Dr. Joseph Austin Holmes, late director of the Bureau of Mines at Washington, says: "Coal was opened up between 1855 and 1858 in Chatham County at a place called Egypt, under the advice of Dr. Ebenezer Emmons, then State geologist. The coal was at that time regarded as of considerable promise.

"During the year 1858 an examination was made of the Deep River region, one of the principal tributaries of the Cape Fear, by Captain Wilkes and other officers of the United States Navy, in compliance with a Senate resolution adopted on April 13, 1858. As a result of this investigation, and in a report published as an executive document early in 1859, Captain Wilkes and his associates reported favorably on the proposition that the Deep River region was a suitable one for the establishment of foundries and other plants for the production of naval ordnance and supplies."

Captain Wilkes made the following statement in regard to the coal:

"It is a shining and clean coal, resembling the best specimens of Cumberland (Md.). It ignites easily, and burns with a bright, clear combustion, and leaves a very little purplish-grey ash. It is a desirable coal for blacksmiths' use, for the parlor, and superior to most coals for the production of gas, for which it is likely to be in great demand. Its freedom from sulphur is another of its recommendations."

These favorable preliminary reports by Captain Wilkes of the Navy Department, and Dr. Emmons, the State geologist of North Carolina, awakened considerable interest in the development of this coal. But it was found in subsequent operations that the coal, as mined, generally contained a considerable quantity of slate and other black earthy material, that its ash formed a slag on the grate bars, and that it contained no little sulphur. This composition made it a rather difficult coal to use in ordinary furnaces. But during the war, it was extensively used to make coke for the iron works established in the Deep River region. It was also used as a steam coal; but its use on board blockade runners and other ships was found highly objectionable, both on account of the poor quality of the coal and the smoke which resulted from its use.

At intervals between 1870 and 1900 the shaft at the Egypt coal mine (about 465 feet deep) was again opened and the mine worked on a small scale, the coal being shipped to Raleigh, Fayetteville, and other local markets; but it never became a good merchantable coal, and its use remained limited and local.

Besides, the coal itself gave off in the mine considerable quantities of explosive gas, and there were several bad explosions, one of which, in December, 1895, killed thirty-nine men, and another, in May, 1900, killed twenty-three men. The operating company was much discouraged by these disasters, and the mine was closed.

There is probably a considerable quantity of coal still to be obtained in the vicinity of the old Egypt mine, and if the mine were worked with modern safety precautions, to prevent disastrous explosions, and the coal were washed so as to remove the dirt, it would be found to be a fairly satisfactory fuel. If briquetted (as is frequently done in European countries), it would be both suitable and available for domestic use in the adjacent markets.

The formation in which this coal occurs extends from the South Carolina line northward to near Oxford in Granville County, its greatest width being from twelve to fifteen miles. At different points in this formation there are beds of sandstone available for building purposes; but the workable coal seems to be limited to a few thousand acres in that part of Chatham County near the old hamlet of Egypt, formerly known as the "Gulf," but which during the past few years has been called "Cumnock."

FAYETTEVILLE ON THE CAPE FEAR.

Known as Cross Creek and Campbellton up to 1784, the name of this interesting old town was then changed to Fayetteville, in tribute to the services of the Marquis de Lafayette, who visited Fayetteville in 1824.

The people of Fayetteville, between whom and the people of Wilmington there have been for a hundred years the most cordial social and business relations, were ever as thrifty and enterprising as hospitable and cultured. They were among the first in the State to establish cotton factories; and, being at the head of water transportation and having an extensive system of plank roads into the interior, Fayetteville was the great mart of trade in North Carolina, especially for the extensive country lying west to the Blue Ridge, and even for the transmontane country comprising parts of East Tennessee and Southwest Virginia. This trade was carried on by canvas-topped wagons as vehicles of transportation, drawn by two, four, and even six horses, for mules in those days were seldom employed. Said Mr. J. H. Myrover, the historian of Fayetteville:

"The starting point of all this vast back-country carrying trade was the wharves and Water Street in Wilmington, though in the early part of the last century wagoning was done by

stages, or relays, between Fayetteville and Philadelphia, before
the first steamer was put on the Cape Fear. Among the pioneers of steamboat building and operating on the Cape Fear
River, though perhaps not the first, was Mr. Seawell. One of
the first boats to ply the stream bore the same name as one of
the last—the *City of Fayetteville.* It was launched not far
from the Clarendon Bridge, and it has been related that some
one having prophesied that it would 'turn turtle' when it
reached the water, the architect boldly rode its bow as it slipped
off the ways, and the event justified his faith in his work.

"It is impossible, with the lapse of time, to enumerate all the
craft that formed the Cape Fear merchant marine. The *Henrietta, Fanny Lutterloh, Cotton Plant, Zephyr, Magnolia, Halcyon,
Governor Worth, North State, A. P. Hurt, D. Murchison,* and
R. E. Lee are recalled as leading among the passenger and
freight steamers from the thirties up to and for some time
after the War between the States. Equally impossible would
it be to give the names and record of the services of the faithful
captains.

"Notable commanders in the history of Cape Fear navigation
were Captains John P. Stedman, who lost his life by the explosion of the boiler of the *Fanny Lutterloh,* Rush, A. P. Hurt,
after whom a steamer was named, Phillips, Skinner, Green,
Worth, Smith, Garrason. The captain's rule on board was
autocratic but patriarchal. He sat at the head of the table and
served the passengers as the father of a family would his children. The fare was plain but wholesome and abundant, and,
with good weather and a fair depth of water, the trip between
Fayetteville and Wilmington was very pleasant. The river
goes on its way to the sea with many a wind and bend, its
banks steep and heavily wooded, the wild grape climbing the
tall trees, and the wild jasmine and flowering honeysuckle giving forth their fragrance. Those veteran captains knew the
river well and most of the people on either bank clear to Wilmington; the pilots, many of whom were negroes, knew every
crook and eddy of the stream. Dan Buxton, an esteemed colored
man of this city, has a record of fifty years faithful service as
a pilot on the Cape Fear. The late Col. Thomas S. Lutterloh,
always a large boat owner, is said to have been the first Cumberland man to become sole owner of a steamer on the river.
Many of the business men of Fayetteville and Wilmington were
stockholders in these boat lines.

"The oldest inhabitants still look back on those times as the 'good old days' of Fayetteville. The merchants were not the progressive men of the 20th century; they were conservative and cautious and honest as the day, with their word as bond. They made money slowly, but they lived simply, and gradually accumulated modest fortunes."

Mr. Myrover overlooked in his sketch a very prominent Cape Fear mariner, who, during his long and useful career, commanded successively the well-known river steamers *Henrietta, Brothers, Scottish Chief, James R. Grist, James T. Petteway,* and *John Dawson.* A hearty, genial, bright-eyed Scotsman of superior attainments was Capt. John Banks, in some respects the most notable of all the river captains. He was a highly esteemed citizen of Wilmington and he owned a valuable residence on the corner of Market and Seventh Streets, where he reared an interesting family, several members still surviving. Other commanders were Capt. James Barry, of the *A. P. Hurt;* Captain Driver of the *Flora Macdonald;* Capt. Roderick Mac-Rae, of the *Rowan;* Captain Stedman, of the *Kate McLaurin;* Capt. Jesse Dicksey, of the *Black River;* Captain Peck, of the *Nellie Hart,* and Captain Jones, of the *Enterprise.* There were two other boats, the *North Carolina* and the *T. S. Lutterloh,* the names of whose commanders I have forgotten.

United States Minister E. J. Hale says:

"From the close of the Revolution and up to the building of the Wilmington and Raleigh [Weldon] Railroad and the Raleigh and Gaston Railroad (about 1838), the great mail stage lines from the North to the South passed through Fayetteville. There were four daily lines of four-horse post and passenger coaches to Raleigh, Norfolk, Charleston, and Columbia; and, in addition, two tri-weekly lines to New Bern and Salisbury.

"The Legislature sat in Fayetteville in 1788, 1789, 1790, and 1793. At the convention at Hillsborough in 1788, called to deliberate on the acceptance or rejection of the United States Constitution, Fayetteville failed to secure the location of the permanent capital by one vote, that of Timothy Bloodworth, of New Hanover, who subsequently was elected to the United States Senate. The ordinance adopted fixed the location of the capital on Joel Lane's plantation in Wake, on the ground that this point was nearer the centre of the State than Fayetteville."

Notable Incidents

VISITS OF PRESIDENTS OF THE UNITED STATES TO WILMINGTON BEFORE THE WAR.

"Wilmington," said Iredell Meares, Esq., in an interesting pamphlet, "has been honored by the visits of five of the Presidents of the United States—Washington, Monroe, Polk, Fillmore, and Taft." We may now add the name of Wilson, who, as stated elsewhere, once lived in Wilmington.

GENERAL WASHINGTON, in 1791, made a tour of the Southern States. One of his biographers relates that "no royal progress in any country ever equaled this tour in its demonstrations of veneration and respect." His visit to Wilmington was preserved in the traditions of the people for many years. The old folks used to tell of its incidents, and the ladies of "ye olden times" of an elaborate ball given in his honor. In the possession of Mr. Clayton Giles, of this city, is a letter in excellent state of preservation giving some account of this interesting incident. It was written by Mrs. Jane Anna Simpson to her sister on the day of the reception, and is dated the "25th April, 1791." The letter, among other things, says:

"Great doings this day. General Washington arrived yesterday. The Light Horse went to meet him. The artillery were ready to receive him with a round from the batteries, four guns. This day he dines with the Gentlemen of the town; in the evening a grand ball and illumination; tomorrow takes his leave. I believe the Light Horse are to escort him a day's journey on his way to Chas'ton.

"Half-past four—just going to dinner—cannons firing; Chrissy and the children all gone to see the procession. I don't go to the ball this evening, as Mary can not accompany me. She desires me to ask if you have many beaux at the Marsh. Adieu. I must get the candles.

"Mrs. Quince has given up her house to the General and she stays with our uncles. * * *"

The place at which the Light Horse met General Washington was at the Rouse House, about fifteen miles out on the New

Bern Road. Here was fought, during the Revolutionary War a small battle between the Patriots and the English forces under the command of Major Craig. It is described as a massacre by the historian Caruthers, for Craig gave no quarter and killed every one of the Patriots, who were overwhelmed by numbers, save one boy, who escaped.

It is a tradition handed down by the old folks that upon the occasion of General Washington's visit to the residence of General Smith, at his plantation Belvidere, which is situated across the river in Brunswick County, he was met at the river landing by a group of thirteen young ladies, all dressed in white and representing the thirteen colonies, who preceded him up the avenue of old trees leading from the river to the brick residence, bestrewing his path with flowers as he approached.

The ball which was given to him by the people of Wilmington was held in what was then known as the Assembly Hall, also called "Old '76," because of having been built in 1776. In time it was used as a sailor boarding-house, and was subsequently taken down in 1876 to make way for the present building. It stood on Front Street, east side, between Orange and Ann Streets, where now stands a two-story brick tenement house.

"Wilmington," wrote President Washington in his diary, "has some good houses, pretty compactly built—the whole under a hill, which is formed entirely of sand. The number of souls in it amount by enumeration to about 1,000.

"Wilmington, unfortunately for it, has a mud bank—miles below, over which not more than ten feet of water can be brought at common tides. Yet it is said vessels of 250 tons have come up. The quantity of shipping which loads here annually amounts to about 12,000 tons. Exports are Naval stores and lumber; some tobacco, corn, rice, and flax seed and pork."

"Monday, 25th. Dined with the citizens of the place—went to a Ball in the evening at which there were 62 ladies—illuminations, bonfires, &&."

JAMES MONROE, the fifth President of the United States, visited Wilmington on the 12th day of April, 1819.

In an old copy of the *Raleigh Minerva,* bearing date April 23, 1819, we find a letter from Wilmington, giving an account of the visit of President Monroe and his suite:

"The Presidential cortege was met about twelve miles from town, on the old New Bern Road, somewhere near Scott's Hill,

14

and escorted into the city by the Wilmington Light Horse, a volunteer organization, under the command of Colonel Cowan. The entrance into the town was made on Market Street, the boundary being on Fifth. They then proceeded down Market to Front and up Front to the Wilmington Hotel, where the usual formalities of a grand reception were tendered to the President.

"His Excellency was the guest, while here, of Robert Cochran, Esq., who resided on Second Street, between Chestnut and Mulberry; and John C. Calhoun, the Secretary of War, and his Lady, received the hospitalities of Dr. A. J. DeRosset, sr., at the brick house standing on the corner of Market and Third Streets. It was on Thursday that the President arrived here, and on Friday, accompanied by Judge Murphey, he paid a visit to Wrightsville. On his return he partook of a dinner with the citizens at the Wilmington Hotel and the next day left this place on the steamer *Prometheus* for Fort Johnston, from whence he proceeded immediately to Georgetown, S. C."

At the dinner given in his honor, Hanson Kelly, Esq., presided, assisted by Robert Cochran, Esq. The former was magistrate of police (now the office of mayor), and the latter was the collector of customs for the district of Cape Fear. There were a number of patriotic toasts drunk, the list being published in the papers of the day, and among those who responded were the President, Hon. John C. Calhoun, J. R. London, Esq., Gen. James Owen, Judge Archibald Murphey, Colonel Cleary, Robert Cochran, Esq., John D. Jones, Esq., Gen. Thomas Davis, William B. Meares, Esq., and Alfred Moore, Esq., all prominent citizens of the Cape Fear in that day and time.

In a formal letter addressed to the President by Hanson Kelly, Esq., on behalf of the citizens, occurs this sentiment: "Events, the most propitious, have rendered your administration an epoch of national security and aggrandizement. The united voice of your country, from Maine to Mexico, proclaim the wisdom of councils honorable to you; and in their result, glorious to our extended empire." To this letter, the President responded, as follows:

SIR: On the principle on which I have thought it proper to visit our Atlantic frontier, this town, with its relation to the ocean, had a just claim to attention. It was always my intention to visit it when I should be able to examine the Southern coast; and I am much gratified in having done it, as, in addition to the satisfaction of having performed an interesting part of my public duty, it has afforded me an opportunity of becoming acquainted with a portion of my fellow-citizens, whose kind reception and obliging attention I shall always recollect with great interest. To secure you in peace, and all the advantages in commerce which a kind Providence has enabled you to enjoy, and all the protection in war, to which your situation may expose you, are objects which will never fail to receive the unwearied attention of the General Government in all its branches, according to their respective powers. On my exertions, in those concerns which fall within the department which I have the honor to fill, you may confidently rely. In the late event to which you allude, I concur in all the favorable anticipations which you have suggested of its happy effects on the best interests of our country. In contemplating this epoch we must all derive peculiar satisfaction from the reflection that it was the result of an arrangement by which our differences were settled with a friendly power, and our peace secured against the prospect of early interruption, on conditions equally honorable to both parties.

Should I be able by my future conduct in the public service to carry with me into retirement the same favorable opinion of my fellow-citizens which you have kindly expressed of the past, it will afford me the high consolation to which I have invariably aspired.

JAMES MONROE.

JAMES K. POLK, the eleventh President of the United States, just after his retirement, visited Wilmington, upon invitation of its citizens. The files of the newspapers published here at the time, which will be found in the Wilmington Public Library, contain reports of his reception. From the *Commercial,* issue of Thursday, March 8, 1849, we clip this mention of his visit:

"The ex-President, Mr. Polk, and Lady and Niece, together with Mr. Secretary Walker and Niece, and Mr. Grahame, solicitor of the Treasury, and Lady, reached our town at 10 o'clock yesterday morning. Their arrival was heralded by the booming of cannon, the ringing of bells, and the floating aloft of banners and streamers from stalls, housetops, and mastheads. The magistrate of police, Col. James T. Miller, the Committee of Arrangements, and a large concourse of citizens were ready at the railroad to receive the ex-President and suite, and they were greeted by Colonel Miller in a brief and cordial address, to which the ex-President warmly responded. The whole suite was then escorted, according to the program heretofore published, to Mrs. Swann's boarding-house, on the balcony of which, in view and hearing of the assembled crowd, Mr. William Hill welcomed the ex-President and suite in a cordial, chaste, and eloquent address, during which he alluded to the birth and education of the ex-President in North Carolina, and to many of the leading measures of his administration. Mr. Polk's response was feeling and patriotic. He fondly acknowledged his attachment to North Carolina, and the gratification which it gave him to receive from the archives, and to transmit to our State Executive, the recorded evidence of the early disloyalty and independent resolves of different portions of North Carolina. He spoke of the inestimable value of our Union, and of the bright destiny in store for our country, provided we shall adhere to this glorious Union, and the teachings of the Father of the Republic. When he had closed, General Marstellar announced to the crowd that at 12 o'clock Mr. Polk and suite would be happy to see their fellow-citizens at the Masonic Hall. And, accordingly, at that hour, hundreds repaired thither and offered their salutations to our distinguished guests."

MILLARD FILLMORE, the thirteenth President of the United States, after his retirement, visited Wilmington on the 12th day of May, 1854. He had contemplated a tour of the South in 1853, and on March 10, 1853, the citizens of the town met and passed the following resolution:

Resolved, That a Committee of twenty-four persons, and the magistrate of police, be appointed to correspond with Millard Fillmore, late President of the United States, and such of the members of his late cabinet as may accompany him on his projected visit to the South, and tender to him and to them the hospitalities of our town.

Under this resolution the following gentlemen were appointed: Talcott Burr, jr., John L. Holmes, William A. Wright, William C. Bettencourt, R. H. Cowan, R. H. Beery, George Davis, S. J. Person, James S. Green, John Walker, John MacRae, R. Strange, jr., J. G. Wright, Gaston Meares, E. Kidder, S. D. Wallace, A. A. Brown, E. W. Hall, D. Dupre, Miles Costin, J. J. Lippitt, P. M. Walker, O. P. Meares, and J. T. Miller.

A sub-committee consisting of Messrs. James S. Green, John L. Meares, S. J. Person, and Adam Empie, jr., were appointed to go to Richmond and tender the hospitalities of the town to the ex-President, who was supposed to be on a visit there at the time, and to his suite. The death of Mrs. Fillmore caused the postponement of Mr. Fillmore's tour in the South that year, but in 1854 he fulfilled his desire to make such a tour, with the assurance to the public that he "earnestly wished to avoid the pomp and pageantry of a public reception." In the *Daily Journal,* issue of Friday, May 12, 1854, the files of which are in the local library, is an account of the ex-President's visit, as follows:

"Ex-President Fillmore, of New York, and Mr. Kennedy, of Maryland, Secretary of the Navy under his administration, arrived here this morning on the Manchester cars from Columbia. A very large number of our citizens of both parties have called upon our distinguished visitors at their rooms at Mr. Holmes's hotel [now a store, southeast corner Market and Front Streets]. Owing to the illness of Mrs. Kennedy they are anxious to reach Baltimore at the earliest possible moment, and are thus compelled to leave for the North by the 2 o'clock train. In accordance with the earnest wish of the people, Mr. Fillmore had designed to make a short address from the balcony of the hotel at 11 o'clock, but, in consequence of the rain, his intention could not be carried out. We are pleased to see both gentlemen apparently in the enjoyment of high health and spirits. Mr. Fillmore is certainly a gentleman of exceedingly prepossessing appearance and manners; and bears little evidence of the cares of state having pressed heavily upon him.

THE VISIT OF HENRY CLAY.

The happy occasion of a visit by Henry Clay to Wilmington while he was canvassing the South during his presidential campaign in 1844, is described by the *Wilmington Chronicle* as follows:

April 3, 1844.

The Committee of Arrangement for the reception and entertainment of our distinguished fellow-citizen, Henry Clay, who in compliance with the invitation of the citizens of this town is expected to visit us on Tuesday, the 9th of April, 1844, have adopted the following measures:

[Here follows an elaborate program.]

The following gentlemen are appointed marshals of the day, viz.: O. G. Parsley, Thomas W. Brown, G. B. Alsaps, James Anderson, George W. Davis, James F. McRee, jr., John L. Meares, Nathaniel Hill.

The following gentlemen compose the accompanying committee to wait on Mr. Clay from Charleston, viz.: James Owen, John MacRae, Dr. Thomas H. Wright, Gen. Alexander Mac-- Rae, Gilbert Potter, F. C. Hill, Asa A. Brown, William A. Wright, A. J. DeRosset, jr., George Davis, R. G. Rankin, Porter Strode, Thomas Sanford.

The following gentlemen have been appointed to act as managers of the ball: R. W. Brown, Edward B. Dudley, P. K. Dickinson, James S. Green, G. J. McRee, M. London, James H. Dickson, Thomas D. Meares, John Hall, and Nathaniel Hill.

April 10, 1844.

MR. CLAY IN WILMINGTON.

The publication of the *Chronicle* has been delayed a day to enable us to give some account of the reception and entertainment of Mr. Clay in Wilmington, where he arrived yesterday morning.

On Tuesday afternoon between three and four o'clock, the Committee of Thirteen deputed by the Clay Club to wait upon Mr. Clay at Charleston and escort him to this town, received him on board the fine steamer *Gladiator,* Captain Smith. The steamer had quite a pleasant night for the run, and reached Smithville about sunrise. Mr. Clay was there welcomed to the State by the Committee of Ten, consisting of the chairman of the Whig Central Committee and one gentleman from each of the nine congressional districts. After an hour's delay at Smithville the steamer was again in motion, and reached here at the time named above. From a point three or four miles below town until the boat touched the wharf, a piece of ordnance on board was fired at regular intervals and the reports were answered from numerous other pieces of artillery stationed at various places along the river. The steamer came to on the south side of Market Dock. Here an immense throng had gathered to greet the distinguished man, and as soon as the boat touched the wharf there were repeated bursts of the people's welcome. Mr. Clay was then introduced to the Committee of Arrangements, and, a procession having formed in the prescribed order, he was escorted to his private lodgings at the residence of Mrs. Joseph A. Hill, southeast corner of Front and Dock Streets.

At 11 o'clock Mr. Clay, accompanied by the Clay Club, committees, and citizens, repaired to the new and commodious man-

sion of Capt. Samuel Potter, on Market Street. Here, upon the
balcony of the house facing Market Street, he was addressed in
a most appropriate manner by ex-Governor Dudley, the president of the Clay Club. The address referred to the long and
arduous public services of Mr. Clay, the great debt of gratitude
the country justly owes him, the strong interest and regard the
people throughout the Union have manifested for him on
numerous occasions, the warm affection entertained for him by
so large a portion of the citizens of North Carolina, and appealed to the multitude of upturned faces as furnished evidence
that "Welcome to Henry Clay" were the words then gushing
spontaneously from the hearts of thousands. Mr. Clay made
only a short reply, not exceeding twenty minutes in length.

He said he had long looked forward to this visit to North
Carolina (which he had promised to make when a fitting opportunity should occur) with a pleasing hope, and now having
set foot upon her soil for the first time, his fondest anticipations
were in course of being realized, and the event would form an
epoch in his life. He had for many years wished to visit the
State, and the repeated invitations formed motives of still
weightier influence.

He utterly disclaimed all electioneering designs or selfish
purposes pertaining to his journey. He was traveling on business and to enjoy the hospitality of his friends; the people had
tendered him unexpected civilities, which he could not without
rudeness decline. He had also been brought out on political
topics, and had not hesitated to declare his sentiments, as became an American citizen.

He glanced at the two principal parties of the country, expressing his conviction that both of them are in the main governed by honest views. Men, he said, should act with that party
in whose principles they found the least to condemn, after having given them a thorough examination. None could expect to
find in any party everything exactly as they would have it;
small defects must be overlooked, as are those which a man dis-
covers, perchance, in the woman of his admiration. He had attached himself to the Whig party as the result of his investigations of the great principles of its existence. But every man, he
said, should hold party fealty as subordinate to that due his
country. Properly, parties were but instruments for promoting
our country's good.

Mr. Clay excused himself for the briefness of his discourse

by reference to the fatiguing circumstances of his journey thus far.

The view below and around the place where Mr. Clay stood was striking beyond any effort of ours to portray. The wide street, for a considerable distance on either hand, was one dense mass of human beings, whilst the balconies, windows, etc., were crowded with ladies, all eager listeners to the words of the great statesman of the West. Never was such a scene, or anything approaching to it, witnessed in Wilmington.

His speech ended, Mr. Clay entered the reception room, and was then introduced to a rushing tide of people, made up of both sexes and all ages and conditions. He remained in the reception rooms until one o'clock, and then retired to his lodgings.

At two o'clock a most bountiful collation, prepared by Mr. Keith, was spread out on tables in the open space south of Mr. John Walker's house on Princess Street, to which a general invitation had been given, and of which hundreds partook. Mr. Clay was not present, desiring to have a few hours' rest. The company was, however, highly gratified with able and instructive speeches from Hon. A. H. Stephens, member of Congress from Georgia, who being on his way to Washington was induced to remain over a day; Col. William W. Cherry, of Bertie, an orator of surpassing eloquence; Col. B. F. Gaither, of Burke, and others. Mr. Stephens well sustained the reputation which had preceded him of being an eloquent, humorous, and effective speaker.

At night there was a superb ball and party at the Carolina Hotel and Masonic Hall—all the rooms being connected for the occasion. The whole affair was got up under the superintendency of ladies of Wilmington. It could not, therefore, but be an elegant one. The rooms were beautifully decorated, the refreshments choice, the supper in refined taste and order, the music inspiring, and a hilarious spirit reigned throughout the well-filled apartments. How many hours of the morning heard the festive strains we do not exactly know and will not hazard a conjecture. In the course of the evening Mr. Clay visited the place of gaiety and remained a couple of hours or so.

Between seven and eight this morning Mr. Clay took his departure for Raleigh, by way of the railroad, cheered by many, many, newly-awakened and newly-born wishes for his welfare.

We have thus sketched a meagre outline of Mr. Clay's visit to Wilmington. The glowing lines of the picture the reader's imagination must supply. The enthusiasm, the kindly feeling, the generous good will, all these are to be supposed, for they were all exhibited in an eminent degree.

There was a very great concourse of strangers in town from this and the neighboring counties, Fayetteville, and other parts of the State, who aided us in doing honor to our venerable and beloved guest.

THE VISIT OF DANIEL WEBSTER.

Early in May, 1847, Daniel Webster visited Wilmington as the guest of Gov. Edward B. Dudley. In an old book containing the private correspondence of Mr. Webster I found a letter by him dated Wilmington, May 6, 1847, as follows:

"At one o'clock yesterday, ten miles from this city, we met a special train, with a large deputation, headed by ex-Governor Dudley. The weather was bad, and the wind east, and I was rather easily persuaded to stay over a day. The Governor brought us to his own home, where we were grandly lodged. I go to the hotel to meet the citizens at 11 o'clock, and go off at half-past two this p. m., if the wind goes down. At present it blows rather hard. This is an active little city, built on the east side of the river, on sand-hills. The good people are Whigs, but out of the city, and all around for fifty miles, it is a region whose politics are personified by Mr. McKay.

"There is a thing, Harry, which thou hast often heard of, and it is known to many in this land by the name of *pitch,* etc., etc. We are here in the midst of this very thing, at the very center of the tar and turpentine region. The pines are long-leaved pines. In one of these, a foot from the bottom, a notch is cut, and its capacity enlarged and its shape fashioned a little, so as to hold the liquid, by chiseling, and then it is called the 'box.' Above the box the bark is cut off, for a foot or so, and the turpentine oozes out of the tree on to this smooth surface, and then runs slowly into the box. The box holds about a quart. In a good large tree it will fill five times a season. Sometimes there are two boxes in one tree, so that some trees will yield ten quarts a year. But the greatest yield is the first year; after that it is gradually diminished, and in seven or eight years the tree dies, or will yield no more turpentine. Tar is made by bringing together wood full of turpentine, either trees or knots, and pieces picked up in the woods, and burning it in a pit, just as charcoal is made, then running it off into a hole prepared for it in the ground. At the present price of the article, this is said to be the best business now doing in the State. I am told good, fresh, well-timbered pine lands can be bought for $1.25 to $1.50 per acre.

"One barrel of turpentine distilled makes six gallons of spirits. The residuum, or resin, is not of much value, say twenty-five cents a barrel. Tar and turpentine are now high, and the business is good."

The late Col. Thomas C. McIlhenny, always a welcome guest of Governor Dudley, often entertained me by the recital of important local events of his earlier years, and upon one occasion described the visit of the great Commoner while he was also a guest at the Governor's mansion. The colonel said he was much impressed by the great size of Mr. Webster's head and the powerful penetration of his searching eyes, and by his fancy for the Governor's madeira, of which he kept a pipe of superior quality. After drinking all of the dining room supply, Mrs. Dudley having withdrawn, Mr. Webster laid an affectionate hand upon the colonel's shoulder and said: "Young man, show me where the Governor keeps that wine," and being led to the cellar, he greatly reduced the contents of the cask with much enjoyment, but apparently not altogether with satisfaction, because he seldom knew when he had enough.

With reference to Mr. Webster's visit to Wilmington, the following from the local newspaper, the *Commercial,* Thursday morning, May 6, 1847, is quoted:

HON. DANIEL WEBSTER.

The Hon. Daniel Webster and family arrived at this place yesterday in the cars at a little before 2 o'clock.

Col. John MacRae, magistrate of police, appointed the following gentlemen as a committee to meet our distinguished guest, and to make the necessary arrangements to entertain him while here:

Governor Dudley, John D. Jones, L. H. Marsteller, Alexander MacRae, Dr. W. A. Berry, James T. Miller, Dr. F. J. Hill, R. W. Brown, Samuel Potter, Dr. J. H. Dickson, Gilbert Potter, John Walker, C. D. Ellis, Thomas Loring, A. A. Brown, D. Fulton, R. B. Wood, J. Ballard, H. W. Beatty, J. Hathaway, H. R. Savage, W. C. Bettencourt, Dr. T. H. Wright, Thomas D. Meares, John A. Taylor, James S. Green, W. N. Peden, Owen Fennell, Miles Costin, Alfred Bryant, Dr. J. D. Bellamy, Samuel Black, Henry Nutt, P. K. Dickinson.

A number of the committee started in an extra train at about eleven o'clock and met the regular train at Rocky Point, where they entered the mail train, and through Governor Dudley proffered the hospitalities of our town to Mr. Webster and his family. On arriving at the depot they proceeded to the residence of Governor Dudley on the southwest corner of Front and Nun Streets.

Mr. Webster will leave in the boat today for Charleston.

At the request of the committee appointed by the magistrate of police, Mr. Webster will meet the citizens of Wilmington at the Masonic Hall this morning at eleven o'clock.

The same paper, of May 8, 1847, contained the following:

Mr. Webster.

This gentleman left our place in the boat for Charleston on Thursday evening. The arrangements indicated in our last were carried out by the committee. At the Masonic Hall Mr. Webster made a short address to the many citizens who had assembled to pay their respects to him. We believe men of all parties were very much gratified on the occasion.

Mention has been made to me of Mr. Webster's appreciation of the excellent cooking in the South, and of his preference for a dish of tripe, which leads me to copy a letter on this subject, written in December, 1850, and addressed to his hostess at Richmond, Mrs. Paige.

DEAR MRS. PAIGE:—I sit down to write a letter, partly diplomatic and partly historical. The subject is Tripe—T-R-I-P-E. Your husband remembers Mrs. Hayman, who was Mrs. Blake's cook. Excelling others in all else, she excelled herself in a dish of tripe. I do not know that her general genius exceeded that of Monica McCarty; but in this production she was more exact, more artistical; she gave to the article, not only a certain *gout*, which gratified the most fastidious, but an expression, also, an air of *haut ton*, as it lay presented on the table, that assured one that he saw before him something from the hand of a master.

Tradition, it is said, occasionally hands down the practical arts with more precision and fidelity than they can be transmitted by books, from generation to generation; and I have thought it likely that your Lydia may have caught the tact of preparing this inimitable dish. I entertain this opinion on two grounds: first, because I have been acquainted with very respectable efforts of hers in that line; second, because she knows Mr. Paige's admirable connoiseurship, and can determine, by her quick eye, when the dish comes down from the table, whether the contents have met his approbation.

For these reasons, and others, upon which it is not necessary for the undersigned to enlarge, he is desirous of obtaining Lydia's receipt for a dish of tripe, for the dinner-table. Mrs. Hayman's is before my eyes. Unscathed by the frying pan, it was white as snow; it was disposed in squares, or in parallelograms, of the size of a small sheet of ladies' note paper; it was tender as jelly; beside it stood the tureen of melted butter, a dish of mealy potatoes, and the vinegar cruet. Can this spectacle be exhibited in the Vine Cottage, on Louisiana Avenue, in the City of Washington?

Yours truly, always,

DAN'L WEBSTER.

P. S.—Tripe; the etymon is the Greek word to "turn, to wind," from its involutions, not the same as "tripod," which means "having three feet"; nor the same as "trip," which is from the Latin *tripudiare*, to strike the feet upon the ground; sometimes to stumble; sometimes to go nimbly; to "trip it on the light fantastic toe."

Washington, 29 December, 1850.

THE VISIT OF EDWARD EVERETT.

In 1859 the renowned Edward Everett delivered in hundreds of cities throughout the United States his splendid address on the *Character of Washington,* the receipts being for the benefit of the Ladies' Mount Vernon Association.

Of his visit to Wilmington on that occasion he wrote in his *Mount Vernon Papers:* "Its population, as far as I could judge from a short visit, is intelligent, enterprising, and rather more than usually harmonious among themselves. The river prospects from elevated positions are remarkably fine. An immense audience, assembled in Thalian Hall on the 11th of April last, honored the repetition of my address on the *Character of Washington,* and the net receipts of the evening, $1,091.80, were, in proportion to population, far beyond those of any other place in the Union."

Mr. Everett has also been quoted as saying that at Wilmington alone, during his travels, he was introduced by an orator who surpassed himself, Mr. George Davis.

We copy an interesting account of Mr. Everett's oration in Wilmington from the *Daily Journal* of that date.

April 12, 1859.

MR. EVERETT'S ORATION.

Last evening Thalian Hall was filled by an attentive audience eager to listen to the Washington oration of Hon. Edward Everett, of Massachusetts.

At 8 o'clock Mr. Everett, accompanied by a committee of citizens, appeared upon the stage and was introduced to the audience by George Davis, Esq., whose eloquent though brief remarks formed a fitting prelude to the splendid composition of the distinguished speaker.

Mr. Everett is, we believe, 65 years of age, tall, rather portly than otherwise, his hair, trimmed short, is nearly white, and we learn from those who have heard him before that either advancing years or illness have considerably subdued the vigor of his tones and the energy of his delivery. His features, those of a cultivated gentleman, have been or will be made familiar to most through the portraits of him which have been published.

We have no desire to attempt any sketch of Mr. Everett's address further than to glance at a very few points. He spoke of three eras in Washington's life—when he fought in the old French War, when he took command of the American forces, and when he retired from that command. He spoke of what he denominated the "Age of Washington," reviewed the history of the eighteenth and first half of the nineteenth century; enumerated the great things that had been done, and the great men that had figured within that space of time to which future ages would turn as the Era of Washington; contrasted the character of the American hero and statesman with that of Peter the Great of Russia, Frederick the Great of Prussia, or Napoleon the Great of France.

From Major Washington's visit to Venango down to the last stage of President Washington's life, the speaker followed that great man's career, dwelling with inimitable skill upon the great and good points of his character.

Better still than his comparison and contrast of the character of Washington with that of the great men of his own immediate day, was the episode in which he turned back to John, Duke of Marlborough, the wittiest statesman, the most astute diplomatist, the greatest captain of his day, yet a dishonest man, faithless to his sovereign, a traitor to his country, and a robber of the brave soldiers whose strong arms gave him victory. He pictured in glowing language the beauty and the grandeur of "Blenheim," the seat which national gratitude or kingly extravagance had given to the great bad man, naming it after that famous victory. After all, "Blenheim," with its storied urn and animated bust, its pompous eulogy and lying praise, could only serve to perpetuate the shame and infamy of John Churchill. But away on the banks of the calm Potomac, there rose an humble mansion, bought with no money wrested from the hands of an oppressed and reluctant people, a mansion in which the Father of his Country lived quietly and well with his beloved Martha, and from which he passed away peacefully to the bosom of his God. Around that humble mansion clustered hallowed recollections unstained by aught that could dim their purity. That home the women of America sought to secure, that they might guard it as a sacred trust, restore it to the pristine beauty and simplicity in which its great owner had left it, and transmit it as a sacred heritage to their children forever.

In the course of his oration, Mr. Everett alluded very feelingly to Washington's last and most emphatic advice to his countrymen, to preserve the Union of the States. He drew himself a most painful picture of the probable effect of disunion.

The audience was the fullest we have ever seen in Wilmington. We should think the receipts will not vary much from a thousand dollars. We believe all were pleased, many delighted, none dissatisfied, although some, perhaps, looked for a rather different style of speaking, more, perhaps, of what is generally regarded as oratory, more stirring, more declamatory. The address was highly polished, beautiful in conception, chaste, yet magnificent in execution, the work of a scholar, a rhetorician, faultlessly delivered, too faultlessly for an orator, perhaps, for oratory is never finished, it suggests more than it directly conveys, its apparent failures are sometimes its most effective points, its seeming, mayhaps its real forgetfulness, makes us, too, forget, carries us away, leads our feelings captive; we cease to mark gesture or tone, we feel but do not analyze our feelings. Mr. Everett may be, perhaps is, something more or higher than an orator, but he is also something different.

RECEPTION OF THE REMAINS OF JOHN C. CALHOUN.

In April, 1850, one of the most remarkable demonstrations in the history of Wilmington occurred on the occasion of the death of the illustrious John C. Calhoun. The following excerpts from the local newspapers of that date indicate the profound emotion which stirred the hearts of our people:

Another of the master spirits of the country has passed from time to eternity. John C. Calhoun died in the City of Washington on Sunday morning last. The sad intelligence of his death was to some extent anticipated from recent reports of his dangerous sickness, yet it will strike with heavy force upon the public mind.

The following telegraphic dispatch, dated Washington, March 31st, we copy from the *Charleston Mercury* of Monday: "Mr. Calhoun died this morning at a quarter past seven o'clock in the full possession of his faculties. A few hours previous he directed his son, Dr. John C. Calhoun, to lock up his manuscripts, and just before his death he beckoned him to his bedside and, with his eyes fixed upon him, expired. He died without the slightest symptom of pain, and to the last his eyes retained their brilliancy. With his son, there were at his bedside, Mr. Venable, of North Carolina, and Messrs. Orr and Wallace, of South Carolina. Mr. Venable has been devoted in his attentions to him for weeks, and is entitled to the deepest gratitude. The body will be placed in a metallic coffin and deposited in the Congressional Burial Ground until the wishes of his family are ascertained.

"The Governor of South Carolina has appointed a committee of twenty-five, consisting of citizens of Charleston, to proceed to Washington to receive and convey to his native State the remains of John C. Calhoun."

Wilmington Chronicle.

Wednesday, April 24, 1850.

REMAINS OF MR. CALHOUN.

It is expected that the remains of Mr. Calhoun will reach Wilmington today about 12 o'clock. The Committee of Arrangements publish the following:

Order of Procession.

For escorting the remains of the Hon. J. C. Calhoun.

The procession will be formed in the following order, the right resting on the railroad depot, in open order, for the reception of the corps of attendants on the arrival of the cars.

Order of Procession.

Clergy of the various denominations.
Sergeant at arms and assistants.
Pallbearers.
Coffin.
Pallbearers.
Relations of the deceased.
Committee of the U. S. Senate.
Committee of South Carolina.
Committee of Arrangements.
Citizens of South Carolina.
Judges of the Supreme and Superior Courts.
Members of the bar.
Members of the medical profession.

Magistrate of police and commissioners of the town, collector of customs and officers of the United States service, president and directors of the Wilmington and Raleigh R. R., members of the various societies of the town, in citizen dress, teachers of the schools and academies, captains of vessels and seamen, citizens and strangers.

The Committee of Arrangements recommend the following to their fellow-citizens: A committee of ten, consisting of A. J. DeRosset, sr., James Owen, James F. McRee, sr., Thomas H. Wright, P. K. Dickinson, John Walker, William C. Bettencourt, Thomas Loring, F. J. Hill, of Brunswick, and James Iredell, of Raleigh, will proceed up the line of the Wilmington and Raleigh R. R. to receive the remains, and escort them in their passage through the State. These gentlemen will also act as pallbearers in the procession.

The citizens generally are requested to close their stores, to suspend all operations of business, and to meet at the depot at 12 o'clock. There the procession will be formed, under the direction of William C. Howard as chief marshal, to receive the remains in open order and escort them to the foot of Market Street, where the boat for Charleston, the *Nina,* will be waiting to receive them.

A gun from the wharf of the Wilmington and Raleigh R. R. Co. will give the earliest notice of the arrival of the cars. Immediately upon the firing of this gun, the flags of the public buildings and the ships in port will be struck at half-mast; the bells of the town will commence tolling and minute guns will be fired.

The clergy and the pallbearers are requested to call at Messrs. Dawsons' store for gloves and crape. The citizens will find a supply of crape at the same place.

The steamer will leave for Charleston, it is expected, about five o'clock, p. m.

Wm. C. Howard, *C. M.*

J. G. Green.

Eli W. Hall, *Asst. M.*

Tuesday, April 23, 1850.

The steamer *Nina* arrived here yesterday from Charleston, for the purpose of conveying hence to that city the remains of Mr. Calhoun.

Courtesy: The mayor of Charleston has, on behalf of the city, tendered its hospitalities to the magistrate of police of Wilmington and the committee appointed to receive the remains of Mr. Calhoun on the passage through this place to South Carolina. Colonel Miller, the magistrate of police, has addressed a polite note to the mayor accepting the courteous proffer. The South Carolina State Committee of Arrangements has also invited the Wilmington committee to proceed to Charleston, join in the funeral solemnities, and become the guests of the city.

The committee of the Senate appointed to accompany the remains of Mr. Calhoun to South Carolina has invited three gentlemen of the House to accompany them, to wit: Mr. Holmes, Mr. Winthrop, and Mr. Venable, all of whom have accepted the invitation.

The following is copied from the *Wilmington Chronicle* of May 1, 1850:

On Wednesday last, near 2 o'clock p. m., the cars arrived from Weldon, bringing in the mortal remains of John C. Calhoun, in the special charge of Mr. Beale, the sergeant at arms of the United States Senate, and Senators Mason, of Virginia, Clarke, of Rhode Island, Dickinson, of New York, Davis, of Missouri, and Dodge, of Iowa, and Mr. Berrien, of Georgia. The other members of the Senate Committee joined them in Charleston, having gone on some days before. Mr. Venable, of North Carolina, Mr. Holmes, of South Carolina, members of the House of Representatives, accompanied the committee by invitation. Mr. Winthrop, of Massachusetts, who had likewise been invited to

15

form one of the company, was prevented from doing so. A committee of twenty-five from South Carolina and three of the sons of the deceased also accompanied the remains. The citizens of North Carolina to whom had been assigned the duty of attending on the remains whilst passing through Wilmington, proceeded up the railroad and joined the train some thirty or forty miles above, and in the procession from the depot to the steamer at the wharf acted as pallbearers. The arrangements as to the procession, etc., were carried into effect in accordance with the program published in our last issue.

The following we take from the *Journal:*
On the arrival of the cars, the stores and places of business were closed, the shipping in port struck their colors to half-mast, the bells of the various churches were tolled, and minute guns fired while the procession moved from the depot down Front Street to the steamer *Nina,* lying at Market Dock, where she was waiting to receive the remains of the lamented deceased, and convey them to the city of Charleston.

Notwithstanding the inclemency of the day, the procession was, we think, the largest we have ever seen in this place. Everybody seemed anxious to pay the last respect to the statesman and orator who has so long and so faithfully filled some of the most responsible posts of his country.

The steamer *Governor Dudley,* handsomely decorated for the occasion, accompanied the *Nina,* taking over a portion of the committees and guests to the city of Charleston. Both steamers left the wharf about half past three o'clock p. m.

Wilmington Committee.—The gentlemen whose names follow went to Charleston on Wednesday last with the remains of Mr. Calhoun, as a committee from the citizens of Wilmington, in manifestation of respect for the memory of the illustrious deceased: Dr. A. J. DeRosset, sr., J. T. Miller, Gen. James Owen, C. D. Ellis, Gen. L. H. Marsteller, P. M. Walker, Thomas Loring, A. J. DeRosset, jr., Dr. J. F. McRee, jr., Dr. John Swann, Dr. William A. Berry, James Fulton, James G. Green, Henry R. Savage, William C. Bettencourt, Edward Cantwell, John Cowan, John L. Holmes, Eli W. Hall, Joseph J. Lippitt, Henry Nutt, Robert H. Cowan, and A. A. Brown.

The *Charleston Courier* of Saturday says: "A committee appointed by the citizens of Wilmington came on in the steamer *Nina* and was met at the landing by the chairman of the Committee of Reception, who welcomed them to the city and extended to them its hospitalities, to which Dr. DeRosset, sr., their chairman, responded in an appropriate manner."

We should be greatly lacking in courtesy were we not to express in this public manner the high sense of gratefulness which rests with the Wilmington committee for the manifold attentions and kindnesses bestowed upon them in Charleston by the Committee of Reception and by many others. The profuse and elegant hospitality of which the members of our committee were the objects is very deeply appreciated by them individually and collectively.

DEATH OF GENERAL JAMES IVOR McKAY.

In Mr. Webster's letter from Wilmington, already quoted, he makes reference to a Mr. McKay as personifying political sentiment outside the town of Wilmington.

Gen. James Ivor McKay was born in Bladen County in 1793, and died suddenly at Goldsboro, N. C., the 15th of September, 1853, while on his way home from Tarboro. His name, "Ivor," was altogether appropriate, for he was eminently great. In the campaign of 1844 his report as chairman of the Committee of Ways and Means constituted the Democratic platform on which Polk was elected President; and in 1848 the Democrats of North Carolina presented him as their candidate for the Vice Presidency.

It was said of this distinguished son of the Cape Fear that he was very quiet and reserved in his deportment and held in contempt all manner of base dealing and trickery—a man of such integrity that his presence always inspired confidence and trustfulness in those whose expressions he desired, because they believed in his fidelity.

The Wilmington *Daily Journal* of September 16, 1853, the day after his death, said:

"It becomes our painful duty this morning to announce the unexpected death of one of our most worthy citizens, Gen. James I. McKay, of Bladen County. General McKay arrived here on last Monday night from his residence in Bladen *en route* for Tarboro, in Edgecombe County, as a witness in the case of the State against Armstrong. When we saw him on Tuesday morning he was apparently in better health than for some time previous, and conversed freely. We learn that on his return from Edgecombe yesterday afternoon he was taken suddenly ill on board the cars, and on arriving at Goldsboro it was found necessary for him to stop, where he expired, at Mrs. Borden's hotel, at a quarter before 8 o'clock yesterday evening, of bilious or cramp colic, in the sixty-fifth year of his age.

"As a public man, General McKay was well known to be a firm and consistent Democrat, having served his constituents for eighteen years, from 1831 to 1849, as member of Congress from this district, and during that time, at one period, occupying with marked ability the high and very responsible office of chairman of the Committee of Ways and Means, of which committee he was chairman at the time of the passage of the Tariff Bill of 1846. As a representative, no member of Congress commanded more attention or respect. He might truly be said to have served his constituents 'till he voluntarily retired' as a national representative, always looking to the best interests of the whole country, and discarding all factions and sectional jealousies."

At a meeting of the members of the Wilmington Bar held on Saturday, the 17th day of September, 1853, the following proceedings were had:

"On motion of H. L. Holmes, Esq., Robert Strange, jr., Thomas C. Miller, Mauger London, and David Reid, were appointed a committee to prepare resolutions expressive of the regret of the members of the bar, upon hearing of the death of Hon. James I. McKay, who died suddenly at Goldsboro, on Thursday evening last. Mr. Strange, from the committee, reported the following preamble and resolutions:

This meeting of the members of the Wilmington Bar has heard with deep regret of the sudden and melancholy death of Hon. James I. McKay, of Bladen County. General McKay for many years was a leading practitioner in the courts of this circuit, and since he retired from the bar, has been greatly distinguished in the councils of the nation. The force of his intellect won for him this high position, and strict adherence to his principles and great regard for the honor and safety of his country, combined with almost unparalleled integrity as a public man, secured to him a national reputation, of which North Carolina may justly be proud.

While the death of General McKay is a loss to the whole country, yet we with whom he has been more immediately associated, can not withhold this slight tribute of respect to his memory.

Therefore resolved, That by the death of Hon. James I. McKay, North Carolina has been deprived of one of her most distinguished citizens, and the whole nation of one whose faithful adherence to the Constitution of his country, and whose great ability and honesty of purpose, have won the admiration of men of all parties.

At Wilmington, as his remains were borne through the city, there was a great public demonstration. His body was met by the military, all the bells of the city tolled, and an escort accompanied the remains to their last resting place in the family burying ground on the home plantation in Bladen. The steamboat which conveyed the sad cortége from Wilmington to Elizabethtown was decked in the habiliments of woe, and its wailing monotone resounded continuously through the forests that lined the banks of the river.

GOVERNOR EDWARD B. DUDLEY.

Among the many great men who have adorned the life of our community and contributed to the prosperity of this section of the State, no one has surpassed in usefulness Edward B. Dudley.

On the occasion of his death, Robert H. Cowan was selected by the citizens of Wilmington to deliver an address commemorative of his life and character, and performed that public service on the eighth day of November, 1855. From Colonel Cowan's address we learn that Governor Dudley was born in Onslow County, December 15, 1789, and died in Wilmington on the 30th of October, 1855. When twenty-one years of age he represented Onslow in the House of Commons, and in 1813 and 1814 in the Senate. During the war with England he came to Wilmington, the second in command of the regiment of volunteers who flocked from the neighboring counties to repel threatened British invasion. In 1815 he removed to Wilmington, and in 1816 and 1817 he represented the town of Wilmington in the House of Commons. In politics he was a Republican, as distinguished from the Federalists. Governor Holmes, who was the representative of the district in Congress, having died in November, 1829, Mr. Dudley was elected to fill the vacancy. At that time he was a Jackson man; but not being satisfied with the policy of the administration, in Congress he attached himself to the opposition, and then declined reëlection saying, "I can not, fellow-citizens, forego my own opinion for that of any man. I acknowledge no master but the law and duty—no party but the interests of my country." He was,

more than any other man, the father of the Wilmington and
Weldon Railroad and was its first president. He was elected
governor, in 1836, the first governor chosen by the people—and
doubtless selected because of his advocacy of internal improvements. "He possessed administrative ability of a very rare
order; and his administration as governor was one of the most
efficient and practically useful which North Carolina has ever
known"—and moreover "his hospitality was dispensed so liberally, so graciously, and with such a warm and open heart, that
it will long be remembered by all who had occasion to visit the
capital while he occupied the Executive Mansion. * * * His
whole energies were given to the cause of internal improvements,
for the development of the resources of North Carolina, and for
the building up of her commercial greatness. * * * The
completion of a liberal system of internal improvements and the
establishment of a permanent system of common schools formed
the highest objects of his ambition. His career proves that he is
well entitled to the proud name of Father of Internal Improvements in North Carolina. He was far in advance of his age;
but he lived to see the State arouse from her lethargy and adopt
the measures he had forecast with sagacity and enlarged and
enlightened patriotism."

Addressing the stockholders of the Wilmington and Weldon
Railroad Company, Colonel Cowan said: "You must remember
that yours was the pioneer work in North Carolina, that it was
an experiment, that it was undertaken without sufficient means,
that it was condemned beforehand as a failure, that it encountered troubles, trials, difficulties of the most extraordinary character; that nothing but the most indomitable energy, the most
liberal enterprise, the most unceasing patience, the most determined spirit of perseverance, could have enabled it to surmount
these difficulties. Governor Dudley brought all of these qualifications to the task and commanded the success which he so
eminently deserved. He subscribed a considerable portion of his
large estate to its completion. He devoted all his time, all his
talents, and all his energies, and that too at an immense loss
from the neglect of his private interests, to put it into successful
operation. Nor did his services nor his personal sacrifices stop
there. When your offices, your warehouses and your workshops,
and all of your machinery which was not then in actual use
were laid in ruins by the terrible fire of 1843; when a heap of
smouldering embers marked the spot where all of your posses-

sions in Wilmington the day before had stood; when your most ardent friends had begun to despair; when your own merchants had refused to credit you, and, regarded merely from a business point of view, had justly refused, because they had already extended their confidence beyond the limits of prudence; when your long sinking credit was at last destroyed and your failure seemed inevitable—Governor Dudley came forward and pledged the whole of his private estate as your security, and thus, with renewed confidence in your solvency, you were enabled to go on to that complete success which awaited you entirely through his exertions."

Such was the character of the man—a man of generous sentiments, of high courtesy, of true courage. He set a noble example, was distinguished in all the practical elements of life, and was eminently good in all of his social relations. Thus his death was mourned as a general loss, and his memory is treasured by the people of Wilmington.

THE WILKINGS–FLANNER DUEL.

On the evening of the 30th of April, 1856, the old New Hanover County Courthouse, on Princess Street in Wilmington, was "packed and jammed" by an enthusiastic and excited meeting of the local Democratic association, of which Dr. John D. Bellamy was the president, J. D. Gardner, jr., and C. H. Robinson, the secretaries. Eli W. Hall, Esq., a prominent lawyer, was called to the chair and made an eloquent address upon political affairs out of which had arisen a strong party contest for commissioners of navigation. He showed how Know-Nothing victories had been won over an unsuspecting people, and party issues forced upon a community in whose local affairs they had been previously unknown.

Dr. W. C. Wilkings, a prominent young physician and politician, was loudly called for, and he responded in an animated and stirring address (so runs the *Journal*) in which he portrayed the absurdity, the nonsense, the arrogance of the assumption of exclusive Americanism, made, he said, by the anti-Democratic party. He was followed by Moody B. Smith, a strong speaker, who was listened to with close attention, interrupted by frequent applause.

At the conclusion of his speech, Mr. Ashe moved a vote of thanks to the speakers.

On Saturday, May 3, 1856, another grand rally of the Democrats was held in front of the Carolina Hotel, on Market and Second Streets, and the assembled crowd proceeded thence with torches at a late hour in the evening to "The Oaks," on Dry Pond.

The *Journal* says that insulting reference had been made by the Know-Nothings to the "Sand Hill Tackies." Hon. Warren Winslow was the principal speaker and received the thanks of the assembly for his eloquent address. He was followed by Mr. John L. Holmes, who spoke in earnest and stirring style. The fateful election of commissioners of navigation, which was to include one of the most painful tragedies in the history of Wilmington, occurred on the 5th of May, 1856.

The *Journal* says that by some strange mistake an active and staunch Democrat, in the heat and excitement of the voting, got hold of and put in a Know-Nothing vote, thus in fact electing Mr. Flanner, whereas, had the mistake not occurred, Mr. Costin would have been elected.

In the meantime, intense excitement throughout the town was caused by a rumor that Dr. Wilkings' speech, referred to, had incensed his friend, Mr. J. H. Flanner, who had published a card which resulted in a challenge to mortal combat from Dr. Wilkings. I was then nine years of age, at Jewett's school, and I remember distinctly the excitement of the schoolboys while Mr. Flanner dashed past the schoolhouse behind his two black thoroughbreds on the way to the fatal meeting.

The *Herald* of Monday, May 5, 1856, said: "Our community was painfully startled on Saturday afternoon last by the reception of a telegraphic dispatch from Marion, S. C., to the effect that a hostile meeting had taken place near Fair Bluff, between Dr. William C. Wilkings and Joseph H. Flanner, Esq., both young men and citizens of this place, and that on the third fire the former received the ball of his antagonist through the lungs, and in a very few moments expired. The difficulty grew out of a speech made by Dr. Wilkings on Wednesday evening last at the Democratic meeting at the courthouse. They fought with pistols, at ten paces, Dr. Wilkings being the challenger." The gloom over this dreadful affair hung for many years over those who participated in it, and the principal who survived the duel, and, going abroad as a State agent, survived the four years' war, died some years later, it is said unhappy and under a cloud in a foreign land.

The following cards are taken from the *Daily Journal,* May 5, 7, and 8, 1856, to show something of the temper of the public mind with reference to this sad and exciting affair.

DIED.

Died in Marion district, S. C., on the 3d instant, Dr. W. C. Wilkings, of Wilmington, N. C., aged about 30 years.

Lost to the community in the full promise of a glorious manhood, few men could be more deeply or more generally regretted than our deceased friend. Brave, ardent, and generous, gifted by nature, refined and strengthened by education, there lay before him the prospect of a long, useful, and honorable career. That career has been cut short, the promise of his ripe manhood left unfulfilled, and he has gone down to his grave before his time, but his memory will long survive in the hearts of his friends, and the turf that rests over his cold form be kept green by the unbidden tear starting even from eyes that knew him not in life.

Our intimate acquaintance with Dr. Wilkings was of comparatively recent date, and arose out of community of political feeling. But we soon learned to love and respect the man for himself, and we now mourn him as a personal friend. It is for those who have known him longer and better than we to do justice to his character. We could not omit this feeble and inadequate tribute to his memory.

Yesterday his remains were followed to their last resting place in Oakdale Cemetery by the largest and most deeply affected concourse of people that has ever been seen in Wilmington. Many an eye was wet, although long unused to tears, and as the solemn bell tolled all hearts throbbed mournfully and painfully. When he died, a MAN, a noble, true-hearted man, passed from amongst us.

TODAY.

Saddened by a great calamity in our midst, we have no heart today for political discussion. Overpowered by feelings beyond our ability to express, we know that mere words would be out of place. Standing in heart by the freshly opened grave of a valued friend, whose warm grasp yet thrills through our frame, can we be expected to raise a shout of contest or victory? Duty to our principles alone impels us, but, in sorrow or in joy, that feeling should predominate. We trust that it will prove so today, that, though saddened, the Democrats are not disheartened.

Now is not the time to speak of recent events. Now is not the time to harrow up hearts yet bleeding, and we forbear. That God who tempers the wind to the shorn lamb will be the comforter and sustainer of the bereaved ones in their deep affliction. Let us trust that His helping hand will not be withheld, that He will pour balm into the bleeding wounds, that He will bind up the broken hearts of those whose sorrow is more than they can bear.

WILMINGTON, N. C., May 6, 1856.

As there are reports in circulation calculated to do the undersigned much injustice, in reference to the late unfortunate difficulty between Mr. Flanner and Dr. Wilkings, we feel compelled to state that with the advice of our lamented friend, Dr. Wilkings, we expressed ourselves on different occasions as perfectly willing to agree to any honorable settlement; and under the influence of this feeling, when, after the second exchange of shots, Dr. James F. McRee, jr., who was acting in the capacity of surgeon to both parties (both being present), approached and expressed a warm desire that the matter should be settled, saying that "it had gone far enough, and ought to be settled, that both parties had acted fairly and honorably, and had shown to us, as well as to the world, that they would always be ready to resent any imputation on their honor," and then proposed, for the purpose of giving Dr. Wilkings an opportunity of making an explanation of his remarks made in the courthouse, that Mr. Flanner should withdraw his card published in the *Herald* of the 1st inst., to which we assented, expressing our willingness, if the card was withdrawn, to disclaim for Dr. Wilkings using the language imputed to him by Mr. Flanner. This proposition, coming as it did from a friend of both parties, we sincerely desired would be accepted by the opposite party. It was not, and the matter proceeded to its unfortunate termination.

W. M. WALKER.

F. N. WADDELL, JR.

These are the very words, we think. Dr. McRee doubtless recollects.

The above card, with a few slight alterations, was prepared for publication last evening, but was withheld at the suggestion of a friend, in order, if possible, to make a joint statement by both parties. With that purpose in view, I called upon Mr. O. P. Meares, and handed him the card for his perusal, suggesting at the time that if there was any modification he desired and we approved of it, we would sign it. He objected to the card on the ground that it did not contain a proposition for a settlement of the difficulty which he, Mr. Meares, had offered me; the acceptance of which, on consultation, was declined, because we felt it would sacrifice the honor of our friend. This proposition was not inserted in the original card, because we did not consider it pertinent to our exculpation from the charges now rife in the community. I then requested Mr. Meares to reduce his proposition to writing, which he did, but as we differ so materially in our respective recollections of its character, I thought it but right to publish his as well as my own recollection of it.

W. M. WALKER.

The last conversation held between Mr. Meares and Mr. Walker, before the third fire, was after the following manner and to this effect: Mr. Meares called Mr. Walker to him and said that he was willing to make a fair and honorable settlement, that he, Mr. Meares, would not make an unconditional retraction of Mr. Flanner's card, but he, Mr. Meares, would make in writing a withdrawal or retraction for a specific purpose, and that specific purpose (expressed in the same paper writing) should be to allow an explanation on the part of Dr. Wilkings, to which Mr. Walker replied that he would consult his friends, and then walked to where his friends were, and after conversing with them for a few moments, remarked that we would have to go to work again. Whereupon we immediately loaded the pistols and the third fire was had.

O. P. MEARES.

May 6, 1856, 12 o'clock.

N. B.—Mr. Meares, at the request of Mr. Walker, gives him the above as his statement of his proposition made to Mr. Walker immediately before the third fire.

MR. O. P. MEARES,

Dear Sir:—After having duly considered the above statement, and not being able to reconcile it to my recollection of our conversation, I consulted my friend, Mr. Waddell, to whom I had repeated it word for word in a few moments after its occurrence. I find his recollection accords with my own, and that is, that your proposition made to me on the above occasion, was to the following effect: Dr. Wilkings should request in writing a withdrawal of the card of Mr. Flanner and in the same writing should state what would be the character of his, Dr. Wilkings', explanation. In this event, you furthermore stated you would consent to withdraw Mr. Flanner's card for that specific purpose, viz.: for the purpose of receiving Dr. Wilkings' explanation. This proposition, as friends of Dr. Wilkings, having his honor in our keeping, we felt bound to reject.

W. M. WALKER.

May 6, 1856, 2 o'clock p. m.

To the Public.

I take this method of making a few statements in explanation of the course pursued by me in connection with the recent duel. I can say, with a clear conscience, that I was fully impressed with the responsibility which was attached to my position. I knew that upon one unguarded expression, or one imprudent act of mine, might depend the life of a fellow-being. I can also say that I was not actuated by any feeling of enmity towards the late Dr. Wilkings. We had been born and reared in the same community, and though not intimate friends, we had never had any personal difficulty in our lives. I can say, too, that Mr. Flanner made the declaration before he left town, as he did on the field after the second fire, that he did not desire to take the life of his opponent, and that he hoped a fair and honorable settlement would be made. For these reasons, I went upon the field with the full determination to accept any proposition for a settlement which I could regard as fair and honorable, and during the conversation which occurred after the second exchange of shots, I repeatedly said that I desired a fair and honorable settlement. By way of showing my willingness for such a settlement, I call attention to the fact, that, as the representative of the challenged party, my duty was simply to receive and consider such propositions as might be made by the challenging party, and such is the course usually pursued by persons when placed in the same position, and yet I went beyond my duty by making the proposition for a withdrawal for a specific purpose, as set forth in the card signed by me and published by Mr. Walker in the *Journal* of yesterday.

I deem it due to the public to state, that the first mention which was made of a settlement was immediately after the first fire, when Dr. James F. McRee, jr., who was acting as the surgeon for both parties, remarked that he hoped the difficulty could now be settled, as the parties had taken one fire. Whereupon, I turned to Mr. W. M. Walker, who was the representative of the other party, and asked him the question, in the presence of all the parties: "What have you to say, Mr. Walker?" To which he immediately replied as follows: "Well, sir, we still occupy our former position; you must retract and apologize for your card." I then said, "Is this all you have to say?" He answered, "Yes." And then I said, "We have no retraction or apology to make." We then loaded the pistols and the second fire was made.

The object of this card is not to give a full account of all the facts which occurred upon the field; it is merely to state what is sufficient, and no more, to explain the course which I pursued upon the field. In conclusion, I will say that the position taken by me with regard to a settlement was that I was willing to retract Mr. Flanner's card for a specific purpose, it being so expressed in writing, but that I would not make an unconditional retraction of his card.

I regret the necessity which compels me to publish even this much upon this subject.

O. P. MEARES.

May 8, 1856.

The allegation in Dr. Wilkings' speech that the ticket of the opposition was composed of merchants who would not hesitate to sacrifice the public interests (quarantine, etc.) for the sake of a dollar brought out the publication of Mr. Flanner's card on the following day, that the statement was false, and that Dr. Wilkings knew it was false when he made it. Wilkings promptly challenged Flanner, whose first shot struck Wilkings' hat; the third penetrated his right lung and killed him instantly.

Interesting Memories

OLD SCHOOL DAYS IN WILMINGTON.

Mr. Stephen Jewett, a most amiable and estimable gentleman, cabinet-maker by trade, settled in Smithville about the year 1839, where he was employed in the United States Government service and also as postmaster of that village. While residing there he married Miss Mary Gracie, a Scotch lady of great accomplishments, intimately related to the president of the Bank of Cape Fear, Dr. John Hill. Mr. and Mrs. Jewett subsequently opened a school at Smithville which they conducted jointly, she having been previously engaged in the profession of teaching in Wilmington. Mrs. Jewett died while on her way to Moore County with her husband.

Some years later Mr. Jewett was married to Miss Lucy Bradley, sister of the late Mr. Richard Bradley. He then made his home here, and became cashier of the Bank of Wilmington, in which capacity he served, honored and respected by the community, until his death during the yellow fever epidemic in 1862.

Mr. George W. Jewett, a professional school-teacher of superior attainments, came to Wilmington from Kent Hill, Maine, at the suggestion of his brother Stephen, about the year 1852, and opened the Wilmington Male and Female Seminary in a small frame house on the west side of Third Street, near Ann Street, and later in the old Society Hall in the rear of St. James's Church. He was assisted in the female department by his accomplished wife and two other Northern ladies, Miss Stetson and Miss Whipple. A large majority of Mr. Jewett's boys at that time were sons of the best people of our community, with a reasonable knowledge of the rules of propriety, notwithstanding which his school discipline was marked, under the influence of passion, by frequent acts of unnecessary severity, and, at times, by positive cruelty; which, instead of breaking down his institution, increased the patronage, our fathers in those days evidently regarding such physical treatment as both wholesome and necessary. There were a few very disorderly boys, however, who deserved a whipping as regularly as they got it. Who, among the survivors of the incorrigibles, can forget the stern command: "Walk into the recitation room, sir," over which apartment might have been written, "He who enters here leaves hope behind"; because the unhappy culprit to whom this command was addressed at once gave himself up for lost, reminding us of Marryat's boy, Walter Puddock, who, having been hauled up by his preceptor, O'Gallagher, without remonstrance immediately began to prepare for punishment by the reduction of wearing apparel.

Oft repeated flagellations, according to the testimony of the old-time Eton boys, render the subject callous, and some of these hopeless cases of Mr. Jewett's became so hardened by this process that they ceased to make an outcry, and, in the language of the prize ring, came up smiling after the first round, while the preceptor had evidently the worst of it.

Two habitual offenders, Henry McKoy and William Fergus, however, found it necessary to protect themselves from the neck downwards with padding, which sometimes shifted during the inevitable struggle, causing yells of entreaty which could be heard at a great distance.

Perhaps the most laughable scene in our four years' preparation for college was the startling appearance one morning of one of these boys changed from his attenuated habit of a lean and hungry Cassius to a wonderful state of exaggerated obesity, which Mr. Jewett promptly discovered and proceeded to unroll and reduce before punishment, with the anxious inquiry, "Where on earth did you get all this flannel?"

Many who were Mr. Jewett's pupils will recall the compulsory singing lessons and the noisy demonstrations when the exhilarating and senseless fugues of "Three Blind Mice" and "Scotland's Burning" were rendered in conclusion.

Two or three years later the school was removed to the premises on the east corner of Third and Ann Streets and continued until the commencement of the war, when Mr. Jewett went to Statesville, where he taught for a while. He returned to Wilmington about the close of the war and resumed teaching in the house occupied by the late Captain Divine, and subsequently on the corner of Second and Chestnut Streets, but left about the year 1881 for his former home in Maine, where he died of heart disease. The summons came suddenly, while he was sitting dressed in his chair. He simply straightened out his arms and ceased to breathe.

While teaching in the Wood house, on the corner of Second and Chestnut Streets, an incident occurred which has been treasured by the surviving pupils as one of the few occasions when the boys "got ahead of" their alert preceptor. Doc Nutt and John Cantwell were reckoned as the incorrigibles of the school, and they ceased not to torment the teacher with their irrepressible pranks; it was, therefore, not at all unusual when Mr. Jewett, at the closing hour, ordered them one fine afternoon to remain for punishment. The hours wore away until nightfall, and as the teacher came not, the truth dawned on the delinquents that he had forgotten them. They heard his tread upstairs returning from the lodge meeting, followed by a stillness which convinced them that he had retired for the night. Immediately Doc's fertile brain hatched out a plot; a whispered agreement was made in the semi-darkness of the room; the window on Second Street, which was only a few feet from the ground was raised; the two boys climbed gently to the street and lowered the sash to a chip on the sill, so that they could grip it on the outside. They then proceeded homeward, and after a hearty supper and a sound sleep, they reappeared at school at daylight and noiselessly assumed their places at their desks. When the old woman who made the fires and swept the room appeared later, she was fairly astounded to see them sleepily conning the tasks assigned to them. With a loud exclamation she brought Mr. Jewett down in his night clothes. He was profuse in his apologies—distressed with the thought of his forgetfulness—and tenderly solicitous for their welfare. They had suffered enough, he said, and were excused from attendance until the following day. The scamps played their part well, and wisely kept their own counsel.

Market Street between Third and Fourth Streets was a busy scene of healthful sport for the boys during the hour of recess; "old hundred," "three-handed cat," games of marbles "for fun" and "for winnance," spinning tops of all descriptions—the most approved and expensive being fashioned by William Kellogg— "jumping frog," walking on the hands with the heels in the air, and other diversions made Jack anything but a dull boy. John Rankin took first distinction in putting a top to sleep; Steve Jewett was most skillful at marbles; little Tom Wright excelled at the bat; Jim Metts jumped without running and turned a somersault in the air; he also walked on his hands a whole block, followed on foot by an admiring throng; and Richard Moore's wonderful skill sent a clamshell straight over St. James's Church tower.

Periodically, good Miss Urquhart, who lived in the house now Dr. Thomas' office, mildly expostulated when the clamor became unbearable; and "sounders," who drove their carts full of ground-peas to market, complained that the leakage in passing the school, caused by large stones placed in the cart ruts by the boys, was intolerable. These were minor incidents of constant recurrence; but when Mr. Jewett himself marked time with his big brass hand-bell, in the chorus of

> Scotland's burning! Scotland's burning!
> Look out! Look out!
> Fire! Fire! Fire! Fire!
> Pour on water! Pour on water!

and the town bell in the market house brought the Howard Relief with their hand engine and Captain Griffith with his Hook and Ladder Company, our joy was unconfined.

Jewett's boys generally turned out well; many became eminent in their professions. One of the most studious, dignified boys was Platt Dickinson Walker, forecasting his elevation to the Supreme Court.

Only two of the forty boys (which was the numerical limit) became a reproach to the school; neither was a fit associate, and both were finally expelled. One became a horse thief, and the other a murderer; both were outlawed. In my youth they were held up to me by my parents as horrid examples of total depravity, in striking contrast with the shining virtues of our neighbors, the Calder boys, whose footsteps I have always endeavored to follow.

A system of monitors was a part of Mr. Jewett's method of discipline. At first, in the old school, these very brilliant examples of his favor were privileged to fire the stove, sweep the room, bring in water, and to take a half holiday on Friday; but later this espionage became offensive and fell into desuetude.

Mr. Jewett always wore rubber shoes, which enabled him to steal with cat-like tread upon an unsuspecting culprit absorbed in the drawing of a caricature and administer a form of punishment upon the ear which we all despised.

The recitation-room floggings were generally severe, but to Mr. Jewett's credit it may be said that there was no leniency shown to his four nephews, who had all "a hard road to travel"; and Bradley Jewett, a bright and genial pupil, was often im-

16

posed upon in order to exhibit the discipline of the academy. On one occasion "Brad" created a sensation by exhibiting a brass pistol, with which he declared he would shoot his uncle; but it was found that the lock was broken, and this bloodthirsty design came to naught.

Eating during school hours was strictly forbidden, but several boys who were incapable of very severe intellectual exercise managed to smuggle apples, pies, cakes, and chunks of molasses candy into their desks, which they bartered for sundry information about the next lesson. Galloway said that Solomon's dog did not bark himself to death trying to keep them out of the Temple of Wisdom.

Archie Worth, beloved by all, was so pestered by his hungry associates while he ate his pie at recess, that he had to climb the gatepost to enjoy his repast in peace. From that day he was known as "'Tato Pie." Years afterwards, while he was limping along the roadside during the war, some strange troops passed him, and one of them exclaimed, "Well, if there ain't old 'Tato Pie from Wilmington!"

Wednesday was given up to lessons and exhibitions in declamation. Bob McRee, in "Robert Emmett's Defense," and Eugene Martin, in "The Sailor Boy's Dream," headed the list and melted us to tears. Clarence Martin, Junius Davis, Gilbert and Fred Kidder, Alexander and John London, Cecil Fleming, Duncan and Richard Moore, Platt D. Walker, John D. Barry, John VanBokkelen, Willie Gus Wright, Levin Lane, Griffith McRee, John Rankin, Tom Meares, Sam Peterson, Sonny West, Eddie and Tom DeRosset, Stephen and Willie Jewett, Willie Meares, Willie Lord, and others not now recalled, gave promise of undying fame, in their fervid renditions of "Sennacherib," "Marco Bozzaris," Patrick Henry's "Liberty or Death," "Mark Antony's Oration over Cæsar's dead Body," "Kosciusko," "The Burial of Sir John Moore," "Hamlet's Soliloquy," and "Hohenlinden" (alas! so few survive), and John Walker and big Tom Wright divided honors on the immortal "Casabianca." Henry Latimer and the writer were "tied" on the same subject, and as I was without doubt the worst declaimer in school, my competitor had an easy victory.

Our teacher endeavored to impress upon our minds, by repeated admonitions, the importance of graceful pose and bearing upon the platform. The declaimers were required to bow to the preceptor and to the audience before proceeding with their speeches. Some of these motions were very ungraceful, and others worse. Willie Martin's bow was like the forward movement of a muscovy duck; whereupon, Mr. Jewett admonished him and directed him to watch Mr. Edward Everett on the occasion of his forthcoming eulogy of Washington, which was the talk of the town. On the following Wednesday Willie was called to the stage to imitate the great speaker in his bow to his audience, which was done with an expression of intense pain in his stomach, to the great delight and derision of the whole school.

One of the most memorable exploits of our school days was that of Walter G. MacRae, who came with his brother Roderick to the old school near "The Castle." He had the most retentive memory I ever knew, and once when a column of the *Daily Journal,* edited by James Fulton, which usually contained (to us) the dryest sort of political twaddle, was read over to him, he repeated it "sight unseen," almost verbatim, to his admiring audience. Many years after, we belonged to a local debating society, and on one occasion MacRae was obliged to comply with his appointment as the principal speaker. Picking up a book from the table, he gave us the finest selection of the season. At its conclusion we took the volume from his hands and found it to be a child's spelling book. He had recited one of Rufus Choate's celebrated orations.

Some of the pupils, mere lads at the commencement of hostilities, fell in battle for the Lost Cause; others have dropped by the wayside in the journey of life, and only a few survive, of whom we recall the names and well-remembered faces of Eugene S. Martin, Leighton Boone, Thomas H. Wright, Gilbert P. Kidder, Richard Moore, Thomas D. Meares, John London, George G. Thomas, Jordan Thomas, Platt D. Walker, J. T. Rankin, N. B. Rankin, A. C. Worth, W. E. Worth, John F. Shackelford, John T. Northrop, James I. Metts, John B. Lord, Stephen Jewett, Henry G. Latimer, John M. Walker. The roll of living and dead is an honorable one and, notwithstanding unpleasant recollections by some who were harshly treated, reflects honor upon the memory of him who trained them. He was always proud of his boys; and well he might be, for it is a well-established fact that Mr. Jewett's pupils were thoroughly prepared for college in all the necessary branches of their matriculation; and that many who were unable, by the intervention of the war, to enter college, owed their comparative success in life largely to the early mental training under that able preceptor.

A characteristic incident occurred in St. John's Lodge of Masons a short time before Mr. Jewett's death. A member of the fellowcraft had just been raised to the sublime degree of Master Mason, after a highly creditable examination, during which he exemplified the work of three degrees with remarkable accuracy, when Mr. Jewett arose, and with apparent pride and emotion expressed his profound satisfaction, remarking that the younger brother had been his pupil for four years prior to the War between the States.

He was most cultivated and refined in his social intercourse, which was characterized by an urbanity entirely at variance with his professional habit.

His estimable wife died some years before him, leaving an only daughter, who was at the close of the war a beautiful and accomplished young lady. Miss Ella married Lieutenant Crosley, of the United States Revenue-Cutter Service, but she died long since, without issue.

For several decades before the war Fort Johnston was garrisoned, and the many officers of the army quartered there added greatly to the social life of the Lower Cape Fear. At that period Smithville, being so easily accessible by steamer, was the favorite summer resort of Wilmington families; and there the belles and epauletted beaux found congenial pastime, as described by Mr. Jewett in the following lines:

THE WAYFARER'S ADIEU.

Farewell, dear Smithville! from thy pleasant halls
I haste reluctant whither duty calls:
But for a moment let me linger here
To trace a grateful word and drop a tear.
For who e'er left thy hospitable shore
And blest and wept thee not forever more?
If rash ambition tempts me to aspire
To seize the poet's pen, without his fire,
And, all unskillful, venture to rehearse
Thy lofty virtues in heroic verse,
Appear, O Muse propitious, and supply
Such words and thoughts as fit the purpose high.
All hail, great Smithville! great in origin:
For did not Smith thy great career begin?
Great in thy old renown, when heroes bore
Their martial honors up and down thy shore,
And, strutting stiff, in yellow epaulettes,
Lured many a fair one to their gaudy nets.

Great in thy battlefield, our garrison,
Where Cupid's contests still are lost and won;
Great in the outspread beauty of thy bay,
Great in the tiny fleets that on it play,
Great in thy sunshine; in thy moonlight, great,
Great in thy risings and thy sittings, late,
Great in thy sandy streets and spreading shades,
Great in fandangoes, frolics, and charades,
Great in thy pig-fish, oysters, trout, and clams,
Great in thy raging tempests, great in calms,
Great in thy tête-à-têtes at dewy e'en,
And great, ah! very great, in crinoline.
What visions rise, what memories crowd around
My toiling pen at that suggestive sound!
But thickest cluster in the haunts of song,
Where crinolines, in scores, are wont to throng.
And thou! oh, sacred temple of The Nine,
Where wit and beauty spread their chains divine,
How shall I style thee? for thy noble name
Hath not been soiled by lips of common fame.
They call thee "cottage," but that name I scout,
And here forever blot the scandal out.
No name plebeian, couched in vulgar words,
Is thy true title: thou'rt a "House of Lords."
What though thou standest on Columbia's soil,
Her sons would scorn thy regal halls to spoil;
Here, noble lords and beauteous ladies meet,
And their fair queen with loyal homage greet:
Here, too, 'twas mine to fill an humble place,
And taste, full oft, the sweets of royal grace.
Methinks I see thee as I oft have seen,
Spangled with beauty, set in crinoline.
The fair Columbia stands with stately grace;
Benignant smiles illumine her queenly face.
Victoria's throne was bootless to confer
Imperial dignity on such as her.
And yet she stooped—what folly to record—
The royal lady stooped—to wed a Lord.
Then we turn to the court; and first observe
The lady yonder, with the restless nerve;
"A female archer": mark her pungent wit,
In random shots, regardless whom they hit.
But most she loves to shoot the pedagogues,
As wanton boys, for pastime, pelt the frogs.
In youth she wore the honored name of Brown;
"My name," sighed she, "is but a common noun."
A son of science, with no heart of stone,
O'erheard her plaint, and offered her his own.
So wit and genius she vouchsafed to link
Forever with the rare name of Frink.

On yonder face, so beautiful to view,
How blend the lily's with the rose's hue;
Her flashing eye, in jetty radiance burns,
And almost scorches him on whom it turns.
Forth fly thy arrowy missiles; maid, beware,
Lest you should pierce the heart you mean to spare.
You may not dream that flickering hopes and fears
Hang trembling on a glance of Addie Meares.
Upon that ample brow, where jeweled thought
Is fashioned and with graceful polish wrought,
O'erhangs an eye of rare intelligence,
Whose lightest glance reveals the solid sense.
Deepest and dark, with grave and pensive ray,
Save when the radiant smiles around it play,
Who does not see through the clear, pure light
That ever guides the steps of Anna (W)right?
My eager pen, impatient to advance,
Compels me hence to take a hastier glance,
And scatter gems along the glowing line,
More brilliant than adorn Golconda's mine.
Brown, Rankin, Cowan, Walker, Prioleau,
Shall in one brilliant constellation glow.
I gaze bedazzled, yet delight me still
My modest "Valley" and the favorite "Hill" (Miss Lossie).
But can we, Muse, the starry sphere portray,
By painting separate every golden ray?
Then let my pen this endless task resign,
And bid our stars in blended glory shine.
But hark! from rosy lips there pour along
The echoing walls the mingled streams of song.
Quick to the soul the conquering floods make way
And song and beauty hold divinest sway.
Apollo could but listen, gaze, admire,
And hate, henceforth, his goddess and his lyre.
Oh sacred, cherished spot! to yield thee up
Is gall and wormwood in my parting cup.
Farewell, farewell! May wintry winds
Strain gently on thy braces and thy pins,
May no rude storm unroof thee and expose
Thy naked ribs to their remorseless blows.
May time and whitewash still thy years prolong
To shelter beauty, genius, worth, and song.
Farewell, ye summer pleasures, bright and brief,
That fade and fall before the early leaf;
With summer suns thy leaves again return.
The life that bare you, there may fill an urn.
Farewell, ye warblers, matrons, maidens, all,
Whose forms are wont to grace our festive hall.
Farewell! May Heaven His sweetest peace diffuse
Through each pure breast as sink the gentle dews.

'Neath all His shielding ægis may you rest,
With life, health, love, and friendship blest.
And when from raging summer's heats
Impelled again to flee,
You grace once more the cool retreats,
May I be there to see.

COLONEL JAMES G. BURR.

Col. James G. Burr, one of our oldest and most highly esteemed citizens, died November 13, 1898, aged 80 years.

He was born in Wilmington and was prominent in all of its stirring events. For many years he was cashier of the Bank of Cape Fear. During the War between the States, he was colonel of the regiment of Home Guards. After the war he resumed his profession as a banker. Later, he was assistant postmaster of Wilmington under O. G. Parsley, Esq., during Cleveland's administration.

Colonel Burr, like his brother Talcott, had fine literary attainments, and possessed a discriminating mind, together with an admirable judgment of men. He was much interested in local history and was regarded as an authority with reference to important dates and deeds on the Cape Fear. He wrote with precision and elegance, and contributed many interesting narratives to the local press over his *nom de plume,* "Senex."

Associated all through life with our leading citizens, he knew them well, and his sketches, valuable for their accuracy, have served to rescue from oblivion the memory of many who, in their day, adorned our community.

Attracted by mutual interest in the tales and traditions of the Cape Fear, many years before his death we became devoted friends; and, in recognition of my high regard for him, he voluntarily made over to me all his manuscripts and publications, of which he had a large accumulation. A few weeks before his last illness, however, he came to my office and confided to me that he had destroyed all his manuscripts.

He explained that he had been prevailed upon to republish the distressing story of the desecration of the Holy Sacrament by a party of twelve local debauchees in the early days of the town, and that he had been reproached repeatedly that morning by some descendants of those involved in that horrible affair; that he had then returned home and made a bonfire in his backyard of all the manuscripts which he had promised to leave me.

The condensation of his sketch of the Thalian Association, and the article on Johnson Hooper and the British consul, however, may serve to keep his memory green.

THE THALIAN ASSOCIATION.

In 1871 Col. James G. Burr performed a grateful service to the community by publishing a pamphlet of fifty pages giving an account of the Thalian Association, together with sketches of many of its members, from which the following has been condensed:

When, during the French and Indian War, Col. James Innes was in command of all the colonial forces in Virginia, he made his will, in which he devised a large part of his estate, after the death of his wife, for the use of a free school for the benefit of the youth of North Carolina. A quarter of a century later the Legislature appointed trustees of "Innes Academy," and in 1788 subscriptions were taken up among the citizens, and the three lots next north of Princess between Third and Fourth Streets were secured, and subsequently, by way of confirming the title, were purchased from the University "as escheated property of Michael Higgins, one of the original settlers of the town of Wilmington."[1]

Before the completion of the academy building a theatrical corps had been organized in Wilmington, and an arrangement had been made between them and the trustees of the academy for the lower part of the building to be fitted up and used exclusively as a theatre; and a perpetual lease was made, conformably, to the Thalian Association. The building was erected about the year 1800, when the town could boast of hardly more than 1,500 inhabitants. Years afterwards, the academy fell into ruin and was not used for educational purposes. The Thalian Association, however, continued to hold possession. Its claim was resisted by the University, and by way of compromise the property was sold and purchased by the town, it being agreed that half the purchase money should be applied to the erection of a building with suitable rooms for theatrical performances.

---

[1]The investigations of W. B. McKoy, Esq., show that this property was escheated, not because it had belonged to Higgins, but to two Tories.

Of the members of the first Thalian Association, the name of Col. Archibald McNeill[1] alone has been preserved. He was the star performer, and in his delineation of the character of Hamlet very few professional actors could excel him.

After some years a second Thalian Association was organized, among the members being Edward B. Dudley, William B. Meares, Charles J. Wright, James S. Green, William M. Green, Julius H. Walker, William C. Lord, James Telfair, Charles L. Adams, Dr. James F. McRee, Col. John D. Jones, Robert Rankin, William H. Halsey, Thomas Loring, John Cowan, and others not now remembered.

Of Governor Dudley mention is elsewhere made. Mr. Meares was a lawyer of commanding influence, at one time coming within one vote of being elected to the Senate of the United States; but, unhappily, he died suddenly, while yet in the full maturity of his powers.

Charles J. Wright was an actor by intuition. He strode the boards with a majesty and grace that Cooper or Cook might have envied in their palmiest days. He was the eldest son of Judge J. G. Wright, and a lawyer, but became president of the Wilmington branch of the Bank of the State. His son, Lieut. William Henry Wright, graduated at the head of his class at West Point, Beauregard being next, and became eminent as an officer of the Engineer Corps.

Julius Walker was an actor of extraordinary merit. He had great fondness for the drama, and had few equals as an amateur performer.

James S. Green, the treasurer of the Wilmington and Weldon Railroad Company from its organization till his death, in 1862, was unequaled as a comedian. He was an admirable type of the Cape Fear gentleman of the olden time, with a fund of anecdote and wit, and as a story-teller unrivaled. Passionately fond of music, he sang the plaintive ballads of the old days with great feeling and expression.

Col. John D. Jones excelled in the character of Hamlet. Reared to the practice of the law, he early abandoned it for the more genial pursuits of literature and agriculture. He was speaker of the House of Commons, and presided with great

---

[1]At that time there were two McNeills, kinsmen, in Wilmington; Archibald, a grandson of Sir Charles Wright, the last royal governor of Georgia, and related to the Hasells and others; and Dr. Daniel McNeill, father of William Gibbs McNeill, the famous engineer, who was the grandfather of the celebrated James Abbott McNeill Whistler.

ability. Later, he was naval officer of the port and president of the Bank of Cape Fear.

Dr. James F. McRee[1] was one of the foremost men in his profession, in this or any other State; a most successful practitioner and a bold and brilliant operator. He had great scholarly attainments, was fond of the classics, wrote with ease and elegance, was equally at home in the researches of philosophy and the mazes of metaphysics, the natural sciences and the polite literature of the day.

William M. Green, later bishop of Mississippi, remarkable for intelligence, suavity of manner, and for a beauty somewhat feminine, and David M. Miller, father of the late lamented Col. James T. Miller, played with success the rôle of female characters.

William C. Lord sustained the rôle of the sentimental gentleman with great dignity and propriety. He was one of nature's noblemen.

John Cowan was admirable in genteel comedy. His fine figure, graceful manner, and correct gesticulations appeared to great advantage on the stage. He was the eldest son of Col. Thomas Cowan, one of the old settlers of the town, and was one of the handsomest men of the day. He became cashier of the Bank of the State.

William H. Halsey frequently appeared on the stage and was as natural as life. He was prominent in his profession, and left the reputation of a lawyer of great learning.

Charles L. Adams played well his part among the choice spirits of those days and added much to the success of their representations by his versatility of talent, knowledge of scenic effects, and unfailing good humor.

Thomas Loring was an excellent performer in the higher walks of tragedy. He had a face of marked expression, a voice deep-chested and sonorous, and in his rendition of the characters of Shylock and of the Duke of Gloucester there was an earnestness and a passion not easily forgotten. Mr. Loring was one of the best known editors in the State.

After an existence of some years this organization ceased, but not until it had been of much service to the community. Not only had it afforded entertainment, but it had been still more beneficial in the development of talent and in fostering an interest in the drama, as well as disseminating culture generally among the citizens. Nor was it long before the association was revived by another set of aspirants for the buskin who did not in point of talent disgrace their predecessors.

Among them were Joseph A. Hill, Dr. Thomas H. Wright, Robert H. Cowan, Dr. James H. Dickson, Dr. John Hill, Lawrence D. Dorsey, John Nutt Brown, and many others. They played with very great success.

Joseph A. Hill shone on the mimic stage, as he did upon the actual stage of life, with unfailing lustre. A son of William H. Hill and a grandson of John Ashe, he had no rival of his age as a debater and orator, and no superior of any age in North Carolina.

Dr. Thomas H. Wright played female characters with great success. He became president of the Bank of Cape Fear.

Robert H. Cowan was a very popular member of the association and bore a prominent part in all their representations. After preparing for the law, he abandoned it for agriculture.

Dr. James H. Dickson was a prominent member of the association, appeared frequently upon the stage, and was regarded as an excellent performer. Embracing the profession of medicine, he sprang at once into a large and lucrative practice. He possessed great power—was a student all his life, a lover of books and a thinker, a man of scholarly attainment and fond of scientific study. He fell at his post of duty, one of the earliest victims of the fearful epidemic of 1862.

Dr. John Hill frequently appeared upon the boards, always in genteel comedy and as the gentleman of the piece, which harmonized well with his graceful figure and easy manner. He was a remarkably handsome man. Endowed with versatile talents, he graced equally the stage and the drawing-room. While eminent as a physician, he achieved a particular fame for his literary accomplishments. He became president of the Bank of Cape Fear, and was known as Dr. John "Bank" Hill, to distinguish him from his kinsman, Dr. James H. Hill.

Eventually this association, like its predecessor, dissolved; but there came along a strolling company of actors who leased the theatre for two or three seasons, and after their departure, interest in theatricals having revived, a third organization was formed.

The members of the new association well sustained the reputation of the former players. For a long time they offered the only source of amusement to the public, and crowded houses always greeted their performances. On the list of members we find the names of William Cameron, John S. James, L. H. Marsteller, Bela H. Jacobs, P. W. Fanning, John MacRae, Augustus Ramousin, Joshua James, E. H. Wingate, J. F. Gianople, J. P. Brownlow, A. A. Brown, J. McColl, W. E. Blaney, E. Withington, Daniel Sherwood, C. Manning, William Lowry, W. N. Peden, Dr. W. J. Price, R. J. Dorsey, Daniel Dickson, Roger Moore, W. A. Allen.

William Cameron was a born actor, possessing great versatility of talents, and was passionately fond of theatrical amusements. Later in life he removed farther South.

Lewis H. Marsteller, a descendant of Col. Lewis D. Marsteller, distinguished in the Revolution and one of the pallbearers of General Washington, at an early age came to Wilmington from Virginia. He played the sentimental gentleman, and was easy and natural on the stage. He was at one time the most popular man in the county and was never defeated before the people. He was collector of customs and clerk of the court.

Price, Jacobs, Wingate, Brown, Moore, Withington, Ramousin, Gianople, Brownlow, and Dickson were all good actors and reflected credit on the association.

There were but few better amateur performers than John S. James. His conception and delineation of the powerfully drawn character of Pescara in *The Apostate,* equaled and in many instances surpassed the best efforts of celebrated performers. P. W. Fanning played the old man with such success that he is still remembered by the play-going people of those days as that "good old man"; while Sherwood, with his fine figure and charming voice, bore off the palm in genteel comedy.

This association after a time met the fate of its predecessors, and the theatre remained closed until about the year 1846, when the fourth and last association was organized. Its first president was Col. James T. Miller; Donald MacRae was secretary and treasurer; S. R. Ford, stage manager, and Dr. W. W. Harriss, prompter. On the roll of members were the names of Thomas Sanford, William Hill, Adam Empie, E. D. Hall, J. G. Burr, E. A. Cushing, John C. MacRae, John R. Reston, John J. Hedrick, Talcott Burr, jr., A. O. Bradley, John Walker, W. W. Harriss, J. T. Watts, J. G. Green, W. H. Lippitt, John L. Meares, Donald MacRae, John Cowan, J. J. Lippitt, George Harriss, Mauger London, W. A. Burr, R. H. Cowan, H. W. Burgwyn, H. P. Russell, Edward Cantwell, J. B. Russell, W. B. Meares, L. H. Pierce, W. D. Cowan, G. L. Dudley,

R. F. Langdon, E. A. Keith, F. N. Waddell, J. S. Williams, Robert Lindsay, Wilkes Morris, Eli W. Hall, W. M. Harriss, S. R. Ford, J. T. Miller, Alfred Martin, Stephen Jewett, A. H. VanBokkelen, T. C. McIlhenny, F. J. Lord, J. A. Baker, A. M. Waddell, C. W. Myers, F. P. Poisson, J. H. Flanner, DuBrutz Cutlar, Edward Savage, Robert Strange, William Reston, J. R. London, George Myers, Henry Savage, James A. Wright, O. S. Baldwin, L. H. DeRosset, J. Hill Wright.

"Of the merits of this company," says Colonel Burr, "it may not be proper for us to speak, as so many of its members are still living in our midst—suffice it to say that in ability and histrionic talent it was fully up to the standard of the preceding associations." After much labor and expense in repairing the building, many delays, disappointments, and discouragements, the opening night at length arrived. The play was *The Lady of Lyons,* the afterpiece *'Tis All a Farce,* with the following cast of characters:

THE LADY OF LYONS.

Claude Melnotte ....William Hill
Beauseant ....A. O. Bradley
Glavis ....Talcott Burr, jr.
Colonel Damas ....Robert Lindsay
Gaspar ....John Walker
Mons. Deschappelles ....E. A. Keith
Landlord ....George Harriss
First Officer ....Donald MacRae
Second Officer ....G. L. Dudley
Madame Deschappelles ....W. B. Meares
Pauline ....J. T. Watts
Widow Melnotte..J. J. Lippitt

'TIS ALL A FARCE.

Numpo ....E. D. Hall
Belgardo ....Adam Empie
Don Gortes ....Mauger London
Don Testy ....E. A. Cushing
Carolina ....J. J. Hedrick

The theatre was filled to its utmost capacity with a brilliant and excited audience, for to add to the interest of the occasion the names of the debutants of popular favor had been kept a profound secret. There was not one among them who had ever appeared in front of the footlights, and the excitement and apprehension, therefore, behind the scenes, incident to a first appearance, can only be appreciated by those who have undergone a similar ordeal. The performance was a great success, each actor was perfect in his part and remarkably correct in the delineation of the character assumed. The machinery of the stage, that most vital adjunct to the success of all theatrical exhibitions, was admirably managed, and the applause, long and continued at the close of the performance, testified in language too plain to be misunderstood the hearty approval of the delighted audience. Many representations followed with equal success, and the association soon became a permanent institution. Allied to the entire community, as nearly all its members were, by the ties of consanguinity or business relations, it was felt that their characters were sufficient guaranty that nothing would be presented that would shock the sensibility of the modest or wound the piety of the devout. The association modestly but confidently appealed to the public for generous support. Need we say how such an appeal was responded to by a Wilmington audience? Their well-known liberality was bestowed with no niggard hand, and the association flourished beyond measure and became immensely popular.

The great ability displayed by the members of this last association was fully recognized and appreciated by all classes of society, but as most of them are still living and are residents of our city, it would be rather indelicate to particularize, and we can therefore only refer to them in general terms of commendation; but, as memory brings up the vanished past and the virtues of the departed, we may surely pause, if but for a moment, to lay a few mosses upon the mounds of some of those who joined with us in sportive glee and shared alike our sorrows and our joys.

James T. Miller, the first president of the association, was very active and instrumental in perfecting the organization, but never appeared upon the stage. He took great interest in its success and was always very busy behind the scenes during every performance. Mr. Miller became quite prominent as a party leader, served in the House of Commons, was mayor of the town and also chairman of the Court of Pleas and Quarter Sessions, and from 1854 till his death was collector of customs. Poor Miller! We miss thy familiar form, thy pleasant greeting, thy hearty laugh, thy harmless idiosyncrasies; we miss thee from the favorite spots where friends did mostly congregate to while away the time in pleasant converse and innocent amusement, and thou, the centre of attraction, making all merry with thy playful humor. In the vigor of stalwart manhood, Miller was struck down by the fearful pestilence of 1862, and our city mourned the loss of a most useful, most popular, and most estimable citizen.

Eli W. Hall was an admirable light comedian, a capital representative of humorous characters and an actor of great promise and versatility of talent. He sometimes essayed the higher walks of tragedy, commanding the attention of the audience by the power of his representations. He became a lawyer and commanded an extensive practice. He was elected to the Senate in 1860, 1862, and again in 1864, and won fame in the legislative halls as a ready and able debater. He possessed a brilliant imagination and vivid fancy, with a wonderful command of language, and few men could address a popular assembly with more eloquence and effect. He was a courteous, honorable, well-read gentleman, of strict integrity, entirely devoid of ostentation or egotism, and justly popular in all classes of society.

Thomas Sanford was the oldest member of the association, and one of the best amateur performers that ever appeared in Wilmington. He was entirely at home upon the stage; his style was easy, graceful, and natural, and his voice, of remarkable power and compass, never failed him under any circumstances. He had had much experience in theatricals, for in early youth he was a member of a Thespian association in Philadelphia. Edwin Forrest, the eminent tragedian, was also a member of the same company, and at that time Sanford was regarded as the better actor of the two. He was the star of the association, always appeared in leading characters, and his appearance in any character and on any occasion was always a success.

Talcott Burr, jr., not only excelled in genteel comedy but was most excellent in the higher branches of dramatic art. Gifted with a strong and discriminating mind, which extensive reading had highly improved and cultivated, he at first devoted himself to the practice of law, but finding it unsuited to his taste, adopted the profession of public journalist, in which so many men have risen to eminence and usefulness.

John R. Reston—who does not remember and who did not love John Reston? One of the most amiable, kindhearted, generous beings that ever lived; guileless as a child, a creature of impulse and of the most unsuspecting generosity; a friend to every one and an enemy only to himself, he was never so happy as when engaged in some disinterested act of kindness or ministering to the pleasure of others.

Nature had been lavish in her gifts to him. No one could be in his company, for however short a time, without feeling the influence of his rich and unctious humor, his genial *bonhomie,* his entire unselfishness, and not admire, also, the exhibition of that virtue which so few of us possess, the desire to avoid, even in the slightest degree, anything that might give pain to others. He had a fine ear for music and sang with wonderful sweetness and expression; his voice was not cultivated, but his tone was singularly soft and perfect, like the mournful sighing of the breeze through the lofty pines of the forest. We were boys together, and I knew him well; "a fellow of infinite jest, of most excellent fancy, whose flashes of merriment were wont to set the table in a roar." Green be the turf above and lightly may it rest upon him, for the earth covers not a heart more generous nor one more entirely unselfish.

Dr. Alfred O. Bradley displayed histrionic talent of a very high order. He was inimitable as Sir Able Handy, most excellent as Max Harkaway, in *London Assurance,* and as Beauseant, in *The Lady of Lyons,* was decidedly the best representative of that character we have ever seen on any stage. In the beautiful play *Feudal Times* he appeared as Lord Angus, a fiery representative of the haughty Douglas, and played it with a vehemence and power that astonished all who witnessed the performance.

James A. Wright was one of the most youthful members of the association, and his career upon the stage, though very brief, was full of promise. Few men in our State—few men in any State of his age—had brighter prospects of a more brilliant future. Descended from one of the oldest and most influential families on the Cape Fear, he inherited in large degree the virtues for which they have always been so justly distinguished. Nature had been kind to him, and education had given polish and brilliancy to the jewels with which he was endowed and that adorned his character. But alas! for human hopes and human calculations. The dark cloud of the War between the States, whose mutterings had been heard for years, at length burst suddenly upon us, and the State called upon her sons to go forth and battle for the right. He was among the first to obey the call, and at the head of his company marched to Virginia to meet the hostile invaders, and at Mechanicsville, at the early age of twenty-six, he sealed his devotion to his country with his heart's blood.

We have not the space to speak, as we would like to do, of the merits of Cushing, Hill, Lippitt, Cowan, Pierce, Waddell, and Stephen Jewett. They played well their parts in the world's great drama, and "after life's fitful fever, they sleep well" in the vast and silent city of the dead.

This association continued to occupy and use the theatre building until the old building was sold, as already mentioned. The authorities of the town had determined upon the erection of a city hall on the site of the Old Academy, and purchased the property for that purpose. The association received one-half of the purchase money. Thalian Hall was the result. Mr. Donald MacRae was at that time president of the association, and to his energy, perseverance, and acknowledged business ability are we indebted for the beautiful theatre which reflects so much credit upon our city. The new building was leased by Mr. Marchant, a well-known theatrical manager, and opened to the public in October, 1859. The members of the association had now grown older and were more averse to appearing upon the stage, and the organization found itself hampered with a heavy debt. Under all these circumstances, a proposition was made to the authorities of the town that if they would assume the responsibilities of the association, all the right, title, and interest in that part of the building used for theatrical purposes would be surrendered. This was acceded to—the transfers made in proper form—and the Wilmington Thalian Association as a theatrical organization ceased to exist.

However, it is worthy of note that before its dissolution, the Wilmington Thalian Association contributed a stone, inscribed with its name, to be placed in the monument to George Washington in Washington City, and that stone, now imbedded in the monument to the Father of his Country, perpetuates its memory.

17

A FRAGMENTARY MEMORY OF JOHNSON HOOPER.

By James G. Burr.

The impressions made upon the mind in childhood and youth are always the most vivid and enduring, and though in the daily pursuits of life, in the arduous struggle for success and the jarring conflicts of adverse elements, those impressions may for a time be obscured or forgotten, yet they are never lost. As age creeps upon us and we live in recollection more than we do in hope, that longing for the past of our boyhood cleaves to us all. Our thoughts fly backward to the scenes and associations of our youth and fasten themselves upon them with a longing that nothing else can satisfy. The present and the future are alike unheeded, for our yearning hearts centre only upon the days that have faded into distance. At such moments, incidents the most trivial will excite emotions to which we have long been strangers—a withered leaf, a strip of faded ribbon that bound the ringlets of a lost and loved one, a line traced by a hand long moulded into dust, a little word in kindness spoken, a motion or a tear, will evoke recollections that genius can not trace or inspiration fathom.

This train of thought has been excited by finding in a package of old papers that had long lain hid, some lines written many, many years ago by one who has long since passed to his rest, Johnson Hooper, a Wilmington boy. He was the son of Archibald Maclaine Hooper, one of the most accomplished scholars of his day, who edited for a number of years the *Cape Fear Recorder*, the only newspaper published in Wilmington for a long period. He was a near relative of William Hooper, one of the signers of the Declaration of Independence. The family removed to Montgomery, Ala., where Johnson became connected with the *Montgomery Mail*, a newspaper of extensive circulation and great influence. He found time, however, from his arduous duties to indulge his humorous fancies, and while connected with that paper, gave the world several humorous works of great merit, viz.: *Taking the Census, Captain Simon Suggs*, and others which gave him rank among the best humorous writers of the day. He died in Richmond, Va., shortly after the transfer of the Confederate Government to that city.

Nearly, if not quite eighty years ago, an Englishman, Mr. Anthony Milan, was British consul at the port of Wilmington.

He was an educated gentleman, but possessed certain peculiarities to an unusual and disagreeable extent, was dogmatic and overbearing in disposition, and exhibited continuously a haughty, aristocratic bearing, which he took no pains to conceal. His "personal pulchritude" was immense, but he was always scrupulously neat in his attire, wearing fine broadcloth and ruffled shirts of spotless whiteness. A gold-framed eyeglass dangled from a ribbon around his neck and was conspicuously displayed upon his breast, while a number of massive gold seals hung pendant from his watch fob. He was altogether English, haughty and presumptuous, with a growl at everything and at almost everybody, and could not tolerate democracy in any form. He was an exaggerated type of class intolerance in the official life of the town, and his pompous air and personal decorations were the delightful derision of the small boy.

Upon one occasion, at the corner of Market and Front Streets, Mr. Milan was discussing with an important functionary a question of public affairs in the presence of the newly elected constable—the only policeman—who incautiously interjected the remark that in his opinion, etc. Mr. Milan stared at him with unmitigated contempt—"And pray, sir," said he, "what right have *you* to an opinion?" (*Tempora mutantur, et nos mutamur in illis.*)

About that time a ship had been built at the southern extremity of the town, and the day appointed for the launching had arrived. As the building of a ship in those days was quite an event in the history of the town, almost the entire population turned out to witness the launching, and an immense crowd gathered on the wharves and the surrounding hills. Of course, the British consul was there in full dress. The tide unfortunately was too low at the time for the ship to float when she left the ways; she grounded, and just then Mr. Milan, by some accident, fell overboard, but was quickly hooked up out of the river all dripping wet, with his bald head glistening in the sun like burnished gold. He was not at all injured by his involuntary ducking, but excessively chagrined. Of course, the boys were delighted, for he was exceedingly unpopular with them, and the next day Johnson Hooper, one of the youngsters, produced the following lines, which exhibit, even at that early age, his playful fancies:

ANTHONY MILAN'S LAUNCH.

Ye who pretend to disbelieve
In fixed degrees of fate,
Give, I beseech you, listening ear
To what I now relate.

It is about the launching of
A stately ship I tell,
And of a fearful accident
That then and there befell

To one well known to all in town,
A man of portly size,
Who carries watch seals in his fob
And glasses in his eyes.

He holds a high position from
His Majesty Britannic,
And claims to be a member
Of the breed aristocratic.

He looks with sovereign contempt
On those whose daily toil
Brings out in rich abundance
The products of the soil.

He does not care a pin for him
Who weareth not fine clothes,
And he uses linen cambric
With which to wipe his nose.

He has no need for comb or brush,
For his cheeks are rosy red,
And a microscopic lens can find
No hair upon his head.

His boots are always polished bright,
His beaver sleek as silk,
His ruffled shirt is clean and white
As a bowl of new-skimmed milk.

But to our fate—the morning sun
Shone bright upon that day,
When all our people through the streets
Most gaily took their way

Down to the docks, where on the stocks
The gallant ship was seen,
Decked out in brilliant colors
Of blue and red and green.

A monstrous crowd was gathered there,
In feverish excitement,
To see the ship glide off the ways
Into the watery element.

The British consul with his glass
  Stuck in his nether eye,
Was there in force, for could the ship
  Be launched, and he not by?

She starts, she's off, a shout went up
  In one tumultuous roar,
That rolled o'er Eagles' Island and
  Was heard on Brunswick shore.

Full royally the ship slid down
  Towards the foaming tide,
While cheer on cheer from every lip
  Went up on every side.

She passed along towards the stream,
  Majestically grand—
When suddenly she stopped. Alas!
  She grounded in the sand.

And there she would have always stuck
  And never more have stirred,
Had not the scene I now relate
  Most happily occurred.

Just at that moment when she stopped,
  With many a shake and shiver,
The pompous British consul slipped
  And tumbled in the river.

The Cape Fear rose three feet or more
  As Anthony went under,
The waves they beat upon the shore
  In peals of living thunder.

The ship was lifted from the sand,
  And like the lightning's gleam,
She glided out into the deep,
  And floated in the stream.

"All honor then to Anthony!"
  Was heard on every side.
And should we build another ship
  And scant should be the tide,

May he be there, and gently drop
  His carcass in the sea;
That ship will float, it matters not
  How low the tide may be.

JOSEPH JEFFERSON.

(From the Autobiography of Joseph Jefferson.)

After mentioning that he had engaged a comedian, Sir William Don, an English nobleman six feet six inches tall, Jefferson wrote:

"Sir William went with us to Wilmington, North Carolina, where we opened with the stock, he appearing at the beginning of the second week. The audience here did not like his acting; they seemed to prefer our domestic goods to the imported article. He saw this, but did not seem to mind it, and so bowed to the situation. He became very much attached to the company and remained with us some time, joining in our fishing and boating parties. His animal spirits were contagious; and as we had no rehearsals, the mornings at least were devoted to amusement. We would do the most boyish and ridiculous things. Three or four of us, himself the central figure, would go through extravagant imitations of the circus and acrobatic feats that were then in vogue. *The Bounding Brothers of the Pyrenees* was a particular favorite with him. We would pretend to execute the most dangerous feats of strength—lifting imaginary weights, climbing on one another's shoulders, and then falling down in grotesque and awkward attitudes, and suddenly straightening up and bowing with mock dignity to an imaginary audience. Once he did an act called *The Sprite of the Silver Shower,* pretending to be a little girl, and tripping into the circus ring with a mincing step. Then, with a shy look, he would put his finger in his mouth, and mounting a table would go through a daring bareback feat. Nothing that I ever saw was more extravagant. * * *

"The next fall, 1852, we resolved to make another trial of our fortunes in the Southern circuit. Our limited means compelled us to adopt the most economical mode of transportation for the company. It was settled, therefore, that we, the managers, should arrive at least a week in advance of the opening season; our passage must be by rail, while the company were to proceed by sea. There was in those days a line of schooners that plied between Wilmington, N. C., and New York. The articles of transportation from the South consisted mainly of yellow pine tar and resin, which cargo was denominated 'naval stores.' Feeling confident that we could procure passage for our company by contracting with one of these vessels to take them to Wilmington, we determined to conclude a bargain with the owners. The day was fixed for their departure, and Mr. Ellsler and I went down to the wharf at Peck Slip to see them off. It was an ill-shaped hulk, with two great, badly repaired sails flapping against her clumsy and foreboding masts. The deck and sides were besmeared with the sticky remnants of her last importation, so that when our leading actor, who had been seated on the taffrail, arose to greet his managers, he was unavoidably detained. There was handsome John Crocher, our juvenile actor, leaning with folded arms and a rueful face against an adhesive mast; Mrs. Ray, the first old woman, with an umbrella in one hand and a late dramatic paper in the other, sitting on a coil of rope, and unconsciously ruining her best black dress, etc., etc. It was a doleful picture. Our second comedian, who was the reverse of being droll on the stage, but who now and then ventured on a grim joke off it with better success, told me in confidence that they all had been lamenting their ill-tarred fate. As we watched the wretched old craft being towed away to sea, we concluded that we should never forgive ourselves if our comrades were never heard of again. On our arrival in Wilmington the days were spent in preparing the dusty old rat-trap of a theatre for the opening, and our nights in wondering if our party were safe. The uneasiness was not lessened, either, by the news that there had been bad weather off Hatteras. Within a week, however, they arrived, looking jaded and miserable. Another week for rest and rehearsal, and our labors began.

"Comedy and tragedy were dished up, and I may say, hashed up, alternately, as, for instance, Monday, Colman's comedy of *The Poor Gentleman,* fancy dances by the soubrette, comic songs by the second comedian, concluding with the farce of *The Spectre Bridegroom.* The next evening we gave *Romeo and Juliet.* I felt that the balcony scene should have some attention, and I conceived a simple and economical idea that would enable me to produce the effect in a manner 'hitherto unparalleled in the annals of the stage.' Skirmishing about the wharves and the ship-chandlers, I chanced to light upon a job lot of empty candle boxes. By taking a quantity the cardboards were thrown in, and nothing makes a finer or more imposing but unsubstantial balustrade than cardboard. The boxes, placed one by one on top of each other and painted a neat stone color, form a pleasing architectural pile. The scene opened with a backing of something supposed to represent the distant city of Verona, with my new balcony in the foreground. All seemed to be going well till presently there came the sound of half-suppressed laughter from the audience. The laughter increased, till at last the whole house had discovered the mishap. Juliet retreated in amazement and Romeo rushed off in despair, and down came the curtain. I rushed upon the stage to find out what had occurred, when to my horror I discovered that one of the boxes had been placed with the unpainted side out, on which was emblazoned a semicircular trade-mark, setting forth that the very cornerstone of Juliet's balcony contained twenty pounds of the best 'short sixes.' "

IMMORTALITY.

By Joseph Jefferson.

(Written by Mr. Jefferson for his friend Mr. H. M. Flagler, and given by Mr. Flagler to his friend Mr. James Sprunt.)

Two caterpillars crawling on a leaf
By some strange accident in contact came;
Their conversation, passing all belief,
Was the same argument, the very same,
That has been "proed and conned" from man to man,
Yea, ever since this wondrous world began.

    The ugly creatures
      Sluggish, dull, and blind,
    Devoid of features
      That adorn mankind,

Were vain enough, in dull and wordy strife,
To speculate upon a future life.
The first was optimistic, full of hope;
The second, quite dyspeptic, seemed to mope.
Said number one, "I'm sure of our salvation."
Said number two, "I'm sure of our damnation;
Our ugly forms alone would seal our fate
And bar our entrance through the golden gate.
Suppose that death should take us unawares,
How could we climb the golden stairs?
If maidens shun us as they pass us by,
Would angels bid us welcome in the sky?
I wonder what great crimes we have committed
That leave us so forlorn and so unpitied;
Perhaps we've been ungrateful, unforgiving:
'Tis plain to me that life's not worth the living."
"Come, come, cheer up," the jovial worm replied,
"Let's take a look upon the other side;

Suppose we can not fly like moths or millers,
Are we to blame for being caterpillars?
Will that same God that doomed us crawl the earth,
A prey to every bird that's given birth,
Forgive our captor as he eats and sings,
And damn poor us because we have not wings?
If we can't skim the air like owl or bat,
A worm will turn 'for a' that.' "
They argued through the summer; autumn nigh,
The ugly things composed themselves to die;
And so to make their funeral quite complete,
Each wrapped him in his little winding-sheet.
The tangled web encompassed them full soon;
Each for his coffin made him a cocoon.
All through the winter's chilling blast they lay,
Dead to the world, aye, dead as human clay.
Lo, Spring comes forth with all her warmth and love;
She brings sweet justice from the realms above;
She breaks the chrysalis, she resurrects the dead;
Two butterflies ascend, encircling her head.
And so this emblem shall forever be
Unfailing sign of immortality.

THE JENNY LIND INCIDENT.

By Walker Meares.

In 1850, when the great showman, P. T. Barnum, announced
that he had arranged with Jenny Lind for an American tour,
the country went wild with excitement, and when she arrived
in New York on a Sunday afternoon in September of that year,
the metropolis turned out *en masse* to greet her, while the Stars
and Stripes and the Swedish ensign floated above the scene in
commingled glory. The *New York Herald* of the following day
devoted six columns to the event—a mere prelude to the volumes
to be written later, as the triumphal passage of the great singer
swept southward to Cuba. Had the racy *Punch* not said: "To
call Jenny Lind the Swedish Nightingale is a compliment to the
bird, which will put an additional feather in his cap—or rather
in his tail—for the remainder of his existence"? And had not
the whole world heard of the sweetness of the spirit that found
expression in that marvelous voice? Jenny Lind's coming was
more than a visit—it was a most blessed visitation.

If any evidence of appreciation was lacking the box-office
failed to record it. Not only in numbers but in prices was the
highest satisfaction realized. At the auction of seats at Castle

Garden, it will be remembered, the hatter Genin made himself famous, and later, rich, by paying $225 for the choice of seats, described as "a very handsome spring cushion, crimson velvet chair, placed right against the front of the centre post, and just opposite to Jenny Lind," in order that he might ever after be thus visualized to the purchaser of hats. And the singer Ossian F. Dodge outdistanced Genin by paying $625 for a similar choice in Boston. But so far was Jenny Lind from mercenary intent, that during the first eight weeks of her American tour she gave more than $18,000 to charities—a magnificent scale of benevolence kept up during her two years' tour in this country.

December found her in Richmond, and her next engagement was in Charleston, S. C., for the 26th and 29th of that month. Wilmington was in feverish excitement, especially as the diva must pass through this town. Should her neighbors, Richmond and Charleston, so far o'ertop her? Not without supreme effort on her part. Accordingly, at a meeting of prominent ladies and gentlemen, a committee was appointed, and when the train from Richmond arrived at Wilmington this committee appeared at the depot with smiling countenances and a cart-load of flowers. The elegant and genial spokesman, Mr. James S. Green, presented a bouquet in a gracious speech of welcome, and the charming Jenny smiled her appreciation. The journey from the Virginia city to Wilmington is described as the most uncomfortable she had made thus far in America, the Wilmington and Weldon Railroad having the reputation of being the worst in the United States. A traveling companion of the famous singer, however, described it as being newly laid, and, save for a short distance over which the old timbers of the road were plainly felt, remarkably easy. The car the party occupied as far as Weldon he described as new, approximating somewhat the style in vogue on other roads, but from Weldon to Wilmington they are said to have been stowed away in a sort of caravanserai, described at one time as "a huge and comfortless box with shelves for bedsteads, something like the cabin of a Dutch sloop," and at another as "a gigantic clothes press." With these and other discomforts graphically named by her biographer freshly in mind, it is likely that Jenny Lind valued all the more the compensation of a gracious reception at the end of her journey and that she listened with gratifying interest to the momentous question of the committee. Would she sing for Wilmington? She would gladly if Mr. Barnum could arrange it, and Mr. Barnum pleasingly acquiesced. "But, gentlemen," said he, "what is the capacity of your opera house?" "About one hundred and fifty seats, but by utilizing the aisles two hundred can be provided," they told him, to which the showman laughingly replied, "Gentlemen, my orchestra would fill a large part of that space!" They withdrew to consider possible adjustments and shortly returned with complaisancy, saying it was all arranged, they would erect a platform in the centre of the street immediately in front of the theatre, so that everybody might hear! The idea was diverting and the fair Swede laughed uncontrollably at being asked to sing to an open-air audience in the public streets, but her warm heart quickened its beats at the thought of the simplicity that conceived the plan. Her contract with Mr. Barnum stipulated that she be allowed to hold concerts for charity when she saw fit. If they had only told her that Wilmington had its orphans, its poor, and its sick, no doubt the open-air performance would have received serious consideration.

They did not hear her sing, but they heard that marvelous voice in speech and they saw her. And she—she saw them, a people whose hospitality, simplicity, and inherent kindliness have never been surpassed. She declined an invitation by Queen Victoria to sing at a festival at court to come to America, largely, as she said, to see the American people, and we fancy that in the *potpourri* of precious impressions she carried away went a bit of fragrance from Wilmington. Perhaps, too, she regretted not accepting the open-air suggestion and waiting over a day, for on the night she sailed south on the steamer *Gladiator* from the Cape Fear city, there occurred one of the worst storms ever known along these shores. Three ships were lost on the Carolina coast about that time, and it was rumored that the *Gladiator* had grounded on Cape Romain. She was thirty-four hours making the trip to Charleston, which then took but seventeen under ordinary weather conditions. She was reported lost, and the news was telegraphed to New York, but corrected a dozen hours later; for, notwithstanding wind and weather, the exceptional seamanship of Capt. J. B. Smith took her at last into port at Charleston. Her tiller ropes were broken and she was sweeping in on shore. Another half hour, it is said, would probably have effected her complete destruction with all on board, but Captain Smith steered her safely in and deposited Jenny Lind and two hundred other passengers on shore, where they were in a position to feel that seasickness is, after all, a little better than drowning.

The War Between the States

ON THE EVE OF SECESSION.

In a memorial of Mr. George Davis, the beloved leader of the Lower Cape Fear, the writer, whose affectionate admiration has continued with increasing veneration, said for his committee, on the occasion of a large assembly of representative citizens to honor Mr. Davis' memory by suitable resolutions of respect:

"In 1861 the shadow of a great national calamity appeared—the whole country was convulsed with conflicting emotions. The political leaders of North Carolina were divided upon the issue. Mr. Davis loved the Union, and steadfastly counseled moderation. His appointment by the Legislature as a member of the Peace Commission, to which further reference is made, created a feeling of absolute confidence in the minds of the conservative citizens.

"The desire of the people of North Carolina was to see peace maintained, whether the Union was preserved or not, and for this purpose the Legislature on January 26, 1861, appointed commissioners to conventions to be held at Montgomery, Alabama, and Washington City. These commissioners were Hon. Thomas Ruffin, Hon. D. M. Barringer, Hon. David S. Reid, Hon. John M. Morehead, Hon. D. L. Swain, J. R. Bridgers, M. W. Ransom, and George Davis. Mr. Davis went to Washington City as a member of the Peace Congress, which assembled on February 4, 1861. The moral weight of the position and the character of the gentlemen then and there assembled gave to the significance of the occasion portentous aspects. The Congress sat with closed doors; ex-President Tyler was elected president, and on taking the chair made one of the most eloquent and patriotic speeches ever heard. This conference was in session until February 27, 1861, when Mr. Davis telegraphed: 'The convention has just adjourned *sine die,* after passing seven articles of the report of the committee, much weakened. The territorial articles passed by a majority of one vote. North Carolina and Virginia voted against every article but one.'

"It is difficult for those of us who remember only the intense unanimity of the Southern people after the war was fairly inaugurated to realize how in those previous troublous days the minds of men were perplexed by doubts. Up to this time the Union sentiment in North Carolina had been in the ascendant. The people waited upon the result of the Peace Congress, and in this section especially was the decision of many reserved until Mr. Davis should declare his final convictions. His announcement of them marked an epoch in his life, and in the lives of countless others, for weal or woe."

Immediately upon his return home, the following correspondence took place:

WILMINGTON, 2d March, 1861.

DEAR SIR:—Your friends and fellow-citizens are exceedingly anxious to hear from you with reference to the proceedings of the Peace Congress, and to have your opinion as to their probable effect in settling the distracting questions of the day.

Will you be kind enough to give them a public address at such time as may suit your convenience?

Respectfully yours,

JAMES H. DICKSON.
ROBERT H. COWAN.
D. A. LAMONT.
THOMAS MILLER.
DONALD MACRAE.
ROBERT G. RANKIN.
JAMES H. CHADBOURN.
A. H. VANBOKKELEN.

To GEORGE DAVIS, Esq. O. G. PARSLEY.

WILMINGTON, 2d March, 1861.

GENTLEMEN:—Being under the necessity of leaving home tomorrow, I will comply with the request of my fellow-citizens, as intimated in your note, by addressing them at such hour and place this evening as you may appoint. Respectfully yours,

GEO. DAVIS.

To DR. JAMES H. DICKSON, and others.

The newspaper reports of the public meeting and of Mr. Davis' powerful speech which followed do not convey to our minds the overwhelming sensations of those who listened to this masterpiece of oratory. Mr. Davis was obliged to close before he had finished his address. The people were profoundly moved, and the hearts of all were deeply stirred. Many left the hall while he was speaking, for they could not restrain their emotion.

The *Daily Journal* of March 4, 1861, said: "In accordance with the general desire, George Davis, Esq., addressed his fellow-citizens on last Saturday, March 2, at the Thalian Hall in reference to the proceedings of the late Peace Congress, of which he was a member, giving his opinion as to the probable effect of such proceedings in settling the distracting questions of the day. Although the notice was very brief, having only appeared at midday in the town papers, the hall was densely crowded by an eager and attentive audience, among whom were many ladies."

The report of the speech is full, and deals with all the vital questions which were discussed at the Peace Congress. Mr. Davis said that he shrunk from no criticism upon his course, but, indeed, invited and sought for it the most rigid examination. He had endeavored to discharge the duties of the trust imposed in him faithfully, manfully, and conscientiously, and whatever might be thought of his policy, he felt that he had a right to demand the highest respect for the motives which actuated him in pursuing that policy.

Referring to his own previous position, what he believed to be the position of the State, the course of the Legislature in appointing commissioners, and the objections to the action of the Peace Congress, Mr. Davis said he had gone to the Peace Congress to exhaust every honorable means to obtain a fair, an honorable, and a final settlement of existing difficulties. He had done so to the best of his ability, and had been unsuccessful, for he could never accept the plan adopted by the Peace Congress as consistent with the rights, the interests, or the dignity of North Carolina.

Mr. Davis concluded by emphatically declaring that the South could never—never obtain any better or more satisfactory terms while she remained in the Union, and for his part he could never assent to the terms contained in this report of the Peace Congress as in accordance with the honor or the interests of the South.

When Mr. Davis had concluded Hon. S. J. Person moved that the thanks of the meeting be tendered to him for the able, manly, and patriotic manner in which he had discharged the duties of his position as a commissioner from North Carolina. The motion was enthusiastically carried.

On June 18, 1861, Mr. Davis and Mr. W. W. Avery were elected by the State Convention delegates for the State at large to the Confederate Congress, and they took their seats in the Senate. In alluding to his election the *Journal,* the organ of the Democratic party in this section, said:

"Mr. Davis, in old party times, was an ardent and consistent member of the opposition, and was opposed to a severance from the North until he felt satisfied by the result of the Peace Conference that all peaceful means had been exhausted." At the following session of the Legislature he and W. T. Dortch were elected Confederate States Senators, and later he became a member of the Cabinet.

Through the courtesy of Mrs. Parsley, whose husband, Col. William M. Parsley, of Wilmington, gave his brilliant young life to the cause of the Confederacy, I include as worthy of all honor the following narrative, to which her well-known devotion as one of the leaders of the Ladies' Memorial Society and as president of the Daughters of the Confederacy gives added authority and interest:

"In 1861, when, amid great popular excitement and enthusiasm, South Carolina seceded from the Union of States, the people of Wilmington were deeply stirred by conflicting emotions. Meetings were held at various local points, and speakers for and against secession swayed the multitudes which attended them. At a town meeting, an address by Dr. James H. Dickson, urging moderation and advising against hasty action as to secession, was regarded with close attention and respect, for Dr. Dickson was a man universally trusted and beloved, and one of the foremost to act in any movement for the welfare of Wilmington.

"His speech was followed by one from Mr. O. P. Meares, afterwards a colonel in the Confederate Army, and later a judge. He was an ardent secessionist and a fiery speaker, and the younger element was carried away by his eloquence, but the older citizens, devoted to the Union, were loath to break the bonds, and the community seemed equally divided until Mr. George Davis returned from the Peace Conference in Washington City, with his full account of the utter failure to arrive at an agreement, and gave as his judgment that the Union could only be preserved with dishonor to the South. The immense crowd gathered in the opera house received his words in profound silence, as though the speaker's judgment settled that of each one who heard him.

The Response to Lincoln's Call for Troops.

"Later, when Lincoln's call was made for 75,000 men 'to put down the rebellion,' the whole of the Cape Fear section was fired, and with scarcely an exception looked upon secession and war as the inevitable outcome.

"The young men wore secession rosettes and badges made of small pine burs. The military companies already organized greatly increased their ranks, and drilled vigorously. Other companies were organized and men of Northern birth who did not join some military organization were regarded with suspicion. Many of this class slipped away to the north of Mason and Dixon's line during the next few months.

"Men too old for service in the field formed a cavalry company under Capt. William C. Howard, for home defense, and one company of quite elderly gentlemen was known popularly as the 'Horse-and-Buggy Company,' and though they did not drill, they held themselves in readiness to do what they could when called upon. They did assist in the equipment of companies sent to the field, and many of them aided and supported, during the whole of the war, families of men in the service.

"School boys drilled constantly in the streets with wooden guns and tin swords, and those owning a real gun or a good imitation were sure of being officers, no matter about their other qualifications, though to do them justice they did strive like men.

"When a rumor came that the *Harriet Lane,* a small Revenue Cutter, had been sent to reinforce Fort Caswell, which was under command of Sergeant Reilly, the excitement was overwhelming. The *Harriet Lane* did not come, but when Fort Sumter was bombarded on the 12th and 13th of April, several companies of volunteers were ordered to the fort. Sergeant Reilly, the lonely custodian of the fort, calling all present to witness that he was compelled by superior force, surrendered it in due form and with military honors. He afterwards served with signal courage and devotion in the Confederate service with the rank of major of artillery."

WILMINGTON COMPANIES.

As soon as the Eighth Regiment of Volunteers was organized, it was ordered to encamp at Confederate Point, near New Inlet, the name having been changed from Federal Point. A few months later they were ordered to Coosawhatchie, South Carolina, and moved to several other points to meet expected attacks, and later they were ordered to Virginia. After the ten regiments of State Troops were organized, the Eighth Regiment of Volunteers became the Eighteenth North Carolina State Troops.

Company G of this regiment was organized in Wilmington in

1853 as the Wilmington Light Infantry. They went into the war nearly two hundred strong, under Capt. William L. DeRosset, who was soon promoted. His successor was Capt. Henry Savage. Their records show that fifty-seven commissioned officers of the Confederate States were former members of this company. The regiment reached the seat of war in Virginia just in time for the Battle of Mechanicsville, late in June, 1862.

From first to last there were sent from the immediate vicinity of Wilmington twenty companies of infantry, two of cavalry, and six battalions of artillery, numbering in all nearly 4,000 men, divided as follows:

				No. of men.
Co. C,	1st	Infantry,	Captain J. S. Hines..................	196
Co. E,	1st	Infantry,	Captain James A. Wright............	147
Co. D,	3d	Infantry,	Captain Edward Savage..............	164
Co. F,	3d	Infantry,	Captain William M. Parsley..........	159
Co. K,	3d	Infantry,	Captain David Williams..............	174
Co. C,	7th	Infantry,	Captain Robert B. McRae............	159
Co. A,	18th	Infantry,	Captain Christian Cornehlson.........	211
Co. E,	18th	Infantry,	Captain John R. Hawes..............	169
Co. G,	18th	Infantry,	Captain Henry R. Savage............	194
Co. I,	18th	Infantry,	Captain O. P. Meares...............	186
Co. D,	36th	Infantry,	Captain Edward B. Dudley...........	131
Co. G,	61st	Infantry,	Captain J. F. Moore................	106
Co. A,	51st	Infantry,	Captain John L. Cantwell...........	132
Co. C,	51st	Infantry,	Captain James Robinson.............	87
Co. E,	51st	Infantry,	Captain Willis H. Pope.............	89
Co. G,	51st	Infantry,	Captain James W. Lippitt...........	93
Co. H,	51st	Infantry,	Captain S. W. Maultsby.............	75
Co. K,	66th	Infantry,	Captain William C. Freeman.........	140
Co. A,	41st	Regt. Cavalry,	Captain A. T. Newkirk........	94
Co. C,	59th	Regt. Cavalry,	Captain R. M. McIntire.......	89
Co. A,	1st	Batt. Artillery,	Captain Robert G. Rankin.....	147
Co. B,	1st	Batt. Artillery,	Captain Charles D. Ellis.......	208
Co. C,	1st	Batt. Artillery,	Captain Alexander MacRae.....	177
Co. D,	1st	Batt. Artillery,	Captain James L. McCormack..	127
Co. C,	5th	Batt. Artillery,	Captain James D. Cumming....	142
Co. D,	5th	Batt. Artillery,	Captain Z. T. Adams..........	205
Co. D,	72d	Junior Reserves,	Captain J. D. Kerr............	91
Co. H,	73d	Junior Reserves,	First Lieutenant D. J. Byrd.....	91
Enlisted for the Navy....................................				250

The officers and many of the men of the Third Regiment of Infantry were from New Hanover County, and that regiment (like the 18th) has always seemed to belong peculiarly to Wilmington. Its history, compiled by two of its surviving officers, Captains Metts and Cowan, and embodied in Clark's *Regimental*

Histories, shows that its whole career was "special service," and
the instances of signal bravery, daring, and endurance related
were so constant that they were looked upon as all in the day's
work, and no special notice was taken of them.

This regiment, which went to Virginia in 1861 with 1,500
men, took part in every battle, in the thickest of the fray, from
Mechanicsville to Appomattox. Very much reduced by forced
marches and hard fighting, with no chance for recruiting, only
300 men went into the Battle of Gettysburg, and when the
regiment was mustered after the battle, 77 muskets were all
that responded in the ranks and "they lost no prisoners, and
had no stragglers."

The compilers of the history of the Third Regiment say modestly that they "were not in a position, nor of sufficiently high
grade, to write anything beyond the range of their own vision,
but that the history of one regiment of North Carolina troops is
the history of another, save in the details which marked their
achievements."

An incident told in Captain Denson's *Memorial Address on
General Whiting,* delivered in Raleigh on Memorial Day, 1895,
is interesting. It was written to Captain Denson by Sergeant
Glennan:

"During the bombardment of Fort Fisher, there was at headquarters a detail of couriers, consisting of youths fifteen to
eighteen years of age—the bravest boys I have ever seen; their
courage was magnificent. They were on the go all the time,
carrying orders and messages to every part of the fort. Among
them was a boy named Murphy, a delicate stripling. He was
from Duplin County, the son of Mr. Patrick Murphy. He had
been called upon a number of times to carry orders, and had
just returned from one of his trips to Battery Buchanan. The
bombardment had been terrific, and he seemed exhausted and
agitated. After reporting, he said to me with tears in his eyes,
'I have no fear physically, but my morale is lacking.' And
then he was called to carry another order. He slightly wavered
and General Whiting saw his emotion. 'Come on, my boy,' he
said, 'don't fear, I will go with you,' and he went off with the
courier and accompanied him to and from the point where he
had to deliver the order. It was to one of the most dangerous
positions and over almost unprotected ground.

"The boy and the general returned safely. There was no
agitation after that, and that evening he shouldered his gun

when every man was ordered on duty to protect the fort from a charge of General Terry's men. The boy met death soon after and rests in an unmarked grave, but his memory will ever be treasured."

THE MEMORIAL ASSOCIATION.

The band of faithful women who had worked under Mrs. A. J. DeRosset as the Soldiers' Aid Society organized in July, 1866, a permanent Memorial Association, with the purpose of rescuing from oblivion the names and graves of the gallant Confederates who lie buried near Wilmington. Mrs. Julia A. Oakley was made president. The first memorial observance was on July 21, 1866. Many citizens and a number of old Confederate soldiers were present, and the ladies went from grave to grave in Oakdale, bringing their floral tributes to the dead. A beautiful and touching address was delivered by Maj. Joseph A. Engelhard, and prayer was offered by Rev. George Patterson, who had been chaplain of the Third Regiment.

The Memorial Association afterwards obtained a charter from the Legislature through Col. William L. Saunders in order that they might hold the deed for a "Confederate lot," which was given them by the directors of the Oakdale Cemetery Company.

Five hundred and fifty bodies of Confederate soldiers, buried at various points where they fell in the vicinity of Wilmington, were brought and reinterred in this lot. Only a few of the names were known.

In 1870, Memorial Day was observed for the first time on the 10th of May, the anniversary of Stonewall Jackson's death, which was afterwards made a legal holiday.

In 1872, the beautiful memorial statue to the Confederate heroes was unveiled. Self-denial, work, prayers, tears and heart's blood went into the building of that monument.

In 1899, a neat stone was placed, marking the grave of Mrs. Greenhow, who lost her life in the service of the Confederate States. This same year mention was made for the first time of the fact that the bronze statue of a soldier on the monument was cast from cannon captured during the war.

In 1875, the Memorial Association, having been greatly weakened by death and the age of its members, decided to merge into the Daughters of the Confederacy, an organization then newly formed, in which they could still carry on their sacred work "buoyed up and assisted by the fresh enthusiasm of the younger association." They were made the Memorial Committee of the Daughters of the Confederacy, and some of them still assist in placing the fresh laurel wreaths on Memorial Day.

Besides the five hundred and fifty graves in the Confederate lot, there are scattered about Oakdale three hundred and eighty graves, and in Bellevue, the Roman Catholic Cemetery, and private burial grounds about one hundred more. These are all marked with stone markers and, as far as possible, are adorned with a laurel wreath upon each recurring 10th of May.

A CAPTURE BEFORE THE WAR.[1]

BY JOHN L. CANTWELL.

The fact that the State of North Carolina was slow to follow the secession movement of her more southern sister States was the cause of much chafing among her people in the eastern counties, and especially along the seacoast, where it was urged that the Federal Government was likely, at any moment, to garrison the forts commanding Cape Fear River and Beaufort Harbor.

The people of Wilmington were particularly exercised over the possibility of such a step being taken, and it is likely that the knowledge of this strong feeling, and the impression that it would be regarded as an act of coercion, alone deterred the Washington Government from sending down strong garrisons and ample munitions of war.

Fort Caswell, commanding the main entrance to Cape Fear River, was a bastioned, masonry fort of great strength and in thorough order, but without mounted guns. Once occupied and armed, it would have been impossible for the Confederates, without command of the sea, to have retaken it, and the port which afterwards proved of such inestimable value to them would have been effectually sealed. The Federal fleets having free entrance there, would have held the shores on either side of the river for some distance up, and commanded, from a safe interior base, the entrance through New Inlet, for the defense of which Fort Fisher was afterwards built, and that historic and epoch-making earthwork would probably never have been constructed.

---

[1]From Clark's *Regimental Histories.*

In the State at large the Union sentiment was at this time slightly in the ascendant. In the Lower Cape Fear the secessionists were probably in the majority. These regarded delays as dangerous, and anticipated with forebodings the occupation of the forts by the Union forces.

Early in January, 1861, alarmed by the condition of affairs in Charleston Harbor, they determined to risk no longer delays. A meeting of the citizens of Wilmington was held in the courthouse, at which Robert G. Rankin, Esq., who afterwards gave his life for the cause on the battlefield of Bentonville, presided. A Committee of Safety was formed, and a call made for volunteers to be enrolled for instant service under the name of "Cape Fear Minute Men." The organization was speedily effected, John J. Hedrick being chosen commander.

On the 10th of January Major Hedrick and his men embarked on a small schooner with provisions for one week, the Committee of Safety guaranteeing continued support and supplies, each man carrying such private weapons as he possessed. Arriving at Smithville at 3 p. m., they took possession of the United States barracks known as Fort Johnston, and such stores as were there in charge of United States Ord. Sergt. James Reilly, later captain of Reilly's battery. The same afternoon Major Hedrick took twenty men of his command, reinforced by Capt. S. D. Thurston, commander of the Smithville Guards, and a number of his men and citizens of Smithville, but all acting as individuals only, and proceeded to Fort Caswell, three miles across the bay, where they demanded, and obtained, surrender of the fort from the United States sergeant in charge.

Major Hedrick assumed command and prepared to make his position as secure as possible. About twenty-five strong, armed only with shotguns, but sure of ample reinforcements should occasion arise, these brave men determined to hold Fort Caswell at all hazards. In bitter cold weather, they stood guard on the ramparts and patrolled the beaches, reckoning not that, unsustained even by State authority, their action was treasonable rebellion, jeopardizing their lives and property. There were only two 24-pounder guns mounted, one on the sea face and one on the inner face, both carriages being too decayed to withstand their own recoil; but, such as they were, with them they determined to defy the United States Army and Navy. The smoke of an approaching steamer being once descried below the horizon, the alarm was signaled, and, believing it to be a man-of-war, the brave men of Smithville flew to arms, and soon the bay was alive with boats hurrying them to the aid of their comrades within the fort. Women, as in the old days, armed sons and fathers and urged them to the front. But the steamer proved to be a friendly one.

Upon receipt of unofficial information of this movement, Gov. John W. Ellis, captain general and commander-in-chief of the North Carolina Militia, on the 11th of January, 1861, addressed a letter to Col. John L. Cantwell, commanding the Thirtieth Regiment North Carolina Militia, at Wilmington, in which, after stating his belief that the men were "actuated by patriotic motives," he continued:

"Yet, in view of the relations existing between the General Government and the State of North Carolina, there is no authority of law, under existing circumstances, for the occupation of the United States forts situated in this State. I can not, therefore, sustain the action of Captain Thurston, however patriotic his motives may have been, and am compelled by an imperative sense of duty to order that Fort Caswell be restored to the possession of the authorities of the United States.

"You will proceed to Smithville on receipt of this communication and communicate orders to Captain Thurston to withdraw his troops from Fort Caswell. You will also investigate and report the facts to this department."

Upon receipt of this order on the 12th, Col. J. L. Cantwell notified the Governor that he would proceed at once to Fort Caswell, accompanied by Robert E. Calder, acting adjutant, and William Calder, acting quartermaster, two staff officers temporarily appointed for that duty. Transportation facilities between Wilmington and Smithville were very limited. Colonel Cantwell and his aides embarked on a slow-sailing sloop which became becalmed within four miles of Smithville. They were put into shallow water, out of which they waded and walked to Smithville, where they secured, with difficulty, because the populace was almost unanimously opposed to their supposed mission, a pilot boat in which they sailed to Fort Caswell, arriving there after dark.

After some parleying, and not without reluctance, they were admitted and conducted to Major Hedrick, to whom the following order was delivered:

To MAJOR JOHN J. HEDRICK, Commanding Fort Caswell:

SIR:—In obedience to the order of His Excellency, John W. Ellis, governor, etc., a copy of which I herewith transmit, it becomes my duty to direct that you withdraw the troops under your command from Fort Caswell and restore the same to the custody of the officer of the United States whom you found in charge.

Respectfully,   JOHN L. CANTWELL,
                    Colonel Thirtieth North Carolina Militia.
ROBERT E. CALDER, *Acting Adjutant.*

The garrison asked until the next morning to consider what reply should be made, and, on the morning of the 13th, this was returned:

COLONEL JOHN L. CANTWELL:

SIR:—Your communication, with the copy of the order of Governor Ellis demanding the surrender of this post, has been received. In reply, I have to inform you that we, as North Carolinians, will obey his command. This post will be evacuated tomorrow at 9 o'clock a. m.

JOHN J. HEDRICK,
Major Commanding.
GEORGE WORTHAM, *Acting Adjutant.*

The fort was evacuated on the next day. Colonel Cantwell and his aides returned to Wilmington and reported the facts to Governor Ellis. The United States sergeant again assumed control of the government property.

Thus matters remained in this section until April of the same year, the State in the meantime drifting steadily towards secession and war, and the people sternly arming and preparing. The local military companies in Wilmington were fully recruited, and the former minute men permanently organized as the Cape Fear Light Artillery, under which name they served throughout the war.

On the 12th of April came the firing upon Fort Sumter, followed on the 15th by a call from the Secretary of War upon the Governor of North Carolina for "two regiments of military for immediate service." Immediately the Governor telegraphed orders to Col. J. L. Cantwell, at Wilmington, "to take Forts Caswell and Johnston without delay, and hold them until further orders against all comers." Colonel Cantwell, as commander of the Thirtieth Regiment North Carolina Militia, promptly issued orders to "the officers in command of the Wilmington Light Infantry, the German Volunteers, and the Wilmington Rifle Guards, to assemble fully armed and equipped this afternoon" [15th], which orders were promptly obeyed.

On the morning of the 16th the Governor telegraphed Colonel Cantwell to proceed at once to the forts, "and take possession of the same in the name of the State of North Carolina. This measure being one of precaution merely, you will observe strictly a peaceful policy, and act only on the defensive." The force under Colonel Cantwell's orders moved promptly. It consisted of the Wilmington Light Infantry, Capt. W. L. DeRosset; the German Volunteers, Capt. C. Cornehlson; the Wilmington Rifle Guards, Capt. O. P. Meares; and the Cape Fear Light Artillery, Lieut. James M. Stevenson, commanding. At 4 p. m., United States Ord. Sergt. James Reilly surrendered the post at Fort Johnston, where Lieutenant Stevenson, with his company, was left in command. The remainder of the battalion, under Col. J. L. Cantwell, proceeded to Fort Caswell and took possession at 6.20 p. m., Sergeant Walker, of the United States Army, being placed in close confinement in his quarters "in consequence of the discovery of repeated attempts to communicate with his government."

Officers and men worked with vigor to mount guns and prepare for defense, and the work never ceased until the fall of Fort Fisher in 1865, and the necessary abandonment of the defense of the lower harbor. The Wilmington Light Infantry were soon after sent to Federal Point, where, in Battery Bolles, they began the first defensive works, which afterwards grew into Fort Fisher and its outlying batteries.

Thus was war inaugurated in North Carolina more than a month prior to the act of secession; and it is a noteworthy fact that the news of the act dissolving connection with the Union, and the call upon her sons to arm themselves was first made known to the pioneer troops of the Cape Fear on the parade ground at Fort Caswell.

EARLY WAR TIMES.

The day following the fall of Sumter, Maj. W. H. C. Whiting hastened to Wilmington and by courtesy took command of the defenses of the Cape Fear. He at once formed a staff, organized the Quartermaster and Commissary Departments, and assigned Capt. F. L. Childs, of the old army, to duty as chief of Artillery and Ordnance, and he appointed S. A. Ashe a lieutenant, and assigned him to duty with Captain Childs. Capt. John C. Winder, who bore a commission from Governor Ellis as chief engineer, reported to Major Whiting. So all of the departments were speedily organized, and the work of preparing for defense was begun. It was a time of unremitting work.

To command New Inlet, Capt. C. P. Bolles threw up the first battery on Confederate Point. It was called Battery Bolles. The Wilmington Light Infantry, Capt W. L. DeRosset, which had been drilled at the cannon at Caswell, was its first garrison. The most interesting of these early batteries was a casemate battery constructed by Captain Winder out of railroad iron and palmetto logs cut on Smith's Island. It was located near the river bank and a short distance higher up than Battery Bolles. Captain Winder's plan of defense for Confederate Point embraced a strong fortification to command the inlet; and in order to guard against a land attack there was a redoubt at the head of the sound, another halfway to the point, and a covered way was planned from the sound to the point, affording protection from the guns of the fleet to the riflemen while they should be engaged with any force that might attempt to land.

Major Whiting was soon promoted to the rank of general and ordered to Virginia, and Col. S. L. Fremont had general charge of the Cape Fear. After some months, Colonel Brown of the Regular Army succeeded Colonel Cantwell. Captain DeRosset was promoted and ordered to Virginia, and Maj. J. J. Hedrick had command at Confederate Point. This officer early became distinguished for energy and efficiency, and was especially remarkable for his skill in erecting batteries. His work at Confederate Point and also at Fort Johnston excited admiration. In October, 1861, when an attack was expected, Gen. Joseph R. Anderson, of Richmond, an old West Pointer, was assigned to the command of the district, and brought with him a full staff of Virginians. Major Lamb, of Norfolk, was assigned to the command of Confederate Point and fortunately proved himself to be a most capable, efficient, and acceptable officer.

Later in the war the importance of Wilmington to the Confederacy became manifest, and General Whiting, doubtless the best engineer officer in the army, and a gentleman of most remarkable intellect and attainments, was assigned to the command of the district. General Hebert had command of the lower defenses. His headquarters were at Fort Johnston. It was here that he narrowly escaped being captured. One dark night young Lieutenant Cushing, of the Federal Navy, who achieved great fame by blowing up the ram *Albemarle,* made a raid on Hebert's private quarters, and came near carrying off the general to the blockading squadron. On another occasion, Cushing passed up the river to the vicinity of Wilmington and spent a day within sight of the town, without, however, gaining any information.

In 1863, Col. Thomas M. Jones, a brother of Capt. Pembroke Jones of the navy and associated with the Cape Fear by his marriage with Miss London, was given command of Fort Caswell, but, his health failing, in 1864 he was succeeded by Col. C. H. Simonton.

One of the amusing incidents connected with the early days of the war is recorded by Dr. W. G. Curtis in his *Reminiscences of Smithville-Southport:*

"Much confusion prevailed at first, and the old citizens of the town proposed the establishment of a 'home guard' for the protection of their home interests. Consequently, a public meeting was called at the courthouse, and after much discussion an organization was formed. Mr. John Bell was elected captain, his chief qualification being that he was good-natured and not likely to enforce any military discipline whatever. Much wisdom was apparent in the conversation of these ancient gentlemen, who proposed a great number of things hitherto unheard of in any military organization, the principal one being that they were liable to become fatigued by the exertion of marching. Inquiring of the citizens if they were well and listening to their replies that 'they were not to say well, that they had a mighty hurting in their heads and a misery in their backs,' which being duly reported to Captain Bell, he would reply by saying that he was 'sorry for their infirmities but that mustang liniment was a good thing, and that a small quantity of plantation bitters taken internally would finish the cure.' Upon the occasion of the first meeting Captain Bell issued orders that they should all come together for drill the next morning, and one member of the force proposed to the captain that the soldiers of the 'home guard' should be required to bring camp stools with them, so that when they were tired they could sit down and rest. Captain Bell put them through the various drills marching around the town, and it was observed that when one of the company got opposite to his own home he left the ranks and was no more seen. The 'home guard' being thus weakened so that they could not face any kind of an enemy, it was moved and seconded by one of the members that the organization be now discontinued, to which motion Captain Bell remarked that he thought so, too, and the motion being unanimously carried, thus ended the famous 'home guard.' "

CHANGES DURING THE WAR.

Wilmington, the principal seaport of North Carolina, also became the most important in the Southern Confederacy. Prior to the beginning of hostilities it had sustained a large traffic in naval stores and lumber, and now it was to be for a time the chief cotton port of America. A startling change in the aspect of the port soon became apparent. The sailing vessels, even to the tiny corn-crackers from Hyde County, had vanished; likewise the two New York steamers. The long line of wharves was occupied by a fleet of nondescript craft the like of which had never been seen in North Carolina waters. A cotton compress on the western side of the river, near Market Street ferry, was running night and day to supply these steamers with cargoes for Nassau and Bermuda, while other newcomers were busily discharging their anomalous cargoes of life-preserving and death-dealing supplies for the new Confederacy.

The good old town was sadly marred by the plagues of war and pestilence and famine. Four hundred and forty-six of the population, reduced by flight to about three thousand, had been carried off by the epidemic of yellow fever brought from Nassau by the steamer *Kate;* and hundreds more of the younger generation, who gave up their lives in the Confederate cause, had been brought to their final resting place in Oakdale Cemetery. Suspension of the civil law, neglect of sanitary precautions, the removal of nearly all the famine stricken women and

children to safer places in the interior, and the coming of
speculators and adventurers to the auction sales of the blockade-
runners' merchandise, as well as the advent of lawless and de-
praved characters attracted by the camps and shipping, had
quite changed the aspect of the whole community. The military
post, including all the river and harbor defenses, was under
the command of Maj. Gen. W. H. C. Whiting.

THE YELLOW FEVER.

The distress of Wilmington during the yellow fever epidemic
was described as follows by the late Dr. Thomas F. Wood in
his biographical sketch of one of the heroes of that fearful
scourge, Dr. James H. Dickson, who died at his post of duty:

"The month of September, 1862, was one of great calamity
to Wilmington. The alarming forebodings of the visitation of
yellow fever in a pestilential form had ripened into a certainty.
Depleted of her young and active men, there was only a military
garrison in occupation, and when the presence of fever was
announced the soldiers were removed to a safer locality. The
country people, taking panic at the news of the presence of the
fever, no longer sent in their supplies. The town was deserted,
its silence broken only by the occasional pedestrian bound on
errands of mercy to the sick, or the rumbling of the rude funeral
cart. The blockade was being maintained with increased vigor.
The only newspaper then published was the *Wilmington Journal,* a daily under the editorship of James Fulton, and its issues
were maintained under the greatest difficulties, owing to the
scarcity of paper and to sickness among the printers. All eyes
were turned anxiously toward the physicians and those in authority for help. To all the resident physicians the disease was
a new one; not one in the number had ever seen a case of yellow
fever, and among them were men of large experience. The
municipal authorities recognized their helplessness; the town
was neglected, for it had been overcrowded with soldiers and
visitors since the early days of the spring of 1861. The black
pall of smoke from the burning tar barrels added solemnity to
the deadly silence of the streets; designed to purify the air and
mitigate the pestilence, it seemed more like fuliginous clouds of
ominous portent, a somber emblem of mourning. Panic, distress, mute despair, want, had fallen upon a population then
strained to its utmost, with the bleeding columns of its regi-

ments dyeing the hills of Maryland with their blood, until the whole air was filled with the wail of the widow and the orphan, and the dead could no longer be honored with the last tribute of respect.

"The *Wilmington Journal* of September 29, 1862, gave all its available editorial space to chronicle, for the first time, the character of the epidemic, and in a few brief words to notice the death of some of the more prominent citizens. One paragraph in the simple editorial notice ran as follows: 'Dr. James H. Dickson, a physician of the highest character and standing, died here on Sunday morning of yellow fever. Dr. Dickson's death is a great loss to the profession and to the community.' Close by, in another column, from the pen of the acting adjutant, Lieutenant VanBokkelen, of the Third N. C. Infantry, numbering so many gallant souls of the young men of Wilmington, was the list of the killed and wounded on the bloody field of Sharpsburg.

"Distressed and bereaved by this new weight of sorrow, Wilmington sat in the mournful habiliments of widowhood, striving, amidst the immensity of the struggle, to make her courageous voice heard above all the din of war to nerve the brave hearts who stood as a girdle of steel about beleaguered Richmond.

"James Fulton, the well-known proprietor of the *Journal,* the wary politician and cautious editor, striving to keep the worst from the world, lest the enemy might use it to our disadvantage, often ruthlessly suppressed from his limited space such matters as in these days of historical research might be of the greatest service. There were two predominant topics which eclipsed all the impending sorrow and distress: first, foreign intervention, for the purpose of bringing about an honorable peace; second, warnings to the State government of the inadequacy of the defense of Wilmington Harbor against the enemy. The former topic was discussed with unvarying pleasure. The horizon of the future was aglow with the rosy dreams of mandates from the British and French Governments which would bring independence to the Confederacy and peace and quietness to the numerous homes, from the sea to the mountains, where sorrow and death had hung like a pall. It is not strange, therefore, that the few publications that had survived the scarcity of printing material should have contained so little biographical matter. Comrades dropped on the right and on the left, but the ranks were closed up, the hurried tear wiped away, and the line pushed steadily forward. The distinguished physician, or general, or jurist, as well as the humble private, got his passing notice in the meagre letters which a chance correspondent sent to one of the few newspapers, and in a short time he was forgotten in the fresh calamity of the day."

The following may be added to Dr. Wood's interesting account:

In August, 1862, the military occupation, the laxity of municipal control, the constant movement of troops, the utter neglect of sanitary precautions, the non-enforcement of quarantine regulations, practically invited the introduction of yellow fever from Nassau by the daily arrival of blockade runners with frequent cases of infection.

The first victim was a German wood-and-coal dealer named Swartzman, whose place of business was on the wharf quite near the landing place of the blockade runner *Kate,* which brought the infection. My father was informed promptly of this by our physician, Dr. James H. Dickson, who advised him to remove his family at once to the country. As my father had seen much of this terrible scourge in the West Indies and in South America, he recognized the gravity of the situation, and sent us all to Duplin County, where he had relatives. Before we left, a ludicrous incident occurred which has stuck in my memory. One of my brothers having kept to his room from indisposition, was at once the object of much solicitude. My father, being a bit of a medico, directed the boy to put out his tongue, which he did with evident reluctance, to the horror of my father, who declared he had symptoms of yellow fever. A shame-faced confession that the patient had been secretly chewing tobacco, which had caused his sickness, relieved the situation and calmed our fears. The year 1862 is still remembered by our older people as a period of terror and dismay. The date of frost was delayed nearly a whole month that fall and nothing but frost would stay the fearful pestilence.

Among the devoted band of Christians who remained at their post of duty and yielded up their lives while rendering succor to those who could not leave, were Rev. R. B. Drane, rector of St. James's parish, aged 62 years; James S. Green, treasurer of the Wilmington and Weldon Railroad, aged 63 years; Dr. James H. Dickson, an accomplished physician and man of letters, aged 59 years; John W. K. Dix, a prominent merchant, aged 30 years; Isaac Northrop, a large mill owner, aged 67 years;

James T. Miller, a prominent citizen and the collector of the
port, aged 47 years; Rev. John L. Pritchard, a Baptist minister,
who fell at his post, never faltering, aged 51 years. Thomas
Clarkson Worth, an eminent merchant, after laboring among
the sick and destitute, yielded his life to the plague November
1, 1862; Cyrus Stowe Van Amringe, one of nature's noblemen,
who refused to leave and remained to help the sick, died at his
post, aged 26 years. Rev. Father Murphy, a Roman Catholic
priest, a hero among heroes, worked night and day until nearly
the last victim had died, and then fell on sleep. Rev. A. Paul
Repiton was the only minister remaining in the city who survived. He worked unceasingly for the sick and buried the
dead. His name is blessed in the annals of Wilmington. Hundreds of others bravely met the issue and remained to nurse the
sick during the horror, and few survived. Of about 3,000 inhabitants who remained in the city, about 446 died within three
months.

In a sketch of Wilmington in 1867, the late Joshua T. James
wrote of the epidemic as follows:

"In August, 1821, the yellow fever appeared here, introduced
by means of the brig *John London* from Havana. It raged
with great violence for about six weeks and a large proportion
of the citizens of the little town, then numbering only about
2,500 inhabitants, was swept away by it. In the autumn of
1862 its ravages were terrible. It began August 6 and ended
November 17, 446 persons having died of the plague within
that time. In this instance, as in the former, it was imported
from the Indies, and on this occasion by the steamship *Kate,* a
blockade runner, trading between this port and Nassau. For
over ten weeks it raged with terrible violence, and at a period,
too, when it was most difficult to combat its effects. Medicines
and provisions were both scarce and high in price, and the little
luxuries needed for the convalescent were most difficult to obtain.
Those of the frightened inhabitants that were able to do so fled
the town; all business was abandoned, and the closed stores and
silent streets gave the place the appearance of a deserted city.
It was then, in that time of distress and suffering, that a few
of the noble spirits of Wilmington arose equal to the emergency.
Regardless of self, many of our oldest and most valued citizens
remained behind to minister to the wants of those who were
unable to leave. Distributing food to the poor, medicine and
attendance to the sick, consolation to the dying, and holy burial

to the dead, they remained behind when many others had fled, and nobly fulfilled the trust they had assigned themselves. Many of them escaped, but some fell, and those from the ranks of the most honored and esteemed citizens of the town. Rest they well, and rest they calmly. They need no monument above their tombs; that is to be found in the hearts of those who knew them."

War Prices in Wilmington.

As the war progressed the prices of food and clothing advanced in proportion to the depreciation of Confederate money; the plainest necessities were almost unobtainable—$50 for a ham, $500 for a barrel of flour, $500 for a pair of boots, $600 for a suit of clothes, $1,500 for an overcoat, and $100 a pound for coffee or tea, were readily paid as the fortunes of the Confederacy waned. Coffee was perhaps the greatest luxury and was seldom used; substitutes of beans, potatoes, and rye with "long sweetening"—sorghum—having been generally adopted. Within a mile or two of our temporary home in the country there lived two unattractive spinsters of mature age, one of whom, in the other's absence, was asked by an old reprobate of some means in the neighborhood to marry him, a preposterous proposal, which she indignantly rejected. Upon the return of the absent sister, however, she was made to feel that she had thrown away the golden opportunity of a lifetime; for, said the sister, "Didn't you know he has a bag of coffee in his house?"

Another true incident will also serve to illustrate the comic side of the great crisis. Our evening meal consisted of milk, rye coffee, yopon tea, honey, and one wheaten biscuit each, with well-prepared corn muffins and hominy *ad libitum*. The biscuit, however, were valued beyond price, and the right of each individual to them was closely guarded by the younger members of the family. One evening there appeared just before supper an itinerant preacher, who was made welcome to the best we had. Addressing himself with vigor to the tempting plate of biscuit, and ignoring the despised muffins, which were politely pressed upon him by the dismayed youngsters at his side, he actually devoured the entire dozen with apparent ease and great relish. Upon being informed at the hour of retiring that it would be inconvenient to serve his breakfast at daylight, when he desired to depart, he said, to our amazement, that, rather than disturb us in the early morning, he would take his breakfast then and there before going to bed. But there were no more biscuit to serve.

SOUTHERN RAILROADS IN WAR TIMES.

The following incidents illustrating the physical condition of the railroads in the South resulting from the incessant war strain, which could not be remedied nor repaired because of inadequate facilities and lack of material, may be worth recording.

A few weeks after the termination of the four years' war, I was returning to our temporary home in Robeson County by way of the Wilmington, Charlotte, and Rutherford Railroad, now a part of the Carolina Central and Seaboard Air Line. The track had been partly destroyed and the roadbed and rolling stock were in a dangerous state of disruption and decay. Our speed at five miles an hour was really perilous; during the frequent stops, we were repeatedly passed by an old darkey laden with farming implements, who preferred the footpath to the rickety railroad train. To each and every invitation from the passengers to get on the train as we overtook him, he politely responded, "Much obleeged, Boss, but I hain't got time."

Captain Hobart, of the British Navy, who subsequently became admiral-in-chief of the Turkish Navy, commanded the blockade runner *Don,* and made eight or ten successful runs to Wilmington. He describes in the following incident a railroad trip to Charleston during the war.

"I determined this time to have a look at Charleston, which was then undergoing a lengthened and destructive siege. So, after giving over my craft into the hands of the owners' representatives in Wilmington, who would unload and put her cargo of cotton on board, I took my place in the train, and after passing thirty-six of the most miserable hours in my life traveling the distance of one hundred and forty miles, I arrived at Charleston, South Carolina, or rather near to that city, for the train, disgusted I suppose with itself, ran quietly off the line into a meadow about two miles from the station. The passengers seemed perfectly contented, and shouldering their baggage walked off into the town. I mechanically followed with my portmanteau, and in due course arrived at the only hotel, where I was informed I might have half a room.

"Acting on a hint I received from a waiter that food was

19

being devoured in the dining-room, and that if I did not look out for myself I should have to do without that essential article for the rest of the day, I hurried into the *salle-à-manger,* where two long tables were furnished with all the luxuries then to be obtained in Charleston, which luxuries consisted of lumps of meat supposed to be beef, boiled Indian corn, and I think there were the remains of a feathered biped or two, to partake of which I was evidently too late. All these washed down with water, or coffee without sugar, were not very tempting; but human nature must be supported, so at it I set, and having swallowed a sufficient quantity of animal food, I went off to my room to take a pull at a bottle of brandy which I had sagaciously stored in my carpet-bag. But alas, for the morals of the beleaguered city. I found, on arriving there, a darkey extended at full length in happy oblivion on the floor, with the few clothes I had with me forming his pillow, and the brandy bottle rolling about alongside of him, empty.

"I first of all hammered his head against the floor, but the floor had the worst of it; then I kicked his shins (the only vulnerable part), but it was of no use; so, pouring the contents of a water pitcher over him, in the hope that I might thus cause awful dreams to disturb his slumbers, I left him, voting myself a fool for leaving the key in my trunk.

"Having letters of introduction to some of General Beauregard's staff, I made my way to headquarters, where I met with the greatest courtesy and kindness."

Col. Alfred Moore Waddell wrote in his very interesting reminiscences of a railroad tragedy during the war on what is now a part of the great Atlantic Coast Line system, in which he narrowly escaped death, but which involved a ludicrous scene, as follows:

"The yellow fever was brought to Wilmington by a blockade runner in August, 1862, and raged with terrible effect for two or three months. Happening to be going from Richmond, Va., to Augusta, Ga., and stopping for a day or two in Wilmington, just before the fever broke out, and hearing that a poor fellow named Swartzman, a young German, was sick and alone, I called at his room and sat by his bedside and tried to cheer him, holding his hand in the meantime. I observed that he had a very yellow appearance and supposed he had jaundice. After sitting some time, I bade him good-bye, and a few hours later left the city for Augusta. He died with black vomit within forty-eight hours, and his was the first case of the dreadful scourge, or at least it was the first recognized case. My escape was a signal mercy; and there was cause for additional gratitude when, on my return home, which was delayed until the fever had disappeared, a dreadful railroad accident occurred in which two young ladies sitting immediately behind me were killed and every person in the car except one was hurt, while I crawled out with slight injury. The railroad was in a very dilapidated condition, as the war was going on and no means of repairing it was available, and the engine 'jumped the track' twice after the accident, the last time being about ten miles from Wilmington, whereupon, with several others, I left it and walked to town. I have frequently related the circumstances attending this fatal accident for the purpose of proving that, according to my experience, there seldom occurs a tragedy without some comic incident. In this case the comic incident was as follows: Provisions of all kinds were hard to get, and seeing an old 'aunty' at one of the stations with a box of ten dozen eggs, I bought them, paying her five (Confederate) dollars per dozen for them, and placed them under the seat in front of me, on which Mr. James Dawson, of Wilmington, and another gentleman were sitting. When the accident occurred all the lights in the car were extinguished, and, the night being very dark, it was impossible to distinguish persons. Just after I crawled out of the wreck, and while the cries and groans of the victims were still going on, a feeble voice cried, 'Gentlemen, I am bleeding to death.' At once recognizing the voice as that of Dawson and expressing the hope that he was mistaken, he replied, 'No, just feel my head and my clothes.' I did so, and the wet, slimy clothes certainly seemed to verify his assertion. About that time a lantern was brought by the conductor (Harry Brock) and the revelation it made, in spite of the solemnity of the surroundings, was ludicrous in the extreme. My box of eggs, when the car turned over, had fallen on Dawson's head and shoulders, and the contents were streaming from his battered hat—an old 'stove-pipe'—and from his hair and face and arms in a yellow cascade. His change of expression upon the discovery was even more ridiculous than the plight he was in."

MRS. ARMAND J. DeROSSET.

(From the Confederate Veteran.)

This noble character deserves prominent record for her services to the South. She was president of the Soldiers' Aid Society, of Wilmington, from the beginning to the end of the war.

Endowed with administrative ability, which called forth the remark, "She ought to have been a general," gifted with unusual largeness of heart and breadth of sympathy, she was a leader of society, yet ever alive to the wants and the sufferings of the poor and needy. Under her direction the Soldiers' Aid Society was early organized, and for four years did its work of beneficence with unabated energy.

The North Carolina coast was especially inviting to the attacks of the enemy, and Mrs. DeRosset's household was removed to the interior of the State. Her beautiful home in Wilmington was despoiled largely of its belongings; servants and children were taken away, but she soon returned to Wilmington, where her devoted husband was detained by the requirements of business, and here devoted herself to the work of helping and comforting the soldiers.

Six of her own sons and three sons-in-law wore the gray. The first work was to make clothing for the men. Many a poor fellow was soon without a change of clothing. Large supplies were made and kept on hand. Haversacks were home-made. Canteens were covered. Cartridges for rifles, and powder-bags for the great columbiads were made by hundreds. Canvas bags to be filled with sand and used on the fortifications were required for Fort Fisher—and much more was in requisition. The ladies would daily gather at the City Hall and ply their busy needles or machines, with never a sigh of weariness.

When the troops were being massed in Virginia, Wilmington, being the principal port of entry for the Confederacy, was naturally an advantageous point for obtaining supplies through the blockade, and Mrs. DeRosset, ever watching the opportunity to secure them, had a large room in her dwelling fitted up as a store-room. Many a veteran in these intervening years has blessed the memory of Mrs. DeRosset and her faithful aids for the comfort and refreshment so lavishly bestowed upon him. Feasts without price were constantly spread at the depot. Nor were the spiritual needs of the soldiers neglected. Bibles, prayer-books, and hymn books were distributed. Men still live who treasure their war Bibles among their most valuable possessions.

Mrs. DeRosset's ability to overcome difficulties in getting all she needed for the men was the constant wonder of those who daily assisted her in her labors. An incident of her surpassing executive power is worthy of record. After the first attack on Fort Fisher, the garrison, under the command of the gallant officers Whiting and Lamb, was in great peril and in need of reinforcements, which came in Hoke's division of several thousand men—Clingman's, Kirkland's, Colquitt's, and Hagood's brigades—with some of the North Carolina Junior Reserves. The wires brought the news that in a few hours they would arrive, hungry and footsore. Mrs. DeRosset was asked if the ladies could feed them. The ready reply was flashed back: "Of course we can"; and she proved equal to the task. Through her energies and resources, and those of her able corps of assistants, she redeemed her pledge.

The harrowing scenes of hospital life followed, and here, as elsewhere, Mrs. DeRosset's labors were abundant. The sick were ministered to by tender hands, the wounded carefully nursed, and the dead decently buried. The moving spirit in all these works of beneficence was the Soldiers' Aid Society, directed by Mrs. DeRosset.

When all was over, Mrs. DeRosset was the first to urge the organization of the Ladies' Memorial Association for perpetuating the memory of the brave soldiers who died for our cause. Though persistently refusing to accept office, she remained a faithful member of the association as long as she lived.

A sketch of Mrs. DeRosset's work during the Confederacy would not be complete without some recognition of the valuable assistance given her by all her colleagues, and especially by Mrs. Alfred Martin, the vice president. That she was looked up to as their leader does not in the least degree detract from the value of their services, for without strong hands and willing hearts the head would be of little avail, and she never failed to give due meed of appreciation to all who helped her in her work. From her own countrywomen such devotion was to be expected, but the German women of the city entered into the work, zealously giving their means as well as their time to the call of their president. Were it not open to a charge of invidiousness, a few names might be singled out as especially helpful and interested in serving the country of their adoption, with the unwearied fidelity of true-hearted women of every land.

Her labors ended, Mrs. DeRosset has for years rested peacefully under the shade of the Oakdale trees, waiting her joyful resurrection. The daughters of the South could have no better, purer model, should their beloved country ever call on them, as it did on her, in time of need.

Of her own sons, one noble boy of seventeen sleeps in Oakdale Cemetery, with "Only a Private" inscribed on a stone marking his resting place.

Her oldest son, Col. William L. DeRosset, of the gallant Third North Carolina Infantry, was wounded nigh unto death at Sharpsburg.

Her second son, Dr. M. John DeRosset, assistant surgeon at Bellevue Hospital, New York, with most flattering offers of promotion in a New York regiment, resigned his commission, came South, and was commissioned assistant surgeon, with orders to report to Jackson, in whose command he shared the perils of the famous Valley campaign of 1862. Later, he was one of the surgeons in charge of the hospital in the Baptist College, Richmond.

Another son, Capt. A. L. DeRosset, of the Third North Carolina Infantry, was several times disabled by slight wounds, and at Averasboro was left for dead on the field. He owes his recovery to the skill and care of a Federal surgeon, into whose hands he fell.

Louis H. DeRosset, being physically incapacitated for active duty, was detailed in the Ordnance and Quartermaster's Departments, and was sent to Nassau on business connected with the latter.

Thomas C. DeRosset, the youngest of the six, a boy at school, enlisted before the call for the Junior Reserves, and was detailed for duty under Maj. M. P. Taylor, at the Fayetteville arsenal. He died in 1878 from sunstroke when in command of the Whiting Rifles, attending the memorial services at Oakdale Cemetery.

CONFEDERATE HEROES.

From personal knowledge and from available records I have added to this narrative the following names of the living and the dead identified with Wilmington, which are held in grateful remembrance by those who recall their devotion to the Lost Cause. Hundreds of others, equally meritorious, are upon the roll of honor, but because of limited space I can include only the names of company and regimental leaders of the Lower Cape Fear, and some others whose record is known to me.

As has been said elsewhere, prior to the formal secession of the State of North Carolina from the Union, affairs in Charleston had taken such a turn that the citizens of Wilmington anticipated the occupation and strengthening of Forts Caswell and Johnston at the mouth of the Cape Fear by the Federal Government. To prevent that, a Committee of Safety was organized in Wilmington, and a call made for volunteers to enlist for immediate service. This call was promptly answered, and John J. Hedrick was chosen commander. These minute men embarked on January 10, 1861, for the mouth of the river and, being joined by a Smithville detachment, speedily took possession of the two forts.

The Cape Fear Light Artillery was recruited from the local military companies, and especially from the body of minute men that took possession of Forts Caswell and Johnston prior to the formal secession of the State. Under this name the company served throughout the war.

Gen. W. H. C. Whiting was a distinguished West Point engineer, a man of great ability. His wife was a Miss Walker, of Wilmington, and at the outbreak of the war he was a Wilmingtonian by adoption, well-known and highly esteemed. The day after the fall of Fort Sumter, he came to Wilmington and by courtesy assumed command, and for some weeks directed the preparations for defense. He was, however, needed at the front and was chief engineer with Gen. Joseph E. Johnston at Harper's Ferry and at Manassas. After brilliant service in Virginia, on November 17, 1862, he again assumed command of the defenses of the Cape Fear.

Wilmington was the most important port of the Confederacy for the receipt of supplies and munitions of war, and an officer recognized in both armies as without a superior as an engineer was entrusted with its defense. General Whiting entered the army with the highest record ever made by any graduate at West Point. Having been before the war in charge of the improvements of the harbor and the lower part of the river, he was entirely familiar with the topography of the country, and he exerted every energy for a successful defense. Later, he was assigned to the command of a division in Virginia, but in the summer of 1864 he returned to the Cape Fear.

General Whiting was mortally wounded in the second attack on Fort Fisher, when he exposed himself with unsurpassed heroism. He died a prisoner at Fort Columbus, New York Harbor, March 10, 1865. His remains were brought home, and now rest in Oakdale Cemetery beside those of his most estimable wife, who after some years followed him.

Col. Gaston Meares was appointed colonel of, the Third Regiment on its first organization, with Robert H. Cowan, lieutenant colonel, and William L. DeRosset, major.

Mr. Meares, when quite a young man, moved to the West from Wilmington, and engaged in the Mexican War, attaining the rank of colonel. On the secession of North Carolina, he reported to the Governor for duty, and was at once commissioned as colonel and given command of the Third Regiment, then just organized. Colonel Meares was a man of marked individuality, respected by his superior officers, beloved by his subordinates, and commanded the admiration and confidence of the men of his regiment, for he was always intrepid, and in him they recognized a leader who would lead.

At Malvern Hill, July 1, 1862, while on foot in front of the line and from a slight elevation surveying the enemy through his field glasses, he was instantly killed by a slug from a shrapnel fired from a battery directly in front and not over seventy-five yards distant.

Major DeRosset succeeded his brother-in-law, Colonel Meares, in command of the regiment; Lieutenant Colonel Cowan having been promoted before that to the colonelcy of the Eighteenth Regiment.

William Lord DeRosset was a member of one of the oldest and most prominent families of Wilmington, being the eldest of six sons of Dr. Armand J. DeRosset, all of whom served in the Confederate Army except one, who, being physically incapacitated for active duty, was detailed to the Ordnance and Quartermaster's Departments. In 1861 William L. DeRosset was captain of the Wilmington Light Infantry. When Fort Sumter was bombarded, several volunteer companies were ordered to occupy Fort Caswell, the Light Infantry being among them. Later, when the Constitutional Convention authorized the organization of ten regiments, enlisted for the war and known as State Troops, he was commissioned major of the Third Regiment. Succeeding Colonel Meares in command when the latter fell at Malvern Hill, he led the regiment into the Battle of Sharpsburg in September, 1862. He was seriously wounded; and, finding himself permanently disabled, he resigned, and was enrolled in another branch of the service.

When Fort Caswell was first occupied, January 10, 1861, the Smithville Guards, a volunteer company, of which Stephen D. Thurston was captain, joined the men enrolled in Wilmington, and took part in occupying Forts Johnston and Caswell. Captain Thurston was a few months later appointed captain of Company B. of the Third Regiment, and before Sharpsburg he had risen to the rank of lieutenant colonel. At Sharpsburg when Colonel DeRosset fell wounded, Lieut. Col. Stephen D. Thurston took immediate command of the regiment, and proved a brave and valiant soldier, leading the Third in gallant style during the rest of the battle, where they "were in the vortex of the fire, and proved their endurance, tenacity, and valor." Of the twenty-seven officers who went into action on that memorable morning all save three were disabled, seven being killed. Colonel Thurston was disabled for several months, but returned to his command in September, 1864. He was again seriously wounded on the 19th of September, at Second Winchester. Meanwhile, Lieutenant Colonel Parsley was in command during the absence of Colonel Thurston.

William Murdock Parsley, in April, 1861, was commissioned captain of a company he organized and which was composed chiefly of the young men of Wilmington. They had formed a company in the fall of 1860, under the name of "Cape Fear Riflemen," and were among those who occupied Fort-Caswell. After North Carolina seceded, the Cape Fear Riflemen returned to Wilmington and disbanded. They were almost immediately reorganized under Captain Parsley and completely uniformed by his father, Mr. O. G. Parsley, sr. The captain was just twenty years old, and many of his men were not much older. The company was attached to the Third Regiment, one of the ten organized as State Troops and enlisted for the war. They were ordered to Richmond in June, and, arriving just after the Battle of Seven Pines, Mechanicsville was their first engagement. They took part in the Seven Days' Battle, and on July 1, at Malvern Hill, Captain Parsley was severely wounded through the neck by a minie ball; but, after a three-months' furlough, he returned to his command and was in every battle up to Sharpsburg, September 17, 1862.

Before that time he had by regular gradation reached the rank of major, and, subsequently, on the resignation of Colonel DeRosset and the promotion of Lieutenant Colonel Thurston, he became lieutenant colonel. In the campaign of 1863, known as the Pennsylvania Campaign, Colonel Parsley had command of the regiment. He led it in the charge at Culp's Hill on the 3d of July, when, with the Maryland Battalion, they took possession of the enemy's works. The Third was greatly reduced by severe fighting at Chancellorsville and had had no chance to recruit its ranks since. This proud regiment that went into the field over a thousand strong in the Seven Days' Battle was, after Gettysburg, so much reduced that the major at the head of the column and the assistant surgeon, at the foot, could carry on a conversation without effort. Every officer of Major Parsley's old company, the Cape Fear Riflemen, was killed.

One of the original members of this old company, writing in 1898 of Colonel Parsley, says, "As brave as the bravest, kind and considerate towards inferiors in rank, he was at all times thoughtful and careful of his men in every way. I believe all loved him. I know I loved him, for he was my good friend." Another comrade says: "The major himself, only twenty-two or twenty-three years old, had been in every engagement from the Seven Days' Battle to Gettysburg. His training had been under the eye of Col. Gaston Meares, and, as promotion followed promotion, Colonel Parsley was always a disciplinarian of the progressive type. On occasion he could be a boy and enter a wrestling match in camp with all the zest of a schoolboy, but woe to the officer who presumed upon this to take official liberties."

Between Gettysburg and Chancellorsville he received two slight wounds, one being a narrow escape from death by the glancing of a ball on the button of his coat. At Spottsylvania,

May 12, 1864, Colonel Thurston being absent, wounded, Lieutenant Colonel Parsley led the regiment, and with the greater part of it, after a desperate hand to hand fight at the "Horseshoe," or "Bloody Angle," he was captured and confined at Fort Delaware. From there, with fifty other officers, he was transferred to Charleston Harbor on the prison ship *Dragon* and anchored in the line of fire from Charleston, "in retaliation" for the quartering of some Federal officers, prisoners, in the city of Charleston as a protection to the city, full of non-combatants, against the Federal firing from the "Swamp Angel Battery."

The prisoners on the *Dragon* were kept between decks, overcrowded, near a stove where all the cooking for the whole ship was done. Ventilation was bad, and the suffering from the heat almost unbearable. They were supplied scantily with the coarsest of food and subjected to all kinds of indignities. From here they were exchanged on the 3d of August. Colonel Parsley returned to the army not long afterwards, taking with him a number of recruits for his regiment. He shared the fortunes of the Third till April, 1865. Just three days before Lee's surrender, in the engagement at Sailor's Creek during the retreat to Appomattox, when only twenty-four years old, he met his death by a minie ball fired by a sharpshooter, falling with his face to the foe.

Capt. W. T. Ennet, originally of Onslow County, was promoted to be major after the resignation of Colonel DeRosset, and always after that commanded the regiment in the absence of Colonel Parsley. He was unfortunately captured at Spottsylvania and sent to Fort Delaware, and was among those taken to Charleston Harbor on the prison ship *Dragon,* suffering the hardships of imprisonment with the rest. Major Ennet was by profession a physician and highly accomplished. He was also a brave soldier and a warm friend.

Col. Robert H. Cowan was first chosen lieutenant colonel of the Third Regiment, but in the spring of 1862 was elected colonel of the eighteenth. The Third Regiment parted with sincere regret from Colonel Cowan. The whole command, both rank and file, loved him and recognized him as one of those by whom the regiment had been brought to its fine efficiency. The esteem in which he was held was manifested on his departure by the presentation to him by the regiment of a very fine horse.

Colonel Cowan was a native of Wilmington and was prominent in the politics of the State. No man was more loved and admired than he. His gallantry was unequaled, while his charming personality and graceful manners are well remembered by all who knew him. He was wounded severely at the last of the Seven Days Battles around Richmond, and being disabled from service, resigned in November, 1862.

Col. John L. Cantwell saw active service in the Mexican War, in the War between the States, and subsequently in the Spanish-American War. The records say "that seldom has the flag of a country waved over a braver soldier." His service as colonel of the Thirtieth Regiment, North Carolina Militia, in taking possession of Forts Caswell and Johnston on April 16, 1861, is told elsewhere. On its organization, April 13, 1862, Colonel Cantwell was elected colonel of the Fifty-first Regiment, but resigned and enlisted as a private in Company F, Third Regiment, North Carolina Infantry, Capt. William M. Parsley, on whose promotion after the Battle of Sharpsburg, he became captain of the company, and was a most efficient and gallant officer in that famous regiment. Unfortunately, he was captured in the "Bloody Angle" at Spottsylvania Courthouse on May 12, 1864, along with nearly the entire regiment, during the course of the most terrible engagement of the war. His military training was manifest throughout his civil life, in which, as agent of the Adams Express Company, as a produce broker, as secretary of the Wilmington Produce Exchange, and for many years secretary of the Chamber of Commerce, he maintained a careful and sometimes exaggerated regard for official detail.

During the War between the States he kept a diary of important events in which he, with other Wilmingtonians, was engaged, and this precious little book, which he carefully guarded for nearly fifty years and always carried in his pocket, was a veritable *vade mecum,* or last resort, on any disputed point of military history. It contained particularly a careful record of the names and incidents connected with the Federal retaliation upon six hundred Confederate officers, including Colonel Cantwell and Capt. John Cowan, of the Third Infantry, Capt. Walter G. MacRae, of the Seventh Infantry, Capt. T. C. Lewis, of the Eighteenth Infantry, Capt. J. D. McMillan, of the First Infantry, Capt. F. F. Floyd, of the Fifty-first Infantry, Capt. J. W. Moon, of the Third Cavalry, and Capt. J.

H. Bloodworth, of the Fourth Cavalry, from Wilmington, as well as Capt. G. M. Crapon, of the Third Infantry, and Capt. H. Earp, of the Twenty-fourth Infantry, from Southport, who, by Secretary Stanton's order, were removed from their quarters in the North as prisoners of war and placed under double cross fire on Morris Island, exposed to almost certain death.

When Chief Justice Clark was completing the fifth volume of his most valuable *Regimental Histories,* he requested me to persuade Capt. Walter G. MacRae, then mayor of Wilmington, to write an account of that expedition for his history. This Captain MacRae consented to do, and when the narrative was completed, he wisely asked Colonel Cantwell to listen to its recital in order that its accuracy might be clearly established. The colonel, who was afflicted with deafness, nodded his approval until, in describing the incident of the separation of the transport from its armed convoy while off Wrightsville Beach, and a hurried discussion by the prisoners of a proposed attempt to escape through the surf and its final rejection because of the great risk of life involved, Captain MacRae fell into a habit he has of quoting obscure Bible characters and said that the counsel of Ahithophel prevailed. Instantly the colonel held up a restraining hand, and, with the other cupped to his ear, demanded to know the name of that man. "Ahithophel" repeated Captain MacRae. "No, no," said the colonel, "there was no such person abroad." "But let me explain," said MacRae. "No explanation can falsify this book," said the colonel, as he ran his fingers down the list of the six hundred. "Ahithophel, Ahithophel! No such person aboard, sir, he was doubtless a rank impostor"; and failing to make his meaning clear, Captain MacRae was obliged to delete his quotation from the sacred book of Samuel.

Colonel Cantwell's old-time affability and gentle courtesy won him many friends, but while he was patient and responsive to polite advances, he was quick to resent a fancied or real affront. A few years before his death he attended with his accustomed regularity a prominent church service in a neighboring city. As no usher approached him, he quietly walked up the centre aisle, looking smilingly from right to left, expecting an invitation to be seated, but, no man regarding him, he turned back at the chancel rail and walked quietly out. Presently he reappeared in the vestibule with a short piece of scantling, which he had found near by, and with this improvised seat under his arm, marched solemnly up to the chancel rail and deliberately sat in the aisle on the wooden block throughout the sermon. Then, as he entertained a strong objection to the offertory formality in the service as an idolatrous innovation, he walked quietly out again, to the evident relief of the congregation, who feared he might brain the parson with the piece of timber. He bore himself bravely throughout his long and honored life and met the infirmities of old age with a smiling countenance.

Besides these, a host of others whose services should not be forgotten crowd the memory. Brave Maj. Alexander MacRae, of age far too advanced for service in the field in Virginia, accepted command of the First Battalion of Heavy Artillery in General Hebert's brigade, and did duty at the mouth of the Cape Fear until the fall of Fort Fisher. The gallant old father was worthily followed by his brave sons, whose record appears elsewhere.

John J. Hedrick was major of engineers. He was a brave and skillful artillery commander, and had been in active service since the beginning of the war. In the early days of the conflict he had charge of the erection of batteries at Confederate Point and in the vicinity, one small fort on Bald Head being named Fort Hedrick in his honor. When the Fortieth Regiment (Third Artillery) was organized in December, 1863, Major Hedrick was appointed its colonel. This regiment took part in the defense of Fort Fisher, December 24 and 25, 1864, and January 13, 1865, and on January 17 it was ordered to Fort Anderson, about ten miles up the river, where the garrison of about 900 men was under the immediate command of Colonel Hedrick. On February 17, the enemy attacked the fort in the rear with about 10,000 infantry, while Porter, with a fleet of sixteen gunboats and ironclads, lying within a few hundred yards of the fort, quickly demolished the guns. In this fight, under Colonel Hedrick's leadership, great bravery and heroism were shown; but, finding the command in danger of being cut off by a heavy column of infantry in the rear, Colonel Hedrick determined to evacuate the fort. Carrying all the light guns, including the Whitworth cannon, they fell back towards Wilmington. Later, while on the way to meet the enemy advancing from New Bern, there was a battle at Jackson's Mills, in which about 2,000 Federal prisoners were captured; but the Confederate loss was heavy. Here, while gallantly leading his regiment in a charge upon the enemy, Colonel Hedrick was seriously wounded.

John D. Barry enlisted as a private in Company I, Eighth Regiment, and on the reorganization was elected captain of the company. On the fall of the gallant Colonel Purdie, of Bladen County, in June, 1863, he became colonel of the regiment. He was a valiant and dashing officer, and nobly upheld the traditions of his family, one of the best of the Cape Fear section, his grandfather being Gen. Thomas Owen and his great uncle, Gov. James Owen. The companies composing the Eighth Regiment of Volunteers (afterwards the Eighteenth North Carolina State Troops) were:

The Wilmington Light Infantry, Capt. Henry Savage; the Wilmington Rifle Guards, Capt. Robert Williams; the Scotch Boys, Capt. Charles Malloy; the German Volunteers, Capt. C. Cornehlson; and the companies of Capt. George Tait, of Bladen County; Capt. Robert Tait, of Bladen County; Captain Norment, of Robeson County; Captain Gore, of Whiteville, Columbus County; Capt. J. R. Hawes, of Long Creek, New Hanover County.

About the first of August, 1864, General Lane being wounded, Colonel Barry was appointed temporary brigadier general and commanded the brigade, skirmishing almost daily till the 28th. Subsequently, while on a reconnoitering tour, Colonel Barry was wounded by a sharpshooter. Some time in the latter part of 1864, when General Lane returned to the brigade, Colonel Barry, on account of his wounds and impaired health, was assigned to departmental duty with his regular grade of colonel.

After the close of the war, he returned to Wilmington and, in partnership with William H. Bernard, began the publication of the *Dispatch*. Only a few years of broken health remained to him, and nearly fifty years ago he died in the old house he had left in vigorous youth and with high hopes in 1861.

A few years ago, Col. John D. Taylor passed from our midst, leaving a great name as a soldier and a Christian gentleman, with an affectionate memory of his manly figure, his gentle, sympathetic smile, and the empty sleeve he wore. He was captain in the Thirty-sixth Regiment (Second Artillery), was promoted to lieutenant colonel, and served at different points in defense of the Cape Fear. After the fall of Fort Fisher, Colonel Taylor fought at Fort Anderson and Town Creek, on the retreat to Wilmington, and at Kinston; and he and a part of his regiment made their way to the field of Bentonville and took part in that battle, covering themselves with glory as part of the "Red Infantry," Colonel Taylor there losing his left arm.

Upon the death of Colonel Taylor, the following tribute of a devoted friend was published in the *Star,* May 22, 1912:

"A fellow-townsman recently said to the writer: 'I never passed Colonel Taylor upon the street without exercising the privilege of shaking his hand, because I believed that he exemplified in his daily life, to a remarkable degree, those virtues which adorn the character of the Southern Christian gentleman.'

"His old-time urbanity, his winsome smile, his almost womanly tenderness, his gentle patience, his childlike faith, drew him to our hearts and we loved him. Probably no citizen of our community was more generally respected. There was a quiet dignity in this serene, devout Christian, which told of conflicts won while learning to endure hardness as a good soldier, and of a peace which passes the understanding of this world, which enabled him to look o'er heights of toil and sacrifice and find his chief meed in thoughts of duty done.

"During his long and honored life he inspired the hearts and guided the steps of worthy sons and daughters in the way of life, to the end that they might 'glorify God and enjoy Him forever.' His children rise up and call him blessed.

"In public life he discharged his official duties with diligence, ability, impartiality, and uprightness. Party lines vanished in the pure light of his moral excellence, and his return to office at the expiration of each term, without a dissenting vote, attest the abiding confidence of his fellow-citizens.

"Eminent among the local leaders of the Lost Cause, he believed, with his great chieftain, that Duty is the sublimest word in our language, 'and by it as a pilot star, he ever steered his steadfast course.' He went into his last battle at Bentonville with Company A, Captain Rankin, Company B, Captain Taylor, Company C, Captain Brown, and Captain McDougal's company, and a remnant of the Thirty-sixth Regiment, in all 350 men; and he emerged with nineteen other survivors, an honorable record, and an empty sleeve. Rankin, Taylor, McDougal and Brown were desperately wounded, and Colonel Taylor was the only officer who survived the desperate and bloody charge of the 'Red Infantry.'

"He sheathed his sword when the cause for which he fought was lost, but he put on the invisible armor of the soldier of the Cross, and has fought a good fight and laid hold on eternal life. The greater number of his devoted comrades have crossed over the river and rest with their commander under the shade of the trees.

"We read that at the roll call of the flower of Napoleon's army, the Imperial Guard, as silence fell upon the utterance of a name which death had claimed from the arms of victory, a comrade would step forward from the ranks, and, raising his hand in grave salute, would answer, 'Died on the field of honor!' The thin gray line of Appomattox, diminishing day by day as it yields to the call of the great Conqueror, still closes up its broken ranks of hoary heads and feeble knees. Soon it will vanish away and there will be no reverent comrade's voice to answer the roll call of the dead. But 'Death's truer name is Onward. No discordance in the roll of that eternal harmony whereto the worlds beat time!'

'The glory born of goodness never dies,
Its flag is not half-masted in the skies!'

"In the sessions of his beloved church, our friend will be greatly missed—in no circle beyond his beautiful home life was he more welcome than in that of the church of his fathers.

"David Worth, DuBrutz Cutlar, Kenneth Murchison, William DeRosset, Alfred Waddell, John D. Taylor, classmates all at Chapel Hill, were of the flower of Wilmington, and they are gone; but to live in the hearts of those we love is not to die. 'By the light of their lofty deeds and kindly virtues, memory gazes back into the past and is content; by the light of Revelation, hope looks beyond the grave into the bright day of immortality and is happy.' "

Edward D. Hall organized at Wilmington, in the spring of 1861, a company composed principally of Irishmen; and no better or more loyal men or braver soldiers could be found. When work or fighting was to be done they were always ready. This company was first stationed at Fort Caswell; was later sent to Weldon and attached to the Second Regiment, North Carolina Infantry, and ordered to Richmond, and from there to various points in Virginia until the spring of 1862, when it

20

was returned to North Carolina with General Holmes's division, and was afterwards detached and sent to the Cape Fear and stationed at fortifications on the river.

In March, 1862, Captain Hall was made colonel of the Forty-sixth Regiment, organized at Camp Mangum near Raleigh. Ordered to Virginia, this regiment bore a conspicuous part in the Battle of Sharpsburg, calling forth from the division commander especial mention of its gallant colonel and staff for distinguished bravery and coolness under fire. During that day the regiment occupied several positions of importance and great danger, and on every occasion it exhibited that steadiness and coolness which characterized its record. In October, at Bristow Station, General Cooke fell, and the command of the brigade devolved on Colonel Hall. An unequal struggle was waged, and disaster was averted only by Colonel Hall's skillful management of his command. Late in 1863, Colonel Hall resigned to accept a civil office in North Carolina, and the regiment lost its brilliant commander, a brave man, a good disciplinarian, a most valuable and efficient officer. It was with much regret that his regiment bade him farewell.

Alexander Duncan Moore, who at first commanded a battery of light artillery from Wilmington, was made colonel of the Sixty-sixth Regiment, organized in August, 1863. Colonel Moore had been at West Point and was a brilliant young officer of remarkable appearance and soldierly bearing. The Sixty-sixth was ordered to Virginia in May, 1864, where, in "its first baptism of fire on the 15th of May, its gallantry was conspicuous and favorably commented upon by commanding officers." A series of battles followed, and on the 3d of June, 1864, Colonel Moore was mortally wounded, a ball striking him in the neck. The memory of his heroic courage was ever after present with the officers and men of his command, and comments were made upon his gallantry and the soldierly qualities he always exhibited.

In the attack on Petersburg Colonel Moore was told that his regiment was advancing too rapidly ahead of the right and left, and he was directed to preserve the alignment. On receiving this order, Colonel Moore seized his colors, planted the staff upon the ground, and lifted his sword in the air above his head, the well known signal; his command halted and dressed on the colors, until the regiments on the right and left came upon the same line—then, with a yell, all three sprang forward and rushed upon the enemy. The movement was successful and the foe retreated.

George Tait, of Bladen County, who was elected major of the Eighth Regiment in July, 1861, resigned his commission, and was, with Company K, of the Fortieth Regiment, stationed at a battery near Federal Point Lighthouse. On the 1st of December, 1863, when the Fortieth Regiment was organized as Third Artillery, Captain Tait was appointed lieutenant colonel. In January, 1865, he resigned this commission to take one as colonel of the Sixty-ninth North Carolina Regiment. Colonel Tait was a fine disciplinarian. He remained detached from the Fortieth Regiment after it had been formed in order to train, drill, and discipline the officers and men of the Thirty-sixth; and then he drilled and disciplined the Fortieth, which was afterwards pronounced by the inspector general, Colonel Tansill, "the best drilled regiment of Confederate soldiers" that he had ever seen.

Colonel Tait was a good and brave officer and in his rank had no superior.

Maj. James Dillard Radcliffe, then connected with the Engineer Department of the Cape Fear defenses, was elected colonel of the Eighth Regiment of Volunteers, on its first organization in 1861. Colonel Radcliffe, who had been principal of a military school in Wilmington for several years previous to the war, was an excellent drillmaster and disciplinarian, and soon had the regiment well drilled. On the reorganization in 1862, the regiment then being the Eighteenth State Troops, he was not re-elected; but he became colonel of the Sixty-first Regiment when it was organized, in August, 1862.

Alfred M. Waddell, lieutenant colonel of the Forty-first Regiment (Third Cavalry) was a scion of one of the old and venerated families of the Cape Fear. He was commissioned lieutenant colonel in August, 1863, having previously served as adjutant. His regiment was scattered over an extended field of operations, and operated as detached cavalry, or partisan rangers. In August, 1864, Colonel Waddell resigned. After the war, as long as he lived, he always used his brilliant talent and eloquence in behalf of his comrades and his fellow-citizens of the Cape Fear.

In August, 1863, Roger Moore, a descendant of "King" Roger Moore, was appointed major of the Third Cavalry. He was a brave soldier, maintaining the honor of his ancestors upon the field. In August, 1864, when Colonel Waddell resigned, Major Moore became commanding officer of the regiment, which was looked upon as a bulwark of protection for the railroad from Weldon to Wilmington and of all that portion of thirty counties east of it which was not in the hands of the enemy. Protecting the villages and settlements from forays, guarding the cross-roads and bridges, and checking the approach of the enemy whenever he advanced beyond his gunboats, this regiment daily and hourly did service of vital importance. In 1864 the regiment was ordered to Virginia and took part in the brilliant attack on Reams Station, August 25, 1864, following which General Lee wrote to Governor Vance: "If those men who remain in North Carolina have the spirit of those sent to the field, as I doubt not they have, her defense may be securely entrusted to their hands."

John Grange Ashe entered the Confederate service in April, 1861, as lieutenant under Gen. Braxton Bragg, at Pensacola. He was appointed acting adjutant general to Gen. Robert Ransom in June, 1862, and later in the same year was made major of sharpshooters. He also participated in the Red River campaign with Gen. Dick Taylor, in 1864. He died in Texas in 1867.

William S. Ashe was appointed major quartermaster July 17, 1861, and colonel quartermaster, September 25, 1861. He had in charge all Confederate transportation east of the Mississippi River. Desiring more active service, in the summer of 1862 he was authorized by President Davis to raise a legion of artillery, cavalry, and infantry, but before he had been able to do so, he was killed in a railroad accident in September, 1862.

Dr. Alexander Ashe served as assistant surgeon in the Confederate Navy. He died in Texas, 1866.

Samuel A. Ashe was appointed lieutenant of artillery on April 17, 1861, by Major Whiting, who had assumed command of the Cape Fear defenses, and in May was commissioned by the State. Although all North Carolina staff appointments ceased on the transfer of our troops to the Confederacy on August 20, 1861, he and Capt. John C. Winder continued at their work until November, when he was relieved. Captain Ashe then joined, as a volunteer, Company I, Eighth Regiment, at the front at Coosawhatchie, S. C.; and later enlisted regularly as a private in that company. But in December, the President appointed him in the Regular Army, and in March, 1862, the commission came to him through Gen. R. E. Lee, then commanding at the South. He was assigned to duty at the Charleston arsenal, where he remained until the middle of July, when he was appointed acting adjutant general to General Pender, and joined Pender's brigade in Virginia. The night following the Battle of Second Manassas, he fell into the enemy's hands and was confined in the Old Capitol Prison until October, when he was exchanged. In November he was assigned to duty with General Clingman's brigade, and in July, 1863, became ordnance officer of Battery Wagner, and continued so until the fall of that fort in September, when he was ordered to the arsenal at Fayetteville, where he served as assistant to the commanding officer until the end of the war. On the day General Johnston surrendered, Captain Ashe's chief, General Gorgas, at Charlotte, in the most appreciative terms gave him orders to join him across the Mississippi, but later told him he could go home and govern himself according to circumstances.

At the election in 1870, he was elected a representative from New Hanover and became a very active member of the Legislature, chairman of the Finance Committee, and leading member of the Judiciary and other committees. In 1874 he edited at Raleigh a daily paper, the *Evening Crescent,* which probably did more than any other one instrumentality in bringing about the redemption of the State, the Democratic majority that year being 12,000. In 1879 he purchased the *Observer,* and in 1881 he consolidated the *News* with it, founding the *News and Observer,* of which he was editor until 1894. In 1903 he became editor of a *Biographical History of North Carolina,* of which seven volumes have been printed, and in 1908, his *History of North Carolina* (1584-1783) was published.

Col. John Wilder Atkinson entered the service of the Confederate States in 1861 as captain of a volunteer company, which was assigned as Company A to the Fifteenth Virginia Infantry. With this regiment he took part in the action at Big Bethel in 1861, and at the Battle of Seven Pines served on the staff of General McLaws, who took occasion to mention his services in his official report. He was then promoted to be major and transferred to the Nineteenth Virginia Regiment of Artillery. To this the Tenth Virginia was added in 1863, and he was promoted to colonel of the consolidated command. He took part in the Seven Days' Battle before Richmond, and subsequently remained on duty in the Richmond defenses, where he was, toward the last, in frequent and arduous service combating the Federal raids and defending the city against regular siege. He took a prominent part in the defeat of the raider Dahlgren, and buried the body of that evil-minded man. For some time he was in command of a part of the defenses about the Confederate Capital. His last battle was at Sailor's Creek, where he was captured. Thence he was taken to Johnson's Island, but through the influence of his kinsman, Gen. Winfield Scott, was soon released without taking the oath. In 1866, Colonel Atkinson made his home in Wilmington, where he recently died, leaving the heritage of an honored name.

Capt. Edward H. Armstrong, of New Hanover: In 1862 this brilliant student of the University at Chapel Hill was orderly sergeant of Company G, Third Regiment, North Carolina Troops. Very soon afterwards he was promoted to be second lieutenant of that company, and went through the Seven Days' Battle at Richmond, and with his regiment he participated in the Battle of Sharpsburg with great credit and was made captain of the company, the captain, E. H. Rhodes, and Lieut. W. H. Quince, having been killed in that engagement. His subsequent career was conspicuous at Fredericksburg, Chancellorsville, Gettysburg, and Mine Run, and he met a soldier's death at the Horseshoe, Spottsylvania Courthouse, lamented by his comrades for his modest, beautiful character and for his soldierly qualities. It was said of him that he was fitted to command a division. During the Gettysburg campaign, his shoes having worn out, he marched barefoot.

Louis S. Belden ran away as a youth and enlisted at the beginning of the war in Moore's Battery, Light Artillery, Tenth Regiment, North Carolina Troops, which was, after Moore's promotion to be colonel of the Sixty-sixth Regiment, commanded by Capt. John Miller. Sergeant Belden remained with the battery until the end of the war, rendering at all times excellent service. On his return home, destitute but determined to make his way, he appeared in a suit of clothes which his sister had made of bedticking, the only available material, and he was not long in obtaining honorable employment which led to comparative independence. He still retains, in his advanced years and impaired health, the esteem and confidence of the community.

Charles P. Bolles had been employed on the Coast Survey by the United States Government for many years previous to the war, and was a man of marked ability. In April, 1861, he was assigned to duty as an engineer, and constructed the first battery at Confederate Point, called in compliment to him, "Battery Bolles." For a year or more he was employed with the engineers, and then transferred to the Fayetteville Arsenal. His professional skill was exemplified in the preparation of bolts for Whitworth guns. An English firm presented a battery of Whitworth guns to the Confederate Government through Colonel Lamb at Fort Fisher, by whom they were effectively used at long range against the blockaders and for the protection of the blockade runners. The guns were unfortunately received without ammunition or projectiles, and were worthless until Captain Bolles devised at the Fayetteville armory the peculiar bolts which were used as projectiles and for which he had no pattern. At the arsenal, he was captain of Company A, Sixth Battalion, Armory Guards.

J. H. Boatwright was one of the "Seed Corn" cadets, of Charleston, S. C., when the order was issued by the hard-pressed Confederacy that boys under the military age would be permitted to go to the front and do a man's work. He was offered a lieutenancy at the age of seventeen, but his father declared that he was too young to command, and so he enlisted as a private in Company B, Citadel Guards. He saw service at Coosawhatchie, and at "Tulafinny," and in one of the engagements he was struck by a musket ball. His lieutenant, Mr. Coffin, hearing the bullet strike him, assisted in examining the wound, which was found to be the mutilation of a small Testament in young Boatwright's breast-pocket. The interesting bullet is still preserved by his family.

A year or so afterwards he was sent home on sick leave, and he found Columbia sacked and burned, but his mother and sister safe. Governor McGraw sent for him and, informing him that his secretary had taken fright and departed, offered him the position, which he promptly accepted. Later, when the Governor was arrested by the Federals, his secretary was not regarded as of sufficient importance to be placed under guard. This resulted in his taking charge of all the State archives, which he placed in an old vault, and he kept them in careful custody until after the war, when he delivered them to the first legislature.

Gabriel J. Boney, of Wilmington, enlisted in Company H of the Fortieth Regiment in March, 1864, at the age of eighteen, and was on duty until the war was practically ended, completing his service in a Northern prison. He was in the fight with the Federal gunboats at Fort Anderson, and at Town Creek, having been promoted to be corporal, was in command of twenty men on the line. He was also at Bentonville, where the North Carolina soldiers made their last demonstration of heroic valor. Being captured by the enemy, he was transported to Point Lookout, Md., and confined until June 4, 1865.

Lieut. Alexander Davidson Brown, a native of Scotland, earnestly supported the cause of the State during the great war, and for four years wore the Confederate gray. Although he came to Wilmington as late as 1860, in April, 1861, he enlisted as a private in the artillery company of Capt. James D. Cumming, known as Battery C, of the Thirteenth Battalion. In this gallant command he was successively promoted to corporal and lieutenant. During his military career he participated in the fighting at New Bern and on the Petersburg lines in numerous engagements, and took part in the desperate encounters on the retreat from Petersburg, and at Appomattox Courthouse previous to the surrender.

Thomas O. Bunting enlisted in the Twentieth North Carolina Infantry in May, 1861, though only about sixteen years of age, but in July following withdrew and entered the University of North Carolina, where he studied one year. Returning to the Confederate service, he became a private in Company C, of the Sixty-third Regiment, or Fifth Cavalry, and shared the subsequent gallant career of this command, taking part in the engagements at White Hall and Goldsboro, in 1862, and then, in Virginia, under the leadership of Baker, Gordon, Barringer, Hampton, and Stuart, meeting the enemy on many a field. On April 3, 1865, at Namozine Church, he was captured by the Federals, and was confined at Point Lookout until June 28. Throughout his gallant career he was once seriously wounded, receiving a shot through the ankle on the Ground Squirrel Road near Petersburg, which disabled him for three months.

Samuel R. Bunting was captain of Company I, Tenth Regiment of State Troops, Light Artillery, which was organized at Wilmington in May, 1861. This company served at first as coast guard at Wrightsville and Masonboro Sounds and in March, 1862, moved to Kinston and saw active service in that vicinity; then returned to Fort Fisher. After the fall of Fort Fisher and the evacuation of Wilmington, the regiment joined Gen. Joseph E. Johnston, and fought and surrendered with him.

Bunting's Battery was engaged for three days at Spring Bank, and lost nineteen men killed and wounded.

James G. Burr was colonel of the Seventh Regiment, Home Guards, but did not see actual service in the field.

Thomas Jefferson Capps was a private in Company E, Third North Carolina Infantry, and was in charge of the field ambulances at the Battle of Chancellorsville when a captain ordered him to go to the front, which he refused to do because he was under Dr. McRee's orders and could not leave his post. Finally, the officer reluctantly told him that Stonewall Jackson was wounded and required immediate attention, but he must act with great secrecy. Mr. Capps then drove down the road under heavy fire, lifted the general into his ambulance, and brought him from the field. He was kept under guard all night in order to prevent the possibility of conveying the distressing news and thereby demoralizing the troops.

Robert E. Calder was elected lieutenant of Company B (of Wilson County), which was part of the Second Regiment, and served with distinction in this command throughout the war. He was severely wounded, losing the sight of an eye. Further mention of Lieutenant Calder is made in Colonel Cantwell's narrative of the capture of Fort Caswell.

Lieut. William Calder was born in Wilmington, May 5, 1844. In 1859 he entered the military academy at Hillsboro, and left there in May, 1861, having been appointed drillmaster by Governor Ellis, and assigned to the camp of instruction at Raleigh. Upon the organization of the first ten regiments of State Troops, he was commissioned a second lieutenant of the Third Regiment. He served as drillmaster at Garysburg about four months, and was then transferred to the Second Infantry as second lieutenant of Company K. With this command he participated in the Seven Days' Battle about Richmond; and at Malvern Hill he was wounded in the left thigh, causing a disability that continued until after the Battle of Sharpsburg. He was in battle at Fredericksburg and Chancellorsville, and in most of the engagements of Jackson's and Ewell's corps; and during the three days' fighting at Gettysburg he was in command of the sharpshooters of Ramseur's brigade. On the return to Orange Courthouse he was appointed adjutant of the First North Carolina Battalion, Heavy Artillery, and subsequently was on duty with his command at Fort Caswell, until that post was evacuated. He was in the Battles of Fort Anderson, Town Creek, and Kinston, and at the Battle of Bentonville he served as acting assistant adjutant general on the staff of Colonel Nethercutt, commanding the brigade of Junior Reserves. From that time until the end of hostilities he was with his artillery battalion in outpost duty on the upper Cape Fear River.

James Carmichael, rector of St. John's Episcopal Church, Wilmington, was devoted to the Confederate cause during the great struggle. He was compelled to retire from his studies at the Alexandria Theological Seminary by the advance of the invading armies in 1861. In May of that year he was commissioned chaplain of the Thirtieth Virginia Infantry, and was with this command on the field of duty until the spring of 1862, when he was disabled by lung trouble and was sent on furlough to Greensboro. There he remained, unfit for duty, until November following, when, at the request of Dr. James L. Cabell, post surgeon at Danville, he was assigned as post chaplain at the latter place. In this capacity he served until July 3, 1865.

Anthony D. Cazaux, a well-known citizen of Wilmington, was appointed captain and assistant quartermaster of the Eighteenth Regiment, North Carolina Troops. The Eighteenth Regiment was of the Branch-Lane brigade, and Captain Cazaux acted as one of its quartermasters. For many years after the war Captain Cazaux was actively and prominently engaged in the business affairs of Wilmington and contributed largely to the development of its commerce. His genial, kindly nature won for him many devoted friends.

Columbus L. Chestnutt was appointed assistant quartermaster of the Thirteenth Battalion, which was organized December 1, 1863.

John Cowan joined the Wilmington Rifle Guards (afterwards Company I, Eighteenth Regiment), and took part in the capture, April 16, 1861, of Fort Caswell by order of Governor Ellis. After a few months he was promoted to lieutenant of Company D, Third North Carolina Regiment of Infantry.

He was present at Fredericksburg, Chancellorsville, and various other battles, and served through the Gettysburg campaign. Once, in the absence of Captain VanBokkelen, he was left with his company to hold a line which had been captured the evening before, and he defended his position with great tenacity and held it until he was ordered out. At Spottsylvania he was captured, along with the entire brigade, and sent to Fort Delaware. Subsequently he was placed under fire at Morris Island, after which he was returned to Fort Delaware, where he remained until the end of the war. During all his life Captain Cowan was exceedingly kind to the sailors of this port. He became one of the trustees of the Seamen's Friend Society, and never failed to be present at the Bethel meeting on Sunday afternoons.

The following tribute by a fellow-citizen, on the occasion of a memorial meeting after his death, illustrates the character of this highly esteemed Cape Fear gentleman:

"We are called today to add the honored name of John Cowan to the long roll of the majority, and to pay our tribute of respect to the memory of one of the few members of our society who was faithful unto death.

"For years he has sat with us during our Sabbath service, inspiring us by his devout attention and unswerving loyalty with more zeal in our sacred cause, and uniting our handful of supporters in a closer bond of union and sympathy with the thousands of seafaring men, who, 'like ships that pass in the night and speak each other in passing,' have heard the friendly warning voice of our preacher and vanished from our sight. His beaming face, full of sympathetic courtesy, will be sadly missed in our assemblies.

"Like the great leader in the wilderness, whose presence reflected the glory of his God, he wist not that his face so shone. That face, so deeply lined of late by weariness and pain, is, I believe, radiant now in the presence of Him with whom there is fullness of joy. Buffeted by the storms of life and disabled by disease and suffering, this sailor's friend has met his great Pilot and cast his anchor within the haven of eternal rest.

"His eminent public service as a soldier of the Confederacy is a part of its history. His native modesty forbade the mention by him of his heroic deeds, but who of you will forget the valor of that thin line of twenty-five muskets, the remnant of his shattered but intrepid command, which held an overwhelming force in check at Gettysburg? When he surrendered his sword at the 'Bloody Angle,' he retained that invisible armor for the good fight of faith from which he has come off more than conqueror through Him that loved him and gave Himself for him.

"I am requested by our recent chaplain, the Rev. Dr. James

Carmichael, who could not be present with us today, to add his loving testimony to the work and faith of our dead comrade, who for many years encouraged and sustained him as a colaborer at the Bethel service. He mourns with us the loss of one of the truest friends and supporters whom this society has ever known."

William A. Cumming joined the famous Third Regiment, the record of which has been given in several sketches, and, about a year later, after a fatiguing day's march, he was exposed all night to a soaking rain, which brought on an attack of rheumatism. He was sent to the hospital and, deriving no benefit, was later sent home so emaciated that his father did not at first recognize him. Later, he returned to the army, but he never fully recovered his health, and he was given a commission in the Commissary Department, in which he remained during the war. He never recovered from the first exposure in the field and died after the war from rheumatism, which attacked his heart. He had many warm friends in the Third North Carolina Infantry and in civil life, for he was a kindly, unselfish, Christian gentleman, of fine presence and old-time urbanity.

Preston Cumming, a survivor of the Cape Fear Artillery, enlisted in October, 1861, as a private in the artillery company commanded by his brother, James D. Cumming, and known as Cumming's battery. During his service he was promoted to sergeant, participated in the fighting on the Petersburg lines several months, and was in the Battles of Washington, Kinston, and Bentonville, and finally surrendered with Johnston at Greensboro.

James D. Cumming was second lieutenant of one of the companies that took possession of Fort Johnston and Fort Caswell at the outbreak of the war. This company was assigned soon after to the defense of Confederate Point, and in April, 1862, was reorganized, with Lieutenant Cumming as captain. A battery of field artillery was provided for it, and it bore the name of Cumming's battery. It became part of the Thirteenth Battalion in December, 1863. In May, 1864, a section of it was ordered to Petersburg, Va., and assigned to Moseley's battalion of artillery. The battery, therefore, gave active service to the Confederacy both in Virginia and in eastern North Carolina.

Roger Cutlar, a brother of DuBrutz Cutlar, served throughout the war in Moore's battery. After the war he removed to California. He was a courageous and gallant soldier.

Champ T. N. Davis: Among the officers of Company G, Sixteenth Regiment, on its organization June 17, 1861, appears the name of Capt. C. T. N. Davis, of Rutherford County. The Sixteenth was ordered to Virginia soon after its mobilization, proceeded to Valley Mountain, and assisted in holding the gap against the Federals under General Rosecrans. Afterwards, it was attached to Hampton's legion around Fredericksburg and Yorktown, where it was reorganized, and Captain Davis elected its colonel. At the Battle of Seven Pines the regiment was exposed to a galling fire from several Federal batteries and lost some of its bravest and best officers and men, among whom was the gallant Colonel Davis.

Graham Daves was appointed private secretary to Governor Ellis on January 1, 1859, and held that position until the outbreak of the War between the States. He then joined the army as first lieutenant of the Twelfth Volunteers, Col. J. Johnston Pettigrew, afterwards known as the Twenty-second Regiment, North Carolina Troops, of which he was appointed adjutant, July 24, 1861. With this regiment he served until April, 1862, being on duty at different times at Raleigh, Richmond, and Brooke Station, Va., but most of the time at Evansport, now called Quantico, where the regiment was employed in erecting batteries, which some of the companies occupied and served. These were the batteries that so long blockaded the Potomac River at that point. Lieutenant Daves having resigned his commission on November 16, 1863, was enrolled as a private and assigned to duty in the conscript office, Raleigh, where he remained until July, 1864. He served in various other positions until the surrender of General Johnston's army to General Sherman near Greensboro.

Junius Davis, born June 17, 1845, was a son of George Davis and his first wife, Mary Polk. He was in school at Bingham's Institute, in Alamance County, when North Carolina decided to cast her lot with the Confederate States, and in the spring of 1863, being nearly eighteen years of age, he left his books to enter the military service. He enlisted as a private in Battery C, Third Battalion, North Carolina Artillery, Capt. J. G. Moore, and served until the close of the war. For nearly a year he was about Petersburg, and was in the Battles of Drewry's Bluff and Bermuda Hundred, and of Fort Harrison lines. In the last day's fight at Petersburg he was slightly wounded, but continued on duty during the retreat. The battery being at first a part of the rear guard was almost constantly engaged and was roughly handled; but later it became a part of the van, and at the end, Corporal Davis and a small squad escaped without surrendering. In civil life, Mr. Davis wore well the mantle of his distinguished father.

After the war he came to the bar and was associated with his father, and, like him, became recognized as eminent in his profession and particularly distinguished for his learning in corporation law and for his admirable management of the affairs of the corporations entrusted to his care.

In 1853, Mr. George Davis became counsel for the Wilmington and Manchester Railroad and continued as such after that property was acquired by the Wilmington and Weldon Railroad. Later, he was general counsel of the Atlantic Coast Line, his son, Junius Davis, being associated with him, and when he died the latter's professional connection with the company continued. In time Junius Davis retired from active practice and his son, Thomas W. Davis, a lawyer of recognized ability, who had been associated with him, assumed the connection with the company from which his father resigned. Thus, for more than sixty years, have Mr. George Davis, his son, and his grandson retained the position as counsel for this property, a record, as far as known, without a parallel in the United States.

Besides his admirable work as a lawyer, following further in the footsteps of his illustrious father, Junius Davis made contributions to historical literature and won a high reputation for research into local history and as an entertaining and versatile writer. In particular must be mentioned his masterful address on Locke's *Fundamental Constitutions* and his exhaustive and conclusive article on John Paul Jones, which has been accepted as explaining John Paul's reason for assuming the name of Jones. On its publication in the *South Atlantic Quarterly*, Col. A. M. Waddell, Bishop Robert Strange, Prof. J. G. deRoulhac Hamilton, Mr. James Sprunt, and others united in the following request:

"The undersigned, your fellow-citizens, having read with great interest and satisfaction your admirable contribution to North Carolina history, published in the *South Atlantic Quarterly,* and desiring that this unique elucidation of the mystery of Chevalier Jones's adopted name be published in pamphlet form, in order that it may be placed in public libraries and in private collections for future guidance, most cordially felicitate you upon its production and request your permission for its more extended circulation."

In this article Mr. Davis shows that John Paul, when in need of friends, found them in Allen and Willie Jones, and that he assumed the name of Jones because of his association with them. The Navy Department, in giving chronological data of the life of John Paul Jones, refers to this fact and to Mr. Davis' article, and it may be considered that Mr. Davis has set at rest all doubts on the subject.[1] He was a lovable man. There was a dignity and charm about Junius Davis by which he came naturally, and he had an old-fashioned felicity of expression that delighted his friends. He loved their companionship and that of his books, of which he possessed a wonderful store, for his was indeed a rich and well-stored mind, described by his illustrious father, and in the recent years of his retirement from the greater activities of life, it created its own beauty, wealth, power, and happiness. He had wisdom and insight, and whatever subject he touched he illumined. He thought deeply upon matters pertaining to his legal profession, upon literature and politics, and upon the current affairs of life, and when he spoke we felt that he had received a vision of the truth, for truth was ever his guiding star.

Another old-time Cape Fear gentleman and soldier of the South has crossed over the river and rests under the shade of the trees.

> "The sweet remembrance of the just
> Shall flourish when he sleeps in dust."

Horatio Davis, a half-brother of Mr. George Davis, served in the Confederate Army and later became a judge in Virginia, and finally moved to Florida. He was a brave and fearless soldier.

Armand L. DeRosset was elected captain of Company B at the formation of the Sixth Battalion, called the Armory Guards, which was stationed at the Fayetteville Arsenal and Armory during the War between the States.

Moses John DeRosset was on duty as surgeon in the hospitals at Richmond in 1861, and became surgeon of the Fifty-sixth Regiment on its organization in the summer of 1862. Dr. DeRosset stood high in his profession, having taken a course in Europe and being besides an accomplished French and German scholar.

---

[1]New evidence, more recently discovered, however, again unsettles the question.

Edward B. Dudley was captain of Company D, Anderson Artillery, of the Thirty-sixth Regiment. This regiment was stationed at various points of defense along the Cape Fear. On November 22, 1864, Captain Dudley was sent with his company and others under Maj. James M. Stevenson to Georgia to join the Confederate forces opposing Sherman's advance to Savannah. Later he returned to Fort Fisher and performed his part in the epic defense.

Guilford L. Dudley: The First Regiment was organized near Warrenton in the spring of 1861. G. L. Dudley was appointed one of the two quartermasters, and was second lieutenant of Company E, First Regiment. He served with distinction throughout the Seven Days' Battle, the South Mountain campaign, and at Sharpsburg, Fredericksburg, Chancellorsville, Gettysburg, and in other battles. The last volley fired by the Army of Northern Virginia was fired by North Carolina troops, and the First Regiment was among the number.

Charles D. Ellis: Shortly after the outbreak of the war the Legislature of North Carolina, coöperating with the Confederate Government in defending the entrance of the Cape Fear River and Wilmington, passed an act authorizing the formation of a battalion of heavy artillery (Ninth Battalion, Heavy Artillery), to be composed of three companies, to man the defenses constructed for the protection of the harbor and the shores close to the Cape Fear Bar.

The second company (Company B) was organized by Capt. Charles D. Ellis, and its members were mostly from Brunswick, Duplin, and other counties near New Hanover. Capt. Ellis, however, resigned October, 1862, and was succeeded by Capt. Jacob W. Taylor. In 1863, the three companies were organized into what was known thereafter as the First Battalion of Heavy Artillery.

Z. Ellis was one of the three lieutenants in Company B, raised by C. D. Ellis, and he served with this company throughout the war.

Henry G. Flanner was originally second lieutenant in Company F, Thirteenth Battalion. A section of this company served in the winter of 1863-64 and in the spring of 1864 attached to MacRae's (Tenth) battalion in western North Carolina. This battery, under Capt. H. G. Flanner, was ordered to Virginia in 1862, and served continuously, with the above exception, in General Lee's army. It served on the lines around Petersburg with great credit. It surrendered at Appomattox. Flanner's battery is entitled to the credit of preventing the Federal Army from entering Petersburg on the morning of the springing of the mine (July 29).

Capt. Owen Fennell entered the Confederate service as second lieutenant of Company C, First Regiment, under Col. M. S. Stokes, in June, 1861. The regiment did good service during the Seven Days' Battles around Richmond and in the Maryland campaign, and Lieutenant Fennell shared its marching and fighting until just after the Battle of Sharpsburg, when he was made acting assistant commissary of subsistence, with the rank of captain. He continued in this service until the office was abolished after the Gettysburg campaign.

Clayton Giles joined Company I, Sixty-third Georgia Volunteers, in 1863, and served in that command throughout the war, surrendering at Greensboro under Gen. J. E. Johnston.

Norwood Giles enlisted as a youth in Moore's battery, Light Artillery, Company E, Tenth Regiment North Carolina Troops, afterwards (on Moore's promotion to colonel) commanded by Capt. John Miller. Endowed by nature with a most genial, pleasing personality, he endeared himself throughout the war and for years afterwards to a wide circle of devoted friends. His untimely death, December 11, 1899, was greatly mourned in our community, and the following lines of appreciation were written by one who esteemed him very highly:

"We mourn the death of one in the flower of his manhood who served so well the purpose of his Creator, and who filled so completely the hearts of his friends with loving trust and admiration, that the name of Norwood Giles should be inscribed upon the record of our noblest and best. Who can measure in this world the quiet influence of a Christian man? He was the truth of God impersonated, living and moving among men in daily deeds of goodness, shining in the image of his Maker, and quietly fulfilling a great and noble purpose.

"Such was his character. A thousand sympathetic hearts will pay the tribute of a sigh that he is gone, and many lives will be the better for his unsullied life, which combined the freedom and joyousness of a child with the chivalry and strength and self-control of a Christian gentleman. Endowed with superior intellectual gifts, his scope of knowledge was varied and extensive. Exact and methodical in all the details of his business, which he conducted with marked ability and skill, he was also a

21

close observer of men and affairs and well informed upon the important questions of the day.

"He ever found solace and joy in the freedom of country life. He loved to breathe the clear air of heaven; the ocean and its wonders and the marvelous flora of our region were sources of delight to him, for he found more pleasure in the lilies of the field and in the shells of the sea than in all the arts of man's device. The joyous notes of the mocking-bird, the sighing of the pines, and the voices of the deep were music to his ear, and the modest *Drosera* and *Dionæa* were to his admiring eyes among the masterpieces of creation.

"In all the manly sports and healthful pleasures of the sound he was an ardent and successful leader. His sprightly, generous nature, his exquisite wit and humor, made him ever welcome in social life, and his charming pen sketches of the annual regatta, which were as fresh and breezy as the salt sea air, were always read with feelings of pleasure and delight.

"The kindly, beaming smile is gone, the joyous laugh is hushed, and the captain of the winning boat has met his Pilot on the boundless tide. Sincerity and simplicity went hand in hand with him, who was to rich and poor, to lowly and exalted, the same in high-bred courtesy and never-failing kindliness."

William Henry Green entered the service as a private in the Branch Artillery, Capt. A. C. Latham, in July, 1862. In the following year he was detailed as sergeant major of the battalion of Maj. J. C. Haskell, to which Latham's battery was attached, and he served in this capacity during the remainder of the war. He had an active career as artilleryman, participating in the famous Battles of Cedar Run, Second Manassas, Chantilly, Warrenton Springs, Fredericksburg, Gettysburg, Spottsylvania, and Second Cold Harbor, and throughout the siege of Petersburg and the retreat to Appomattox, where he was paroled.

Maj. Edward Joseph Hale volunteered as a private in the Bethel Regiment, of which D. H. Hill was colonel, the day after Lincoln's proclamation calling for troops. He was in the first pitched battle at Big Bethel, June 10, 1861. When that regiment was disbanded, Governor Clark appointed him a second lieutenant of North Carolina Troops. In 1862 he was appointed first lieutenant and adjutant and assigned to duty with the Fifty-sixth North Carolina Regiment, Ransom's brigade. He participated in all the engagements of that command in Virginia and eastern North Carolina, and distinguished himself for his coolness and bravery. Though little over twenty-one years of age, General Longstreet recognized his ability and appointed him judge advocate of the Department of Court-martial. His ability, fighting record, and general qualifications were known to Brigadier General Lane, and that officer, after the death of Capt. George B. Johnston, tendered him the position of adjutant general of his brigade of veterans in the fall of 1863. Captain Hale displayed such strong character in the conduct of his duties that before the close of the terrific campaign of 1864 he was the idol of the troops. His behavior on the battlefield was extraordinarily cool and courageous. In the Wilderness, at Spottsylvania, and Turkey Ridge; in many battles before Petersburg, after Grant had crossed to the south side of the James; at Deep Bottom, Gravelly Hill, Riddle's Shop, and Fussell's Mill; at Reams Station; in the battles of the 2d of April, 1865, in the morning, and later at Battery Gregg and Battery 45; at Amelia Courthouse, Farmville, and other engagements on the retreat to Appomattox, he distinguished himself, fighting with conspicuous gallantry. Not long before the close of the war a remarkable tribute was paid to Captain Hale's bravery and skill. Upon the petition of the major commanding the Twenty-eighth North Carolina Regiment and all of its officers present, he was recommended by his brigade, division, and corps commanders for the colonelcy of that regiment because of conspicuous gallantry and merit. Later, he was appointed major on the staff.

B. Frank Hall served throughout the war as a member of the Duplin Rifles, or Company A of the Forty-third Regiment, North Carolina Infantry. He entered the service as a private, but soon rose to the rank of first sergeant. Sergeant Hall was on duty with his regiment in Daniel's brigade during the Seven Days' Battle before Richmond, was under fire at Malvern Hill, and afterwards at Drewry's Bluff and Suffolk, and from December, 1862, to June, 1863, he was on duty in North Carolina, participating in the affair at Deep Gulley. He took part in the terrific fight of July 1 at Seminary Ridge and the next two days of the Battle of Gettysburg, and in the affair at Hagerstown, on the retreat from Pennsylvania. Subsequently being attached to Hoke's brigade, he served in North Carolina at the Battle of Bachelor's Creek, the siege and capture of Plymouth, and the skirmishes before New Bern. Returning thence to Virginia, he participated in the battles at Hanover Junction and Bethesda Church; and on March 25, 1865, he took part in the assault upon the Federal works at Hare's Hill. On the morning of April 2, prior to the evacuation of Petersburg, he was in command of a squad of twelve men, which, with a similar squad from the Forty-fifth, entered Fort Mahone, then in the hands of the enemy, capturing 100 prisoners, and he aided effectively in the gallant fighting which forced the Federals from the lines. During the retreat, Sergeant Hall was in the battle at Sailor's Creek; and at Appomattox, Sunday morning, he joined in the last assault upon the enemy.

Dr. William White Harriss was born in 1824, and was graduated from the University of North Carolina in 1842. He entered the Confederate service as surgeon of the Sixty-first Regiment, North Carolina Volunteers, and was on duty chiefly around Charleston until 1863, when General Whiting appointed him surgeon of the City Garrison at Wilmington, where he remained until the surrender. When Wilmington was evacuated he was appointed by General Bragg to remain there as surgeon to take care of the sick and wounded Confederate soldiers.

Maj. Gabriel H. Hill, son of Dr. John Hill, of Kendal, appointed a lieutenant in the United States Army in 1855, came home and served with high distinction at the Battle of Roanoke Island, and afterwards across the Mississippi. He was a very fine officer. After the war he lived in Virginia.

Lieut. John Hampden Hill enlisted early in the winter of 1863, at Smithville, in Company H, Fortieth Regiment, and was commissioned second lieutenant by Governor Vance. He was with his command at Fort Anderson during the bombardment, and in the Battles of Town Creek, Wilmington, Northeast River, Wise's Fork, Kinston, and Bentonville, receiving a wound in the left leg in the last battle.

Thomas Hill, M.D., entered the Confederate service in April, 1861. He was commissioned assistant surgeon, Confederate States Army, in July, 1861, and from that date until March, 1862, was in charge of the general hospital at Fredericksburg, Va. Subsequently he was in charge of the general hospital at Goldsboro until May, 1862, when he was promoted to surgeon in the Confederate Army and appointed to the presidency of the medical examining board at Raleigh; he was also put in charge of General Hospital No. 8, at Raleigh, the building now known as Peace Institute. Remaining there until April, 1864, he was then assigned as surgeon to the Fortieth Regiment, North Carolina Troops, and in December following was appointed chief surgeon of the North Carolina Reserves, on the staff of General Holmes. After this distinguished career, which was brought to a close by the surrender at Greensboro, he resumed the practice of his profession.

In April, 1861, Lieut. George W. Huggins was mustered into military service as a private in the Wilmington Rifle Guards, which was later assigned as Company I to the Eighth (Eighteenth) North Carolina Regiment, one of the volunteer regiments of the State first organized. Private Huggins was promoted to first corporal in September, 1861, and to second lieutenant in April, 1862. With his regiment, in the Army of Northern Virginia, he took part in the following battles: Hanover Courthouse, Mechanicsville, Cold Harbor, Fraser's Farm, and Malvern Hill. At the close of the bloody Seven Days' Battles around Richmond, at Harrison's Landing, he received a severe wound in the foot, which disabled him until July, 1863. He then returned to his regiment in Virginia, but was detailed for duty in the Quartermaster's Department at Wilmington, where he remained until the city was evacuated, when he made his way to Johnston's army and was paroled with it at Greensboro.

James B. Huggins was second lieutenant of Company G, Thirteenth Battalion, and was later assigned to service in the Quartermaster's and Paymaster's Departments, with the rank of captain.

John Christopher James entered the Confederate service in 1863, at the age of sixteen, in Company B, Third Junior Reserves, afterwards the Seventy-second Regiment, North Carolina Troops, Colonel Hinsdale commanding. He was made orderly sergeant of Company D, under Captain Kerr, and later commissioned third lieutenant, and served in the first bombardment of Fort Fisher, in the engagement at Kinston (Hoke's division), and also at the Battle of Bentonville. He surrendered with General Johnston's army at Bush Hill, April 26, 1865, and was paroled with his regiment, May 2, 1865.

He possessed in common with his brother Theodore, to whom eloquent reference was made in the sketch of the Third Regiment by Capt. John Cowan and Capt. James I. Metts, a most attractive personality; and in his devoted, useful life were blended the finest characteristics of the old-time Southern gentleman. Beloved by all who knew him, his memory still lives in the hearts of his friends.

Theodore C. James was an adjutant in the Third Regiment. In writing of him Captain Cowan and Captain Metts say: "Adjutant Theodore C. James has also crossed the narrow stream of death. Our pen falters when we attempt to pay tribute to his memory; companion of our youth, friend of our manhood. For him to espouse a cause was to make it a part of his very self. Intrepid, no more courageous soldier trod the soil of any battlefield upon which the Army of Northern Virginia encountered a foe. The impulses of his nature were magnanimous; no groveling thoughts unbalanced the equity of his judgment. True to his friends and to principle, he remained as

'Constant as the Northern Star
Of whose true, fixt, and resting quality
There is no fellow in the firmament.'

Leaving his right arm upon a battlefield in Virginia, and exempt for that cause from further military duty, he disdained any privilege which such disability brought to him, and continued in active service until the last shot had been fired, 'arms stacked' forever."

Stephen Jewett, when sixteen years of age, joined Ripley's brigade, Forty-fourth Georgia Regiment of Infantry, near Richmond, July 1, 1862, just after the Seven Days' Battle; and he served with that regiment until May 10, 1864, never missing a day's service, skirmish, or battle in which his regiment participated. He was in the engagements at South Mountain, Sharpsburg, Fredericksburg, Chancellorsville, Warrenton Springs, Morton's Ford, the Wilderness, Gettysburg, and Spottsylvania, where he was captured, May 10, 1864, and taken to Fort Delaware. He remained a prisoner of war until March 10, 1865, when he was sent back to Richmond on parole, and was on parole furlough when the surrender of the Army of Northern Virginia ended the war. He entered the army as a private when he could scarcely carry a musket, and he continued to serve throughout the war in that capacity with ever increasing efficiency. Steadfastness, tenacity of purpose, cheerfulness in devotion to duty, a high sense of integrity, have marked his career from boyhood to comparatively old age.

J. Pembroke Jones, a prominent officer in the United States Navy, resigned his commission and joined the Confederate Navy. He was first lieutenant commanding on the iron-clad sloop-of-war *Raleigh*, which carried four guns, and which attacked and broke the Cape Fear blockade. He served with distinction in several departments of the Confederate Navy, and after the war was employed by the Argentine Republic upon important military defenses.

James G. Kenan: "Man must endure his going hence even as his coming hither, ripeness is all."

On the 9th of January, 1912, James G. Kenan went, as must all mortal men, back upon the pathway by which he came—back to the great unknown. His sun went down after it reached the zenith and began receding toward the west. When it set beyond our vision, darkness fell upon thousands of devoted and admiring friends, and many hearts were sad.

Some men flower early; others late. Captain Kenan was a noted man in early life, and was at his best when the final summons came. When he passed away he left an enviable record as a soldier, public official, and private citizen, and the work he did will grow brighter and brighter as the years pass until it becomes his lasting monument, more enduring than marble and brass and forever sacred in the hearts of his grateful countrymen. His deeds of kindness, of charity, and of generosity will ever keep alive his memory and frequently call to recollection the glory of his name.

Captain Kenan was a true man, a lover of justice, a believer in the supremacy of the law, a friend of every cause that lacked assistance. In his views he was broad and liberal, had charity for all, trusted the people, and never lost faith in humanity.

He was a fine type of the Southern gentleman of the old school, being the descendant of a long line of Southern ancestry; but still he was a plain, simple man, who loved his fellow-man, a friend of the toiler and an eloquent advocate of the oppressed. He had faith in his Creator sufficiently abiding to illumine his soul when he reached the river which all of us must some day cross. Not given to loud professions or vain boastings of a religious experience, yet deep down in his heart was a well of love and trust which was constant in its flow towards the Saviour of mankind. During all his life he exemplified the human side of religion by doing what he believed to be right. In this respect his faith was fixed. His purposes were strong. His constant effort was to lift all persons with whom he associated to higher conceptions of life and duty.

His personal character was as spotless as a maiden's, and as unsullied as a ray of light. The memory of his just, virtuous, and upright life will linger in the minds of all who knew him.

Upon the occasion of his death the James G. Kenan Chapter, Daughters of the Confederacy, and the Confederate Veterans of Warsaw, in convention assembled, passed the following resolutions:

1st. That by the death of Captain Kenan, the chapter of the Daughters which bears his name has lost a devoted friend and counselor; the Confederate Veterans, a noble comrade and an ever-ready champion of the cause which they so nobly espoused, and his bereaved family, a devoted husband and loving father.

2d. That a copy of these resolutions be spread upon the minutes of the Daughters, a copy be sent the family, and a copy to each county paper, and one to some State paper.

Captain Kenan was the last of a family of three sons and a daughter of the late Owen R. Kenan and was born near Kenansville, of Scotch-Irish parentage, being descended from Thomas Kenan, who settled in Duplin County about one hundred and seventy-five years ago. The family has been for years one of the most prominent in the State of North Carolina.

He served the county of Duplin several terms as sheriff and enjoyed the confidence and esteem of his fellow-citizens in every walk of life. At the outbreak of the war, with his distinguished brothers, William Rand Kenan and Thomas S. Kenan, he early enlisted in the cause of the Confederacy, and was captain of a company in the Forty-third Regiment, North Carolina Troops, Confederate States Army. He was captured at Gettysburg and confined later in a Federal prison. He was a gallant soldier and numbered among his comrades many of the veterans of the war throughout Eastern Carolina.

Captain Kenan was about seventy-two years old. He is survived by his wife, three sons, and one daughter, his children being Dr. Owen Kenan of New York, resident physician for the season at the chain of Palm Beach hotels, Mr. Thomas S. Kenan, of Atlanta, Graham Kenan, Esq., of the law firm of Kenan & Stacy, in Wilmington, and Miss Emily Kenan, of Kenansville.

Thomas S. Kenan: In 1735, when Henry McCulloh and a number of Irish gentlemen obtained from the King grants in the province of Carolina for more than one million acres of land, several large tracts were laid off for them in upper New Hanover, now embraced in Duplin and Sampson Counties, in which settlers from the north of Ireland located, among them Colonel Sampson and Thomas Kenan. From that day the Kenan family has remained in the settlement, or near to it, where their ancestors in America first located. "A race of gentlemen," writes Captain Ashe in his *Biographical History of North Carolina,* "ever observant of their obligations, they have always been held in high esteem and have taken a prominent part in regard to all great questions that have concerned the public welfare." The Kenan family came from Scotland to Ireland in 1700; thence to the Cape Fear in 1735; and in the succeeding generation James Kenan was a zealous, daring, and brilliant patriot officer during the War of Independence. His son, Thomas, after serving in the General Assembly, was a member of the United States Congress from 1805 to 1811, and his grandson, Owen R. Kenan, the father of Col. Thomas Stephen Kenan, also served several terms in the General Assembly and was a member of the Confederate Congress.

Thomas Stephen Kenan obtained his early education at the old Grove Academy, of Kenansville, under the venerated Rev. James Menzies Sprunt. This was an institution that educated many of the brightest young men of the Cape Fear section. He was afterwards at the Central Military Institute in Selma, Alabama, and later entered Wake Forest College. In 1857 he was graduated from the University of North Carolina with the degree of A.B., and the next year the University conferred upon him the degree of A.M. Having determined to become a lawyer, he spent two years studying with Chief Justice Pearson, at Richmond Hill, and entered upon the practice of law at Kenansville in 1860. In 1859 the Duplin Rifles was organized in Kenansville, and in 1861 this company volunteered under Thomas Stephen Kenan as its captain, and was assigned to the First, or Bethel, Regiment, and afterwards to the Second Regiment. At the end of the year, it was reorganized and assigned to the Forty-third Regiment, and Colonel Kenan was made lieutenant colonel, on April 24, 1862, becoming colonel. His regiment was assigned to Daniel's brigade and was engaged in the operations before Richmond, Colonel Kenan winning high laurels. The next year, as a part of Rhodes's division, the Forty-third under Colonel Kenan carried the flag to Carlisle, Pa. Returning to Gettysburg on the first of July, Colonel Kenan was in the hard fight on Seminary Ridge that day and was under fire all the next day, his regiment supporting a battery of artillery on Seminary Ridge, and on the third day he participated in the desperate assault on Culp's Hill. While leading a charge, he fell severely wounded, and, while being borne to the rear in an ambulance train the next day, he was captured. He was confined on Johnson's Island, a prisoner of war, until March, 1865, when he was paroled, together with a number of other prisoners, but he was never exchanged.

The war over, he returned to Kenansville to the practice of law and served in the Legislature of 1865-66 and 1866-67, and his wisdom was shown in those sessions of the General Assembly, made up of the best men in the State, who sought patriotically to conform the laws of the State to the changed conditions that resulted from the war. Of course when Reconstruction came on he was retired to private life, but then, as during the war, he was regarded as the natural leader of his people. In 1868 he led the party fight as the Democratic candidate for Congress in his district.

In 1869 he moved to Wilson to practice his profession, and shortly afterwards he became mayor of the town and the most progressive citizen of that growing community. To this day the people of Wilson point with pride to the fact that he was the first mayor to introduce progressive measures, to light the town, to improve the streets, and to make it what he always loved to think it, "the village beautiful."

In 1876, in the great campaign led by Vance for governor, the campaign that redeemed North Carolina, the Democrats put up a ticket of superior men. "There were giants in those days." The ticket made up of Vance and Jarvis and Kenan and Saunders and Worth and Love and Scarborough represented the brains and chivalry and sterling worth of the State, and the character of those men had much to do with the victory that was won in the election. Vance, of course, towered above all, but none of that great combination stood higher in all the virtues of noble manhood than Thomas Stephen Kenan. When he was elected attorney general, he measured up to the duties of that great office and broadened and deepened the respect of the people of the State, which had been given him in full measure in every community in which he had lived and in every station to which he had been called. For eight years he was attorney general, and upon the conclusion of this period returned to Wilson to the practice of his profession. But in February, 1886, Colonel Kenan was selected by the Supreme Court as clerk of that court. He was learned and wise enough to preside over the court itself. He made a distinguished and faithful official. Conscientious in the highest degree, faithful in the smaller as well as the greater duties, a master of detail, he let nothing come between him and public duty, and he set an example of official conduct worthy of lasting emulation.

In 1904 he was elected president of the State Bar Association, and his address upon that occasion contained words of wisdom as the result of long experience and wide observation. He held the highest ideals of his profession, and by precept and example sought to inspire a devotion to the highest ethics in its practice.

Colonel Kenan was a trustee of the University College of Medicine, at Richmond, Va., took deep interest in the organization of the Oxford Orphan Asylum, of which he was a director, and held the highest offices in the gift of the Masonic Order, of which he became a member in early life.

On the 20th of May, 1866, Colonel Kenan married Miss Sallie Dortch, a daughter of the late Dr. Lewis Dortch, of Edgecombe County, and their home was ever the center of a delightful social life illustrative of the best hospitality and happiness of the South. Having no children of their own, the home of Colonel and Mrs. Kenan was the home of their nieces and nephews, to whom Colonel Kenan maintained a fatherly relationship that was most beautiful and endeared him to them as if he had been in truth their father. His niece, Mrs. Henry M. Flagler, during childhood and young womanhood was always in his home, and was to him as a daughter.

Colonel Kenan was the oldest of five children, the sons of Owen Rand Kenan and Sarah Graham. He was born February 12, 1838, and was nearly 73 years old at the time of his death.

From the day he graduated at Chapel Hill in 1857 the master passion of his life, outside his own family, was his love for the University of North Carolina. He was one of those who led in the reopening of the University in 1875, after its doors had been closed under Reconstruction, and he was one of its trustees thirty years or more. Never when in health did he miss attending a meeting of the trustees of the University or a commencement at Chapel Hill. For many years he was a member of the Executive Board. For nearly a quarter of a century he was also the president of the Alumni Association and looked forward to its annual meetings with joy and delight. Except Dr. Kemp P. Battle, no one in the State did as much for the University as Colonel Kenan.

Knowing for months that the end was near, Colonel Kenan not long before his death selected in Oakwood Cemetery, in

Raleigh, the city in which he lived over twenty-five years, a lot in which he wished to be buried. It is as near as he could secure it to the Confederate Cemetery, where his comrades sleep in honored, though some in unknown, graves.

Capt. William Rand Kenan enlisted as a private in the Forty-third Regiment in November, 1863, while attending the University of North Carolina. He was at once detailed as sergeant major. In May and June, 1864, he was acting adjutant of his regiment, and after that, on account of his gallantry at the Battle of Bethesda Church, he was ordered by General Grimes to take command of the sharpshooters from his regiment, with the rank of lieutenant. While serving in this capacity, he was shot through the body in the fight at Charles Town, in the Shenandoah Valley, August 22, 1864, which compelled him to remain at home sixty days. On recovery, he was assigned to the command of Company E, Forty-third Regiment, by Colonel Winston, who sent in an application for his promotion to second lieutenant on account of distinguished gallantry. This bore the warm endorsement of General Grimes and was approved by General Early. After three weeks service in command of Company E, he was appointed adjutant of the regiment, the rank which he held to the close of hostilities. Among the battles and skirmishes in which he was engaged were the following: Plymouth, Drewry's Bluff, Bethesda Church, Gaines's Mill, Cold Harbor, Harper's Ferry, Monocacy, Washington, D. C., Snicker's Ford, Kernstown, Winchester, Hare's Hill, Petersburg, Sailor's Creek, Farmville, and Appomattox Courthouse.

George W. Kidder was a lieutenant in Company A, First North Carolina Battalion, until he resigned in 1862 or 1863.

Charles Humphrey King entered service in the Wilmington Rifle Guards, in April, 1861, serving in the occupation of Fort Caswell. This company was assigned to the Eighth Regiment, North Carolina Infantry, and he continued with it, earning promotion to corporal and fourth sergeant, until June, 1862, when the period of enlistment expired. He then became a private trooper in the Scotland Neck Rifles; and eight or ten months later he was transferred to the Sixty-first Regiment, North Carolina Infantry, as quartermaster sergeant. He was on duty with this command until the surrender of Johnston's army.

Lieut. William Emmett Kyle enlisted at the first call to service in the famous First Regiment of Volunteers, under Col. D. H. Hill, and shared the service of that command at Big Bethel. After the disbandment of that regiment, he entered the Fifty-second Regiment of State Troops, and was commissioned lieutenant of Company B. With this regiment, in Pettigrew's brigade, he fought in the Army of Northern Virginia, at Franklin, Hanover Junction, Gettysburg, Hagerstown, Falling Waters, Bristow Station, Culpeper, Mine Run, the Wilderness, Spottsylvania Courthouse, Cold Harbor, Petersburg, Drewry's Bluff, Hatcher's Run, Southerland's Station, Reams Station, Amelia Courthouse, and Farmville, and he surrendered at Appomattox, April 9, 1865. Lieutenant Kyle was wounded three times—at Gettysburg, Spottsylvania Courthouse, and Petersburg—in the head, hip, and leg, and was taken prisoner at Petersburg, but managed to escape a few hours later. At the time of the surrender at Appomattox he was in command of the sharpshooters of MacRae's brigade.

Col. William Lamb came to Wilmington with General Anderson, and at first was quartermaster. His great efficiency caused him to be elected colonel of the Thirty-sixth Regiment, which was formed of ten artillery companies for local defense. On July 4, 1862, he was assigned to the command of Confederate Point, succeeding Major Hedrick. He advanced the construction of Fort Fisher, greatly enlarging and strengthening the works and making it, by 1865, one of the strongest fortifications in the world. In particular he constructed the Mound Battery, of a great height, commanding the inlet and intended to protect the blockade runners and to keep the port open, both of these objects being successfully accomplished. He was at every point a most efficient officer, and his defense when the fort was assaulted in 1865 was heroic.

As a man Colonel Lamb was of the most attractive personality. A comrade says of him: "Lamb was one of the most lovable men in existence, a fine, dashing young Confederate officer." After the war he returned to Norfolk, where he lived for many years an active, useful life.

John R. Latta was adjutant of the Fifty-first North Carolina Regiment, organized at Wilmington, April 13, 1862. About December 1, this regiment was on picket duty near New Bern, and was under fire for the first time near Goldsboro on December 17.

In February, 1863, the Fifty-first Regiment proceeded to

Charleston, thence to Savannah, and later camped on James Island, returning to Wilmington on May 1, along with the other regiments of Clingman's brigade. About July 1, the regiment was sent to Morris Island as a part of the garrison for Battery Wagner. Remaining at Charleston until November 24, it returned to North Carolina, and was stationed at Foster's Mill in Martin County. On January 5, 1864, the regiment went to Petersburg, but later in the month it returned to North Carolina, and engaged in a sharp skirmish at Bachelor's Creek, driving the enemy into New Bern. On May 12, the Fifty-first marched to Drewry's Bluff, and on the 18th and 19th to Cold Harbor, where on June 1 the Battle of Cold Harbor was fought.

From August 19 to December 24, the Fifty-first Regiment was engaged in meeting a raiding party operating on the Wilmington and Weldon Railroad, and in assaulting Fort Harrison; after which it proceeded to North Carolina, where it was needed on account of Butler's threatening Fort Fisher. After the fall of Fort Fisher, the regiment went to Kinston, where it engaged in three days' fighting, March 7, 8, and 9, 1865. The advance of the enemy from Wilmington and the near approach of Sherman's army from Fayetteville caused it to proceed to Bentonville, where the Confederate forces met and checked Sherman. The regiment surrendered with Johnston's army at Bush Hill, and was paroled May 2, 1865. Adjutant Latta was with the regiment from the beginning to the end, without once returning home, having participated in the campaigns mentioned above.

Lewis Leon, a well known resident of Wilmington and a veteran of the Confederate States service, was born in Mecklenburg, Germany, November 27, 1841. Three years later he was brought by his parents to New York City, whence he moved to Charlotte in 1858, and engaged in mercantile pursuits as a clerk. Becoming a member of the Charlotte Grays, he entered the active service of that command, going to the camp of instruction at Raleigh on April 21, 1861. The Grays were assigned to Col. D. H. Hill's regiment, the First, as Company C, and took part in the Battle of Big Bethel, in which Private Leon was a participant. At the expiration of the six months' enlistment of the Bethel Regiment, he reënlisted in Company B, Capt. Harvey White, of the Fifty-first Regiment, commanded by Col. William Owen. He shared the service of this regiment in its subsequent honorable career, fighting at Gettysburg, Bristow Station, Mine Run, and the Wilderness, receiving a slight wound at Gettysburg, but not allowing it to interfere with his duty. During the larger part of his service he was a sharpshooter.

On the 5th or 6th of May, 1864, the sharpshooters of his regiment were much annoyed by one of the Federal sharpshooters who had a long-range rifle and who had climbed up a tall tree, from which he could pick off the men, though sheltered by stumps and stones, himself out of range of their guns. Private Leon concluded that "this thing had to be stopped," and taking advantage of every knoll, hollow, and stump, he crawled near enough for his rifle to reach, and took a "pop" at this disturber of the peace, who came tumbling down. Upon running up to his victim, Leon discovered him to be a Canadian Indian, and clutching his scalp lock, he dragged him back to the Confederate line.

At the Battle of the Wilderness he was captured, and from that time until June, 1865, he was a prisoner of war at Point Lookout and Elmira, N. Y. Upon being paroled he visited his parents in New York City, and then worked his way back to North Carolina. He is warmly regarded by his comrades of Cape Fear Camp, U. C. V., and has served several terms as its adjutant. When Col. James T. Morehead prepared a sketch of his regiment, the Fifty-third, Private Leon furnished him with a copy of a diary which he had kept from the organization of the regiment up to the 5th of May, 1864, when he was captured.

Richard F. Langdon was one of the second lieutenants of Company E (New Hanover County), First Regiment North Carolina Troops, and was subsequently appointed captain and quartermaster of the Third North Carolina Infantry.

Capt. Thomas C. Lewis became a member of the Wilmington Rifle Guards and went on duty with that organization early in the conflict. When it became Company I of the Eighth Regiment he was appointed a sergeant, and after the reënlistment in 1862 he served as quartermaster sergeant until the Battle of Second Manassas, when he became second lieutenant of his company. At this battle he received a severe wound in the hip which disabled him for half a year. Upon rejoining his command he was promoted to be captain. He served with his company until he was captured in the disaster to Johnston's division at Spottsylvania Courthouse. He was confined at Fort

Delaware and shared the bitter experience of the 600 officers held under fire at Morris Island. He was not released until June, 1865. It is much to the credit of Captain Lewis' memory, that, although efforts were made by his Northern kinsmen to induce him to take the oath of allegiance while he was a prisoner at Fort Delaware, he manfully refused and remained a prisoner of war until the final surrender.

Capt. J. W. Lippitt was captain of Company G, Fifty-first Regiment, North Carolina Troops, and commanded the regiment at the surrender at Bush Hill.

Maj. Charles W. McClammy joined a cavalry company commanded by Captain Newkirk at the beginning of hostilities in 1861, and was elected lieutenant of this organization. This company did good service in eastern North Carolina, among its achievements being the capture of a gunboat of the enemy which had grounded in New River in Onslow County. Upon the resignation of Captain Newkirk, Lieutenant McClammy was promoted to the captaincy. His subsequent gallant career is well described in the following extract from an address delivered by Colonel Moore: "From the time he gave his services to his State and country, he was all enthusiasm and dash, and never lost an opportunity to do his best. In nearly every fight in which our regiment was engaged he was present in glorious service. His services were so meritorious that Colonel Baker, before his capture, spoke of wanting to promote him. When he was promoted, he was the ninth captain in rank and one of the youngest, if not the very youngest. He was complimented in general orders for gallant services in battles on the White Oak and Charles City Road."

During the Holden-Kirk War, in 1870, favored by the local factions and divisions of the dominant Republicans, Major McClammy and Capt. Samuel A. Ashe were elected to the Assembly, and became leaders in the important work of that body, remedying many of the excesses of the Reconstruction period, impeaching and deposing the Governor, pacifying the State, and measurably unifying the discordant elements of the white people of the State. Many years then elapsed before New Hanover had another Democratic representative in the Assembly. Later, Major McClammy represented the Cape Fear district in the Congress of the United States.

William Dougald McMillan enlisted in the spring of 1861, at the age of sixteen years, in the Topsail Rifles, with which he served one year on the coast. In the spring of 1862 he became a member of Rankin's heavy artillery; but, after a few months' service, he provided a substitute for that command and volunteered as a private in the Fifty-first Regiment of Infantry, in which he served in 1863 as sergeant major, and during 1864-65, while able for duty, as acting adjutant. His regiment was attached to Clingman's brigade and did gallant service in North Carolina and Virginia. He shared its fortunes in battle at Plymouth, Bermuda Hundred, Drewry's Bluff, Cold Harbor, Port Walthall Junction, in the trenches at Petersburg and the fighting on the Weldon Railroad, and at Fort Harrison and the Crater. He was slightly wounded at Drewry's Bluff, Second Cold Harbor, Bermuda Hundred, and Petersburg, and seriously at Fort Harrison. He was last in battle in the defense of Fort Fisher. He surrendered at High Point in the spring of 1865.

Alexander MacRae: Shortly after the outbreak of the war in 1861, the Legislature of North Carolina, coöperating with the Confederate Government in defending the entrance to the Cape Fear River, passed an act authorizing the formation of a battalion of heavy artillery, to be composed of three companies. One of the companies was raised by Capt. Alexander MacRae, of Wilmington. Captain MacRae had been president of the Wilmington and Weldon Railroad Company, and was then well advanced in age. Captain MacRae's company was on duty at Fort Anderson and at Fort Fisher. In 1863, four companies were organized into a battalion, with Alexander MacRae as major, the companies being known as Companies A, B, C, and D, of the First Battalion of Heavy Artillery. This, with the Thirty-sixth and Fortieth Regiments, and attached companies, formed Hebert's brigade. After participating in the defense of the Lower Cape Fear, this brigade returned to Goldsboro and fought at Bentonville. Major MacRae was paroled in May, 1865.

Henry MacRae: The Eighth Regiment, North Carolina State Troops, was organized at Camp Macon, near Warrenton, N. C., in August and September, 1861, and Henry MacRae was commissioned captain of Company C. Captain MacRae died while in service.

Capt. Walter G. MacRae, a gallant North Carolina soldier, was born in Wilmington, January 27, 1841. He was educated in New England, entering a private school in Boston in 1856,

22

and was graduated from the English High School in that city in 1860, receiving the Franklin medal. He then studied law at the Harvard Law School until the outbreak of hostilities in 1861, when he returned home to fight for his State. Joining the Eighth North Carolina, he accompanied it to South Carolina, and a few months later was transferred to the heavy artillery and stationed at Fort Fisher. Subsequently he became a member of McNeill's Partisan Rangers and, after an adventurous career of thirteen months with that command, joined Company C of the Seventh North Carolina Infantry, with a commission as lieutenant. From that time he was in command of his company, with promotion to captain after the Battle of Gettysburg. Among the engagements in which he participated were the encounters at Thompson's Bridge, on the Neuse River, the skirmish near Pollocksville, and the Battle of Chancellorsville, where he was slightly wounded in the right thigh. Afterwards, he was in command of three companies of skirmishers during the fighting on the Rappahannock River. At Gettysburg he was in battle three days, and on the evening of the third day received a severe wound in the left thigh. While being carried to Richmond he was sick three weeks with fever at Newton, Va., and on reaching the Confederate Capital he was granted a furlough for forty days. In May, 1864, he participated in the death grapple of the armies in the Wilderness and had the misfortune to be captured. He was held at Fort Delaware, and in the following August was one of the 600 officers placed under fire at Morris Island, thence being returned to Fort Delaware and held until the close of hostilities.

Gen. William MacRae was a man of commanding gifts, but very strong prejudices. The severity of his discipline in his regiment was universally known. He was elected lieutenant colonel of the Fifteenth Regiment, and afterwards, on June 22, 1864, was appointed brigadier general and assigned to the command of Kirkland's brigade. An officer of the regiment speaking of General MacRae, said: "General MacRae soon won the confidence and admiration of the brigade, both officers and men. His voice was like that of a woman; he was small in person and quick in action. History has never done him justice. He could place his command in position quicker and infuse more of his fighting qualities into his men than any other officer I ever saw. His presence with his troops seemed to dispel all fear and to inspire every one with a desire for the fray. The brigade remained under his command until the surrender. General MacRae, on being assigned to the brigade, changed the physical expression of the whole command in less than two weeks, and gave the men infinite faith in him and in themselves which was never lost, not even when they grounded arms at Appomattox."

General MacRae distinguished himself in the Battle of Reams Station, August 25, when with a small force he captured several flags and cannon, killed a large number of the enemy, and took 2,100 prisoners. He was one of the best of Lee's brigadiers and won a most enviable reputation.

Capt. Robert B. MacRae was captain of Company C (New Hanover County), Seventh Regiment, and was wounded in the Battle of Hanover Courthouse, May 27, 1862. Colonel Haywood was wounded in the Battle of Second Manassas, and Captain MacRae took command of the regiment, and right gallantly did he discharge the duties imposed upon him. In this battle he was severely wounded. Later, he was promoted to be major of the regiment.

MacRae's battalion, commanded by Maj. James C. MacRae, was better known as the Eighteenth Battalion. It was organized in the summer and fall of 1863 for the protection of the counties of western North Carolina against the bushwhackers and partisan leaders. No general engagement between the whole force and the enemy ever occurred, but there were frequent encounters between the detached companies and parties of bushwhackers who infested the mountains. There were many stirring adventures and brave and venturesome acts by these men, whose history ought to have been better preserved.

Capt. Robert M. McIntire, of Rocky Point, raised a cavalry company in the spring of 1862, afterwards known as Company C, Fourth Regiment of Cavalry. He furnished sabres, saddles, and twelve horses, and he was elected first lieutenant, while his uncle, Dr. Andrew McIntire, became captain. In September, 1863, Lieutenant McIntire was promoted to be captain of his company.

The service of Company C was first near Suffolk, Va., and then in eastern North Carolina. It was a part of the force that in December, 1862, repelled Foster's army, which threatened to capture Goldsboro, and pursued it until the Federal column found shelter in New Bern. Some months later the regiment was ordered to Virginia and, along with the Fifth North Carolina Cavalry, formed Robertson's cavalry brigade, which was a part of the great cavalry division under the command of that brilliant and dashing leader, Gen. J. E. B. Stuart.

Company C shared all the vicissitudes and endured all the hardships of the Gettysburg campaign. Its history is a part of the history of the regiment. At Middleburg it struck the First Rhode Island Regiment, and "then commenced a series of cavalry battles continuing through several days, in which the regiment was an active participant, suffering great loss in killed, wounded, and captured." Then, on the 21st of June, near Upperville, "the fighting became desperate, often hand to hand, with severe loss. * * * All the companies were engaged in this fight and sustained losses."

The Fourth Regiment passed through Hagerstown, and on July 1, reached Chambersburg, Pennsylvania, and then moved towards Carlisle, but soon hurried to Gettysburg, arriving on the morning of the 3d, when, at once becoming engaged, it charged and routed the Federal Cavalry. But this hard contest was the end of Captain McIntire's fine, active career. Like many others, he fell into the enemy's hands at South Mountain, Pennsylvania, and, along with Colonel Kenan and hundreds of other brave soldiers of the Cape Fear, he suffered all the terrible hardships of a long captivity on Johnson's Island. It was not until the war had virtually closed, March 15, 1865, that he was paroled.

John C. McIlhenny was a first lieutenant in Company E, Light Artillery, Tenth Regiment, North Carolina Troops; a fine officer.

Thomas Hall McKoy, of Wilmington, entered the army early in the war and saw active service throughout the campaigns of the Branch-Lane brigade, of which he was one of the two commissaries, with rank of major.

His devotion to the cause, and his eminence as a merchant of Wilmington are worthy of honorable mention. He engaged in the mercantile business at the close of hostilities and died some years ago, respected and honored by his friends and associates.

Dr. James F. McRee, jr., was a surgeon in the Third North Carolina Infantry, and was faithful and well beloved. He was commissioned May 16, 1861, from New Hanover County.

Sergt. Maj. Robert McRee, son of Dr. James F. McRee, jr., was killed at Spottsylvania Courthouse; a gallant soldier.

Henry C. McQueen was born in Lumberton, North Carolina, July 16, 1846. His ancestors were of the Highland Scotch who adhered with romantic loyalty to the cause of the Pretender, and after his final defeat at Culloden, emigrated to America, where their descendants have been distinguished and widely known. Enlisting when a mere lad as a private in the First North Carolina Battery, Henry McQueen, by the faithful discharge of every duty devolving upon him, won the esteem and admiration of all his comrades. On the 15th of January, 1865, when Fort Fisher fell, he was wounded and captured, remaining in prison until the close of the war.

His business career, which has been one of uninterrupted honor and success, began in Wilmington, in January, 1866. In 1869 he entered the employ of Williams & Murchison, in New York, and twelve years later became a partner in this firm. In 1899 he became president of the Murchison National Bank, of Wilmington, and its success, which has been unexcelled in the financial history of the State, has been due in large measure to his exceptional ability and superior management. From its organization in 1900 until he resigned in 1915, he was president of the People's Savings Bank, and he is still chairman of its Board of Directors. Under his wise control, this bank has reached a degree of prosperity which makes it a marvel to the public. The same success has marked his presidency of the Bank of Duplin, at Wallace, North Carolina, which he helped to organize. He served two terms as president of the Chamber of Commerce, was for many years commissioner of the Sinking Fund of Wilmington and chairman of its Board of Audit and Finance. At present he is president of the Carolina Insurance Company and vice president of the Jefferson Standard Life Insurance Company, which is the largest insurance company in the South and which has kept millions of dollars in this section.

A man of dignity, gentleness, courtesy, modesty, and unselfishness, Mr. McQueen has the most attractive personality, while his unswerving integrity, moral firmness, and frank sincerity have won for him universal confidence and respect. He is a member of the First Presbyterian Church of Wilmington and one of its ruling elders.

In 1871, he married Miss Mary Agnes Hall, a daughter of Avon E. Hall, of Fayetteville, and until her death in January, 1904, their life together was completely happy, with no discordant note.

Capt. Eugene S. Martin was fourth sergeant of the Wilmington Rifle Guards, a company formed before the war and which entered service on April 15, 1861, on the occupation of Fort Caswell. Captain Martin was assigned to duty as sergeant major, and afterwards as adjutant of the post, and served as such until June 20, 1861, when he resigned the office and returned to his company. In the meantime, the Eighth Regiment was formed, and the Wilmington Rifle Guards became Company I of that regiment, Captain Martin being second sergeant, in which capacity he served until he was mustered out, April 15, 1862. He was commissioned in May, 1862, first lieutenant of artillery, and assigned to Company A, First North Carolina Battalion of Heavy Artillery.

In the spring of 1864 he was detached from the company and ordered to Fort Caswell as ordnance officer, where he served until the fort was evacuated and blown up in January, 1865, upon the fall of Fort Fisher. He served at Fort Anderson during the bombardment in February, 1865, as ordnance officer, and at the Battles of Town Creek, Kinston, and Bentonville, as ordnance officer of Hagood's brigade; and afterwards was ordered to the brigade of Junior Reserves, as ordnance officer, to assist in organizing that brigade. He never received his commission of captain, but ranked as captain during the time he was at Fort Caswell and until the end of the war. He surrendered in Wilmington in May, 1865, to General Hawley, commanding that post, and afterwards took the oath of allegiance.

Clarence D. Martin, a younger brother, left the University in 1861 and enlisted in Company C, Thirteenth North Carolina Regiment, serving as sergeant of his company. He was wounded at the Battle of Williamsburg in May, 1862, and carried to a hospital in Richmond. Later, he was removed to Kenansville, where his father was residing temporarily, and died there on his eighteenth birthday, June 27, 1862. His comrades and officers praised him as a fine soldier, and his memory is cherished by all who knew him.

John E. Matthews: When Fort Sumter was bombarded by Beauregard, Dr. Matthews was a member of the Elm City cadets, of New Bern, which were ordered at once to take possession of Fort Macon. He remained there for two months under Col. C. C. Tew, who was in command, and returned with the company to New Bern, where he remained until ordered to Garysburg, when the company became a part of the Second Regiment, North Carolina Troops, under Colonel Tew. Dr. Matthews served continuously and actively with this regiment throughout the war.

After the Battle of Fredericksburg, in December, 1862, the first corps of sharpshooters for Ramseur's brigade was organized, which was the beginning of this branch of the service, and Dr. Matthews was made second sergeant of the corps, participating at Chancellorsville, Gettysburg, and Kelly's Ford, where, while on picket duty, he was captured. He was confined at Point Lookout, but was exchanged in February, 1865, returned to duty at Petersburg, and took part in the subsequent battles around Petersburg and on the retreat at Sailor's Creek, where he was again captured and again confined at Point Lookout until July 1, 1865, months after the surrender.

Thomas D. Meares has the honor of being one of the boy soldiers of North Carolina during the closing scenes of the great struggle. In December, 1864, being about sixteen years of age, he enlisted as a private in the Junior Reserves, but within a few weeks his soldierly qualities led to his selection as a courier on the staff of Gen. Wade Hampton, between Hillsboro and Durham, and he began a service as courier for that gallant cavalry commander which continued until the end of the war.

Col. Oliver Pendleton Meares was captain of the Wilmington Rifle Guards, which was one of the companies that occupied Fort Caswell on April 16, 1861. This company was composed of all the best young men of Wilmington who were not members of the older company, the Wilmington Light Infantry. At one time it had on its rolls more than a hundred men, ranging from sixteen to twenty-two years of age, and only one married man among them.

On the formation of the Eighth Regiment of Volunteers, the Rifle Guards became Company I of that Regiment. The organization was effected at Camp Wyatt on July 1, 1861, and Colonel Radcliffe was elected colonel and Oliver P. Meares, lieutenant colonel. The Rifle Guards, like the Wilmington Light Infantry, furnished a large number of officers to other organizations of the State.

On the expiration of the twelve months for which the volunteer companies had originally enlisted, the regiment was reorganized, and Colonel Meares retired as lieutenant colonel. On the formation of the ten regiments of State Troops, enlisted for three years, or the war, they were called the First Regiment, North Carolina State Troops, and so on; and the Eighth Regiment Volunteers became the Eighteenth, and so on.

In August, 1862, Colonel Meares became commissary of the Sixty-first Regiment. After the war he became a judge. Wilmington never had a truer son than Colonel Meares, and his memory is justly revered.

Capt. E. G. Meares, of Company D, Third North Carolina State Troops, was killed in the Battle of Sharpsburg. He was "a good soldier, a brave man, discharging his duty under all conditions." He was a young man of fine character and was greatly lamented.

Capt. James I. Metts was born at Kinston, N. C., March 16, 1842, but has lived in Wilmington since he was six years old. Early in 1861 he left the State University to enlist in the Rifle Guards, organized in anticipation of war, and on April 15 was with his company in the seizure of Fort Caswell. Soon afterwards his company was assigned to the Eighth Regiment, and he was made corporal and was one of the color guard of the regiment when it was ordered to Coosawhatchie, S. C. After this he was given charge of the regimental colors, which he carried until the twelve months' term of service expired. Reënlisting, he became fifth sergeant of Company G, Third Regiment, Col. Gaston Meares. His bravery and ability won for him distinction in the Seven Days' Battle, and were specially manifested at Cold Harbor, where he re-formed part of the regiment, and when in command of a detail in Chickahominy Swamp. After Malvern Hill, where he was among those receiving the last orders of Col. Gaston Meares, he was promoted to orderly sergeant, and was assigned to the main work of drilling the recruits for his company. During the Maryland campaign he was disabled by illness, but rejoined his company at Bunker Hill, and in the promotions following the death at Sharpsburg of Captain Rhodes and First Lieutenant Quince, Sergeant Metts became senior second lieutenant. At Winchester he was detailed as commissary of the regiment, and after Front Royal he discharged the duties of adjutant. His coolness at Fredericksburg attracted the attention of superior officers. Afterwards he was in the hospital at Richmond ill of pneumonia, but joined his regiment in the fighting around Winchester, where his brigade, Stuart's, did much at Jordan Springs towards the victory over Milroy.

In the Confederate assault at Culp's Hill, on the evening of the second day at Gettysburg, he led his men within seventy-five yards of the Federal breastworks, and here, while hotly engaged, a boy soldier approached him and said, "Lieutenant, my father is killed." He could only answer, "Well, we can not help it," and the brave boy, replying, "No, we can not help it," turned and resumed firing as rapidly as he could at the enemy, which he continued to do until exhausted, and the next day his face was black with powder. In this engagement, while standing with Lieut. Col. William M. Parsley, Adjutant James, and Capt. Edward H. Armstrong, three as brave men as ever stepped to the tap of a drum, Lieutenant Metts was wounded in the left lung, and experienced excruciating pain as he was hauled two miles over a rough road in an ambulance. But for a Sister of Charity, he would have died in the field hospital. Many people from Baltimore and elsewhere visited the wounded Confederates at Gettysburg, bringing clothing and delicacies of food. An elderly lady, accompanied by two charming young lady friends, finding Lieutenant Metts without a sheet, removed her petticoat, tore it in two, and pinning it together, said, "Don't mind me, boys, I'm a mother, and he shall have a good sheet tomorrow." The same kindness followed him in the general camp hospital and in the West Building Hospital in Baltimore, where he found his kinsmen, Col. Thomas S. Kenan and James G. Kenan, also wounded on Culp's Hill. He was transferred to Johnson's Island, Lake Erie, where for thirteen months Colonel Kenan was his bunkmate. Their sufferings here during the winter were very severe, with cruel guards, insufficient food, scanty clothing, in houses neither ceiled nor plastered, and with but one stove for about sixty prisoners. During the night of January 1, 1864, when the mercury registered twenty degrees below zero and even the guard was forced to take shelter, Maj. John Winsted and three or four others escaped and made their way across the ice to the mainland, but the excessive cold prevented all but Major Winsted from going farther. He reached Canada, and returned to the Confederacy on a blockade runner. In August, 1864, Lieutenant Metts was selected as one of the most enfeebled and delicate of the prisoners, for exchange, and he soon reached Richmond, rejoicing in a new lease of life, for he had been assured that he could not survive another winter on Johnson's Island. He found that Captain Armstrong, an amiable gentleman, a fine scholar, and one of the bravest of men, had been killed at Spottsylvania, and he had been promoted to the captaincy of his company, which he took command of, together with Company E, and served in Cox's brigade, Grimes's division, notwithstanding his delicate health, until detailed to serve on the staff of Major General Grimes as special instructor of division. The night before arms were stacked at Appomattox he accompanied a band from division headquarters to serenade General Lee, who was too much affected to say much, but gave each of the boys a warm pressure of the hand and an affectionate good-bye. Joining his family, who had lost all of their property, Captain Metts went to Wilmington to begin the struggle of civil life. His first engagement was with two Federal sutlers, who treated him kindly. Since then his exertions have been rewarded with the success that is the just desert of a brave patriot.

Dr. James A. Miller, surgeon of the Eighth (Eighteenth) Regiment, became surgeon of the brigade and then division surgeon, and finally district surgeon of the district of the Cape Fear.

Capt. John Miller, a son of Mr. Tom Miller, commanded A. D. Moore's battery after Moore's promotion to the colonelcy of the Sixty-sixth Regiment. He moved to California.

Capt. Julius Walker Moore was instrumental in raising a company of cavalry early in the war. Later, he became captain of a cavalry company raised chiefly in Onslow County, called the "Humphrey Troop," and borne on the roll as Company H, Forty-first Regiment. Captain Moore, along with a considerable number of his company, fell into the hands of the enemy, and was confined in Fort Delaware and on James Island until the end of the war, when he returned home broken in health and fortune, and he soon died at Charlotte.

James Osborne Moore became a purser in the Confederate Navy. After the war he became a civil engineer. He died at Charlotte. A still younger brother, Alexander Duncan Moore, enlisted in Company I, Eighth Regiment of Volunteers, and was sergeant major of the regiment when he fell on one of the battlefields in Virginia. He was a bright young man, with the finest characteristics, and was imbued with the noble spirit of his Revolutionary forefathers.

Charles D. Myers was one of the members of the Wilmington Light Infantry of ante-bellum times, and served in that company until he was made adjutant of the Eighth Regiment,

North Carolina Troops. He subsequently served upon the staff of Gen. Samuel G. French, who commanded the Confederate forces in the vicinity of Wilmington, with the rank of captain.

Kenneth McKenzie Murchison[1] was born near Fayetteville, February 18, 1831, the son of Duncan Murchison, who was born in Manchester, Cumberland County, May 20, 1801, and the grandson of Kenneth McKenzie Murchison, for whom he was named, and who came to this country from Scotland in 1773. Duncan Murchison became prominent in the planting and manufacture of cotton.

Colonel Murchison, the second son of Duncan, was graduated at Chapel Hill in 1853, after which he was engaged in business pursuits in New York City and Wilmington until the spring of 1861, when he disposed of his business in the North, assisted in the organization of a company at Fayetteville, and entered the service as second lieutenant. He commanded Company C, of the Eighth Regiment, which was captured at Roanoke Island, a disaster which Lieutenant Murchison escaped by his fortunate absence on military detail. He then organized another company in Cumberland County, which was assigned to the Fifty-fourth Regiment, with himself as captain. Upon the organization of the regiment he was elected major, was soon promoted to lieutenant colonel, and after the death of Col. J. C. S. McDowell, at Fredericksburg, became the colonel of the regiment. He was especially commended by Gen. E. M. Law, commander of his brigade, for gallant service at Fredericksburg. He commanded his regiment at Chancellorsville, and in the Battle of Winchester against Milroy. Subsequently he was ordered to convey the prisoners taken on that occasion to Richmond, after which he returned to Winchester and served in guarding the wagon trains of Lee's army. On July 6, in command of his regiment, he gallantly repulsed the enemy's advance on Williamsport. He served in Hoke's brigade during the subsequent operations in Virginia, and when the brigade was cut off by the enemy at Rappahannock Station, November 7, 1863, he was among those captured. He was held a prisoner of war on Johnson's Island, Lake Erie, from that time until July, 1865, an imprisonment of twenty months. Upon his release he resumed business in New York, and formed a brief partnership under the firm name of Murray & Murchison, but dissolved it

---

[1]Sketch by Col. Alfred M. Waddell, in the *Biographical History of North Carolina.*

in June, 1866, and established the firm of Murchison & Company, the members of the firm being himself, his brother, David R. Murchison, George W. Williams, of Wilmington, and John D. Williams, of Fayetteville. This firm did a very large and profitable business for some years, the New York house being managed by Colonel Murchison, under the name of Murchison & Company. The Wilmington house was known as Williams & Murchison, and the Fayetteville connection was known as John D. Williams & Company.

Colonel Murchison lived in New York after the war, but generally spent the winter in North Carolina. In the year 1880 he bought the old historic plantation called "Orton," the family seat of "King" Roger Moore, situated about sixteen miles below Wilmington, on the west side of the Cape Fear, and the southernmost of all the old rice plantations on that river, and he expended a large amount of money in restoring it to its former condition and improving it in various ways to satisfy his taste. Within its boundary was the colonial parish church and churchyard of St. Philip's, and this interesting ruin with its consecrated grounds was conveyed in fee simple by Colonel Murchison and his brother, David R. Murchison, to the diocese of North Carolina. It is now carefully preserved by the North Carolina Society of Colonial Dames of America. Orton has always been a paradise of sportsmen, and the colonel was very fond of hunting. It was his custom to bring some of his friends down from the North every winter, and give them the opportunity to enjoy the old-time hospitality, which he dispensed with a lavish hand. It was here that those who loved him best and who were loved by him spent their happiest days. The restful seclusion of this grandest of all colonial homes, with its broad acres and primeval forests, was most grateful to him and to his intimate associates after the storm and stress of war and the subsequent struggles of business life. It was here that the austerity of worldly contact was relaxed and the manifold humanities of a gentle, kindly life unfolded. He never spoke of his own exploits, nor did he willingly recall the horrors of the four years' war. He loved to roam the woods with his faithful dogs, to linger for hours in the secluded sanctuary of the game he sought so eagerly, and the sight of his triumphant return from an exciting chase, with Reynard at the saddlebow, surrounded by his yelping pack of English hounds, would rouse the dullest of his guests to exclamations of delight.

Colonel Murchison was also the joint owner with his brother David of the celebrated Caney River hunting preserve, in the wildest part of the mountains of North Carolina, where they spent the summers of several happy years along the fourteen miles of trout streams of icy waters. Within this splendid domain is some of the most picturesque of American mountain scenery, including Mount Mitchell and the neighboring peaks. It is the scene of big Tom Wilson's hunting and trapping exploits, and Wilson still survives as the custodian of the magnificent forest and stream, to tell the curious stranger in his own peculiar way how he found the body of the great naturalist whose name Mount Mitchell bears.

Colonel Murchison's striking personality was likened by those who knew him to that of the great German chancellor, Prince Bismarck, in his younger years. The commanding figure and uncompromising expression, which characterized his outward life, suggested a military training beyond that of his war experience, and this was in strange contrast to his inner life, a knowledge of which disclosed a sympathetic tenderness for all suffering or afflicted humanity. He preferred and practiced the simple life; his wants were few and easily supplied. A notable characteristic was his exceeding devotion to his five surviving children; he was proud of them and of their loyal love to him, and he made them his constant companions. He gave to worthy charities with a liberal and unostentatious hand. His patriotic spirit responded quickly to every public emergency, and his local pride was manifested in the building and equipment, at a great expense, of "The Orton," when a good hotel was needed in Wilmington, and when no one else would venture the investment.

During the last fifteen years of his honored life, Colonel Murchison gradually withdrew from the activities of strenuous business cares, and with the first frosts of autumn resumed control at Orton Plantation. He left it in June of 1904 in the vigor and spirits of abounding health, to meet, a few days later, the sudden call of the Messenger of Death, whom he had never feared. So lived and died a man of whom it may be said, "We ne'er shall see his like again." He was an example of splendid physical manhood, of broad experience, of unyielding integrity, pure in heart and in speech, with the native modesty of a woman and the courage of a lion. He was especially sympathetic and generous to his negro servitors, who regarded him with loving veneration.

Another of the long line of proprietors of Orton, where the soft south breezes, which brought from their island home the first Barbadian settlers, bring to the listening ear the murmured miserere of the sea, has "crossed over the river to rest under the shade of the trees."

David Reid Murchison[1] was born at Holly Hill, Manchester, N. C., December 5, 1837. He spent his boyhood days at Holly Hill and received his early education in Cumberland County. Later, he was a student at the University of Virginia. In 1860 he commenced his business career as a member of the firm of Eli Murray & Co., of Wilmington, which was interrupted in 1861 by the commencement of the War between the States. He enlisted at once in the Seventh North Carolina Regiment and remained with that command one year, when he was transferred to the Fifty-fourth North Carolina Regiment and assigned to duty with the rank of captain. With this regiment he saw active service, and his conduct always reflected honor and credit upon him as a brave and efficient officer. He was taken from the Fifty-fourth North Carolina Regiment and made inspector general of the Commissary Department of North Carolina, having been appointed to this position by President Davis on account of his executive ability, which was then, despite his early age, recognized as of a very high order. The change from active service to his new duties was very distasteful to him and against his wishes. Brave himself, and born of heroic blood, with a firmness and fortitude which faltered in no crisis, he had an apitude for war, and doubtless would have risen high in the profession of arms had he been allowed to see active service in the field to the close of the war, as was his wish and desire. One of his chief characteristics, however, was a high sense of duty, which always prompted him to do whatever work was before him as best he knew how. He filled the position to which he was assigned until the close of the war with great credit to himself and benefit to the soldiers of North Carolina. His papers for advancement to the grade of major were prepared, but were not executed because of the close of hostilities.

He was a singularly brave man, devoid of fear. Cool and self-reliant under all circumstances, he gave confidence and strength to the weak and timid. He was generous, full of sympathy and of kindness to the poor and needy, to whom he

---

[1]Sketch by Major C. M. Stedman.

gave with an open and liberal hand. He was a sincere man, abhoring deception and hypocrisy and looking with scorn upon all that was base and mean. He died in New York, where he had gone for medical treatment, February 22, 1882. He was in the full meridian of his intellectual powers and his nobility of mind and heart was never more clearly manifested than in his last days. He went to his rest, his fortitude unshaken by long-continued and severe suffering, his chief desire to give the least possible pain and trouble to others, solicitous not for himself, but for the happiness of those he loved. His gentleness and self-abnegation were as beautiful as his iron nerve was firm and unyielding. North Carolina has furnished to the world a race of men who by their great qualities have shed lustre upon the State which gave them birth. In the elements of character which constitute true greatness—courage, honor, truth, fidelity, unselfish love of country and humanity—Capt. David Reid Murchison will rank with the best and noblest of her citizens.

He was a man of extraordinary business sagacity, which was made manifest about the year 1880, when, after being appointed receiver of the Carolina Central Railway, he startled the community by buying out the whole road, and he conducted it successfully until his health began to fail, when he sold it at a profit.

Col. John R. Murchison, the oldest of the sons of Duncan Murchison, had a career brilliant with heroic deeds and personal sacrifice. Beloved at home by his fellow-countrymen and upon the field by his devoted followers, as colonel of the Eighth North Carolina Regiment, Clingman's brigade, Hoke's division, he took part in the Battles of Hatteras Inlet and Neuse Bridge, and after camping for two months at Camp Ashe, Old Topsail Sound, he won distinction at Morris Island, and fought so bravely at Plymouth and Drewry's Bluff, that he was recommended for honors, and was promoted to be brigadier general a few hours before his untimely death. In the Battle of Cold Harbor, while personally leading a second charge of his regiment, he was mortally wounded and fell within the enemy's lines. This final sacrifice of his noble life was marked by an armistice between General Grant and General Lee, during which several officers and men of the Eighth Regiment, seeking the body of their beloved commander, were, through a misunderstanding by General Grant, made prisoners and sent to the rear of the Federal Army, and the body of Colonel Murchison was never recovered. The official correspondence on that occasion is as follows:

COLD HARBOR, VA., June 7, 1864—10.30 a. m.

GENERAL R. E. LEE,

    Comdg. Army of Northern Virginia.

I regret that your note of 7 p. m. yesterday should have been received at the nearest corps headquarters to where it was delivered after the hour that had been given for the removal of the dead and wounded had expired. 10.45 p. m. was the hour at which it was received at corps headquarters, and between 11 and 12 it reached my headquarters. As a consequence, it was not understood by the troops of this army that there was a cessation of hostilities for the purpose of collecting the dead and wounded, and none were collected. Two officers and six men of the Eighth and Twenty-fifth North Carolina Regiments, who were out in search of the bodies of officers of their respective regiments, were captured and brought into our lines, owing to this want of understanding. I regret this, but will state that as soon as I learned the fact I directed that they should not be held as prisoners, but must be returned to their comrades. These officers and men having been carelessly brought through our lines to the rear, I have not determined whether they will be sent back the way they came or whether they will be sent by some other route.

Regretting that all my efforts for alleviating the sufferings of wounded men left upon the battlefield have been rendered nugatory, I remain, &c.,

U. S. GRANT,
Lieutenant General.

HEADQUARTERS ARMY OF NORTHERN VIRGINIA,

LIEUT. GEN. U. S. GRANT,   July 7, 1864—2 p. m.

    Commanding U. S. Armies.

GENERAL:—Your note of 10.30 a. m. today has just been received. I regret that my letter to you of 7 p. m. yesterday should have been too late in reaching you to effect the removal of the wounded.

I am willing, if you desire it, to devote the hours between 6 and 8 this afternoon to accomplish that object upon the terms and conditions as set forth in my letter of 7 p. m. yesterday. If this will answer your purpose, and you will send parties from your lines at the hour designated with white flags, I will direct that they be recognized and be permitted to collect the dead and wounded.

I will also notify the officers on my lines that they will be permitted to collect any of our men that may be on the field. I request you will notify me as soon as practicable if this arrangement is agreeable to you. Lieutenant McAllister, Corporal Martin, and two privates of the Eighth North Carolina Regiment, and Lieutenant Hartman, Corpl. T. Kinlaw, and Privates Bass and Grey were sent last night, between the hours of 8 and 10 p. m., for the purpose of recovering the body of

Colonel Murchison, and as they have not returned I presume they are the men mentioned in your letter. I request that they be returned to our lines. Very respectfully, your obedient servant,

R. E. LEE,
General.

June 7, 1864.

Referred to General G. G. Meade, commanding Army of the Potomac. I will notify General Lee that hostilities will cease from 6 to 8 for the purposes mentioned. You may send the officers and men referred to as you deem best. Please return this. U. S. GRANT,
Lieutenant General.

COLD HARBOR, VA., June 7, 1864—5.30 p. m.

GENERAL R. E. LEE,
Commanding Army of Northern Virginia.

Your note of this date just received. It will be impossible for me to communicate the fact of the truce by the hour named by you (6 p. m.), but I will avail myself of your offer at the earliest possible moment, which I hope will not be much after that hour. The officers and men taken last evening are the same mentioned in your note, and will be returned. U. S. GRANT,
Lieutenant General.

Commodore W. T. Muse was an officer in the North Carolina Navy. The State of North Carolina, immediately after the adoption of the ordinance of secession, began the defense of her inland sounds by the construction of forts at Hatteras and Ocracoke Inlets and by the purchase of several small steamers, which were converted into gunboats. Those of her sons who were in the United States Navy tendered their resignations and placed their services at the disposal of their native State; prominent among them being William T. Muse, who was ordered by the Naval and Military Board, of which Warren Winslow was president, to Norfolk, to take charge of, and fit out, as gunboats at the navy yard at Portsmouth the steamers purchased by the State. Commander W. T. Muse sailed from Norfolk, August 2, 1861, with the *Ellis,* arriving off Ocracoke Inlet the 4th. North Carolina's naval force consisted of seven vessels, but she sold them to the Confederate Navy in the fall of 1861, and her naval officers were then transferred to the Confederacy.

A. W. Newkirk was commissioned as captain of Company A (originally known as the "Rebel Rangers"), New Hanover County, Forty-first Regiment, the 19th of October, 1861. A brilliant exploit performed by the Rebel Rangers is reported by Gen. W. H. C. Whiting, commanding the district of Wilming-

23

ton. He says that in November, 1862, Captain Newkirk's cavalry and Captain Adams with a section of a field battery captured a steam gunboat of the enemy on New River. Her crew escaped, but her armament, ammunition, and small arms were captured.

Capt. William Harris Northrop, a prominent business man of Wilmington, who served in the Confederate cause in various capacities throughout the war, was born in that city in 1836, and there reared and educated. In 1855 he became a member of the Wilmington Light Infantry, with which he was on duty before the secession of the State at Fort Caswell, and later at Fort Fisher. In June, 1865, he was commissioned lieutenant and assigned to the Third North Carolina, then stationed at Aquia Creek, on the Potomac. He served in the line about eighteen months and was then commissioned captain quartermaster. After six months of this duty with his regiment, he was transferred to the Second Corps, Engineer Troops, and stationed at Wilmington and vicinity. After the evacuation of that city he was attached to the staff of General Bragg until the surrender. Among the engagements in which he participated were Aquia Creek on the Potomac, the Seven Days' Battle before Richmond, Frederick City, Boonsboro, Sharpsburg, and Bentonville. Both as a company officer and as a staff officer, his service was marked by bravery and entire devotion to the cause. After the close of hostilities Captain Northrop constantly resided at Wilmington.

Capt. W. P. Oldham was captain of Company K, Fortyfourth Regiment, North Carolina Troops. At the Battle of Reams Station Captain Oldham sighted one of the guns repeatedly, and when he saw the effect of his accurate aim upon the masses in front, he was so jubilant that General MacRae, with his usual quiet humor, remarked: "Oldham thinks he is at a ball in Petersburg."

Rev. George Patterson, D.D., of the Protestant Episcopal Church, was commissioned on the 30th day of December, 1862, chaplain of the Third Regiment. He was faithful to the last. He preached in Wilmington for years after the war, and afterwards in Memphis, Tenn., where he recently died.

One of our venerable survivors of war times who retains the respect and admiration of all who know him, and they are legion, is Richard P. Paddison,[1] of Point Caswell, whose mili-

---

[1] Captain Paddison has since died.

tary record is told in his own words. A chapter of his humorous experiences can appropriately be added, as the tragedies of these fearful years of bloodshed were not without a comic point of view.

He tells us that in the month of March, 1861, "this part of North Carolina was wild with excitement and rumors of war, and a public meeting was called at Harrell's Store, in Sampson County, for the purpose of organizing a military company to be tendered the Governor. In a short time an organization was effected, and a man named Taylor was elected captain. At the next meeting they voted to call the company the 'Wild Cat Minute Men.' Next the question came up as to where the company should go. After considerable talk it was voted that the company should remain around Wild Cat as a home protection. There were a number of us, however, who did not take to the Wild Cat idea, and quietly withdrew and marched to Clinton, where a company was being organized by Capt. Frank Faison, called the 'Sampson Rangers,' composed of the flower of the young men of the county. I joined as a private in this company. We had a good time drilling and eating the best the country could afford, and every fellow was a hero in the eyes of some pretty maiden. But this easement was suddenly cut short by orders to go with utmost dispatch to Fort Johnston. The whole town was in excitement. We were ordered to get in marching order, and to my dying day I shall remember that scene—mothers, wives, sisters, and sweethearts all cheering and encouraging their loved ones to go forth and do their duty; such love of country could only be shown by true Southern womanhood. After a good dinner and a sweet farewell under the inspiring strains by the band of 'The Girl I Left Behind Me,' we took up our march to Warsaw, where we boarded the train for Wilmington and arrived before night. We were met by the officials and marched up Front Street to Princess and Second; here we halted and the fun began. On the northeast corner stood a large brick house built for a negro jail and operated, I think, by a Mr. Southerland. We were informed that this was to be our quarters for the night. Now picture in your mind, if you can, a hundred and twenty wealthy young men, most of them Chapel Hill and high-school boys, whose combined wealth could purchase half the city of Wilmington, being forced to sleep in a negro jail. We marched into the house and deposited our luggage, which in after years would have been sufficient for

Stonewall Jackson's army. The rumbling noise of discord and discontent rose rapidly. We held a council of war and informed our officers that we would not submit to quarters in that house. We were to take the steamer next morning at nine o'clock for Fort Johnston. This was rather a critical situation for both officers and men. At this juncture, Judge A. A. McKoy, who was a private, said he would stand sponsor for the boys to be on hand next morning on time. This was accepted, and there was a hot time in the old town that night. Next morning, promptly on time, every man was present. We boarded a river steamer, I think the *Flora Macdonald,* and arrived in good shape at our destination, where we had a good time until the organization of the Twentieth North Carolina Regiment, when our trouble began. Our captain was elected lieutenant colonel, and an order was issued for the election of a captain. The candidates were James D. Holmes and William S. Devane. There was a strong feeling on both sides in the company. The Devane men, of whom I was one, said we would not serve under Holmes. I can not remember how long this trouble lasted, but the matter was carried to Governor Ellis, who settled it by ordering each faction to send out recruiting officers and make two companies, which was done. I was sent out, and had ten recruits in three or four days. Both candidates were elected, Captain Holmes's company going to the Thirtieth Regiment; and Captain Devane's company was detached for quite a long time doing service at Fort Caswell and Fort Johnston. In 1862 the Sixty-seventh Regiment was organized, and Captain Devane was made lieutenant colonel. About this time I was appointed hospital steward by Hon. James A. Sedden, Secretary of War. I remained at Fort Johnston during the epidemic of yellow fever in 1862, and of smallpox in the winter of the same year; after this I was transferred to General Hospital No. 4, Wilmington, which comprised the Seamen's Home building and buildings on the opposite side of Front Street. Thomas M. Ritenour was surgeon and A. E. Wright and Josh Walker, assistant surgeons. This was one of the largest and best equipped hospitals in the State.

"After the fall of Fort Fisher we had orders to send our sick and wounded to Fayetteville and Goldsboro. By the aid of Captain Styron and his assistant, Mr. I. B. Grainger, who was the best organizer and disciplinarian I ever knew, we succeeded in getting all except thirty-two removed to safety. These were so badly wounded that it was impossible to move them. I placed these wounded in ward No. 2 with Mrs. McCauslin, matron, in charge. Supplies were very scarce. Dr. Josh Walker was the last one to leave. He went out on Tuesday night, and Wednesday morning the streets were swarming with Federal soldiers. About 10 a. m. a surgeon came to our hospital and inquired who was in charge. I replied that I was in charge. He said: 'I want you to move everything out. I want this hospital for our use.' I replied that I had nowhere to go, and no way to move. 'You must find a house,' he replied, 'and at once, and report to me at headquarters. I will furnish you with transportation.' I did not stand on the order of my going. I found a house on Fourth Street near Red Cross, owned by David Bunting, whose family had left the city. I made the report, and the Federal surgeon general ordered three ambulances. The transfer was soon made. I wish to state that we had courteous treatment from the authorities, but of course we were very short of supplies. The first genuine treat we had was by Mr. F. W. Foster, who was acting as sanitary agent. He drove up one morning, came in and inquired about the sick, and asked if I would like to have some milk punch for the men. I said, 'Yes,' as it had been a long time since we had had any such luxury. He went out and soon returned with two large pails and a dipper, and personally served to each all they could stand. This he continued to do for several weeks. On one of his visits he asked me if I would like to have some canned goods for the hospital. I replied, 'Yes,' and he said, 'The steamer *General Lyon* is unloading a cargo of hospital supplies. If you will go down there you can get what you want.' I replied that I had no way to get them and no money to hire with. He said, 'I will send you an ambulance; go down and get what you want.' I said, 'Won't you give me an order?' to which he replied, 'No, if any one says anything to you tell them Foster sent you.' The ambulance came. I didn't want any help. The vessel was unloading near where Springer's coal yard is now. We backed up and I began to select what I wanted. I was not at all modest, and thinking that this would be the last haul I would get from Uncle Sam, I loaded to the limit. Strange to say, no questions were asked, and it is safe to say our boys fared well while things lasted. As the men improved they went home, and on the 5th of June I closed the doors. The last hero had gone to rebuild his broken fortunes and I felt a free man once more.

I came out of the army as I had entered it—without one dollar, but with a clear conscience, having performed my duty to my country as I saw it. From April 20, 1861, to June 5, 1865, I never had a furlough or a day's absence from duty.

"I can not close without saying a word about the splendid women of Wilmington for their devotion and attention to our destitute sick and wounded during those trying times. I have tried to recall the names of some of them, but can not do so. I fear few, if any, are living today."

Capt. Elisha Porter, of Company E, Third North Carolina Regiment, served from the beginning of the war up to and including the Battle of Chancellorsville. During that engagement he penetrated within the enemy's breastworks and was bayoneted by a Federal soldier. Finding that he was about to be killed, he attempted to scale the breastworks and succeeded in doing so, but was shot in the thigh and apparently mortally wounded. After the battle he heard the voice of a friend, by whom he was taken to the Confederate field hospital. Dr. Porter survived for many years after the war, but was always crippled.

Joseph Price was one of the first lieutenants in Company H, Fortieth Regiment, which was organized at Bald Head, at the mouth of the Cape Fear River, the 1st of December, 1863, from heavy artillery companies already in the service. Company H was composed principally of Irishmen, and no better or more loyal men or better soldiers could be found in any company. Whether work or fighting was to be done, they were always ready and went wherever ordered. Lieutenant Price's capture of the United States steamer *Water Witch,* by boarding in a night attack, was one of the most brilliant of the Confederate exploits on the water. His modest official report of this affair was characteristic of the man.

Capt. Richard W. Price entered the Confederate service in October, 1864, at the age of seventeen, in the Junior Reserves, afterwards the Seventy-second Regiment. He served chiefly at Fort Fisher, and when the fort fell he was captured and taken a prisoner to Fort Delaware, where he remained until after the general surrender. When the Fort Fisher Survivors' Association, composed of the Blue and the Gray, was organized, Captain Price was made secretary, and held that position to the time of his death.

Capt. Robert G. Rankin was chairman of the Safety Committee before the outbreak of the war. At the beginning of the war he was made quartermaster of Wilmington, and was afterwards made captain of the First Battalion, Heavy Artillery. This battalion went into the Battle of Bentonville with 260 men and came out with 115. Every officer except two was killed, wounded, or captured. Captain Rankin was among the killed, stricken by eight balls.

Capt. John T. Rankin entered the Confederate Army as a private, and at the youthful age of nineteen was made first lieutenant of Company D, First Battalion, North Carolina Heavy Artillery, under Captain McCormick. He was at Fort Fisher during the first battle and was highly complimented by General Whiting for gallantry. During the second battle Captain McCormick was killed and Lieutenant Rankin became captain.

He fought at Fort Anderson, and on February 20, 1865, was wounded in the thigh at Town Creek and taken prisoner. He was treated with great courtesy by Colonel Rundell, of the One Hundredth Ohio Regiment, and carried to the Old Capitol Prison at Washington, where he saw the crowd and commotion caused by the second inauguration of President Lincoln. He was afterwards sent to Fort Delaware, where he remained until released after the war.

Maj. James I. Reilly: General Whiting, in his report of the fall of Fort Fisher, says: "Of Major Reilly, with his battalion of the Tenth North Carolina, who served the guns of the land face during the entire action, I have to say he has added another name to the long list of fields on which he has been conspicuous for indomitable pluck and consummate skill." Colonel Lamb, in his official report, says: "Major Reilly, of the Tenth North Carolina Regiment, discharged his whole duty. To the coolness of Major Reilly we are indebted for the defense of the land face." Maj. William J. Saunders, chief of artillery, says: "I would beg particularly to call attention to the skill displayed by that splendid artillerist, Maj. James Reilly, of the Tenth North Carolina Regiment."

James Reilly was a sergeant in the old United States Army, and was in charge of Fort Johnston, when, on January 10, 1861, it was hastily occupied by some ardent Southerners from Wilmington. After the State seceded he was appointed captain of a light battery and won fame in Virginia. On September 7, 1863, he was promoted to major, and John A. Ramsay became captain of the company. Major Reilly was one of the bravest and most efficient defenders of Fort Fisher.

A. Paul Repiton, a son of Rev. A. Paul Repiton, joined the Corps of Engineers in 1863. He was a man of fine spirit and a very efficient soldier.

C. H. Robinson enlisted early in the war, having given up a good business to respond to the call of his adopted State, and became quartermaster sergeant of the Fifty-first Regiment, North Carolina Troops, in which capacity he served throughout the war.

His regiment was organized at Camp Mangum, near Raleigh, September 18, 1862, Col. J. V. Jordan, commanding; E. R. Liles, lieutenant colonel; J. A. McKoy, major; W. H. Battle, surgeon; John W. Cox, quartermaster; and C. H. Robinson, quartermaster sergeant.

Frederick G. Robinson, a native of Bennington, Vermont, joined his prominent relatives on the Cape Fear prior to the war of 1861, and, full of enthusiasm for his adopted State, enlisted at the beginning of hostilities in the Wilmington Rifle Guards, which became Company I of the Eighth Regiment, North Carolina Volunteers, and with it, and later with the Fortieth, he did valiant service through all the campaigns to the Battle of Bentonville, where he was captured. He remained a prisoner of war until after the general surrender.

The writer, an intimate, lifelong friend, who admired his brave and generous nature, recalls a characteristic incident in Sergeant Robinson's military career. A contemptible comrade having behind his back questioned his loyalty to the South on account of his Northern birth, Sergeant Robinson stepped out of the ranks and publicly denounced the base insinuation, and offered to fight each and every man then and there who dared to repeat the allegation.

Beloved by many of his associates, his memory is still cherished in the hearts of his friends.

Capt. Edward Savage was captain of Company D, Third Regiment, a company raised by him. In May, 1862, Lieutenant Colonel Cowan having been promoted to the colonelcy of the Eighteenth North Carolina Infantry, Captain Savage was made major. Major Savage was wounded in the Battle of Mechanicsville. After the death of Col. Gaston Meares at Malvern Hill, Major Savage became lieutenant colonel. He resigned after the battles around Richmond on account of continued ill health.

Capt. Henry Savage was one of the organizers of the Wilmington Light Infantry, in 1853, in which he held the rank of junior second lieutenant. With this command, which became Company G of the Eighth, later the Eighteenth, North Carolina Regiment, he entered the Confederate service in April, 1861, and in June was promoted to be captain of his company. He served in Virginia, in the brigade of General Branch, and participated in the Battle of Hanover Courthouse and the Seven Days' Battle before Richmond. He escaped serious injury from the enemy's bullets, though hit several times; but, falling a victim to disease as the result of arduous service and exposure, he was sent to a hospital in Richmond, and a few days later allowed to go home on furlough. Four or five months afterwards, having in a measure recovered strength, he attempted to rejoin his regiment, but, suffering a relapse en route, he returned home and accepted an honorable discharge. In the early part of 1863 he was appointed by President Davis collector of customs at the port of Wilmington and depositary for the Confederate States Treasury, and the duties of this position occupied him until the close of the struggle for independence. After the fall of Fort Fisher he retired to Raleigh, and, establishing his office in a box car, moved west as necessity demanded until the fall of the government.

Daniel Shackelford enlisted with Company I, Eighth Regiment, and served in it for twelve months. He reënlisted in the Sixty-first Regiment and became first lieutenant, and was killed at the Battle of Fraser's Farm. His brother Theodore, who was in the same command, and who was also in the hospital with him, died literally of a broken heart, grieving because of the death of his brother.

Dr. Joseph C. Shepard, of Wilmington, was born in New Hanover County in 1840. Early in the fall of 1861 he enlisted in the Confederate States service and, being commissioned assistant surgeon, was assigned to duty on the coast, with Adams' battery. In the fall of 1864 he was transferred to Fort Fisher, where he remained through the first bombardment and the second, at the latter being captured with the brave defenders. He was sent as a prisoner of war to Governor's Island and held there until early in March following, when he was returned to duty in North Carolina and assigned to the hospital at Greensboro, where he remained until after the surrender.

Rev. James A. Smith as a boy participated in the War between the States, manifesting the same courage and energy which characterized his subsequent life. At the age of seventeen he enlisted as a private in the Confederate service in Company D, First North Carolina Heavy Artillery, January 13, 1865, and was given a position as courier for Major General Whiting. While serving in this capacity he was with the troops at Fort Fisher, and on January 15, 1865, during the bombardment and assault of that stronghold, was wounded. He was taken prisoner with the garrison and confined for six months at Point Lookout, being released June 9, 1865.

Maj. James Martin Stevenson entered the Confederate Army at the beginning of the war as first lieutenant of a company raised by Capt. J. J. Hedrick.

Soon after the seizure of Fort Johnston, Lieutenant Stevenson was ordered to Fort Caswell as ordnance officer, and while there three young men from Sampson County raised a company and offered him the captaincy, which he accepted. This company was attached to the Thirty-sixth Regiment and ordered to Fort Fisher, where Captain Stevenson was made major of the regiment. Major Stevenson remained at Fort Fisher until he was ordered to reinforce General Hardee in Georgia. There he was highly complimented for his cool bravery and tact in covering General Hardee's retreat. He took with him to Georgia five companies from the Thirty-sixth Regiment.

Major Stevenson was again remanded to his regiment at Fort Fisher, where he arrived just after the attack in December, 1864. On the 13th of January, 1865, the attack was renewed. In the battle Major Stevenson was hurled from the parapet by the explosion of an eleven-inch shell. He fell bleeding in the fort below the battery and was carried a prisoner to Fort Columbus, Governor's Island, N. Y., where he died. He did his whole duty and did it well. Wilmington had no nobler son.

James C. Stevenson and Daniel S. Stevenson were worthy sons of Maj. James M. Stevenson, of Wilmington. Both enlisted in the Confederate Army when they were much below the service age limit. James, for a time, was employed on the North Carolina steamer *Advance;* afterwards he served in the field as a private in Company A, Thirty-sixth Regiment, North Carolina Troops. He survived the war, and was for many years a prominent merchant, a most estimable citizen, and an active Christian worker. He died April 13, 1907, lamented by the community.

Daniel Stevenson was an efficient member of the Confederate States Signal Corps, and was detailed for active service with the blockade runners, on several of which he served with great coolness under fire. He was captured in 1865 off Galveston and imprisoned until the war ended. His last exploit was running through the blockade in daylight in the steamer *Little Hattie,* which drew the fire of the whole fleet, but anchored comparatively uninjured under the guns of Fort Fisher. Dan Stevenson was a young man of most amiable, generous impulses, and was greatly esteemed by his associates for his many excellent qualities. He died shortly after the termination of the war.

Capt. William M. Stevenson was elected one of the lieutenants of Company B, Sixty-first Regiment of North Carolina Troops, of which James D. Radcliffe of Wilmington was colonel and William S. Devane lieutenant-colonel and subsequently colonel. At the Battle of Fort Harrison, in Virginia, September, 1864, while in command of the company, to which position he had succeeded, he was captured and taken to Fort Delaware, where he was confined until the surrender.

Captain Stevenson's service in the field was continuous from his enlistment in 1861 up to the last of 1864, including the action at Fort Hatteras and the campaigns of the Army of Northern Virginia.

Rev. Dr. James Menzies Sprunt, who was principal of the Grove Academy, went to the front with the Duplin Rifles and became chaplain of the Twentieth Regiment, North Carolina Troops, commanded by Colonel Iverson, in Garland's brigade, D. H. Hill's division, under Stonewall Jackson. General Hill, who greatly admired him, said he was one of the few chaplains always at the front on the battlefield. He served throughout the war, revered by the men of his regiment, and was greatly beloved at his home in Duplin County throughout his honored life.

Maj. Matthew P. Taylor was major of the Sixth Battalion, Armory Guards. The battalion was as well drilled and as thoroughly disciplined as any command in the Confederate service.

Capt. John F. S. VanBokkelen left Harvard College in 1861 and returned to Wilmington, where he aided in raising a company which was assigned to the Third North Carolina Infantry as Company D, Edward Savage, captain; E. G. Meares, first lieutenant; and John F. S. VanBokkelen, second lieutenant. He served through the Seven Days' Battles around Richmond, and at Sharpsburg, Fredericksburg and Chancellorsville with conspicuous bravery.

After the Seven Days' Battles around Richmond he was promoted to first lieutenant, and he acted as adjutant of the company for some time. After the Battle of Sharpsburg he was promoted to be captain of the company, Captain Meares having been killed. Capt. VanBokkelen was wounded at the Battle of Chancellorsville, and died within a month afterwards.

It was with genuine grief that the death of Capt. Van-Bokkelen, which occurred in Richmond, was announced to the regiment while on the march in the campaign of 1863. He was universally popular and almost idolized by his own men. He was but twenty-one years of age, and full of youthful ardor, intelligent, and with an acute conception of his duties and an indomitable energy in pursuing the line of conduct which a discriminating judgment dictated to him. To him, probably more than to any other officer, was due the high morale which the company attained. His surviving classmates of Jewett's school still remember the sterling character of this worthy son of the Cape Fear, who was generally beloved for his unselfish, kindly nature and genial humor.

Rev. Dr. Alfred A. Watson was chaplain of the Second Regiment, and, besides his clerical duties, gave valuable service as a scout. His acquaintance with the topography of the country was of great value to the commanding officer. He had the profound respect of every man. He was commissioned the 21st of June, 1861, and resigned in 1862. He preached in Wilmington many years after the war, and was bishop of the diocese of East Carolina from 1884 until his death.

Capt. O. A. Wiggins, a gallant veteran of Lane's brigade, entered the service as a private in the Scotland Neck Mounted Riflemen, organized in his native county, and subsequently was promoted to lieutenant of Company E, Thirty-seventh Regiment, in the brigade then commanded by General Branch, and later by General Lane. With this command he went through the entire war, participating in the battles at Hanover Courthouse, Mechanicsville, Cold Harbor, Fraser's Farm, Cedar Run, Second Manassas, Ox Hill, Sharpsburg, Harper's Ferry, Shepherdstown, Fredericksburg, Chancellorsville, Gettysburg, Falling Waters, Bristow Station, Mine Run, the Wilderness, Spottsylvania Courthouse, Reams Station, Jones's Farm, Hare's Hill, and the fighting on the Petersburg lines until they were broken. He was wounded at Chancellorsville. At Spottsylvania Courthouse, May 12, he was promoted to captain on the field, and was wounded on the same field May 21; at Petersburg, April 2, he was shot in the head and made prisoner. While being conveyed to Johnson's Island, he escaped by jumping from a car window while the train was at full speed, near Harrisburg, Pa., after which he disguised himself and worked his way back to Dixie.

Capt. J. Marshall Williams, of Fayetteville, entered the Confederate service in the Bethel Regiment as a private. When the regiment was disbanded he and Col. K. M. Murchison organized a company of 125 men, which was assigned to the Fifty-fourth Regiment. After the Fifty-fourth Regiment was organized, it was sent immediately to Lee's army and assigned to Hood's brigade. When Hood was promoted, Gen. Robert F. Hoke succeeded to the command. The brigade was composed of the Sixth, Twenty-first, Fifty-fourth, and Fifty-seventh Regiments and was in Jackson's corps. This brigade was under six or eight different commanders, but was always known as Hoke's old brigade. It was in most of Lee's battles. When the regiment was captured at Fredericksburg, Captain Williams was absent on detached service.

Having no command, he was then detailed to command sharpshooters in different regiments until his regiment was exchanged. He had the rank of captain and was adjutant and inspector general. He saw his regiment overpowered and captured twice, and on the latter occasion made his escape by swimming the Rapidan River near Brandy Station. He was wounded once, and had his shoulder dislocated by a fall. He surrendered at Appomattox as second senior officer of the regiment, and rode home on a horse that had been with Hoke's staff for two years and wounded twice.

Capt. A. B. Williams, of Fayetteville, entered the Confederate service at the age of eighteen as second lieutenant of Company C, Light Battery, Tenth Regiment, organized at Charlotte, May 16, 1861, and was promoted to captain March 1, 1864. He was first ordered to Raleigh, then to New Bern and various other places in eastern North Carolina, and was in many of the great battles, including Malvern Hill, Gettysburg, the Wilderness, Spottsylvania Courthouse, where he was severely wounded, Petersburg, and Appomattox Courthouse. He was attached to Pogue's battalion, Third Corps, Army of Northern Virginia, and went with Lee's army to Maryland and Pennsylvania.

His battery is supposed to have fired one of the last, if not the last, shots at Appomattox. He was subsequently mayor of Fayetteville, chairman of the Board of County Commissioners, captain of the Lafayette Light Infantry, president of the Centennial Celebration, and delegate to State and National conventions.

From a eulogy by Colonel Broadfoot, a fellow-member of the United Confederate Veterans' Camp, the following is taken:

"Comrades:—This time it is an artilleryman—Capt. Arthur Butler Williams, of Brem's battery, Army of Northern Virginia, Company C, Tenth Regiment, North Carolina Troops, whose guns fired the last shot at Appomattox, which will echo and reëcho to the last syllable of recorded time, and gladden all hearts ready and worthy to do and die for country. In the sixty-first year of his age he passed quietly to his rest.

"He was of fine presence, good manners, pleasing address, and withal plain as a pikestaff. His habits were exemplary, his principles sound, his character the highest; in the community, in fact, in this part of the State, everybody knew him, everybody respected, and those who knew him best, loved him.

"We shall miss his manly form, his cheerful greeting—the eyes that looked you squarely in the face, but always pleasantly. The open hands are now folded, palm downward; the tongue that always voiced the bright side, and was never—no never— known to grumble, has been hushed.

"Comrades, let us speak more often the kindly word, extend more readily the helping hand to each other; and let each soldier keep his armor bright against that day, when each in turn shall be called to pass inspection before the great Captain—'Close up.' "

Capt. Robert Williams became captain of the Rifle Guards, but later, resigning, was appointed purser of the blockade runner *Index,* and died of yellow fever while in that service.

Capt. David Williams, of the Burgaw section of New Hanover, raised Company K of the Third Regiment of State Troops, and was one of the most valued officers of that regiment. He had the esteem, confidence, and affection of his soldiers to a remarkable degree.

Thomas Fanning Wood, in April, 1861, joined the Wilmington Rifle Guards, which later became Company I, Eighth Regiment of Volunteers. In November, 1861, the regiment was hurried to Coosawhatchie to confront the Federals who had landed on the South Carolina coast; and in the spring of 1862, it joined Jackson's corps in Virginia.

Dr. Wood was often called on to help the sick soldiers in the hospitals, and after the Seven Days' Battles around Richmond he was ordered to hospital duty. When Dr. Otis F. Manson, of Richmond Hospital, learned that he was a medical student, he secured from the Secretary of War an order detailing him for duty at the hospital, with the privilege of attending lectures at the Virginia Medical College. Doctor Manson had brought his library to Richmond with him, and gave Dr. Wood free access to it. In 1862, after passing the examination by the Medical Board, Dr. Wood was appointed assistant surgeon and served in that capacity until the end of the war.

After the war, Dr. Wood attained eminence in his profession. He served many years as secretary of the State Medical Society, and he established and edited until his death the *Medical Journal,* a publication, highly valued by his professional brethren.

John L. Wooster was first lieutenant of Company E, First Regiment. He was wounded in the shoulder at one of the Seven Days' Battles around Richmond in 1862, and disabled from further service.

William A. Wooster, private, Company I, Eighteenth Regiment, was killed in the Seven Days' fight in Virginia. He was one of the brightest young men of the Cape Fear. He had been commissioned lieutenant before he was killed.

Adam Empie Wright was commissioned the 20th of July, 1862, as assistant surgeon of the New Hanover County Hospital, in Wilmington.

Thomas Charles Wright, sergeant major, was one of the brightest and best of the Wilmington boys who went from Jewett's school to the War between the States. Fired with the enthusiasm of youth and manly courage, he served with great credit in the Virginia campaigns and was mortally wounded in the head and died at a hospital in Richmond.

Capt. James A. Wright, son of Dr. Thomas H. Wright, was captain of Company E, First Regiment. He was killed in the battles around Richmond. He was the most brilliant young man of Wilmington—and of the State—and his early death was greatly deplored.

Lieut. Joshua Grainger Wright first enlisted for military duty in the spring of 1862, becoming the orderly sergeant of an independent cavalry company. But he was with this command not more than four or five weeks when he became a member of the First North Carolina Infantry, which had been on duty in

Virginia since July, 1861. In this regiment he was commissioned first lieutenant of Company E. The regiment was part of Ripley's brigade, D. H. Hill's division, and served with great credit in the Battles of Boonsboro, or South Mountain, Sharpsburg, Fredericksburg, and Chancellorsville. At the last battle, while participating in the gallant assault by Jackson's corps, he was seriously wounded, a shot passing through his left hip. This caused his entire disability until the spring of 1864, when he attempted to reënter the service, but soon found it impossible to undertake duty in the field. Returning to Wilmington, he was assigned to duty in the office of the provost marshal for several months. He made two more attempts to enter the field, but without success.

Charles W. Yates enlisted in 1862 in an independent cavalry company organized from several counties, which became Company E, of the Forty-first Regiment, North Carolina Troops. During nearly the whole of his service he acted as courier for Col. John A. Baker and his successor, Col. Roger Moore. Among the cavalry engagements in which he took part were those at New Bern, Kinston, Hanover Courthouse, Reams Station, Ashland, Chaffin's Farm, Drewry's Bluff, and Petersburg. He was slightly wounded in the skirmish near Kinston; and just after the fall of New Bern in June, 1862, he was captured and imprisoned in a jail at that place several months, and afterwards held nearly two months at Governor's Island and Fort Delaware before he was exchanged. During the retreat at Appomattox Courthouse, he was captured in the fight at Namozine Church, April 6, and after that was a prisoner of war at Point Lookout until June, 1865.

ROSTER OF CAPE FEAR CAMP, U. C. V.

Doubtless many examples of faithful, efficient, and ever heroic service have been overlooked in the preparation of this record, although diligent inquiries have been made in order that it might be as nearly complete as possible. To this end I have been permitted to copy the roster of Cape Fear Camp, U. C. V., although it may be said that it comprises only a part of that great number of Wilmington men who served the Confederacy in the War between the States.

Alderman, Allison

*   *   *   *   *   *   *

Alderman, G. F.
Private, Co. I, 10th N. C...
Atkinson, John W.
Colonel, 10th Va. Artillery ....Died Oct. 26, 1910.
Baldwin, A. M.
Private, Co. K, 40th N. C...
Barry, John
Sergeant, Co. E, 1st N. C........................Died Mar. 28, 1914.
Bear, Solomon
Private, Howard's Cavalry.......................Died Feb. 24, 1904.
Bellamy, W. J. H.
Private, Co. I, 18th N. C...........................Died Nov. 18, 1911.
Belden, Louis S.
Sergeant, Co. E, 10th N. C........................Died June 8, 1914.
Bernard, W. H.
Private, Co. H, Bethel Regiment......................................
Bishop, C. W.
Private, Co. I, 10th N. C...
Bishop, H. M.
Private, Co. H, 3d N. C..
Blackwell, Rev. C. S.
Sergeant, Co. F, 2d Va....................Removed to Norfolk, Va.
Blanks, William
Non-Commissioned, Staff, 61st N. C.................Died Feb. 26, 1904.
Bolles, C. P.
Captain, P. A. C. S...............................Died 1910 or 1911.
Boatwright, J. L.
Captain, P. A. C. S..
Boatwright, J. H.
Private, 1st Bat. S. C. Cadets....................Died Jan. 27, 1911.
Boney, G. J.
Corporal, Co. H, 40th N. C..
Bowden, W. B.
Private, Co. H, 3d Cavalry........................Died Mar. 15, 1903.
Brown, A. D.
Lieutenant, Co. C, Cumming's Battery...............................
Brown, E. A.
Private, Co. C, 4th Artillery.....................Died June 26, 1905.

24

Brown, George L.
Hart's Battery, Va............................Sent to Richmond 1909.
Brown, I. H.
Private, Co. K, 3d N. C.............................Died May 5, 1892.
Brown, T. A.
Sergeant, 36th N. C................................Died Aug. 14, 1902.
Bunting, T. O.
Private, Co. C, 5th Cavalry.......................Died June 20, 1913.
Burr, Ancrum
Lieutenant, Co. D, 36th N. C.............................Removed.
Burr, James G.
Colonel, 7th Batt. H. G..........................Died Nov. 13, 1898.
Calder, William
Adjutant, 1st Batt. Artillery..
Cantwell, J. L.
Colonel, 51st N. C.................................Died Dec. 21, 1909.
Capps, T. J.
Corporal, Co. E, 3d N. C..
Carman, Samuel
Private, Co. E, 56th N. C..........................Died Apr. 17, 1902.
Carmichael, Rev. James
Chaplain, 30th Va.................................Died Nov. 25, 1911.
Cazaux, A. D.
Captain, A. Q. M., 18th N. C..
Chadwick, Robert
Private, Co. K, 3d N. C...
Chapman, Louis
Private, Co. D, 2d Cavalry..
Cobb, John G.
Private, Co. C, 1st Batt. Artillery..................................
Collier, Sam P.
Sergeant Major, 2d N. C...
Cook, A. B.
Sergeant, Co. I, 18th N. C.........................Died Jan. 12, 1908.
Corbett, R. A.
Private, Co. C, 4th Cavalry...
Cornish, F. W.
Private, Co. H, 51st N. C...
Cornish, W. A.
Private, Co. H, 18th N. C...
Cowan, M. S.
Captain, Co. I, 3d N. C............................Died Mar. 24, 1900.
Cowles, Charles L.
Captain, Co. B, 56th N. C...........................Died Oct. 9, 1901.
Cox, R. E.
Private, Co. B, S. C. Cavalry.......................................
Crapon, George M.
Lieutenant, Co. H, 3d N. C..
Crow, J. E.
Sergeant, Co. E, 12th Va...........................Died Nov. 4, 1907.
Cumming, J. D.
Captain, Cumming's Battery.........................Died Nov. 26, 1901.
Cumming, Preston
Sergeant, Cumming's Battery...
Currie, John H.
Private, 5th Cavalry............................To Fayetteville Camp.

Casteen, J. B.
Orderly Sergeant, Co. D, 3d N. C.......................................

Cannon, J. W.
Private, Co. G, 20th N. C...

Cannon, Alfred
* * * * * * *

Cox, T. B.
Private, Co. F, 67th N. C..

Cox, A. F.
* * * * * * *

Daves, Graham
Major, P. A. C. S..............................Resigned, Feb. 1, 1890.

Davis, Jackson
Sergeant, Co. K, 5th N. C........................Died Mar. 12, 1902.

Davis, Junius
Corporal, Co. E, 10th N. C.......................Died April 11, 1916.

Davis, M. T.
Private, Co. A, 35th N. C..

DeRosset, A. L.
Captain, P. A. C. S................................Died Feb., 1910.

DeRosset, William L.
Colonel, 3d N. C.................................Died Aug. 14, 1910.

Dickey, J. J.
Private, Co. D, 3d N. C..........................Died Nov. 11, 1911.

Dicksey, J. W.
Private, Co. E, 10th N. C.........................Died Aug. 31, 1899.

Divine, J. F.
Captain, A. Q. M., C. S. A........................Died Aug. 20, 1909.

Dixon, W. M.
Private, Co. G, 10th N. C..

Dowdy, W. R.
Private, Co. I, 10th N. C.........................Died Dec. 19, 1911.

Darden, R. J.
Goldsboro Provost' Guard...

Elliott, W. P.
Private, Co. I, 10th N. C.........................Died May 20, 1894.

Evans, A. H.
....Died 1911 or 1912.

Everett, John A.
Private, Co. I, 10th N. C..

Farrior, S. R.
Lieutenant, Co. A, 43d N. C..

Farrow, J. A.
Private, Co. E, 10th N. C...........................Died Feb., 1911.

Farrow, Benjamin
Private, Co. E, 10th N. C.........................Died Oct. 14, 1911.

Fennell, Owen
Lieutenant, Co. C, 1st N. C.......................Died July 6, 1910.

Fillyaw, DeLeon
Corporal, Co. A, 40th N. C........................Died Jan. 27, 1904.

Fillyaw, O. M.
Private, Co. A, 40th N. C..

French, W. R.
Private, Co. E, 51st N. C..........................Died............

Gaither, W. W.
Surgeon, 28th N. C................................Died............

Ganzer, C. H.
Private, Howard's Cavalry.........................Died May 22, 1899.

Garrell, Jacob F.
Private, Co. I, 10th N. C...........................Died May 29, 1891.

Giles, Clayton
Private, Co. I, 63d Ga. Volunteers.....................................

Giles, Norwood
Private, Co. E, 10th N. C..........................Died Dec. 11, 1899.

Goodman, William
Private, Co. A, 1st Batt. Artillery...................Died Apr. 3, 1911.

Gore, D. L.
Private, Co. D, 72d N. C...

Gray, Jesse W.
Private, Co. B, 3d Cavalry.........................Died Apr. 18, 1911.

Green, W. H.
Sergeant Major, Starr's Battery...................Died Jan. 12, 1914.

Hall, B. F.
Sergeant, Co. A, 43d N. C...

Hall, E. D.
Colonel, 46th N. C................................Died June 11, 1896.

Hall, S. G.
Private, Co. E, 21st N. C...........................Died July 31, 1911.

Hamme, R. F.
Private, Co. G, 30th N. C...

Hanby, John H.
Private, Co. B, 16th Va............................Died Apr. 22, 1910.

Hanby, Joseph H.
Private, Co. B, 16th Va............................Died Sept. 8, 1905.

Hancock, J. T.
Private, Co. I, 10th N. C...

Hankins, J. A.
Private, Co. C, Starr's Battery......................Died July, 1910.

Hankins, A. G.
Lieutenant, Co. H, 3d Cavalry...

Hankins, W. M.
Private, Co. H, 3d Cavalry..

Harper, John H.
Private, Co. H, 3d N. C.............................Died............

Harriss, W. W.
Assistant Surgeon ....Died............

Hawkins, J. W.
Private, Co. A, 1st Batt. Artillery....................................

Hayden, P. H.
Private, Co. C, 19th Va.............................Died............

Heide, A. S.
Private, Co. A, 5th Cavalry.....................Resigned Feb. 4, 1901.

Heide, R. E.
Private, Co. H, 1st N. C...........................Died June 13, 1905.

Heinsberger, P.
Private, Co. C, Starr's Battery.......................................

Henderson, T. B.
Lieutenant, Co. H, 3d Cavalry.....................Died Mar. 10, 1890.

Hewett, James H.
Sergeant, Co. F, 3d N. C..........................Died Mar. 20, 1913.

Hicks, James H.
Private, Co. F, 3d N. C............................Died Nov. 9, 1908.

Hill, A. J.
Sergeant, Co. C, 4th Cavalry..........................Died............

Hill, Owen C.
Private, Co. G, 3d N. C.............................Died Sept. 2, 1904.

Hines, John W.
Private, Co. D, 3d N. C.............................Died Feb. 27, 1906.

Hodges, L. W.
Private, 16th Va..

Hodges, T. A.
Company E, 15th Batt. Artillery......................................

Huggins, George W.
Lieutenant, Co. I, 18th N. C...

Huggins, J. B.
Captain, A. Q. M., C. S. A.........................Died May 16, 1910.

Hawes, J. J.
Sergeant, Co. G, 20th N. C...

James, Josh T.
Lieutenant, Co. I, 18th N. C.......................Died Nov. 13, 1899.

Jewett, Stephen
Private, Co. K, 44th Ga..

Jones, George T.
Lieutenant, Co. E, 50th N. C...

Keeter, Elijah
Private, Co. D, 3d N. C.............................Died............

Kelly, D. C.
Private, Co. B, 36th N. C..

Kelly, James E.
Private, Co. K, 20th N. C..........................Died Nov. 2, 1910.

Kenly, John R.
Private, Co. A, 1st Md. Cavalry......................................

Kenan, W. R.
Adjutant, 43d N. C................................Died Apr. 14, 1903.

King, Charles H.
Q. M. Sergeant, 61st N. C.........................Died 1909 or 1910.

King, James A.
Private, Co. A, 3d Cavalry...

King, James A.
Private, Co. B, 10th N. C..

King, James M.
Private, Co. F, 3d N. C..

King, John M.
Private, Co. I, 10th N. C..........................Died Dec., 1912.

King, T. E.
Sergeant, Co. I, 10th N. C.........................Died Dec. 1, 1911.

King, W. H.
Private, Co. A, 3d Cavalry...

Latta, John R.
Adjutant, 51st N. C...............................Died June 30, 1898.

Lee, J. B.
*   *   *   *   *   *   *

Leon, L.
Private, Co. C, 1st N. C...

Leslie, Alexander
Private, Co. G, 18th N. C..

Leslie, Joseph H.
Private, Co. G, 18th N. C.........................Died Sept. 13, 1896.

Lewis, Thomas C.
Captain, Co. I, 18th N. C. ....Died Nov. 14, 1909.
Lippitt, Thomas B.
Lieutenant, Co. G, 51st N. C. ....Died Dec. 21, 1898.
Littleton, D. C.
Private, Co. H, 41st N. C. ....
Loftin, Dr. I. C. M.
Company E, 20th M ....Died............
Love, Richard S.
Sergeant, Co. C, 4th Cavalry.......................Died............
Love, Thaddeus D.
Major, 24th N. C. ....Died Jan. 6, 1892.
Lumsden, H. C.
Private, Co. E, 1st N. C. ....
MacRae, W. G.
Captain, Co. C, 7th N. C. ....
Manning, E. W.
Chief Engineer, C. S. N. ....Died Dec. 10, 1900.
Martin, E. S.
Lieutenant, 1st Batt. Artillery..
Marshall, J. R.
Private, Co. E, 3d N. C. ....
Mason, W. H.
Private, Co. E, 3d N. C. ....
Matthews, D. W.
Private, Co. C, 1st Batt. Artillery....................................
Matthews, J. E.
Sergeant, Sharpshooters.............Dropped by request, Apr. 9, 1910.
Meares, O. P.
Lieutenant Colonel, 18th N. C. ....Died Nov. 21, 1906.
Meares, T. D.
Courier to Gen. Wade Hampton.......................................
Merritt, Joseph
Private, 18th N. C. ....Died Aug. 12, 1904.
Merritt, L. W.
*   *   *   *   *   *   *
Metts, J. I.
Captain, Co. G, 3d N. C. ....
Mitchell, Frank H.
Private, Co. I, 18th N. C. ....Died Feb. 28, 1899.
Mintz, W. W.
Private, Co. I, 10th N. C. ....Died Sept. 15, 1897.
Montgomery, James A.
Private, Co. B, 36th N. C. ....
Moore, Benjamin R.
Lieutenant Colonel, Gen. Bates's Staff...............Died Apr. 12, 1894.
Moore, E. H.
Lieutenant, Co. D, 7th N. C. ....
Moore, Edward J.
Sergeant, Co. G, 18th N. C. ....Died May 12, 1891.
Moore, Roger
Lieutenant Colonel, 3d N. C. ....Died Apr. 21, 1900.
Moore, W. A.
Private, Co. K, 36th N. C. ....Died Apr. 25, 1906.
Moore, W. H.
Private, Co. A, 1st Cavalry..

Morton, Rev. P. C.
Chaplain, 23d Va.................................Died Feb. 28, 1903.
Mott, A. J.
Private, Co. G, 61st N. C...
Munn, D.
Captain, Co. B, 36th N. C............................Died Feb., 1905.
Myers, Charles D.
Captain, P. A. C. S.................................Died Oct. 2, 1892.
Myrry, R. S.
    *   *   *   *   *   *
McClammy, Charles W.
Major, 3d Cavalry.................................Died Feb. 26, 1896.
McClammy, Charles W.
Private, Co. F, 3d N. C................................Died Nov. 19, 1900.
McEvoy, John
Lieutenant, Co. A, 2d N. C.........................Died Nov. 21, 1896.
McGirt, A. G.
Private, Co. D, 46th N. C..........................Died Aug. 22, 1890.
McGowan, James M.
Captain, A. Q. M.................................Died June 20, 1903.
McIntyre, R. M.
Captain, Co. C, 4th Cavalry........................Died Apr. 17, 1913.
McIver, J. T.
Private, Co. G, 48th N. C..........................Died Feb. 24, 1907.
McKeithan, R. W.
Corporal, Co. E, 10th N. C..
McKoy, T. Hall
Major Lane's Staff.................................Died May 10, 1902.
McMillan, W. D.
Sergeant Major, 51st N. C...
McQueen, H. C.
Private, Co. D, 1st Batt. Artillery....................................
Nobles, S. W.
Captain, Co. K, 61st N. C...........................Died Feb. 16, 1904.
Northrop, W. H.
Captain, A. Q. M., 3d N. C..
Oldham, William P.
Captain, Co. K, 44th N. C...
Ormsby, James O.
Private, Co. I, 10th N. C..
Ortman, F. W.
Private, Co. A, 25th S. C...........................Died Apr. 22, 1911.
Pearce, E. L.
Captain, Co. E, 26th Ga..............................Died...........
Percy, A. B.
Lieutenant, Co. F, 56th Regiment...................Died Oct. 13, 1893.
Pickett, J. H.
Private, Co. B, 1st Batt. Artillery....................................
Pinner, J. L.
Private, Co. A, 1st Batt. Artillery....................................
Poisson, J. D.
Sergeant, Co. G., 18th N. C.........................Died Jan. 11, 1911.
Porter, Elijah
Captain, Co. E, 3d N. C.............................Died July 1, 1907.
Potter, Dr. F. W.
Surgeon, 50th N. C.................................Died June 1, 1893.

Pratt, D.
Private, Co. I, 10th N. C..............................Died............

Prempert, H. C.
Sergeant, Co. H, 2d N. C.........................Died Sept. 17, 1896.

Price, Joseph
Commander, C. S. N..............................Died May 15, 1895.

Price, R. W.
Private, Co. D, 72d N. C...........................Died Nov. 25, 1909.

Primrose, John W.
Captain, A. C. S., 1st Cavalry...................Resigned Dec. 29, 1890.

Rankin, R. G.
Private, Co. A, 1st Batt. Artillery..................Died June 28, 1913.

Rankin, J. T.
Lieutenant, Co. D, 1st Batt. Artillery..............................

Reaves, Calvin
Private, Co. G, 61st N. C..

Reaves, J. F. A.
Private, Co. F, 3d N. C...........................Died June 27, 1908.

Reaves, R. M.
Private, Co. E, 18th N. C..

Rivenbark, W. W.
Private, Co. F, 20th N. C.........................Died Nov. 25, 1904.

Roberts, B. M.
Private, Co. C, 13th Battery........................Died Feb. 4, 1903.

Robinson, Charles H.
Quartermaster, 31st N. C..

Rogers, J. M.
Private, Co. B, 1st Batt. Artillery.................................

Ruark, J. H.
Sergeant, Co. F, 3d N. C...

Russell, B. R.
Assistant Engineer, C. S. N........................Died Dec. 15, 1906.

Savage, Henry
Captain, Co. G, 18th N. C.........................Died Aug. 1, 1904.

Scharf, E.
Private, 1st Batt. Ala. Cavalry.................Removed to New York.

Schenck, N. W.
Captain, A. C. S...

Schriver, Eli
Private, Co. H, 3d N. C. Cavalry...................................

Sharp, John H.
Private, 13th Batt. Va. Artillery..................................

Shepard, Dr. J. C.
Assistant Surgeon, C. S. A.........................Died Mar. 4, 1903.

Shepard, T. A.
Lieutenant, Co. G, 18th N. C.......................Died July 5, 1899.

Shutte, John T.
Corporal, Starr's Battery......................Removed to New York.

Sikes, R. J.
Private, Co. H, 3d N. C..

Skipper, Joshua G.
Private, Co. I, 10th N. C..........................Died Dec. 18, 1904.

Smith, H. H.
Lieutenant, Co. A, 5th N. C........................Died Aug. 24, 1908.

Smith, Rev. J. A.
Private, Co. I, N. C. Artillery....................................

Smith, M. K.
Private, Co. D, 72d N. C..

Smith, Peter H.
Private, Co. F, 3d N. C.............................Died...........

Smith, T. Jefferson.
Private, Co. I, 18th N. C...

Sneeden, S. J.
Private, Co. A, 3d N. C............................Died Dec. 7, 1910.

Southerland, D. D.
Private, Co. I, 10th N. C..........................Died June 14, 1900.

Southerland, T. J.
Captain, Co. I, 10th N. C.........................Died Feb. 18, 1891.

Spooner, W. T.
Company F, 3d N. C..

Stedman, C. M.
Major, 44th N. C..................................Greensboro, N. C.

Stevenson, J. C.
Private, Co. A, 36th N. C.........................Died Apr. 13, 1907.

Stevenson, W. M.
Captain, Co. B, 61st N. C..

Stolter, Henry
Private, Co. A, 18th N. C.........................Died Oct. 5, 1896.

Stolter, John F.
Private, Co. A, 18th N. C.........................Died Dec. 27, 1903.

Story, S. A.
Private, Co. 1, 10th N. C..........................Died...........

Sutton, D. M.
Private, Co. K, 18th N. C.........................Died...........

Swain, S. A.
Private, Co. C, 1st Batt. Artillery...............Died Feb. 11, 1899.

Sykes, Thomas P.
Private, 3d N. C. Cavalry..

Taylor, James H.
Adjutant, 51st N. C...

Taylor, John D.
Lieutenant Colonel, 36th N. C.....................Died May 21, 1912.

Taylor, J. J.
Private, Co. H, 3d Cavalry........................Died Apr. 29, 1902.

Taylor, Lewis
Private, Co. B, 1st Batt. Artillery...............Died Oct. 8, 1912.

Taylor, M. P.
....Died...........

Tilley, George F.
Private, Co. H, 18th N. C.........................Died May 9, 1905.

Turrentine, J. R.
Hart's Battery, Light Artillery....................................

Ulmer, J. H.
....Died Sept. 2, 1910.

Van Amringe, Stacy
Captain, Co. G, 61st N. C.........................Died Jan. 2, 1897.

Voss, John G.
Private, Co. A, 18th N. C.........................Died July 19, 1890.

Waddell, A. M.
Lieutenant Colonel, 3d N. C.......................Died Mar. 17, 1912.

Walker, J. Alvis
Private, Co. E, 2d Eng., C. S. A..................Died Sept. 29, 1912.

Walker, John M.
Orderly Sergeant, Co. F, 2d N. C. Batt. Artillery.....................
Walker, J. P.
Private, Co. E, 18th N. C...........................Died 1909 or 1910.
Wallace, J. P.
Color Corporal, Co. C, 51st N. C.......................Died Oct., 1911.
Ward, C. H.
Private, Co. G, 10th N. C..
Warrock, E. S.
Corporal, Ga. Artillery.....................................Removed.
Warrock W. S.
Captain, Co. B, 1st Ala. Cavalry..................Died Mar. 19, 1900.
Watkins, L. A.
Private, Co. D, 5th N. C. Batt. Artillery............................
Watson, Rt. Rev. A. A.
Chaplain, 2d N. C..................................Died Apr. 21, 1905.
Watson, A. W.
Private, Co. F, 7th N. C..
Weill, Abram
Medical Department ....Withdrawn.
West, John W.
Sergeant, Co. D, 36th N. C..
White, B. F.
Lieutenant, Co. I, 18th N. C........................Died June 23, 1903.
Wiggs, Alexander W.
Sergeant, Co. D, 36th N. C.........................Died Aug. 30, 1906.
Wiggins, O. A.
Captain, Co. E, 36th N. C......................Resigned May 10, 1902.
Wilder, Jesse
Lieutenant, Co. C, 4th Cavalry ....
Wilkins, W. L.
Corporal, Co. F, 3d N. C...........................Died Aug. 31, 1908.
Williams, George W.
Private, Co. F, 3d N. C...
Williams, J. A.
Private, Co. G, 3d N. C. Cavalry......................................
Williams, J. R.
Sergeant, Co. H, S. C. V...
Wood, Dr. Thomas F.
Assistant Surgeon, 3d N. C........................Died Aug. 22, 1895.
Woodcock, George W.
Lieutenant, Co. E, 18th N. C.......................Died Feb. 10, 1896.
Woodcock, Henry M.
Private, Co. E, 18th N. C.......................Removed to Georgia.
Woodward, W. J.
Private, Co. H, 1st N. C............................Died Oct. 11, 1907.
Wooten, Edward
Lieutenant, Co. B, 5th Cavalry...........................Withdrawn.
Wright, Joshua G.
Lieutenant, Co. E, 1st N. C........................Died Dec. 30, 1900.
Yates, C. W.
Company E, 3d Cavalry..
Yopp, F. V. B.
Lieutenant, Co. G, 51st N. C.......................Died Dec. 29, 1894.

FORT CASWELL.

The work at Fort Caswell at the mouth of the Cape Fear River was commenced by the government in the year 1826. Maj. George Blaney, of the United States Engineer Corps, was in charge of it for several years until his death at Smithville in 1836 or 1837. He was born in Boston, Massachusetts, and was an accomplished officer. His remains were brought to Wilmington, and the Wilmington Volunteers, a uniformed company and the only one then existing in the town, formed at Market Street dock to receive them, and escorted them to the old burial ground adjoining St. James's Church, where they were interred with military honors and where they still repose.

Major Blaney's assistant in building the fort was Mr. James Ancrum Berry, a native of Wilmington, a natural engineer, the bent of whose mind was strongly mathematical. He was thoroughly competent for the position he held, and took great pride in the work—so much so, indeed, that he had a small house erected on the river front of the fort and resided there with his family for a year or two until the encroaching waters rendered his habitation untenable, when he returned to Smithville. He died suddenly in 1832. He was hunting with the late Mr. John Brown, and, while crossing a small stream on a log, lost his footing and his gun came in contact with the log and was discharged, the contents entering his brain, killing him almost instantly. He was an honorable gentleman, high-toned, chivalric, and was greatly mourned.

It is probable that Capt. A. J. Swift, son of the distinguished chief of the Engineer Corps, Gen. Joseph Swift, succeeded Major Blaney. It is known that he had charge of the works at the mouth of the river for quite a long time, and it is believed they were finished under his supervision.

Captain Swift was regarded as one of the ablest engineer officers in the army and, though dying quite young, left behind him a reputation second to none in that branch of the service.

It is a remarkable fact that, notwithstanding its exposed position to the Federal fleet, no general engagement occurred at Fort Caswell during the four years' war. The fort was of great service, however, in defending the Main Bar and the garrison at Smithville, although the fighting was confined to an occasional artillery duel with the United States blockading fleet.

The defenses of Oak Island during the War between the States were composed of Forts Caswell and Campbell, the latter a large earth fort situated about one mile down the beach from Fort Caswell, and Battery Shaw, with some other small works, all at the close of the war under the command of Col. Charles H. Simonton. With Colonel Simonton were the following members of his staff: Capt. E. S. Martin, chief of ordnance and artillery; Capt. Booker Jones, commissary; Capt. H. C. Whiting, quartermaster, and Captain Booker, assistant adjutant general.

Fort Fisher fell about nine o'clock Sunday night, January 15, 1865, and by midnight orders had been received at Fort Caswell to send the garrisons of that fort and Fort Campbell down the beach and into the woods before daylight in order to conceal them from the Federal fleet. The troops were immediately withdrawn from the forts, and under cover of darkness marched away. Orders were also received to spike the guns in those two forts and destroy the ammunition as far as possible. Accordingly, during Monday, the 16th of January, the chief of ordnance and artillery, Capt. E. S. Martin, was employed with the ordnance force of the forts in carrying out this order, preparing to burn the barracks—large wooden structures built outside and around Fort Caswell—and to blow up the magazines.

About one o'clock on the morning of Tuesday, January 17, the order came to evacuate and blow up the magazines. Thereupon Col. C. H. Simonton, Lieut. Col. John D. Taylor, and Capt. Booker Jones, who had remained up to this time, departed, leaving Captain Martin to destroy the barracks and forts. The buildings without the fort and the citadel within were at once set on fire and were soon blazing from bottom to top. Trains had been laid during the day to each of the seven magazines at Fort Caswell and the five magazines at Fort Campbell, and under the lurid glare of the burning buildings the match was applied to the trains, and magazine after magazine exploded with terrific report. One of the magazines in Fort Caswell contained nearly one hundred thousand pounds of powder, and when it exploded the volume of sound seemed to rend the very heavens, while the earth trembled, the violence of the shock being felt in Wilmington, thirty miles distant, and even at Fayetteville, more than one hundred miles away. The sight was grand beyond description. Amidst this sublime and impressive scene the flag at Fort Caswell was for the last time hauled down. It was carried away by Captain Martin, who, with his men, silently departed, the last to leave the old fort, which for four long years of war had so effectually guarded the main entrance to the river.

FORT FISHER.

Col. William Lamb, who was in command of Fort Fisher, in his admirable report of its defense, says:

"The indentation of the Atlantic Ocean in the Carolina coast known as Onslow Bay and the Cape Fear River, running south from Wilmington, form the peninsula known as Federal Point, which during the Civil War was called Confederate Point. Not quite seven miles north of the end of this peninsula stood a high sandhill called the 'Sugar Loaf.' Here there was an intrenched camp for the army of Wilmington under Gen. Braxton Bragg, the department commander, that was hid from the sea by forest and sandhills. From this intrenched camp the river bank, with a neighboring ridge of sand-dunes, formed a covered way for troops to within a hundred yards of the left salient of Fort Fisher. Between the road and the ocean beach was an arm of Masonboro Sound, and where it ended, three miles north of the fort, were occasional fresh-water swamps, generally wooded with scrub growth and in many cases quite impassable. Along the ocean shore was an occasional battery formed from a natural sandhill, behind which Whitworth guns were carried from the fort to cover belated blockade runners or to protect more unfortunate ones that had been chased ashore.

"About half a mile north of the fort there was a rise in the plain, forming a hill some twenty feet above the tide on the river side, and on this was a redoubt commanding the approach to the fort by the river road. Thus nature, assisted by some slight engineering work, had given a defense to Confederate Point which would have enabled an efficient commander at the intrenched camp, coöperating with the garrison of Fort Fisher, to render the point untenable for a largely superior force at night, when the covering fire of the Federal Navy could not distinguish between friend and foe."

The plans of Fort Fisher were Colonel Lamb's, and as the work progressed they were approved by Generals French, Raines, Longstreet, Beauregard, and Whiting. It was styled by Federal engineers the "Malakoff of the South." It was built solely with the view of resisting the fire of a fleet, and it stood uninjured, except as to armament, in two of the fiercest bombardments the world ever witnessed. The two faces to the works were 2,580 yards long. The land face was 682 yards long, and the sea face 1,898 yards long.

The Land Face of Fort Fisher.

At the land face of Fort Fisher the peninsula was about half a mile wide. This face commenced about one hundred feet from the river with a half bastion, and extended with a heavy curtain to a full bastion on the ocean side, where it joined the sea face. The work was built to withstand the heaviest artillery fire. There was no moat with scarp and counterscarp, so essential for defense against storming parties, the shifting sands rendering such a construction impossible with the material available.

The outer slope was twenty feet high and was sodded with marsh grass, which grew luxuriantly. The parapet was not less than twenty-five feet thick, with an inclination of only one foot. The revetment was five feet nine inches high from the floor of the gun chambers, and these were some twelve feet or more from the interior plane. The guns were all mounted in barbette on Columbiad carriages, there being no casemated gun in the fort. There were twenty heavy guns on the land face, each gun chamber containing one or two guns, and there were heavy traverses, exceeding in size any before known to engineers, to protect from an enfilading fire. They extended out some twelve feet or more in height above the parapet, running back thirty feet or more. The gun chambers were reached from the rear by steps. In each traverse was an alternate magazine or bombproof, the latter ventilated by an air chamber. The passageways penetrated traverses in the interior of the work, forming additional bombproofs for the reliefs of the guns.

As a defense against infantry, there was a system of subterranean torpedoes extending across the peninsula, five to six hundred feet from the land face, and so disconnected that the explosion of one would not affect the others; inside the torpedoes, about fifty feet from the berm of the work, extending from river bank to seashore, was a heavy palisade of sharpened logs nine feet high, pierced for musketry, and so laid out as to have an enfilading fire on the center, where there was a redoubt guarding

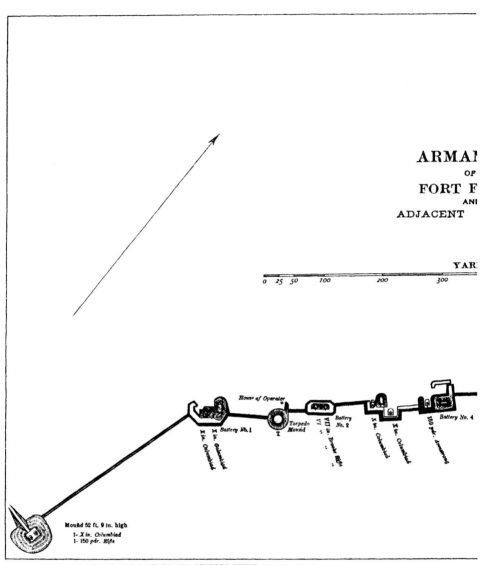

ARMA...
OF
FORT F...
AND
ADJACENT...

YAR...

0   25 50   100   200   300

House of Operator

Battery No. 1

X in. Columbiad

X in. Columbiad

Torpedo Mound

VII in. Brooke Rifle

Battery No. 2

X in. Columbiad

X in. Columbiad

150 pdr. Armstrong

Battery No. 4

Mound 52 ft. 9 in. high
1- X in. Columbiad
1- 150 pdr. Rifle

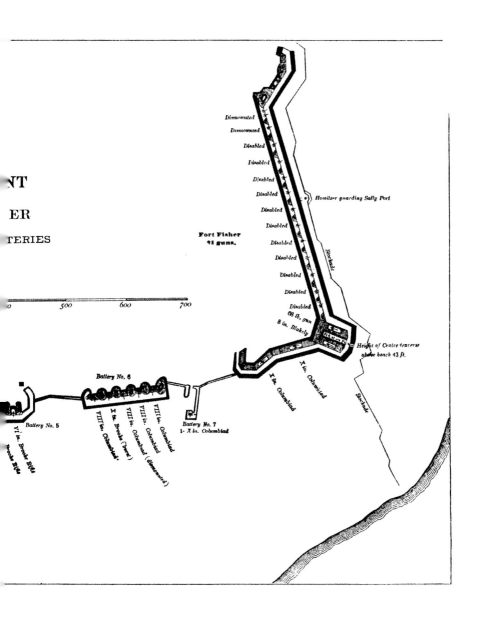

NT

ER

TERIES

Fort Fisher
41 guns.

Dismounted
Dismounted
Disabled
Disabled
Disabled
Disabled
Disabled
Disabled
Disabled
Disabled
Disabled
Disabled
Disabled
68 lb. gun
8 in. Blakely

Howitzer guarding Sally Port

Stockade

X in. Columbiad

X in. Columbiad

Height of Centre traverse
above bench 43 ft.

Stockade

500   600   700

Battery No. 6

VIII in. Columbiad.
VIII in. Columbiad
X in. Brooke
X in. Columbiad (dismounted)
VIII in. Columbiad
VIII in. Columbiad

Battery No. 5
VI in. Brooke Rifle
Brooke Rifle

Battery No. 7
1- X in. Columbiad

a sally-port, from which two Napoleons were run out as occasion required. At the river end of the palisade was a deep and muddy slough, across which was a bridge, the entrance of the river road into the fort; commanding this bridge was a Napoleon gun. There were three mortars in the rear of the land face.

THE SEA FACE OF FORT FISHER.

The sea face, for one hundred yards from the northwest bastion, was of the same massive character as the land face. A crescent battery intended for four guns joined this, but it was converted into a hospital bombproof. In the rear a heavy curtain was thrown up to protect the chamber from fragments of shells. From the bombproof a series of batteries extended for three-quarters of a mile along the sea, connected by an infantry curtain. These batteries had heavy traverses, but were not more than ten or twelve feet high to the top of the parapets, and were built for ricochet firing. On the line was a bombproof electric battery connected with a system of submarine torpedoes. Farther along, where the channel ran close to the beach, inside the bar, a mound battery sixty feet high was erected, with two heavy guns which had a plunging fire on the channel; this was connected with a battery north of it by a light curtain. Following the line of the works, it was over one mile from the mound to the northeast bastion at the angle of the sea and land faces, and upon this line twenty-four heavy guns were mounted. From the mound for nearly one mile to the end of Confederate Point, was a level sand plain scarcely three feet above high tide, and much of it was submerged during gales. At the point was Battery Buchanan, four guns, in the shape of an ellipse commanding New Inlet, its two 11-inch guns covering the approach by land. An advanced redoubt with a 24-pounder was added after the attack by the forces on the 25th of December, 1864. A wharf for large steamers was in close proximity to these works. Battery Buchanan was a citadel to which an overpowered garrison might retreat and with proper transportation be safely carried off at night, and to which reinforcements could be sent under the cover of darkness.

THE FORT FISHER FIGHT.

General Whiting, in his official report of the taking of Fort Fisher on the night of the 15th of January, 1865, after an assault of unprecedented fury, both by sea and land, lasting from Friday morning until Sunday night, says:

"On Thursday night the enemy's fleet was reported off the fort. On Friday morning the fleet opened very heavily. On Friday and Saturday, during the furious bombardment of the fort, the enemy was allowed to land without molestation and to throw up a light line of field-works from Battery Ramseur to the river, thus securing his position from molestation and making the fate of Fort Fisher, under the circumstances, but a question of time.

"On Sunday, the fire on the fort reached a pitch of fury to which no language can do justice. It was concentrated on the land face and front. In a short time nearly every gun was dismounted or disabled, and the garrison suffered severely by the fire. At three o'clock the enemy's land force, which had been gradually and slowly advancing, formed in two columns for assault. The garrison, during the fierce bombardment, was not able to stand to the parapets, and many of the reinforcements were obliged to be kept a great distance from the fort. As the enemy slackened his fire to allow the assault to take place, the men hastily manned the ramparts and gallantly repulsed the right column of assault. A portion of the troops on the left had also repulsed the first rush to the left of the work. The greater portion of the garrison being, however, engaged on the right, and not being able to man the entire works, the enemy succeeded in making a lodgment on the left flank, planting two of his regimental flags in the traverses. From this point we could not dislodge him, our own traverses protecting him from the fire of our most distant guns. From this time it was a succession of fighting from traverse to traverse, and from line to line until nine o'clock at night, when we were overpowered and all resistance ceased.

"The fall both of the general and the colonel commanding the fort—one about four and the other about four-thirty o'clock p. m.—had a perceptible effect upon the men, and no doubt hastened greatly the result; but we were overpowered, and no skill or gallantry could have saved the place after the enemy effected a lodgment, except attack in the rear. The enemy's loss was very heavy, and so, also, was our own. Of the latter, as a prisoner, I have not been able to ascertain.

"At nine o'clock, p. m., the gallant Major Reilly, who had

fought the fort after the fall of his superiors, reported the enemy in possession of the sally-port. The brave Captain Van Benthuysen, of the marines, though himself badly wounded, with a squad of his men picked up the general and the colonel and endeavored to make his way to Battery Buchanan, followed by Reilly, with the remnant of the forces. On reaching there, it was found to be evacuated, by whose order and by what authority I know not. No boats were there. The garrison of Fort Fisher had been coolly abandoned to its fate. Thus fell Fort Fisher after three days' battle unparalleled in the annals of the war. Nothing was left but to await the approach of the enemy, who took us about 10 p. m. The fleet surpassed its tremendous efforts in the previous attack. The fort had fallen in precisely the manner indicated so often by myself, and to which your attention has been so frequently called, and in the presence of the ample force provided by you to meet the contingency."

Colonel Lamb, in his report, says he had half a mile of land face to defend with 1,900 men. He knew every company present and its strength. This included the killed, wounded, and sick.

To capture Fort Fisher, the enemy lost, by their own statement, 1,445 killed, wounded, and missing. Nineteen hundred Confederates with 44 guns contended against 10,000 men on shore and 600 heavy guns afloat, killing and wounding almost as many of the enemy as there were soldiers in the fort, and not surrendering until the last shot was expended.

The garrison consisted of two companies of the Tenth North Carolina under Major Reilly; the Thirty-sixth North Carolina, Col. William Lamb, ten companies; four companies of the Fortieth North Carolina; Company D, First North Carolina Artillery Battalion; Company C, Third North Carolina Artillery Battalion; Company D, Thirteenth North Carolina Artillery Battalion, and the naval detachment under Captain Van Benthuysen.

General Whiting had been assigned to no duty by General Bragg, although it was his right to command the supporting troops. He determined to go to the fort and share its fate. The commander, Colonel Lamb, offered to relinquish the control, but General Whiting declined to take away the glory of the defense from him. He remained with him, however, and fought as a volunteer. It is related that during the fight, when one hundred

25

immense projectiles per minute[1] were being hurled at the fort, General Whiting was seen "standing with folded arms, smiling upon a 400-pound shell, as it lay smoking and spinning like a billiard ball on the sand, not twenty feet away, until it burst, and he then moved quietly away." During the fight General Whiting saw the Federal flag planted on the traverses. Calling on the troops to follow him, they fought hand to hand with clubbed muskets, and one traverse was taken. Just as he was climbing the other, and had his hand upon the Federal flag to tear it down, he fell, receiving two wounds. Colonel Lamb, a half-hour later, fell with a desperate wound through the hip. The troops fought on. Lamb, in the hospital, found voice enough, though faint unto death, to say: "I will not surrender"; and Whiting, lying among the surgeons near by, responded: "Lamb, if you die, I will assume command, and I will never surrender."

After the fort was captured and General Whiting was made prisoner, he was taken to Fort Columbus, on Governor's Island, and there died, March 10, 1865. The fearless defender of the last stand at Fort Fisher, Maj. James Reilly, in after years lived not far from the scene of his exploits until his death, November 5, 1894.

---

[1]Rear-Admiral Porter's official report of the second attack on Fort Fisher contains the following statement: "We expended in the bombardment about 50,000 shells," but in commenting on this the compilers of the *Official Records of the Union and Confederate Navies in the War of the Rebellion*, Series 1, Vol. XI, p. 441, say "An examination of reports and logs shows that in the first attack on Fort Fisher by the Federal fleet there were expended 20,271 projectiles, weighing 1,275,299 pounds. In the second attack there were expended 19,682 projectiles, weight, 1,652,638 pounds. It is estimated that the above statement includes between 90 and 95 per cent of the projectiles actually expended."

Blockade Running

FINANCIAL ESTIMATES OF BLOCKADE RUNNING.

Some idea of the magnitude of the blockade-running interests involving the Cape Fear alone may be gathered from Badeau's statement that "in little more than a year before the capture of Fort Fisher, the ventures of British capitalists and speculators with Wilmington alone had amounted to sixty-six million dollars in gold, and sixty-five million dollars worth of cotton in gold had been exported in return."

In the same period 397 steamers had run the blockade at Wilmington. Ridpath says that the number of prizes of blockade runners made during the four years' war was 1,504 vessels captured, stranded, or destroyed.

Admiral Porter, who directed the naval operations against Fort Fisher, says that a telegraphic dispatch from General Lee to Colonel Lamb at Fort Fisher was captured which read as follows: "If Fort Fisher falls, I shall have to evacuate Richmond."

In "Tales of the Cape Fear Blockade," published in the *North Carolina Booklet,* February 10, 1902, page 20, under the caption "Financial Estimates," the writer said:

I have not been able to obtain an approximate estimate of the value of supplies brought by blockade runners into the Confederacy during the four years' war, nor the amount of the losses by shipowners who failed to make a successful voyage through the Federal fleet. I have, however, carefully computed the actual sum realized by the United States Government from public sales of prizes, recorded by Admiral Porter in his *Naval History of the Civil War,* which aggregates $21,759,595.05; to which may reasonably be added $10,000,000 for prizes to my knowledge not included in this report, and $10,000,000 more for valuable ships and cargoes stranded or destroyed by design or accident while attempting to escape from the blockading squadron. This total of $42,000,000 represents only a part, perhaps one-half, of the capital invested. Many successful steamers ran up their profits into millions. A steamer carrying 1,000 bales of cotton sometimes realized a profit of a quarter of a million dollars on the inward and outward run within two weeks. Cotton could be purchased in the Confederacy for three cents per pound in gold, and sold in England at the equivalent of forty-five cents to one dollar a pound, and the profits on some classes of goods brought into the Confederacy were in the same proportion. It is probably within the bounds of truth to say that the blockade-running traffic during the war, including the cost of the ships, amounted to about one hundred and fifty million dollars, gold standard.

The Confederate States steamer *R. E. Lee,* under Captain Wilkinson, ran the blockade at Wilmington twenty-one times and carried abroad nearly seven thousand bales of cotton, worth at that time about two million dollars in gold; and she also took into the Confederacy equally valuable cargoes.

The steamer *Siren,* most successful of all, made sixty-four runs through the blockade, and her profits ran into millions.

Montesquieu has said that it is not the number killed and wounded in a battle that determines its general historical importance, and Creasy, in *Fifteen Decisive Battles of the World, from Marathon to Waterloo,* says: "It is not because only a few hundred fell in the battle by which Joan of Arc captured the Tourelles and raised the seige of Orleans that the effect of that crisis is to be judged."

Napoleon said that an army moves upon its belly. The resources of the Confederate Army commissariat, steadily depleted by the incessant drain upon the food producers and by the blockade of the Southern ports, were largely sustained during the war by the successful blockade runners from the West Indies to Wilmington, whence cargoes of increasing value were immediately transported to our starving Confederates in the field; but when the multiplied arms of the new navy, like the deadly tentacles of the octupus, reached into every hiding-place of these fugitives of the sea, they gradually brought to an end, in the capture of Fort Fisher, this wonderful epoch in our naval and commercial history.

New Inlet, since closed by harbor and river improvements, was more frequently used by the blockade runners than the Main Bar, under the guns of Fort Caswell, It was protected for four years by Fort Fisher, which commanded the last gateway between the Confederate States and the outside world. Its capture, with the resulting loss of all the Cape Fear River defenses and Wilmington, the *entrepôt* of the Confederacy, effectually ended blockade running and compelled the subsequent surrender of the Confederate Army in the field.

It was, therefore, not the valor of the Federal or of the Confederate forces in the contest at Fort Fisher that made it most memorable in the history of the war. It was the fatal blow to the Confederate commissariat, the cutting off of supplies, the starvation of Lee's army, the closure of the last hope of the Confederacy, which gives to the victory of Curtis, the gallant leader of the Union forces at Fort Fisher, its lasting importance as an historical event.

THE PORT OF WILMINGTON DURING THE WAR.

When Beauregard fired that fateful bombshell which burst over Fort Sumter at half past four on the morning of April 12, 1861, it sent a thrill of dismay into every Southern port, and panic-stricken master mariners hurriedly prepared their ships for sea, and welcomed any wind that would blow them away from the impending danger.

In a short time the Cape Fear was deserted, and the occupation of pilots and longshoremen was gone. At that time there were sixty or seventy licensed bar and river pilots and apprentices, who had no thought of the rich harvest of golden sovereigns which Fortune was to pour into their pockets in the strange commerce of the beleaguered city that became the gateway of the Southern Confederacy.

The Blockade.

On the nineteenth of April, 1861, President Lincoln declared by proclamation a military and commercial blockade of our Southern ports, which was supplemented by the proclamation of the 27th of May to embrace the whole Atlantic coast from the capes of Virginia to the mouth of the Rio Grande. This was technically a "constructive," or "paper," blockade, inasmuch as the declaration of the great powers assembled in congress at Paris, in 1856, removed all uncertainty as to the principles upon which the adjudication of prize claims must proceed by declaring that "blockades, in order to be binding, must be effective; that is to say, must be maintained by a force sufficient really to prevent access to the enemy's coast."

It was obviously impossible at that time for the Federal Government to enforce a blockade of the Southern coast, measuring 3,549 miles and containing 189 harbors, besides almost innumerable inlets and sounds through which small craft might easily elude the four United States warships then available for service, the remaining 38 ships of war in commission being on distant stations.

Measures were, therefore, taken by the Navy Department to close the entrances of the most important Southern ports, notably those of Charleston and Savannah, by sinking vessels loaded with stone across the main channels or bars. Preparations were also made on a more extensive plan to destroy the natural roadsteads˜of other Southern ports and harbors along the coast by the same means; but, although twenty-five vessels were sunk in the smaller inlets, it does not appear that this novel method of blockade was generally adopted.

In the meantime, urgent orders had been sent recalling from foreign stations every available ship of war; and by December of the same year the Secretary of the Navy had purchased and armed 264 ships, which, with their 2,557 guns and 22,000 men, rendered the "paper blockade" comparatively effective. A sorry looking fleet it was as compared with our modern navies; ships, barks, schooners, sloops, tugs, passenger boats—anything that would carry a gun, from the hoary type of Noah's Ark to the double-end ferry boat still conspicuous in New York waters.

"The blockading fleet," says Judge Advocate Cowley, "was divided into two squadrons; the Atlantic Blockading Squadron of 22 vessels, carrying 296 guns and 3,300 men, and the Gulf Blockading Squadron of 21 vessels, carrying 282 guns and 3,500 men." This force was constantly increased as the two hundred specially designed ships of war were built by the Navy Department. The squadron reached its highest degree of efficiency during the fourth year of the war by the acquisition of many prizes, which were quickly converted into light draft cruisers and rendered effective naval service, frequently under their original names.

THE BLOCKADERS.

The first blockader placed upon the Cape Fear Station was one bearing the misnomer *Daylight,* which appeared July 20, 1861. Others soon followed, until the number of the blockaders off New Inlet and the Main, or Western, Bar of the river was increased thirty or more; these formed a cordon every night in the shape of a crescent, the horns of which were so close in shore that it was almost impossible for a small boat to pass without discovery. Armed picket barges also patrolled the bars and sometimes crept close in upon the forts. For a year or more the fleet was largely kept upon the blockading stations; then a second cordon was placed across the track of the blockade runners near the ports of Nassau and the Bermudas, the cruisers of which sometimes violated the international distance restriction of one league—three geographical miles— from neutral land. At last a third cordon was drawn on the edge of the Gulf Stream, to which the hunted and harassed blockade runner often became an easy prey in the early morning after a hard night's run in the darkness, during which no lights were visible to friend or foe, even the binnacle lamp being carefully screened, leaving only a small peephole by which the ship was steered.

The Cruisers.

Some of the later cruisers were faster than the blockade runners and were more dreaded than the blockading squadron, not only because of their greater speed, but chiefly because of the proximity of their consorts, which kept them always in sight, often to the discomfiture of their unhappy quarry, headed off and opposed in every direction. The prospective division of big prize money, running into millions of dollars, was, of course, the most exciting feature of the service on the Federal side. Occasionally there was comparatively trifling compensation, but great enjoyment in the capture of some small-fry blockade runners, consisting of pilot boats or large yawls laden with two or three bales of cotton and a crew of three or four youths, that sometimes came to grief in a most humiliating way. These small craft, upon one of which the writer was at sea for two weeks, were too frail for the risk of the longer voyages, and were usually projected from the small inlets, or sounds, farther South, which gave them a short run of about a hundred miles to the outer Bahama Keys, through whose dangerous waters they would warily make their way to Nassau. A boat of this description sailed over a Florida bar on a dark night under a favorable wind; but, failing to get out of sight of land before morning dawned, was overhauled at sunrise by a blockader and ordered to come alongside, where, with their own hands, these miniature blockade runners were obliged to hook on to the falls of the Federal davits, by which they were ignominiously hoisted—boat, cargo and crew, to the captor's deck.

The desertion of negro slaves from tidewater plantations and their subsequent rescue as "Intelligent Contrabands" by the coasting cruisers formed an occasional incident in the records of their official logs; but it is a noteworthy fact, deserving honorable mention, that comparatively few of the trusted negroes upon whom the soldiers in the Confederate Army relied for the protection and support of their families at home were thus found wanting. A pathetic and fatal instance is recalled in the case of a misguided negro family which put off from the shore in the darkness, hoping that they would be picked up by a chance gunboat in the morning. They were hailed by a cruiser at daylight, but in attempting to board her their frail boat was swamped, and the father alone was rescued, the mother and all the children perishing.

A PORT OF REFUGE.

The natural advantages of Wilmington at the time of the War between the States made it an ideal port for blockade runners, there being two entrances to the river, New Inlet on the north, and the Western, or Main, Bar, on the south of Cape Fear.

For miles the slope of our beach is very gradual to deep water. The soundings along the coast are regular, and the floor of the ocean is remarkably even. A steamer hard pressed by the enemy could run along the outer edge of the breakers without great risk of grounding; the pursuer, being usually of deeper draft, was obliged to keep further off shore. The Confederate steamer *Lilian,* of which I was then purser, was chased for nearly a hundred miles from Cape Lookout by the United States steamer *Shenandoah,* which sailed a parallel course within half a mile of her and forced the *Lilian* at times into the breakers. This was probably the narrowest escape ever made by a blockade runner in a chase. The *Shenandoah* began firing her broadside guns at three o'clock in the afternoon, her gunners and the commanding officers of the batteries being distinctly visible to the *Lilian's* crew. A heavy sea was running which deflected the aim of the man-of-war, and this alone saved the *Lilian* from destruction. A furious bombardment by the *Shenandoah,* aggravated by the display of the *Lilian's* Confederate flag, was continued until nightfall, when, by a clever ruse, the *Lilian,* guided by the flash of her pursuer's guns, stopped for a few minutes; then, putting her helm hard over ran across the wake of the warship straight out to sea, and on the following morning, passed the fleet off Fort Fisher in such a crippled condition that several weeks were spent in Wilmington for repairs.

THE CHASE.[1]

[After Homeward Bound.]

Freed from the lingering chase, in devious ways
 Upon the swelling tides
 Swiftly the *Lilian* glides
Through hostile shells and eager foemen past;
The lynx-eyed pilot gazing through the haze,
And engines straining, "far hope dawns at last."

Now falls in billows deep the welcome night
 Upon white sands below;
 While signal lamps aglow
Seek out Fort Fisher's distant answering gleams,
The blockade runner's keen, supreme delight,—
Dear Dixie Land, the haven of our dreams!

JAMES SPRUNT.

CAPE FEAR PILOTS.

The four years of blockade running, from 1861 to 1865, were so crowded with incidents and adventures of an extraordinary and startling nature that each day brought a new and novel experience.

I recall my first day under fire, the trembling knees, the terrifying scream of the approaching shells, the dread of instant death. Again, the notable storm at sea in which our ship was buffeted and lashed by the waves until the straining steel plates cut the rivets, the fireroom was flooded and the engines stopped, while the tempest tossed us helpless upon the mountainous waves, and all hope of saving our lives was gone until we were mercifully cast upon a reef which extends about

[1]First published in the *North Carolina Booklet.*

thirty miles from Bermuda. And later, when our party of five persons endeavoring to reach the Confederacy in a small launch after the fall of Fort Fisher was cast away the second day upon Green Turtle Cay, an obscure island of the Bahamas, where we dwelt in a negro's hut for three weeks, and then foolishly risked our lives again for two weeks at sea in a small boat which landed us in the surf among the man-eating sharks off Cape Canaveral, Florida.

Strangely enough, as I was writing these reminiscences of long ago, a benevolent old gentleman presented himself at my office door and said, "I want to see my old friend, Mr. Sprunt, who was purser of my ship fifty years ago, and whom I have not seen since then." It was gratifying to see again in the flesh my brother officer, Andrew J. Forrest, of Baltimore, who was first assistant engineer with us when Fort Fisher was captured and our occupation as blockade runners terminated. Among many other incidents which our meeting brought to mind was a ludicrous scene recalled by my friend. "Do you remember," said Andy, "how annoying it was to the captain when his belated slumbers, after a night at poker, were disturbed in the early morning by the usual holy-stoning and washing-down-decks which Chief Officer Carrow was so particular about? Do you recall the occasion when, having finished breakfast, we were strolling about the quarter-deck, and a rooster got out of the coop near the galley and, perching himself upon the bridge-deck near the captain's stateroom, crowed and crowed, until with a savage oath the skipper burst out of the door in his pajamas with a big Colt's revolver and chased that rooster all over the ship in a rage that fairly choked us with laughter?"

My friend tells me that we two are the only survivors of the fifty-two officers and men upon the muster roll of the old ship, which was subsequently used as a transport in the South American wars.

The stirring scenes recalled in these reminiscences occurred more than a half-century ago. But few of those who participated in blockade running still survive, and their hoary heads and feeble knees attest the measure of their days. One, whose moral excellence commands universal respect, still heeds the call of the sea, and none of his profession is more skillful in piloting the big steamers with their valuable cargoes through the devious Cape Fear Channel over the bar to the city's harbor.

Fifty years ago he and I were captured, man and boy together, in the same ship, under the Confederate flag; and we suffered together the privations, discomforts, and trials of prisoners of war. Upon the return of peace our vocations cemented a friendship which has extended unbroken to the present time. Some years ago he was called by the Master who once walked upon the sea to the higher service of a minister of the gospel, in which he has been signally blessed.

The writer, for twenty-six years a member of the Board of Commissioners of Navigation and Pilotage, having ample means of observation at home and abroad, believes that our pilots compare most favorably with those of the order elsewhere in all the essential qualifications of this dangerous calling.

The story of their wonderful skill and bravery in the time of the Federal blockade has never been written, because the survivors were modest men, and because time obliterated from their memories many incidents of that extraordinary epoch in their history.

Amidst almost impenetrable darkness, without lightship or beacon, the narrow and closely watched inlet was felt for with a deep-sea lead as a blind man feels his way along a familiar path, and, even when the enemy's fire was raking the wheelhouse, the faithful pilot, with steady hand and iron nerve, safely steered the little fugitive of the sea to her desired haven. It might be said of him as it was told of the Nantucket skipper, that he could get his bearings on the darkest night by a "taste" of the lead.

We recall the names of some of the noted blockade runners and their pilots, so well known in Smithville about fifty years ago: *Cornubia,* afterwards called the *Lady Davis,* C. C. Morse; *Giraffe,* afterwards known as the *R. E. Lee,* Archibald Guthrie; *Fanny,* Henry Howard; *Hansa,* J. N. Burruss; *City of Petersburg,* Joseph Bensel; *Old Dominion,* Richard Dosher; *Alice,* Joseph Springs; *Margaret and Jessie,* Charles W. Craig; *Hebe,* George W. Burruss; *Advance,* C. C. Morse; *Pet,* T. W. Craig; *Atalanta,* Thomas M. Thompson; *Eugenia,* T. W. Newton; *Ella and Annie,* J. M. Adkins; *Banshee,* Thomas Burruss; *Venus,* R. Sellers; *Don,* William St. George; *Lynx,* J. W. Craig; *Let Her Be,* J. T. Burruss; *Little Hattie,* R. S. Grissom; *Lilian,* Thomas Grissom; *North Heath,* Julius Dosher; *Let Her Rip,* E. T. Burruss; *Beauregard,* J. W. Potter; *Owl,* T. B. Garrason; *Agnes Fry,* Thomas Dyer; *Kate,* C. C. Morse;

Siren, John Hill; *Calypso,* C. G. Smith; *Ella,* John Savage; *Condor,* Thomas Brinkman; *Coquette,* E. T. Daniels; *Mary Celeste,* J. W. Anderson; *Susan Bierne,* Richard Dosher.

Many other steamers might be named, among them the *Britannic, Emma, Dee, Antonica, Victory, Granite City, Stonewall Jackson, Flora, Havelock, Hero, Eagle, Duoro, Thistle, Scotia, Gertrude, Charleston, Colonel Lamb, Dolphin,* and *Dream,* the names of whose pilots may or may not be among those already recalled. These are noted here because there is no other record of their exploits extant.

Some of the steamers which were run ashore by the blockaders may still be seen: The *Ella* on Bald Head, the *Spunky* and the *Georgiana McCall* on Caswell Beach, the *Hebe* and the *Dee* between Wrightsville and Masonboro. The *Beauregard* and the *Venus* lie stranded on Carolina Beach; the *Modern Greece,* near New Inlet; the *Antonica,* on Frying Pan Shoals. Two others lie near Lockwood's Folly Bar; and others whose names are forgotten lie half-buried in sands, where they may remain for centuries to come.

JAMES WILLIAM CRAIG, A VETERAN PILOT.

He is now the Rev. James William Craig, Methodist preacher, but I like to think of him as Jim Billy, the Cape Fear pilot of war times, on the bridge of the swift Confederate blockade runner *Lynx,* commanded by the intrepid Captain Reed, as she races through the blackness of night on her course west nor'west, straight and true for the Federal fleet off New Inlet, in utter silence, the salt spray of the sea smiting the faces of the watch as they gaze ahead for the first sign of imminent danger.

Soon there is added to the incessant noise of wind and waves the ominous roar of the breakers, as the surf complains to the shore, and the deep-sea lead gives warning of shoaling water. "Half-speed," is muttered through the speaking tube; a hurried parley; a recognized landfall—for Reed is a fine navigator—and "Are you ready to take her, Pilot?" "Ready, sir," comes from Jim Billy in the darkness. Then the whispered orders through the tube: "Slow down," as there looms ahead the first of the dread monsters of destruction. "Starboard," "Steady," and the little ship glides past like a phantom, unseen as yet. Then "Port," "Port," "Hard a'port," in quick succession, as she almost touches the second cruiser. She is now in the thick of the blockading squadron; and suddenly, out of the darkness and close aboard, comes the hoarse hail, "Heave to, or I'll sink you," followed by a blinding glare of rockets and the roar of heavy guns. The devoted little Confederate is now naked to her enemies, as the glare of rockets and Drummond lights from many men-of-war illuminate the chase. Under a pitiless hail of shot and shell from every quarter, she bounds full speed ahead, every joint and rivet straining, while Jim Billy dodges her in and out through a maze of smoke and flame and bursting shells. The range of Fort Fisher's guns is yet a mile away. Will she make it? Onward speeds the little ship, for neither Reed nor Jim Billy has a thought of surrender. A shell explodes above them, smashing the wheelhouse; another shell tears away the starboard paddle-box; and as she flies like lightning past the nearest cruiser, a sullen roar from Colonel Lamb's artillery warns her pursuers that they have reached their limitations; and in a few minutes the gallant little ship crosses the bar and anchors under the Confederate guns. The captain and his trusty pilot shake hands and go below, "to take the oath," as Reed described it—for the strain must be relaxed by sleep or stimulation. "A close shave, Jim," was all the captain said. "It was, sir, for a fact," was the equally laconic answer.

My shipmate, Jim Billy, is growing old, and so am I. Our lives have been united all these years in a bond which death only can divide; and as we talk, as we often do, about old times and those who took part with us in the stress of war, all of whom have gone out upon the boundless tide, we are thankful that we are in the convoy of Him who walked upon the sea, and that we will be guided to our desired haven by His good hand upon us. Some days ago I drew out of Jim Billy the following narrative, which I have set down as nearly as may be in his own words, and I trust it may serve to interest and instruct some readers who do not often hear a true sailor's yarn:

"I was born in May, 1840, and piloted my first vessel into the Cape Fear River when I was seventeen years of age. At that time Mr. P. W. Fanning, of Wilmington, was chairman of the Board of Commissioners of Navigation and Pilotage, and the present custom of issuing branches, or licenses, was not in vogue.

"I acted under the protection of my father, who was a full branch pilot; in other words, he was permitted to carry in vessels of any depth suitable for the water then available. I was an apprentice to him.

"When the war broke out I was twenty-one years of age and, in view of certain circumstances favorable to my reputation, I was given by the Board of Commissioners of Navigation and Pilotage a license for twelve feet, the laws having been changed a year or two before the war in respect to the method of issuing licenses.

"My father, James N. Craig, lived a short distance from Fort Fisher on the river side at a place called Craig's Landing, and his house and landing were both used later by the commander of Fort Fisher, Col. William Lamb, who was so intimately engaged with my father that he gave him general charge of the duty of setting lights for the benefit of blockade runners, under certain restrictions which had been provided. I was therefore engaged for nearly two years after the outbreak of the war in assisting my father, and became more familiar with the channel and the approaches of the channel than many other pilots who had not the opportunity of sounding, as we had frequently, under government instructions.

"The first proposal made to me to take a ship through the blockade was by Capt. E. C. Reed, commander of the celebrated cruiser *Sumter*. This vessel had been dismantled of her guns on account of her slow speed and general unfitness for a cruiser, after her destruction of many vessels of the enemy, and she was sent into Wilmington with a cargo of war stores, conspicuous among which were two enormous Blakely guns, which were subsequently used in the defense of Charleston.

"After the discharge of the cargo at Wilmington, the *Sumter* was loaded with cotton, and Captain Reed brought her down to Old Brunswick landing and anchored before he made arrangements for the engagement of a pilot to take him out.

"In coming into the Cape Fear Captain Reed had, through a successful ruse, passed through the blockading fleet by hoisting the United States ensign and pretending to be one of the fleet. The blockaders did not discover his true character until he was under the guns of Fort Fisher, and consequently they were very eager to capture him on his voyage outward.

"At that time of the tide it was impossible to take over the Rip Shoal or across either of the bars a ship drawing more than eleven feet. The *Sumter* drew eleven feet of water and grounded repeatedly in attempting to go out. Captain Reed offered me $1,000 in gold if I would take the ship out successfully and reach Bermuda, where he would discharge me and proceed to England with his cargo.

"I made several ineffectual attempts to get the *Sumter* outside, but, owing to the lack of water and the vigilance of the blockading fleet, we were baffled repeatedly. At last I took her out successfully over the bar at New Inlet, the fleet in the meantime having concentrated at the Western Bar, expecting to capture her there, and Captain Reed subsequently told me that he proceeded to Bermuda and to England without sighting a single hostile vessel during the whole voyage.

"A short time after that I piloted in the Steamship *Orion* over New Inlet Bar successfully, the vessel having arrived off the bar without a pilot and, very luckily for the ship as well as for me, hailed me while I was setting some lights for another vessel, the *Cornubia,* ready to go out in charge of Pilot C. C. Morse.

"Just as Morse was passing us, he called out, 'Don't take your lights in too soon, because if we run afoul of a blockader outside, he may run us in again, and we want the benefit of the lights.'

"Sure enough, a few minutes after the *Cornubia* had faded from our sight beyond the bar, we were surprised by the sudden looming up of another large steamer, which at first we supposed was a blockader chasing the *Cornubia.*

"We were still more surprised, and really frightened, when they lowered a boat and pulled close up to us in the semi-darkness and demanded to know who we were, Pilot Thomas Newton being with me. They asked if we were pilots, which we admitted was the case. The voice, which proved to be that of the chief officer of the blockade runner *Orion,* a very fine ship, then replied, 'We have been trying to run into Charleston, and failed to do so. We are groping around for the New Inlet Bar. Will you take us in?' We at once agreed, and proceeded to the ship and brought her in over the bar and anchored her in safety under the guns of Fort Fisher.

"Strangely enough, the captain of the *Orion,* who claimed to be a Baltimorean, recognized me, and reminded me that I had taken him over the bar before the war, when he commanded a schooner from Baltimore.

"Some months afterwards a very fine blockade runner called the *Don,* under command of Captain Roberts (whose real name was Hobart, a son of the Earl of Buckinghamshire, and a post captain in the British Navy, who had obtained leave of absence in order to try his skill at blockade running), was brought successfully to Wilmington by Pilot St. George, who was there taken sick, and I was requested to assume his place.

"On my return to Wilmington in the *Don,* I relinquished this vessel to her former pilot, St. George, and made a contract with the agent in Wilmington of a firm which owned a number of blockade runners—a notable one being the *Hansa*—to pilot any vessels which he might designate and be subject to his orders at any moment, the term of engagement being three months.

"Immediately afterwards, I was ordered to proceed to Nassau in the blockade runner *Fanny* (formerly the *Orion*), and report to Captain Watters, of the blockade runner *Annie,* for duty on that ship.

"I remember that we left in the *Fanny* on Saturday night and arrived in Nassau before daylight on Tuesday morning, where I found the *Annie,* fully loaded and ready for sea, waiting for me. We accordingly left about 4 o'clock that afternoon and arrived without incident inside the Cape Fear Bar on the Friday night following.

"I made a second voyage through the blockade in the *Annie,* passing within a cable-length of two of the Federal fleet that failed to observe us.

"We again loaded the *Annie* in Nassau and cleared for Wilmington, but fell in with a hurricane shortly afterwards, and were obliged to heave to for about forty hours, and so lost our reckoning. Failing to get observations for three days, we waited until the gale subsided, and then anchored the ship in smooth water, by a kedge, until the captain succeeded in getting an observation of the North Star, by which he worked out his position. We then shaped our course straight for the blockade fleet off Fort Fisher.

"At that time, and subsequently, it was the custom for the flagship of the blockading squadron to carry a large light, and this, being the only one visible, often served the purpose of guiding the blockade runners until they could get the bearings of the Mound Light. On this particular night of May 6, 1864, we came very near running afoul of the Confederate iron-clad ram *Raleigh* outside of the bar, but, supposing her to be one of the blockaders, got out of her way as quickly as possible.

"My term of three months' service having expired, I was proceeding in my skiff from Craig's Landing to Wilmington when I was overtaken by a very swift blockade runner, with two rakish funnels, a perfect model of its kind, called the *Lynx,* and, having been given a towline, climbed aboard and found, to my great surprise and delight, that the ship was commanded by my old friend, Captain Reed, who immediately requested that I would arrange to go with him, as his engagement of a pilot was only for the voyage inward.

"To this I consented on condition that General Whiting would approve it, and I received a few days afterwards a telegram to go on board the *Lynx* at Fort Fisher. I was in a hurricane on this ship in which she fared badly, her paddle-boxes, sponsons, and bridge-deck being partly washed away; but we at last limped into Bermuda and, after repairing damages, proceeded again to Wilmington.

"The longest chase of which I was a witness during the war occurred while I was on the *Lynx,* which was chased for fifteen hours by that very fast cruiser, *Fort Jackson.* The *Fort Jackson's* log and official report subsequently showed that she was making sixteen knots an hour, which at that time was considered phenomenal speed (the average blockade runner seldom exceeding fourteen knots an hour), and on this occasion I remember that the safety-valves of the *Lynx* were weighted down by the iron tops of the coal bunkers, which of course imperiled the life of every one on board, but increased the speed of the *Lynx* to more than sixteen knots an hour and enabled her ultimately to escape.

"After making two round passages in the *Lynx* and running the blockade four times in this vessel, several times under fire, I joined at Wilmington the Confederate steamer *Lilian* under the following peculiar circumstances:

"Quite a number of the Wilmington pilots had been captured by the enemy, and the force available for ships belonging to the Confederate Government waiting in Bermuda and Nassau was in consequence greatly reduced. The regular pilot of the *Lilian* was Thomas Grissom, and I was one of four extra pilots (the three others being Joseph Thompson, James Bell, and Charles Craig), who were ordered by General Whiting to proceed to Bermuda and take charge of certain ships to be designated by Maj. Norman S. Walker, the Confederate agent at that port.

"Trouble began before we got outside. An armed barge from the fleet had come close inside the Western Bar and lay in our track in the channel, and immediately upon our approach, sent up a rocket and fired a gun, which was instantly answered by the whole fleet outside, and I remember that we crossed the bar in a bright flash of Drummond lights and rockets which made the night as bright as day. Every one of the blockaders was firing at us or over us as we headed out to sea, and when the next morning, Sunday, dawned, we had just succeeded in dropping the last of the cruisers, which had chased us all night.

"We were congratulating ourselves after breakfast that morning that we would have a clear sea towards Bermuda—and, by the way, the sea was as smooth as glass—when the lookout in the crow's nest reported a vessel of war ahead, shortly afterwards another on the starboard bow, and a little later a third on our port bow, and in a few minutes a fourth on our beam. We had unfortunately run into the second line of blockaders, called the Gulf Squadron, and it was not more than two hours before they were all in range and pelting us with bombshells.

"The chase lasted until half-past one in the afternoon, when a shell from the cruiser on our starboard beam, called the *Gettysburg,* formerly the blockade runner *Margaret and Jessie,* struck us below the water line, making a large hole through which the water rushed like a mill-stream.

"All our efforts to stop the leak with blankets were unavailing. We had previously thrown over our deck-load of cotton, but it was impossible to reach the aperture from the inside, as the hold was jam full of cotton; and in a short time the vessel began to steer badly and gradually sank almost to the level of the deck. Finding further efforts to escape utterly fruitless, the captain stopped the ship and surrendered to the boats which immediately surrounded us.

"I remember that when the ship was hove to and the Federal officers came on board, our sullen and dejected commander was standing on the starboard paddle-box, with his arms folded and his back turned to the approaching Federals. One of them, with a drawn sword, approached and asked if he was in command of the ship. Captain Martin responded with an oath: 'I was in command, but I suppose you are captain now.'

"Although every effort had been made to escape, those of us

who knew Captain Maffitt, the former commander of the *Lilian,* regretted very much his absence on this occasion, as he would most likely have been more fortunate in getting away.

"Knowing how eager the Federals were to identify the pilot of the ship, they being in blissful ignorance that there were no fewer than five Wilmington pilots on board, we all agreed to personate firemen or members of the crew, and succeeded in passing ourselves off as such. Subsequently all of us escaped except the ship's pilot, who was detained at Point Lookout until the end of the war.

"Our ship's company numbered forty-eight men, and now, after a lapse of forty-eight years, we two, James Sprunt, purser, and J. W. Craig, pilot, are the only survivors of them all.[1]

"After our escape from prison, we made our way to Halifax, Nova Scotia, through the medium of some gold coins, which I fortunately kept next to my body in a waistband and which paid the passage of four of my companions, including Mr. Sprunt. I joined the steamer *Bat* at Halifax, and proceeded as her pilot to Wilmington. When off the bar, and in the midst of the blockading fleet, which was firing heavily upon us, the captain lost his nerve and, notwithstanding my expostulations, persisted in stopping the *Bat.* The cause of the captain's excitement was due to this remarkable incident: One of our sailors was a survivor of the desperate battle between the *Alabama* and the *Kearsarge* off Cherbourg some months before, serving on the *Alabama;* but, instead of proving to be, as might be expected, a very brave man, under the fire of the blockading fleet he became terrified and hid himself as far forward under the turtleback in the eyes of our ship as he could squeeze himself. During the firing of the fleet a shot struck the exact spot where this poor fellow was hiding and cut off his leg, causing him to utter such shrieks as to demoralize the captain, who ignobly stopped and anchored his ship in the midst of the enemy, when he might just as well have gone on, with less risk of destruction. The ship that took us that night was the United States steamer *Montgomery.*

"For the second time I was made a prisoner of war and under the following circumstances, which I have never mentioned but once before.

"Before I became engaged in the blockade-running service, I was acting as mate on the Confederate steamer *Flora Mac-*

---

[1]Mr. Craig has since died.

donald, a transport on the Cape Fear River, and when the Confederate privateer *Retribution* sent into Wilmington a prize schooner, which she had captured at sea, in charge of one of the *Retribution's* officers named Jordan, who had shipped with Capt. Joseph Price in Wilmington, I assisted in towing that vessel from the bar to Wilmington, and of course saw much of Jordan.

When I was captured by the *Montgomery,* I was taken to Portsmouth Navy Yard, where we were boarded by a Federal officer in a captain's uniform, who proved to be none other than my quondam Confederate friend Jordan, who had gone over to the enemy, and who immediately recognized me and informed against me.

"I was then put in irons and sent on board the U. S. man-of-war *Sabine,* where I was most kindly treated by its commander, Captain Loring, and while a prisoner on his ship I was repeatedly approached by the Federal officers, who offered to pay any sum I would name if I would join their fleet off Fort Fisher and take part as a pilot in their attack against my home. I told them that the United States Government did not have enough money to induce me to accept such a proposition, and I accordingly remained a prisoner at Point Lookout until after the war was over.

"I may add that while I was a prisoner on the *Sabine,* two of the Cape Fear pilots, C. C. Morse and John Savage, were brought on board as prisoners, under suspicion of being pilots, and, although they were intimate friends of mine, I took particular pains to treat them as total strangers and paid no attention to them, lest it might get them into further trouble. They were much relieved when they discovered my purpose. Savage was subsequently released, but Morse, having been identified later by some other means, was made a prisoner with me until the end of the war.

"The monotony of prison life affords so few incidents that my experience is hardly worth recalling, and yet I remember some diversions, which gave us much merriment at the time.

"While our friends of the *Lilian* were confined for several weeks in a casemate of Fort Macon, that garrison consisted of what the Yankees called the First Regiment of North Carolina Volunteers. These men were known to us, however, as 'Buffaloes,' and they were a mean lot, as can be imagined from their having turned against their native State in time of great stress of war. Every day an officer and a guard took us outside our gloomy casemate and permitted us to stretch our legs along the beach, while we gazed with longing eyes across the intervening sound to Dixie Land. The marsh grass was full of sand fiddlers, which scuttled away at our approach. I pretended to be surprised and asked the guard what these things were, saying that they would be called lobsters in my country if they were much larger. The old renegade looked at me with a most contemptuous expression and replied: 'You know what they are; you've got millions of them at Smithville, whar you come from.'

"Another daily experience was the persistent, though unsuccessful, effort of the officer of the day to tease out of our young purser, James Sprunt, whom he thought an easy mark on account of his youth (17 years), betrayal of our pilot, little dreaming that we were five Wilmington pilots.

"A warm attachment began in that prison life between Mr. Sprunt and myself, which has been true and steadfast through all these intervening years. We little thought then that our lives would be so long united in the bonds of Christian fellowship and commercial enterprise.

"During my subsequent confinement on the *Sabine* as a prisoner of war, a large number of blockade runners who had been captured at sea were brought to that school-ship for confinement, and Captain Loring tried in every way to surprise those suspected of being pilots into an admission of the fact. One fine day, while the prisoners were lying on the deck, he, looking like an old sea dog, bluff and hearty, paced up and down among them, and suddenly turning on his heel called out: 'All you North Carolinians stand up quick!' I cast my eyes over a number of our pilots, fearing they would be taken by this surprise and betray themselves, but not a man stirred, and old Loring, who was really a good fellow and kind to us, went on his way.

"I hope it may not be amiss, in the conclusion of these reminiscences, to allude to the fact that, although I have been all these years engaged as a Cape Fear pilot, in the duties of my vocation, it has pleased God to call me also to the higher duty of preaching His gospel, as a Methodist minister, and to make me the humble instrument, in His hands, of guiding some of my fellow-men to their eternal rest, as I have guided the ships to their haven.

"There was a moral lesson, to those who heeded, in the

devious path of our hunted fugitives of the sea in war time,
for the Christian warfare is a running fight with many adver-
saries of the soul, and if we will but follow the lead of the
Great Pilot, He will bring us safe at last to 'an anchor within
the vail, whither our Forerunner is already entered.'

"There is a beautiful figure in this Scripture which few
landsmen recognize. The approach by sailing vessels in the
olden time to the inlets of the Mediterranean Sea was often
baffled by adverse winds, or calms; a little boat was then
lowered, which carried into the harbor a kedge anchor that was
dropped overboard. To this small anchor was attached a line
by which the vessel was warped by the windlass into the haven.
The man who carried the anchor in was the forerunner, and,
in the figure, he is Christ, the Captain of our Salvation; the
line is the line of faith, and the man at the windlass is a human
soul who trusts in God."

CAPTAIN DANIEL W. LEE.

A few weeks ago I spent a pleasant day with Capt. Daniel
W. Lee, in Virginia, the sailor nephew of the illustrious leader
of the Lost Cause, who served as an officer on board the Confederate States cruiser *Chickamauga,* which, under the command of Capt. John Wilkinson, spread consternation up and
down the Northern coast during the last ninety days of the
war.

Across the historic Rappahannock lay the famous town of
Fredericksburg, the home of Washington and Mercer, the
cradle of American independence, so often swept by fire and
sword in the scourge of war. Beyond this, like two great
armies, were the serried ranks of 30,000 to 40,000 Confederate
and Federal dead, waiting for the trumpet call; and farther
still, the ancient house of Brompton on Marye's Heights, around
which the iron hail and storm of battle swept, leaving many
thousand bullet-scars which time has not effaced.

From these familiar scenes which fill the contemplative mind
with sad emotions, Captain Lee turned with kindling eyes to
the recital of his daring runs through the Cape Fear blockade,
and courteously inquired for the welfare of his old shipmates
at Wilmington and Southport, nearly all of whom have gone
out on their last voyage. With characteristic modesty he declined to write a narrative of his war-time experience; but as

he was a subordinate under Captain Wilkinson, the latter's narration of cruises in which they were engaged will serve to connect the sea life of this distinguished gentleman with a unique epoch in Cape Fear history.

Pilot Burruss.

A familiar face and figure in the strenuous days of 1861 to 1866 was Pilot Ned Burruss, of Smithville. He was reckoned one of the coolest and bravest of men under fire and also a pilot of great ability. I recall a characteristic story of Burruss. When Captain Reed, of the *Sumter,* aroused him from a deep sleep with the exclamation, "Ned, we are surrounded by the Yankees and can not escape; we must either be sunk or run ashore," Burruss rubbed his eyes and remarked in a matter-of-fact tone, "Well, I guess I'd better put on a clean shirt." For years after the war he held a steady engagement as pilot on the Clyde steamers, and when he gave it up his employers parted with him regretfully, because they regarded him as a most trustworthy and capable man. Mr. Burruss always inspired his shipmates with confidence. His quiet, kindly disposition and his well-known skill made many friends. His death recently was greatly deplored.

Captain Steele.

I recall an instance of extraordinary nerve on the part of Captain Steele, of the blockade runner *Banshee,* who found himself at daylight close alongside a Federal cruiser. The captain of the warship *Nyphon* simply had the *Banshee* in the hollow of his hand, and desiring to capture this valuable prize without the risk of sinking her and thereby losing the prize money, he commanded Steele to heave to immediately or he would sink him. Steele, standing on the paddle-box, presented a ludicrous spectacle as he coolly shouted back that he didn't have time to stop, because he was in a hurry. Thereupon issued a cross fire of vituperation, while Steele's engineers were piling on steam in a desperate effort to escape. The Federal commander, still unwilling to destroy his prize and lose its value, continued to threaten, until he saw the *Banshee* gradually drawing away from him, when he shot away one of her masts and raked the little ship from stem to stern with grapeshot, while

Steele's men were lying flat on the deck for shelter.   The quartermaster abandoned the wheel and the little ship ran into the breakers, but was brought safely through by her intrepid pilot, Tom Burruss, a brother of Ned Burruss.

John William Anderson.

John William Anderson was a Smithville mariner, engaged, as all of them were, in running the blockade.   His name will live in the hearts and minds of the Lower Cape Fear people, because his last voyage splendidly illustrated the heroism and fidelity to duty of a Cape Fear pilot.   Although I remember the incident in all its details, I prefer to relate it in the words of the late Alfred Moore Waddell, the gifted writer of Wilmington, whose spirit has also taken its "flight to the undiscovered country":

"Among these blockade runners in 1863 was a steamer called the *Mary Celeste*.   Her pilot was John William Anderson, of Smithville, and he, like all the best pilots, was as familiar with the channels over the bars, both at New Inlet (where Fort Fisher stood, and which is now closed) and at the mouth of the river, as a farmer is with the roads over his land.   One night, in the month of August, 1863, Anderson took the *Mary Celeste* out over New Inlet Bar, and, gliding past the blockading fleet, which was always watching for such valuable prizes, escaped under cover of darkness and reached Nassau in safety. He only escaped one danger to run into another more fearful. Yellow fever was raging there, and the victims of that scourge were most numerous among the sailors and other non-residents. Anderson was stricken with the fever just before the *Mary Celeste* weighed anchor for her return voyage, and by the time she neared the North Carolina coast it was evident he must die.

"An entrance through the blockading fleet could, of course, only be made between sunset and sunrise and, as Anderson was the only Cape Fear pilot on board, great anxiety prevailed as to the safety of the ship.   At last the critical hour arrived, when, in the uncertain light of the dawn, they found that they had run near a blockader and had been seen by her.   The blockader opened fire on the *Mary Celeste* and pursued her.   Like a scared greyhound she made straight for New Inlet Bar, then visible several miles away, and after her steamed the blockader, from whose bow gun every few minutes would leap a flame followed by a shell which would pass over or through her rigging and burst in the air, or, striking the sea, would flash a great column of spray towards the sky. By this time poor Anderson was dying in his berth, and the officers of the ship began to realize the terrible situation in which they found themselves, with the enemy in pursuit and before them a bar over which it was almost certain destruction for any one aboard except Anderson to attempt to steer the *Mary Celeste.* Anderson heard the firing and knew what it meant before they told him. He knew, too, that he was dying and had no further interest in this world's affairs; but the sense of duty asserted itself even in the presence of death.

"He was too weak to go up, but he demanded to be taken on deck and carried to the man at the wheel. Two strong sailors lifted him and carried him up to the wheelhouse. They stood him on his feet and supported him on either side. His face was as yellow as gold, and his eyes shone like stars. He fixed his unearthly gaze upon the long line of breakers ahead, then upon the dim line of pines that stood higher than the surrounding forest, then at the compass for a moment, and said calmly, 'Hard starboard.' Quickly revolved the wheel under the hands of the helmsman; slowly veered the stem of the rushing steamer, and a shell hurtled over the pilot-house and went singing towards the beach.

"Anderson kept his gaze fixed on the breakers, and in the same calm tone said, 'Steady.' On ploughed the steamer straight for her goal, while the group of men in the pilot-house stood in profound silence but fairly quivering with suppressed excitement. The blockader, finally seeing that it was impossible to overtake her and not desiring to come within range of the big guns of Fort Fisher, abandoned the chase with a farewell shot, and the *Mary Celeste,* now nearly on the bar, slackened her pace a little, and nothing but the swash of the sea and the trembling thud of the ship under the force of the engine could be heard. The dying pilot, though failing fast, continued in the same calm tone to give his directions. They were now crossing the bar, but had passed the most dangerous point, when he bent his head as if to cough, and the horrified men saw the last fatal symptom which immediately precedes dissolution—black vomit—and knew that the end was very near. He knew it, too, but gave no sign of fear and continued at his post. His earthly home was now visible to his natural eye—he was almost there, where loved ones waited his coming—but nearer still to his spiritual vision was the 'house not made with hands, eternal in the heavens.' At last the bar was safely crossed, smooth water was reached, the engine slowed down, the *Mary Celeste* glided silently into the harbor, stopped her headway gradually, lay still, loosed her anchor chains, dropped her anchor, and as the last loud rattle of her cable ceased, the soul of John William Anderson took its 'flight to the undiscovered country.' "

NARRATIVES OF DISTINGUISHED BLOCKADE RUNNERS.

CAPT. JOHN WILKINSON, C. S. N.

One of the most intelligent and successful commanders in the blockade-running fleet was Capt. John Wilkinson, who entered the United States Navy as a midshipman in 1837, and, after an honorable and distinguished career, tendered his services to the Confederacy upon the secession of his native State, Virginia.

Having received a commission in the Confederate States Navy, he served in various responsible positions, and eventually was ordered upon special service in command of the Confederate States steamer *R. E. Lee.*

In his interesting book entitled *Narrative of a Blockade Runner,* with reference to the citizens of Virginia who resigned their commissions in the old service, he says: "They were compelled to choose whether they would aid in subjugating their State, or in defending it against invasion; for it was already evident that coercion would be used by the General Government, and that war was inevitable. In reply to the accusation of perjury in breaking their oath of allegiance, since brought against the officers of the army and navy who resigned their commissions to render aid to the South, it need only be stated that, in their belief, the resignation of their commissions absolved them from any special obligation. They then occupied the same position towards the government as other classes of citizens. But this charge was never brought against them until the war was ended. The resignation of their commissions was accepted when their purpose was well known. As to the charge of ingratitude, they reply their respective States had contributed their full share towards the expenses of the General Government, acting as their disbursing agent; and, when these

States withdrew from the Union, their citizens belonging to the two branches of the public service did not, and do not, consider themselves amenable to this charge for abandoning their official positions to cast their lot with their kindred and friends. But, yielding as they did to necessity, it was nevertheless a painful act to separate themselves from companions with whom they had been long and intimately associated, and from the flag under which they had been proud to serve."

With reference to his experience in blockade running at Wilmington, Captain Wilkinson writes:

"The natural advantages of Wilmington for blockade running were very great, owing chiefly to the fact that there were two separate and distinct approaches to Cape Fear River, *i. e.*, either by New Inlet to the north of Smith's Island, or by the Western Bar to the south of it. This island is ten or eleven miles in length; but the Frying Pan Shoals extend ten or twelve miles farther south, making the distance by sea between the two bars thirty miles or more, although the direct distance between them is only six or seven miles. From Smithville, a little village about equidistant from the two bars, both blockading fleets could be distinctly seen; and the outward-bound blockade runners could take their choice through which to run the gauntlet. The inward-bound blockade runners, too, were guided by circumstances of wind and weather, selecting that bar over which they would cross after they had passed the Gulf Stream, and shaping their course accordingly. The approaches to both bars were clear of danger, with the single exception of the 'Lump' before mentioned; and so regular are the soundings that the shore can be coasted for miles within a stone's throw of the breakers.

"These facts explain why the United States fleets were unable wholly to stop blockade running. It was, indeed, impossible to do so. The result to the very close of the war proves this assertion; for, in spite of the vigilance of the fleet, many blockade runners were afloat when Fort Fisher was captured. In fact, the passage through the fleet was little dreaded; for, although the blockade runner might receive a shot or two, she was rarely disabled; and, in proportion to the increase of the fleet, the greater we knew would be the danger of its vessels firing into each other. As the boys before the deluge used to say, they would be very apt to 'miss the cow and kill the calf.' The chief danger was upon the open sea, many of the light cruisers having

great speed. As soon as one of them discovered a blockade
runner during daylight, she would attract other cruisers in the
vicinity by sending up a dense column of smoke, visible for
many miles in clear weather. A cordon of fast steamers stationed ten or fifteen miles apart, inside the Gulf Stream, and
in the course from Nassau and Bermuda to Wilmington and
Charleston, would have been more effective in stopping blockade running than the whole United States Navy concentrated
off these ports. It was unaccountable to us why such a plan did
not occur to good Mr. Welles, but it was not our business to
suggest. I have no doubt, however, that the fraternity to which
I then belonged would unanimously have voted thanks and a
service of plate to the Honorable Secretary of the United States
Navy for this oversight.

"I say inside the Gulf Stream; because every experienced
captain of a blockade runner made it a point to cross the Stream
early enough in the afternoon if possible to establish the ship's
position by chronometer, so as to escape the influence of that
current upon his dead reckoning. The lead always gave indica-
tion of our distance from the land, but not, of course, of our
position; and the numerous salt works along the coast, where
evaporation was produced by fire, and which were at work night
and day, were visible long before the coast could be seen. Occasionally, the whole inward voyage would be made under adverse
conditions. Cloudy, thick weather and heavy gales would prevail so as to prevent any solar or lunar observations, and reduce
the dead reckoning to mere guesswork. In these cases, the
nautical knowledge and judgment of the captain would be taxed
to the utmost. The current of the Gulf Stream varies in veloc-
ity and, within certain limits, in direction; and the Stream
itself, almost as well defined as a river within its banks under
ordinary circumstances, is impelled by a strong gale towards
the direction in which the wind is blowing, overflowing its
banks, as it were. The counter current, too, inside of the Gulf
Stream is much influenced by the prevailing winds.

"Upon one occasion, while in command of the *R. E. Lee,*
formerly the Clyde built iron steamer *Giraffe,* we had experienced very heavy and thick weather, and had crossed the Stream
and struck soundings about midday. The weather then clearing, so that we could obtain an altitude near meridian, we found
ourselves at least forty miles north of our supposed position, and
near the shoals which extend in a southerly direction off Cape

MAP OF THE
CAPE FEAR RIVER
AND THE
APPROACHES
TO
WILMINGTON, N.C.

From C.S.A. Engineer Surveys.
Scale of Miles

Confederate Defenses

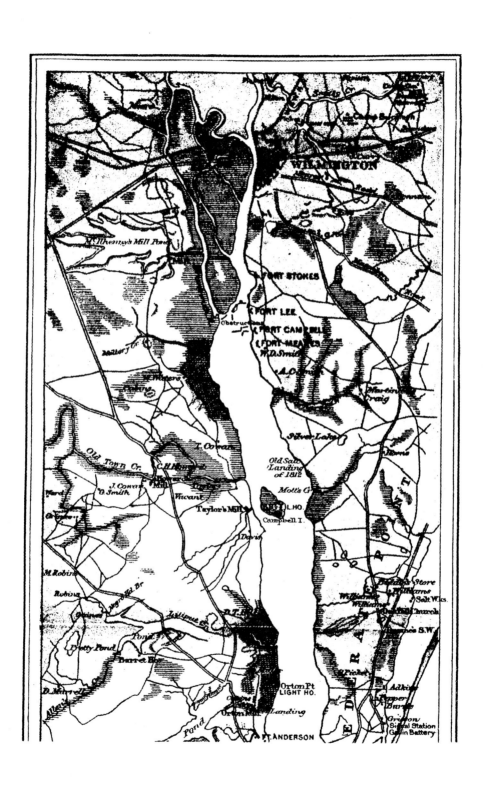

Lookout. It would be more perilous to run out to sea than to continue on our course, for we had passed through the off-shore line of blockaders, and the sky had become perfectly clear. I determined to personate a transport bound to Beaufort, a port which was in possession of the United States forces and the coaling station of the fleet blockading Wilmington. The risk of detection was not very great, for many of the captured blockade runners were used as transports and dispatch vessels. Shaping our course for Beaufort, and slowing down, as if we were in no haste to get there, we passed several vessels, showing United States colors to them all. Just as we were crossing the ripple of shallow water off the 'tail' of the shoals, we dipped our colors to a sloop-of-war which passed three or four miles to the south of us. The courtesy met prompt response; but I have no doubt her captain thought me a lubberly and careless seaman to shave the shoals so closely. We stopped the engines when no vessels were in sight; and I was relieved from a heavy burden of anxiety as the sun sank below the horizon, and our course was shaped at full speed for Masonboro Inlet.

"The staid old town of Wilmington was turned 'topsy-turvy' during the war. Here resorted speculators from all parts of the South to attend the weekly auctions of imported cargoes; and the town was infested with rogues and desperadoes, who made a livelihood by robbery and murder. It was unsafe to venture into the suburbs at night, and even in daylight there were frequent conflicts in the public streets between the crews of steamers in port and the soldiers stationed in the town, in which knives and pistols would be freely used; and not infrequently a dead body with marks of violence upon it would rise to the surface of the water in one of the docks. The civil authorities were powerless to prevent crime. *'Inter arma silent leges'!* The agents and employees of different blockade-running companies lived in magnificent style, paying a king's ransom (in Confederate money) for their household expenses, and nearly monopolizing the supplies in the country market. Towards the end of the war, indeed, fresh provisions were almost beyond the reach of every one. Our family servant, newly arrived from the country in Virginia, would sometimes return from market with an empty basket, having flatly refused to pay what he called 'such nonsense prices' for a bit of fresh beef or a handful of vegetables. A quarter of lamb, at the time of which I now write, sold for $100; a pound of tea, for $500. Confederate money which in September, 1861, was nearly equal to specie in value, had declined in September, 1862, to 225; in the same month, 1863, to 400, and before September, 1864, to 2,000.

"Many of the permanent residents of the town had gone into the country, letting their houses at enormous prices; those who were compelled to remain kept themselves much secluded, the ladies rarely being seen upon the more public streets. Many of the fast young officers belonging to the army would get an occasional leave to come to Wilmington, and would live at free quarters on board the blockade runners or at one of the numerous bachelor halls ashore.

"The convalescent soldiers from the Virginia hospitals were sent by the route through Wilmington to their homes in the South. The ladies of the town were organized by Mrs. DeRosset into a society for the purpose of ministering to the wants of these poor sufferers, the trains which carried them stopping an hour or two at the station that their wounds might be dressed and food and medicine supplied to them. These self-sacrificing, heroic women patiently and faithfully performed the offices of hospital nurses.

"Liberal contributions to this society were made by both companies and individuals, and the long tables at the station were spread with delicacies for the sick to be found nowhere else in the Confederacy. The remains of the meals were carried by the ladies to a camp of mere boys—home guards—outside of the town. Some of these children were scarcely able to carry a musket, and were altogether unable to endure the exposure and fatigue of field service; and they suffered fearfully from measles and typhoid fever. General Grant used a strong figure of speech when he asserted that 'the cradle and the grave were robbed to recruit the Confederate armies.' The fact of a fearful drain upon the population was not exaggerated. Both shared the hardships and dangers of war with equal self-devotion to the cause. It is true that a class of heartless speculators infested the country, who profited by the scarcity of all sorts of supplies; but this fact makes the self-sacrifice of the mass of the Southern people more conspicuous; and no State made more liberal voluntary contributions to the armies, or furnished better soldiers, than North Carolina.

"On the opposite side of the river from Wilmington, on a low, marshy flat, were erected the steam cotton presses, and there the blockade runners took in their cargoes. Sentries were posted on the wharves, day and night, to prevent deserters from getting on board and stowing themselves away; and the additional precaution of fumigating the outward-bound steamers at Smithville was adopted; but, in spite of this vigilance, many persons succeeded in getting a free passage abroad. These deserters, or 'stowaways,' were, in most instances, sheltered by one or more of the crew; in which event they kept their places of concealment until the steamer had arrived at her port of destination, when they would profit by the first opportunity to leave the vessel undiscovered. A small bribe would tempt the average blockade-running sailor to connive at this means of escape. The 'impecunious' deserter fared worse, and would usually be forced by hunger and thirst to emerge from his hiding place while the steamer was on the outward voyage. A cruel device employed by one of the captains effectually put a stop, I believe—certainly a check—to this class of 'stowaways.' He turned three or four of them adrift in the Gulf Stream, in an open boat, with a pair of oars, and a few days' allowance of bread and water."

CAPTAIN M. P. USINA.

During my intercourse with officers of celebrated blockade-running ships in the years 1863 and 1864, I met a mariner named M. P. Usina, from Charleston, familiarly known as Mike Usina, whose skill and daring made him famous in Nassau and Bermuda and in all of the Atlantic States. The American consul at Nassau, Mr. Whiting, eager for his capture by the cruisers which hovered near the British islands, bought Usina's portraits from a local photographer, and sent them broadcast among the Federal commanders in order to identify him when captured, as many Southerners escaped long confinement by claiming to be Englishmen. Captain Usina seemed to have a charmed life, but he was in reality so cool under fire and so resourceful in a tight place or situation, that he slipped through their fingers frequently when his capture seemed certain.

I remember some of the incidents connected with his blockade experience which stirred my blood long years ago and which I still recall with something of the old-time enthusiasm. In a speech before the Confederate Veterans' Association of Savannah, July 4, 1893, which I have carefully preserved, Captain Usina told a number of thrilling stories of his career which deserve honorable mention in the history of the strenuous times which he most graphically described. On that occasion he said:

"The men who ran the blockade had to be men who could stand fire without returning it. It was a business in which every man took his life in his hands, and he so understood it. An ordinarily brave man had no business on a blockade runner. He who made a success of it was obliged to have the cunning of a fox, the patience of a Job, and the bravery of a Spartan warrior. The United States Government wanted at first to treat them as pirates, and was never satisfied to consider them contrabandists. The runners must not be armed and must not resist; they must simply be cool and quick and watchful and, for the rest, trust to God and their good ship to deliver them safely to their friends.

"The United States blockade squadron on the Atlantic coast consisted of about 300 vessels of all kinds—sailing vessels, three-deckers, monitors, iron-clads, and swift cruisers—most of them employed to prevent the blockade runners from entering Charleston and Wilmington, these being the ports where most of the blockade running was done. At each of these ports there were three lines of ships anchored in a semicircle, so that our vessels had to run the gauntlet through these three lines before they had the enemy astern and their haven ahead. Besides these, the ocean between the Confederate ports and the Bermudas and the West Indies was policed by many of the fastest ships that money could buy or build, so that we had practically to run two blockades to reach a Southern port. The swiftest of the captured blockade runners were put into this service, and I have more than once been chased by ships of which I had myself been an officer.

"A few instances will suffice to illustrate the fact that the risks to be taken by the blockade runners were not confined to our own coast, and they will also illustrate the impunity with which the Federal blockaders practically blockaded friendly ports in violation of the neutrality laws governing nations at peace with each other.

"English steamers, with an English crew and without cargo, bound from one English port to another, were taken as prizes simply because they were suspected of being brought to the islands to be used as blockade runners.

"During the afternoon of March 3, 1863, while going from Nassau to Havana in the steamer *Stonewall Jackson,* we were sighted by the *R. R. Cuyler,* which chased us for thirteen hours along the Cuban coast until early the next morning, when we passed Morro Castle flying the Confederate flag, with the *Cuyler* a short half-mile astern of us flying the Stars and Stripes.

"In 1864, the *Margaret and Jessie,* bound from Charleston to Nassau, was chased and fired into while running along the coast of Eleutheria, within the neutral distance—an English league—the shot and shell passing over her falling into the pineapple fields of the island. She was finally run ashore by her captain to prevent her sinking from the effects of the enemy's shot.

"On one occasion I was awakened by the sound of cannon in the early morning at Nassau, and imagine my surprise to see a Confederate ship being fired at by a Federal man-of-war. The Confederate proved to be the *Antonica,* Captain Coxetter, who arrived off the port during the night and, waiting for a pilot and daylight, found when daylight did appear that an enemy's ship was between him and the bar. There was nothing left for him to do but run the gauntlet and take his fire, which he did in good shape, some of the shot actually falling into the harbor. The Federal ship was commanded by Commodore Wilkes, who became widely known from taking Mason and Slidell prisoners. After the chase was over Wilkes anchored his ship, and when the Governor sent to tell him that he must not remain at anchor there, he said: 'Tell the Governor, etc., etc., he would anchor where he pleased.' The military authorities sent their artillery across to Hog Island, near where he was anchored, and we Confederates thought the fun was about to begin. But Wilkes remained just long enough to communicate with the consul and get what information he wanted, and left.

"All this vigilance on the part of the Yankees made the trip a very hazardous one, and the man who failed to keep the sharpest kind of a lookout was more apt to bring up in a Northern prison than in a Confederate port. Then, too, the Yankee cruisers managed to keep pretty well posted as to our movements through the American consuls stationed at the different ports frequented by our vessels.

"Having occasion to go from Nassau to Bermuda, and there being no regular line between the islands, I chartered a schooner to take me and part of my crew there, and we had sailed within about sixty miles of our destination when, at daylight, we were spoken by the United States man-of-war *Shenandoah.* Her officer asked: 'What schooner is that, where from and where bound to?' Our captain was below and I answered him:

27

'Schooner *Royal*, bound from Nassau to Bermuda.' He ordered: 'Lower your boat and come alongside.' I said: 'I'll see you,' etc., etc., and then, 'I won't.' Nothing further was said, but in about twenty minutes they sent an armed boat alongside.

"In the meantime I had our captain called and the English ensign hoisted. Upon coming on deck the officer, quite a young lieutenant, was shown below, and after examining the vessel's papers, which he found O. K., he was about to return to his ship when I invited him to have a glass of wine with me. I have never forgotten his answer: 'I hadn't oughter, but I reckon I will.' After a little wine he grew talkative. He asked if I had not answered their hail, and when I replied 'Yes,' said 'I thought so, it sounded like you.' 'Why, what do you know about me?' I asked. 'Oh, I know enough to surprise you.' 'That is something no one has ever done yet.' 'Would you be surprised if I told you that your name is Usina?' 'Oh, no, my name is Marion Robinson.' 'How about the man who sat on the rail near you when I came on board? He is your man Irvin.' 'You have it bad this morning,' said I; 'Does wine usually affect you that way?' 'You know that I am giving it to you straight,' said he. 'Oh, no, you're badly mixed.' 'Will you think I'm mixed when I tell you that that little Frenchman is John Sassard, your chief engineer; that red-headed fellow over there is Nelson, your chief officer; these are all your men, and you are going to Bermuda to take charge of a new ship?' 'Well,' said I, 'you certainly have it bad, you had better not take any more wine.' 'Will you acknowledge I am right now?' said he, and produced my photograph with my history written on the back of it. I had to acknowledge it then; but I was under the protection of Her Most Gracious Majesty, and he had to admit his inability to take me now, though he promised to capture me before long and boasted that he had come very near me often before. But 'close' didn't count any more then than it does now, and he promised to treat me well if he should ever have the chance, and so we parted good friends.

"I afterwards found out that his ship had called at Nassau shortly after our leaving there, and the consul had given him my picture and the information which he sprung on me. I learned then that the photographers there had been making quite a nice thing selling the pictures of blockade runners to the United States authorities, together with what information they could gather about the originals; and the result was that, with but one exception (Captain Coxetter, who was too wise to have his picture taken), the Yankees had all our pictures, which did then, and perhaps do still, adorn the rogues' gallery in Ludlow Street Jail, New York City. Thus many a poor fellow who thought he was successfully passing himself off as an Englishman was identified and sent to Lafayette or Warren, two winter resorts that are not too pleasantly remembered by some of my old shipmates.

"The enemy's ships were provided with powerful calcium searchlights, which, if a blockade runner was in reach, would light her up about as well as an electric light would at the present time, and make her a perfect target for the enemy's fire. I have several times been just far enough to be out of reach of the light and by circling around it dodged them in the darkness. Another plan they adopted was to throw rockets over the ship occasionally, showing to all the vessels of the fleet the course taken by the fugitive. I think one of the worst frights I had during the war was the landing of a rocket on deck close to where I was standing. While we could not circumvent their searchlights, I succeeded in making the rocket scheme useless by providing myself with a quantity of them, firing back at them whenever they fired at us, or firing them in every direction, making it impossible to tell in which direction the chased ship was going.

"Among the vessels blockading Wilmington in 1864 was the little side-wheel steamer *Nansemond,* after the war a revenue cutter, and stationed at this place. She had a rifle gun mounted at each end, and being quite fast made several valuable captures. I remember that among the craft captured by her was the steamer *Hope,* Capt. William Hammer, of Charleston, with 1,800 bales of cotton and more men on board the *Hope* than there were on board the *Nansemond,* but, unfortunately, while the *Hope* was a stronger and larger ship and had more men, she was not allowed to defend herself and had to submit to the inevitable.

"One afternoon, while in command of the *Atalanta* and approaching Wilmington, I was sighted by the *Nansemond* and was being chased away from my port. Although I had the faster vessel, I realized that if the chase continued much longer I would be driven so far from my destination that I would not be able to get back that night, and so determined that, although

I had no guns to fight with, I might try a game of bluff. Hoisting the Confederate flag, I changed my course directly for him, and in a few minutes the tables were turned and the chaser was being chased, the *Nansemond* seeking with all possible speed the protection of the ships stationed off the bar, and that night the *Atalanta* was safe once more in Dixie.

"Several years afterwards I was a passenger on board the little revenue cutter *Endeavor,* better known as the *Hunkey Dory,* bound from Tybee to Savannah, and a stranger to every one on board. The conversation drifted into war reminiscences. Mr. Hapold, the officer in charge of the *Hunkey Dory,* had been an engineer on board the *Nansemond* when stationed on the blockade off Wilmington, and while giving his experience, among other incidents, he told of the narrow escape they had when the *Nansemond* was decoyed away from the fleet by a cruiser, under the guise of a blockade runner, that, when she thought the *Nansemond* was far enough away from her friends, ran up the Confederate flag and attempted to make a prize of her. 'But,' said he, 'the little *Nansemond's* speed saved her.' You can imagine their surprise when I informed them that I was in charge of the Confederate vessel, which was an unarmed ship chasing one that was armed—a clear case of 'Run, Big 'Fraid, Little 'Fraid'll catch you!'

"As a rule, the blockade runners were ships very slightly built, of light draft and totally unfit to brave the storms of the Atlantic. Yet the worse the weather the better it was liked, since a rough sea greatly reduced the danger from the enemy's guns. In most of the ships the boilers and engines were very much exposed, and a single shot to strike the boiler meant the death of every one on board. We had no lighthouses or marks of any kind to guide us, except the enemy's fleet, and had to depend upon our observations and surroundings on approaching the coast. Our ships were painted gray, to match the horizon at night; some were provided with telescopic funnels, and masts hinged, so that they could be lowered, and others had the masts taken out altogether. A great source of danger, and one which was unavoidable, was the black smoke caused from our fires, and for this sign the blockaders were always on the lookout. The United States Government having forbidden the exportation of anthracite coal, there was nothing for us to do but use bituminous and take all precautions possible to prevent the issuing of black smoke from our funnels.

"On dark nights it was very difficult to discern their low hulls, and moonlight nights, as a rule, were nights of rest, few ships venturing to run the gauntlet when the moon was bright. No lights were used at sea. Everything was in total silence and darkness. To speak above a whisper or to strike a match would subject the offender to immediate punishment. Orders were passed along the deck in whispers, canvas curtains were dropped to the water's edge around the paddles to deaden the noise, and men exposed to view on deck were dressed in sheets, moving about like so many phantoms on a phantom ship.

"The impression always prevailed, and still prevails to a great extent, that the South has no sailors, but the record of the Southern sailors during the war is second to none that the world has ever produced, and should the emergency arise again, the descendants of the same men will emulate the example set by their fathers. I do not think their services have ever been understood or appreciated, from the fact that so little of their authentic history has ever found its way into the hands of the reading public.

"Most of them had all their relatives and friends in the Southern service, suffering untold hardships and exposing their lives daily, and they felt it their duty to risk their ships and their lives to bring food to our starving countrymen, determined if their ship was stopped that it must be by the enemy and not by their own order.

"During the first two years of the war the blockade runners were almost exclusively officered by English and Scotch, but during the last two years the danger was very much increased, and while there can be no question as to the bravery of the British sailor, it required the additional incentive of patriotism to induce men to venture into the service. It is noticeable that nearly all the officers during the last two years were Confederates.

"The first steamship to which I was attached was the side-wheel steamer *Leopard*. She was officered entirely by Southern men: Captain Black of Savannah, commander; Capt. Robert Lockwood, of Charleston, pilot, and as gallant a man as the war produced. Cool, quiet, and never losing his wits, he was an ideal blockade pilot. In the engine room were Peck, Barbot, Sassard, and Miller, four splendid mechanics and gallant fellows all. The deck officers were Bradford, Horsey, and myself, three boys, twenty-four, twenty-three and twenty-two years of age, respectively, but each had received his baptism of fire in Virginia—Bradford, with a Virginia artillery company; Horsey, with the Washington Artillery, of Charleston; and I, with the Oglethorpe Light Infantry, of Savannah. Yet, though long in the service, not one of us three ever saw the inside of a Federal prison. Such were the men who supplied the munitions of war, clothing, and food for our armies up to the close of the war, while the United States Government, with an immense fleet of ships and the whole world to draw upon, was powerless to prevent it.

"When I was promoted to the command of the *Mary Celeste,* I was fortunate to have associated with me as brave and faithful a set of officers as ever fell to the lot of any man; and I needed them, for I was the boy captain, the youngest man to command a blockade runner. My chief engineer was John Sassard, of Charleston, and I have never known a better engineer nor a more conscientious Christian gentleman. I never knew him to take a drink, and I never heard an oath issue from his lips. Shrinking from anything like notoriety, he was a true Confederate and as brave as brave could be. I think one of the best illustrations of his nerve was an incident that occurred on my first voyage in command. We had succeeded in getting through the blockade off Wilmington and shaped a course for Bermuda. Daylight found us in the Gulf Stream, the weather dirty, raining, and a heavy sea, our ship small and heavily loaded. The rain clearing away, there was disclosed to our view a large brig-rigged steamer within easy gunshot, with all her canvas set, bearing down upon us. I found out afterwards that she was the steamship *Fulton,* a very fast ship built for the passenger trade between New York and Havre, France.

"We altered our course head to wind and sea, causing the chasing steamer to do the same and to take in her sails, which gave us a little advantage; but she was a large, able ship, and made good weather, while our little craft would bury herself clean out of sight, taking the green seas in over the forecastle. Calling Mr. Sassard, I said: 'John, this will never do. That ship will soon sink us or catch us unless we do better.' He answered in his quiet manner: 'Captain, I am doing all that a sane man dare do.' 'Then,' said I, 'you must be insane, and that quick, for it is destruction or Fort Lafayette for us, and I would rather go to the former. I am going to lighten her forward, so that she will go into the sea easier, and you *must* get more revolutions out of the engines.' He went below, and I took forty-five bales of cotton from forward, rolled them abaft the paddles, cut them open, so that the enemy could make no use of them, and threw them overboard. The loose cotton floating in our wake caused him to deviate from his course occasionally, which helped us some. About this time Sassard sent for me to come down to the engine-room, where he said: 'Captain, I am getting all the revolutions possible out of the engines. I am following steam full stroke; this is a new ship, first voyage; these boilers are, I hope, good English iron. All there is now between us and eternity are these boilers. How much steam there is on them I don't know.' He had a kedge anchor made fast to the safety valve. In my opinion it takes a mighty brave man to do that. I went on deck, threw the log and found the ship to be making seventeen miles an hour, into a heavy head sea. 'All right,' I said, 'keep that up a little while, and there is no ship in the United States Navy that can catch her.' We were soon out of range of the enemy's guns and enabled to reduce the pressure on the boilers. Sassard and I never separated until after the surrender. My first assistant engineer, Middleton, was chief of the ill-fated *Lelia,* and lost his life when she went down at the mouth of the Mersey with very nearly all hands. My second assistant engineer was the heroic McKay, who afterwards drove the *Armstrong* for seven hours, while three ships were raining shot and shell at her. My pilot, Thomas M. Thompson, of Wilmington, was another officer who knew no fear.

"To illustrate more fully the kind of men with whom I was associated, I will relate a few incidents that occurred on board the *Atalanta* on her last run into Wilmington, when she was turned over to the naval authorities and converted into the cruiser *Tallahassee.*

"Just before leaving Bermuda for Wilmington, several of our fastest ships returned after unsuccessful attempts to get into the Confederacy and reported that the ocean and coast were alive with the enemy's ships and that it was impossible to get through. We were ready for sea, however, and I determined to make the trial. We approached the entrance to Wilmington Harbor on a beautiful moonlight night in July, only one day before the full moon. Before approaching the blockaders the officers and men were notified that the attempt was about to be made, with the chances very much against us. (There were thirty-five blockaders anchored there the afternoon before, counted from Fort Caswell.) But, I said that we had four hundred tons of meat for starving soldiers and I intended to make a run for it, and if any of them were unwilling to take the risk, they were at liberty to take the small boats and try to reach the beach. To their credit, be it said, not one man availed himself of the privilege. When I said to Mr. Thompson, our fearless pilot, 'Tom, I am going to make the attempt, what do you think of it?' his answer was, 'I am ready, sir, whenever you are'; and not another word was said except the necessary orders for the management of the ship.

"Slowly approaching the vessel I supposed to be the flagship, which we used as a point of departure to find the inlet, there being no lights or other marks to find the entrance, I was notified by the engineer that he could not hold his steam, and that we must either go faster or he would be obliged to open his safety valve, something never allowed when the enemy was within hearing. I told him to hold on a few moments and he would have a chance to work his steam off. We could distinctly see the ships in the beautiful moonlight, and they were so many that we had to steer directly for and through them. As we neared the big flagship she fired a blank cartridge and then a solid shot across our bows; and when near enough to hail us, her officer ordered us in very emphatic language to stop that ship or he'd blow us out of the water.

" 'Hold on,' I said, 'until I speak to the engineer,' which I did through the speaking tube; but instead of stopping the engines, he threw her wide open and she almost flew from under our feet. Our neighbors soon found that we were not doing very much stopping and attempted to do the stopping themselves; but, fortunately for us, they failed to do so.

"My chief officer, a Virginian named Charles Nelson (and well named), was ordered by me to ascertain the depth of the water, as our ship was approaching shoal water very rapidly. In his deliberate manner he went to the leadsman, found out, and reported so slowly that I reproached him for it. Said I, 'Can not even a shell make you move faster?' (Two of them had exploded between us in the meantime.) His answer was, 'What is the use, sir? I might go just fast enough to get in the way of one of them.' This man was afterwards in command of the *Armstrong,* bound from Wilmington to Bermuda, about the middle of November, 1864, when, after successfully

eluding the vigilance of the blockaders around the inlet, she
was sighted at 7 o'clock in the morning and then began—in my
opinion—the most memorable chase in the war. She was first
seen by the *R. R. Cuyler,* which was soon joined by two other
ships; and the *Armstrong* was soon in the position of the little
hare and three large hounds in pursuit. The *Cuyler* was a
large screw steamer built for the passenger trade between Savannah and New York. She was named after a former president
of the Central Railroad, and before the war was considered the
fastest steamer out of New York. At 10 a. m., the first shot
was fired from the *Cuyler,* and for seven long hours Nelson
walked the bridge, cool and collected, not more excited, in fact,
than if the *Armstrong* were moored to a dock in a safe harbor.
The *Cuyler* alone fired 195 shot and shell. The top of the
paddle-box was shot away; Nelson, covered up with the wreck,
shook himself clear. An exploding shell set fire to the cabin;
the hose was let down, the pumps turned on, and the fire put
out with less excitement than would be seen at a fire in any
city in time of peace. The anchors and chains were thrown
overboard, and the masts were cut away. More than 400 bales
of cotton were dumped into the sea, and everything possible was
done to lighten the ship and increase her speed; but of no avail,
the sea was too rough for the little fugitive to compete with the
large ships that were chasing her.

"At 5 p. m. the captain of the *Cuyler* hailed Nelson and
ordered him to stop the ship or he would blow them out of the
water, which seemed to be a favorite way the blockaders had of
expressing themselves. Just about that time the *Armstrong's*
engine-frame broke in two and she was a prize.

"The first boat that boarded her had in it a lieutenant and a
surgeon; the latter, before leaving his boat to go on board the
Armstrong, asked: 'How many killed and wounded?' and,
strange to say, not a man was scratched. It seemed miraculous
when we consider that all hands, about forty men, were on deck
engaged in throwing the cargo overboard. One of her crew
afterwards told me that he could have filled a peck measure with
the grapeshot that were gathered up about the decks, and that
the pieces of shell were shoveled overboard. An officer of the
Cuyler said to one of the prisoners, 'We have captured twenty-
two blockade runners, and I think I know whereof I speak when
I say your captain is the bravest man that runs the blockade.'
The *Armstrong* made a trip to Savannah from New York after
the war and was called the *Savannah.*

"The leadsman on board a blockade runner occupied a very responsible position; he had to have great physical endurance and courage. When shoal water was reached, the safety of the ship and the lives of all on board depended upon his skill and faithfulness. Were he disposed to be treacherous, he could, by false soundings, put the ship in the hands of the enemy or run her in the breakers and endanger the lives of all.

"My leadsman was a slave owned by myself. On the last trip of the *Atalanta,* while under fire, the ship going very fast toward shoal water, I thought possibly he might get rattled, and to test him I said: 'Irwin, you can't get correct soundings, the ship is going too fast, I'll slow her down for you.' He answered: 'This is no time to slow down, sir, you let her go, I'll give you the bottom'; and he did, he being a leadsman without a peer. I have had him in the chains for hours in cold winter weather, with the spray flying over him cold enough to freeze the marrow in his bones, the ship often in very shoal water, frequently but a foot to spare under her, and sometimes not that. Yet I never knew him to make a mistake or give an incorrect cast of the lead. He is the man to whom, when pointing to the island of New Providence, I said: 'Every man on that island is as free as I am, so will you be when we get there.' He answered: 'I did not want to come here to be free, I could have gone to the Yankees long ago if I had wished.' And afterwards, when the war was over, I said to him: 'I am going to England, perhaps never to see Savannah again, you had better go home.' His answer was: 'I can not go without you'; and he did not. The feeling that existed between us can only be understood by Southern men; by a Northern man, never.

"My brave old quartermaster, William Cuthbert, who had been with me in the chances and changes of blockade running, always took his place at the wheel on trying occasions. He had the courage necessary to steer a ship without flinching through the whole United States fleet. He was a sailor, every inch of him. He it was who, when I heard a crash and asked him if he was hurt, answered: 'We are all right, sir, but I do not know how much wheel there is left, and the compass is gone; give me a star to steer by.' A shot fired by a ship astern of us had passed the two men at the wheel, taken out two spokes, destroyed the compass, and buried itself in the deck. He was steering the ship as though nothing unusual had happened.

"While in command of the *Armstrong,* a very poorly built,

light draft, side-wheel ship, on a trip from Nassau to Wilmington, having experienced very heavy weather, our steam-pipe was injured to such an extent that we found it impossible to make more than three miles an hour. At that rate of speed we could not reach the entrance to Wilmington before daylight, and to remain at sea would place us at the mercy of the cruisers, then as thick as bees. So we shaped our course to make the land in the neighborhood of Georgetown, S. C.

"When daylight broke, the weather bitterly cold, we found ourselves among three of the enemy's ships lying at anchor near the entrance to Georgetown, the farthest not more than two miles from us. We, of course, ran away from them as fast as our crippled condition would allow, expecting to be chased and captured in short order; but, to our surprise and delight, they remained quietly at anchor, and we continued on our course and, when far enough to feel safe, circled around them and came to anchor ourselves under the beach near Little River Inlet, about twenty miles from the mouth of the Cape Fear. This remarkable luck can only be accounted for by the extreme cold, which must have prevented the Yankee ships from keeping a proper lookout.

"After making all preparations for setting fire to the ship and landing the people if we should be discovered by the Federals, we blew off our steam and proceeded to make temporary repairs to the steam-pipe.

"Before coming to anchor my attention was attracted to a party of six men on shore making signals to us. I sent a boat and brought off the men, who proved to be Federal prisoners escaped from Florence, S. C., and who, after many days of suffering in a strange country, had succeeded in reaching the coast, only to find themselves prisoners on board a blockade runner instead of one of Uncle Sam's gunboats, which they fondly imagined us to be. One poor fellow remarked: 'I believe the dogs would catch a fellow in this country; this is the third time I have escaped, only to be recaptured each time.'

"I had on board at this time seven Confederates who had escaped from Johnson's Island, and whom it was my good fortune to come across in Halifax, N. S. Having been on board ship some time, they were anxious to get on shore, so I landed and found that we had anchored in the neighborhood of some salt works, which were quite numerous on this coast, and whose fires at night frequently served us in lieu of lighthouses.

"While ashore I secured transportation by wagons, and sent my prisoners in charge of the seven Confederates across to the railroad and to Wilmington, where they met me the next day. While lying at anchor with no steam and perfectly helpless, three of the enemy's ships passed us almost close enough to see the men on deck, but took no notice of us, evidently mistaking us for one of their own ships. At dark, having completed the necessary repairs to the steam-pipe, we weighed our anchor and at 11 p. m. were safely anchored under the guns of Fort Caswell.

"At one time I was one of a party of four who were waiting at the island of Bermuda for a new ship. We became tired of the poor hotel, kept by a Northern man of whom we were not very fond, but whose hostelry was the only one there. Having an opportunity to do so, we rented a furnished cottage, and for a little while enjoyed the comforts of a bachelors' hall. Among our visitors were the officers of the British Army and Navy stationed there, and we became very good friends with most of them. They professed to be warm Southern sympathizers while under *our spiritual influence,* and it was not long before I had an opportunity to test the good will of one of them.

"Some time in October, 1864, I was anchored a few miles from Nassau, taking in a lot of arms and ammunition from a schooner alongside. We were all ready to sail, with the exception of this lighter load, and had our fires banked, ready to get steam at a moment's notice. The American consul found out and notified the British authorities that we were taking in contraband of war, and an officer was sent from the British frigate then in port to investigate. As soon as the unwelcome visitor was seen approaching, the engineer was ordered to pull down his fires, and to be prepared to leave at once. Anxiously watching the approaching boat, I recognized the officer to be an old Bermuda acquaintance, Lieutenant Wilson, who had partaken of our hospitality at our bachelors' cottage. As he came alongside I said: 'Hello, Wilson! What brought you here?' He answered: 'It is reported that you are taking in contraband of war, and I am sent to look after you.'

"As he came over the side a case of rifles was being hoisted in from the other side. 'What have you there?' he asked. 'Hardware,' I said. 'Would you like to examine that case now, or will you come below and have a glass of wine first?'

"He decided to take the wine first, and spent quite a while sampling some excellent 'green seal' and indulging in reminiscences of the pleasant days spent together at Bermuda, and when it was time to return to his ship he had forgotten to examine the cases of hardware, which were being hurried over the side in the meantime. Returning to his boat, not without some assistance, as he did not seem to have his sea-legs aboard, he bade me farewell, saying, 'Usina, take good care of that hardware—that hardware, you know.'

"Before he reached his ship and another boat could be sent, the hardware was all on board, and the *Armstrong* was steaming for Dixie, where the hardware was soon in the hands of men who knew something about that kind of hardware.

"While blockade runners dreaded moonlight, and gladly availed themselves of dark nights and stormy weather to run into the Confederate ports or out of them, yet on several occasions the gauntlet was run successfully in the daytime.

"On one occasion we reached the neighborhood of the blockaders off Wilmington in a gale of wind. The sea was so heavy that if we should get ashore it meant the destruction of the ship and the loss of all hands, so we determined, if we could live the night through (of which there was considerable doubt), to make a dash for it at daylight.

"Just as the day dawned we found ourselves alongside the United States steamship *Huntsville* (an old Savannah trader), which immediately gave chase and commenced firing at us. The noise of the guns attracted the attention of the other vessels, and we soon found ourselves in a hornet's nest. In consequence of the rough sea, however, their firing was very inaccurate, and the batteries near Fort Caswell soon began firing over us at them as fast as they came within range, causing them to keep at a respectful distance, to cease firing at us, and to haul off as we neared the fort, so that it was not very long before we were in a position to receive the congratulations of our friends over our lucky escape.

"On another occasion I made the land between Georgetown and Wilmington in the afternoon, and as the night would soon be upon us I thought I would get a look at the enemy before dark. Accordingly, I steamed slowly towards them, keeping a bright lookout.

"As we approached Lockwood's Folly Inlet, twelve miles from Fort Caswell, it became apparent that the ship stationed there to guard that point was absent from her post, and if we could reach there without being seen by the other ships, there was a

chance that we could gain the protection of our batteries before
they could head us off, and we determined to try it. As we
rounded the point of shoals off Lockwood's Folly, we came in
full view of all their ships; it seemed to me that there were
hundreds of them. They at once recognized our character and
purpose, and then began a most exciting race for a given point,
our ship going for all she was worth, hugging the shore and
depending upon the leadsman to keep her afloat; the enemy's
ships were coming in to head us off and the booming of their
guns reminded me of the music of a pack of hounds in full
chase, but on this particular occasion I failed to appreciate the
music. The signal station, located between Lockwood's Folly
and Fort Caswell, signaling the fort, the commanding officer
rushed a couple of Whitworth guns down the beach in our direction, and in a little while we heard the welcome sound of their
shots going over our heads, and we were safe. From the time
we were seen by the enemy until we were under the protection
of our guns did not occupy more than forty-five minutes, but to
us it seemed an age.

"One of the most valuable cargoes ever brought into the Confederacy was brought in by the old cruiser *Sumter,* converted
into a blockade runner and commanded by E. C. Reed. Her
cargo consisted of arms, ammunition, clothing, cloth, medicines,
and not the least important articles were the two big Blakely
guns, which some of you now present may have seen mounted
at Charleston. They were so large and unwieldly that they
were loaded with their muzzles sticking out of the hatches.

"The *Sumter* was a slow ship, and could not make more than
nine miles an hour. Unable to get in during the night, Reed
found himself near the enemy's ships at daylight. To attempt
to go off shore with so slow a ship meant a chase and certain
capture. So he determined to try a game of bluff. Hoisting
the American ensign, he steamed in amongst them, paying not
the least attention to their signals or movements, and when they
awoke to the fact that the *Sumter* was not one of themselves, she
had the inside track and was soon welcomed by the guns of
Fort Fisher.

"The devotion of the women of the Confederacy, and their
heroic conduct during our struggle for existence, will always be
held in grateful remembrance by the veterans of the Lost Cause.
In my career as a blockade runner I chanced to see several
instances of nerve displayed by them, which would do honor to

an old soldier. On one of our trips from Bermuda to Wilmington I had with me as a passenger a lady from Richmond. On nearing the blockaders I sent her down to the cabin, which was below the water line and comparatively safe while we were under fire. A little later, during the hot chase and fire which we had to take, I heard a voice at my elbow and, turning, saw her at my side. I said: 'I told you to go below and stay there'; but she answered: 'I could not remain there in the darkness, hearing the guns; if you will let me stay here I'll give you no trouble.' 'Well, you may remain,' I told her, 'but you must not speak to any one.' She never left the bridge until we were safely anchored under the guns of Fort Caswell, and I think was the coolest person on board the ship.

"Upon another occasion the steamer *Lynx*, Capt. E. C. Reed, while attempting to get into Wilmington, was completely riddled by the enemy's ships, and, finding her in a sinking condition, she was run ashore near Fort Fisher, to prevent her sinking in deep water, the crew escaping to the beach in small boats. A lady passenger, a resident of Wilmington, was sent below when the firing began, where she remained until the boats were ready to land on the beach; she was found standing knee-deep in the water, obeying orders 'to remain until sent for.'

"One more incident and I am done with the ladies. During the bombardment of Sumter our ship was selected, on account of her speed, to take important dispatches from the Confederacy to Europe, and we had on board as passengers a bridal couple. We had to pass out through a terrible cross-fire from the batteries on Morris Island and James Island and the ironclads anchored in Morris Island Channel, which was returned by Sumter, Moultrie, Ripley, Castle Pinckney, and the Confederate vessels. After passing through the fireworks display in the neighborhood of Sumter, the vessels outside the bar made it lively for us, but daylight found us well to sea with no enemy in sight. At the beginning of the firing, my attention was attracted to the bridal couple. The groom had himself spread out upon the deck-load of cotton, while the bride was standing quietly near by. I said to her: 'Are you not frightened, Mrs. B.?' 'Yes, I am frightened,' she said; 'this is terrible, but we are in the hands of the Almighty.' You can imagine the respect I entertained ever after for the gentleman who, with such an example before him, displayed such arrant cowardice.

"Sailors have always been charged with being superstitious;

but while I do not think there is any superstition in my composition, yet I think blockade running was a business well calculated to develop it, as is indicated, for instance, in the names of some of the ships, the *Phantom, Will-o'-the-Wisp, Banshee, Whisper, Dream, Owl, Bat,* and others of like character, the usual objection to sailing on Friday, the carrying of a corpse, etc. One of the funniest notions that came under my observation was that if passage could be obtained for freight shipped with a certain cross-eyed Captain K., it would be a success.

"While, as I said, I do not think I am given to superstition, yet I had with me a mascot that, I believe, was at that time one of the most widely known dogs that ever existed. I was known as the man that owned the dog! He was photographed at Bermuda, and the artist realized quite a neat sum from the sale of his pictures. He was left with me by a shipmate who died at sea, and when dying frequently called for 'Tinker.' I cherished him for his master's sake, and afterwards became warmly attached to him for his own. He was a terrier, a great ratter, and fond of the water. He was my constant companion. He seemed to know when we were approaching the enemy and to be on the alert, and when under fire would follow me step by step.

"It was our custom, in anticipation of capture or destruction of the ship, to prepare the boats for leaving the ship the afternoon before running through the fleet. Tinker seemed to inspect the work and to devote most particular attention to the captain's boat. The sailors wondered how he knew one boat from another, but he certainly did.

"When I placed my chief officer, Nelson, in command of the *Armstrong,* I induced some of my men whom I knew could be depended upon to go with him, as I was more than anxious to have him succeed. Among those that I approached was my old stand-by, William Cuthbert. His answer was, 'I do not like to refuse you, but I am too old a man now to go to Fort Lafayette in the wintertime; and if you leave the ship and take Tinker with you I know we will be captured.' I said to him, 'I am surprised to hear a man of your intelligence express yourself in that way. What has the dog to do with the safety of the ship? I am ashamed of you.' 'Well, sir,' he replied, 'you may call it superstition, or anything you please, but as sure as you leave the ship and take Tinker with you we will be captured.' After considerable persuasion he consented, very unwillingly, to go, saying, 'I'll go in the ship to please you, sir, but, I know how it will be.' The ship was captured; and when we met again his first words were: 'I told you so, sir.'

"I had with me as chief officer an Englishman, who was a very intelligent shipmaster. He was promoted to command, and when about to try his luck, came to me, saying, 'Captain, let me have Tinker just for one trip and here is five hundred dollars in gold.' I said, 'Green, two fools, you and I'; but I did not let him have the dog. I could relate a great number of incidents to illustrate the value placed upon Tinker by blockade runners, but I'll inflict only one more upon you.

"I sailed for Wilmington from Bermuda in the steamship *Rattlesnake* about the 20th of January, 1865. Eight hours after I left Bermuda, Captain Maffitt, in command of the *Owl*, arrived at Nassau with the news that the forts at the mouth of the Cape Fear River had fallen. My friends at the island thought I was sure to be captured. Col. James Crenshaw, who before the war was a criminal lawyer, practicing in Richmond, and at this time was part owner and agent of our ships at the islands, had been a sailor in his young days, and certainly not an ignorant one. When told of the great danger of capture to which we were exposed, he told my wife to make herself easy; as I had Tinker with me, I was all right. Upon approaching Nassau a few days afterwards, pointing to my flag, he said: 'There is the *Rattlesnake;* didn't I tell you so?' I was lying at anchor in the harbor. I think this was the last attempt made to get into Wilmington, and an account of it may interest you.

"We reached the coast early in the night, in fact before it was yet dark, but quite hazy; so much so that we could not see a ship any distance, when suddenly I found myself surrounded by a great number of lights. When you remember that the ships of the blockade squadrons were always in darkness, with no lights set, you can imagine my surprise. Proceeding toward the entrance, we found our passage almost obstructed by the enemy's ships, they were so many, and, stranger than all, not a shot fired at us, and no one demanding that we either 'stop that ship, or he'd blow us out of the water.' We approached Fort Fisher near enough to call the signal officer, who responded instantly. I remarked to my signal officer: 'There is something up, I never had so prompt an answer before; they are on the alert tonight.'

"We reported: 'Steamship *Rattlesnake,* bound in, set range

28

lights.' An answer came as quick as thought: 'All right, the lights will be set.' We signaled our respects to Colonel Lamb, and asked about his health. The answer was: 'The colonel is quite well. (He was then lying dangerously wounded.) How are all on board, and what is the news from Bermuda?' I instructed the officer to amuse himself talking to them, that I was going aloft, which I did, and as I reached the masthead and could look over the low sandhills which line the North Carolina coast, I could see the camp fires of the armies, and decided that either there had been an attack on Fort Fisher, or there soon would be one. Upon reaching the deck I said to the pilot: 'The tide is falling, and I think we will not take the risk on a falling tide. I will wait until the flood tide makes, and go in just before daylight. I remained among the fleet the best part of the night. I counted seven monitors; we came very near colliding with three of them, and not a word was said and not a shot was fired. I concluded that we had met with a very cool reception, and it was not a healthy place for us just then; so, at 2 a. m., I shaped our course for Nassau. When, upon arrival there, I asked the pilot what was the news from Wilmington, he answered: 'Wilmington has gone up the spout, sir.' I learned afterwards that several ships had gone in and congratulated themselves upon getting in so easily; but to their dismay, when the boarding officer came on board, he wore the blue instead of the gray. At the fall of Fort Fisher our signal-book fell into the hands of the enemy, and all that was necessary was to draw the ships in and take possession, which accounted for our not being shot at.

"After the surrender, on my way to England, I buried my faithful Tinker among the icebergs of the North Atlantic, and every man on board stood with uncovered head when he was consigned to his watery grave. When blockade running ceased, his spirits drooped, his occupation gone, and he soon sickened and died.

"His master felt much the same way, but survived. It was one of the saddest moments of my life—the Confederacy, of whose success I had never lost hope, no longer in existence; leaving my native land, as I then thought never more to return. I felt that all the ties that I had formed during my childhood and youth were become mere memories; that all the fast friends I had made during our bitter fight were to be only as some much-beloved hero of a favorite novel, with whom we become very familiar until the tale is all told, and who then passes out of mind and is never heard of more. But it was ordained otherwise, and I am happy now to be in my old home, meeting everywhere men whose sympathies in that grand struggle were the same as my own, and who feel as I do, that though our fighting days are over, the memory of our dead comrades is strong enough to bind us to each other until we all shall be called away to join them in the land of eternal peace."

Thomas E. Taylor.

Several large and important shipping firms in Liverpool were interested in blockade running at Wilmington, and each of these houses owned and operated from five to ten of the most successful boats.

A young gentleman, Thomas E. Taylor, scarcely twenty-one years of age, was sent out from England to represent a firm which ultimately designed and ran some of the finest ships engaged in this perilous, though profitable, business; but it may be doubted if the company with whom he was associated or any other owners realized, in the end, large profits on their ventures, because, while the returns were very large under favorable conditions, the frequent losses by capture and the final fall of the Confederacy, which left them with ships unsalable for ordinary trade, so reduced their earnings that the game was scarcely worth the candle.

In 1896 Mr. Taylor published a most readable book entitled *Running the Blockade,* in which he tells most graphically some of his extraordinary experiences. He was much liked by all who were fortunate enough to know him, and I well remember his genial, happy spirits and his masterful leadership into danger when duty called him in the interest of his employers. I quote from his narrative an exciting incident which made a sensation in blockade-running circles at the time:

"The reason for my leaving the *Banshee* was the arrival at Nassau of a new steamer, which my firm had sent out to me. This was the *Will-o'-the-Wisp,* and great things were expected from her. She was built on the Clyde and was a much larger and faster boat than the *Banshee,* but shamefully put together and most fragile. My first introduction to her was seeing her appear off Nassau, and receiving a message by the pilot-boat from Capper, the captain, to say that the vessel was leaking badly and he dare not stop his engines, as they had to be kept going in order to work the pumps. We brought her into the harbor, and having beached her and afterwards made all necessary repairs on the slipway, I decided to take a trip in her.

"As soon as the nights were sufficiently dark we made a start for Wilmington, unfortunately meeting very bad weather and strong head winds, which delayed us; the result was that instead of making out the blockading fleet about midnight, as we had intended, when dawn was breaking there were still no signs of them. Capper, the chief engineer, and I then held a hurried consultation as to what we had better do. Capper was for going to sea again, and if necessary returning to Nassau; the weather was still threatening, our coal supply running short, and, with a leaky ship beneath us, the engineer and I decided that the lesser risk would be to make a dash for it. 'All right,' said Capper, 'We'll go on, but you'll get d—d well peppered!'

"We steamed cautiously on, making as little smoke as possible, whilst I went to the masthead to take a look around; no land was in sight, but I could make out in the dull morning light the heavy spars of the blockading flagship right ahead of us, and soon after several other masts became visible on each side of her. Picking out what appeared to me to be the widest space between these, I signaled to the deck how to steer, and we went steadily on, determined when we found we were perceived to make a rush for it. No doubt our very audacity helped us through, as for some time they took no notice, evidently thinking we were one of their own chasers returning from sea to take up her station for the day.

"At last, to my great relief, I saw Fort Fisher just appearing above the horizon, although we knew that the perilous passage between these blockaders must be made before we could come under the friendly protection of its guns. Suddenly we became aware that our enemy had found us out; we saw two cruisers steaming towards one another from either side of us, so as to intercept us at a given point before we could get on the land side of them. It now became simply a question of speed and immunity from being sunk by shot. Our little vessel quivered under the tremendous pressure with which she was being driven through the water.

"An exciting time followed, as we and our two enemies rapidly converged upon one point, other ships in the distance also hurrying up to assist them. We were now near enough to be within range, and the cruiser on our port side opened fire; his first shot carried away our flagstaff aft, on which our ensign had just been hoisted; his second tore through our forehold, bulging out a plate on the opposite side. Bedding and blankets to stop the leak were at once requisitioned, and we steamed on, full speed, under a heavy fire from both quarters. Suddenly, puffs of smoke from the fort showed us that Colonel Lamb, the commandant, was aware of what was going on and was firing to protect us; a welcome proof that we were drawing within range of his guns and on the landside of our pursuers, who, after giving us a few more parting shots, hauled off and steamed away from within reach of the shells, which we were rejoiced to see falling thickly around them.

"We had passed through a most thrilling experience; at one time the cruiser on our port side was only a hundred yards away from us, with her consort a hundred and fifty on the starboard, and it seemed a miracle that their double fire did not completely sink us. It certainly required all one's nerve to stand upon the paddle-box, looking without flinching almost into the muzzles of the guns which were being fired at us; and proud we were of our crew, not a man of whom showed the white feather. Our pilot, who showed no lack of courage at the time, became, however, terribly excited as we neared the bar, and, whether it was that the ship steered badly, owing to being submerged forward, or from some mistake, he ran her ashore whilst going at full speed. The result was a most frightful shaking, which of course materially increased the leaks, and we feared the ship would become a total wreck; fortunately, the tide was rising, and, through lightening her by throwing some of the cargo overboard, we succeeded in getting her off and steamed up the river to Wilmington, where we placed her on the mud.

"After repairing the shot holes and other damage, we were under the impression that no further harm from running ashore had come to her, as all leaks were apparently stopped and the ship was quite tight. The result proved us to be sadly wrong on this point. After loading our usual cargo we started down the river all right, and waited for nightfall in order to cross the bar and run through the fleet. No sooner had we crossed it and found ourselves surrounded by cruisers, than the chief engineer rushed on the bridge, saying the water was already over the stoke-hole plates, and he feared that the ship was sinking. At the same moment a quantity of firewood which was stowed around one of the funnels (and which was intended to eke out our somewhat scanty coal supply) caught fire, and flames burst out.

"This placed us in a pretty predicament, as it showed our whereabouts to the two cruisers which were following us, one on each quarter. They at once opened a furious cannonade upon us; however, although shells were bursting all around and shot flying over us, all hands worked with a will, and we soon extinguished the flames, which were acting as a treacherous beacon to our foes. Fortunately, the night was intensely dark and nothing could be seen beyond a radius of thirty or forty yards, so, thanks to this, we were soon enabled, by altering our helm, to give our pursuers the slip, whilst they probably kept on their course.

"We had still the other enemy to deal with; but our chief engineer and his staff had meanwhile been hard at work and had turned on the 'bilge-injection' and 'donkey-pumps.' Still, the leak was gaining upon us, and it became evident that the severe shaking which the ship got when run aground had started the plates in her bottom. The mud had been sucked up when she lay in the river at Wilmington, thus temporarily repairing the damage; but when she got into the seaway the action of the water opened them again. Even the steam pumps now could not prevent the water from gradually increasing; four of our eight furnaces were extinguished, and the firemen were working up to their middles in water.

"It was a critical time when daylight broke, dull and threatening. The captain was at the wheel and I at the masthead (all other hands being employed at the pumps, and even baling), when, not four miles off, I sighted a cruiser broadside on. She turned around as if preparing to give chase, and I thought we were done for, as we could not have got more than three or four knots an hour out of our crippled boat. To my great joy, however, I found our alarm was needless, for she evidently had not seen us, and, instead of heading, turned her stern towards us and disappeared into a thick bank of clouds.

"Still we were far from being out of danger, as the weather became worse and worse and the wind increased in force until it was blowing almost a gale. Things began to look as ugly as they could, and even Capper lost hope. I shall never forget the expression on his face as he came up to me and said, in his gruff voice, 'I say, Mr. Taylor, the beggar's going, the beggar's going,' pointing vehemently downwards. 'What the devil do you mean!' I exclaimed. 'Why, we are going to lose the ship and our lives, too,' was the answer. It is not possible for any one unacquainted with Capper to appreciate this scene. Sturdy, thickset, nearly as broad as he was long, and with the gruffest manner but kindest heart—a rough diamond, and absolutely without fear. With the exception of Steele, he was the best blockade-running captain we had.

"In order to save the steamer and our lives we decided that desperate remedies must be resorted to, so again the unlucky deck cargo had to be sacrificed. The good effect of this was soon visible; we began to gain on the water, and were able, by degrees, to relight our extinguished fires. But the struggle continued to be a most severe one, for just when we began to obtain a mastery over the water the donkey-engine broke down, and before we could repair it the water increased sensibly, nearly putting out our fires again. So the struggle went on for sixty hours, when we were truly thankful to steam into Nassau Harbor and beach the ship. It was a very narrow escape, for within twenty minutes after stopping her engines the vessel had sunk to the level of the water.

"After this I made a trip in a new boat that had just been sent out to me, the *Wild Dayrell*. And a beauty she was, very strong, a perfect sea-boat, and remarkably well engined.

"Our voyage in was somewhat exciting, as about three o'clock in the afternoon, while making for the Fort Caswell entrance (not Fort Fisher), we were sighted by a Federal cruiser, which immediately gave chase. We soon found, however, that we had the heels of our friend, but it left us the alternative of going out to sea or being chased straight into the jaws of the blockaders off the bar before darkness came on. Under these circumstances what course to take was a delicate point to decide, but we solved the problem by slowing down just sufficiently to keep a few miles ahead of our chaser, hoping that darkness would come on before we made the fleet or they discovered us. Just as twilight was drawing in we made them out; cautiously we crept on, feeling certain that our friend astern was rapidly closing up on us. Every moment we expected to hear the shot whistling around us. So plainly could we see the sleepy blockaders that it seemed almost impossible we should escape their notice. Whether they did not expect a runner to make an attempt so early in the evening, or whether it was sheer good luck on our part, I know not, but we ran through the lot without being seen or without having a shot fired at us.

"Our anxieties, however, were not yet over, as our pilot (a new hand) lost his reckoning and put us ashore on the bar. Fortunately, the flood tide was rising fast, and we refloated, bumping over stern first in a most inglorious fashion, and anchored off Fort Caswell before 7 p. m.—a record performance.

"Soon after anchoring and while enjoying the usual cocktail, we saw a great commotion among the blockaders, who were throwing up rockets and flashing lights, evidently in answer to signals from the cruiser which had so nearly chased us into their midst.

"When we came out we met with equally good luck, as the night was pitch dark and the weather very squally. No sooner did we clear the bar than we put our helm aport, ran down the coast, and then stood boldly straight out to sea without interference; and it was perhaps as well we had such good fortune, as before this I had discovered that our pilot was of a very indifferent calibre, and that courage was not our captain's most prominent characteristic. The poor *Wild Dayrell* deserved a better commander, and consequently a better fate than befell her. She was lost on her second trip, entirely through the want of pluck on the part of her captain, who ran her ashore some miles to the north of Fort Fisher; he said in order to avoid capture—to my mind a fatal excuse for any blockade-running captain to make. 'Twere far better to be sunk by shot, and escape in the boats if possible. I am quite certain that if Steele had commanded her on that trip she would never have been put ashore, and the chances were that she would have come through all right.

"I never forgave myself for not unshipping the captain on my return to Nassau; my only excuse was that there was no good man available to replace him, and he was a particular protégé of my chief. But such considerations should not have weighed, and if I had had the courage of my convictions it is probable the *Wild Dayrell* would have proved as successful as any of our steamers.

"About this time I had two other new boats sent out, the *Stormy Petrel* and the *Wild Rover,* both good boats, very fast, and distinct improvements on the *Banshee No. 1* and the *Will-o'-the-Wisp.* The *Stormy Petrel* had, however, very bad luck, as, after getting safely in and anchoring behind Fort Fisher, she settled, as the tide went down, on a submerged anchor, the fluke of which went through her bottom, and despite all efforts she became a total wreck; this was one of the most serious and unlucky losses I had. The *Wild Rover* was more successful, as she made five round trips, on one of which I went in her. She survived the war, and I eventually sent her to South America, where she was sold for a good sum.

"We had in the early part of the war a depot at Bermuda as well as at Nassau, and Frank Hurst was at that time my brother agent there. I went there twice, once in the first *Banshee,* and once from Halifax, after a trip to Canada in order to recruit from a bad attack of yellow fever; but I never liked Bermuda, and later on we transferred Hurst and his agency to Nassau, which was more convenient in many ways and nearer Wilmington. Moreover, I had to face the contingency, which afterwards occurred, of the Atlantic ports being closed and our being driven to the Gulf. The Bermudians, however, were a kind, hospitable lot and made a great deal of us, and there was a much larger naval and military society stationed there than in Nassau. They had suffered from a severe outbreak of yellow fever, and the Third Buffs, who were in garrison at the time, had been almost decimated by it.

"It was on my second trip to the island that one of the finest boats we ever possessed, the *Night Hawk,* came out, and I concluded to run in with her. She was a new side-wheel steamer of some 600 tons gross, rigged as a fore-and-aft schooner, with two funnels, 220 feet long, 21½ feet beam, and 11 feet in depth; a capital boat for the work, fast, strong, of light draught, and a splendid sea-boat—a great merit in a blockade runner that sometimes has to be forced in all weathers. The *Night Hawk's* career was a very eventful one, and she passed an unusually lively night off Fort Fisher on her first attempt at blockade running.

"Soon after getting under way our trouble began. We ran ashore outside Hamilton, one of the harbors of Bermuda, and hung on a coral reef for a couple of hours. There loomed before us the dismal prospect of delay for repairs, or, still worse, the chance of springing a leak and experiencing such difficulties and dangers as we had undergone on the *Will-o'-the-Wisp,* but fortunately we came off without damage and were able to proceed on our voyage.

"Another anxiety now engrossed my mind: the captain was

an entirely new hand and nearly all the crew were green at the work; moreover, the Wilmington pilot was quite unknown to me, and I could see from the outset that he was very nervous and wanting in confidence. What would I not have given for our trusty pilot, Tom Burruss! However, we had to make the best of it, as, owing to the demand, the supply of competent pilots was not nearly sufficient, and towards the close of the blockade the so-called pilots were no more than boatmen or men who had been trading in and out of Wilmington or Charleston in coasters. Notwithstanding my fears, all went well on the way across, and the *Night Hawk* proved to be everything that could be desired in speed and seaworthiness.

"We had sighted unusually few craft, and nothing eventful occurred until the third night. Soon after midnight we found ourselves uncomfortably near a large vessel. It was evident that we had been seen, as we heard them beating to quarters, and we were hailed. We promptly sheered off and went full speed ahead, greeted by a broadside which went across our stern.

"When we arrived within striking distance of Wilmington Bar, the pilot was anxious to go in by Smith's Inlet, but as he acknowledged that he knew very little about it, I concluded it was better to keep to the New Inlet passage, where, at all events, we should have the advantage of our good friend Lamb to protect us; and I felt that as I myself knew the place so well, this was the safest course to pursue. We were comparatively well through the fleet, although heavily fired at, and arrived near to the bar, passing close by two Northern launches, which were lying almost upon it. Unfortunately, it was dead low water, and although I pressed our pilot to give our boat a turn around, keeping under way, and to wait a while until the tide made, he was so demoralized by the firing we had gone through and the nearness of the launches, which were constantly throwing up rockets, that he insisted upon putting her at the bar and, as I feared, we grounded on it forward, and with the strong flood tide quickly broached-to, broadside on to the northern breakers. We kept our engines going for some time, but to no purpose, as we found we were only being forced by the tide more on to the breakers. Therefore, we stopped, and all at once found our friends, the two launches, close aboard; they had discovered we were ashore, and had made up their minds to attack us.

"At once all was in confusion; the pilot and signalman rushed to the dinghy, lowered it, and made good their escape; the captain lost his head and disappeared; and the crews of the launches, after firing several volleys, one of which slightly wounded me, rowed in to board us on each sponson. Just at this moment, I suddenly recollected that our private dispatches, which ought to have been thrown overboard, were still in the starboard lifeboat. I rushed to it, but found the lanyard to which the sinking weight was attached was foul of one of the thwarts; I tugged and tugged, but to no purpose, so I sung out for a knife, which was handed to me by a fireman, and I cut the line and pitched it overboard as the Northerners jumped on board. Eighteen months afterwards that fireman accosted me in the Liverpool streets, saying, 'Mr. Taylor, do you remember my lending you a knife?' 'Of course I do,' I replied, giving him a tip, at which he was mightily pleased. Poor fellow! he had been thirteen months in a Northern prison.

"When the Northerners jumped on board they were terribly excited. I don't know whether they expected resistance or not, but they acted more like maniacs than sane men, firing their revolvers and cutting right and left with their cutlasses. I stood in front of the men on the poop and said that we surrendered, but all the reply I received from the lieutenant commanding was, 'Oh, you surrender, do you? * * * ' accompanied by a string of the choicest Yankee oaths and sundry reflections upon my parentage; whereupon he fired his revolver twice point-blank at me not two yards distant. It was a miracle he did not kill me, as I heard the bullets whiz past my head. This aroused my wrath, and I expostulated in the strongest terms upon his firing upon unarmed men. He then cooled down, giving me into the charge of two of his men, one of whom speedily possessed himself of my binoculars. Fortunately, as I had no guard to my watch, they didn't discover it, and I have it still.

"Finding they could not get the ship off, and afraid, I presume, of Lamb and his men coming to our rescue, the Federals commenced putting the captain (who had been discovered behind a boat!) and the crew into the boats; they then set the ship on fire fore and aft, and she soon began to blaze merrily. At this moment one of our firemen, an Irishmen, sang out, 'Begorra, we shall all be in the air in a minute, the ship is full of gunpowder!' No sooner did the Northern sailors hear this than a panic seized them, and they rushed to their boats, threatening to leave their officers behind if they did not come along. The men who were holding me dropped me like a hot potato, and to

my great delight jumped into their boat, and away they rowed
as fast as they could, taking all our crew, with exception of the
second officer, one of the engineers, four seamen, and myself,
as prisoners.

"We chuckled at our lucky escape, but we were not out of the
woods yet, as we had only a boat half stove in with which to
reach the shore through some 300 yards of surf, and we were
afraid at any moment that our enemies, finding there was no
gunpowder on board, might return. We made a feeble effort
to put the fire out, but it had gained too much headway, and
although I offered the men with me £50 apiece to stand by me
and persevere, they were too demoralized and began to lower the
shattered boat, swearing that they would leave me behind if I
didn't come with them. There was nothing for it but to go, yet
the passage through the boiling surf seemed more dangerous to
my mind than remaining on the burning ship. The blockaders
immediately opened fire when they knew their own men had left
the *Night Hawk,* and that she was burning; and Lamb's great
shells hurtling over our heads and those from the blockading
fleet bursting all around us formed a weird picture. In spite of
the hail of shot and shell and the danger of the boiling surf, we
reached the shore in safety, wet through, and glad I was in my
state of exhaustion from fatigue and loss of blood to be welcomed by Lamb's orderly officer.

"The poor *Night Hawk* was now a sheet of flame, and I
thought it was all up with her; and indeed it would have been
had it not been for Lamb, who, calling for volunteers from his
garrison, sent out two or three boatloads of men to her, and
when I came down to the beach, after having my wound dressed
and after a short rest, I was delighted to find the fire had sensibly decreased. I went on board, and after some hours of hard
work the fire was extinguished. But what a wreck she was!

"Luckily, with the rising tide she had bumped over the bank,
and was now lying on the main beach much more accessible and
sheltered. Still, it seemed an almost hopeless task to save her;
but we were not going to be beaten without a try, so, after having ascertained how she lay and the condition she was in, I
resolved to make an attempt to get her dry, and telegraphed to
Wilmington for assistance.

"Our agent sent me down about 300 negroes to assist in
bailing and pumping, and I set them to work at once. As good
luck would have it, my finest steamer, *Banshee No. 2,* which had

just been sent out, ran in the next night. She was a great improvement on the first *Banshee,* having a sea speed of 15½ knots, which was considered very fast in those days; her length was 252 feet, beam 31 feet, depth 11 feet, her registered tonnage 439 tons, and her crew consisted of fifty-three men in all. I at once requisitioned her for aid in the shape of engineers and men, so that now I had everything I could want in the way of hands. Our great difficulty was that the *Night Hawk's* anchors would not hold for us to get a fair haul at her.

"But here again I was to be in luck. For the very next night the *Condor,* commanded by poor Hewitt, in attempting to run in stuck fast upon the bank over which we had bumped, not one hundred yards to windward of us, and broke in two. It is an ill wind that blows nobody good, and Hewitt's mischance proved the saving of our ship. Now we had a hold for our chain cables by making them fast to the wreck, and were able gradually to haul her off by them a little during each tide, until on the seventh day we had her afloat in a gut between the bank and the shore, and at high water we steamed under our own steam gaily up the river to Wilmington.

"Considering the appliances we had and the circumstances under which we were working, the saving of that steamer was certainly a wonderful performance, as we were under fire almost the whole time. The Northerners, irritated, no doubt, by their failure to destroy the ship, used to shell us by day and send in boats by night; Lamb, however, put a stop to the latter annoyance by lending us a couple of companies to defend us, and one night when our enemies rowed close up with the intention of boarding us, they were glad to sheer off with the loss of a lieutenant and several men. In spite of all the shot and shell by day and the repeated attacks at night, we triumphed in the end, and, after having the *Night Hawk* repaired at heavy cost and getting together a crew, I gave May, a friend of mine, command of her, and he ran out successfully with a valuable cargo which made her pay, notwithstanding all her bad luck and the amount spent upon her. Poor May! he was afterwards governor of Perth gaol, and is dead now—a high-toned, sensitive gentleman, mighty proud of his ship, lame duck as she was.

"When she was burning, our utmost efforts were of course directed towards keeping her engine-room and boilers amidships intact, and confining the flames to both ends; in this we were successful, mainly owing to the fact of her having bunkers athwart-ship; but as regards the rest of the steamer she was a complete wreck; her sides were all corrugated with the heat, and her stern so twisted that her starboard quarter was some two feet higher than her port quarter, and not a particle of woodwork was left unconsumed. Owing to the limited resources of Wilmington as regards repairs, I found it impossible to have all of this put right, so her sides were left as they were, and the new deck put on with the slope I have described, and caulked with cotton, as no oakum was procurable. When completed she certainly was a queer-looking craft, but as tight as a bottle, and as seaworthy as ever, although I doubt if any Lloyd's surveyor would have passed her. But as a matter of fact she came across the Atlantic, deeply immersed with her coal supply, through some very bad weather, without damage, and was sold for a mere song, to be repaired and made into a passenger boat for service on the East Coast, where she ran for many years with success.

"It had been a hard week for me, as I had no clothes except what I had on when we were boarded—my servant very cleverly, as he imagined, having thrown my portmanteau into the man-of-war's boat when he thought I was going to be captured—and all I had in the world was the old serge suit in which I stood. Being without a change and wet through every day and night for six days consecutively, it is little wonder that I caught fever and ague, of which I nearly died in Richmond, and which distressing complaint stuck to me for more than eighteen months. I shall never forget, on going to a store in Wilmington for a new rig-out (which, by the way, cost $1,200), the look of horror on the storekeeper's face when I told him the coat I had purchased would do if he cut a foot off it; he thought it such a waste of expensive material.

"The *Tristram Shandy* had a very short and unfortunate career; after being reloaded subsequent to a compulsory return, she started on her second attempt and steamed safely in. But in coming out, her funnels, owing to the peculiar construction of her boilers, flamed very much, and it appears that a gunboat followed her by this flame all night, and when morning broke was seen to be about three miles astern. The captain at once ordered extra steam to be put on, but owing to this having been done too suddenly, one of her valve spindles was wrenched off, and she lay helpless at the mercy of the chaser, who speedily came up and took possession.

"She had on board a very valuable cargo of cotton, and in addition $50,000 in specie belonging to the Confederate Government; this, according to agreement with the government, Doering, the purser, proceeded to throw overboard, but some of the crew, determined to have a finger in the spoil, rushed aft and broke open the kegs. In the *mêlée* a quantity of gold pieces were strewn among the cotton bales on deck, and when the Northerners came on board they were very irate to think they had lost a considerable portion of their prize money. The steamer was taken into Philadelphia and condemned, and the crew were kept prisoners in New York for several months.

"In addition to the worries and anxieties I have detailed, we had to fight that demon, Yellow Jack, which raged with fearful mortality both at Nassau and Wilmington. In Nassau I have counted seventeen funerals pass my house before breakfast, and in one day I have attended interments of three intimate friends. In Wilmington it was worse; in one season alone, out of a total population of 3,000 remaining in the city, 446 died. No wonder the authorities were scared and imposed heavy penalties on us in the shape of quarantine. On two occasions I have been in quarantine for fifty days at a time. Think of that, you modern luxurious travelers, who growl if you are detained three days!

"On the first occasion, out of a crew of thirty-two, twenty-eight were laid low, and we had seven deaths; only the captain, chief engineer, steward, and myself were free from fever. On the second, we had no sickness, and only suffered from the ennui consequent upon such close confinement and short rations, as latterly we had nothing but salt pork and sardines to eat. We were saved from a third dose of quarantine by almost a miracle.

"It happened that the Southern agent in Egypt had sent a very valuable Arabian horse to Nassau, as a present for President Jefferson Davis. Heiliger, the Confederate agent there, asked me if I would take it through the blockade. I at once consented, and it was shipped on board the *Banshee*. We got through all right, but when the health officer came on board and ordered us to quarantine, I said: 'If we have to go there, the horse will certainly have to be destroyed, as we have no food for it.' Thereupon he telegraphed to Richmond, and the reply came back that the *Banshee* was to proceed to the town, land the horse, and return to quarantine. When we were alongside the wharf, a large number of our crew jumped on shore and disappeared. I said to the general, who was a friend of mine, 'There is no use of our going back to quarantine after this, you either have the infection or not,' and I induced him to telegraph to Richmond again. The answer came back, '*Banshee* must discharge and load as quickly as possible, and proceed to sea; lend all assistance.'

"The general acted on these instructions, and upon the third day we were gaily proceeding down the river again with an outward cargo on board, passing quite a fleet of steamers at the quarantine ground, whose crews were gnashing their teeth. We got safely out and returned, after making another trip, to find the same boats in quarantine, and, as it was raised three days after our arrival, we steamed up the river in company, much to the disgust of their crews.

"Good old horse! he saved me from a dreary confinement in quarantine, and made the owners of the *Banshee* $100,000 to $150,000 extra, but he was nearly the cause of our all being put in a Northern prison and losing our steamer. On a very still night, as we were running in and creeping noiselessly through the hostile fleet, he commenced neighing (smelling the land, I suppose). In an instant two or three jackets were thrown over his head, but it was too late; he had been heard on board a cruiser very close to which we were passing, and she and two or three of her consorts immediately opened fire upon us. We had the heels of them, however, and our friend, Colonel Lamb, at Fort Fisher, was soon protecting us, playing over our heads with shell.

"On a subsequent occasion, disaster might have overtaken the *Banshee* under somewhat similar circumstances had a cruiser happened to be near. A game cock which we kept on board as a pet suddenly began to crow. But this time the disaster was to the game cock and not to the *Banshee,* for, pet as he was, his neck was promptly twisted. Such experiences as these show how easy it was to increase the risks of blockade running; absence of all avoidable noise at night was as essential as the extinction of all lights on board ship."

Upon this remarkable incident so graphically described by Mr. Taylor, there hangs a local story which proves the ready wit of the children of Israel under all circumstances.

A day or two after the landing of the Arabian horse, which was the most docile, most beautiful animal ever seen in Wil-

mington, a well-known dry-goods merchant, who had prospered
on Confederate contracts, and who had often tried unsuccess-
fully to obtain General Whiting's permission to visit Nassau,
sauntered into Mr. John Dawson's store near the foot of Market Street, and obtained permission to search the loft above the
store for anything worth while which might be put to good use
during the stress of war and famine. He found nothing but
a soiled and greasy horse blanket which had been used upon
Mr. Dawson's well-known race horse, and afterwards thrown
aside when he parted with him a year or so before. It was
originally of fine blue padded silk, with Mr. Dawson's monogram, "J. D.," in large letters tastefully embroidered on it.
Our friend having been assured by Mayor Dawson that he was
quite welcome to the blanket, proceeded with the assistance of
his accomplished wife to renovate and repair it until, under
their skillful manipulation, it was made almost as good as new.
Having obtained through a friend a letter of introduction to
Mrs. Jefferson Davis, he proceeded to Richmond and was
ushered into the presence of that distinguished lady. With his
most engaging smiles he said he was about to depart on a visit
to Nassau and that he hoped he might be favored with an order
from Mrs. Davis for any articles of personal or household use
which were then unobtainable in the Confederacy. What appeal
to the feminine heart could be more potent! While she graciously responded to this attractive proposal, the President himself entered the room, to whom, in another courteous speech,
the Wilmington merchant presented, with complimentary allusions to the Arabian horse, a beautiful silk blanket bearing the
President's monogram, "J. D.," which was as graciously accepted in token of our friend's personal loyalty and devotion.
The subsequent details included a pass to Nassau signed by
the highest authority in the Confederacy, which was brought
back to Wilmington in triumph, and a few days afterwards a
favored son of the Scattered Nation was a very seasick man
on a voyage to Nassau through the Cape Fear blockade.

29

RESCUE OF MADAME DeROSSET.

In the summer of 1864, while the *Lilian* was undergoing repairs, we found at the shipyard in Wilmington the noted blockade runner *Lynx,* commanded by one of the most daring spirits in the service, Captain Reed. This officer has been described in a Northern magazine as a pirate, but he was one of the mildest mannered of gentlemen, a capital seaman, and apparently entirely devoid of fear. He had previously commanded the *Gibraltar,* formerly the first Confederate cruiser *Sumter;* and he brought through the blockade in this ship to Wilmington the two enormous guns which attracted so much attention at that time. One of them exploded, through a fault in loading; the other was used for the defense of Charleston, and rendered effective service.

A thrilling incident occurred in the destruction of the *Lynx,* a few weeks after we left her at Wilmington, which nearly terminated the life of a brave and charming lady, the wife of Mr. Louis H. DeRosset, and of her infant child, who were passengers for Nassau. At half past seven o'clock on the evening of September 26, 1864, the *Lynx* attempted to run the blockade at New Inlet, but was immediately discovered in the Swash Channel by the Federal cruiser *Niphon,* which fired several broadsides into her at short range, nearly every shot striking her hull and seriously disabling her. Notwithstanding this, Captain Reed continued his efforts to escape, and for a short time was slipping away from his pursuers; but he was again intercepted by two Federal men-of-war, the *Howquah* and the *Governor Buckingham.*

Mrs. DeRosset, describing the scene a few days afterwards, said: "Immediately the sky was illuminated with rockets, and broadside upon broadside, volley upon volley, was poured upon us. The captain put me in the wheelhouse for safety. I had scarcely taken my seat when a ball passed three inches above my head, wounding the man at the wheel next to me; a large piece of the wheelhouse knocked me violently on the head. I flew to the cabin and took my baby in my arms, and immediately another ball passed through the cabin. We came so near one of the enemy's boats that they fired a round of musketry and demanded surrender. We passed them like lightning; then our vessel commenced sinking! Eight shots went through and through below the water line. I stayed in the cabin until I could no longer keep the baby out of the water."

The *Howquah* then engaged the *Lynx* at close quarters, and her batteries tore away a large part of the paddle-boxes and bridge deck. The *Buckingham* also attacked the plucky blockade runner at so short range that her commander fired all the charges from his revolver at Captain Reed and his pilot on the bridge. The continual flashing of the guns brightly illuminated the chase and, escape being impossible, Captain Reed, much concerned for the safety of his passengers, headed his sinking ship for the beach. In the meantime Fort Fisher was firing upon his pursuers with deadly effect, killing and wounding five men on the *Howquah* and disabling one of the guns. The sea was very rough that night, and the treacherous breakers with their deafening roar afforded little hope of landing a woman and a baby through the surf; nevertheless, it was the only alternative, and right bravely did the heroine meet it. Through the breakers the *Lynx* was driven to her destruction, the shock, as her keel struck the bottom, sending her crew headlong on the deck. Boats were lowered with great difficulty, the sea dashing over the bulwarks and drenching the sailors to the point of strangulation. Madame DeRosset, with the utmost coolness, watched her chance, while the boat lurched and pounded against the stranded ship, and jumped to her place; the baby, wrapped in a blanket, was tossed from the deck to her mother ten feet below, and then the fight for a landing began; while the whole crew, forgetful of their own danger, and inspired with courage by the brave lady's example, joined in three hearty cheers as she disappeared in the darkness towards the shore. Under the later glare of the burning ship, which was set on fire when abandoned, a safe landing was effected, but with great suffering. Soaking wet, without food or drink, they remained on the beach until a message could reach Colonel Lamb at Fort Fisher, five miles distant, whence an ambulance was sent to carry the passengers twenty miles up to Wilmington. The baby blockade runner, Gabrielle, survived this perilous adventure, and also an exciting run through the fleet in the Confederate steamer *Owl*. She is now the widow of the late Col. Alfred Moore Waddell, formerly mayor of Wilmington.

IMPROVED SHIPS AND NOTABLE COMMANDERS.

The last year of the war evolved a superior type of blockade runner of great speed, many of which were commanded by celebrated men of nerve and experience. Of these may be mentioned at random and from memory: the *Lilian,* Captain Maffitt; the *Little Hattie,* Captain Libby; the *Florie,* named for Captain Maffitt's daughter; the *Agnes E. Fry,* commanded by that noble but unfortunate naval officer, Capt. Joseph Fry; the *Chicora,* still running in Canadian waters; the *Let Her Rip;* the *Let Her Be;* also the fleet of three-funnel boats, one of which, the *Condor,* was commanded by the famous Admiral Hewitt, of the British Navy, who won the Victoria Cross in the Crimea, and who was knighted by Queen Victoria for his distinguished services as special envoy to King John of Abyssinia. The *Falcon,* another, was commanded for one voyage by Hobart Pasha; the *Flamingo,* the *Ptarmigan,* and the *Vulture,* were also of the three-funnel type.

Another notable British officer who ran the blockade was the gallant Burgoyne, who was lost in the iron-clad *Captain* in the Bay of Biscay, which vessel he commanded on that unfortunate voyage.

Captain Carter was a notable naval officer of the Confederacy; he commanded the blockade runner *Coquette.*

Capt. Thomas Lockwood, a North Carolinian, was, perhaps, the most noted of the commercial class. His last command was the celebrated steamer *Colonel Lamb,* named for the defender of Fort Fisher. This was the largest, the finest, and the fastest of all the ships on either side during the war. She was a paddle-steamer, built of steel, 281 feet long, 36 feet beam, and 15 feet depth of hold. Her tonnage was 1,788 tons. At the time she was built, 1864, she was the fastest vessel afloat, having attained on her trial a speed of sixteen and three-fourth knots, or about nineteen miles an hour. Captain Lockwood made several successful runs in this fine ship, and escaped to England at the close of the war. The *Colonel Lamb* was sold to the Greek Government, and subseqently, under another name, was blown up while in the Mersey loaded with war supplies. Other fast boats were the *Owl, Bat, Fox, Dream, Stag, Edith, Atalanta, Virginia, Charlotte, Banshee* and *Night Hawk.*

Another merchant commander of distinction was Captain

Halpin, who was very skillful and successful. He afterwards commanded the famous leviathan, *Great Eastern,* while she was engaged in laying the Atlantic cable.

It is a remarkable fact that, although speed was regarded the first essential to success, some of the slowest vessels engaged in the traffic were the most fortunate. The *Pet,* for example, was a very slow steamer, yet she made the runs, over forty of them, through the blockade with the regularity of a mail boat. I think this was due to the superior skill of her commander, who exercised great caution and never became excited in a tight place. The *Antonica* was another slow, lumbering boat, but it was said of her that when she was fairly set on her course between Nassau and Wilmington they could simply lash her wheel and she would go in or out "by herself." The *Scotia,* the *Greyhound,* and others were equally slow coaches, but had for a time, it seemed, a charmed life.

The loss of the *Merrimac* was, like that of the *Bat,* as related by Pilot Craig, a notable example of cowardice on the part of the captain. This fine, large steamer, which had successfully run into Wilmington, was ordered to be sold in this port, and she was bought by a number of prominent citizens and merchants, one of whom was Mr. Edward Kidder. She was laden with a very valuable cargo of cotton and tobacco and put to sea for Nassau. On the second day out she was chased, as they thought, by a cruiser which steadily gained on her, and when the stranger fired a small gun, the captain of the *Merrimac* ignominiously surrendered to an *unarmed passenger steamer,* whose little popgun, containing a blank cartridge used for signals in those days, would not have harmed a fly. This incident caused much merriment on board the passenger steamer, which profited largely in the prize money.

THE NORTH CAROLINA BLOCKADE RUNNER "ADVANCE."

The following communication, prepared for me by the late Col. James G. Burr, of Wilmington, will be read with interest:

"In the month of August, 1862, Zebulon B. Vance, then colonel of a North Carolina regiment serving in the Army of Northern Virginia, and quite a young man, was elected governor of the State by a large majority. He did not seek the

office. In fact, he objected to the use of his name, for the reason
that he preferred the position that he then held in the army,
and for the further reason that he thought he was too young to
be governor. The people, however, thought differently and he
was borne into office by a popular upheaval. With what energy
and vigor he discharged his duties, how true he was in every
way to his State and his people, are matters of history and
need not be referred to here. He was inaugurated the ensuing
September, and early in his administration he conceived the
idea of purchasing for the State a steamer to run the blockade
at Wilmington, bringing in supplies for our soldiers in the
field and for our suffering people at home.[1]

"Capt. Thomas N. Crossan, formerly of the United States
Navy, was accordingly sent to England with Mr. Hughes, of
New Bern, where, in conjunction with Mr. John White, the
agent of the State in England at the time, they purchased the
fine side-wheel steamer *Lord Clyde,* then running between Glasgow and Dublin, which name before her advent into Southern
waters was changed to that of *Advance* or *Ad Vance,* the latter
in compliment to the distinguished war governor, through whose
instructions and active influence the purchase had been made.

"In the spring of 1863 the *Advance* made her first successful
trip through the blockaders and arrived safely in the harbor of
Wilmington, bringing a large amount of much-needed supplies.
The Governor was informed of her arrival and came to Wilmington immediately, and the next day, Sunday, went down on
one of the river steamers with a number of his friends to the
ship, which was lying at the quarantine station about fifteen or
sixteen miles below the city. After spending several hours on
board examining the ship and partaking of the hospitalities of
its officers, it was determined to take her up to the city without
waiting for a permit from the health officers, as it was assumed
the Governor's presence on board would be a justification for
the violation of quarantine regulations. Accordingly, steam
was raised and she came up to the city and was made fast to
the wharf in front of the custom house. This was objected to
by Major Strong, aide-de-camp to General Whiting, as being in

---

[1]During the Revolution the State made heavy importations and had
vessels engaged in running the blockade; and early in 1861 that precedent was again recommended, especially by Gen. J. G. Martin, the
adjutant general of the State, and ample funds were provided. When
Vance came in as governor the time was ripe for it, and he wisely
carried the plan into execution.

violation of quarantine regulations, and he ordered the vessel to return to her quarantine berth. But the chairman of the Board of Commissioners of Navigation was sent for, and he gave a permit for the vessel to remain where she was, and for all persons who wished to land to do so.

"The *Advance* was a first-class ship in every respect and had engines of great power and very highly finished, and her speed was good. With a pressure of twenty pounds to the square inch she easily averaged seventeen knots to the hour, and when it was increased to thirty pounds she reeled off twenty knots without difficulty. Her officers were Captain Crossan, commander; Captain Wylie, a Scotchman, who came over with her, sailing master; Mr. Hughes, of New Bern, purser; Capt. George Morrison, chief engineer. The only objection to her was her size and heavy draught of water, the latter rendering it difficult for her to cross the shoals, which at that time were a great bar to the navigation of the river, and in consequence of which she could never go out or return with a full cargo of cotton or supplies.

"She ran the blockade successfully seven or eight trips, bringing in all kinds of supplies that were much needed by our troops and people, thanks to the energy and wise foresight of our patriotic war governor. The regularity of her trips was remarkable and could be forecast almost to the very day; indeed, it was common to hear upon the streets the almost stereotyped remark, 'Tomorrow the *Advance* will be in,' and when the morrow came she could generally be seen gliding up to her dock with the rich freight of goods and wares so greatly needed by our people. In the meantime, however, she had several narrow escapes from capture. Coming from Nassau on one occasion, the weather being very stormy and a heavy fog prevailing, she ran ashore opposite Fort Caswell and remained there for two days. The sea was so rough that the blockaders could not approach near enough to do her damage, and after discharging part of her cargo she was relieved from her perilous position and got safely into port. But the most exciting trip was one made in the month of July, 1864, from Bermuda. She had on board as passengers a number of prominent gentlemen, among them Marshall Kane, of Baltimore, Rev. Dr. Moses D. Hoge, of Richmond, Va., and others who had come down from St. Johns, New Brunswick, and joined the ship at Bermuda, and who were extremely anxious to reach the Confederate States. By some error in calculation, instead of making Cape Fear Light at 3 a. m., as was intended, they made the light on Cape Lookout, a long distance out of their course. What was best to be done was the question to be solved, and to be solved at once, for daylight comes very soon in July. The ship had scarcely enough coal in her bunkers to take her back to the port she had left and almost certain capture stared them in the face should they attempt to run in. It was determined, however, to make the attempt to get in. The ship was headed for New Inlet and, hugging the shore as closely as possible, with all steam on, she dashed down the coast with the speed of a thoroughbred on a hotly contested race-course. Fortunately, at that time many persons were engaged in making salt on the coast, and the smoke rising from the works created a cloud, or mist, which concealed the ship from the blockaders, although it was broad day; but as she neared the inlet she was compelled to change her course further out to sea on account of a shoal, or spit, that makes out into the ocean at that point, and she was immediately discovered by the blockading fleet, that opened fire upon her and gave chase like a pack of hounds in eager pursuit of a much coveted quarry. It was a most trying situation, for the ship was compelled to keep her course, although it carried her nearer and nearer to the enemy, until she could round the shoal and run in towards the land, when she would be in comparative safety. Round shot and shell were flying around her in every direction, but she held steadily on, though rushing, as it seemed, to certain destruction, when suddenly a roar was heard from the fort—the heavy guns upon the mound had opened upon the pursuers and with such effect as to check their speed and force them to retire; and the gallant ship, which had been so hard pressed, soon rounded the shoal and was safe beneath the sheltering guns of the fort.

"But the pitcher that goes often to the fountain is broken at last, and the time came when the career of the *Advance,* as a blockade runner, was to cease forever. She was captured on her outward trip a few miles from our coast, owing to an inferior quality of coal she was compelled to use, which was very bituminous and emitted a black smoke that betrayed her to the watchful eyes of the fleet, and, being surrounded by them, she was obliged to surrender with her cargo of cotton, her officers and crew becoming prisoners. She was a noble ship, greatly endeared to the people of our State, and her capture was felt by all as a personal calamity.

"In 1867 she made her reappearance in the waters of the Cape Fear as the United States man-of-war *Frolic,* sent to this port to prevent the Cuban warship *Cuba* from leaving Wilmington, which duty was successfully performed. It happened on that occasion that Capt. George Morrison, her former engineer, met some of her officers and was asked by them her rate of speed while he had charge of her engines. He replied, 'Seventeen knots, easily.' 'Impossible,' they said, 'for we have not been able to get more than eight or nine out of her.' 'Something wrong then,' said the captain, 'and, unless you have made some alterations in her machinery, I will guarantee to drive her to Smithville at a rate of seventeen knots an hour.' He was cordially invited on board to examine, did so, and found that they had placed a damper where it ought not to be, which prevented the generation of steam. He removed it, and then ran down to Smithville at a rate of nineteen knots an hour, to the great surprise of all on board.

"As Captain Morrison held such an important position on the *Advance* and was so competent and reliable, it is thought that a brief sketch of his early life will not be out of place in this volume. He was born in Philadelphia, served four years in a machine shop, and at the expiration of his service removed to Baltimore, where he was appointed engineer on one of the Chesapeake Bay boats; subsequently he was chief engineer of a steamer plying between Norfolk, Old Point Comfort, and the eastern and western shores of the peninsular counties of Virginia. He came to Wilmington about 1840 and was appointed assistant engineer on the steamer *Gladiator,* running between Wilmington and Charleston. When the boat was sold, he became a conductor on the Wilmington and Weldon Railroad, and served with great acceptability for a number of years. He made six trips on the *Advance,* but was not on board when she was captured. For more than fifty years he was a citizen of Wilmington and enjoyed in his ripe old age, as in earlier years, the general esteem of the community.

"Another engineer on the *Advance* was Capt. James Maglenn, an Irishman, who on her last trip was chief engineer. After her capture, the *Advance* was carried into New Bern, where Captain Maglenn escaped and got to Baltimore. There some friends aided him to escape to Canada. When he was on the train he observed an officer and a guard come into the car, and he was very apprehensive. But the officer engaged himself in ascertaining how the passengers would vote, and while many voted for McClellan, Maglenn observed that the officer's eyes brightened when any one voted for Lincoln. When, therefore, the officer stopped opposite to him and asked, looking at him very intently, 'Who do you vote for?' in a voice loud enough to be heard throughout the car, he answered, 'I cast my vote for President Lincoln.' The officer slapped him on the shoulder, and said, 'You are the right sort, my friend.' Several passengers then came up and shook hands with him. Maglenn was very happy when he had got well into Canada.

"After the war he was engineer on the Coast Line, master mechanic of the Carolina Central, and superintendent of motive power of the Seaboard. In all walks of life and in every association with his fellow-men he was honest, true, and faithful. He lived many years in Raleigh, where he recently died."

OTHER VESSELS FAMOUS IN BLOCKADE RUNNING.

In the second stage of blockade running, when steam was at a premium, a number of walking-beam boats of excellent speed, which had plied regularly between Southern ports and which had been laid up since the proclamation, were bought by Southern business men who became prominent in blockade running, and, after the removal of passenger cabins and conspicuous top hamper, were placed in this dangerous traffic. Of these may be mentioned the steamer *Kate,* previously known as the *Carolina,* upon the line between Charleston and Palatka; the *Gordon,* which was built to run between Charleston and Savannah; also the *Nina, Seabrook, Clinch,* and *Cecile,* which had plied on the same line. The *Cecile,* loaded at Nassau with a cargo of powder, rifles, and stores for Gen. Albert Sidney Johnston's army at Shiloh, struck a sunken rock off the Florida coast and went to the bottom in ten minutes. The officers and crew escaped.

Two steamers which formerly ran between New Orleans and Galveston became prominent as Cape Fear blockade runners; the *Atlantic,* renamed the *Elizabeth,* and the *Austin,* which became the famous Confederate steamer *Ella and Annie.* In the early morning of November 9, 1863, the *Ella and Annie,* under command of Capt. F. N. Bonneau, of Charleston, was intercepted off New Inlet, near Masonboro, by the United States steamer *Niphon,* which attempted to press her ashore. Several other cruisers preventing the escape of the *Ella and Annie,* Captain Bonneau at once resolved upon the desperate expedient of running the *Niphon* down. He accordingly ran his ship at reckless speed straight at the war vessel, and struck it with great force, carrying away the bowsprit and stem and wounding three of the men. The *Niphon,* by quick movement, avoided the full effect of the blow, and fired all her starboard guns into the *Ella and Annie,* wounding four of her men. As soon as the vessels came together the *Niphon* carried the *Ella and Annie,* by boarding, and made her a prize. She afterwards became the United States flagship *Malvern.*

The *Governor Dudley,* of the Wilmington and Charleston route before the completion of the Wilmington and Manchester Railroad, which, prior to the war, had been put on the summer run between Charleston and Havana, made one or two successful voyages through the blockade to Nassau.

A Nassau correspondent of the *New York Times* on February 15, 1862, wrote: "On Tuesday last, the 11th of February, 1862, the old steamer *Governor Dudley* arrived from Charleston with 400 bales of cotton. The captain, fearing the cotton would go North if sold here, refused to take any price for it. After taking out a British register and changing her name to the *Nellie,* he left for Havana with a Nassau pilot on board to carry him across the [Bahama] Banks. He intends taking a return cargo to Charleston, and expects to be back here in about a month with more cotton. The *Nellie* is an old boat, nearly used up both in hull and machinery. Her speed is not over 8 or 10 knots, with a full head of steam." The other boats formerly comprising the Wilmington and Charleston line were probably too old for blockade-running service. The *Wilmington* was sold to run on the Gulf of St. Lawrence. The *Gladiator* went to Philadelphia, and the *Vanderbilt,* having been sold to New Orleans, foundered in the Gulf of Mexico while running the blockade.

Another old friend of the New York and Wilmington line, which was managed here by the late Edwin A. Keith, the *North Carolina,* rendered an important service to the Confederate Government by carrying through the blockade, as a passenger, the distinguished Capt. James D. Bulloch, naval representative of the Confederacy in Europe during the War between the

States. On February 5, 1862, she completed the loading of a
cargo of cotton, rosin, and tobacco at Wilmington, under her
new name, *Annie Childs,* named for the wife of Col. F. L.
Childs, and proceeded through the blockade by Main Bar, arriving at Liverpool, via Fayal, Madeira, and Queenstown, Ireland,
early in March. Her supply of coal was quite exhausted when
she sighted Queenstown, and she barely reached that port of
call by burning part of her rosin cargo with spare spars cut in
short lengths. Captain Bulloch said that she was badly found
for so long a voyage, but she weathered a heavy northwest gale,
and proved herself to be a fine sea boat. I am informed that she
returned to other successful ventures in blockade running under
the name of *Victory.*

The fleet of runners was augmented by old-fashioned steamers,
partly from the Northern ports, bought by foreigners and sent
via neutral ports, where they went through the process of "white-
washing," a change of name, ownership, registry, and flag. A
much greater number, however, came from abroad; a few of
these formerly having been fast mail boats, but the majority
freighters on short routes in Europe, bought at big prices for
eager speculators, who were tempted by the enormous profits of
blockade running.

A few of those of the better class became famous, as the
North Carolina steamer *Advance,* before known as the *Lord
Clyde;* the Confederate steamer *R. E. Lee,* formerly the *Giraffe;*
and the *Lady Davis,* previously the *Cornubia.* Some of the
others were the *Alice, Fanny, Britannia, Ella, Pet, Sirius,
Orion, Antonica, Hansa, Calypso, Duoro, Thistle, Scotia, City
of Petersburg, Old Dominion, Index, Caledonia, Dolphin, Georgiana McCall, Modern Greece, Hebe, Dee, Wave Queen,
Granite City, Stonewall Jackson, Victory, Flora, Beauregard,
Ruby, Margaret and Jessie, Eagle, Gertrude, Charleston, Banshee, Minna,* and *Eugenie,* all of which were more or less
successful.

The beach for miles north and south of Bald Head is marked
still by the melancholy wrecks of swift and graceful steamers
which had been employed in this perilous enterprise. Some of
the hundred vessels engaged in this traffic ran between Wilmington and the West Indies with the regularity of mail boats, and
some, even of the slowest speed—the *Pet,* for instance—eluding
the vigilance of the Federal fleet, passed unscathed twenty,
thirty, and forty times, making millions for the fortunate

owners. One little beauty, the *Siren,* a fast boat, numbered nearly fifty voyages. The success of these ships depended, of course, in great measure upon the skill and coolness of their commanders and pilots. It is noteworthy that those in charge of Confederate naval officers were, with but one exception, never taken; but many were captured, sunk, and otherwise lost, through no fault of the brave fellows who commanded them. The *Beauregard* and the *Venus* lie stranded on Carolina Beach; the *Modern Greece,* near New Inlet; the *Antonica,* on Frying Pan Shoals; the *Ella,* on Bald Head; the *Spunky* and the *Georgiana McCall,* on Caswell Beach; the *Hebe* and the *Dee,* between Wrightsville and Masonboro. Two others lie near Lockwood's Folly Bar; and others, whose names are forgotten, are half-buried in the sands, where they may remain for centuries to come. After a heavy storm on the coast, the summer residents at Carolina Beach and Masonboro Sound have occasionally picked up along the shore some interesting relics of blockade times which the heaving ocean has broken from the buried cargoes of the *Beauregard, Venus, Hebe,* and *Dee.* Tallow candles, Nassau bacon, soldiers' shoes, and other wreckage comprise in part this flotsam yielded up by Neptune after nearly fifty years' soaking in the sea.

The *Venus* was commanded by a prominent officer of the Royal Navy on leave of absence, Captain Murray-Aynsley, known by blockade runners as Captain Murray. He is now an admiral in the British Navy on the retired list. He was a great favorite with the prominent people, and especially with Colonel Lamb, of Fort Fisher, whose description of the veteran naval officer on the bridge of the *Venus,* running through the Federal fleet in broad daylight, hotly pursued by the enemy, with coat sleeves rolled up to his armpits, but cool and defiant, is well worth recording.

The loss of the *Georgiana McCall* is associated with a horrible crime—the murder of her pilot. When the ship was beached under the fire of the blockaders, Mr. Thomas Dyer did not go with the retreating crew who sought safety ashore; he seems to have been left behind in the rush. It was known that he had a large amount of money in gold on board, and it was thought that he remained to secure it. A boat returned for him, but found his bloody corpse instead. His skull was crushed as by a blow from behind; there was no money on his person. Another man was found on board, unhurt, who professed ignorance of his fellow. This person was the watchman, and it is said he carried ashore a large amount of money. He was arrested on suspicion, but there was no proof. He still lives on the river, but the cause of poor Dyer's death will probably never be known until the Great Assize.

Examples of dash and daring on the part of noted Cape Fear blockade runners in this phase of their history could be multiplied, if the limited scope of this paper would permit of their narration—instances so thrilling that it still stirs one's blood to recall them after an interval of fifty years. I shall, however, select from memory and from published accounts of others, whom I remember as participants, only a few exploits of the many which might be recorded, and, finally, some illustrations of the closing scenes when the false lights of the conquerors of Fort Fisher decoyed the unwary into the snare of the fowler or hastened the retreat of the few that escaped to a neutral port.

A Close Call.

The following interesting narrative, which is true in all its details, was told to the writer by the late George C. McDougal, of Rosindale, N. C., who by a clever expedient kept out of Fort Lafayette, and made some forty voyages as chief engineer in the little steamer *Siren* before his former shipmates were released:

"The well-known blockade-running steamer *Margaret and Jessie* left Nassau heavily laden for Wilmington, and made a good run across to the North Carolina coast. About 12 meridian she was in the latitude of New Inlet, and she ran on the western edge of the Gulf Stream until sundown, when she headed for the beach and made land to the northward of the blockading fleet of the Cape Fear. While tracking down the beach, one of the cruisers sighted us and sent up rockets, which made it necessary for us to run the remainder of the distance under fire from the whole line of the blockaders. Just as we got the lights in range at the inlet and were about to head the ship over the bar, we distinguished a gunboat anchored in the channel under cover of the wrecked steamer *Arabian*. We immediately put the ship about, and, with the whole fleet trailing after us, ran off shore. At daylight none of our followers was in sight, but away offshore to the southward we sighted the armed transport *Fulton*. As we could not cross her bow, Capt. Robert Lockwood, who commanded our ship, hauled to the northward and eastward, unfortunately driving us across the bows of all the cruisers which had run offshore in chase. We had to run the fire of five of these warships as we crossed their bows and dropped them astern. During all this time the *Fulton* kept the weather gauge of us; and after a hard day's chase from New Inlet to Hatteras, we were at last compelled to surrender late in the afternoon, as the *Fulton* seemed determined to run us down, there being hardly a cable's length between us when we hove to and stopped the engines. Before doing this, however, we were careful to throw the mail bags, government dispatches, and ship's papers into the furnace of the fireroom, where they were quickly consumed.

"While our ship's company was being transferred to the *Fulton,* the United States steamer *Keystone State* and two other cruisers came up, and sent several boats' crews aboard the *Margaret and Jessie,* who looted her of all the silver, cutlery, glassware, cabin furniture, tablecloths, and napkins—doubtless everything they could carry off in their boats. The *Fulton,* having sent a prize crew on board, took us in tow for New York, where, immediately on our arrival, we were confined in Ludlow Street Jail. Two days after, the officers and crew of the blockade runner *Ella and Annie* were brought in, she having been captured off Wilmington after a desperate resistance by her brave commander, Captain Bonneau. During our incarceration we were visited frequently by United States deputy marshals, who tried to identify some of us suspected of holding commissions in the Confederate service and of being regularly engaged in blockade running, as distinguished from those less harmful members of the crew who would be only too glad to abandon further attempts on regaining their liberty. These officers were immediately assailed with questions from all quarters. 'What are you going to do with us here?' 'Are you going to let us out?' to which they would respond, 'We can not tell—the crew lists have been sent to Washington for inspection; you will have to wait until they are returned.'

"We were kept in this state of suspense for about three weeks, when a squad of deputy marshals came to the jail and mustered the entire company. We soon ascertained that the crew lists had come from Washington, and that we were to go down to the marshal's office, where the names of those who were to be released were to be called out, and the unfortunate ones remaining prepared for a long term of imprisonment at one of the well-known prison-pens so dreaded by those who afterwards realized all their horrors. We were, accordingly, marched down to the marshal's headquarters in Burton's old theatre, on Chambers Street, opposite City Hall Park, where we were ordered to select our baggage and prepare to be searched for contraband articles. The entire office force of clerks had been drawn by curiosity from their desks to the other end of the large room, where the inspection was going on; and, while my baggage was being examined by an officer, I asked him if he knew who were to be released; to which he replied that he did not know, but that the list of those who would be released could be found in a large book on that desk, pointing his finger to the other end of the room. When his inspection was completed, I asked if I might go and read the names to satisfy my curiosity. He said there could be no harm in doing so, and asked if I could read. I said, yes, that I thought I could make out the names. Whereupon, I walked with forced indifference to the desk, and found a big journal laid open upon it, containing the names of the men belonging to the *Ella and Annie's* crew who were to be discharged. This did not interest me; and looking further down I saw, also, the names of those of my own ship who were to be released, but from the top to the bottom there was no George C. McDougal. You may depend upon it, I felt very sad as Fort Lafayette loomed up in all its dreariness. Looking furtively over my shoulder, I saw that the desk was so placed that my back shielded me from the eyes of the marshals at the moment, and also that the officers and clerks were very busy seeing what they could confiscate, each man for himself, out of the baggage of the unfortunate prisoners; and, feeling that no worse fate could overtake me, I slipped my hand cautiously along the desk, took up a pen and, imitating as closely as possible the character of the writing before me, inscribed my own name at the bottom of the list, and immediately returned to the crowd at the other end of the room. The deputy asked me if I saw my own name, to which I promptly responded, 'Yes.' 'Then you are all right,' said he, 'and will be turned out tonight.' Shortly afterwards, we were marched off to a neighboring place to get our supper at the expense of Uncle Sam, after which the chief marshal and Judge Beebe appeared, and in due form separated those who were to be released from the unfortunate ones remaining. I waited, with feelings that can be imagined better than they can be described, as the names were read; and at last my own name was called without detection of my expedient, which was, doubtless, owing to the fact that the room was badly lighted and darkness had already set in. Promptly responding to my name, I at once passed out into the night, leaving my commander, Capt. Robert Lockwood, Mr. Charles Craig, the Wilmington pilot, Billy Willington, our engineer, and several others of the *Margaret and Jessie,* who, together with Capt. Frank Bonneau, his Wilmington pilot, and his chief engineer, Alexander Laurence, were sent to Fort Lafayette, where they remained until about the end of the war."

THE KATE'S ADVENTURE.

In the spring of the year 1862, the Confederate Government, desiring to arrange for the importation of supplies for the War Department, and finding the principal ports of the South Atlantic coast so well guarded by the blockaders that the new undertaking of blockade running was considered extra hazardous, decided to use the smaller inlets, which were less carefully watched by the enemy, and dispatched the steamer *Kate* from Nassau with a cargo of ammunition to Smyrna, Florida, where an entrance was safely effected by that vessel, and the cargo immediately discharged and transported across the country to a place of safety.

The *Kate* was commanded by Capt. Thomas J. Lockwood, of Smithville, on the Cape Fear River, who was well known to our river pilots and seafaring people as a man of very superior skill and seamanship, and as thoroughly familiar with the bars and inlets along the Southern coast.

A second voyage by the *Kate* had been completed, and the cargo successfully discharged and transported, before the movement became known to the blockading squadron; but, while the *Kate* was waiting for the return of Captain Lockwood from Charleston, whither he had proceeded to bring his family to the ship at Smyrna Inlet, a Federal man-of-war discovered her hiding place, which forced the chief officer of the *Kate* to proceed to sea at once, leaving the captain behind. The Federal cruiser landed a boat's crew, who burned the house of Mr. Sheldon, the pilot who had assisted in bringing the *Kate* to an anchorage, shortly after which, Captain Lockwood arrived with his family, to find that the ship had already departed. Mr. Sheldon, however, furnished him with an ordinary whaleboat, which had escaped the scrutiny of the Federal man-of-war's

30

men, and Captain Lockwood at once determined to undertake
the voyage in this frail craft, and overtake the *Kate* at Nassau.
The boat was only sixteen feet long and not at all well found for
such a perilous voyage.

After a short delay, the captain, his brave wife, their two
children, and a hired boy, found themselves safe over the bar
and headed for the Bahamas. The following account of this
remarkable voyage was written by Mrs. Lockwood, and has been
kindly furnished by her brother, Mr. McDougal:

"After the baggage was safe on board, I was carried in a
man's arms through the surf and placed in the boat, and we
started over the sea in our frail little craft. A few yards from
shore, we discovered that she was sinking, but turned back in
time to reach the beach, to which I was again transferred just
as the boat went down. With some difficulty she was recovered,
when it was found that the plug had come out of the bottom
while drawing the boat over the beach. We soon found a remedy
for this trouble, and proceeded to cross the Gulf Stream. On
the following morning, the wind blew a gale. The waves dashed
high over us all day, while the wind increased in fury. For
fifteen hours we waited and prayed, thinking that every moment
would be our last. About five o'clock in the evening, we discovered a reef and steered along the rocks to find an opening,
so that we might cross the line of breakers and get into calm
water. Oakie told us to sit still and hold fast to the boat, as we
must go over the rocks or sink. As each enormous wave came
towards us it seemed to reach the sky and break over our frail
craft, deluging us with water. For several moments in succession I would sit under these huge waves, holding on with one
hand and clasping my baby with the other. Breaker after
breaker burst over us, and at the same time lifted the boat
farther and farther on to the rocks, until at last we were plunged
ahead into the smooth water of the bay beyond. By some means,
I cannot tell how, we reached one of the vessels lying at anchor,
when they lifted us all on board and carried us into the cabin.
We could not walk for cold and cramp. On Sunday, the 23d,
the schooner upon which we had taken refuge sailed for Nassau,
and on Monday we landed on Elbow Cay, one of the Bahama
Islands, the wind not being favorable for us to continue farther
that day. On the 25th, with a fair wind, we again proceeded
towards Nassau, and arrived on Wednesday, after being three
weeks on the journey from Charleston."

Mr. McDougal adds in his journal, that he was then chief engineer of the steamer *Kate,* of 500 tons, in the Gulf Stream, about 150 miles from where Captain Lockwood was cruising in the little boat; and that the gale was so severe that this large vessel was obliged to lie to, and suffered considerable damage in consequence of the severity of the storm, and that it seems a miracle that a small boat like Captain Lockwood's should have lived through such a fearful gale.

THE BRITISH FLAG.

A majority of the blockade runners bore British certificates of registry and sailed under the British flag because they were owned and manned by British subjects, and traded with British ports. This did not save them from capture and condemnation if caught with contraband cargoes between Nassau or Bermuda and the coast of the Southern States, whether they attempted to break the blockade or not. But if they were bound from a British port, say Nassau or Bermuda, to a home port in Great Britain, loaded with cotton, they would be protected from capture by their flag and register and their manifest of British ownership; or, if they were bound from Great Britain to Nassau or Bermuda with arms or war supplies and certified British ownership, although ultimately intending to run the blockade, their papers would protect them from molestation by the Federal cruisers. Not so with those under the Confederate flag, which were liable to capture whenever found on the high seas.

When the War between the States began Mr. Donald MacRae was British vice consul at Wilmington. He resigned, however, and Mr. Alexander Sprunt was appointed by Consul Henry Pinckney Walker at Charleston to act in his place; but the function was suspended by General Whiting because there were no diplomatic relations between the foreign powers and the Confederacy, Great Britain having only recognized our belligerent rights.

It is remarkable that during the entire war the British flag was the only foreign colors flown in the ports of the Confederacy.

THE LAST DAYS OF BLOCKADE RUNNING.

By Captain John Wilkinson, C. S. N.

In the early part of December, 1864, I was summoned again, and for the last time during the war, to Richmond. There now remained to the Confederacy only the single line of rail communication from Wilmington, via Greensboro and Danville, to Richmond. The progress of demoralization was too evident at every step of my journey, and nowhere were the poverty and the straits to which the country was reduced more palpably visible than in the rickety, windowless, filthy cars, traveling six or eight miles an hour, over the worn-out rails and decaying road-bed. We were eighteen hours in making the distance (about one hundred and twenty miles) from Danville to Richmond. As we passed in the rear of General Lee's line and I saw the scare-crow cattle there being slaughtered for the troops, the game seemed to be at last growing desperate. We were detained for perhaps an hour at the station where the cattle were being slaughtered. Several soldiers who were on the train left us there; and as soon as they alighted from the cars, they seized portions of the offal, kindled a fire, charred the scraps upon the points of their ramrods, and devoured the unclean food with the avidity of famished tigers.

It was arranged in Richmond that I should take command of the *Tallahassee* and proceed with all dispatch to Bermuda for a cargo of provisions, my late experience with the governor of the island rendering it quite probable that he would prevent the *Chickamauga* from even discharging her cargo as a merchant vessel. That steamer (the *Tallahassee*), of so many aliases, had just returned from a short cruise under Captain Ward, of the Confederate States Navy. She was now christened again, and bore, thenceforward, the appropriate name of *Chameleon*. Her battery was dismounted, her officers and crew detached, and she was ostensibly sold to the navy agent at Wilmington. A register and bill of sale were prepared in legal form, the crew shipped according to the laws relating to the merchant service, and regular invoices and bills of lading made out of her cargo of cotton. The vessel, indeed, was so thoroughly whitewashed that she subsequently passed a searching examination in Bermuda; but my recent experience there had convinced me of the necessity of adopting every precaution, and I was left to my own discretion with regard to all the details; the instructions under which I was acting requiring me only to bring in a cargo of provisions with all dispatch.

The *Chameleon* was in nearly all respects like the *Chicka-mauga,* only a few feet longer, and drawing a few inches more water.

On the afternoon of December 24, the United States fleet opened fire upon Fort Fisher, the heavy cannonading continuing during the two following days. The booming of the heavy guns could be distinctly heard in Wilmington.

There was a complete panic there; the non-combatants moved away and fright and confusion prevailed everywhere. The co-operating land forces, under General Butler, had almost completely invested the fort, and the communication between it and Wilmington was at one time interrupted, so that it was impossible to ascertain the condition of affairs below. In the midst of the turmoil, we cast off from the wharf about two o'clock in the afternoon of December 26 and anchored off Smithville after dark, the tide not serving for crossing the bar that night.

Next morning the *Agnes Fry,* an inward-bound blockade runner, was discovered aground on the Western Bar. Towards evening two or three of the blockading fleet stationed off that bar steamed in and opened fire upon her. The bombardment of the fort was still in progress. A little after dark, just as we were weighing our anchor, General Whiting, who was then in Fort Fisher, telegraphed to us that the United States land forces were embarking, the attack upon the fort having been abandoned. We were under way in a few minutes, closely followed by the *Hansa,* Captain Murray, and parting from her just as we crossed the bar. I had known the captain for many months, under his assumed name, and it was quite generally understood that he held a commission in the British Navy. While I was living in Nova Scotia, some years afterwards, the card of Captain A., commanding H. B. M.'s ship *J——n,* was brought to me, and I was surprised to find in the owner of it my old friend Murray. Several British naval officers of rank and high character were engaged in the same exciting and lucrative occupation of blockade running; among them the gallant Captain Burgoyne, who commanded afterwards the unfortunate ship *Captain,* of the British Navy, and who perished together with nearly the whole crew when she foundered at sea.

We crossed the bar under such favorable circumstances that

we were not discovered; nor did we see any of the fleet until we cleared the Frying Pan Shoals, when we easily avoided several vessels which had participated, no doubt, in the attack upon Fort Fisher, and were now about to take their stations off the Western Bar.

We made a rapid, though very rough voyage to Bermuda, a stormy northwest gale following us nearly the whole distance. The Prussian Major Von Borcke, who had served on General "Jeb" Stuart's staff and who afterwards published (in *Blackwood's*) his experience of the war, was a passenger. The major was no sailor, and his sufferings from seasickness were much aggravated by a gunshot wound in his throat. As the engines of the *Chameleon* would "race" in the heavy sea following us, and her whole frame would vibrate, he declared in military phraseology ("our army swore terribly in Flanders") that he would rather encounter the dangers of a "stricken field" than voluntarily endure an hour of such torture.

We arrived at St. George's on the 30th of December; and our troubles immediately commenced. It was the 5th of January before permission was received to land our cargo of cotton, His Excellency, the governor, having called upon the law officers of the Crown for aid in the dire dilemma. When the vessel's papers were at last pronounced correct, we discharged our cargo; and then arose the perplexing question of loading. I haven't the slightest doubt that the American consul was sadly bothering His Excellency all this time; however, permission was finally granted to us to take in provisions, but no munitions of war. As we did not want "hardware," as munitions of war were then invoiced, we proceeded to load. But a great deal of time had been lost, and we did not take our departure for Wilmington till the 19th of January. We had on board as passengers General Preston and staff, returning from Europe.

Our voyage across was very rough, and the night of our approach to New Inlet Bar was dark and rainy. Between one and two o'clock in the morning, as we were feeling our way with the lead, a light was discovered nearly ahead and a short distance from us. As we drew closer in and "sheered" the *Chameleon,* so as to bring the light abeam, I directed our signal officer to make the regular signal. No reply was made to it, although many lights now began to appear looming up through the drizzling rain. These were undoubtedly camp fires of the United States troops outside of Fort Fisher; but it never occurred to me as possible that a second attack could have been made, and successfully, in the brief period of time which had elapsed since our departure from Wilmington. Believing that I had made some error in my day's observations, the *Chameleon* was put to sea again, as the most prudent course in the emergency. The night was too far spent to allow of any delay. Orders were therefore given to go at full speed, and by daylight we had made an offing of forty or fifty miles from the coast. Clear and pleasant weather enabled me to establish our position accurately (it was my invariable custom at sea, during the war, to take my own observations), and early in the night we made the Mound Light ahead, for which I had shaped our course. The range lights were showing, and we crossed the bar without interference, but without a suspicion of anything wrong, as it would occasionally happen, under particularly favorable circumstances, that we would cross the bar without even seeing a blockader. We were under the guns of Fort Fisher, in fact, and close to the fleet of United States vessels, which had crossed the bar after the fall of the fort, when I directed my signal officer to communicate with the shore station. His signal was promptly answered, but turning to me, he said, "No Confederate signal officer there, sir; he can not reply to me." The order to wear round was instantly obeyed; not a moment too soon, for the bow of the *Chameleon* was scarcely pointed for the bar before two of the light cruisers were plainly visible in pursuit, steaming with all speed to intercept us. Nothing saved us from capture but the twin screws, which enabled our steamer to turn as upon a pivot in the narrow channel between the bar and the Rip. We reached the bar before our pursuers, and were soon lost to their sight in the darkness outside. Our supply of coal being limited, the course was shaped for Nassau as the nearer port, where we arrived without accident. A day or two after our arrival the news came of the fall of Fort Fisher.

Several narrow escapes, besides our own, were made. Maffitt, in command of the *Owl*, crossed the Western Bar a night or two after the fall of Fort Fisher, and while our troops were evacuating Fort Caswell and other military stations along the river. Crossing the bar and suspecting no danger, he continued on his way up to Smithville, where he anchored. He was boarded a few moments afterwards by a boat from our military post there. The officer in command of the boat informed him of the capture of Fort Fisher, and that our troops were then evacuating Fort

Caswell, adding that several vessels of the Federal fleet had crossed the New Inlet Bar, and were at anchor in the river almost within hail of him. Maffitt was about to give the order to slip the chain, "not standing upon the order of his going," when his pilot begged for permission to go ashore, if only for ten minutes. He represented the situation of his wife, whom he had left ill and without means of support, in such moving terms, that Maffitt granted permission, upon condition that he would return speedily. The pilot was faithful to his promise, returning in fifteen or twenty minutes. During his absence, steam was raised and the chain unshackled. As the pilot's foot touched the deck of the *Owl,* the boat was hooked on and run up the davits, the chain slipped, and the *Owl* upon her way to sea again.

Another blockade runner is said to have been not so fortunate. She had run the gauntlet safely and come to anchor off Smithville. The tarpaulins had been removed from the hatches, the lamps lighted, and a cold supper spread upon the table, at which the passengers were seated, two or three officers of the British Army among them. A toast to the captain having been proposed, they had just tossed off a bumper of champagne to his health and continued successes, and he was about to reply to the compliment, when the officer of the deck reported that a boat was coming alongside. The captain received the officer at the gangway. The mail-bag, according to the usual routine, was given to the latter for transportation to the shore; and the customary inquiries made after the name of the vessel, cargo, number of passengers, etc. The astounded captain was then informed that his vessel was a prize to the United States ship, then at anchor near him!

Charleston was now the only harbor on the Atlantic coast at all accessible, and that must evidently soon fall; but a cargo might be landed there before that inevitable catastrophe, and, fully appreciating the exigency, I determined to make the effort. Even after the occupation of Wilmington by the United States troops, there would remain an interior line of communication between Charleston and Virginia. The facts of history prove that the importance of carrying in a cargo of provisions was not exaggerated, for the Army of Northern Virginia was shortly afterwards literally starving; and during their retreat from the position around Petersburg, the country adjacent to their line was swarming with soldiers who had left the ranks in search of food.

But it was the part of prudence to ascertain, positively, before sailing, that Charleston was still in our possession. This intelligence was brought by the *Chicora,* which arrived at Nassau on the 30th of January; and on February 1, the *Owl, Carolina, Dream, Chicora,* and *Chameleon* sailed within a few hours of each other for Charleston.

We passed Abaco Light soon after dark and shaped our course direct for Charleston. At early dawn the next morning, while I was lying awake in my room on the bridge, I heard the officer of the deck give the quick, sharp order to the helmsman, "Hard a-port." The steering wheel in all of the blockade runners was upon the bridge and immediately forward of the captain's stateroom, and the officer of the deck kept his watch upon the bridge. As I never undressed at night while at sea in command during the war, I was out upon the deck in a moment; and then I saw, distant two or three miles and directly in our former course, a large side-wheel steamer. From her size and rig I guessed her to be the *Vanderbilt;* and I was afraid that the *Chameleon* had at last found more than her match, for the *Vanderbilt* enjoyed the reputation of great speed. We were around before we were discovered, but as the strange steamer's bow was pointed in our direction a few moments afterwards, it was plain that we would have to make good use of our heels, and that the race would be a trying one. The *Chameleon* was in fine condition for the ordeal, and the usual precaution of cleaning fires and raising the steam had been taken before daylight. My staunch old quartermaster, McLean, who had been with me in nearly all the chances and changes of blockade running, always took his place at the wheel on trying occasions. He had nerves of steel, and would have steered the vessel without flinching against a line of battleships, if so ordered. Upon one occasion, after we had crossed the Western Bar, and were steaming at full speed along the coast, we suddenly discovered a long, low blockader on our starboard bow, and at the same instant distinctly heard the order from the stranger's deck, to "pass along the shell." I called out to my old helmsman, "Port, and run her down," and if the strange vessel had not moved out of our way with alacrity, she would assuredly have been cut in two. We grazed her stern by a hair's breadth as we shot by her at the rate of thirteen knots. Before they had recovered from the confusion on board of her, we had passed into the darkness beyond, and the shell which they sent after us flew wide of its mark.

McLean was now placed at the wheel. It was a close race for hours, neither apparently gaining or losing a foot; but Providence again befriended us. As the day advanced, the breeze, which was very light from the northward at daylight, continued to freshen from that quarter. We soon set all of our canvas, and so did the chaser, but as the latter was square-rigged, and we carried fore and aft sails, our sheets were hauled flat aft, and the *Chameleon* was kept close to the wind by the steady old helmsman. I do not doubt that we would have been overhauled but for this favorable contingency. Head to wind, our pursuers would certainly have overtaken us, and off the wind her chances would have been almost equally good. But she began to drop gradually to leeward as the wind continued steady, and by two o'clock in the afternoon she was five or six miles distant on our lee quarter. Although we had not increased the distance between us much, if any, since the commencement of the chase, we had weathered upon the chaser until her sails had become useless about twelve o'clock, when she furled them. As the snowy cloud of canvas was rolled up like magic, and the tall, tapering spars were seen in its place, I supposed the cruiser was about to retire from the contest; but she still followed with the tenacity of a bloodhound. Apparently to no purpose, however, till about two o'clock, when the chief engineer, Mr. Schroeder, appeared on the bridge with the report that the journals were heated, and it was absolutely necessary to stop in order to ease the bearings. This was a predicament, indeed, but when I looked down into the hold and saw the clouds of vapor rising from the overheated journals, as a stream of water was being pumped upon them, I saw that Schroeder was right in the assertion that unless the bearings were instantly eased the machinery would give way. I had implicit confidence in Schroeder, and it had been justly earned, for he had served long under my command, and had always displayed, under trying circumstances, great coolness, presence of mind, and ability. He made every preparation for the work before him, taking off his coat, and when everything was in readiness, the order to stop the engines was given. In a few moments we lay like a log upon the water, and the chaser was rapidly lessening the distance between us. The suspense became almost intolerable. Our fate was hanging by a thread; but in ten minutes the journals had been cooled off, the bearings eased, and the *Chameleon* again sprang ahead with renewed speed. The steamer in chase had approached nearly within cannon shot—probably within long range—but in the course of the next hour we had gained so rapidly in the race that the pursuit was abandoned as hopeless; and as the stranger wore around, to resume her station under easy steam, we followed in her wake till dark, when we evaded her without difficulty and continued on our course toward Charleston.

But another precious day had been lost, and subsequent unfavorable weather still further retarding our progress, we did not reach the coast near Charleston Bar till the fifth night after our departure from Nassau. The blockading fleet had been reinforced by all the light cruisers from the approaches to the Cape Fear River; and, as we drew in to the land, we were so frequently compelled to alter the course of the *Chameleon* in order to evade the blockaders, that we did not reach the bar till long after midnight, and after the tide had commenced to fall. I was tempted to force the pilot to make the attempt, but finally yielded to the assurances that access was impossible under the circumstances. As this was the last night during that moon, when the bar could be crossed during the dark hours, the course of the *Chameleon* was again, for the last time, shaped for Nassau. As we turned away from the land, our hearts sank within us, while the conviction forced itself upon us that the cause for which so much blood had been shed, so many miseries bravely endured, and so many sacrifices cheerfully made, was about to perish at last.

The closing scenes of blockade running are described by Colonel Scharf in his *History of the Confederate States Navy* as follows:

"The military and naval expeditions against Wilmington in December, 1864, and in January, 1865, resulted in the capture of the forts and the closing of the port. Eight vessels left the port of Nassau between the 12th and 16th of January, one of which took four one-hundred-pounder Armstrong guns; and at the time of their sailing there were over two and a half million pounds of bacon stored at Nassau awaiting transportation. The confidence reposed in the defense of Wilmington continued unabated on the part of the blockade runners, and the *Charlotte,* the *Blenheim,* and the *Stag,* all British steamers, ran in after the fall of Fort Fisher, and were captured by the Federal cruisers in the river. The blockade runner *Owl,* Capt. John N. Maffitt, C. S. N., in command, succeeded in passing over the bar near Fort Caswell, and anchored at Smithville on the night the forts were evacuated; but immediately returned to Bermuda, arriving on the 21st, and carrying the news of the fall of Fort Fisher and the end of blockade running at Wilmington. Her arrival was timely, stopping the *Maud Campbell, Old Dominion, Florence, Deer,* and *Virginia.* Most, if not all, of these steamers now turned their prows towards Charleston, the last harbor remaining accessible; and, though the fall of that city was impending, yet a cargo might be safely landed and transported along the interior line to the famishing armies of the Confederate States. To that end Captain Wilkinson determined to make the effort, which was a brave and gallant one, but was ineffectual. The blockading fleet, reinforced from that off Wilmington, now closed every practical entrance; but it was not until after assurances from the pilot that entrance was impossible, that Captain Wilkinson turned back. The *Chicora,* more fortunate than the *Chameleon,* ran into Charleston, but, finding the city evacuated, ran out, despite the effectiveness of the blockade, and reached Nassau on the 28th. The *Fox,* less fortunate, ran into Charleston in ignorance of its capture and was seized by the Federal cruisers.

"Capt. John N. Maffitt, C. S. N., in the *Owl,* left Havana, about the middle of March, within a quarter of an hour after the United States ship *Cherokee* steamed out of the harbor. Passing Morro Castle, the *Owl* hugged the coast towards the west, followed by the *Cherokee,* the chase continuing for an hour or more. The *Owl* had speed, and Maffitt had the seamanship to 'throw dust into the eyes' of his pursuer by changing her coal from hard to soft, thus clouding the air with dense black smoke, under cover of which the *Owl* turned on the *Cherokee,* and, steaming away to the stern of the cruiser, disappeared in the darkness of night and storm."

THE CONFEDERATE NAVY.

If the Federal Government was unprepared for naval warfare at the beginning of the civil strife, the Confederacy was even less prepared, for it could not claim the ownership of a single ship. In a conversation shortly after the war, our distinguished naval officer, Capt. John Newland Maffitt, said:

"The Northern Navy contributed materially to the successful issue of the war. The grand mistake of the South was neglecting her navy. All our army movements out West were baffled by the armed Federal steamers which swarmed on Western waters, and which our government had provided nothing to meet. Before the capture of New Orleans, the South ought to have had a navy strong enough to prevent the capture of that city and hold firmly the Mississippi and its tributaries. This would have prevented many disastrous battles; it would have made Sherman's march through the country impossible, and Lee would have been master of his lines. The errors of our government were numerous, but the neglect of the navy proved irremediable and fatal.

"Nobody here," he continued, "would believe at first that a great war was before us. South Carolina seceded first, and improvised a navy consisting of two small tugboats! North Carolina followed suit, and armed a tug and a small passenger boat! Georgia, Alabama, and Louisiana put in commission a handful of frail river boats that you could have knocked to pieces with a pistol shot! That was our navy! Then came Congress and voted money to pay officers like myself, who had resigned from the Federal Navy, but nothing to build or arm ships for us to command. Of course, it woke up by and by, and ordered vessels to be built here, there, and everywhere; but it was too late.

"And yet," said the captain, with a momentary kindling of the eye, as the thought of other days came back to him, "the Confederate Navy, minute though it was, won a place for itself in history. To the Confederates the credit belongs of testing in battle the invulnerability of ironclads and of revolutionizing the navies of the world. The *Merrimac* did this; and, though we had but a handful of light cruisers, while the ocean swarmed with armed Federal vessels, we defied the Federal Navy and swept Northern commerce from the seas."

Colonel Scharf, in his admirable *History of the Confederate States Navy,* says: "In many respects the most interesting chapter of the history of the Confederate Navy is that of the building and operation of the ships-of-war which drove the merchant flag of the United States from the oceans and almost extirpated their carrying trade. But the limitations of space in this volume forbid more than a brief review of the subject. The function of commerce-destroyers is now so well admitted as an attribute of war between recognized belligerents by all nations of the world, that no apology is necessary for the manner in which the South conducted hostilities upon the high seas against her enemy; and, while Federal officials and organs styled the cruisers 'pirates' and their commanders 'buccaneers,' such stigmatization has long since been swept away, along with other rubbish of the War between the States, and their legal status fully and honorably established. We have not the space for quotations from Professor Soley, Professor Bolles, and other writers upon this point; but what they have said may be summed up in the statement that the government and agents of the Confederacy transgressed no principle of right in this matter, and that if the United States were at war today, they would strike at the commerce of an enemy in as nearly the same manner as circumstances would permit. The justification of the Confederate authorities is not in the slightest degree affected by the fact that the Geneva Tribunal directed Great Britain to pay the General Government $15,500,000 in satisfaction for ships destroyed by cruisers constructed in British ports.

"Eleven Confederate cruisers figured in the Alabama Claims settlement between the United States and Great Britain. They were the *Alabama, Shenandoah, Florida, Tallahassee, Georgia, Chickamauga, Nashville, Retribution, Sumter, Sallie,* and *Boston.* The actual losses inflicted by the *Alabama,* $6,547,609, were only $60,000 greater than those charged to the *Shenandoah.* The sum total of the claims filed against the eleven cruisers for ships and cargoes was $17,900,633, all but about $4,865,000 being caused by the *Alabama* and the *Shenandoah.* The tribunal decided that Great Britain was in no way responsible for the losses inflicted by any cruisers but the *Alabama, Florida,* and *Shenandoah.* It disallowed all the claims of the United States for indirect or consequential losses, which included the approximate extinction of American commerce by the capture of ships or their transfer to foreign flags. What this amounted to is shown in the 'Case of the United States' presented to the tribunal. In this it is stated that while in 1860 two-thirds of the commerce of New York was carried on in American bottoms, in 1863 three-fourths was carried on in foreign bottoms. The transfer of American vessels to the British flag to avoid capture is stated thus: In 1861, vessels 126, tonnage 71,673; in 1862, vessels 135, tonnage 64,578; in 1863, vessels 348, tonnage 252,579; in 1864, vessels 106, tonnage 92,052. Commanders of the Confederate cruisers have avowed that the destruction of private property and the diversion of legitimate commerce in the performance of their duty were painful in the extreme to them; but in its wars the United States had always practiced this mode of harassing an enemy, and had, indeed, been the most conspicuous exemplar of it that the world ever saw."

Since the foregoing was written by Colonel Scharf in 1887, there has been a growing aversion to privateering on the part of the principal commercial powers. A press association dispatch from Washington during the late Boer War said:

"The report from Brussels that former President Kruger is being urged to notify the powers that unless they intervene in the South African contest he will commission privateers is not treated seriously here. It is well understood, as one outcome of the war with Spain, that the United States Government will never again, except in the most extraordinary emergency, issue letters of marque; and the same reasons that impel our government to this course would undoubtedly operate to prevent it from recognizing any such warrants issued by any other nation, even if that nation were in full standing.

"In the case of the Spanish War, both the belligerents by agreement refrained from issuing commissions to privateers, and it now has been many years since the flag of any reputable nation has flown over such craft."

About the beginning of the year 1862, the Confederate States Government began the construction of an ironclad ram, named *North Carolina,* on the west side of Cape Fear at the shipyard of the late W. B. Beery, the drawings and specifications of the vessel having been made by Capt. John L. Porter, chief naval constructor of the Confederate States Navy, with headquarters at Portsmouth, Virginia.

The armament of the *North Carolina* consisted of one 10-inch pivot gun in the bow and six broadside guns of about 8-inch calibre. The timbers of the vessel were heavy pine and hardwood covered with railroad iron, giving the ram, when launched, the appearance of a turtle in the water.

The *North Carolina* was subsequently anchored for a long time off Smithville, as a guard vessel commanding the entrance to the river at the Main Bar, until she was gradually destroyed by the teredo, or sea-worm, and sank at her moorings, where, I believe, she still remains.

The *Raleigh,* a vessel of light construction, was built later at the wharf near the foot of Church Street; and after being launched was completed at Cassidy's shipyard. Her construction and armament were similar to that of the *North Carolina,* but she was covered with heavy iron plates of two thicknesses running fore and aft and athwart ship.

The star of the Confederacy was waning in the spring of 1864; a depreciated currency and the scant supply of provisions and clothing had sent prices almost beyond the reach of people of moderate means. In Richmond, meal was $10 per bushel; butter, $5 per pound; sugar, $12 per pound; bacon, hog round, $4 per pound; brogan shoes, $25 per pair; felt hats, $150; cotton cloth, $30 per yard; and it was a saying in the Capital of the Confederacy, that the money had to be carried in the market basket and the marketing brought home in the pocketbook.

Early in May the condition of the commissariat was alarming; but a few days' rations were left for Lee's army, and only the timely arrival of the blockade runner *Banshee* with provisions saved the troops from suffering.

Wilmington was the only port left to the blockade runners, and the blockade of the mouths of the Cape Fear had become dangerously stringent. Some twenty steamers guarded the two inlets, besides two outer lines of fast cruisers between this city and the friendly ports of Nassau and the Bermudas. On dark nights, armed launches were sent into the bar to report outgoing steamers by firing rockets in the direction taken by them. The ceaseless vigilance of the forts could scarcely make an exit for friendly vessels even comparatively free from danger. An hour after dark, Fort Fisher, having trained its sea-face guns upon the bar, would ricochet its Columbiad shot and shell upon that point, so as to frighten off the launches; and then the blockade runners would venture out and take their chances of running the gauntlet of the blockading fleet.

In this emergency, Commodore Lynch, commanding the Confederate fleet in the Cape Fear River, determined to raise the blockade of New Inlet, the favorite entrance of the blockade runners.

The ironclad ram *Raleigh,* already described, Lieut. J. Pembroke Jones commanding, and two small wooden gunboats, *Yadkin* and *Equator,* were chosen for the purpose. Our late townsman, Capt. E. W. Manning, chief engineer of the station, and the late Engineer Smith, Confederate States Navy, of Fayetteville, were in charge of the machinery of the *Raleigh*. On the afternoon of May 6, 1864, the commodore visited Fort Fisher, to take a reconnaissance and obtain as far as practicable the coöperation of the fort. Seven vessels were at anchorage at sundown: the *Tuscarora, Britannia, Nansemond, Howquah, Mount Vernon, Kansas,* and *Niphon.* He arranged a distinguishing signal for his vessels—a red light above a white one—so that they would not be fired upon by the fort.

Fort Fisher had its sea-face guns manned after dark by experienced artillerists, and about eight o'clock the range lights were set on the mound and the Confederate flotilla put to sea. The commander of the fort, Col. William Lamb, with some of his officers, repaired to the ramparts opposite the bar and awaited the result.

Within thirty minutes after the vessels had disappeared from the vision of the anxious garrison, a few shots were heard from seaward, and some Coston blue lights were seen in the offing; then all was dark as Erebus and silent as the grave. Speculation was rife among the Confederates who manned the guns. Had the foe been dispersed or destroyed? Why were no rockets sent up to announce a victory, to cheer the thousand hearts which beat with anxious hope within Fort Fisher? A long night of waiting was spent without any sign save the occasional twinkle of a distant light at sea. The gunners were relieved at midnight, but all continued dark and silent.

At last day dawned, the breakers on the bar became visible, the *Raleigh* and her consorts appeared, and then outside of them, at long range, the enemy's fleet. Shots were exchanged between the combatants after daylight; one of the Federal vessels fired rapidly at the *Raleigh,* approaching as she fired, but, receiving a shot from the ironclad through her smokestack, withdrew to a safer distance.

Then the seven blockaders came closer to the Confederate fleet, showing fight, and probably with the intention of trying to run the *Raleigh* down; but that vessel and her consorts headed for the fort and steamed slowly in, the enemy prudently keeping beyond range of the guns of Fort Fisher. It was a great disappointment that the garrison saw the *Raleigh, Yadkin,* and *Equator* come over the bar and under the guns of the fort, leaving the blockading squadron apparently unharmed.

The *Yadkin* and *Equator* came safely into the river, but the *Raleigh,* after passing the mound and rounding Confederate

31

Point, grounded on the Rip at the mouth of the river. Efforts were made to lighten her and get her off, but the receding tide caused her to hog and break in two, on account of the heavy armor, and, becoming a wreck, she subsequently sank and went to pieces. Little was saved from her; but the crew were not endangered, as the weather was calm.

The following is the account of the incident given by the *Daily Journal* of Tuesday, May 10, 1864, omitting, however, mention of the accident to the *Raleigh:*

The Iron-Clad "Raleigh" at Sea.

Fort Fisher, N. C., May 7, 1864.

The monotony of garrison life has been disturbed by an act of gallantry on the part of our navy. Last evening, the iron-clad *Raleigh,* Lieut. Pembroke Jones commanding, bearing the broad pennant of Flag Officer Lynch, steamed out of New Inlet in quest of the enemy. Not long after leaving the bar the *Raleigh* met a blockader cruising about, and gave her a seven-inch shot crashing through her sides; the Federal vessel being unused to such an encounter, immediately left, making signals to the fleet. The iron-clad continued her cruise until after midnight, when an unsuspecting blockader, taking her for a blockade runner, fired a shot and ran down to pick up a prize, but, instead of receiving the surrender of an unarmed blockade runner, Jonathan was complimented by a ball that was more surprising than agreeable. Thinking in wonder that they had been fired on by one of the squadron through mistake, the blockader displayed the usual signal of a bright blue light, when the *Raleigh,* being very near, sent a rifle shell whistling through her bulwarks. The Yankee "doused his glim" with unexampled alacrity. Very soon the red-and-blue signals of the enemy were seen flashing in different directions, giving the alarm to each other. Nothing more was seen or heard during the night, and we who awaited the result on the ramparts of Fort Fisher were relieved when the dawn commenced to roll the curtain from the scene. Daylight first disclosed the small steamers *Yadkin* and *Equator* about two miles from shore awaiting the orders of the *Raleigh,* which they accompanied over the bar. Soon the horizon was clear, and we discovered the iron-clad eight miles to sea, in quiet possession of the blockading anchorage. Soon after, the blockaders that had run off to sea appeared on the horizon, and the little black dots developed themselves into gunboats.

First, came two well in view, and one, approaching within range of the *Raleigh,* was greeted by a shot; a long-taw engagement now commenced, in which the second blockader joined; but the enemy was soon sufficiently amused and ran off, giving the flag officer a wide berth. Six sails now appeared, but only one had the temerity to exchange shots with the iron-clad, and she soon decamped beyond range. About 6 o'clock eight blockaders came in sight, but notwithstanding the *Raleigh* steamed defiantly around their anchorage, eight miles from the guns of Fort Fisher, not one dared to take up the gauntlet. At 7 o'clock the flag officer, wishing to save the tide on the bar, signalled for his steamers and turned the *Raleigh's* prow to shore. The little trio formed in line some five miles out, and steamed slowly in, the Confederate flag waving saucily above their decks. The fort greeted the *Raleigh* with a salute as she passed in.

What damage the iron-clad did to the two vessels she struck is not known. She was not struck.

WILMINGTON DURING THE BLOCKADE.
(By an Ex-Confederate Officer.[1])

After the Capital of the Confederacy there was not in the South a more important place than the little town of Wilmington, North Carolina, about thirty miles from the mouth of the Cape Fear River, noted in peace times for its exports of tar, pitch, turpentine, and lumber.

Previous to the War between the States Wilmington was very gay and social. But the war sadly changed the place—many of the old families moving away into the interior, and those who remained, either from altered circumstances or the loss of relatives in battle, living in retirement. When we first knew it, Maj. Gen. W. H. C. Whiting was in command. He had been a United States Army officer, who for a long time had been stationed at Smithville, near the Old Inlet at the mouth of the river, where, prior to the war, there had been a fort and a garrison, though for some years disused. Whiting was one of the

---

[1] In a Northern magazine after the war.

most accomplished officers in the Southern Army. He was a splendid engineer, and having been engaged in the Coast Survey for some time on that portion of the coast, knew the country thoroughly, the capability of defense, the strong and the weak points. He was fond of the social glass, and may have sometimes gone too far. He was not popular with many of the citizens, as he was arbitrary, and paid little attention to the suggestions of civilians. He was a very handsome, soldierly-looking man, and though rough sometimes in his manners, he was a gentleman at heart, incapable of anything mean or low, and of undaunted courage. Peace to his ashes!

On Whiting's staff were three young officers of great promise: his brother-in-law, Maj. J. H. Hill, formerly of the United States Army, now an active express agent at Wilmington; Maj. Benjamin Sloan, his ordnance officer, now teaching school somewhere in the mountains of South Carolina; and Lieut. J. H. Fairley, a young Irishman, who had been many years in this country, and who hailed from South Carolina. Fairley was noted in the army as a daring scout and a very hard rider, withal one of the quietest and most modest of men. He is now drumming for a dry-goods house in New York instead of inspecting the outposts. We wonder if he recollects the night when the writer picked up a rattlesnake in his blanket at Masonboro Sound.

Whiting scarcely ever had enough troops at his command to make up a respectable Confederate division. In 1864 he had at Wilmington Martin's brigade, which was a very fine and large one, composed of four North Carolina regiments, remarkably well officered; two or three companies of heavy artillery in the town, doing provost and guard duty; at Fort Caswell at the mouth of Old Inlet on the Western Bar, a battalion of heavy artillery and a light battery; at Smithville, a similar battalion; at Bald Head, an island opposite Fort Caswell, Hedrick's North Carolina regiment, about 600 effective men; at Fort Fisher, Lamb's North Carolina regiment, about 700 effective men; a company at Fort Anderson; a company of the Seventh Confederate States Cavalry at the ferry over New River, sixty miles northeast of Wilmington, on the sound; two companies of cavalry, a light battery, and a company of infantry at Kenansville, forty miles north of Wilmington and seven miles east of the Weldon Railroad. These, with two or three light batteries scattered along the sound, from a little above

Fort Fisher up to Topsail, constituted in the spring of 1864 the whole Confederate force in the Department of Cape Fear.

With this force and Whiting's skill and bravery, we military men thought we could hold Wilmington, for we justly regarded the general as one of the few eminently fit appointments that the War Department had made. In Whiting, we had implicit faith. So, though there were constant rumors of expeditions against the place, we scarcely believed they were coming, so long had the thing been delayed, and, in fact, an attack was wished for by the youthful Hotspurs to relieve the monotony of garrison life at Caswell, Bald Head, and Fisher. Thus we had lapsed into a dream of security, or thought, at least, the evil day was far off. We ate, drank, and were merry, and there was marrying and giving in marriage, as in the days before the flood.

It seemed singular to us that the United States should so long neglect to close almost the only port of the Confederacy into which, every "dark of the moon," there ran a half-dozen or so swift blockade runners, freighted with cannon, muskets, and every munition of war, and with medicines, cloth, shoes, bacon, etc. Through that port were brought, till January, 1865, all the stores and material needed by the indefatigable Colonel Gorgas,[1] the Confederate chief of ordnance, the most efficient bureau officer the Confederacy had. Through it came those famous Whitworth and Armstrong guns sent us by our English friends. Into Wilmington was brought by Mr. Commissary General Northrup that rotten, putrid bacon called "Nassau," because it had spoiled on the wharves of that place before being reshipped for Wilmington. It was coarse Western bacon, bought by Confederate emissaries at the North; and many a time have we imprecated curses both loud and deep on poor old Northrup's devoted head as we worried down a piece of the rancid stuff. We must say, in all candor, that he was impartial in his distribution of it, and ordered it given to both Confederate trooper and Federal prisoner. Northrup himself ate none of it; he lived on rice, of which he would buy a hogshead at a time from the commissariat. We became so vitiated in our taste by eating it that at last we came to prefer it to good bacon, and liked the strong, rancid taste. We could not afford to permit our stomachs to cut up any shines, and forced them to stand any and everything by breaking them into it.

---

[1]The father of the present distinguished officer of that name.

But the cargoes of those white-painted, bird-like-looking steamers that floated monthly into Wilmington, producing such excitement and joy among its population, unfortunately for the Confederates, did not contain government stores and munitions of war alone, bad as the bacon and much of the stuff bought abroad by worthless Confederate agents were. The public freight compared with the private was small. By them were brought in the cloth that made the uniforms of those gaily-decked clerks that swarmed the streets of Richmond with military titles, and read the battle bulletins and discussed the war news. From that source came the braid, buttons, and stars for the host of "majors," who were truly fifth wheels and did not even have the labor of "following the colonel around," with which the Confederacy was afflicted.

As for ourselves, we never had the pleasure of this sort of thing but twice. Once by invitation of our friend George Baer, alias Captain Henry, who immortalized himself by writing that celebrated protest concerning the capture of the *Greyhound,* and by his escape from his captors in Boston. Baer invited us to a fashionable 10 o'clock breakfast on the *Index,* which he then commanded, and the consequence was we nearly stuffed ourselves to death, and came near having an apoplectic fit.

The Confederate Government used to send some queer agents abroad at the expense of the people. A Mrs. Grinnell was sent out by the surgeon general—so she stated—to get bandages, etc., which nobody else, we suppose, but Mrs. Grinnell could get. She was an English woman of that class and with those manners which any man, if he has traveled much, has often seen. She gave herself out as a daughter of an English baronet, and had first come to New York several years prior to the war. Then there was Belle Boyd, who represented herself, we believe, as an agent sent out by Mr. Benjamin. She was captured, with our friend George Baer, on the *Greyhound.* Another was a Mrs. Baxley, of Baltimore. She represented herself, we believe, as an agent of old Mr. Memminger.

Mr. Mallory's navy was always the laughing-stock of the army, and many were the jeers that the Confederate "mud-crushers" let off at his iron-clads, formidable things as they were, had he properly managed the Confederate Navy. Captain Lynch was the flag officer of the Cape Fear squadron when we first went there. His fleet consisted of the ironclad ram

North Carolina, which drew so much water that she could never get over the bars of the Cape Fear River inlets, except, possibly, at the highest spring tide, and then the chances were against her ever getting back again; the *Raleigh,* another iron-clad, not completed until late in the spring of 1864; and two or three little steam-tugs. They all came to grief. The *North Carolina,* the bottom of which was neither sheathed nor prepared to resist the worms, was pierced by them till her hull was like a honeycomb, and finally she sunk opposite Smithville. The *Raleigh* was beached and lost on a bar near Fort Fisher. The tugs were burned on the river subsequent to the evacuation of the town.

Whiting and Lynch, from some cause or other, never were on good terms, jealous of each other's authority, we suppose. It finally came near culminating seriously. There had been an order sent by Mr. Mallory to Lynch, in pursuance of an act of the Confederate Congress, not to let any vessel go out without taking on a certain proportion of government cotton. Lynch was commander of the naval defenses of the Cape Fear. By some oversight the Adjutant General's office at Richmond had sent no such order to Whiting, who commanded the department, and consequently the port and its regulations. One of Collie's steamers was about to go out without complying with the law. Old Lynch sent a half company of marines on board of her and took possession. This Whiting resented rather haughtily as an unwarrantable interference with his authority as commander of the port, and, marching in a battalion of the Seventh North Carolina Regiment, under Lieut. Col. John C. Lamb, ejected the marines and took possession of the steamer, hauling her up stream to her wharf. Lynch said he did not care how far Whiting took her up the river, but he vowed if any attempt was made to take her to sea, he would sink her, and he shotted his guns. Matters looked squally and excitement was high. A collision was feared. They were both summoned to Richmond to explain, and both returned apparently satisfied. Lynch, however, was shortly afterward relieved, and Commodore Pinckney took his place.

We had often wondered why the port was not more effectually closed. To tell the truth it was hardly closed at all. Many of the blockade runners continued their career till the fall of Fisher. An experienced captain and a good engineer invariably brought a ship safely by the blockading squadron. Wilkinson

and Carter never failed—good sailors, cool, cautious, and resolute, they ran in and out without difficulty many times. The
great danger was from the exterior line of the blockade some
forty or fifty miles out.

But owing to the configuration of the coast it is almost impossible to effect a close blockade. The Cape Fear has two
mouths, Old Inlet, at the entrance of which Fort Caswell
stands, and New Inlet, nine miles up the river, where Fort
Fisher guards the entrance. From the station off Old Inlet,
where there were usually from five to six blockaders, around
to the station off New Inlet, a vessel would have to make an arc
of some fifty miles, owing to the Frying Pan Shoals intervening, while from Caswell across to Fisher was only nine miles.
The plan of the blockade runners coming in was to strike the
coast thirty or forty miles above or below the inlets, and then
run along (of course at night) till they got under the protection of the forts. Sometimes they got in or out by boldly running through the blockading fleet, but that was hazardous, for,
if discovered, the ocean was alive with rockets and lights, and
it was no pleasant thing to have shells and balls whistling over
you and around you. The chances were, then, that if you were
not caught, you had, in spite of your speed, to throw a good
many bales of cotton overboard.

The wreck of these blockade runners not infrequently occurred by being stranded or beached, and highly diverting
skirmishes would occur between the blockaders and the garrisons of the forts for the possession. The fleet, however, never
liked the Whitworth guns we had, which shot almost with the
accuracy of a rifle and with a tremendous range. The soldiers
generally managed to wreck the stranded vessels successfully,
though oftentimes with great peril and hardships. It mattered
very little to the owners then who got her, as they did not see
much of what was recovered, the soldiers thinking they were
entitled to what they got at the risk of their lives. But a
wreck was a most demoralizing affair—the whole garrison generally got drunk and stayed drunk for a week or so afterwards.
Brandies and fine wines flowed like water; and it was a month
perhaps before matters could be got straight. Many accumulated snug little sums from the misfortunes of the blockade
runners, who generally denounced such pillage as piracy, but
it could not be helped.

We recollect the wrecking of the *Ella* off Bald Head in December, 1864. She belonged to the Bee Company, of Charleston, and was a splendid new steamer, on her second trip in, with a large and valuable cargo almost entirely owned by private parties and speculators. She was chased ashore by the blockading fleet and immediately abandoned by her officers and crew, whom nothing would induce to go back in order to save her cargo. Yankee shells flying over and through and around her had no charms for these sons of Neptune. Captain Badham, however, and his company, the Edenton Battery, with Captain Bahnson, a fighting Quaker, from Salem, N. C., boarded and wrecked her under the fire of the Federals—six shells passing through the *Ella* while they were removing her cargo. The consequence was that for a month afterwards nearly the whole garrison were on "a tight," and groceries and dry-goods were plentiful in that vicinity. The general demoralization produced by "London Dock" and "Hollands" seemed even to affect that holy man, the chaplain, who said some very queer graces at the headquarters mess-table.

Seldom, however, was there any loss of life attending these wrecks. But there was one notable case of the drowning of a famous woman, celebrated for her beauty and powers of fascination. We allude to the death of Mrs. Greenhow, so well known for many years in Washington circles. Before she even crossed the Confederate lines, she had undoubtedly rendered valuable service to the authorities in Richmond, and was in consequence imprisoned by the Federal authorities in Washington. After coming to Richmond and laboring in the hospitals there for some time, she sailed for Europe from Wilmington, and it was on her return trip that she was drowned, just as she reached the shores of the South. She had lived past her beauty's prime, had drunk deep of fashion's and folly's stream of pleasure, had received the admiration and adulation of hundreds of her fellow-mortals, and had reached that point in life when those things no longer please, but pall on the senses. Her time had come. The *Condor,* a blockade runner on which she was coming as a passenger, was beached a short distance above Fort Fisher, and Mrs. Greenhow, fearing capture and the treatment of a spy, pleaded with the captain to send her ashore. He refused, saying that he would protect her; but she finally prevailed upon him; and manning a boat, he made an effort to have her taken to the shore. Unfortunately, the boat capsized. She alone was drowned. It was supposed the gold she had

sewed up in her clothing weighted her down and was the cause
of her drowning. Her body was found on the beach at daylight
by Mr. Thomas E. Taylor, who afterwards took it to Wilmington. She was laid out in the Seaman's Bethel, where we saw
her. She was beautiful in death. After her funeral, her ward-
robe and a great many articles that she had brought over for
sale, and which had been rescued from the wreck, were sold
at auction in Wilmington. It was very splendid, and the "venture" she had brought in for sale was most costly. It was said
that an English countess or duchess had an interest in this
venture, and was to have shared the profits of the speculation.

But the storm was soon to rain on our devoted heads. Those
white-painted steamers, clipping the water so nimbly, with the
British and Confederate flags flying, with their brandies and
wines, their silks and calicoes, their bananas and oranges, glad-
dening the hearts of the dwellers on the banks of the Cape Fear,
were soon to disappear from its waters, and the glory of Wilmington to depart.

Day after day we had watched the blockading fleet with the
naked eye and a glass, and often thought what a lonely time
those fellows must be having, and longed for some northeast
storm to send them on the coast, in order that we might have
the pleasure of their acquaintance. Cushing's acquaintance, by
the way, we came very near making, when that daring officer
came up the Cape Fear in June, we think it was 1864, passing
through the New Inlet by Fort Fisher, with a boat's crew of
some eighteen or twenty sailors and marines, and, landing
half-way between the town and the fort, concealed his boat in
a creek, and laid *perdu* on the Wilmington and Fisher road,
waiting for Whiting or Lamb to come along. A mere accident
enabled us to escape him; and, though of no importance ourself,
we had papers with us at the time that would have been highly
interesting to the United States Government. We all of us
admired his courage, and thought it deserved success. We well
remember delivering Cushing's message to General Whiting,
repeated to us by an old citizen whom he caught and released,
that "he had been in Wilmington, and would have him or
Colonel Lamb shortly."

On December 24, 1864, the armada commanded by Butler and
Porter appeared off the coast, and the bombardment of Fisher
commenced, and such a *feu d'enfer* as was poured on that devoted fort was never seen. Coming up the river from Smith-

ville on a steamer that afternoon, we witnessed it, and such a
roar of artillery we never heard. Those large double-enders
seemed to stand in remarkably close to the fort, and deliver their
fire with great accuracy, knocking up the sand on the ramparts.
It seemed a continuous hail of shot and shell, many of them
going over Fisher and dropping into the river. But Fisher
was a long sand fort, stretching in an obtuse angle from the
river bank around to the mouth of the New Inlet, that opened
into the ocean. It was over a mile from point to point. Though
it was thus heavily bombarded for two days, little or no impression was made on its works except to give them a ragged
appearance, and very few casualties occurred, the garrison
sticking mostly to their bomb-proofs, which were very complete.
Whiting was there in command in person, having been sent there
by Bragg.

The next day, Christmas, was Sunday, and all day Porter's
guns were thundering away at Fisher, and shaking the windows
in Wilmington, where the citizens were offering up their prayers
for our protection from the enemy. Communication with Fort
Fisher by land or telegraph was then cut off—messages had
been sent up to that time. Toward night sensational messages
commenced to be brought up from below—one to the effect
that the enemy were on the parapet at Fisher (in truth and in
fact they never got closer than the stables, at least two or three
hundred yards from the fort). Bragg sent Mrs. Bragg away
that night at 9 p. m., in a special train up the Weldon Railroad,
and an officer who saw him at about 11 p. m. reported that the
old gentleman seemed to be quite unnerved, and that his hand
was very tremulous. Of course there was a great exodus of
civilians from the place early the next morning, the fact that
Mrs. Bragg had gone off acting as a keynote of alarm to others.
By midday, Monday, however, these sensational reports and
stories were all quieted by the authenticated news that the
enemy had reëmbarked on the fleet and that the attack had
ceased. Then the fleet sailed, and everything quieted down.
The general impression was that there would not be another
attack till after the spring equinox, say in May or June.

When Whiting returned to the city, Bragg still continued in
command, and his friends and himself evidently took the credit
of having foiled Butler's attempt. Bragg was a friend and
favorite of Mr. Davis. He had sided with General Taylor in
Taylor's quarrel with General Scott, and Mr. Davis was a man

who never forgot his friends nor forgave his enemies. He seemed determined to sustain Bragg at all events, though the feeling throughout the whole army, and, in fact, the South, was against that general. When Wilmington was known to be threatened and Bragg was sent there, the *Richmond Examiner* simply remarked, "Good-bye, Wilmington!" and the prediction was verified.

Whiting, after the first attack, wrote to Bragg, suggesting that in case of another attack, which would probably be made, to prevent surprise he would advise that Hagood's South Carolina brigade, numbering about 2,000 effective men, be thrown into Fort Fisher, the garrison of which consisted of one raw, inexperienced regiment, that had never smelled powder except in the first attack, and which did not number over 700 effective men. Hagood's troops were veterans, and had been in many a battle. He also advised that the three other brigades of Hoke's division be placed along about the spot where the Federals had first landed, and be intrenched so as to prevent a landing above the fort. Wise precautions, if they had been adopted. Bragg endorsed on the letter of advice from Whiting that he saw no necessity in carrying out those suggestions. It was the failure to carry out those suggestions that caused the loss of Wilmington. Had they been followed, Wilmington would not have fallen when it did, nor Fisher have been taken. Instead, Bragg brought Hoke's division up about half a mile back of Wilmington, over twenty miles from the Fort, and had a grand review there, in which he paraded himself in a new suit of uniform, presented to him by his admirers in Wilmington.

Whiting's prediction about a surprise was shortly to be verified. Thursday night, the 12th of January, 1865, the fleet again appeared off Fisher. This time, through Bragg's imbecility, it did its work effectually. Friday morning the citizens of Wilmington were aroused by the booming of Porter's cannon, a second time opening on Fisher. When the news came up at midnight that the fleet had again appeared, the band of Hoke's division was in town serenading, the officers were visiting, and the men scattered about—Bragg, no doubt, asleep in fancied security.

Of the capture of Fort Fisher, and the subsequent inevitable loss of Wilmington, I shall not speak. These events have passed into history. My purpose has been simply to portray the aspect of Wilmington when blockaded.

THE FIRST AND SECOND ATTACKS UPON FORT FISHER.

On the morning of December 20, 1864, a Federal fleet began to assemble at New Inlet. It bore the force General Grant had sent under Gen. B. F. Butler to reduce Fort Fisher, and the Federal Navy, under Admiral Porter, was coöperating with 52 warships, the greatest flotilla ever brought together in American waters. But General Butler hoped for the practical destruction of the fort by means of an explosion of powder on a vessel, the *Louisiana.* All being in readiness, on the night of the 23d the *Louisiana* was brought in, and at 1.52 a. m. the explosion occurred. To the amazement of Butler nothing happened. Colonel Lamb, the next morning, reported: "A blockader got aground near the fort, set fire to herself and blew up." So little was the explosion noticed that its purpose was not conjectured.

During the 24th a terrific bombardment was kept up by the Federal fleet, but without much damage, Colonel Lamb noting that the greatest penetration into his sand defenses was not more than five feet perpendicularly. On Christmas day, Sunday, a large force of infantry was landed at Battery Anderson, three miles up the beach. These, being unopposed by infantry and well beyond the fire of the fort, prepared for the assault. The beach was swept by the guns of the fleet and had there been an infantry force to attack the Federal troops it could not have approached them. At 4.30 p. m. the expected assault was made, but successfully repulsed; and the next morning, General Butler, admitting failure, withdrew his troops to his ships; and, although the bombardment continued, this first attack ended in disaster for the Federals, the defense being a glorious victory.

Admiral Porter and General Grant were much disappointed at Butler's fiasco, and they arranged to make another attempt. General Grant enjoined the utmost secrecy, and a new force was quietly collected under General Terry and transported to Beaufort. The Confederates were jubilant at the defeat of Butler, and General Bragg, who did not expect an early renewal of the attack, moved Hoke's division to Wilmington, en route to make an effort to capture New Bern. General Whiting, however, was of a different opinion and looked for the return of the Federal forces. On the 8th of January the new expedition had reached Beaufort, and, all the details having been arranged by General Terry and Admiral Porter, on the 12th the vessels sailed for New Inlet. Early on the morning of the 13th, the fleet opened fire on the fort, and by 2 o'clock 8,000 troops, with 12 days rations and intrenching tools, had been landed at Battery Anderson, and General Terry at once began to intrench himself from the beach to the river. Hoke's division was hurried from Wilmington, but arrived too late to be of use in the defense. Hagood's brigade was ordered to reinforce the garrison, and two of his regiments succeeded in reaching the fort in time. The arrangement was for an assault on the afternoon of the 15th, and on the evening of the 14th Admiral Porter threw 2,000 sailors and marines ashore, who quickly intrenched themselves in the sand near the fort, ready to coöperate with the infantry. At 3 o'clock, on the 15th, all the whistles of the fleet united in the signal, and the assault was made under cover of a fierce bombardment. The sailors being close to the front of the fort, and in such numbers, were mistaken for the principal attacking force, and the garrison was concentrated to meet them. They were swept off the approach to the fort as leaves by a whirlwind. But the troops under Terry were more successful. Although suffering heavy losses, and meeting stern resistance, they were able to gain possession of a traverse at the river end of the fort, and then by the aid of the fleet, which threw its shells into the traverses held by the garrison, the Federal infantry gradually progressed until by 9 o'clock it had carried the fort. Whiting and Lamb and scores of officers and many men lay either terribly wounded or dead, and at length, after hours of fierce fighting in the black night, all the blacker from the smoke of battle, the survivors withdrew to Battery Buchanan, in the hope of finding boats as a means of escape. But the boats were no longer there, and nothing remained but to surrender.

NOTE: In the accompanying drawing of the second attack upon Fort Fisher is seen the *Lilian*, the blockade runner on which the author, when but eighteen years of age, was purser.

The *Lilian* was a beautiful little ship, a model of a yacht, and very fast. She made many successful trips, eluding the vigilance of the blockading fleet or showing them her heels; but, finally, on August 23, 1864, during a chase for five hours under fire, she was struck by several shells, one of which, fired by the *Gettysburg*, penetrated her starboard bow below the water-line, making steering impossible. Three of the Federal cruisers now overhauled her, and when they came along side,

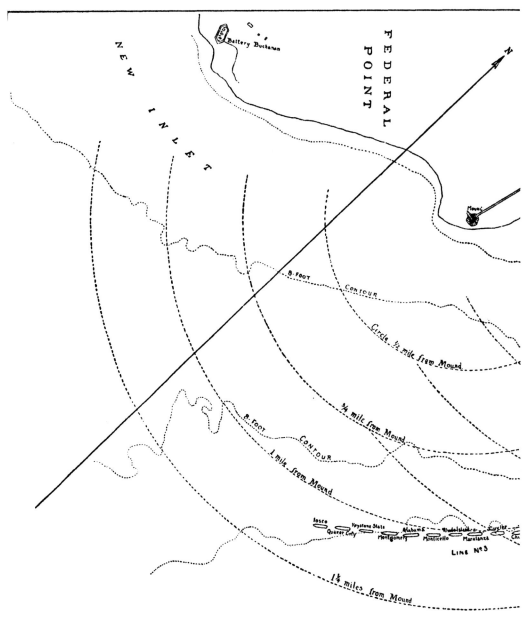

PLAN
or
SECOND ATTACK
on
FORT FISHER
Jan. 13, 14, 15, 1865.
Showing the Position of Vessels

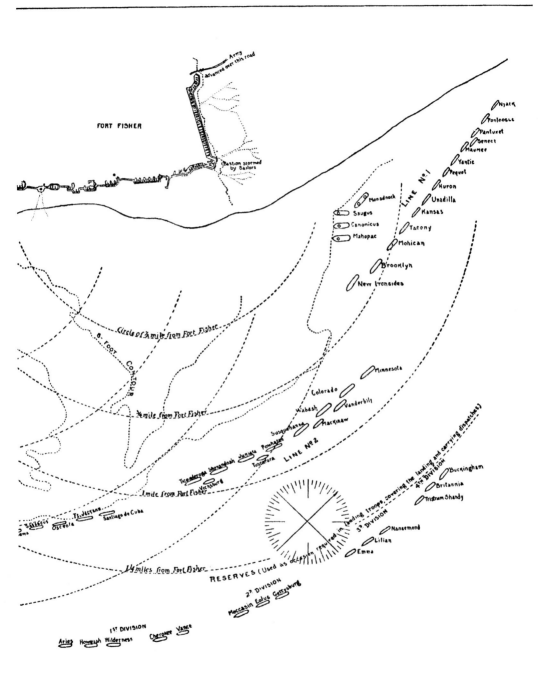

FORT FISHER

Army
advanced over this road

Bastion stormed
by Sailors

LINE Nº1

Nyack
Pontoosue
Pawtuxet
Seneca
Maumee
Yantic
Pequot
Huron
Unadilla
Kansas
Tacony
Mohican
Brooklyn
New Ironsides

Monadnock
Saugus
Canonicus
Mahopac

Circle of a mile from Fort Fisher

6 FOOT CONTOUR

½ mile from Fort Fisher

¾ mile from Fort Fisher

1 mile from Fort Fisher

1¼ miles from Fort Fisher

Minnesota
Colorado
Vanderbilt
Wabash
Mackinaw
Susquehanna
Powhatan
Juniata
Tuscarora
Ticonderoga
Shenandoah
LINE Nº2
Vicksburg

Seneca
Osceola
T. Jefferson
Santiago de Cuba

Buckingham
Britannia
Tristram Shandy
4ᵗʰ DIVISION
3ᵈ DIVISION
Occasion required in landing troops, covering the landing and carrying dispatches
Nansemond
Lilian
Emma

RESERVES (Used as occasion required in landing troops, covering the landing and carrying dispatches)

2ᵈ DIVISION
Moccasin Eolus Gettysburg

1ˢᵗ DIVISION
Aries Howquah Wilderness Cherokee Vance

the *Lilian* was down so much by the head that she was almost submerged forward. The author with forty-eight men was taken aboard the U. S. S. *Keystone State*, which the next day joined the blockading fleet at New Inlet. The *Lilian* was towed into Beaufort and repaired at Philadelphia. She was then equipped by the Federals with an armament of two heavy guns and took part in the second attack upon Fort Fisher.

THE CAPTURE OF WILMINGTON.

Fort Fisher fell January 15, 1865. General Hoke, with 4,500 veteran troops, was intrenched in the sand-hills, opposite Fort Anderson, and General Terry, deeming his force too weak, awaited reinforcements before advancing.

At length, on February 11, his strength being 8,000, he moved forward, but was checked by Hoke. On the night of the 14th, he sought to turn Hoke's left flank, but again failed. Abandoning the plan of a direct movement, he then threw Cox's division to the western shore of the river, purposing to approach Wilmington from that direction. The ironclads began a brisk bombardment of Fort Anderson, and Cox made a feint as if to attack the fort in its front, but moved a brigade around Orton Pond to gain the rear of the fort and possess himself of the open road to Wilmington. This movement being discovered, General Hagood at once abandoned the fort and took post beyond Town Creek. The right and rear of his position thus being opened to the fire of the Federal fleet, General Hoke fell back to a more secure position, four miles from the town. On the 19th General Cox advanced to Town Creek, and Terry followed Hoke on the east side of the river. The following day Cox crossed Town Creek below the Confederate position, and was able to reach Hagood's rear, after a stiff fight, capturing Colonel Simonton, who was in temporary command, a large number of officers, and 395 men. Two days later Cox reached Eagle's Island, and Wilmington was at his mercy. Hoke thereupon destroyed such property as would be of use to the Federal Army, and retreated towards Goldsboro. On the morning of the 22d, General Terry entered and took possession of the town.

The following is an abstract from the journal of Maj. Gen. Jacob D. Cox, United States Army, with reference to daily events after the capture of Fort Fisher. We quote from Wednesday, February 15, 1865, up to Wednesday, February 22, 1865, when he entered Wilmington and took possession of the town.

Wednesday, February 15:—We started last night at dark and found the pontoons were very slow in getting up even with our lines. A division of Terry's command preceded mine, having the pontoons in charge. The train became much scattered before it reached our advanced line of works, and part of the boats did not get any farther. It was nearly midnight when the train reached the Half-Moon Battery, about a mile in front of our line, where our outer picket is placed. We got about a mile beyond this on our former trip, and on this occasion we succeeded in getting about a mile farther than then. Only eighteen of the boats would be got up, and it became evident that no crossing could be effected before daylight, even if the rest of the boats could be got up by that time. It also appeared that the enemy were on the *qui vive,* and we could see their camp fires on the other side of the sound. As we had not boats enough to make a bridge, and the appearance was that the passage would be disputed, General Schofield again determined to give up the plan, and we countermarched to camp, getting back about 2.30 o'clock in the morning. The weather was pleasanter than we had reason to expect, for it grew milder all night and ended by raining hard this morning. The clouds partly concealed the moon, but it seems to me impossible that the enemy should not have seen us, as the strip of sand is so narrow and the line of surf makes such a white background for the dark masses of the moving column. My own preference would have been to give up the movement as soon as it was evident that the pontoons would be behind time, so as not to let the enemy have any idea of the movement, which from that time was certain to prove a failure. I suspect, however, that the plan was a suggestion of Colonel Comstock, one of Grant's staff, who is with us as engineer, and that General Schofield on that account thought it best not to stop till it had been well tried. The fleet bringing our Second Division is said to have arrived yesterday. The delay of the pontoons above spoken of was owing to the impossibility of dragging a heavily loaded truck in the soft sand with scant teams.

Thursday, February 16:—Moved the command by steamboat to Smithville, on the other side of the bay, with a view to operate on that side of Cape Fear River. Baggage did not get down till dark. Orders given to move up the river at 8 a. m. tomorrow.

Friday, February 17:—March up the river, meeting the

enemy's cavalry as soon as we get three miles from the village. Drive them back till we get within two miles of Fort Anderson, where we go into camp according to orders, and open signal communications with General Schofield on his headquarters steamship, and with the fleet under Admiral Porter. Advanced ten miles today.

Saturday, February 18:—Move at 7 o'clock, driving back the enemy and establishing a line of investments on the south side of the fort. Have a lively skirmishing fight. The enemy open with artillery along their line, while our fleet opens heavily on the fort. At 1 o'clock I withdraw Casement's and Reilly's brigades (Colonel Sterl commanding the latter) and move them to the left and rear around the head of Orton Pond. Reach the head of the pond about 5.30 o'clock and find there a strong party of the enemy's cavalry, who oppose our passage. Moore's Creek, running into the pond, has wide, marshy banks, the marsh being filled with thick tangled undergrowth, through which it was almost impossible for skirmishers to make their way. The road is a narrow causeway, only wide enough for one wagon, and the enemy had rifle-pits commanding the exits from the swamps, as well as a second line a little farther back. We are delayed here about an hour. Succeed finally in driving off the rebels with a loss to us of seven men wounded and one killed. Just as we gained the opposite bank General Ames, with his division of Terry's men, came up and reported to me under General Schofield's orders, and we go into camp for the night, the rebel cavalry retreating in the direction of Fort Anderson.

Sunday, February 19:—The train of supplies which was to have come up last night didn't report till 10 o'clock this morning. We resumed our march up the west bank of Orton Pond to turn the enemy's position at Fort Anderson. March about half-way, when we meet Captain Lord of General Schofield's staff, who informs us that the fort is evacuated, the enemy having left it in the night, after hearing of our movement around the pond. General Ames proceeds to the fort with his division, whilst I go on up the river with my command, the two brigades left in front of the fort joining me. I put Henderson in advance, and press the enemy rapidly to Old Town Creek, where we find him in a strong line of works, the bridge being destroyed and the creek being both unfordable and difficult of approach by reason of the marshy banks so common in this

32

region. I learn that there is no ford at which men or horses can pass for fifteen miles above, but find a flatboat about a mile down the stream which I secure for tomorrow's operations.

Monday, February 20:—Order Henderson to keep the enemy amused by pressing as closely as possible in front, and direct Casement to take opposite side of the creek, and thence around to the enemy's rear. A little later I order Moore's brigade, which is temporarily in my command, to follow Casement, and go with it myself. We overtake Casement before he reaches the road to Wilmington behind the rebels. I order Moore across to the old Wilmington Road, so called, to stop any retreat in that direction, and with the two brigades under Casement push down upon the rear of the enemy. They are evidently taken by surprise and we charge over them, capturing their two pieces of artillery and nearly 400 prisoners, including the colonel commanding the brigade. We also take three battle flags. Our loss was about 30, caused chiefly by the few discharges of cannon they were able to make before our men could reach their lines. Moore fails to come to time on the old Wilmington Road, and the remainder escape that way. The action ended just at nightfall. I have the bridge repaired during the night, ready to move in the morning.

Tuesday, February 21:—Marched toward Wilmington, meeting no opposition. The bridges along the road were destroyed, causing much delay in repairing them, but in spite of delays my advance reached the Brunswick Ferry, opposite Wilmington, a little after noon. The enemy had a few skirmishers on Eagles' Island, between us and the city, and had sunk and partly destroyed their pontoon bridge at this place. We get up some of the boats and with them ferry over a regiment (Sixteenth Kentucky). These skirmish across the island, about one mile and a half, and find some of the enemy on the farther side of it with a piece of artillery posted so as to rake the road, which is very straight and flanked by impassable swamps on both sides. I keep the regiment there, ordering them to make the best cover they can and set to work to raise and repair the rest of the pontoon boats. The rebels immediately begin to burn the supplies and stores in Wilmington, the smoke rising in columns more immense than any I have ever seen. I send a dispatch to General Schofield, informing him of my progress and of these indications of evacuation by the enemy, but before I can get an answer I receive his dispatch, sent earlier, in which he informs me that General Terry has made no headway, and orders me to withdraw my command and cross the river to Terry's support. I start one brigade, and send him a dispatch urging him not to remove all of my troops, as I am sure the enemy is evacuating. A second dispatch reiterates the order to move, and I start another brigade at midnight, and prepare to move the rest, when, to my great satisfaction, I got a third dispatch countermanding the order as to two of the brigades, and stating that my dispatches had not come to hand when the orders to move were sent.

Wednesday, February 22:—As I expected, we enter Wilmington this morning without opposition, and as it is Washington's birthday we hail the event as a good omen. The enemy has retreated up the road to Goldsboro. I complete the repair and relaying of the rebel pontoon bridge, and by noon cross the Brunswick River and the island to the ferry across Cape Fear River (the channel on the west of the island is called Brunswick River), and so into Wilmington with my troops. General Terry, being on the same side of the river, marches through in pursuit of Hoke. My troops are put in camp around the town, and I assume command of the place. Assigned One Hundred and Fourth Ohio to duty as provost-guard, and fix my headquarters temporarily at the house of a Dr. Bellamy, a fugitive rebel.

USE OF TORPEDOES IN THE CAPE FEAR RIVER DURING THE WAR.

Shortly after the occupation of Fort Anderson by the advancing Federals and the supposed clearing of the river of Confederate mines and torpedoes, the Federal transport *Thorn,* laden with army supplies, was proceeding up the river towards Wilmington when she struck a torpedo which had been planted in the channel in Orton Cove and was blown up and sunk. This vessel was subsequently raised and floated by the Baker Wrecking Company, of Norfolk. The *Thorn* was piloted by a well-known negro man from Smithville, who before the war had served on board a United States Coast-Survey schooner.

With reference to the use of torpedoes in the Cape Fear at the time, Capt. E. S. Martin, ordnance officer, Confederate States Army, has furnished the following information:

"I do not recollect that torpedoes were used until the fall of 1864, when they were sent to Fort Caswell to be placed on or near the bar. They were placed there by me, connected by wire with electric batteries in the fort, to be exploded as occasion required. They were never exploded, however. I tried to explode them when the fort was evacuated, but did not succeed, as the batteries would not work. These torpedoes were large, carrying 400 pounds of powder. I think the Federal Government took them up after the war.

"Just before or during the attack on Fort Anderson, in January, 1865, a number of so-called floating torpedoes were sent to Fort Anderson to be placed between the fort and the fleet of the enemy, and were so placed by me under order of General Hagood, commanding at that place. These torpedoes were attached to floats of just sufficient buoyancy to keep them near the surface of the water and were provided with sensitive fuses, so that if touched they would explode. Twenty or more of them were taken down the river at night and located, as I have said, at different points in the channel. I think that a vessel, probably the transport *Thorn,* was blown up by one of these torpedoes after we evacuated the fort, and the rest were removed by the Federal Government. There were no torpedo boats used in the Cape Fear."

Since the above information was furnished by Captain Martin, I learn that during the war a number of torpedoes were chained and anchored by the Confederates in the following named channels of Cape Fear River, leaving open a limited space for the passage of blockade runners under the pilotage of specially detailed men who were entrusted with the secret knowledge of these mine fields. Capt. E. D. Williams, the present harbor master of the port of Wilmington, was one of the persons entrusted with this secret defense against the Federal fleet. He tells me that the first mine was planted three miles below Wilmington at a point in the ship channel opposite Hart's Vineyard, the second was at Orton Cove, near Fort Anderson at Old Brunswick. This one blew up the Federal transport *Thorn.* The third mine was anchored outside New Inlet Rip near Fort Fisher. A fourth and last one was outside the Rip near Fort Caswell.

A number of these torpedoes were brought up with the anchors of merchant vessels for two years after the war, but no premature explosions occurred. A torpedo boat named *General Whiting* was brought into the Cape Fear the last year of the war by a blockade runner, from England, but proved to be too small for effective use. At the end of the war she was sunk in the river near Point Peter.

Peace Restored

After the four years' war, the trade and commerce of the Cape Fear gradually returned to normal conditions. At first there was a large coastwise trade by sailing vessels, chiefly schooners of 150 to 600 tons, and a larger volume of business direct with Europe and the West Indies in foreign bottoms, consisting of brigs, barques, and sometimes of full-rigged ships, of British, German, and Scandinavian origin. The exports were naval stores—spirits turpentine, rosin, tar—and some cotton to Europe, and lumber to the West Indies.

For many years after the war Wilmington maintained first place in the turpentine and lumber trade, and there were as many as a hundred sailing vessels in port at one time. As the cotton trade increased it was taken up by this class of vessels; but in 1881 the new era of steam appeared in the arrival of the British steamer *Barnesmore,* chartered by Alexander Sprunt & Son, which loaded a cargo of 3,458 bales of cotton, 673 casks of spirits turpentine, and 550 barrels of rosin. Much ado was made of this occasion, and a banquet and speech-making accentuated its importance to the community; but in his letter of acknowledgment to the president of the Chamber of Commerce, under whose auspices the event was celebrated, Captain Trenery, of the *Barnesmore,* regretted to say that the depth of water in the Cape Fear was not sufficient to encourage further steamer trade. He, however, complimented his enterprising agents for loading into his ship in nine days 3,458 bales of cotton. A few weeks ago the same firm loaded one of many cargoes within nine days, and this cargo consisted of 20,300 bales of cotton valued at a million and a half dollars, yet it caused scarcely a ripple of remark in these progressive times; but the contrast of the *Barnesmore* with the *Holtie* is an object lesson in the development of Cape Fear commerce. The *Barnesmore's* draft was 14 feet. The draft of the *Holtie* is 20 feet, with seven to eight feet to spare underfoot in the river channel, which now shows 27 to 28 feet from Wilmington to the sea.

REPORTS ON WILMINGTON TRADE 1815-1872.

The following reports on the trade of Wilmington at intervals of about thirty years, beginning with 1815 and ending with 1872, will give some idea of the domestic and foreign commerce for the half-century preceding the War between the States and the period immediately following it, when every effort was made to recover from the paralyzing effects of the great struggle.

THE TRADE OF WILMINGTON, 1815.

BY JOSHUA POTTS.

(A commercial statement which came into the possession of the Chamber of Commerce, Wilmington, North Carolina, through the courtesy of Mrs. W. H. C. Whiting, widow of General Whiting.)

Wilmington, though but a small port, affords in season and in proportionate quantities nearly all the various kinds of produce that are to be found in the growth of the United States, collectively—such is the effect of an intermediate climate, an extensive territory of different soil, and diversity of occupation of numerous inhabitants.

Portable articles of produce are brought from the interior country by land carriage to inland towns at the head of boating navigation; thence they are carried down to Wilmington in large flatboats, calculated for that purpose.

In the lower part of the country transportation of lumber, naval stores, timber and spars is facilitated by rafts, conducted by a few hands down numerous rivers and creeks.

In times of uninterrupted commerce, many ships and vessels of considerable burthen were annually loaded here and bound for European ports with cargoes of naval stores, tobacco, flaxseed, cotton, rice, and large timber of pitch pine; their cargoes were dunnaged and stowed with staves.

Our produce is particularly adapted for the markets of the West India Islands, and when we have a free trade, many vessels of Wilmington and the Northern States during winter and spring load here, and depart for the West Indies in as many directions as there are islands, their cargoes assorted with lumber, flour, rice, pork, bacon, lard, butter, tobacco, tar, livestock, etc.

A proportion of our produce is transported coastwise to various ports, but that of New York the principal—and vice versa, the merchants and dealers of Wilmington and Fayetteville are generally furnished with a variety of merchandise from sundry ports on the northern coast, especially from New York. Regular packets ply between Wilmington and New York.

Excellent crops of various kinds of produce are annually produced throughout this country. Our market opens in November, is brisk in December, increases in January, February, and March, slackens in April, declines in May, and ends in June. The summer and fall months in regard to trade, are dull, and the fall sickly.

Those kinds of our produce of the first importance are noted for the present year as follows:

Tobacco is raised only in the upper country; it is brought and inspected at Fayetteville, at the head of boating navigation, ninety miles above Wilmington. It may be had at Fayetteville at almost any time of the year; but it is more plentiful between December and March. Of late years the quantity has been reduced, and the culture of cotton substituted, as being less precarious, less toilsome, and of more profit than tobacco. Within the last fifteen years, tobacco has been lessened in culture more than one-half of former crops. Its quality is said to have been inferior to that of Virginia, but of late it has been produced of amended goodness, and some of it prime. In the first place, it is uniformly purchased from the planters by merchants of Fayetteville, and by them either exported to Europe or sold again in the United States.

Cotton, upland, is but of recent cultivation in this State, and is increasing in quantity; the quality is said to be equal to that of South Carolina or Georgia. The planters at first put up their cotton in round bags, but of late much of it is packed in square bales. There is no inspection of cotton.

Rice: A fine crop is raised chiefly in the vicinity of Wilmington, near tidewater, of quality equal to any in the Southern States; and a charge for the rough casks which contain it is always made by the planters.

Flour: The usual crop of considerable quantity; of late years subject to a good inspection and marked under several qualities; the superfine is said to be equal to that of the Middle States.

Corn is seldom either plentiful or cheap in Wilmington. The country around does not produce it in sufficient quantity for exportation.

Tar is not made in as large quantity as formerly, nor is it produced and brought to market with the same ease; it is an article subject to waste, and the price generally low. Countrymen, in many instances, have paid attention to cotton and timber; and numerous inhabitants of that description have removed to the Western States. Since the return of peace, however, the demand for tar and turpentine has raised the value of those articles to an encouraging price. It is rafted to Wilmington, and after having been coopered and inspected, is transported coastwise, and a proportion shipped for European ports.

Turpentine is seen at market from June to December. In consequence of the late war, the quantity has been reduced and prices depressed; the present demand, however, has enhanced the value. There is a scarcity at present.

Flaxseed, as well as tobacco and flour, is raised in the interior of this country. It is first contained in bags and brought in wagons to Fayetteville, and there measured and sold by the bushel, usually from 90 to 120 cents, according to prospect. The purchasers at Fayetteville have it there perfectly cleaned in machines for that purpose, and put up in casks of oak, well made, each containing seven bushels. When commerce is free, the price of a cask of flaxseed at Wilmington is generally between ten and eleven dollars. There is no inspection on flaxseed.

Lumber, many kinds and of superior quality, is brought plentifully to market during the winter and spring—plenty of sawed boards, planks, and scantling, of fine grained pitch and yellow pine. Pine timber and spars of any size may be had. Shingles of cypress, 22 inches in length, are plentiful, generally thin and light, but proportionately cheap. Shingles of juniper, well drawn and rounded, may be had from a distance, on timely notice.

Staves are not to be had here in quantity sufficient to furnish cargoes for vessels; they are, however, to be had during winter and spring, and wherewith cargoes of other produce are dunnaged and stowed. Staves are, however, at times so plentiful as to compose the principal part of a vessel's cargo. White oak hogshead and barrel staves are never plentiful; the growth of the tree is confined to narrow limits on the borders of the River Cape Fear. Red oak hogshead staves are to be had in larger numbers than those of the white oak, and are always more than proportionately cheap.

It is unadvisable, and often disadvantageous, for a merchant in a distant State or foreign port to dispatch a ship to Wilmington under orders for a cargo of our produce without having written his correspondent of particulars required. Four to six weeks previous notice to the agent is always requisite, that he may have time and opportunity to procure the produce described at the best advantage and have it in readiness by the time of arrival of such ship. Great detention and disappointment often happen in consequence of voyages being abruptly commenced; as but seldom peculiar kinds of produce can be had on sudden notice.

Inspection of produce is established by law throughout North Carolina. A clause enacts that the shippers thereof shall pay the fees of inspection on the several articles as follows: Rice, flour, pork, lard, beef, butter, tar, turpentine, pitch, and rosin. The rates are low.

On lumber, the buyer and seller equally sustain the charges of inspection and delivery. Custom supersedes a law for inspection of lumber. The fee is small.

Cash or suitable bills (commonly drafts on New York) are the only funds that will command either tobacco, rice, cotton, or flaxseed.

Considerable quantities of Liverpool salt were formerly imported, but during our Restrictive Acts and nearly three years continuance of the late war with England scarcely any has been brought in. Coarse salt of late has arrived tolerably plentiful, and although subject to a duty of about 30 cents per bushel, the last sales per cargo were per bushel 65 cents.

Liverpool ground salt is always preferred at Fayetteville to any coarse salt, at the same price, owing to weight of wagonage up the country, Liverpool being the lightest, per bushel.

For a few years since, while commerce was under restriction, and during the late war, sundry salt works were erected on the sound, near Wilmington, which, towards the last of the war, highly rewarded their several proprietors. But, since the return of peace, the price of home-made salt has, consequently, fallen to that of similar quality imported. Notwithstanding, the domestic works will be continued in operation. They will be productive of profit, so far at least as the duty on foreign salt may be extended.

The manner of producing what is here called "sound" salt is by means of vats constructed with boards, into one of which the salt water is brought by pumps worked with wind. Three vats constitute one set, and the sea water under evaporation, after having deposited the druggy and slimy parts, is timely drawn from one reservoir into another, by which process the crystallized salt becomes of the purest quality. The grain is of the size called hominy salt, or larger, and the quantity annually produced, within eight to twenty miles of Wilmington, is already more than 30,000 bushels.

Main Bar of Cape Fear, high water at 7 o'clock at full and change of the moon, depth 18 feet.

New Inlet Bar, high water at 7 o'clock at full and change of the moon, depth 11½ feet.

Tides on each bar, perpendicular, 5 to 6 feet.

Flatts, ten miles below Wilmington, to town, 11½ feet.

Course in, over the Main Bar: When in five fathoms water, the lighthouse used to bear north half east, but, unfortunately, a couple of years since the sea encroached on the shore[1] and destroyed the lighthouse; and within a few years an angle to the westward has been formed in that part of the channel which was formerly straight, by which circumstance the navigation over the Main Bar has become difficult. Pilots generally attend in time to conduct vessels in safety.

Lighterage, between the Flatts and Wilmington, comes on all vessels above 11½ feet.

Also, between the Main Bar and the Flatts, at high water, are shoals of 14½ feet.

Wilmington is situated on the east side of Cape Fear, or Clarendon, River, and lies north 30 miles above the Main Bar, and 20 miles above New Inlet.

THE TRADE OF WILMINGTON, 1843.

BY ROBERT W. BROWN.

(A commercial statement which came into the possession of the Wilmington Chamber of Commerce through the courtesy of Major M. P. Taylor.)

Portable articles of produce are brought from the interior country by land carriage to Fayetteville, at the head of boating navigation; thence they are carried down to Wilmington by well constructed steamboats and their numerous towboats, com-

---

[1]Why? Because the river current had been depreciated to such extent in volume and force by the opening at New Inlet as to be overcome by the current and force of waves of the ocean; thus permitting the ocean waves and currents to gradually wear away the shore.

H. NUTT.

prising a flotilla on an extensive scale, qualified to carry large quantities of merchandise up and produce down; and when the river is not too low for steamboats to run all the way, greater dispatch is not given in any part of our country. At those periods of low water which occasionally happen, transportation is facilitated by the smaller flat towboats, aided by steamboats, so far as the latter can proceed.

In the course of many years practice of the author in his agency for numerous merchants of the interior, and since the establishment of steamboats, he has had goods delivered at Fayetteville within a week or ten days from New York, and the merchants and farmers of the back country, hitherto trading extensively with South Carolina, must find their way to the convenient seaport of their own State, and Wilmington can produce a market, for export and import, with all necessary facilities. The larger vessels for foreign trade and the smaller for coasting have the advantage of two bars—the New Inlet and the Main Bar to pass in and out.

Regular packets ply between Wilmington, New York, and Philadelphia. Steamboats of good capacity ply on the river below Wilmington for passengers, freighting, and towing. The healthy summer retreat at Smithville is much resorted to.

The summer and fall months, in regard to trade, are dull; rivers generally low; crop season with the country people; a relaxation in town; and consequently business generally is less active, except the ordinary preparations for renewal of the fall trade, and the importation of large quantities of goods for their passage to the interior, which is a steady employment from July to November. This business demands the constant vigilance, care, and presence of the consignees and parties entrusted with it during the most unfavorable period of the season.

A new route is now established by the Wilmington and Raleigh Railroad through the northeastern counties of the State, leading to Weldon, on the Roanoke, and thence to Norfolk or Petersburg. Splendid steamboats, built for the purpose, and second to none in the United States, ply between Wilmington and Charleston, conveying with great comfort and comparatively no risk the mail and passengers, which route, as already ascertained, is admitted to be one of the best in the whole country, avoiding the great hazard of Capes Hatteras, Lookout, and Frying Pan, in a short seascope between Cape Fear and Charleston Bars, so far as passengers are concerned.

Trade, too, has commenced upon this route with the rich and fertile counties of the east, whose inhabitants are ready to embrace the great facility in prospect of finding at Wilmington a market for their valuable productions. It is only necessary to have the supply to insure demand.

Cotton: Upland in moderate supply the last year or two. It is now packed mostly in square bales, and delivered at market in excellent order. Freight to England, chiefly Liverpool, varies as to circumstances ½ to ⅝d., and it often occurs that cotton purchased by order is shipped coastwise to New York, where it takes the chances of a good market, or is forwarded by packet to England or France. Shipments to France direct are made from Wilmington. Both cotton and rice can be obtained and shipped.

Rice: We have often heard a preference expressed for the rice on this river. Charleston dealers send for it, to clean there and export in the rough, etc. The quantity made is about 200,000 bushels. There is now an extensive steam mill, besides sundry water mills, which enable us to furnish in due season the whole crop of this article, and greatly add to our supply of clean rice for export from the port of Wilmington. The quantity may now be fairly estimated at about ten thousand tierces. In consequence, dealers may expect less disappointment in supplies and at fair prices. A steam mill recently erected at New York has made demands upon our rough rice and takes it coastwise. By custom, the purchaser pays 50 cents for each cask and 8½ cents for inspection. The casks are of various sizes, from 300 to 600 pounds net. About the middle of November to the first of December we get the first new rice to market.

Flour is expected to be fine this year—the crops of wheat throughout are represented as excellent. It is inspected and branded at Fayetteville, under several qualities, and at present no charge of inspection to the shipper here. The cross middling, fine and superfine, are generally sent down together. It is not always practicable to procure superfine alone. Quality good. Inspection improved.

Wheat is brought into Fayetteville by wagons, where it is bought, cleaned at mills, and put up in casks of seven bushels or bags, and sent down to Wilmington for sale or to ship.

Corn: We have it frequently from the northern counties in this State, brought round in vessels, and also from Maryland. The demand this year has been uniformly good, and sold at full prices. The adjoining counties have had satisfactory accounts—the consumption seems to have increased.

Tar is rafted to Wilmington down rivers and creeks, and bought of the country people by the raft, from 20 to 300 barrels, afloat; after which, it is landed on a wharf, inspected and coopered—the purchaser always paying inspection of 2 cents per barrel, cooperage, wharfage, and the landing charge; the whole expense about 12 cents per barrel, including one week's wharfage. Our cooperage is good, and attention is paid to pumping, in order to clear it of water as much as possible. January to May is the season when tar is most plentiful.

Turpentine is seen in market from June to April. We generally get the greatest quantities from the 20th of November until about the last of February. Before and after these periods it comes in smaller parcels. After heavy rains and during high freshets we have considerable quantities down at once; and often at such time the supply offered for sale reduces the price. Turpentine is rafted and sold as tar, subject to inspection and like expenses. The buyer, from custom, pays for the whole raft, as landed, including hard or scrapings as well as soft; the hard, however, at less price—one-half the rate paid for soft. By custom and law of the State, it is weighed, taking 320 pounds gross as the barrel. Our barrels are generally large, and when packed overgo that weight. The usual crop has been 100,000 to 140,000 barrels. I will further add, in regard to this article, that on inspection, after the inspector has tried each cask at the bung with a rod, he weighs a small portion of the lot, by which the whole purchase is averaged. Inspection, 3 cents per barrel. The crop of 1843-44 is expected to reach 200,000 barrels. The railroad route delivers a large proportion of turpentine to market, which is in addition to the rafting process. The several distilleries now established for working up turpentine in the home market consume weekly 1,500 barrels of the raw material, and such distilling has become a great item of business here. They produce rosin, spirits turpentine, and make varnish and pitch.

Flaxseed is an article in regard to the quantity of which an accurate estimate can not be formed. The seed is sown with no other view than to produce flax for domestic purposes; gathered in quantities and brought to market from the first of September to the fifteenth of January—principally in November and December. In common, the quantity received depends materially upon the price. Crops of former years, about 3,000 tierces. Of the last season's, the quantity exported and shipped coastwise, only about 9 to 1,500 casks. There is no other market in the Southern States where it is purchased to any extent. No inspection.

Lumber: Many kinds and of a superior quality are rafted plentifully to market during winter and spring from water mills; say, sawed boards, plank and scantling, of fine grained pitch and yellow pine, promiscuously sawed, however, unless previously contracted for, and thus sold by the raft, at a rate to be agreed on, turn out as it may; refuse at half-price, and is commonly so shipped altogether. Expenses of rafting or landing and inspection paid by the purchaser. Pine timber and spars of any size may be had upon previous notice by contract with the country people; and at a time when the waters are sufficiently up for rafting. Five well-constructed steam sawmills are erected in the vicinity of the town and now in operation, where lumber of any lengths or sizes may be furnished, and delivered to vessels bright from the saws. The quality is excellent—sawed from square logs of good timber. The increasing demand for our lumber, coastwise and steady calls for it throughout the West Indies, has vastly increased the trade and employment of vessels. Half the inspection is charged at those mills, and their prices are uniform. The lumber trade is also benefited by the establishment at Orton, fifteen miles below Wilmington, of two excellent sawmills, carried by a never-failing water power from a pond seven miles in extent, supplying lumber from square timber equal to that of the steam mills and at the same rates. In a contract with those mills, vessels meet as good dispatch as at any other.

An extensive planing mill is also erected at this place, where flooring and all other descriptions of boards are supplied for domestic use as well as foreign demand.

Shingles of cypress, 22 inches in length, are plentiful and often good, and may be contracted for to be brought of better quality and larger size. Demand the past season was good. Demand this summer has been less, and a corresponding falling off in supply—ruled from $1.50 to $4 per thousand. Shingles of juniper, 18 inches, may be had on timely notice during the winter.

Pipe staves are never made here. All our staves are generally very good. In the further progress of railroads and opening to the country, we shall expect to find our stave supply revived.

Main Bar of Cape Fear, high water at 7 o'clock, at full and change of the moon; depth formerly 18 feet, but pilots now say only 13½ to 15 feet.

New Inlet Bar, high water at 7 o'clock, at full and change of the moon, 10 to 11½ feet.

Tides on each bar, perpendicular, 5 to 6 feet.

Flatts, five or six miles below Wilmington, 10 to 11½ feet.

Pilots generally attend in time to conduct vessels in safety; and there are now two decked boats in use, besides many open boats.

The course in, over Main Bar, is much more direct and less difficult than formerly: a lighthouse on Bald Head Island, as also a lighted beacon at New Inlet.

Lighterage comes on all vessels above 10 to 12½ feet at present, in consequence of some operations on the river below town, which were commenced with a view to improvement.

Also, between Flatts and Smithville, at high water, are shoals 14 feet; consequently, vessels that load deeper than 14 feet, must go down to Smithville to complete their cargoes. Thirteen and a half to 15 feet water may be carried out over Main Bar; 10 to 11 feet, New Inlet.

The Trade of Wilmington, 1872.

(Extracts from a commercial statement made by the Chamber of Commerce.)

Taking the harbor as it was, and as it is confidently expected by those who have studied the matter it will be again, by a judicious management of the government works now going on, and completed, we have a capacious harbor, easy of access, with winds from almost any quarter, perfectly land-locked, and the approaches to the bar well protected from the principal storms on our coast, with good anchorage outside. Lying to the southward of all the dangerous capes on the coast which would interfere with navigation or voyages to and from all Southern, West Indian, and South American ports, as well as to Europe, a considerable saving in the single item of marine insurance is made.

By reference to the report of exports hence, it will be seen that we furnish cargoes of everything required in the markets of the West Indies and South America, with perhaps the single exception of flour, which will soon be within our grasp. Hence we are enabled to furnish full cargoes outward, and the return voyage with cargoes of sugar, coffee, fruits, molasses, and other tropical products would be laid down in our market cheaper than in any other on the coast. Again, being "headquarters" for spirits of turpentine, rosin, tar, pitch, lumber, timber, etc., we are enabled to furnish the European markets with these products on the best terms and to receive cargoes in return of their products and manufactures laid down at as low cost as in any other port.

This being a great railroad center, with one line extending southward and westward through the Gulf States, with another, in course of completion, extending its arms almost in an air line to Cincinnati, Louisville, St. Louis, Chicago, and other cities of the great Northwest; another extending northward and connecting with lines to every point of the country, Wilmington offers every facility for the safe and rapid distribution of importations, and for the return of the products of the whole country for exportation.

Steam communication on the Cape Fear River is had with Fayetteville, and by a comparatively small outlay for improvement of the navigation of the upper rivers, which is in part complete, would put us in easy reach of the great deposits of iron, coal, and various other minerals in which the valley of Deep River abounds. The development of these mining interests only awaits the restoration of our harbor. Then the value of this port to the General Government as a coaling and naval station can hardly be estimated.

The trade of this port is steadily and constantly increasing, and as our harbor improves will continue to do so in more rapid proportion.

Since the late War between the States, the article of rice, which was at one time among our principal articles of export, has almost ceased to be produced, owing to the indifferent, hard-to-be-controlled labor. The crop will not now exceed 10,000 bushels, not enough for home demand.

The production of cotton in this State has been very largely increased, and although no accurate figures can be given, in consequence of a large portion leaving the State via the ports of Virginia and South Carolina, it is believed that the crop amounts to at least 200,000 bales. At this port is handled cotton from Georgia and South Carolina, as well as our own State, and during the year 1871 there were exported, principally coastwise, over 95,000 bales. The extension of the Wilmington, Charlotte, and Rutherford Railroad and its completion will, it is estimated, at least double our receipts of the staple.

Spirits of turpentine is manufactured to a considerable extent in the city, and the whole pine region of this State and South Carolina is dotted with numerous distilleries worked by owners or tenants of the forests. Most of the products find their way to this market.

Exports of naval stores for the past year from this port have been as follows:

	Coastwise.	Foreign.
Spirits turpentine, barrels........	64,862	47,162
Rosin, barrels	441,341	127,100
Tar, barrels.....................	31,993	5,874
Turpentine, barrels	17,126	836

Leaving stocks in port of spirits turpentine, 7,299 barrels; rosin, 72,166 barrels; tar, 2,640 barrels, and crude turpentine, 2,842 barrels.

Pitch is manufactured in sufficient quantity only to supply the demand, and the reputation of "Wilmington pitch" is excelled by none. The manufacture of this article is confined to the distillers of turpentine in this city, very little being made in the country.

These articles alone show material to occupy quite a fleet of vessels. In this connection it should be stated that no vessel has ever been obliged from choice to leave this port in ballast.

The timber and lumber trade, though not what it was fifteen years since, has steadily increased since the war, and should reach and exceed its former figures. Our shingles (cypress and juniper or cedar) have an established reputation in the Northern and West India markets, and may be had in quantity to suit any demand from the very extended and heavily timbered swamps on our water courses and railways. Staves could be had of the best white or red oak to supply any demand. At present they are called for almost entirely for home consumption.

Our principal supplies of corn reach us by sea from the eastern counties; but our rail connections with the West will soon throw the corn and other grain from that section into competition.

Peanuts are produced to considerable extent in the surrounding country and form quite a feature in our domestic exports.

33

The crop of 1870-71 amounted to about 100,000 bushels, of an aggregate value of $200,000. The crop this year is largely in excess.

Among the manufactures of interest and value should be mentioned cane fibre, by a patented process from the swamp cane, with which our swamps abound, and which is reproduced in three years after cutting and of a quality superior to the original growth. The prepared fibre is used in the manufacture of paper and *papier-mâché* goods.

Barrel shooks are manufactured to a great extent and shipped to Northern markets for the reception of syrups from sugar manufactories.

Fuel for manufacturing purposes is very cheap, and principally of the surplus sawdust and shavings from steam saw and planing mills, which may be had for the asking. Pine wood is in abundance at low prices.

Banking facilities are by no means sufficient to meet the demands of trade; but as our people recuperate more steadily from the disastrous effects of their late struggle, this want is being supplied.

In the present condition of our bar and river, vessels drawing over 12 to 12½ feet require to be lightered to and from a point outside the Rip, whence they can always sail with 15½ to 16 feet. Our harbor restored, we confidently expect to find at least 20 feet at mean low tide on the bar (with a rise of tide 4 to 5 feet), and the removal of obstructions in the river will give us ample water for our docks.

CUBAN MAN-OF-WAR INCIDENT.

Early in October, 1869, a remarkable incident occurred in Cape Fear waters which drew the attention of the civilized world upon the port of Wilmington. Cuba was in a state of insurrection against the Spanish Government and, although there was no established seat of government, the Cubans proclaimed a republic. Neither the United States nor any foreign power, except some South American States, had recognized the Cuban Republic or accorded the rights of belligerents.

Therefore, when the Cuban man-of-war *Cuba,* alias *Hornet,* alias *Lady Stirling,* alias *Prince Albert,* for she had assumed all of these names in order to escape detection at sea, arrived on a quiet Sunday morning in the Cape Fear River, she made quite a sensation, which was increased when two of her officers appeared at the First Presbyterian Church in Wilmington and called from his devotions, in front of this writer, the late Mr. David G. Worth, the only dealer in coal in the town at that time, with a request that he deliver at once a supply of coal for the Cuban man-of-war. The requisition upon the straight-laced Presbyterian was promptly rejected, much to the disgust and dismay of the applicants, who were told that he did not sell nor deliver coal on Sunday. Meantime, the Washington Government was informed by wire that the *Cuba,* a propeller of 1,800 tons register, with two smokestacks, two masts, brig-rigged, pierced for 18 guns, two of which were pivots of very heavy caliber, with a strange flag, commanded by Captain Higgins, with 300 men and 30 officers, was waiting in the port of Wilmington for needed supplies with which to prey upon Spanish commerce.

Prompt action followed this news. The United States gunboat *Frolic* (formerly the North Carolina blockade runner *Advance*) and two other war vessels were dispatched to the Cape Fear to intercept the stranger, and the Federal Court subsequently seized and disarmed her.

BOARD OF COMMISSIONERS OF NAVIGATION AND PILOTAGE.

To the efforts of the Board of Commissioners of Navigation and Pilotage, with the coöperation of the Chamber of Commerce and with the aid of our representatives in Congress, are largely due the development of the river and harbor improvement, the marking of the river and bar channels, the building and establishment of the new lightship on Knuckle Shoal—the finest lightship in the service of the United States—the important aid to river navigation in the thirty-one powerful new lights (for which the board obtained, through great perseverance, an appropriation from Congress), the construction of the best pilot service on the coast, the systematic monthly soundings of the bar by competent pilots, the quarterly charted soundings of the bar and river (which are posted in the Chamber of Commerce), the reduction of bar and river casualties until they are almost unknown, the minimizing of the rates of marine insurance, and the establishment by subscription of a fund for the benefit of the widows and children of deceased pilots of the Cape Fear River and Bar, amounting now to about $6,000 and which it is the ambition of the chairman to raise to $20,000.

These are some of the things which the Board of Commissioners of Navigation and Pilotage has done for Wilmington; and all of this work, and much more, has been done without emolument or reward, beyond the satisfaction of serving well the port of Wilmington and the Commonwealth of North Carolina. The aim of the board has always been to build up, and in this constructive work it has received the constant support and coöperation of practically all the working pilots.

The board consists of four commissioners residing in Wilmington and one residing in Southport, all being appointed every four years by the Governor of North Carolina. This is the oldest commercial organization in the State, having been established more than eighty years ago, and it has always been composed of reputable, experienced men, familiar with maritime affairs pertaining to the port of Wilmington and to the Cape Fear River and Bar.

The commissioners have authority in all matters appertaining to the navigation of the Cape Fear waters from seven miles above Negrohead Point downward and across the bar. They license and control the pilots, and have authority to make regulations, and to impose reasonable fines, forfeitures, and penalties for the purpose of enforcing their rules and regulations. They elect the harbor master and port wardens.

The board meets for the transaction of routine business at 11 o'clock on the first Wednesday of every month, and the chairman calls special meetings in cases of urgency for official action.

Bar pilotage is compulsory and, although river pilotage is optional, the services of a river pilot are employed in nearly all cases.

CAPE FEAR AIDS TO NAVIGATION.

The aids to the navigation of the Cape Fear, which are effective in the steady expansion of our commerce, are largely due to the watchful care and cordial coöperation of our Commissioners of Navigation and Pilotage and to our Chamber of Commerce, supported by our representatives in Congress, and I may add that they are more particularly due to the untiring devotion of our junior senator, Lee S. Overman, whose powerful personality has repeatedly prevailed in the securing of special appropriations when other means which had been employed failed to interest the department officials at Washington.

Our acknowledgments are specially due Senator Overman for his excellent service to Wilmington in procuring the greatly improved river lights, and the new lightship *Number 94,* on Frying Pan Shoals, after our former light vessel had been arbitrarily removed, and in safeguarding by special act of Congress this most important aid from a second removal to a much less important position to us, thirty miles at sea. He has proven the adage, "A friend in need is a friend indeed."

A prominent master mariner has well said: "If we want to mark a dangerous hole in the public highway, we do not place a lantern on the next block away from the danger, but we put a light on the spot where the danger lies." Therefore, why should we permit the removal of our lightship from the Frying Pan Shoals, on which it has been moored as a beacon for half a century, to a point thirty miles at sea for the benefit of coastwise traffic which does not come to Wilmington at all? With the lightship ahead, the careful mariner makes the port in safety; with the lightship invisible behind him, he gropes in darkness and in danger of disaster.

Comparatively few of the citizens of our commercial community are interested in the detail work of the Department of Commerce at Washington, or in its Lighthouse Service, so important to those who go down to the sea in ships and do business upon its great waters. This is probably due chiefly to the technical nature of the information regularly published and easily obtained from the obliging inspector of the Sixth District, who has given me the following comprehensive review of the aids to navigation along our dangerous coast and up the Cape Fear River to the port of Wilmington.

With general depths of 7 to 14 feet, Frying Pan Shoals extend in an unbroken line 10 miles south-southeastward from Cape Fear; for a distance of 5½ miles farther in the same direction the shoals are broken, the depth over them ranging from 10 to 24 feet. Frying Pan Shoals light vessel is moored off the end of this part of the shoals, and a red whistling buoy is moored off the western side of the shoals, nearly 8½ miles northwestward of the light vessel.

Broken ground with depths of 6 to 7 fathoms extends 7 miles eastward and 12 miles east-southeastward from the light vessel; the least depth is 3¾ fathoms, and lies 9 miles, 99 degrees true E. by S. of the light vessel. The outer end of the shoals is marked by a gas-and-bell buoy (flashing white light), which lies 12 miles, 118 degrees true SE. by E. ¼ E. of Frying Pan Shoals light vessel. Large, deep-draft vessels generally pass southward of the gas-and-bell buoy.

Light vessel *Number 94* was built for the station on Frying Pan Shoals in the Sixth Lighthouse District. The vessel is 135 feet 9 inches over all, with a beam of 29 feet and a draft of 12 feet 9 inches; the displacement at this draft is 660 tons. The hull is built of mild steel, with two wooden deck-houses on the spar deck serving the purpose of pilot-house and bridge-and-radio house. One steel lantern mast, of diameter sufficient to contain a ladder giving access to the lantern, and a wooden mainmast, carrying a fore-and-aft sail, are fitted.

The signal light is carried on the lantern mast. It consists of an incandescent oil-vapor light mounted in a lens of the fourth order, and gives a light of 2,900 candlepower.

The fog-signal apparatus consists of a 12-inch deep-toned chime whistle connected to the main boilers. Steam is supplied through a reducing valve, and a specially designed vertical engine is arranged to cut off steam to the whistle so as to give the characteristic: Blast, 5 seconds; silent, 55 seconds. A submarine bell, actuated by compressed air, strikes one stroke every 3 seconds.

This vessel was equipped with radio outfit before being placed on the station, so that its effective date would be coincident with the establishment of the vessel. This installation has an effective radius of about 200 miles, and besides being of great value to passing vessels, it is of great aid to the Lighthouse Service in keeping the vessel to the highest state of efficiency as an aid.

The propelling machinery consists of one vertical, direct-action, surface-condensing, fore-and-aft compound engine, having cylinders 16 and 31 inches in diameter by 24 inches stroke, driving a cast-steel propeller 8 feet in diameter by ten-foot pitch, and supplied by steam under a pressure of 110 pounds per square inch of heating surface. The machinery and boilers are located amidship. The vessel is fitted throughout with all modern appliances, including steam windlass, sanitary plumbing and fixtures, and drainage system, but has no electric-lighting system.

The complement of this vessel is four officers and ten men. The officers' quarters, mess-room, pantry, and bathroom are located as far as practicable on the main deck. Quarters for the crew, including the galley, are located on the main deck just forward of the boilers and machinery. The oil-room and stores are located on the lower deck and in the hold forward and aft. The hull is yellow, with "Frying Pan" in large black letters on each side. This vessel was constructed under the Act of May 27, 1908, appropriating $115,000. The vessel was built under contract at Muskegon, Michigan, and the cost was $104,080.37. Construction was commenced on May 28, 1909, and was completed and the vessel delivered to the government on June 13, 1911. On November 15, 1911, the light vessel was placed on the station in the Sixth Lighthouse District.

The cape is a low, sharp point of sand beach forming the southern extremity of Smith's Island. The island, lying on the eastern side of the entrance to Cape Fear River, is mostly low and marshy, but has a thick growth of trees on its western side. Near the southern end of the island is Cape Fear Lighthouse, which will usually be the first object seen in approaching the cape.

The lighthouse on the cape is a white, iron, skeleton tower, upper part black. The light is flashing white (light 2.3, eclipse 7.7 seconds), 159 feet above the water, and visible 19 miles. The light is incandescent oil vapor, using a mantle 2¼ inches in diameter, and the intensity of the flash through the lens, which is six feet in diameter, is 160,000 candles. This light was built in 1903, and is, with one exception, the newest and most modern first-class lighthouse in the district.

On the west side of Smith's Island, east side of the entrance to the Cape Fear River, is Bald Head Lighthouse. The structure is a white, octagonal, pyramidal tower. The light is flashing white, with a dark sector between 220 degrees and 308 degrees, 99 feet above the water, and visible 16 miles. This light has recently been converted from an oil light with a keeper to an unwatched gaslight, and now forms a part of the system described below.

Cape Fear River has a total length of above 371 miles, and empties into the sea immediately west of Cape Fear. It is the approach of the city of Wilmington, which is 27 miles above its mouth. Frying Pan Shoals light vessel, Cape Fear Lighthouse, and Bald Head Lighthouse are the principal guides for the approach.

The entrance of the river is obstructed by a bar which extends about two miles off-shore. The channel is under improvement to secure a depth of 26 feet from the sea to Wilmington, with a width of 400 feet across the bar, 300 feet in the river, and an increased width at the bends. In June, 1912, the full depth had been obtained, but not the full width in places. The channel is well marked by range lights and buoys, and with the aid of a chart it could not be difficult for a stranger of 16-feet draft to navigate it on a rising tide.

CAPE FEAR RIVER LIGHTS.

These aids consist of thirty-three lights marking the dredged channels of the Cape Fear River. They replace twenty-nine lights, mostly of the oil-burning post-lantern type, on old wooden structures, and not properly placed to mark the new channels. Ten of the new lighted beacons were established December 1, 1912, and the remainder November 15, 1913.

The aids extend along the Cape Fear River from the entrance to Wilmington, a distance of about twenty-nine miles. The sites are (except in three cases) submarine, the depth of water averaging six feet. The bottom is hard sand, underlaid in a few cases with rock.

The substructures built on marine sites (thirty in all) consist each of four reinforced concrete piles and connecting beams. These are surmounted by skeleton towers of galvanized iron pipe, carrying slatted wooden daymarks. Towers for rear range lights are thirty feet high and for front lights and others ten feet high.

A variety of illuminating apparatus has been installed, as follows:

No.	Apparatus	Illuminant	Characteristic	Candlepower
1	Reflector	Oil	Fixed	3,100
1	Range lens	Acetylene	Flashing every second	3,000
1	4th Order lens	Acetylene	Occulting every 2 seconds	830
7	300 mm. lens lanterns	Acetylene	Flashing every second	200
1	300 mm. lens lanterns	Acetylene	Flashing every 3 seconds	200
6	300 mm. lens lanterns	Acetylene	Occulting every 2 seconds	200
16	300 mm. lens lanterns	Oil	Fixed	170

In general, acetylene is used as the illuminant, where possible, for a distance of about twenty miles from the entrance, and oil from there to Wilmington. All acetylene lights are white, rear lights being occulting every two seconds and front lights flashing every second. All oil lights are fixed, rear lights white, and front lights red.

Eight of the white range lights which could be suitably located abreast of turns in the channel are provided with red sectors of 30 degrees covering these turns.

There have been no quarters provided, all lights being unwatched. The change of illuminant in Bald Head Light, which constitutes a unit of this system, makes quarters no longer necessary in connection therewith. The entire group of lights is cared for by two post light keepers, one resident near Southport, close to the entrance, having charge of three oil and sixteen gas lights, and one at Wilmington, at the other end of the group of lights, having charge of fourteen oil lights. All gas lights are so located that gas tanks can be landed from a launch directly upon the structure, except at Bald Head Light.

These improvements in the lighting of the Cape Fear River are being made under the Act of March 4, 1911, appropriating $21,000, and the Act of August 26, 1912, appropriating $30,000 additional. The total expenditures and obligations for the thirty-three lights to September 30, 1913, is $50,076.30, with a probable further expenditure of $500 for one additional light, and $300 for clearing timber which partially obstructs one range line.

Other aids supplementing the lighting aids mentioned above are, Frying Pan Shoals Whistling Buoy, westward of the outer end of the shoals; Cape Fear Entrance Whistling Buoy,[1] about two and one-half miles off the bar; Cape Fear Entrance Bell Buoy, at the entrance to dredged channels, and thirty-three iron buoys and five beacons marking turns and other critical points in the dredged channels in the river. Two other iron buoys mark the quarantine anchorage, and one marks a wreck on the middle ground at the mouth of the river.

---

[1]Notice to mariners:

"On November 2, 1915, Cape Fear River Entrance Gas-and-Whistle Buoy CF, painted in perpendicular stripes, was established in 6½ fathoms of water, in place of Cape Fear River Entrance Whistle Buoy CF, which was discontinued. The gas-and-whistle buoy is cylindrical, with skeleton superstructure, and shows a flashing white light of 390 candlepower every three seconds, thus, 0.3 seconds; eclipse 2.7 seconds, 16 feet above the water."

GENERAL CHARACTER OF THE COAST.

Between Cape Hatteras and Charleston, three dangerous shoals extend seaward at right angles to the coast, namely, Diamond Shoals, Lookout Shoals, and Frying Pan Shoals. These shoals reach out from the shoreline to an average distance of twenty miles, and have an average width of 1.5 miles. A fourth shoal exists in the vicinity of Cape Romain, but of less extent and of less dangerous character than any of those just mentioned.

The prevailing winds on the North Carolina coast are from the northeast around to southeast and southwest. The attendant currents generally set directly on the three great shoals between Hatteras and Cape Fear, and it is in the vicinity of these shoals that practically all the maritime disasters on the coast of the Carolinas occur.

The treacherous currents along this stretch of coast are largely responsible for the sweeping of vessels upon the shoals. From Cape Lookout Bight to Frying Pan lightship, Capt. G. L. Carden, commanding the *Seminole,* has usually found it necessary to allow for at least five miles westerly set of current on a run of eighty-nine miles. Below Frying Pan, there is also a strong set into the bight, and this is especially noticeable in the run from Cape Fear Bar to the entrance of Winyah Bay.

According to Captain Carden, there is a safe rule for all navigators to follow on this station; that is, never get inside of ten fathoms, unless sure of one's position. The ten-fathom curve will carry one clear of all the great shoals from Hatteras to Romain. The same eminent authority said to the writer: "A stranger approaching this section of the coast will, on finding himself in thick weather inside of ten fathoms, do well to let go an anchor at once."

The end of Frying Pan Shoals is marked by our lightship, *Number 94,* and the present position of this craft is most advantageous to vessels making for the Cape Fear Bar. It is a fact that Cape Fear Light is not seen from the extreme end of Frying Pan Shoals, and it is the end of the spit which masters of ships are so anxious to determine. A gas buoy, 12 miles SE. by E. ¼ E. off Frying Pan lightship, marks the end of the broken ground. This gas buoy is a favorite mark for coasting vessels, and is also available for ships coming in from seaward, but before shaping into the Cape Fear, safe navigation demands that one should find the end of Frying Pan, and it is this useful function which the present lightship serves. From the Frying Pan lightship, two courses only are necessary, one to clear the Knuckle Buoy, and a second course direct to the Whistling Sea Buoy. Then from the sea buoy one has only to run right down to the bell buoy marking the commencement of the bar. Nowadays, crossing the Cape Fear Bar is a very different matter from what it was under the ten to twelve feet conditions of blockade-running days, when there were no lights, nor buoys, nor any guide save the lead, the line of breakers, and possibly an outline of shore.

Wilmington's approach from the sea is a magnificent thoroughfare, both across the two miles of bar and the twenty-seven miles of river stretch inland. The channel across the bar is well lighted and furnished with buoys. The prevailing winds being from northward to northeast, the Frying Pan Shoals and Cape Fear Spit protect the bar entrance during the major part of bad weather, making it a better entrance than the former New Inlet Channel, which led past Fort Fisher.

To maintain the magnificent thoroughfare of two miles of Cape Fear Bar, it is necessary for the engineers directing the river and harbor improvement to keep a suction dredge constantly employed upon the bar, as the currents are continually sweeping the sandy bottom into the ship channel, thereby endangering navigation, but as long as continued appropriations are available for this important aid, the work can be done effectively.

A project for the permanent maintenance of deep water by stone jetties, similar to those employed on Charleston Bar, has been discussed by our local Board of Commissioners of Navigation and Pilotage, and the matter has been taken up with the United States Corps of Engineers.

The Frying Pan Shoals must be rounded before a vessel can stand to the northward. The depth along the Frying Pan Spit varies from 7 to 14 feet, and the shoals extend in an unbroken line 10 miles south-southeast from Cape Fear. Following the same general direction of the primal shoal are numerous patches running out for a distance of 5½ miles farther. The depth over these patches varies from 10 to 24 feet. It is just beyond these patches that the Frying Pan lightship is anchored, and by keeping to seaward of the Frying Pan lightship, there will be no depth of water encountered less than 3¾ fathoms; and the patches can be avoided by deep-draft ships by shaping a course which will carry them to the southward and eastward of Frying Pan lightship until the position of the present lighted bell buoy is reached. The 3¾ fathom patch referred to above lies 9 miles east by south (mag.) of the Frying Pan lightship. For deep-draft vessels the practice in running the coast is to pass outside the gas buoy, but the practice on the *Seminole,* when coming from the northward, is to shape straight to the Frying Pan lightship, making allowance for fully five miles inset of current on a ninety-mile course.

In general terms, a stranger approaching the coast between Hatteras and Frying Pan can determine his position by recourse to the lead. The depths are very regular, and from 4 to 6 fathoms can be taken to within one mile of the beach. The ten-fathom curve follows the curve of the coast at an average distance of eight miles from the shore until in the vicinity of Cape Fear, and there it bends around Frying Pan.

There is a mighty carrying trade from north to south past these dangerous shoals. Practically all steam craft to and from the Gulf follow the coast, and this trade promises to be greatly augmented since the opening of the Panama Canal.

The *Seminole* keeps eyes and ears open on that part of this great thoroughfare which has been assigned to her, and night and day trained wireless operators are listening for a call. At the first call for help the cutter must start, and to be prepared for emergency call at any hour, and for any stage of weather, demands the constant attention of officers and crew.

The headquarters of the *Seminole* are at Wilmington, where the Revenue-Cutter Service possesses its own wharf and storehouses, and at this port the cutter is provisioned after each cruise. The officers of the *Seminole* during the year 1912-13 were:

> Captain Godfrey L. Carden, U. S. R. C. S.
> First Lieutenant L. C. Covell, U. S. R. C. S.
> Second Lieutenant L. T. Chalker, U. S. R. C. S.
> Third Lieutenant T. S. Klinger, U. S. R. C. S.
> Third Lieutenant C. H. Abel, U. S. R. C. S.
> First Lieutenant Engineers R. B. Adams, U. S. R. C. S.
> Second Lieutenant Engineers W. P. Prall, U. S. R. C. S.
> Third Lieutenant Engineers C. C. Sugden, U. S. R. C. S.

The wireless has contributed wonderfully to the effectiveness of the patrol. The *Seminole* has picked up messages at the first call from distressed craft, and long after the cutter had started confirmations were being received via official sources from land. It is not too much to say that ordinarily the *Seminole* will pick up any distress call from a modern wireless installation which may be sent out on her station. What the *Seminole* may miss will in all probability be picked up by either one of the United States powerful wireless stations at Beaufort or Charleston, and the *Seminole* is always in touch with one or the other of these two stations.

UNITED STATES REVENUE–CUTTER SERVICE.[1]

An important arm of great reach and efficiency is the admirable Revenue-Cutter Service on this station. At no time in its history has this service been more effective in life-saving and in the rescue of imperiled ships from imminent destruction than during the past five years. Within the writer's memory more than a hundred vessels have been totally lost on or near Cape Fear and many brave seamen went down with them; but such is the equipment and efficiency of the cutter *Seminole* and the professional skill and daring of her commander, his well-tried officers and men, that valuable ships and crews, given up for lost in the terrific winter gales of our dangerous coast, have been drawn out of the teeth of the destructive elements and restored to usefulness, and this without reward or the hope of reward beyond the consciousness of duty done.

Repeated recognitions of rescue work have been made by Lloyd's and other important underwriters, and two services of silver plate have been presented to the commander and officers of the *Seminole,* and quite recently, with the approval of the Secretary of the Treasury, a gymnasium has been presented, by friends of this valuable service, to the crew of that vessel as a mark of appreciation by shipowners and underwriters and as a reward of distinguished merit.

The quality of mercy is not strained by the fine fellows who

---

[1] In January, 1915, the United States Congress passed an act creating the Coast Guard by combining the Revenue-Cutter Service and the Life-Saving Service, and all duties previously performed by the two latter services are now performed by the former, with equipment, officers, and administration suited to the combined activities of the two.

respond so quickly and eagerly to the S.O.S. wireless call for help. An unwritten law compels them to succor a fellow seaman in distress even at the risk of their own destruction, and it stirs the blood of all humanity to read of ships like the *Seminole,* tossed upon a raging sea, yet standing by a sinking ship until every man is rescued from the jaws of death.

During the past decade the President of the United States has annually designated vessels of the Revenue-Cutter Service to patrol actively the Atlantic coast during the winter months for, the purpose of rendering aid to distressed merchant craft. The patrol extends from Maine to the Gulf of Mexico and has numbered as many as ten cutters. From the first day of December of each year to the first day of April following, the patrolling force is constantly cruising.

The littoral lying between Cape Hatteras and Charleston has for several years constituted the station of the revenue-cutter *Seminole.* Measured between lightships, or over the course usually followed by coasting steamers, the distance between the northern and southern extremities of this station is 270 nautical miles. This stretch of coast during the winter months is noted for the disasters which occur to shipping. The *Seminole's* record for the winter season of 1912-13 is typical. During the four months from December 1, 1912, to April 1, 1913, the cutter assisted, in all, nine craft, comprising both steamers and sailing vessels, and representing a value of floating property of $993,000, a cargo value of $573,000, or a total vessel-and-cargo valuation of $1,566,000. A tenth vessel, the *Savannah,* a dangerous derelict, was destroyed with a mine.

About six weeks before a recent season's winter cruising commenced, the *Seminole* made a run of over 100 miles in a northeast gale to the burning steamship *Berkshire,* of the Merchants and Miner's Line, took off the passengers, put out the fire, and saved both vessel and cargo from total loss—representing for cargo and vessel fully $500,000.

It may be asked why private wrecking craft are not available to render some of the service performed by the cutters. The fact is that they are not in evidence. Nor can private enterprise hope to cope with a government service in which there is high *esprit de corps* such as characterizes the Revenue-Cutter Service. Risks and hazards are cheerfully assumed by the Revenue-Cutter Service, the sole object to be attained being relief for the distressed and the performance of duty.

CAPE FEAR LIFE–SAVING SERVICE.[1]

A public service which measures its efficiency by the number of human lives saved from the perils of the sea is to be classed among the highest humanities of a great government.

Through the courtesy of its general superintendent, the Hon. S. I. Kimball, I have obtained the following information with particular reference to the Life-Saving Service in the neighborhood of Cape Fear.

The equipment of the Cape Fear and Oak Island Stations, which are located in the vicinity of Cape Fear, consists of apparatus, including line-throwing guns, projectiles, lines, beach lights, signaling devices, and power boats, as well as other boats. The Cape Fear Station has a Beebe-McLellan self-bailing surfboat, an open Beebe surfboat, and a Beebe-McLellan self-bailing power surfboat, with horizontal engine; and the Oak Island Station is equipped with a Beebe-McLellan self-bailing surfboat and a 36-foot self-righting and self-bailing power lifeboat. The Beebe-McLellan self-bailing power surfboat and the 36-foot self-righting and self-bailing power lifeboat are the latest developments in power life-saving boats, and are as good as any in the world. A constant watch is kept from the lookout towers of the stations and a beach patrol is maintained at night, and during the day when the weather is thick or stormy.

The recent instances of service at wrecks by the Cape Fear and Oak Island Life-Saving Stations have been as follows:

On December 8, 1912, the steamer *Aloha,* tonnage 42, value $15,000, with four persons on board, was rendered assistance by the Life-Saving Station at Oak Island; also on December 16, 1912, the schooner *Dohemo,* value $7,500, with two persons on board, and in the same day, the launch *Anerida II.,* value $1,700, with two persons on board, was saved.

On December 27, 1912, the schooner *Savannah,* tonnage 584, value $44,000, which was a total loss, with nine persons on board, and on March 26, 1913, the British steamer *Strathardle,* tonnage 4,377, value $120,000, with thirty-three persons on board, were rendered assistance by the Life-Saving Stations at Cape Fear and Oak Island.

On October 10, 1913, the schooner *John Twohy,* tonnage

---

[1]See Note on Revenue-Cutter Service, page 525.

1,019, value $30,000, which was a total loss, with ten persons on board, was rendered assistance by the Life-Saving Station at Cape Fear.

The total value of property involved in the above disasters was $218,200; the total value of property lost was $74,000, and the total number of persons on board was sixty. No lives were lost.

The rescue of the crew of the schooner *Savannah,* which was stranded on the western edge of Frying Pan Shoals, is illustrative of the value of this work. It is indicative of the service of these stations.

On December 27, 1912, the 584-ton, four-masted schooner *Savannah,* bound from Jacksonville, Florida, to Portland, Maine, with a cargo of pine lumber, and carrying a crew of 9 men, all told, stranded about noon on the western edge of Frying Pan Shoals, in a westerly gale and thick weather. The vessel and cargo, valued together at more than $40,000, were totally lost. The ship's crew, however, were saved by the crews of the Cape Fear and Oak Island Stations.

As the schooner lay on the shoals, with the mountainous seas dashing against her and over her, she was discovered by Keeper Brinkman of the Cape Fear Station. To make sure that she was aground the keeper climbed the tower of the Cape Fear Light to get a look at her through a spyglass. On leaving the tower he asked the lightkeeper to set a signal, which, according to a previous understanding, would convey to the station crew at Oak Island and to the revenue-cutter *Seminole* the information that a vessel was in trouble offshore.

The Cape Fear crew put off the beach in their surfboat without loss of time, and covered the eight miles to the schooner in two and a half hours. The Oak Island crew also appeared about the same time in their power lifeboat. It was agreed that Keeper Brinkman should undertake the work of rescue, a boat under oars being more readily and safely handled than a power boat, in broken water about a wreck. This arrangement was duly carried out, the Oak Island crew standing by, ready to assist their comrades should the surfboat meet with misfortune while alongside. "After a hard battle with wind and sea," says Keeper Brinkman in his report, "we took the captain and eight men off."

The rescue accomplished, the sailors were transferred to the power boat, which thereupon proceeded ashore with the surfboat in tow.

The ship's crew were cared for at the Oak Island Station until the following morning, when they were placed aboard the *Seminole,* which had appeared off the station during the night. The cutter and two tugs attempted to float the schooner, but without success.

The total approximate cost of maintaining the Cape Fear and Oak Island Stations and for salaries during the fiscal year which ended June 30, 1913, was $17,430, the expense being about evenly divided between the two stations. The amounts expended for salaries were $7,089.10 and $6,940.80 for the Cape Fear and Oak Island Stations, respectively. The expense for maintaining the stations averaged about $1,700 each during the year. The cost of rebuilding the Cape Fear Station, now under way, will amount to between four and five thousand dollars.

USE OF OIL TO PREVENT BREAKING SEAS.

About the year 1870 the late Alexander Sprunt, founder of the firm of Alexander Sprunt & Son, demonstrated in a magazine article published abroad the efficacy of the use of oil at sea in stormy weather. He subsequently endeavored to induce the British Admiralty to provide every ship with his simple device for protection against breaking seas while lying to, and received some recognition.

At that time, in the winter, he loaded a small brig of about two hundred tons register with a heavy cargo of naval stores for Europe. The captain was induced to provide a barrel of crude oil, two canvas bags perforated with a large needle, and a twenty-foot spar with block and tackle, to be used in case of need. On his return to Wilmington some months later, he gratefully acknowledged that his ship and crew had been providentially saved from destruction by this simple and effective provision.

He was obliged to lay to for several days in a hurricane. The heavy waves smashed the boats and threatened to destroy the vessel. He thought of the oil and at once applied it. Running the spar out on the weather side, he filled the bags with oil and hauled them out to the end of the spar. Immediately a thin covering of oil spread over the advancing waves and, although the brig rose and fell upon the mountainous seas, the water did not break, and the little vessel rode out the gale in safety.

34

In the *Hydrographic Bulletin* of the United States Navy, December 31, 1913, the following reference is made to the use of oil to calm seas:

"Imperial Transport (Br. ss.), Capt. E. R. Frankland:

"On November 25, 1913, during the voyage from Narvik toward Philadelphia, a hurricane struck the vessel from the southwest, gradually shifting to the westward. The hurricane was of such force that it was found impossible to steam against it. The engines, therefore, were stopped, and the vessel, losing headway, fell off beam-on to the sea. During this operation oil was used plentifully, several pints being thrown on the deck, and the same washing overboard to windward smoothed the tops of the seas, thus stopping them to a great extent from breaking on board. When the vessel was drifting, two oil-bags were hung overboard to windward, one at each end of the bridge deck, each bag being attached to fifteen fathoms of line, this usage greatly assisting in arresting the force of the seas. One oil-bag was hung in the forward lavatory at the break of the forecastle head, and the flush left open, the oil thus coming in contact with the sea without being blown to leeward. The same operation was repeated in the lavatory amidships. A hand was stationed in each of these places replenishing the oil-bags. During the squalls a little oil was also poured down the pipes from a can. The seas, although breaking heavily to windward, had the force taken out of them when coming in contact with this second distribution of oil. We subsequently encountered seven hurricanes, and oil was used in the same manner and with the same effect. The oils used were fish, colza, engine, and linseed, and no apparent difference in effect was noticed. All of the hurricanes started from the south and veered to north through west, and then backed from north to south through west. The same was experienced in the storms of lesser violence. At no time during the passage was the wind from the eastward unless at the beginning of the storm, when sometimes it was SSE. I might add that the vessel came through with the minimum of damage, considering the terrific weather encountered."

A more recent test of this device was made by the revenue-cutter *Seminole*. In reply to my inquiry, Capt. G. L. Carden says, under date of January 11, 1914:

"I am attaching herewith a memorandum relative to the use of oil by the *Seminole* when working on the schooner *Thomas*

Winsmore. As a further proof of the efficacy of oil, I had occasion during the month of October, 1910, when commanding the *Manning* in the Pacific, to have recourse to it. We had left Kodiak Island for a run across to the Alaska coast, shaping for Cape Ommaney. It had been blowing a gale of wind for three days from the northwest and, not long after clearing the lee of Kodiak, I encountered a tremendous sea. Nothing like it had been seen during the entire past five months in the far North. The *Manning* was put before the seas, but it seemed as if every moment they must break aboard. In the mouths of the forward closet bowls, on either side of the bow, canvas bags filled with oakum were placed. The bags were punctured with ordinary sail needles, and a plentiful supply of fish oil was poured into the oakum-filled bags. The closet traps were then raised and very soon a thin film of oil was seen to reach out on either side of the ship for a distance of about ten feet, spreading out fan-tail fashion as it worked aft. At a distance of twenty feet abaft the stern, I should say, the width of the oil space was fully fifty feet. The effect was marvelous. The big seas would come up right to the edge of the oilfield and then dive under the ship and pass away forward. The film of oil alongside kept the seas from slapping aboard. I ran the *Manning* very slowly throughout the greater part of the night, but towards morning the wind and sea abated and we were able to head up on our regular course. During the entire night I do not believe we used over ten gallons of oil."

"*Memorandum:*—The American schooner *Thomas Winsmore* was found at 7.30 a. m., January 4, 1914, close to the breakers on Lookout Shoals. The *Seminole* at the time was in charge of First Lieut. Eben Barker. A fresh westerly gale was blowing. The *Thomas Winsmore* was displaying her ensign union down. The seas were breaking completely over the schooner. The *Seminole* anchored to windward of the *Winsmore*, veering down chain so as to bring the cutter near the schooner. Efforts to shoot a line aboard by means of a line-firing gun proved abortive. Oil was used freely through the closets forward. The oil formed a slick astern of the *Seminole* and prevented the seas from breaking. After a plentiful use of the oil, a pulling boat was lowered and a four-inch line was run to the *Winsmore*. By means of the four-inch line a ten-inch hawser was later gotten aboard the distressed craft. The *Winsmore* was then towed into the lee of Lookout Bight."

VISITS OF THE CRUISER RALEIGH TO THE CAPE FEAR.

Soon after the United States steamship *Raleigh* went into commission, in 1895, she came into the Cape Fear River to receive a service of silver, which was presented to her on behalf of the State by the Hon. Elias Carr, then governor of North Carolina.

Later, after our war with Spain, about the first of May, 1899, the *Raleigh,* returning from the Philippines, commanded by Captain Coghlan, again visited the Cape Fear for the purpose of delivering to the city of Raleigh some trophies of war, including several Spanish cannon, which were formally received by a delegation sent from Raleigh on behalf of the State of North Carolina.

The cruiser and her officers and men were honored by an enthuiastic welcome to Wilmington, and Captain Coghlan was deeply touched by his cordial reception. The *Raleigh,* under the command of Captain Coghlan, had joined in the attack upon the Spanish forts and war vessels in Manila Bay, and our people, desiring to mark this incident by a special compliment, presented another very handsome and valuable service of silver plate to Captain Coghlan and the ship. Mr. William Calder made the presentation speech, and the commander responded in a felicitous address which was long remembered by those who were present.

FEDERAL GOVERNMENT IMPROVEMENTS ON UPPER CAPE FEAR RIVER.

The present project for the improvement of the upper Cape Fear River was adopted by Congress in the River and Harbor Act of June 25, 1910. This project contemplates an improvement by canalization and dredging to obtain a navigable depth of water between Wilmington and Fayetteville, a distance of 115 miles, of eight feet. To accomplish this it is planned to put in two locks and dams. The first lock and dam, known as "Lock and Dam No. 1," is under construction at King's Bluff, 39 miles above Wilmington ; and the second, or "Lock and Dam No. 2," is to be located at Brown's Landing, near Elizabethtown, 72 miles above Wilmington. The 8-foot channel between Wilmington and King's Bluff has already been obtained by dredging, and it is only necessary now to maintain it. The locks will be of concrete, with pile foundations and steel-mitering gates. The lock at King's Bluff will be about 294 feet long over all, with a maximum width at the base of about 84 feet. The walls will be 28 feet high, and the chamber will take vessels about 200 feet long and 40 feet wide. The dam will be of the timber-crib type filled with stone, with sheet-piling above and below. It will be about 275 feet long and 50 feet wide, and will raise the water eight feet above that in the lower part of the river. The abutment for the dam on the side of the river opposite the lock will be of reinforced concrete pile construction, and will have the same height as the lock walls. As the dam is low, in comparison with the river banks, it will be submerged, and its effect as an obstruction in the river will disappear by the time the river rises to the top of the bank, so that the area of land covered by water during flood times will be practically the same after the dam is put in as it is now. As the lock walls are much higher than the dam, vessels may use the lock during a considerable rise in the river, and when the river drowns out the lock, there will be no fall over the dam and vessels will pass directly over it.

The cofferdam is constructed of steel interlocking piling made by the Lackawanna Steel Company, and is of the same general type as was used in the cofferdam for raising the battleship *Maine*. The piling is 45 feet long, and was driven through from 23 to 28 feet of compact sand and thin layers of rock. This piling is anchored back by heavy steel wire cables to pile anchorages 52 feet from the wall. In addition to the above work on the cofferdam, the dredging inside of the cofferdam and of the approaches has been completed. This dredging involved the removal of 33,000 cubic yards of material. Inside the cofferdam a level bottom was secured about 18 feet below water. Driving the foundation piles is now in progress; this requires the driving of 1,850 piles with a penetration of about 23 feet. When it is completed, concrete will be deposited around the heads of the piles, the cofferdam will be pumped out, and the lock walls built in the dry. Work on the abutment will be started shortly and carried on simultaneously with the construction of the lock, and as soon as these are completed the dam will be built in place.

The same general type of construction is being used for Lock and Dam No. 2, at Brown's Landing as at King's Bluff. Here, however, the dam will raise the water 12 feet above the level of the water between King's Bluff and Brown's Landing, thus requiring heavier construction throughout.

This work is being rapidly prosecuted and its completion in 1917 is dependent only upon sufficient congressional appropriations and favorable stages of water for sinking the dams. The amount expended on locks and dams to June 30, 1915, was $647,635.79; on other improvements, $183,654.10.

The advantages to be derived from this improvement are obvious and are those which would naturally result from certain all-the-year-round navigation with 8-foot navigable depth. It will benefit the cities of Wilmington and Fayetteville, at the two ends of the improved channel, in a commercial way, acting as it will as a steady and increasing feeder to their business activities. In addition to this, not the least important result will be that this stream, with its cheap transportation facilities close at hand, will act as a constant incentive to the development of the agricultural resources of the country through which it flows.

DISASTROUS FIRES.

The following account of a great conflagration on the night of April 30, 1864, taken from the *Daily Journal*, is of particular interest, as it gives us a glimpse of the city during the war—the value of cotton, $1,000 a bale; the interest of the Confederate Government, of the State of Virginia, and of the blockade runners in cotton, and the quantities stored in Wilmington, with other details of the war.

"Yesterday morning at 20 minutes to one o'clock," says the *Journal,* "a fire broke out in a warehouse or shed on the western side of the river, some 200 feet south of the ferry, which is opposite to the Market Dock. From this point it spread with amazing rapidity, and in an inconceivably short space of time, every building on the western side of the river south of the depot of the Wilmington and Manchester Railroad was enveloped in flames.

"When we arrived at the dock the whole western bank of the river for several squares was one line of flame, and it was feared that the railroad depot, with the workshops of the company, would also be destroyed. The destruction of property is very great.. We sum it as nearly as possible as follows:

"The Confederate Government lost 800 bales of cotton burned, of which about 200 bales were Sea Island, say $800,000. It lost, also, in materials and work in progress at Beery's ship-yard, about $100,000. T. Andrea lost 2,500 bales of cotton, 300 of it Sea Island, say $2,430,000. The Nashville and Chattanooga Railroad Company lost 187 bales; J. W. Thomas, thirty-seven bales, say $200,000. In Captain Hallet's sheds there were 850 bales of cotton, forty-seven of it Sea Island, belonging to the State of Virginia and sundry other parties. Also, rope and bagging to the amount of $100,000. All burned. Loss, about $900,000. Rankin and Martin's Rosin Oil Works, about $70,000. Insurance to the amount of $7,000. B. Hallet's loss in shed, about $25,000. Insurance, $3,000. The Southern Express Company lost two cars with merchandise, also some merchandise in a small warehouse. Loss, about $100,000. John A. Taylor, shed, etc., at ferry, $10,000. The damage to the machinery and tools at B. W. & W. L. Beery's ship-yard is comparatively light. Most of the workmen's tools were saved. They expect to be able to resume work in about three weeks. The sheds and sawmill machinery in rear of ship-yard is the principal loss. Estimated loss, $25,000. The Wilmington & Manchester Railroad Company lost the small wooden building in which the president, treasurer, and superintendent had their offices. All the contents were saved. The building was of little value. The chief loss of railroad property was twenty-five freight cars, fifteen of them belonging to the Georgia Central Road, eight to the Wilmington and Manchester Road, and two to the Southern Express Company. Total loss in cars, $150,000.

"Thus far we have a summing up of about $4,800,000, but this does not include the injury to a quarter of a mile of wharfing, mainly ruined, nor the loss of the sheds and buildings belonging to the Confederate Government and to the other parties, nor the injury to the cotton-press. These and other things not necessary to mention can hardly be estimated at the present time, since it may be impossible to replace them and difficult to do without them. We are happy, indeed, to learn that the cotton-press itself is expected to be in operation again in a short time. It is probable that, when the whole loss is known, and the wharves, buildings, etc., have been included, it will fall little, if anything, short of six millions of dollars.

"The usual doubts are expressed as to whether this tremendous fire was accidental or the result of incendiarism. It may have been either. We have not been able to discover anything that will warrant us in saying that it was the one or the other, if we except the astonishing rapidity of its spread, which does look as though it were too rapid to be merely accidental, and gives rise to suspicions of foul play, although the combustibility of the materials the fire had to work upon could hardly have been increased. We doubt whether any human power could have arrested the progress of the fire when it had once gotten under way, still we could not but remark upon the fact that even if the fire had been within reach of control by the exertions of the fire department, there was no fire department to be found by which such exertions could be made. This struck us the more forcibly because of our having noticed the activity and zeal of the firemen on several occasions during the present year—we had seen that they were practicing with their engines, and we know that the town authorities had been making exertions to increase the efficiency of the department and to have its apparatus put in the best order. We believe they succeeded in accomplishing both these objects. We inquired why the present state of things exists, and were told that the white companies are on duty as Home Guards and that the colored companies, mustering 180 men in all, mainly free negroes, have had their members either impressed or scared off by the fear of impressment. Whether incendiaries are abroad or not, we shudder at the thought of a fire breaking out in the closely built part of the town, filled as every place seems to be with cotton—cotton is our next door neighbor—cotton is everywhere."

On Saturday night, April 11, 1880, a store building on Front Street, between Market and Dock Streets, occupied by George A. Peck, was burned. During this fire a volunteer fireman named William Ellerbrook entered the building, followed by his dog, a large Newfoundland. After the fire was over, his body was found crushed by the walls and timbers of the building, and by his side was found the body of the faithful dog. The dog had hold of his master's coat and was evidently trying to drag him out of danger when the crash came. Man and beast were buried together in Oakdale Cemetery, and a stone was erected by the volunteer fire company, of which Ellerbrook was a member, and by his friends.

About 1880 fire was discovered at Colville & Taylor's sawmill, at the foot of Walnut Street. The fire bell rang about twelve o'clock Friday night, and the fire companies were dismissed at six o'clock Sunday afternoon, but while the sawmill was destroyed, a large part of the lumber was saved. The Champion Compress, near by, was saved after a hard fight.

In the early part of 1886 a Fayetteville steamboat, while drifting down the river, caught fire. Her tiller ropes burned in two and she landed at the Clyde Steamship wharf, which is now used by the Springer Coal Company. From this wharf the fire started about two o'clock, February 25, 1886, and swept up to the Champion Compress and destroyed that and the Atlantic Coast Line warehouses; burned the Methodist Church, on the corner of Front and Walnut Streets, and everything on that block except the Methodist parsonage. Everything on the block west of that was also destroyed. The fire crossed Red Cross Street and burned Mr. Henry Nutt's handsome residence, and sparks jumped to Brooklyn, where several frame houses were burned. The fire department was dismissed the next day, and the military placed in charge to keep thieves from looting everything that had been put in the street.

FIRE COMPANIES.

The first Wilmington fire company was organized in 1847 and chartered in 1867, under the name of the Wilmington Hook and Ladder Company. In 1857 the Howard Relief Fire Engine Company was organized and was chartered two years later. The third company was chartered in 1869, and called the Wilmington Steam Fire Engine Company.

On the evening of the 1st of February, 1869, a very fierce and destructive fire occurred in Grant's public stables on the southwest corner of Princess and Third Streets. The Wilmington Hook and Ladder Company, of which Col. Roger Moore was chief, rendered excellent service by tearing down the connecting buildings, thus arresting the progress of the fire towards structures of greater importance. Unhappily, however, several members of the company who ventured too far were caught under the falling walls. In this accident Mr. John T. Rankin suffered injuries which it was feared would be fatal. He recovered slowly, however, but with a permanent lameness. Shortly after this fire, and during the convalescence of Captain Rankin, the first steam fire engine used in Wilmington was purchased by popular subscription and named "John T. Rankin." This belonged to the Wilmington Steam Fire Engine Company. All of these companies were volunteer organizations, and the apparatus for each was purchased and maintained by subscriptions from the business men of the city and by the dues of the members.

In addition to the above named volunteer companies, there was a fire company composed entirely of negroes, and about 1870, with the assistance of the city, it was furnished with a steam fire engine. This company, from its inception, was supported almost entirely by the city; it was a very good company, and did splendid work under the command of Valentine Howe, who was an exceptionally fine negro.

About 1878 the first appropriation was made by the city for the support of these companies, and this was gradually increased until 1898, when the city took over the property of the entire fire department, since which time it has been under the efficient leadership of Chief Schnibben.

THE EARTHQUAKE OF 1886.

On the 31st of August, 1886, I was a passenger in mid-ocean on the Cunard steamer *Etruria,* bound from Liverpool to New York, in company with the Hon. William A. Courtenay, who was then mayor of Charleston. These were the days before the Marconi wireless system of communication with vessels at sea, and we had no thought of the fearful earthquake of that date which shook Wilmington to its foundations and nearly destroyed the city of Charleston.

At the quarantine station in New York Harbor we were handed several telegrams, and, looking up in dismay from the reading of one addressed to me, I saw that Mr. Courtenay had suddenly vanished without a word. Panic-stricken by the terrifying news, he had hurried ashore to catch the first train to Charleston.

On my arrival at Masonboro Sound, where my family was residing, I heard with great thankfulness that my household had escaped injury. My wife had retired early with the two children, and she was awakened by the upheaval of the bed and the falling of glassware from the mantel. Terrified by the thought that the door would be jammed by the twisting framework, she pulled it open with desperate effort and, with a child under each arm, ran to the open ground, on which were soon assembled neighbors and servants in a panic, intensified by the screams of the horses confined in the stables and by the loud lamentations of the negroes, who thought the day of judgment had come.

Several days later our office building was so greatly shaken by a second earthquake that we quickly sought safety in the street.

The newspapers of the day made the following references to this exciting episode.

The *Morning Star* of Wednesday, September 1, 1886, in its account of the earthquake, reported that "It was exactly ten minutes to ten o'clock p. m. when the first shock occurred. It lasted about thirty seconds and was accompanied by a long rumbling sound, like the passage of a railway train over a bridge. The river seemed to be violently agitated, and washed against its banks as if a storm were raging. The first shock was followed ten minutes afterwards by a second shock, and this by a third ten minutes later, neither of them of as great severity as the first. It is impossible to describe the alarm that pervaded the community. People thronged the streets and many of them were greatly agitated. A great crowd centered around the telegraph office, anxiously inquiring as to news from other places.

"As far as known, the damage caused by the shock was slight. Plastering was dislodged and fell in the Commercial Hotel and other houses, and bricks were shaken from chimneys and from the walls of buildings in the process of erection, among the number the chimney of a house on the corner of Second and Princess Streets."

The shock was quite severe at other places. At Smithville the Signal-Service observer reported as follows: "A severe earthquake shock felt here at 9.50 p. m., lasted about ten seconds, came from northwest. Ten minutes after the first shock another came from the west, lasting about three seconds."

The *Star* mentioned the wide extent of territory in which the earthquake made itself evident, with varying degrees of violence, as far north as New York and west to Chicago. The disturbance was greatest at Charleston, and at Laurinburg also the shock was extremely severe.

The *Daily News* had a very graphic account of the earthquake, and enlarged upon the terror and awe of the occasion, but differed slightly from the *Star* in a few comments. The first and most violent shock was claimed to have lasted forty-five seconds, followed by two more at short intervals, and others at one o'clock, four o'clock, and eight-thirty the next morning (September 1). The *Review* of September 2, 1886, reported shocks after the above, occurring at 5.12 p. m. and about midnight of the 1st of September.

The terrible disaster to Charleston cast a deep gloom over our citizens, and generous assistance was immediately organized in the form of a contribution, and a relief committee composed of a number of prominent people was dispatched to the stricken city as soon as the journey could be made.

THE VISIT OF PRESIDENT TAFT.

By IREDELL MEARES.

William Howard Taft, the twenty-seventh President of the United States, visited Wilmington on the 9th day of November, 1909. The occasion was a notable one in the annals of the city. The Governor of the State, with his staff officers, United States Senators and Congressmen, the representative editors of the State press, and a large concourse of visitors from all parts of the State did honor to the occasion. The city was beautifully decorated. The day was ideal in its sunshine and balmy air. The spirit of the people who crowded the streets was splendid. Not an incident occurred to mar the great reception.

On his arrival on the early morning train, the executive committee of the citizens' organization escorted the President and his suite in automobiles from the depot to the elegant residence of Mr. James Sprunt, where a breakfast was given in honor of the President by that hospitable gentleman and his wife. The home was tastefully and appropriately decorated. The approaches to it were guarded by the United States Coast Artillery from Fort Caswell, the band of which, during the breakfast, played patriotic airs. Breakfast was served in the conservatory, which had been transformed into an arbor of green foliage, with vines trailing overhead, from which hung clusters of real grapes. The hostess served a breakfast prepared in the old-fashioned Southern style. There were seated at the table fifty-two guests. On the right of Mr. Sprunt, the host, sat the President, and on his left, Hon. W. W. Kitchin, governor of the State; on the right of the President, United States Senator

Lee S. Overman was seated. Others of the distinguished guests were Gen. J. F. Armfield, the adjutant general of the State, and members of the Governor's staff; Capt. Archibald B. Butt, United States Army, who afterwards lost his life in the wreck of the *Titanic;* Dr. J. J. Richardson, a prominent throat and ear specialist of Washington, D. C., physician to the President; Lieutenant Whitney, of the United States revenue-cutter *Seminole,* and Captain Hancock, of the United States Coast Artillery; Representatives John H. Small, R. N. Page, Charles R. Thomas, and H. L. Godwin, all members of the United States Congress; and Hon. Walter G. MacRae, mayor of the city. The rest of the party consisted of the Citizens' Executive and Reception Committees.

After breakfast, the presidential party was conveyed under the escort of the local military and the Naval Reserves to the corner of Market and Third Streets, where all the school children of the county of New Hanover were assembled in a most beautiful flag formation, and as the President, with bared head, witnessed the scene, they sang the national anthem. He was then driven to St. Stephen's Church, where he reviewed the colored school children of the county, and made them a short address. Next, he was escorted to the United States revenue-cutter *Seminole* for a cruise down the Cape Fear as far as Southport. Accompanying him on the trip were the Governor and his military staff, the Senator and Congressmen mentioned, Mr. H. C. McQueen, chairman of the Citizens' Executive Committee, the late Hon. Alfred M. Waddell, ex-member of Congress, and a large number of representative editors of the State press and citizens of Wilmington. Luncheon was served on the boat, and the President held an informal levee.

On the return, the *Seminole* was met at the Dram Tree, the entrance to the harbor, by all the river craft and steamers in port, with colors flying, and, formed in parade line, the picturesque fleet preceded the *Seminole* to the dock. On landing, a procession was formed consisting of the United States Coast Artillery, detachments from the revenue cutter, and companies of the State Guard and Naval Reserves, including a detachment of Confederate veterans and some twenty-odd different organizations of the city. The President was then escorted to the City Hall, where from a platform he reviewed the military parade of Federal and State troops and the citizens' organizations. He was introduced to the vast audience, estimated from fifteen to twenty thousand people, by Governor Kitchin in cordial and spirited remarks, and delivered a notable address to the people. After a rest in the afternoon, a banquet was served to the President in the Masonic Temple, at which representative citizens of the city and State were present. The menu was prepared and served under the immediate supervision of the Ladies' Committee and in all respects could not have been excelled. The President made a short address after the dinner, and then repaired to his private car at the depot and proceeded to Richmond, at which place he ended the tour he had made of the Western and Southern States.

On the same evening at the Chamber of Commerce, there was given a "smoker" to visiting members of the press, at which many fine and eloquent speeches were made, and this constituted one of the conspicuous entertainments of the occasion. The local papers of the city and State printed elaborate accounts of the reception and illustrated cuts of the scenes which featured the doings of the day.

WOODROW WILSON'S YOUTH IN WILMINGTON.[1]

In the autumn of 1873, when Woodrow Wilson was just reaching his seventeenth year, and while his parents were residing at Columbia, he entered Davidson College. After finishing his examinations at the end of the first year, however, he fell ill and was taken to his home, then in Wilmington, his father having just been called to the pastorate of the Presbyterian Church of that city. He remained in Wilmington throughout the year 1874-75. It had been determined that he should go to Princeton, and he spent the year being tutored in Greek and a few other studies which it was thought might be necessary for entrance to Princeton.

In truth, there was a good deal of play done that year, too. The boy had grown too fast, and was hardly fit for the rigid schedule of college. So he "took it easy" in a city, the first in which he had ever lived that possessed any particular local charm. Wilmington was an old historic place. It was a seaport; for the first time Woodrow saw a ship and caught the smell of the sea. Foreign shipping floated in the noble river

---

[1] Based on Hale's *Life of Woodrow Wilson*.

or lay at the docks. Wilmington was a great depot for naval stores; its lower streets were redolent of the deep. Talk also was still full of adventures of the blockade runners of the war lately ended. What imaginative youth from the interior but would have haunted the docks and made an occasional trip down to the cape, to return with the pilot of an outgoing ship? Here, too, for the first time, the young man began to take part in the social life which is so important an element of existence in the South. He was really too young for the associations into which he was now thrown. Dr. and Mrs. Wilson immediately achieving devoted popularity, the manse swiftly becoming a social rendezvous of the city—a city of gentlemen of good company and women who would have been esteemed brilliant the world over. It was a young man very different from the raw youth of Davidson who, one day in September, 1875, took the Wilmington and Weldon train for the North.

During his senior year at Princeton he concluded that the best path to a public career lay through the law. In the autumn, therefore, he matriculated in the law department of the University of Virginia, that seat of liberal learning organized by Thomas Jefferson.

Just before Christmas, 1880, he returned to Wilmington, and devoted himself to reading law and otherwise preparing himself for the practice of his chosen profession. It was not till May, 1882, that he finally determined where to locate, and then he opened an office in Atlanta. His father continued to reside in Wilmington until April, 1885, when he accepted the position of professor of theology in the Southwestern University, at Clarksville, Tennessee. In the fall of 1898, Dr. Wilson made Wilmington his winter home until his death, January 21, 1903. In 1905 a tablet was unveiled in the Presbyterian Church as a memorial to "Rev. Joseph R. Wilson, D.D., Faithful and Beloved Pastor of This Church."

SOUTHPORT ON THE CAPE FEAR.

This charming little town at the mouth of the Cape Fear River was known in colonial days as Fort Johnston. It was a mere hamlet then, and its only importance pertained to the garrison of a fort, which mounted twenty-four cannon, named in honor of Gabriel Johnston, colonial governor. In 1792 it was

laid off as a town, and called Smithville, in honor of Governor
Benjamin Smith, and it retained that name until 1887 when it
began to be called Southport. Southport has been the home of
most of the Cape Fear pilots for nearly a hundred years. Its
salubrious climate and kindly inhabitants make it one of the
most attractive and wholesome winter and summer resorts in
our country. Its harbor is spacious and its deep water would
float the largest battleship of our navy. Its possible importance
as a coaling station for steamers from the south outward bound,
and its prospective usefulness to the Panama-Canal traffic in
that respect, is attracting attention to it as a convenient port
of call.

Of this interesting town our venerable ex-president of the
University of North Carolina, Hon. Kemp P. Battle, has said:

"Near the mouth of the beautiful Cape Fear River, on its
right bank, is a pleasant little town. It is fanned by the deli-
cious sea breezes; huge live oaks gracefully shade its streets. In
its somber cemetery repose the bodies of many excellent people.
Its harbor is good. It is on the main channel of the river.
From its wharves can be seen not far away the thin white line
of waves as they break on the sandy beach. But the ships to
and from its neighbor, Wilmington, pay little tribute as they
pass and repass. Its chief fame is that it contains the courthouse of the county of Brunswick. Its name is Smithville.

"Opposite the good old town is a desert island composed of
undulating sand-hills, with here and there occasional green flats
and dwarfed pines to relieve the general monotony. It is exposed to the full fury of the Atlantic storms. New Inlet once
poured a rapid stream between the island and the mainland.
But daring and industrious man now seeks to force by walls of
stone the impetuous floods through the river channel to the west,
to float larger ships up the river to the port of Wilmington. Its
southern end forms the dangerous cape which Mr. George Davis
so eloquently describes.

"The University of North Carolina has amid its group of
buildings one in its shape and portico and columns imitating a
Greek temple. Its basement was until recently the home of the
State Agricultural Experiment Station, which has done so much
to protect our farmers from fraud, but now it is the laboratory
of the professor of chemistry. Above is a long and lofty room
containing the library of the University. On its shelves are
many ancient books of great value, but vacant spaces plead

piteously for new books in all the departments of literature and science. The name of this building is 'Smith Hall.'

"What member of the widely spread family of Smith has thus given his familiar name to a county town, an island, and a university hall? His Christian name was Benjamin. He was an active officer of the Revolution, a governor of our State, and the first benefactor of the State University.

"Governor Smith had many vicissitudes of fortune. In his youth he was aide-de-camp to Washington in the dangerous but masterly retreat from Long Island after the defeat of the American forces. He behaved with conspicuous gallantry in the brilliant action in which Moultrie drove the British from Port Royal Island and checked for a time the invasion of South Carolina. A Charleston paper of 1794 says: 'He gave on many occasions such various proofs of activity and distinguished bravery as to merit the approbation of his impartial country.' After the strong Union superseded the nerveless Continental Confederation, when there was danger of war with France or England, he was made general of militia, and when later, on account of the insults and injuries of France, our government made preparations for active hostilities, the entire militia of Brunswick County, officers and men, roused to enthusiasm by an address from him full of energy and fire, volunteered to follow his lead in the legionary corps raised for service against the enemy. The confidence of his countrymen in his wisdom and integrity was shown by their electing him fifteen times to the Senate of the State. From this post he was chosen by the General Assembly as our chief executive in 1810, when war with England was constantly expected, and by large numbers earnestly desired.

"The charter of the University was granted in 1789. The trustees were the great men of that day—the leaders in war and peace. Of this band of eminent men Benjamin Smith was a worthy member. He is entitled to the signal honor of being the first benefactor of the infant institution, the leader of the small corps of liberal supporters of education in North Carolina. For that reason alone his name should be revered by all the long line of students who call the University their Alma Mater and by every one who desires the enlightenment of our people."

The communication between Southport and Wilmington in olden times was by a sloop which carried passengers and probably the United States mails. The daily schedule was protected

35

by the saving phrase "wind and weather permitting." Within the memory of our citizens in middle life, not to say of old age, the daily steamers to and from Charleston, already referred to, afforded the passengers at Smithville and Wilmington, and also the planters along the river, who boarded them from small boats, comfortable and speedy service. Later, on the completion of the Wilmington and Manchester Railroad, the steamer *Spray* plied regularly; but none of these conveyances was more satisfactory to the general public than the steamer *Wilmington,* owned and commanded by Capt. John W. Harper, who, after many years of excellent service, still controls and regulates the river trade and traffic.

The new railroad between Wilmington and Southport, called the Wilmington, Brunswick, and Southport Railroad, runs a daily passenger, mail, and freight schedule between Southport and Navassa, where it connects with the Atlantic Coast Line and the Seaboard Air Line Railroads for Wilmington or for other points on these trunk lines.

The railroad is thirty miles long, and was completed in 1911. The capital stock is $165,000. Its officers are: President, M. J. Corbett; vice president, H. C. McQueen; general manager, M. W. Divine, and traffic manager, H. E. Godwin.

In view of the opening of the Panama Canal and of the manifest destiny that the United States will have closer commercial relations with the countries of South America, whose development is now progressing with such rapid strides, the admirable location of Southport for a government coaling station is apparent, and it will surely become a commercial *entrepôt* of importance. Business is quick to avail itself of superior advantages, and the facilities offered by Southport are unrivaled. Its landlocked harbor, ranging from thirty-five to forty-nine feet in depth, and five miles long, with a width varying from one-quarter to three-quarters of a mile, affords a commodious and secure anchorage for the fleets of commerce and the navies of war, while the frowning ramparts of Fort Caswell assure ample military protection. Its bar is almost perfectly protected from the heaviest gales; for twenty-five years the hurricane signals have been hoisted at Southport only twice, and no hurricane wave can possibly enter the port. Safety of all shipping is thus assured.

While possessing these advantages, Southport enjoys the distinction of being on the direct line between the vast coal fields of

the interior and the points where the coal will be wanted—
Colon and Guantanamo Bay. It is as near Panama as Charleston, and, being south of Hatteras, has evident advantages over
Norfolk. No other Atlantic port is so near to the ports of the
Caribbean Sea or to the ports on the east coast of South America. Its climate is remarkably fine; it has a constant sea breeze
and fogs are almost unknown. Its temperature is free from extremes. For twenty-nine years the mean temperature during
the months of June, July, and August has been 79 degrees, and
for December, January, and February, 44.8 degrees. And its
water supply is excellent.

Located upon the system of inland waterways now in process
of construction, and connected with the great southern railway
lines, it has every facility for commerce, and, directly connected
with the vast coal fields, it offers advantages for a government
coaling station second to no other port on the coast.

FORT CASWELL AT THE PRESENT TIME.

In reply to my request through Senator Overman for particulars of the present defenses at Fort Caswell, which has been
made one of the most important military posts on our coast, the
Assistant Secretary of War says:

"Fort Caswell is situate in Brunswick County, North Carolina, about two miles from Southport and twenty-two miles from
Wilmington. The military reservation includes Oak Island and
contains an area of 2,325 acres. It is the headquarters of the
coast defenses of the Cape Fear, and is garrisoned by three companies of the Coast Artillery Corps. It is commanded by Col.
Charles A. Bennett, Coast Artillery Corps.

"The armament of the post consists of mortars, direct and
rapid-fire guns, and includes a mine defense.

"The batteries have been named in honor of Richard Caswell,
a distinguished member of the Continental Congress, an officer
of the Revolutionary Army, and first governor of the State of
North Carolina; of the late Capt. Alexander J. Swift, Corps of
Engineers, who was employed upon the construction of Fort
Caswell, and who died of disease contracted in the field during
the Mexican War; of the late Ensign Worth Bagley, United
States Navy, of North Carolina, killed in action at Cardenas,
Cuba, May 11, 1898; of the late First Lieut. William E. Shipp,

Tenth Cavalry, killed at the Battle of San Juan, Cuba; of Surgeon William S. Madison, Third United States Infantry, who was killed May 14, 1821, in action with the Indians near Fort Howard, Wisconsin; of First Lieut. Patrick McDonough, Corps of Artillery, United States Army, who was killed August 15, 1814, at the Battle of Fort Erie, Canada; and of Capt. Henry McKavett, Eighth United States Infantry, who was killed September 21, 1846, at the Battle of Monterey, Mexico."

THE PROPOSED COASTAL CANAL.

A great coastal canal system ultimately connecting Boston with the Rio Grande entirely through inland waters would be of importance to the commerce of the Cape Fear River, as to all the Atlantic and Gulf coast. Such a project has received the approval of many of the most thoughtful statesmen of the country, and a beginning has already been made towards its accomplishment. The Cape Cod Canal, constructed by private means, is already finished, and it shortens the distance by water from Boston to New York seventy miles, while it eliminates many of the dangers of the old route. The government has determined to secure possession of the Chesapeake and Delaware Canal with the purpose of converting it into a ship canal connecting the two great bays. A government ship canal has been opened from Norfolk to Beaufort, and at various points along the coast canals are either in course of construction or have been surveyed by the Board of Engineers and recommended to Congress for construction.

The link from the Cape Fear River to the northward, it was hoped, might start above Wilmington, but the surveys showed difficulties that were avoided by a sea-level canal through the sounds, reaching the river by Telford's Creek.

R. A. Parsley, J. A. Taylor, Hugh MacRae, and M. W. Divine, among others, have been active and prominent in presenting the arguments in favor of the construction of the link from the Cape Fear River; and we can reasonably expect that at no distant day this important aid to the commerce of Wilmington will be determined upon by the Federal Government, and when opened its advantages will be of immense benefit to the city.

While the senators and representatives in Congress from the

State, especially the members from this section, have been keenly alive to the advantages that will accrue from the construction of this inland waterway, the work of Hon. John H. Small, the member from the First District, has been of unexcelled importance. He has, indeed, been the genius and guardian spirit of the inland-waterway improvement from its inception, and he is entitled to first distinction in the acknowledgments of all patriotic people who recognize public service unselfishly and effectively rendered. He piloted the project through the shoals and snags of increasing and innumerable difficulties with untiring zeal and discretion, and this tribute is paid with a grateful sense of appreciation and admiration. He conceived a project national in scope, and has been actuated by no considerations of local advantage; his honors will grow with the progress of the work until his name will be known and his worth recognized from the North Atlantic to the Gulf.

MUNICIPAL GOVERNMENT IN WILMINGTON.

The development of the port and city of Wilmington during the last decade has been in line with the general progress of the country at large, and perhaps somewhat ahead of it. The improvement of the streets and the building of tall structures along the principal thoroughfares denote a new era for the old colonial town, which emerged so slowly from the shadows of the War between the States.

Prior to the year 1877, the city of Wilmington had been for years governed by a Board of Commissioners or a Board of Aldermen, elected by the people. In the year 1877, for financially important reasons, the General Assembly provided for a Board of Audit and Finance, to be appointed by the Governor, giving the body so named and constituted almost exclusive control of the revenue and expenditures of the city. Under this dual system, which worked with very little friction, and always in the line of economy, the affairs of the city were managed until 1907, when, in authorizing an issue of $900,000 in bonds for water and sewerage and for street improvements, the General Assembly established two additional boards, a Water and Sewerage Commission and a Street Commission. In 1909 still another was added, a Police and Fire Commission. Under this state of affairs there were four separately constituted boards managing different departments of the municipality, with resulting clash of authority and responsibility. Over them all, the Board of Audit and Finance held control of the purse strings.

The inconvenience of transacting business with so many departments managing the affairs of the city without coördination, and naturally therefore with lack of economy, became so apparent that at an election, when the question was submitted, the people almost unanimously adopted the commission form of government. In 1911, a council of five members superseded all of the boards previously existing, and for nearly five years the city has been under this form of government. Although some good has been accomplished by simplifying governmental methods, much more might be done, it is believed, by the employment of a municipal manager, as is being done in some other cities, and by following more closely the methods adopted by business corporations.

The commission form of municipal government has not proved a success, except in cases where notorious graft prevailed, and the tendency of municipal reform seems to be upon the lines adopted successfully by the Germans of having trained managers and concentrated control. As Price Collier says: "No State can make men. No State can produce wealth and worth. These three—men, and wealth, and worth—are produced, and produced only, where men measure themselves against men for the mastery over the fruits of the earth, without adventitious aids of any kind and under the protection of laws that all make and all obey. Our mistakes and our political troubles have mostly arisen from a wrong interpretation of 'government by the people.' It has never meant, and can never be successful when it is interpreted as meaning, that each individual shall take an active part in government. This is the catch-penny doctrine preached from the platform by the demagogue. The real spirit of 'government by the people' is merely that they should at all times have control, and keep control, of their governors."

Arthur J. Brinton, in the *Dispatch,* says: "When James Bryce, late British Ambassador to the United States, a keen, acute, brilliant observer of American affairs, wrote a quarter of a century ago that the Americans knew how to do some things well, but did not know how to run their city governments, the observation hurt. Here is Mr. Bryce's exact language: 'There is no denying that the government of cities is the one conspicuous failure of the United States. The deficiencies of the National Government tell but little for evil on the welfare of the people. The faults of the State governments are insignificant compared with the extravagance, corruption, and mismanagement which mark the administration of most of the great cities. There is not a city with a population exceeding two hundred thousand where the poison germs have not sprung into a vigorous life. In some of the smaller ones, down to seventy thousand, it needs no microscope to note the results of their growth.'

"Such criticism stung. American cities, feeling the wound, have sought a soothing salve for their hurt feelings in revolutionizing the form of their city governments. Mayors have served them ill; municipal officials have been corrupt. Away with them! Let us get our city governments on a business basis; let us run them as we run our private business."

The present mayor of Wilmington, Parker Quince Moore, is a worthy descendant of the leading spirits of the colonial Cape Fear described by the British Governor Burrington in his official dispatches to the Home Government as the "pestiferous Moore family," who vexed the Royal Government at Brunswick by their revolutionary tendencies, and later, on the 19th of February, 1766, advocated the first armed resistance on the American continent to the authority of their Sovereign Lord, King George.

Mayor Moore is not only to the manner born, but his business training, his patriotic spirit, and the charm of his pleasing personality have established him in the respect and confidence of all classes of our people. To my request for an expression of his observations of municipal government he has kindly responded as follows:

"For some years there has been an increasing demand in this country for better municipal government, and, if the views attributed to an eminent statesman—that we had the worst-governed municipalities in the world—is even approximately correct, there is need for change. While we may not be quite prepared to accede to so severe an arraignment, many of us are fully convinced that the ordinary government of our cities and towns is very far from being noticeable for the effective and economic management usually prevailing in other corporations.

"The first move made in the direction of advantageous change was in Galveston, where what has been popularly called the commission form of government was first instituted. Several hundred cities have since undertaken this method, and as a step forward in the betterment of conditions it is to be highly approved. While not all cities or towns had so wide a margin as Galveston, between corruption and extravagance on the one hand and honest administration on the other, upon which to work, and while therefore the changes made elsewhere have not indicated the same tremendous improvement, it is unquestionably true that there has been a general and decided tendency towards a higher standard in municipal government. That the commission form of government is not in itself a panacea for all ills of municipalities has been ascertained and is admitted, but the method permits of more opportunities for improvement, and offers a better basis upon which to promote the interest of taxpayers, who may be likened to stockholders in a corporation, except that they secure dividends through savings rather than from profits.

"In our own city, the new government had a small field for accomplishment, as the previous ones had been economic and conservative—possibly a little too conservative. It was the result of the infliction on the city of too many commissions, though the establishment of these was due to a desire for the abolition of harmful politics, and was attributable to an effort in the direction of better things. The form as we now have it was intended to simplify and improve. This it has done, but there is more to be accomplished. We should advance further by making our council more of a legislative and less of an executive body, and by consolidating departmental management under one responsible head, following the method forced by experience on all commercial corporations. The appointment of a city manager, having charge of executive and administrative work, subject to the legislative control of the council, would, in my judgment, unify the work of the government, promote harmony of operation, secure economy and effectiveness (which is practically the same thing), and, while not interfering with the right of the people to select their own rulers, would secure management which would approve itself in lower taxes, higher efficiency, less deference to selfish interests. Several cities are trying out the manager plan, already successful in other countries, and it is more than probable that all will adopt it eventually."

J. Allan Taylor, Esq., one of our most eminent publicists and logicians, whose experience as an alderman of the city of Wilmington in former years increases the weight of his excellent opinion, has expressed to me his view of municipal government in the following words:

"Among the expedients tried for the betterment of city government is the commission form, but the principle of this form of administration is only indifferently understood and worse applied. The principle proceeds upon the true conception of municipal government—that the nearer government comes to the control of the citizen in both life and property the more closely it should approach industrial corporate management, and the expedient has proved successful just in the degree that its true conception has been appreciated and its true principle applied. The political element is so ever-present and persistent that capable administration can obtain only under conditions of civic pride and sense of property responsibility, and when it is remembered that of our municipal electorate only about four per cent represent real property owners, the difficulty of administering city government on a business basis would seem an all but insoluble problem.

"In regard to our local government, we have never had the commission form except in name, and the opportunity for giving the theory a practical test was lost when political pressure proved strong enough to dictate the terms of legislative enactment, so that the present system is distinguishable from our old form of aldermanic government only as respects the payment of salary to councilmen and the shearing of the mayor of all magisterial power. Ward lines still mark the political influence that shaped the system, a condition thoroughly inconsistent with the choosing of councilmen with the single idea of fitness, and this is the rock on which our experiment has been wrecked. With ward lines abolished, there is reason to believe that it would be possible to elect men at large qualified to administer the government on business principles, provided the duties of councilmen were made directorial and the salary eliminated.

"The ability of the city to pay salaries commensurate with the undivided services of capable men is obviously impossible, and the only practical alternative is the making of the office of councilman an honorarium. The commission form of government thrives just in proportion as the politician is absent and the business man present."

THE REVOLUTION OF 1898.[1]

"The year 1898 marked an epoch in the history of North Carolina, and especially of the city of Wilmington. Long continued evils, borne by the community with a patience that seems incredible, and which it is no part of my purpose to describe, culminated, on the 10th day of November, in a radical revolution, accompanied by bloodshed and a thorough reorganization of social and political conditions. It is commonly referred to as the Wilmington Riot, and legally and technically it may be properly so termed, but not in the usual sense of disorderly mob violence, for, as was said by an army officer who was present and witnessed it, it was the quietest and most orderly riot he had ever seen or heard of. A negro printing office was destroyed by a procession of perfectly sober men, but no person was injured until a negro deliberately and without provocation shot a white man, while others, armed and defiant, occupied the streets, and the result was that about twenty of them were killed and the rest scattered. It constituted an interesting chapter in the public history of the country, and therefore I will not enlarge upon it further than to say that it was the spontaneous and unanimous act of all the white people, and was prompted solely by an overwhelming sense of its absolute necessity in behalf of civilization and decency."

Conditions in Wilmington were somewhat similar to those described by Woodrow Wilson in his *History of the American People* as existing in the South in Reconstruction days: "Adventurers swarmed out of the North, as much the enemies of one race as of the other, to cozen, beguile, and use the negro. The white men were aroused by a mere instinct of self-preservation." The city government had long been controlled by partizans dependent upon the negro vote and was not at all responsive to enlightened opinion. The ills attending that deplorable condition had operated to check enterprise, arrest development, and produce stagnation. The city had ceased to make industrial and commercial progress. Whatever increase there was in the number of inhabitants was mainly due to the influx of indolent and undesirable negroes, whose attitude towards the whites had become unbearable. Hope of better days had almost faded away when a vile publication in a negro newspaper aroused the whites

---

[1]Based in part on Colonel Waddell's *Memories.*

to action and determined them to rid the city of the pests that had been a menace to its peace and an incubus on its prosperity. It was resolved to purge the city and to displace the inefficient government.

At 11 o'clock on Wednesday, November 9, a remarkable meeting of the leading citizens was held at the courthouse, at which Col. A. M. Waddell, chairman of the meeting, under resolutions adopted, appointed a committee composed of twenty-five of the prominent business men of the city to adopt measures to carry out the purposes of the meeting.

It was demanded that the offending negro editor leave the city within twenty-four hours, never to return, and that the press on which his paper was published be shipped away. A number of negro ministers and other reputable members of the race were asked to use their influence to see that these demands were met peaceably and to respond within a given time. Owing to the failure on the part of a negro to deliver the reply within the specified time, the white citizens, after waiting far beyond the appointed hour, marched to the office of the paper and destroyed the printing press and other equipment. By accident and not by intention, fire resulted, and the building was destroyed, to the regret of the white people. Bloodshed, as Colonel Waddell stated in the foregoing quotation from his *Memories,* was begun by the negroes, it being the purpose of the white people to avoid all bloodshed and needless violence.

On the evening of the day of this revolution, the mayor and board of aldermen then in charge of the city of Wilmington resigned, and their successors were nominated and elected. Thus there was an entire change in the city government, and the order of things then instituted has continued uninterrupted ever since. The effect of the change upon the prosperity of Wilmington was most happy, and the city then took a start in progress which has never ceased.

It was only under stern necessity that the action of the white people was taken, and while some of the incidents were deplored by the whites generally, yet when we consider the peaceable and amicable relations that have since existed, the good government established and maintained, and the prosperous, happy conditions that have marked the succeeding years, we realize that the results of the Revolution of 1898 have indeed been a blessing to the community.

CAPE FEAR NEWSPAPERS.

If we may believe the historian Williamson, the Lords Proprietors and the royal governors during their administration of affairs were extremely hostile to the establishment of newspapers in the colony. Doubtless they knew well the power of an unfettered press, and dreaded its influence upon the minds of the people. Nor did the circumstances and conditions of the early times offer any financial inducement for establishing a printing house. It was not until 1749 that a press was set up in the colony. In that year James Davis erected one at New Bern; and in 1755, some post offices being then established by which newspapers could be distributed, Davis began the publication of a paper in that town. It was called the *North Carolina Gazette,* and was printed on a small sheet, and issued weekly.

The second press set up in North Carolina was at Wilmington, in 1763, by Andrew Stewart, who printed a paper called the *Cape Fear Gazette and Wilmington Advertiser.* That paper was discontinued in 1767, but was succeeded the same year by the *Cape Fear Mercury,* published by Adam Boyd. Boyd was a man of versatile talents, an Englishman, but a true friend to the colonies. He was a member of the Committee of Safety for the town of Wilmington, in 1775, and was a prominent member of the Committee of Correspondence. In 1776 he entered the ministry and was appointed a chaplain of the Continental Line.

We have no means of knowing how long the *Mercury* existed, nor have we been able to find copies of any other publications prior to 1818. In that year, Mr. David Smith, jr., father of the late Col. William L. Smith, formerly mayor of the city of Wilmington, commenced the publication of the *Cape Fear Recorder,* which continued under his management until 1835, when Mr. Archibald Maclaine Hooper succeeded him. Mr. Hooper had fine, scholarly attainments and was fond of the classics. He had the pen of a ready writer, and his style was characterized by ease and elegance. He was felicitous in expression, and clothed his ideas in language chaste and beautiful. He was a near relative of William Hooper, the signer of the Declaration of Independence, and he was the father of Johnson Hooper, in his day so well-known to fame as the author of *Simon Suggs, Taking the Census,* and other humorous works. For a number of years the *Recorder* was the only paper published in this part of the State. The next paper established was the *Wilmington Advertiser.*

About the year 1832, Mr. Henry S. Ellenwood came to Wilmington, and assumed the editorial chair of the *Advertiser.* He was an educated gentleman, and fitted for the duties of a journalist. He courted the muses with considerable success, and much of his work gave ample evidence of wit and fancy and *belles-lettres* culture. His connection with the paper was, however, very brief, as he died suddenly a short time after taking charge. After his death the paper was purchased by Mr. Joshua Cochrane, of Fayetteville, and conducted by him until the summer of 1836, when he died and Mr. F. C. Hill became the editor and proprietor, and continued its publication until about the year 1842, when it ceased to exist.

Contemporary with the *Advertiser* was the *People's Press,* a paper published by P. W. Fanning and Thomas Loring, the latter being the editor-in-chief, which position he held for some time, when he disposed of his interest and purchased the *Standard,* the organ of the Democratic party of the State, issued at Raleigh, and he removed to that city. There he brought to the discharge of his duties great energy, perseverence, marked ability, and a thorough familiarity with political history. He was a man of sanguine temperament and a warm partisan, and in the excitement of controversy often indulged in expression towards his political opponents, which, in his calmer moments, his judgment condemned. He wielded at one time a political influence second to but few men in the State, and was an acknowledged leader of his party; but, differing from them in 1842 in regard to their course towards the banks of the State, he retired from the position he held rather than continue to hold it at the sacrifice of his independence. Returning to Wilmington, he established the *Commercial,* which he conducted for a number of years, until failing health compelled him to discontinue it.

The *Wilmington Chronicle* was established about the year 1838, by Asa A. Brown. It was an exponent of the principles of the Whig party, and advanced them with great zeal and ability. Mr. Brown was a capable editor, a good writer, and a man of more than ordinary ability. In 1851, he disposed of the paper to Talcott Burr, jr., who changed its name to the *Wilmington Herald.*

Under Mr. Burr's management, the *Herald* became one of the leading papers in the State, and but for his untimely death in 1858, would have taken rank with any in the South.

Mr. Burr's peculiar characteristics as a writer were his ready wit and sparkling humor, overlaying a deep vein of strong, impulsive feeling. Quick, vivid, and flashing, never missing its point, yet never striking to wound, abounding in gay and pleasant fancies, and always warm and genial as the summer air, his wit and humor touched the commonest topic of everyday life, and imbued it with new and charming attractiveness. He was struck down by the shaft of the Great Destroyer in the prime of life and in the midst of an active, useful, and honorable career. After his death, his brothers, C. E. and R. Burr, carried on the paper for a year or two, when it passed into the hands of A. M. Waddell, and ceased to exist on the breaking out of the war.

The *Wilmington Journal*: In the year 1844, Alfred L. Price and David Fulton, under the firm name of Fulton & Price, issued the first number of the *Wilmington Journal,* a paper destined to exercise a controlling influence for many years upon the political questions of the day. The editorial department was under the control of Mr. Fulton, and was very ably conducted until his death, which occurred a year or two after the establishment of the paper, when his brother, James Fulton, took charge of its management.

James Fulton was no ordinary man. He possessed a vigorous intellect and a clear judgment, was quick at repartee, and prompt to take advantage of any point exposed by an adversary; but he was always courteous, and rarely indulged in personalities. He wrote with great ease, and his style was chaste, graceful, and vigorous. He had humor, too, and it bubbled up continually—not that keen, pungent wit that stings and irritates, but that which provokes merriment by droll fancies and quaint illustrations. He read much, and remembered what he read, and could utilize it effectively.

The *Journal* quickly became a power in the State. In this section particularly, its influence was unbounded. Mr. Fulton died in the early part of the year 1866, and was succeeded as editor by Maj. J. A. Engelhard, who sustained the high reputation the paper had acquired. Upon the retirement of Mr. Alfred L. Price, about 1873, Col. William L. Saunders became connected with the paper, the editors being Engelhard and Saunders, an intellectual combination in journalism seldom surpassed.

During the troublous times after the close of the war, the utterances of the *Journal* were manly, outspoken, and fearless in condemnation of measures regarded as oppressive to our people. The editors practiced no temporizing policy, but boldly uttered what their convictions prompted them to declare. The paper continued thus until 1876, when adverse circumstances caused its suspension as a daily. It was then published as a weekly, the name *Wilmington Journal* being retained by Joshua T. James, the new editor and proprietor.

But few copies of the earlier papers published in Wilmington are now in existence. Of some, not a copy can be found, hence there may be, and doubtless are, omissions in the present list.

The *Wilmington Post,* a Republican paper, was established in 1866, but about 1872 was discontinued.

The *North Carolina Presbyterian,* weekly, was first established in Fayetteville, January 1, 1858, the Rev. George McNeill and the late Bartholomew Fuller being the editors. It was removed to Wilmington in November, 1874, John McLaurin becoming the editor and proprietor. Mr. McLaurin, who was one of our most exemplary Christian citizens and a gentleman of fine attainments, continued its publication in Wilmington for about twenty-five years, when he sold it to a Charlotte publishing company, which disposed of it later to Dr. A. J. McKelway, of Charlotte, where it is published as the *Presbyterian Standard.*

The *Wilmington Sun* had a place in the morning field of Wilmington journalism, and although short-lived, having its beginning in September, 1879, and its end in April, 1880, it left a pleasing memory in the community, which held in the highest esteem its able editor, Mr. Cicero W. Harris, and his capable staff, Mrs. Cicero W. Harris, Mr. Wade H. Harris, and Mr. Harry P. Russell.

For some years prior to 1879, Mr. and Mrs. Harris, who were of Oxford, N. C., were conspicuous in Wilmington for their literary attainments. Mr. Harris was for some time editor of the *Star,* and Mrs. Harris, who was a woman of most attractive personality and of remarkable energy, published a magazine, the *South Atlantic,* which might have prospered but for the financial depression of the times.

Col. Wade H. Harris, the present editor of the *Charlotte Observer,* although a mere youth at the time, served as local editor of the *Sun,* and today speaks of his experience and training in Wilmington in the warmest terms of appreciation.

Mr. Harry P. Russell shared with Mrs. Harris the duties of the business office. He was a young man of fine attainments, and later was prominently connected with the New York Sugar Exchange and amassed a comfortable fortune. He died in Orange, N. J., some six years ago.

The *Sun* was printed by Messrs. Jackson & Bell, the well-known printers of Wilmington, and had as its capable foreman, Mr. Thomas T. Seeders, whose make-up was said to be the best in the State.

The *Africo-American Presbyterian,* published in the interest of the colored members of that denomination by Rev. D. J. Saunders, a colored man of remarkable attainments, lived for several years.

The *North Carolina Medical Journal* was established by Dr. Thomas F. Wood in January, 1878. It was a monthly publication, ably edited and of great value to the profession.

The *Morning Star,* the State's oldest daily newspaper, was founded September 23, 1867, by William H. Bernard, who came from his home in Fayetteville just at the close of the war, and, on October 1, 1865, with the late Col. John D. Barry, began the publication of the old *Wilmington Dispatch,* a morning daily newspaper, with its offices of publication on the south side of Market Street, between Front and Second Streets. The copartnership existing between Messrs. Bernard and Barry lasted but a few months, and there was a dissolution of the firm, each partner assuming his share of the liabilities. Major Bernard took charge of the job printing department of the business and Colonel Barry continued the publication of the newspaper, which, after two or three years, suspended publication.

The job office included in its equipment the first press on which the *Morning Star* was printed. Major Bernard removed his part of the business to a room over a grocery store, then conducted by Edwards & Hall, on Water Street, between Market and Dock. He did job printing exclusively for several months, but on September 23, 1867, began the publication of the *Star,* which was conducted for some months as an evening paper, but later took the morning field. It has remained in the newspaper firmament of the State as a morning paper until this day, while other papers, started at intervals since, during all these years have, for various reasons, one after another dropped from the morning constellation.

The installation of a faster press necessitated a removal of the plant to what is now known as Custom House Alley, where it was published for nearly ten years. In 1876 the *Star* was removed from that location to Numbers 10 and 11 Princess Street, once an inn of the earlier Cape Fear period. The building at one time housed the late Joseph Jefferson, who, with his theatrical company, came from New York in a sailing vessel, playing in the local theatre and making trips by vessel to the larger port cities of the two Carolinas, maintaining permanent headquarters in Wilmington.

The predominant characteristic of the *Star* under the administration of Major Bernard was its intense loyalty to the Democratic party. Though conservative, it was not unmindful of the need of party reform from time to time. Its greatest service was perhaps during what is known as the "White Government Campaign" in North Carolina in 1898, culminating in the Wilmington Revolution in the same year. Major Bernard never sought office, though for twenty-seven years he was a member of the State Democratic Executive Committee, and, for a part of the time, a member of the Advisory Committee of the party organization in the State.

On May 1, 1909, on account of impaired health and a desire to retire from active journalism, Major Bernard sold the paper to the present owners, the Wilmington Star Company, Inc., composed of some of the leading Wilmington business men, the incorporators being James Sprunt, H. C. McQueen, M. J. Corbett, Col. Walker Taylor, D. C. Love, C. W. Yates, William H. Sprunt, Capt. John W. Harper, J. A. Springer, W. E. Springer, the late James H. Chadbourn, James H. Carr, Joseph E. Thompson, Maj. William H. Bernard, and his son, William Stedman Bernard, the last two named having retained a small interest in the business largely for sentimental reasons.

Upon the purchase of the property by the new owners, in 1909, the paper was moved to quarters fitted up for it in the Orton Building, a perfecting press was installed, and new typesetting machines were added. Within the next four years the paper about doubled its circulation in Wilmington and tributary counties in eastern North Carolina and upper South Caro-

36

lina. It has devoted its energies for the most part since that time to the educational and moral advancement of the community, to advocacy of a commission form of government, enforcement of law, and the general upbuilding of the community. In 1914, its business having outgrown its former quarters, an eligible site was purchased from the Murchison estate, and the paper has moved into a home of its own on Chestnut Street, overlooking the United States post-office grounds and in close proximity to the business district of the city. With the removal into its new home, a modern perfecting, stereotyping press has been added to its equipment and other improvements have been made.

Financially, the paper has prospered and was never upon a sounder basis. The outlook for the future is all that could be desired, and coming years are expected to justify fully the faith that has inspired the present owners.

The *Wilmington Messenger,* which was founded by Julius A. Bonitz, was removed to Wilmington from Goldsboro in May, 1887, at the solicitation of a number of Wilmington's most influential business men, and the first issue was printed June 29 of the same year in the old Journal Building on Princess Street. Mr. Bonitz was induced to move to Wilmington after his plant had twice been destroyed by fire within a few years. It was said that he gave Wilmington the most progressive Democratic daily paper of its period. He continued as owner and editor up to the time of his death, February 7, 1891, and on April 5 of the same year the plant and good will were purchased under foreclosure by Messrs. J. W. Jackson and Benjamin Bell, and the paper was published under the firm name of Jackson & Bell.

The *Messenger* was printed without missing a single issue from Mr. Bonitz's death until it was taken over by the new proprietors, and it was continued as an eight-page publication.

The paper under its new ownership was improved from time to time, and for many years was one of the best edited and most influential newspapers in eastern North Carolina. As a leader in the campaign for white supremacy in 1898, under the editorship of Dr. T. B. Kingsbury, the *Messenger* did commendable service and was recognized throughout the State as a powerful factor in aiding the Democratic party to accomplish the political reforms of that period.

Dr. Kingsbury was succeeded in the editorial chair by Samuel T. Ashe, another experienced editor, who remained with the *Messenger* until its suspension.

The *Messenger* suspended publication June 5, 1907, after serving well its day and generation for twenty years. The proprietors discontinued the paper in order to give closer attention to the job department of the plant, this feature of the business having greatly increased and having become more profitable than the newspaper.

The *Evening Review* was published in Wilmington for several years by its founder, editor, and proprietor, the late Joshua T. James, a prominent member of one of the old substantial families of the Cape Fear, noted for its intelligence and refinement, its public spirit and unselfish devotion to the best interests of our people. Mr. James was a born journalist, alert, intelligent, with the old-time urbanity which was a family characteristic. Emerging from the four years' war, he served for years on the old *Journal* staff, and then, without the necessary means, he bravely undertook a task beset with difficulties and which at times seemed insurmountable—the establishment of an evening daily newspaper.

The *Review* was a clean, dignified newspaper, ably edited. It had the good will of our community, and the lamented death of its proprietor cut short the honorable career of one of the builders of a better Wilmington. It lived from December, 1875, until July, 1898.

The *Evening Dispatch* was begun the 10th of January, 1895, upon the "commonwealth basis" by four printers with very slender pecuniary means, who agreed to work without any compensation until the venture was established upon a paying foundation. After two months' struggle one of the four partners died, and the three survivors secured the services of Mr. R. K. Bryan as editor. For two years the paper had a precarious existence, and dire necessity forced two of the promoters into more remunerative employment. The survivor, Mr. R. P. McClammy, became the sole proprietor, and now after nineteen years of changing fortune he has established it upon a sound, paying basis, with a competent staff of enterprising men under his efficient leadership. It has grown from a mere hand-bill of local items to its present respectable dimensions, and from its original dingy quarters into a home of its own which was specially designed for larger growth and influence. Recently it has been equipped with modern facilities, and its patronage as the only evening daily is increasing by leaps and bounds. Mr. R. P. McClammy is the proprietor, Mr. James H. Cowan is editor, and Mr. William E. Lawson is city editor.

DR. T. B. KINGSBURY.

A chapter on the newspapers of the Lower Cape Fear in these *Chronicles* would be incomplete without particular reference to the career of our veteran journalist and scholar, the late Dr. Theodore B. Kingsbury, whose memory is venerated by those who were his contemporaries and by our citizens generally, who regarded him with great respect and admiration. We learn from Captain Ashe's fine tribute in his *Biographical History of North Carolina,* that early in life after Mr. Kingsbury left the University of North Carolina, he published a literary weekly at Oxford, North Carolina, under the name of the *Leisure Hour,* which attracted much attention and drew high commendation from John R. Thompson, editor of the *Southern Literary Messenger,* then the most meritorious literary magazine published in the South, and from Paul H. Hayne, the poet, then editing *Russell's Magazine,* a large monthly of genuine merit, published in Charleston, South Carolina, and from other gifted editors. In June, 1859, he was elected to the chair of literature in Trinity College; but his thoughts and religious fervor led him into another field, and he entered the ministry, and continued in that calling until 1869. It was about that time, in March, 1869, that he was employed as an associate editor of the *Raleigh Sentinel,* then conducted by Hon. Josiah Turner, and for two years and more he continued in that capacity. While on the *Sentinel,* a momentous crisis in public affairs was precipitated by the Republican administration of the State, and Josiah Turner, with unequaled boldness, made the *Sentinel* the champion of free government and of the traditional liberties of the people. No greater service was ever performed by any press than that rendered to the people of North Carolina by the *Sentinel.* In those exciting and perilous times Dr. Kingsbury wrote much, and with strength and patriotic fervor, for the editorial columns of the paper, and he deserves to share in the great fame that is so justly awarded Josiah Turner for his bold and resolute editorial work. On three occasions Dr. Kingsbury declined the editorship of the *Raleigh Christian Advocate;* but he edited *Our Living and Our*

Dead for several years, a publication of a high order of merit, begun by Col. S. D. Pool; and he also edited the *Educational Journal* in 1874 and 1875, doing much to advance the cause of public education at that time in North Carolina. His contributions to *Our Living and Our Dead* were noteworthy, especially his literary criticisms. About that time he was offered a position as editorial writer on the *Wilmington Star,* and, accepting it, began a long career of journalism that gave great satisfaction to his friends and the patrons of that paper. He continued with the *Star* for nearly thirteen years, when he became editor of the *Wilmington Messenger,* with which he remained for about as long a period, having had an experience in journalism in Wilmington of more than a quarter of a century. As an editor, Dr. Kingsbury brought to the discussion of his subjects a large store of varied learning, and his productions were read with great avidity by a host of admirers and received the warm commendation of many of the ablest men and best thinkers of the State. In particular were his literary articles valued by the most cultured among the readers of his papers. The teachers and the professors of the various colleges, the lawyers, and the ministers of every denomination were generous and unstinted in their praise, while his work was not without the appreciation of the editorial fraternity. His style was clear and perspicuous, elegant in diction and remarkably forceful, and there ran through all his editorials a strain of patriotism, a love of North Carolina, an appreciation of the excellence of her great men, that was a distinctive characteristic of his work. In particular was he as an editor at pains to perpetuate the memory of the great feats performed by the North Carolina soldiers in the War between the States, and to instill into the minds of the present generation a correct understanding of the causes that led to the bloody contest. Indeed, no other editor of the State has been more patriotic than Dr. Kingsbury, and none has excelled him in elegance of diction and in a large vocabulary and literary merit.

THE WILMINGTON BAR.

The Wilmington Bar has always been one of strength and power, even from colonial days. Among the earlier members who stood high were William Hooper and Archibald Maclaine;

later, the eminent Samuel R. Jocelyn, famed as an equity lawyer, Judge J. G. Wright, William Hill, and William K. Halsey; then Joseph Alston Hill, William B. Meares, and Owen Holmes, followed by William A. Wright and Joshua G. Wright. Just before the war, in addition to the two Wrights, were Lucian Holmes, Thomas Miller, Adam Empie, Mauger London, Eli Hall, John L. Holmes, Oliver P. Meares, Moody B. Smith, Griffith J. McRee, DuBrutz Cutlar, Alfred M. Waddell, and Fred Poisson, and on a somewhat different level from any of these were George Davis, Robert Strange, and Samuel J. Person.

After the war the eloquent voice of Joshua G. Wright was heard no more, but his mantle fell on Charles M. Stedman. Other accessions were the brothers William S. Devane and Duncan J. Devane, Judge Robert French, Duncan K. MacRae, Eugene S. Martin, and Marsden Bellamy. While Mr. William A. Wright was accorded a particular eminence, Mr. Davis, Colonel Strange, and Judge Person were without superiors in the profession anywhere in the Union. No other city of only twenty thousand inhabitants could boast of a bar of equal strength, eloquence and learning. And there was never heard any suggestion of scandal among them. The shining lights of that period have passed away, their places being taken by their sons and kinsmen and others of excellent learning, fine attainments, and high character.

Members of the bar now licensed to practice in New Hanover County are: C. C. Bellamy, E. H. Bellamy, J. D. Bellamy, J. D. Bellamy, jr., Marsden Bellamy, W. J. Bellamy, W. M. Bellamy, L. A. Blue, B. H. Bridgers, E. K. Bryan, K. O. Burgwin, E. T. Burton, Robert Branch, W. B. Campbell, C. C. Cashwell, J. O. Carr, A. C. Chalmers, T. W. Davis, Rufus DeVane Dickson, George B. Elliott, B. G. Empie, S. M. Empie, W. P. Gafford, Louis Goodman, R. G. Grady, L. Clayton Grant, Lee Greer, J. F. Head, C. D. Hogue, G. H. Howell, W. F. Jones, Graham Kenan, Woodus Kellum, J. C. King, J. W. Little, C. C. Loughlin, E. S. Martin, Iredell Meares, Thomas D. Meares, jr., H. McClammy, J. G. McCormick, W. B. McKoy, J. A. McNorton, George L. Peschau, L. J. Poisson, A. G. Ricaud, H. E. Rogers, George Rountree, Robert Ruark, P. D. Satchwell, J. H. Scull, K. C. Sidbury, J. A. Smith, W. L. Smith, W. P. Stacey, R. W. Strange, W. A. Townes, W. P. M. Turner, C. D. Weeks, A. S. Williams.

HONORABLE GEORGE DAVIS, CONFEDERATE STATES ATTORNEY GENERAL.

On January 4, 1864, Hon. George Davis, then in the Confederate States Senate, was appointed by President Davis Attorney General of the Confederacy. His fine attainments gave him high eminence in the Cabinet, and his counsel was most helpful in determining the many delicate questions that pressed upon the President for decision, involving not merely the constitutional powers of the government, but also matters of great import in international law. The complications of the war period and the fact that the Confederacy was not recognized as a sovereign nation, made his function as the legal adviser of the government exceptional, and he discharged his high duties with great acceptability and distinction.

The high esteem in which Mr. George Davis was held by his devoted chief is attested in the following letter, addressed by the Confederate President to his faithful Attorney General after the evacuation of Richmond:

CHARLOTTE, N. C., 25th April, 1865.

HON. GEO. DAVIS, *C. S. Attorney General.*

MY DEAR SIR:—I have no hesitation in expressing to you my opinion that there is no obligation of honor which requires you, under existing circumstances, to retain your present office. It is gratifying to me to be assured that you are willing, at any personal sacrifice, to share my fortunes when they are least promising, and that you only desire to know whether you can aid me in this perilous hour to overcome surrounding difficulties. It is due to such generous friendship that I should candidly say to you that it is not probable for some time to come your services will be needful.

It is with sincere regret that I look forward to being separated from you. Your advice has been to me both useful and cheering. The Christian spirit which has ever pervaded your suggestions, not less than the patriotism which has marked your conduct, will be remembered by me when in future trials I may have need for both.

Should you decide (my condition having become rather that of a soldier than a civil magistrate) to retire from my Cabinet, my sincere wishes for your welfare and happiness will follow you; and I trust a merciful Providence may have better days in store for the Confederacy, and that we may hereafter meet, when, our country's independence being secured, it will be sweet to remember how we have suffered together in the time of her sorest trial.

Very respectfully and truly your friend,

JEFFERSON DAVIS.

CHARLOTTE, N. C., April 26, 1865.

HON. GEO. DAVIS, *C. S. Attorney General.*

MY DEAR SIR:—Your letter dated yesterday, tendering your resignation, has been received. While I regret the causes which compel you to this course, I am well assured that your conduct now, as heretofore, is governed by the highest and most honorable motives. In accepting your resignation, as I feel constrained to do, allow me to thank you for the important assistance you have rendered in the administration of the government, and for the patriotic zeal and acknowledged ability with which you have discharged your trust.

Accept my thanks, also, for your expressions of personal regard and esteem, and the assurance that those feelings are warmly reciprocated by me.

With the hope that the blessings of heaven may attend you and yours,

I am most cordially your friend,

JEFFERSON DAVIS.

This affectionate regard for the beloved leader of the Cape Fear was the subject of repeated conversations in late years between the writer of the *Chronicles* and the distinguished lady who bore the honored name of Jefferson Davis, and who was ever faithful and true to him and to the people whom he loved.

Upon the receipt of the sad intelligence of his death, she wrote to me from a sick bed the following tender and sympathetic lines:

"I am able to sit up a little, and regret that I am not strong enough to say as much about dear Mr. George Davis as my heart dictates.

"He was one of the most exquisitely proportioned of men. His mind dominated his body, but his heart drew him near to all that was honorable and tender, as well as patriotic and faithful in mankind. He was never dismayed by defeat, and never dejected. When the enemy was at the gates of Richmond he was fully sensible of our peril, but calm in the hope of repelling them, and if this failed, certain of his power and will to endure whatever ills had been reserved for him.

"His literary tastes were diverse and catholic, and his anxious mind found relaxation in studying the literary confidences of others in a greater degree than I have ever known in any other public man except Mr. Benjamin. Upon being asked one day how he was, he answered: 'I am very much comforted and rested by Professor Holcomb's *Literature in Letters*,' one of the few new books which came out during the Confederacy.

One of the few hard things I ever heard him say was when some one asked him if he had read Swinburne's *Laus Veneris,* and added, 'You know it is printed on wrapping paper and bound in wall paper.' He replied: 'I have never thought wall paper wholesome, and am sorry to know there is enough wrapping paper on which to print it.'

"He was fond of tracing the construction of languages, and the variants from one root were a favorite subject of conversation with him.

"When he fell in love and married a charming woman, the whole of Richmond rejoiced with him, and expressed no doubts of the happiness of either. Mr. Davis' public life was as irreproachable as his private course. Once when my husband came home wearied with the divergence of opinions in his Cabinet, he said: 'Davis does not always agree with me, but I generally find he was right at last.'

"I can not, of course, tell you about his political opinions, except that he was one of the strictest construers of the Constitution, and firmly believed in its final triumph over all obstacles to freedom.

"My husband felt for him the most sincere friendship, as well as confidence and esteem, and I think there was never the slightest shadow intervened between them."

GEORGE DAVIS—AN APPRECIATION.

Very early in life it became known that Mr. George Davis excelled in literary attainments and in oratory. On the death of Henry Clay, he made an address that brought him an enviable reputation; at the commencement of the State University in 1855, he delivered an oration—"Olden Times on the Cape Fear"—that was pronounced extraordinary; and the next year his address before the Greensboro Female College was a most remarkable effort. After the war, he delivered in Wilmington a masterful oration on the political issues of that day. A similar address, delivered in Wilmington in 1876, is thus described by Dr. Kingsbury in the *Morning Star:*

"The speech to which we listened is a very memorable one. It will long abide with us as one of those felicitous, rounded, finished efforts of a highly endowed and noble intellect that are a memory and a joy forever. As a composition, the effort

of Mr. Davis was very admirable. There was humor, there was
sarcasm, there was exquisite irony, there were flashes of wit,
there was an outburst of corosive scorn and indignation, that
were wonderfully artistic and effective. At times a felicity of
illustration would arrest your attention, and a great outburst
of high and ennobling eloquence would thrill you with the most
pleasurable emotions. The taste was exceedingly fine, and,
from beginning to end, the working of a highly cultivated,
refined, graceful, and elegant mind was manifest. There were
passages delivered with high dramatic art that would have
electrified any audience on earth. If that speech had been
delivered before an Athenian audience in the days of Pericles,
in Rome in the day when Cicero thundered forth his burning
and sonorous eloquence, or in Westminster Hall, with Burke
and Fox and Sheridan among the auditors, the speaker would
have received their loudest acclaims, and his fame would have
gone down the ages as one of those rarely gifted men who know
well how to use their native speech and to play with the touch
of a master on that grand instrument, the human heart.

"We could refer at length, if opportunity allowed, to the
scheme of his argument, to his magnificent peroration, in which
passion and imagination swept the audience and led them captive at the will of the magician; to the exquisitely apposite
illustrations, now quaint and humorous, and then delicate and
pathetic, drawn with admirable art from history and poetry and
the Sacred Truth—to these and other points we might refer.
But how can words, empty words, reproduce the glowing eloquence and entrancing power of the human voice when that
voice is one while soft as Apollo's lute, then resonant as the
blast of a bugle under the influence of deep passion? How can
human language bring back a forgotten strain or convey an
exact impression made by the tongue of fire when burdened
with a majestic eloquence?"

From time to time Mr. Davis delivered other addresses on
literary, historical, and political subjects. Especially notable
were those on the death of General Lee and of President Davis.

In the third volume of *Southern Literature,* Dr. Alphonso
Smith, a competent and severe critic, attributes to Mr. Davis
the rare power of the

> "Choice word and measured phrase above the reach
>   Of ordinary men."

"He brought," says Dr. Smith, "an interpretative imagination to bear upon every subject that he discussed; he visualized the scenes and vitalized the events he sought to portray. He had that rarest of gifts—the feeling for the right word in the right place. There was no strained after-effect, but his style was clear, strong, and flexible. He could be dignified without being heavy, and playful without being light." According him great ability as an orator, Dr. Smith adds: "His power over an audience did not rest merely on oratorical gifts, but rather upon the high moral, social, and civic ideals which he exemplified in his daily life."

No man was ever more revered in his community than Mr. Davis. He was regarded as the most illustrious son of the Cape Fear. When he died the Wilmington Chamber of Commerce prepared a memorial of his life and the Daughters of the Confederacy erected the monument to him that stands in the heart of the city. Though he declined the distinction offered him by Governor Vance in January, 1878, of being appointed to the office of Chief Justice, his memory was honored by the Supreme Court when, on the 19th of October, 1915, it accepted a portrait of him. The occasion of the presentation was notable, and Capt. S. A. Ashe delivered an eloquent and masterful address reviewing Mr. Davis' life and work.

Would that the youth of the rising generation who daily pass the bronze effigy of this foremost scholar and statesman of the Cape Fear knew more of one whose wisdom truly illustrated the principles of law and equity, whose eloquence commanded the admiration of his peers, who was beloved for his stainless integrity, and, shining in the "pure excellence of virtue and refinement," exemplified with dignity and simplicity, with gentle courtesy and Christian faith, the true heart of chivalry in Southern manhood. As we contemplate his lofty qualities, we can not repress the sigh of regret that such greatness is no more. The soaring thought, the brilliant imagination, the balanced judgment, the profound learning we do not expect to see every day, nor in every generation. The stainless honor, the broad patriotism, the noble disinterestedness of his public service are unhappily too little seen in our public men. But it is surely not too much to hope that the example of his blameless life will not be lost upon the people among whom he lived so long and so honorably. How well he exemplified in his own career the beautiful message which he brought in his early years to those just entering upon the duties of life:

"Rather be yours the generous ambition to shine only in the pure excellence of virtue and refinement. * * * Go forth, then, into the world and meet its trials and dangers, its duties and pleasures, with a firm integrity of heart and mind, looking ever onward and upward, and walking erect before the gaze of men, fearless, because without reproach. When the glad sunshine is upon you, rejoice and be happy. When the dark hours come, light them with a gentle patience and a Christian faith. "* * * This above all: 'To thine own self be true, and it must follow as the night the day, thou canst not then be false to any man.'"

THE GEORGE DAVIS MONUMENT.

By Mrs. William M. Parsley.

Several years after the death of the Hon. George Davis, the Cape Fear Chapter of the Daughters of the Confederacy conceived the idea of erecting a monument to the memory of this beloved statesman of the Cape Fear. It was not, however, until January, 1904, that the financial condition of the chapter enabled the members to make even a beginning in the cherished undertaking. At that time a small balance of $50 in the treasury was placed in bank to the credit of the George Davis Memorial Fund, and a committee of five ladies was appointed to take charge of the matter. The members of this committee were Mrs. William M. Parsley, chairman; Mrs. Martin S. Willard, president of the chapter, Mrs. James Carmichael, Mrs. Gabriel Holmes, and Miss Mary Calder. Later, the number of members was increased to ten, and Mrs. Jane D. DeRosset was elected chairman, with Mrs. John C. James, secretary.

The first action of the committee was to notify all chapters of the Daughters of the Confederacy and camps of Confederate Veterans throughout the State of the plan, inviting their coöperation and support; but these organizations were busy with their own local work, most of them with inadequate means, and, though expressing the heartiest approval, they were able to contribute but little.

The first voluntary contribution—a ten-dollar gold piece— was made by Mrs. Henry Rehder, who, though not a Daughter of the Confederacy, admired and revered Mr. Davis. Another lady made a contribution of $50—the proceeds from work by her own hands. The Wilmington Light Infantry gave a dramatic entertainment for the benefit of the fund and realized $90. The ever loyal and faithful George Davis Children's

Chapter sent several gifts of $10 each. But the fund grew slowly, and the committee, feeling its inability to cope with the matter, had almost decided to return the amounts subscribed and abandon the hope of erecting the monument. At this critical time, however, one of our leading business men, whose personal admiration for Mr. Davis gave him enthusiasm for the cause, subscribed $1,000 and persuaded a friend to contribute a like amount. Later, he raised the remainder of the $5,500 needed, and the committee was at once enabled to carry out its plans.

The design of the memorial is a portrait statue in bronze on a base of North Carolina granite, executed by Francis H. Packer, of New York City—a chaste, beautiful monument, with a wonderfully accurate likeness of Mr. Davis, standing with his face towards the Cape Fear River and reaching forward in a characteristic gesture of the right hand, while the left rests lightly upon the flag to which he was true to the end of his life.

On October 14, 1909, the cornerstone was laid with imposing ceremonies, Col. A. M. Waddell making the address; and on April 20, 1911, the monument was unveiled by four of Mr. Davis' grandsons—Robert Cowan Davis, Heiskell Gouverneur, George Rountree, and Donald MacRae, jr.

The address of Judge Henry G. Connor in presenting the monument to the city was heartily enjoyed by every one in attendance and was an able and brilliant review of the life of Mr. Davis, scintillating with touches of local history and memories that are ever dear to every patriotic Wilmingtonian. Following Judge Connor, the acceptance on behalf of Wilmington was by Mayor MacRae, who spoke in his characteristically happy, but brief manner, as follows:

Ladies and Gentlemen and United Daughters of the Confederacy: It is my duty for the mayor and aldermen, and for all that is best in Wilmington, to receive this monument. It commemorates the virtues of one of our own fellow-citizens who, through a long life as a great lawyer, never bowed the knee to Baal, never lowered the standard of Right, never stood for anything which his conscience did not approve, never permitted any motive of selfish gain or advancement to move him from his integrity. Though he has crossed over the river, he still survives in the best and broadest sense; for the life that he lived is an inspiration to all. The beauty of righteousness is still crimson in his cheeks and on his lips and Death's pale flag is not advanced there.

If there be any ambitious young men who feel disheartened and discouraged when they see mean men promoted and base actions applauded, let them take heart again and go forward with renewed courage. Behold this statue shall be a witness unto you, lest ye deny your God, and say, in your hearts, that crooked ways are good and bad methods justifiable.

We receive the statue with pride and shall count it among the city's most precious possessions.

ALFRED MOORE WADDELL—AUTHOR.

We feel grateful to the State press for many graceful tributes of respect to the memory of this dead statesman, jurist, scholar of the Cape Fear; but I think that these generous tokens of admiration have not sufficiently emphasized the beautiful expressions of his pen. Colonel Waddell's superior talents, his remarkable power of speech, his pleasing personality, and his courteous address were known to all men, but how few of our people know of his generous contributions to literature.

I have read and reread his three charming books, *A Colonial Officer and His Times, Some Memories of My Life,* and *The History of New Hanover County,* with ever-increasing pleasure and profit.

There are flashes of wit and humor throughout his *Memories,* and even Mark Twain at his best does not surpass him in his description of Haynes Gainey, the bleeding to death of James Dawson in the railroad accident, or the Confederate prisoner's estimate of the damage done to Fort Fisher by Butler's "powder ship"; nor have I read in Clarke Russell's wonderful sea tales anything comparable to Colonel Waddell's thrilling story *Pilots in a Storm.* Its descriptive, dramatic strength reminds one of Victor Hugo's weird "Story of the Gun"; but Colonel Waddell's story is true in all its details, as it tells of a tragedy in which five devoted Cape Fear pilots went down to death, and how five other toilers of the sea in the same gale were saved at the risk of a life freely volunteered for theirs, for the sake of their wives and children, and his hero, Joe Arnold, still survives.

The poetic principle is described in his closing reference to St. Philip's Church, and to Fort Anderson, which enclosed it, at Old Brunswick; and as we read the lines we can almost hear the sighing of the pines as they bend gently in the soft south wind to the call of the sea: "Since then it has again relapsed into its former state, and the bastions and traverses and parapets of the whilom Fort Anderson are now clad in the same exuberant robe of green with which generous nature in that clime covers every neglected spot. And so the old and the new ruin stand side by side, in mute attestation of the utter emptiness of all human ambition, while the Atlantic breeze sings gently amid the sighing pines, and the vines cling more closely to the old church wall, and the lizard basks himself where the sunlight falls on a forgotten grave."

In conclusion, his beautiful verses in reply to Gen. Albert Pike's "Every Year" appeal with peculiar tenderness to those of us who were in sympathy with our dear friend, and who are fast following his footsteps towards "The Better Land."

THE BETTER LAND.

By Alfred Moore Waddell.

"Time, fly he ne'er so fleetly
  Every year,
Only tunes your harp more sweetly
  Every year,
And we listen to its ringing,
And the minstrel swan-like singing,
More melodious numbers flinging,
  Every year.

"Sing on, O grand old master,
  Every year,
Pour thy mellow measures faster
  Every year;
They will make our journey lighter,
And our weary pathway brighter,
As our locks grow thin and whiter
  Every year.

"Yes, our loved ones go before us
  Every year,
And the living more ignore us
  Every year.
It is well; what need for sorrow
If the dawn of each tomorrow
Brighter tints from heaven borrow
  Every year."

BISHOP ROBERT STRANGE.

An eminent divine has said: "Among the great gifts that God has given *to* men is the gift *of* men; and among all the gifts with which God has enriched His Church, one of the greatest has been the gift of consecrated men, for they are the instrumentalities by which the Church has been moulded and guided and prospered in all the generations of the world."

As we contemplate the lofty qualities of many consecrated men of the past in Wilmington, whose chief end was to glorify God, whose self-sacrificing lives were devoted to the temporal and spiritual welfare of our people, we are moved to emotions of profound thankfulness that God has given us such Christ-like examples of His people who through faith and patience have inherited the promises. The honor roll is a long one, but their' record is on high, and the last is of one who was loved with more than fraternal affection by his devoted people.

Those of us who had known Robert Strange from his boyhood and had witnessed the generous impulses of his school life; who had later watched with affectionate interest the moulding of a character that was to shine in the reflected glory of the King in His beauty; whose life was to expand from the narrower to the widest. sphere of activity and usefulness, were proud of this prophet, who was not without honor in his own country, for we believed that he had seen the vision and as his Divine Exemplar's evangel would draw many men from worldliness to the better life. His gentle, genial, kindly nature, his exquisite courtesy of manner, his loving, sympathetic devotion to his people and indeed to all men, for he had an intense yearning for souls, were always manifest; but I think from the time of his great decision, when, like Samuel of old, he humbly responded to the call of Jehovah, the increasing beauty of his personal life was "the fruit of the Spirit—love, joy, peace, longsuffering, gentleness, goodness, faith, meekness, temperance." He was renewed in the image of God and was enabled more and more to die unto sin and to live unto righteousness.

His humanities were manifold and found expression in his constant solicitude for the health and happiness of the children of the city. Several times in the year he made an address to the pupils of the public schools, and he never went unprepared; there was a charm in what he said and in his manner of saying it that greatly pleased his eager listeners, and his appearance was always hailed with expressions of delighted appreciation. He gave much of his valuable time to various schemes for public playgrounds, and his patience and forbearance under repeated disappointments when his plans were almost accomplished are gratefully remembered by those who strove with him to obtain these benefits for the boys of Wilmington.

We were workers together in the Seamen's Friend Society of this port at a critical time in its history, when the forces of evil baffled the efforts of the few who were faithful in promoting the welfare of the toilers of the sea, and it was largely due to his sympathy and support in the earlier days of his ministry that this important service was brought to a higher degree of efficiency.

In many other ways he was devoted to the welfare of the people whom he loved so well, and his constantly increasing activities, linked with the larger responsibilities of his sacred office, gradually undermined a constitution which had been greatly overtaxed. His sudden illness, which from the beginning filled us with sad forebodings, seemed for a time to yield to medical treatment, but the joy this brought to many hearts was evanescent, for it soon became apparent to those who discerned a change that the frail tenement was closing up its windows, and putting out its fires; but as the outward man failed, the inward man was renewed day by day, until his gentle spirit took its flight to be forever with the Lord.

It may be said of him in the dying words of General Havelock, while his devoted son held him in his arms, "For forty years I have tried so to live as to meet death without dismay."

One of Bishop Strange's rare qualities was a cheerful countenance and an abiding spirit of cheerfulness. "He wist not that his face so shone." And even under the inevitable shadow of clouds and darkness which sometimes obscured the light, he was never dismayed. Nor did he ever protest under a sense of injustice or unfairness.

> "One single passion held his heart in sway;
>   An earnest craving for the pure and true.
> And though at times God's face felt far away
>   His earth-dimmed eyes so deeply yearned to view;
>
> "Still in the dark as in the light he smiled,
>   He said the sun was shining all the time;
> And for the things he could not understand
>   He hoped and trusted in a love sublime."

37

NORTH CAROLINA SOCIETY OF COLONIAL DAMES OF AMERICA.

By Rosa Pendleton Chiles.

"There be of them that have left a name behind them."

"For there are deeds that should not pass away, and names that must not wither."

"Did ever a man a valiant deed but a woman arose to sound his praises?"

"As the painter puts upon canvas the images and fancies of his imagination, making them real and tangible, so your society records upon bronze and stone the deeds of a brave people."

Organized in 1894 by the initiative and largely through the enthusiastic efforts of Mrs. George W. Kidder, the North Carolina Society of Colonial Dames of America, in its twenty-two years of patriotic life, has accomplished much of which not only the society but the State may be justly proud. And better than tangible achievement, has been the infusion into its membership and quietly through its membership, as well as by its public acts, into the life of the State an increasing love of the work for which the organization exists—to strengthen patriotism and to preserve in visible memorial and in the heart of an age whose sentiment is in danger of becoming dimmed by the intensity of its practical aims, deepened interest in that heroic past when the foundation of our country's greatness was laid upon a rockbed of lofty purpose and valiant deed.

So rich is North Carolina in colonial achievement, that the effort to perpetuate the memory of it, much of which lay buried in unidentified sites and in unpublished archives, has commanded the most persistent and strenuous activities of the Colonial Dames of this State. Especially has this been true of the Dames of the Cape Fear, where local traditions abound and historic memories are associated with nearly every point on the river.

The State membership is large—now more than five hundred—and among the leaders many have come from the Cape Fear. Not being able to mention all who have aligned themselves with the highest purposes of the organization and through masterful leadership carried those purposes to fulfillment, consideration in this brief account will be given only to the work of three ladies of the Cape Fear who have been presidents of the society—Mrs. George W. Kidder, Mrs. Gaston Meares, and Mrs. James Sprunt.

Mrs. Kidder, the first president, is a descendant of William Hill, whom Josiah Quincy visited at Brunswick in 1773 and found a man of exalted patriotism and warmly attached to the cause for which America was about to take up arms, and of his son, Capt. John Hill, a gallant and distinguished Continental officer of the Cape Fear. As was natural, therefore, she brought to the North Carolina Society of Colonial Dames of America, together with the lovely characteristics of Cape Fear womanhood, the devoted patriotism of her forefathers.

By her successful initiative, her high aims, and her unconquerable determination, Mrs. Kidder accomplished the important work of organization and of giving definite purpose to the labors of the society. In the start she emphasized the fact that the organization should not exist merely for the gratification of ancestral pride and the poetizing of patriotic sentiment, and under her incumbency one of the principal undertakings of the North Carolina Dames was begun—the erection of a monument to Cornelius Harnett and the civic and military heroes of the Revolution. The magnitude of this task was such that thirteen years were spent in its completion, but during this long period there was no lessening of steadfast purpose, no diminution of persistent effort.

Mrs. Kidder was succeeded in the presidency by Mrs. Gaston Meares, a descendant of Moses John DeRosset, mayor of Wilmington when the men of the Cape Fear successfully resisted the Stamp Act in 1766, and the widow of the lamented Col. Gaston Meares, who fell at Malvern Hill in 1862, while commanding the Third Regiment of North Carolina Troops—a woman whose talent and eminent position imparted strength to the society and energized its efforts. Mrs. Kidder says of her that she gave the work of the Monument Committee "fresh impetus, for she brought to it all the influence of a masterful mind and a strong personality." She also did much towards systematizing the work of the society throughout the State by the appointment of committees of research in the counties to coöperate with the head organization in Wilmington. In 1906 Mrs. Meares retired, and was succeeded by Mrs. James Sprunt, who for some time had been vice president.

Mrs. Sprunt was a descendant of the distinguished William Bryan and his wife, Lady Alice Needham, of colonial times, and of the Murchisons and other heroes of the Cape Fear. She was Luola Murchison, and throughout an honored Christian life sustained the virtues implied in her Indian name—"a true woman and good to look upon." From her earliest years she was trained in patriotism, and when only four and a half years old gathered in her grandfather's barn the grains of corn from which her heroic mother—the most beautiful woman in Cumberland County and a devoted patriot—made gruel for the sick and wounded soldiers when Sherman's army devastated her grandfather's plantation, leaving food neither for the family nor for the disabled Federals and Confederates whom they abandoned to their fate. She brought to the office of president an amplitude of mind, a strength of personality, a forceful energy, a voluntary activity, an unlimited perseverance, and a wealth of initiative that bore substantial and permanent fruit. During the first year of her administration the Monument Committee completed its work for the Harnett Memorial, and on May 2, 1907, the beautiful shaft was unveiled. The ceremonies upon this occasion were imposing, but the most interesting feature of the program was the presentation of the monument to the city of Wilmington in the eloquent sentences of Mrs. Kidder as the first monument ever erected in that city to the men of colonial times. Too much can not be said in praise of this laudable undertaking—costly in time and effort and money—and of the ladies who gave themselves so freely to its accomplishment. Of Mrs. Sprunt's part in carrying the work to completion, Mrs. Kidder has recently written:

"The memorial to the 'Men of the Cape Fear' would have had no existence but for the wonderful brain, energy, and foresight of Luola Murchison Sprunt. This idea which I suggested to the society as its specific work would have fallen to naught, languished, and died but for her zeal and untiring work for its completion. Through all her life she was my tower of strength, and without her I could have accomplished nothing. Her withdrawal from the presidency of the North Carolina Society of Colonial Dames on account of failing health, which office she filled with such signal ability, grace, and tact for six years, was a matter of deep concern to the society. She set a high standard for the emulation of the accomplished Dame who succeeded her, Mrs. E. P. Bailey, another admirable daughter of the Cape Fear." Mrs. Bailey's recent death is greatly deplored, but as president of the society she is ably succeeded by Mrs. Waddell, widow of Col. A. M. Waddell.

Mrs. Sprunt's last report as president of the society indicates the active work of the organization during her successful administration. The following account embraces a part only of that work. The report itself, in its clear and succinct presentment, attests the personal strength and ability of its author. After mentioning the Harnett Memorial, Mrs. Sprunt stated that the next undertakings were a contribution of the North Carolina Society to the fund to restore the old church at Jamestown, Virginia; the collecting of relics, including such valuable specimens as old deeds and records, personal heirlooms, rare old furniture, portraits and miniatures for the Jamestown Exposition, though these were not used, owing to the fact that the building intended to receive them was not completed in time; the preparation of an original program celebrating the three-hundredth anniversary of the first permanent English settlement in America, and the personal gift of these programs, which were very elaborate and compiled by prominent men of North Carolina, by Mrs. Sprunt to the State at large.

Following this work was the carrying out of a recommendation by the biennial council of 1906 to the State societies to bring to the next council a detailed report of historic spots not marked by other patriotic organizations. In this task Mrs. Sprunt brought to her assistance some of the ablest men in the State, and seventy-eight such spots belonging entirely to the colonial period were found. For this work, as well as for her report on it, the whole country is indebted to Mrs. Sprunt. The report was so complete and authoritative that it was published in the minutes of the National Society of Colonial Dames, and is now in use by the North Carolina Historical Society as data.

Then came the unveiling of a tablet at Russellborough, commemorating resistance to the Stamp Act by the Cape Fear patriots of 1766, the base of which was built of stones taken from the ruins of Tryon's palace.

The next effort was to mark the site of Fort Johnston, the first fort in the colony, built by act of the Assembly of 1748, completed in 1764, and destroyed by the patriots July 18, 1775, when the province of North Carolina forever laid aside the sceptre of royal rule. For authorization to mark this spot Mrs. Sprunt appealed to the United States Government through the Secretary of War, and, the appeal being granted, the tablet was erected in May, 1911.

In addition, a tablet to Col. Maurice Moore, founder of the

town of Brunswick in 1725, was placed in St. Philip's Church. This was the gift of two of Colonel Moore's descendants—Ida N. Moore and Selina M. Harvey. The Dames of the Cape Fear have devoted themselves in particular to the care and preservation of the ruins of this old church at Brunswick, the site and grounds of which were conveyed to the diocese of North Carolina by the owners of Orton, Col. K. M. Murchison and Capt. D. R. Murchison, and for some time Mrs. Sprunt assumed personal supervision of them. For many years it has been the custom of the Dames to make an annual pilgrimage to this hallowed spot, and there by addresses and religious services they have awakened, perchance, a deeper patriotism and a holier reverence for the past of which this church represents so large a part.

Perhaps the most important work undertaken at any time by the society was the movement to promote original research. At the biennial council in Washington in 1906, Mrs. Sprunt was appointed by the national president a member of the committee on this subject, and with ardent zeal entered upon the important task of promoting interest in the wealth of historical material for which the colonial period of North Carolina is especially noted, but much of which has not been compiled. To further this effort the society offers prizes for competitive essay work, exclusively from original sources and pertaining only to the colonial period of North Carolina, to the upper classmen of the State University at Chapel Hill. The results have been encouraging and the amounts of the prizes have been increased. Mrs. Sprunt's report on this subject is illuminating and valuable, and with her interesting report on old silver and her report on necrology, valued for its depth of spiritual perception and delicate beauty of thought, has, by order of the Board of Managers, been published by the society as literature.

The report on old silver, comprising a description of ecclesiastical silver in North Carolina prior to 1825, was considered of such value that Mrs. Sprunt was requested by the national chairman to read it at the biennial council in Washington. To her assistance in valuing these rare old specimens, Mrs. Sprunt brought the professional knowledge of an English expert, Mr. Jones, who came to North Carolina and examined the pieces in the different places in the State to which they belonged.

Space fails in enumerating the full activities of the Colonial Dames of North Carolina. What has been said pertains chiefly to the Cape Fear, but a brief word here and there has, I trust, indicated in a small way, at least, the work of the society in the State at large, and the assistance it renders, from time to time, to the society in other States, and to the national society.

The expense of these undertakings, especially of the Harnett Memorial, has been large, and to lighten the burden of it, Mrs. Sprunt, during her six years as president, entertained the Cape Fear Dames in their monthly meetings in her beautiful homes in Wilmington and at Orton, saving the rental of a hall for meetings. Her home in Wilmington, built for the first governor elected by the people and sheltering since so many distinguished guests, including President Taft, and, before his election, President Wilson, Secretary Bryan, and Cardinal Gibbons, and beautiful Orton, one of the finest provincial homes in America, in historic association as well as in beauty of adornment, were an inspiration to the work, while her gracious and lavish hospitality and the ardor of her enthusiasm made every effort more delightful. In reference to her resignation, the historian of the society, Elizabeth Stone Strange, widow of Bishop Strange, said:

"We are called upon to bear a heavy loss in the resignation of our beloved president. By her ability, her breadth of view, her untiring devotion to the cause, her gracious personality, and her generous hospitality, she has carried us onward and upward as a society and linked us to herself by the strongest ties of love and loyalty. While we deplore Mrs. Sprunt's resignation as our president, we can but show our appreciation of her by keeping ever before us her high standard of duty, fidelity, and patriotism."

This feeling was shared by all, and, as the recent letter of Mrs. Kidder, already quoted, indicates, the feeling of loss of her exceptional service in the office she filled so admirably constantly increases. Truly was it said of her, "Many daughters have done virtuously, but thou excellest them all."

PLACES OF HISTORIC INTEREST IN NORTH CAROLINA RELATING TO THE COLONIAL PERIOD WHICH ARE STILL UNMARKED.

In accordance with the resolution of the Council of 1906, in which each State society was asked to present, through the chairman of its delegation, a brief and concise statement of any localities still unmarked in the State which are of sufficient historic importance to come within the description of the objects of the society in Article 2 of the constitution, the dates to be strictly colonial, I have to report the following places of historic interest in North Carolina, relative to the colonial period which are still unmarked.

(Signed)   LUOLA MURCHISON SPRUNT,
President North Carolina Society
of Colonial Dames of America.

WILMINGTON, N. C., April 29, 1908.

EXPLORATION AND SETTLEMENT.

1. Landing place of Amadas and Barlowe, Ballast Point, Roanoke Island.

2. Memorial on Roanoke Island of the first Christian rites celebrated on American soil.

3. Memorial at Croatan of the lost colony.

4. Durant's Neck, at the junction of the Perquimans and Little Rivers, the first identified permanent settlement.

5. Site of Massachusetts settlement of 1660 on the Cape Fear River.

6. Crane Island, in the Cape Fear River, scene of the treaty with the Indian chief Wat Coosa in 1663.

7. Hilton River, named by the explorers from the Barbadoes in 1663.

8. Rocky Point, named by the explorers from the Barbadoes in 1663.

9. Site of Charlestown settlement on the Cape Fear River in 1665.

COLONIAL FORTS.

10. Fort Johnston,[1] at Southport, on the Cape Fear River.

11. Fort at Howe's Point, on the Cape Fear River.

12. Fort Dobbs, near Barbour Junction, in Rowan County.

13. Old Fort, McDowell County, built against the Catawba Indians.

14. Fort Reading, on the Pamlico River, near Bath.

15. Remains of the fort at Bath.

16. Fort Defiance, in Happy Valley, Caldwell County.

17. Nahucke Fort, near Snow Hill, in Greene County, a relic of the Tuscarora War.

18. Fort Barnwell, on the Neuse River, in Craven County, a relic of the Tuscarora War.

19. Scene[2] of the execution of John Lawson, on the Neuse River, in Craven County.

---

[1] Marked since the report was made.

[2] A monument to John Lawson has been erected in Goldsboro.

BATTLE GROUNDS.

20. Sugar Loaf, opposite Orton, on the Cape Fear River. Indians defeated by "King" Roger Moore.

21. Repulse of the Spanish at Beaufort in 1746.

22. Repulse of the Spanish at Brunswick in 1748.

CHURCHES AND SCHOOLS.

23. Memorial at Hertford of the first sermon preached in the colony. Preached by William Edmundson, a Quaker, at the residence of Henry Phillips, where Hertford now stands.

24. Memorial of the Episcopal Church at or near Edenton, the first church built in the colony.

25. St. Thomas' Church at Bath.

26. Bethabara Church, in Forsyth County, first Moravian settlement.

27. New Garden, early Quaker meeting house and school, in Guilford County.

28. Shiloh Church, begun by the first Baptist congregation in the colony, organized in Camden County.

29. St. John's, early Baptist Church, in Bertie County.

30. Quanky Church, near Halifax.

31. Site of school in New Bern. First incorporated academy in the colony.

32. Site of Queen's Museum, later Liberty Hall, in Charlotte.

THE REGULATION.

33. Sandy Creek, Randolph County, place of meeting and residence of Herman Husband.

34. Site of courthouse in Hillsboro where Regulator uprising occurred.

35. Place of execution of the Regulators after the Battle of Alamance, in Cameron grounds, at Hillsboro.

36. Phifer's Hill, Rowan County, where the "Black Boys" stopped the relief expedition.

COLONIAL HOUSES AND LOCALITIES OF NOTE.

37. Eden House, on Salmon Creek, opposite Edenton.

38. Tower Hill, now Snow Hill, Greene County, selected for location of colonial capital.

39. Site of Teach's residence at Bath.

40. Site[1] of Tryon's residence at Brunswick.
41. Tryon's residence at Wilmington.
42. Tryon's usual residence at Hillsboro.
43. Site of Tryon's Palace at New Bern.
44. Site of Green House, in Edenton, where the "Tea Party" occurred.
45. Old Government House at Bath.
46. House used for the meeting of the Assembly at Edenton.
47. The old tavern at Hertford.
48. Site of old courthouse in Charlotte.
49. Probable place of meeting of the first Assembly, on White Plantation, in Perquimans County.
50. Spratt's, near Charlotte, where the first court in Mecklenburg was held.
51. Point where Sam Swann came out of the Dismal Swamp.
52. Quaker Meadows, Burke County, McDowell home.
53. Swan Ponds, Burke County, Avery home.
54. Orton, on the Cape Fear River.
55. Kendal, on the Cape Fear River.
56. Lilliput, on the Cape Fear River.
57. Hayes, at Edenton.
58. The Grove, Halifax County, the Jones home.
59. Sedgeley Abbey, on the Cape Fear River.
60. Site of Buncombe Hall, Tyrrell County.
61. Hilton Park, in New Hanover County, residence of Cornelius Harnett.

BURIAL PLACES.

62. Hugh McAden, famous Presbyterian minister, at Red Horse Creek Church, in Caswell County.
63. Alexander Craighead, famous Presbyterian minister, in Sugar Creek Cemetery, Mecklenburg County.
64. Gov. Arthur Dobbs, on his plantation, on Town Creek.
65. Gov. Thomas Pollock, at Edenton.
66. Chief Justice Eleazar Allen, at Lilliput.
67. "King" Roger Moore, at Orton.
68. Abner Nash, at Pembroke, opposite New Bern.
69. Edward Moseley. (To be located.)
70. Hugh Waddell, at Castle Haynes.
71. John Baptista Ashe, at Grovely, the Bellamy place, near Wilmington.

---

[1]Marked since the report was made.

72. Gen. John Ashe, on Colonel Sampson's plantation, near Clinton.

73. Sam Swann, at Swann Point, opposite Castle Haynes.

74. John Swann, at Swann Point, opposite Castle Haynes.

75. Original resting place of William Hooper, at Hillsboro.

76. Richard Caswell, in Lenoir County.

77. Thomas Burke, at Tyaquin, near Hillsboro.

78. Col Maurice Moore, at Rocky Point. (To be located.)

LUOLA MURCHISON SPRUNT—AN APPRECIATION.

"Death is a translation into life."

"Those we call dead
Are breathers of an ampler day
For ever nobler ends."

"All the gifts that were in her, penetrated as they were by spiritual significance, told of immortality. Such a presence as hers, erect and prophetic, was itself a pledge that its life can not be spilt as water."

Once in a far distant time God's messengers to man came in glistening white, and with the majesty of angelic function delivered to those privileged to receive them the commands of the great I Am. Radiant moment! Marvelous privilege! Wonderful experience! this talking face to face with one of the heavenly host, but contact no more vital than is granted many now who live day by day and year by year in close association with spirits as truly messengers of God as the white-winged multitude. Human are they, as we, and yet dwelling on sublimated heights; our companions and intimates, and yet exalted above the incompleteness and the emptiness that mar the fast fleeting days with most of us. Such was Luola Murchison Sprunt. Hers was a life sent from God. If to any this seems a statement borrowed too nearly from the Sacred Word, let them consider for a moment the fruits of her life so in harmony with the requirements of the Sacred Word. Now that the Lord, whose she was and whom she served, has called her to higher tasks, the results of her labors on earth are finding more fully the acknowledgment she endeavored while living to suppress. Here a letter from a factory superintendent, voicing the gratitude of himself and his employes for her education and care of the factory children; here a memorial service in China expressing the deep sense of loss in one whose arm of usefulness stretched in power across the seas to uplift and train the heathen; here letters from patriotic societies acknowledging her exceptional service in furthering their aims and in administering their affairs; here letters from church and charitable organizations telling of the enlargement given their efforts by her personal labors and liberality; here messages from an innumerable company whom she housed, clothed and fed, comforted and gave new hope. The intimate testimony of her friends and acknowledgments from an extended acquaintance, from the highest to the lowliest, all are redolent with fragrant memories of her queenly bearing, her gracious personality, her deep spiritual discernment, her marvelous and fruitful service. Her activities were too numerous to be recorded, for hers was a life that "translated truth into conduct," and she constantly, though unconsciously, measured her life by the service she was able to render others. Treading this royal pathway, she ever traveled heavenward along the way her Saviour trod, and now that she has come to the end of that glorious way and the great white portals have opened to admit her to the presence of her Lord, marvelous will be the tasks He has reserved for a spirit so harmoniously related to heavenly requirements while on earth, and so intimately and richly prepared for more exalted labors in heaven. Sent from God and returned to God; but the memory of the sweetness and strength of her life, the beauty and depths of her character, the great scope and marvelous fertility of her service she has left as a gift in perpetuity to earth, and these shall bear fruit while time shall last. Not only the life but the labors and the influence of the saints are immortal.

SAMUEL A'COURT ASHE.
ROSA PENDLETON CHILES.

THE BOYS' BRIGADE.

"How far that little candle throws its beams."

Company A, First N. C. Regiment, U. B. B. A., the first company of the Boys' Brigade in North Carolina, and doubtless the first in the South, was organized at Wilmington on February 14, 1896, by Col. Walker Taylor, then commanding the Second Regiment of North Carolina State Troops. This company was organized in the basement of Immanuel Presbyterian Church, a mission church located in the southern part of the city, and subsequently Companies B and C were formed to provide for the training of boys between the ages of ten and seventeen. The present membership totals one hundred and thirty.

The home now occupied by the brigade is an armory given as a memorial to a deceased friend of the organization, Capt. William Rand Kenan, and the structure is an ornament to that section of the city. The building is thoroughly equipped for the work, and the organization provides most effective means for physical, mental, moral, and religious training.

For eight years the home of the brigade was in the small basement room of the church, with the streets as drill grounds; and here weekly meetings were held every Monday night and short helpful addresses made by the commander. The rule, most faithfully kept, required the presence of every member, unless unavoidably prevented, and the commander set the standard, which has been lived up to in a most remarkable degree by even the youngest members. From the first the commander took the boys into his confidence, laid his plans before them, expressed his deep interest in their welfare and his abiding faith in their possibilities; and from this humble beginning has grown a force for moral uplift than which nothing greater has ever occurred in the life of the community. The organization is on a strictly non-denominational basis; church membership is not a condition precedent to membership in the brigade, but attendance on Sunday-school is a condition rigidly exacted. Of its membership fully eighty per cent are communicant members of some church, and the light that has gone out from the organization has penetrated into many forbidding corners, and brought hope and courage to many to whom the best prospects in life had been denied. The commander is a leader among men, and doubtless his experience as a military man suggested this form of organization for the development of young men in whom he saw latent possibilities but to whom the fortune of position had not offered equal opportunity for success and advancement. So thoroughly grounded has been the work among these boys, that membership in the organization is a passport to public confidence. In a most pronounced degree has there been developed among them a spirit of loyalty, self-respect, ambition, industry, sobriety, and propriety. To be a member of the brigade imposes a duty, as it offers an opportunity, and the sense of obligation following upon privilege is deeply ingrained into the spirit of the organization.

An account of the Boys' Brigade has been prepared by Rev. Dr. Wells, as follows:

"In connection with the work done by the First Presbyterian Church at Immanuel Church, in the southern part of the city, there has been established one of the most useful institutions in Wilmington. This is the Boys' Brigade, now quartered at the southeast corner of Second and Church Streets.

"On the evening of February 14, 1896, Col. Walker Taylor, then the commander of the Second Regiment of North Carolina State Troops, and an active worker in the Immanuel Presbyterian Sunday-school, met with fifteen boys and organized the first company of the Boys' Brigade in the South. In the charter granted, Col. Walker Taylor was commissioned as captain, E. P. Dudley as first lieutenant, and J. J. Loughlin as second lieutenant of the new company. While growing out of Immanuel Church and connected with it, the work in its scope and influence has been largely undenominational. Every member has been required to attend a Sunday-school. The brigade has been a blessing to every church in our city, and in return has received the cordial support and sympathy of them all.

"For eight years the brigade continued to meet in one of the rooms connected with Immanuel Church. Then in 1904 a splendid armory for the organization was erected by Mrs. Henry M. Flagler as a memorial to her father, Capt. William Rand Kenan, an elder in the First Presbyterian Church, who had been a sympathetic friend and wise counselor of the organization. The building is of concrete, colored to represent gray sandstone. The style is Norman, and the building, sixty by one hundred feet in size and four stories in height, is a very massive and handsome structure. It is complete in every detail, with large gymnasium, ample dressing-rooms and bathrooms, library and reception rooms, offices, large auditorium, dining-room, kitchen and pantry, bowling alleys, and rooms for guns and equipment. The armory was completed in 1905, and was dedicated to the glory of God and opened for the use of the organization on June 22 of that year. On that occasion the principal address was delivered by Hon. R. B. Glenn, then governor of North Carolina.

"A complete and useful library of two thousand volumes was shortly after presented to the brigade by Mr. James Sprunt; and this, with an ample supply of current papers and magazines, has served to make the library of the brigade an attractive and helpful feature of the work.

"In September, 1905, a second company, B, was organized, and in 1911 a third company, C. These companies, while enjoying the training and privileges of the organization, are at the same time 'feeders' from which members pass into the senior company. The brigade now numbers one hundred and thirty members. Mr. Charles Dushan is the efficient secretary and physical director.

"Bible classes, weekly addresses by prominent business and professional men, an annual ten-day encampment, athletic games and contests of all kinds, and a helpful and instructive winter lyceum course are all employed for the instruction and amusement of the members.

"A notable constructive work has been done by the brigade in the community. The little room and the wooden guns have developed into the magnificent building and the complete equipment. The little working boys have developed into some of our city's most valued business leaders and professional men. The whole tone of that part of the city has been lifted, and the community is vastly better for the work done there. And this has been the work of one man—Col. Walker Taylor. The friend and trusted helper of the boys when they were lads, he has continued to be their adviser and confidential friend in their moral, religious, civic, and business life. He has made weekly talks that have been of the greatest influence in moulding their characters. He has taught them in his Sunday-school class with vigor and power. He has visited them in their homes and places of business. His office door has always been open for them to tell him their troubles or joys or to seek his advice upon their problems. And all the while he has been stamping the influence of his strong Christian character upon their plastic lives. He has builded well, not only in concrete but also in character."

PUBLIC BUILDINGS IN WILMINGTON.

By W. B. McKoy.

The first public building erected in the town of Wilmington was situated at the intersection of Market and Front Streets. It was built by private contribution, and was called the Town House. Under the act incorporating the town, 1739, this building became the county courthouse. I have been informed that it was a brick building, with an open area below paved with brick, and with open archways approached from each street; on the second floor was one large hall, with slate roof. The building was of oval shape and is said to have resembled somewhat in appearance the old market house which still stands in the streets of Fayetteville. Here town meetings, the Superior Courts, and the General Assembly of the province were held when they met in the town.

There was no town bell for some time, and a drum was used to assemble people to all meetings. In 1751 a bell was procured, and Mrs. Clay was in the employ of the town for over ten years, to sweep the courthouse above and below, to keep the windows shut, and to ring the bell on necessary occasions.

In 1790 the building was in bad condition, and its situation in the street endangering the spread of fire across the street, an act was passed requiring that it should be rebuilt, on the same spot, of brick as before, of the same size, shape, and dimensions, and that it was to be used for no other purpose than a courthouse.

In 1840 this building was greatly damaged by fire, and the public records were damaged by water, so that in 1845 they all had to be copied. Many of the deeds and papers were utterly lost at the time, as blank pages of the records now testify.

The next courthouse was built on what was then called the new jail lot, on the north side of Princess Street, between Second and Third Streets. To the west of this new building stood the "stocks and whipping post," in open view from the street, and they remained there till removed after our late War between the States, an offensive mark of the barbarity of the times to our now squeamish inhabitants, but no honest man had fear of them.

More recently a new courthouse was built on Third Street, between Princess and Market.

The first jail stood where the McRary house now stands, and the old basement walls of that building are said to be a part of that structure, which gave reason for the local gossip that under that house are dungeons. It is now the most historic building in the city, having been the headquarters of Lord Cornwallis and Major Craig during the Revolution. The old DeRosset house opposite, on Market Street, with its quaint chimney stacks, is also a very old building, and this was the Confederate headquarters in our late War between the States.

A new jail was built in the forties, at the northeast corner of

Second and Princess Streets. This building still stands, but is hardly recognized under its new dress and modern tasteful exterior; should one ever probe its massive stone walls, however, he will find that the heart of the old edifice still stands there. I recall as a small child its massive doors, its cells, and the heavy gratings at the openings and at the steps on each floor, the heavy trap-doors on a level with the floor, the timbers and boards thick and heavy. In my mind I pictured it as resembling the keep of some ancient castle or fortress.

About 1850, a new jail was built on Princess Street, between Third and Fourth.

The market house where meat was sold (not the fishmarket, for that, known as "Mud Market," was at Second and Market, along Jacob's Run, then a considerable stream, where the fish boats came up) stood in the middle of Market Street, halfway between the courthouse and the river. This was a long, one-story brick building, standing there in 1766. The lower end, towards the river, was rented out by the town as a store, and was once occupied by DeRosset & Brown. It was from the roof of this building that the people of Wilmington, after taking the stamp master forcibly from Governor Tryon's residence, on the south side of Market Street, immediately opposite the market, placed a rope around his neck and threatened to publicly hang him if he did not then and there swear not to distribute the stamps, and publicly to resign his office before the face of royal authority.[1] This building was taken down when the courthouse was removed, and replaced by a long shed in the middle of Market Street extending from Front Street towards the river, supported by iron pillars and open on all sides. It was paved with brick and fitted with wooden meat stalls and timber sawed into chopping blocks. At the upper end was a stairway leading to a bell tower. Before the war the bell in this tower was rung at nine o'clock, one o'clock, and seven o'clock; and it rang the nine o'clock curfew, which required all slaves without a pass to leave the street.

Another public institution was at Market Dock, the ancient ducking-stool, a chair attached to a long piece of timber which could be swung around quite easily on a pivot and ducked into the river, a now forgotten instrument of authority, where the scolds of the town had their morals regulated.

---

[1]This tradition does not seem to be in accord with contemporaneous publications.

38

There was but one more building that I can recall belonging to the public. The Innes Academy, later known as the Old Academy Building, was a great brick structure, the first floor of which was used as a theatre and the second as a schoolroom. In the latter, Ghost Elliott, a famous teacher in the early days, at one time taught. It was in this building that the comedian Joseph Jefferson partially laid the foundation of his distinguished career as an actor.

THE NEW CUSTOM HOUSE.

The first government building in Wilmington, the custom house, was built in 1846. It contained the post office, the room used by the Federal Court, and the offices of the collector. In 1891 a new post-office building was erected. Now a new custom house is being built.

In the year 1902 a bill was introduced in Congress to make New Bern the principal port of North Carolina and Wilmington subsidiary thereto. Whatever may have been the purpose of this action, it was followed by an immediate revival of the commerce of Wilmington as the chief port of North Carolina. One of the arguments in favor of New Bern was the fact that the Wilmington Custom House was not paying the cost to the government of its expenses, the salary of the collector, Mr. B. F. Keith, being then $1,000, with commissions increasing it to $1,400 or $1,500. Now the salary is $2,500, and a balance over and above all expenses has been returned to the Treasury Department for several years.

In 1903, the aggregate receipts of the Wilmington Custom House were $4,760, the value of exports $14,966,754 and the imports were $290,822. The cost to the government to collect $1.00 was $1.41. In the year 1913 the aggregate receipts were $24,934, the value of exports $19,510,926, and the imports were $3,460,419. The cost to the government to collect $1.00 was $0.26.

From the above it appears that the receipts of the port of Wilmington increased 423 per cent, the value of exports increased 30 per cent, and the value of imports, 1,089 per cent within ten years.

The following official table illustrates in a condensed form the commerce of the port of Wilmington during the years from

1899 to 1915 inclusive.   It will be observed that the European
War greatly reduced the volume of trade in the port year of
1915.

Fiscal Year, June 30	Vessels Entered, Foreign	Vessels Entered, Coastwise	Vessels Cleared, Foreign	Vessels Cleared, Coastwise	Entries, Merchandise	Total Receipts	Value Exports	Cost to Collect $1.00	Number Employees	Value Imports
1899	69	92	107	65	33	$ 11,093	$ 7,586,526	$ .631	4	$ 158,887
1900	69	85	108	65	31	8,846	10,975,511	.754	4	109,614
1901	71	88	102	70	35	9,053	12,013,659	.773	4	131,475
1902	56	83	88	78	43	7,835	11,102,171	.893	4	258,358
1903	38	101	80	71	23	4,760	14,966,754	1.412	5	290,822
1904	37	95	73	71	27	8,933	19,085,221	.718	5	264,550
1905	30	96	64	78	23	4,598	17,481,566	1.416	5	415,295
1906	33	96	60	78	47	9,588	18,466,929	.663	5	381,890
1907	29	107	53	79	61	22,581	18,566,468	.304	4	805,203
1908	36	88	64	78	63	22,686	30,291,681	.299	4	878,952
1909	27	66	52	71	84	33,093	20,479,726	.227	4	1,228,945
1910	42	60	39	100	113	32,684	20,922,398	.208	4	2,355,253
1911	47	65	45	96	156	43,639	28,804,785	.169	4	3,205,407
1912	54	75	55	90	161	41,272	28,705,418	.172	4	3,159,043
1913	63	39	32	96	154	24,934	19,510,926	.25	4	3,460,419
1914	52	75	35	92	231	28,844	25,870,850	.252	4	4,174,745
1915	47	90	30	109	152	18,786	11,308,535	.39	4	1,990,755

The collector of the port during nearly all of that time was
Mr. B. F. Keith, who has recently resigned, and his successor,
Col. Walker Taylor, appointed by President Wilson, has assumed charge.   A good account will be given of him, for he is
one of our foremost men in a progressive age.   Of the former
incumbent there is much to be said, particularly with respect
to his sagacity and industry in carrying to a successful issue his
scheme, supported by our commercial people, for a new Federal building and extensive grounds in keeping with the dignity
of the port of Wilmington.

Collector Keith first persuaded the Secretary of the Treasury
to purchase the adjacent property, from the present custom
house building to Princess Street up to Wright's Alley.   He
then showed him a sketch which indicated the ground purchased
surrounded by dilapidated buildings, detracting from the value
of the location.   This led the Secretary to send several special
agents to Wilmington, and they reported favorably upon the
collector's suggestion that the government purchase all of the

property from Princess Street to Market Street, from Wright's Alley back to the river wharf, including a portion of the wharf owned by the Kuck and the Calder estates, which gives us one of the most desirable plots for a new custom house at the very small cost of $69,000, the present value of which is estimated at more than double that sum.

When this ground was bought the appropriation for the purchase and for a new building was $300,000. To secure this amount Collector Keith had made persistent effort, supported by the congressmen and senators from the State. Representative H. L. Godwin, of the district in which Wilmington is situated, and Representative Charles R. Thomas, of the Third Congressional District, were particularly helpful, Mr. Thomas, as a member of the House Committee on Public Buildings and Grounds and of the sub-committee having in charge all authorizations for public buildings in North Carolina, being able to write into the section of the bill which finally became a law the item for the Wilmington Custom House and to push the matter in the full committee. To him is very largely due the credit for securing the initial appropriation of $300,000. The amount remaining after the purchase of a site, however, was entirely inadequate for a building and the plans for one were withheld until appeal could be made to Congress for an additional appropriation. At a hearing before the House Committee on Public Buildings and Grounds, December 13, 1912, Representative Godwin, Collector Keith, and Mr. Joseph W. Little, of Wilmington, testified to the need of an additional amount, and the supervising architect of the Treasury, Mr. Wenderoth, who was present, named the amount required. Mr. Keith gave a graphic description of the old building, held together by iron rods to keep it from falling down, and of the lack of facilities for handling the business of the port, which he stated had probably increased more than that of any other port of the Atlantic coast. His remarks included the very pertinent statement that many business firms wanted to come to Wilmington to make it a distributing point, but were unable on account of inadequate facilities. Some difficulty was experienced later in securing the desired amount, but the collector and others kept up their untiring efforts, and eventually, on March 4, 1913, the law was passed which raised the appropriation for the Wilmington Custom House to $600,000.

In retiring to private life with clean hands Mr. Keith is

entitled to the commendation of well done by an appreciative public.

The contracts for the erection of the new custom house were awarded April 15, 1916, the building to cost $368,400 and the mechanical equipment, $37,746. These contracts call for completion within twenty-two months from April 15, 1916. The Secretary of the Treasury states that the plans call for one of the most complete buildings that he has ever had the pleasure of approving, and it is stated by the supervising architect that the room to be used by the United States Court will be one of the handsomest in the entire country; so that Wilmington may justly be proud of the building when completed.

James Walker Memorial Hospital.

By Dr. Robert B. Slocum.

James Walker, stonemason, contractor, and builder, was born at Douglas, Lenarkshire, Scotland, April 29, 1826. He came to this country when twenty years of age and settled in Washington, where he was engaged with his brother, aged 22, upon one of the wings of the Capitol building, later, upon the old Smithsonian building and other important public structures. The two brothers erected several public buildings in Petersburg and other cities of the South, where they were engaged prior to the outbreak of the War between the States.

In 1857 James Walker was sent from Washington to erect the United States Marine Hospital, which is still a prominent building in Wilmington, after which he made his home here, and during the war was engaged in erecting salt works on the sounds near Wilmington, there being a great scarcity of this necessary commodity in consequence of the Federal Blockade of all the Southern ports.

He became a useful citizen, and was regarded as a quiet, wise, and capable master builder. He erected the First Presbyterian Church, the D. R. Murchison residence, on Third Street, and many other notable buildings in Wilmington, and was engaged for nearly ten years upon that model State institution for the insane at Morganton.

A year or two before his death, March 15, 1901, he conferred with his physician, Dr. W. J. H. Bellamy, and with other friends in reference to his desire to establish a public park as a gift to the city of Wilmington, but he was induced to supply a still greater local need, that of a public hospital. The erection of this building employed his waning powers until it was nearly finished, and when the summons for his departure came, he entrusted its completion to his two friends, James Sprunt and William Gilchrist. It was accomplished mainly through the wise management of Mr. Gilchrist, who gave it his unceasing attention to the end. The *Wilmington Star* alluded to the simple transfer of the property known as the James Walker Memorial Hospital as follows:

"The formal transfer to the city and county of the James Walker Memorial Hospital took place yesterday morning at 10 o'clock on the grounds of the new building, on Dickinson and Rankin Streets.

"The exercises attendant upon the transfer were not of an elaborate or public nature, in conformity to the wish of the donor, expressed shortly before his death, but there were assembled at the hospital Mayor A. M. Waddell, members of the City Council, county commissioners, President Elliott and members of the new James Walker Memorial Hospital Board, and Messrs. James Sprunt and William Gilchrist, executors of the estate of the late Mr. Walker, to whom the municipality and county are indebted so much for the munificent gift.

"After an informal inspection of the grounds and building, the party gathered on the front veranda of the hospital and was called to order. Mr. James Sprunt, representing the executors, then made the speech of presentation as follows, paying an eloquent and deserved tribute to the deceased philanthropist, whom he represented.

" '*Mr. Mayor and Aldermen, Mr. Chairman and Commissioners:*

" 'The devisor of this fine property, bequeathed to our city and county for the noble purpose of relieving suffering humanity, was a man of humility and reserve. With characteristic diffidence he laid the cornerstone without the usual ceremonies, and it was his expressed wish that the necessary formalities in the transfer of the completed hospital be free from ostentation. We, his executors, therefore, in simplicity tender you the keys of the James Walker Memorial Hospital, with a grateful sense of the trust which he reposed in us, and with the hope that it may long serve the humane object of its generous donor.'

"Mr. William Gilchrist then formally handed the keys of the

building to Mayor Waddell, who responded very briefly and read the deed making the legal transfer.

"Mr. Elliott next responded with a speech in behalf of the Board of Managers which was highly fitting the occasion and characteristic of the speaker."

From the date of its opening to the present time this laudable benefaction has increased in importance until its benign influence under its wise and beneficent directors has extended with our increasing population to a degree not dreamed of by its original founder.

The James Walker Memorial Hospital is governed by a Board of Managers composed of nine men. The institution is intended for the treatment of acute disorders, not chronic and incurable diseases. It is necessary to draw the line between a hospital, on the one hand, and such eleemosynary institutions as the county home, on the other, as Mr. Walker's intention was to care for persons receiving the benefits of the former and not of the latter.

Both pay patients and charity cases are admitted. Any regular physician residing in New Hanover County may take a pay case to the hospital and treat it. The hospital charges are from $7 per week in the wards to $35 for private rooms (the rooms vary from $17.50 to $35). The resident physician and three internes act as assistants in these cases. Charity cases are admitted upon permit from the county superintendent of health, who must be sure that the patient is a resident of New Hanover County, in indigent circumstances, not afflicted with a chronic or incurable disease nor with an infectious disease. The treatment of all charity cases is in the hands of the resident physician, with the assistance of the internes, and the hospital is under the control of the resident physician. In 1914 the city and county appropriated for the maintenance of the hospital $15,249.99, and this year they will each appropriate $10,000. The receipts from pay cases in 1914 were $17,438.97.

For the year 1914 there were admitted 1,407 patients, 767 white and 640 colored, 772 pay cases and 635 charity cases. There were 19,409 days' treatment, 7,137 being for pay cases and 12,272 for charity cases. The average number of patients in the hospital for any day of the year was fifty-three. The institution can accommodate about eighty patients if they are properly apportioned as to color and sex.

The hospital is composed of three brick structures, the principal one being used for white patients and as an administration building. The kitchen and laundry plants are in the basement of this building. The building for colored patients, which cost $10,000, was given by Mr. W. H. Sprunt. The first floor is used for patients and the second for a nurses' home. There are twenty-eight nurses in training, with a superintendent of nurses and one assistant. The course of training is three years. The building for infectious diseases was given by Mr. Sam Bear, jr., as a memorial to his brother. While it is not the intention of the hospital to receive such cases, they get in sometimes and have to be cared for.

Recently the breadth of its service has been enlarged beyond the most hopeful expectations of the management by a generous benefaction of Mr. and Mrs. James Sprunt, augmented by a trust fund left for this specific purpose by the late Edward Payson George, who propose to build as a memorial to Mr. and Mrs. Sprunt's only daughter, Marion, an annex to the James Walker Memorial Hospital which shall be devoted to the treatment of white women and children. The quality and scope of this loving service to the community command not only the deepest gratitude of the hospital and of those who may share directly in its benefits, but of the medical profession and of the public. The following letter explains the nature and high purpose of this proposed enlargement.

                                                    November 11, 1915.
SAMUEL BEAR, ESQ.,
    President James Walker Memorial Hospital.

DEAR MR. BEAR:—In August of the year 1901, I visited with my family a so-called health resort where we were assigned apartments which we ascertained too late were infected by recent cases of scarlet fever, against the recurrence of which no precautions had been taken for the protection of subsequent occupants. Our only daughter, Marion, aged thirteen years, almost immediately fell a victim to this criminal neglect and died after a very brief illness.

For many years since then my wife and I have desired in testimony of our faith in a covenant-keeping God and in loving sympathy with His suffering children, to erect in His name and as a memorial of our lamented daughter a hospital for the care of maternity cases and sick children, where their suffering might be alleviated or overcome by the employment of modern scientific appliances and expert medical treatment; and while our desire has been primarily the relief of suffering, it was also hoped that the whole community might be benefited by affording our local practitioners the opportunity of studying cases, which can only be properly done in a well-regulated hospital, for, after all, a good hospital is in the highest sense an educational institution of the first order. As Dr. Osler truly says in one of his addresses, "It makes of the hospital a college in which . . . . the students learn for themselves under skilled direction the phenomena of disease. It is the true method, because it is the natural one, the only one by which the physician grows in clinical wisdom after he begins practice for himself." And in another lecture by the same distinguished authority I read years ago: "I wish to plead particularly for the wasted opportunities in the smaller hospitals of our large cities, and in those of more moderate size. There are in this State a score or more of hospitals with from thirty to fifty medical beds offering splendid material for good men on which to build reputations."

From time to time we have by costly experiments attempted to find a way for the fulfillment of our desire, and as you know we have also made overtures to your board to that end, but the lack of your means for its support at the time in conjunction with your general hospital work has been the chief obstacle.

Believing that the development of your splendid charity will now admit of its greater extension along the lines of our endeavor, we propose to erect as an annex to the James Walker Memorial Hospital a modern hospital for maternity and children's cases for both pay and charity patients, to cost between $25,000 and $30,000, completely furnished, in line with the appliances of the best equipped institutions of the United States and with the advice of competent medical and surgical authorities.

The institution is to be a part of your general hospital, supported and maintained under its rules and regulations modified to meet the purposes already defined, to be free from any and all political influence or control, and dedicated and restricted to the benefit of white women and children.

More than one-third of the sum which we propose to expend in this cause has been left to James Sprunt and William H. Sprunt, in trust for this specific purpose, by our daughter's devoted friend, the late Edward Payson George, formerly of Wilmington. The remainder will be paid by James Sprunt and his wife, Luola Murchison Sprunt, and the annex is to be designated and known as the "Marion Sprunt Memorial."

My brother-in-law, Mr. Kenneth M. Murchison, an eminent architect of New York, who drew the original plans, has kindly offered to contribute his time and talents in this cause, and I respectfully request that you will convene a meeting of your Board of Managers at your earliest convenience to discuss this matter with him and with us and inspect the plans and specifications provided for your approval.

Very truly yours,   JAMES SPRUNT.

The Board of Managers responded to this generous offer by the following resolutions expressing fitting and grateful acknowledgment:

Resolved, That this board accept with grateful thanks the offer of Mr. James Sprunt and Mrs. Sprunt to erect, equip, and furnish complete an annex to the hospital building of this hospital to be devoted to the care and treatment of children and maternity cases and to be known as the "Marion Sprunt Memorial."

Resolved, further, That this board express to Mr. and Mrs. Sprunt a keen and sincere appreciation of the generous spirit and Christian purpose which has actuated them in making this gift to the James Walker Memorial Hospital, and through that means to suffering women and children of this community, and that this board further express to Mr. and Mrs. Sprunt its purpose and determination to do all within its power, both now and hereafter, to see to it that the management and administration of the "Marion Sprunt Memorial" shall be such as will in fullest measure accomplish the high purpose for which the gift is made.

Resolved, further, That we honor the memory of the late Edward Payson George, who, before his untimely death, cherished a warm affection for his old home in Wilmington and gave it expression in his deed of trust to James Sprunt and William H. Sprunt of a gift of money which, with its increment to the first of January, 1915, was to be joined with a greater sum from James Sprunt and Luola M. Sprunt, his wife, in the cost of the erection and equipment of a children's hospital as a memorial of his friend, Marion Sprunt, and in testimony of his love for the people of Wilmington.

Resolved, further, That a copy of this resolution of thanks be furnished to Mr. and Mrs. James Sprunt.

This extension will without doubt make of the James Walker Memorial Hospital one of the best equipped institutions of its kind in the South.

Since the reception of this generous donation the death of Mrs. Sprunt has occurred, and more recently that of Mr. Sam Bear, jr., who was associated with the hospital from its organization to the end of his life. After speaking very beautifully of his life and character and his great usefulness as a citizen, the Board of Managers adopted the following resolution in acknowledgment of Mr. Bear's service to the hospital:

Samuel Bear, president of the Board of Managers of the James Walker Memorial Hospital, departed this life in the sixty-third year of his age, on March 3, 1916, at his residence in the city of Wilmington. Since the organization of this hospital, he has been its friend in act and in deed. He was a member of the original Board of Managers, and during the years that have followed, gave himself unreservedly to its service. His interest was vital, and had its origin in a heart that loved his fellow-man and in a genuine desire to lend a helping hand to suffering humanity.

He gave of his time, of his thought, and of his means cheerfully and unsparingly, without ostentation and without desire for praise or approval. He was elected president of this board on October 8, 1912, and served ably and efficiently in that capacity from the day of his election until his death. During times of stress, his great business ability was active in the service of the hospital, and the administration of its affairs was given his close personal attention and study.

His personality was pleasing; his sense of humor keen; his sympathy boundless, and his hand was ever ready to help those in need. He had the affection and respect of his associates. His loss will be felt by the entire community, but especially by the hospital and his associates on this board. His works will live after him.

WILMINGTON CHURCHES.

As the spiritual evolution of any section constitutes the most vital part of its history, no local history would be complete without some record of its churches. It is with distinct satisfaction, therefore, that I have been able to secure from some of the ministers and members of the churches with which Wilmington is blessed the following sketches of the various Christian bodies represented in this city. These sketches all show the deep religious fervor, the holy impulse and righteous endeavor, the unconquerable faith and glorified hope with which the spiritual leaders of the community from early times until now have given themselves to the accomplishment of the Master's work. Trusting in a great transcendent Cause, an omnipotent Energy, a guiding Personality, a rewarding God, they have taken their relation to Him seriously, and with deathless loyalty have sought to work in harmony with His eternal purpose in the upbuilding of His kingdom on earth.

We are not all Presbyterians, but I think the Shorter Catechism furnishes a question and answer to which we can all subscribe: "What is the chief end of man?" "To glorify God and to enjoy Him forever." No wavering philosophy, no uncertain groping here, but profound conviction of a distinct personal relation to the Infinite whereby the purchase of eternal happiness embraces man's glorifying his Creator. And if man must glorify Him, he must, within the measure of his capacity, understand Him, so that Pope's dictum, to the devout, is paraphrased to read, "The proper study of mankind is God." The life that interprets each new experience as a revelation of God in individual existence, each new movement in history as the unfolding of His larger plan; that sees each day more and more of the steadfast purpose, each hour more and more of the infinite love and sweetness of the Eternal, will find itself so dominated by spiritual verities and so held in the thrill of ever-enlarging experience, that it will form the habit of the angels, to glorify its Maker by the song on the lips sounding forth the cadence in the soul, and in this conscious exaltation go forward with joy doing the will of Him who is chiefly glorified by faithful service.

The people of the Southern States throughout most of their history have been more homogeneous than those of the North and West, and have maintained their ancestral faiths with a steadiness almost unknown in some parts of our country. They have clung tenaciously to the great essentials of the Christian system, have been quick to see the insufficiency of modern substitutes for the Gospel of God's grace, and have turned a deaf ear to the exponents of mushroom religions.

The churches of the South have generally maintained the absolute authority of the Bible as the word of God, have insisted upon the exclusively spiritual mission of the church, have refrained from handling in their ecclesiastical courts political questions, have refused to follow the protean theories of an unbelieving criticism, have declined to offer men the stone of mere humanitarianism instead of the bread of divine grace, and as a consequence have enjoyed a rare exemption from the vagaries and religious fads which have mocked the spiritual hunger of many of our people in other parts of the land. It has been so in Wilmington. We are profoundly thankful that no fitful religious fancy, no form of higher criticism or heresy has invaded the counsels of our churches to disrupt them or to mar the usefulness of their membership. Our people "know in whom they have believed." They have answered the question, "Whom say ye that I am?" and have taken hold upon God never to be free, we trust, to consider any new doctrine that might loosen their grasp. They follow the course of humanity and sin like the rest of the world. Held in the rushing tide of modern life, their energies may be diverted at times from the main purpose; but they have laid hold upon real values and permanent ideals and their faith maintains its integrity in the midst of an age too largely given to doubt. May it ever be so! Christian orthodoxy in perpetuity is a rich heritage for any people.

Not only have our people maintained the faith of their fathers, but a very deep spirituality has pervaded our churches, and in the main their spiritual life and activity may be summed up in the words of Dr. Jowett:

"We are fighting to make known the love of the Father in the person and work of his Son, our Saviour, Jesus Christ. We are fighting to disperse the darkness of ignorance, to break the chains of evil habits, to offer a solvent for the bondage of guilt, to make an end of cruelty, to dry the tears no other hand can touch, to transfigure sorrow, to exalt wedlock, to glorify the home, to hallow childhood, to beautify age, to light up death.

"This is the grand commission of the army of the Lord. Is it worth fighting for—to unveil the infinite love of God, to make known the great mother bird of the race, to uncover the riches of forgiveness, to unseal the springs of freedom, to kindle the inspiration of eternal hope, to light up the road which leads to home and to God?"

St. James's Parish.

The early history of St. James's parish, in the town of Wilmington, is very closely interwoven with the history of the town itself. The settlement of the colony by English subjects established the ecclesiastical law of England as the law of the Church in the colony. The bishop of London was made the diocesan of the colony, and the province of North Carolina became thereby a part of the See of London.

Little attention seems to have been given the religious needs of the colonists by the Church in England until the incorporation of The Venerable Society for the Propagation of the Gospel in Foreign Parts in 1701.

It is in the records of the Venerable Society that we find the first official notice of St. James's parish. In 1736 the society records note that "Mr. Marsden had a settlement in the parish, and being a clergyman of the Church of England, had officiated there for several years past." We know, however, from local sources, that thirty years prior to this entry the whole province had been divided into twelve parishes, and several laws had been passed by the colonial Legislature for the support of religion. We also learn from the same sources that the parish of St. James was organized in the year 1730, and that in 1729 the Rev. John LaPierre, "a French Huguenot, who had been ordained by the bishop of London in 1708, and for many years had served a congregation of his own people in South Carolina, called St. Dennis' parish," came into the Cape Fear region, and

served St. James's and St. Philip's, Brunswick, until about
the year 1735. Mr. Marsden served only about one year, when
his appointment as missionary was withdrawn by the Venerable Society, and Mr. Moir was made missionary to the parish.
Mr. Moir's labors were arduous, but his service was most successful. He served the entire parish, from the Cape Fear
to the Neuse River, and during his first year baptized 210
persons, in his second year, baptizing 316 others. In 1742 he
was placed in charge of St. Philip's, Brunswick, in addition to
St. James's, and between 1742 and 1745 he reported 1,316
persons taken into the church through baptism. It will be seen,
therefore, that his labors bore much fruit. This good man
served the parish until 1747, when, because of ill health, he
removed to St. Mary's Chapel, near Tarboro, in Edgecombe
County, where we find record of his further faithful and loving
service as late as 1765.

Prior to the year 1751 the congregation of St. James's had
no church building, and used the county courthouse as a place
of worship. In Dr. Drane's *Historical Notices* of St. James's
parish, it is stated that the lot for the original church was given
by Michael Higgins, "a tried and true churchman." It is
recited, however, by Colonel Waddell, in his *History of New
Hanover County,* that the lot was conveyed by Higgins to
James Smallwood, in June, 1745, in consideration of 200
pounds, and that Smallwood conveyed it to John Rutherford
and Lewis DeRosset, wardens, together with the adjoining lot,
the following year. The lot secured, located near the corner of
Fourth and Market Streets, was not sufficient in size for a
church and burying ground, and to remedy the situation an
act was secured from the colonial Legislature, in 1751, authorizing the church to use thirty feet of Market Street for its
purposes.

There were three commissioners appointed by the act to build
the church. Evidently great difficulties were encountered, for
it was nineteen years after the passage of the act before the
church was completed, in 1770.

The church as built could lay no claims to architectural
beauty. It was of brick and extended thirty feet into Market
Street—a large square building, with neither steeple nor belfry.
There were three entrances, one fronting the river, one open-
ing on Market Street, and another leading into the graveyard.
The aisles were wide, paved with large square brick, and the

pews were of the old English style—"double pews" that would seat a large family, though compelling some to sit with their backs to the chancel. The furniture was plain, with a high reading desk and higher pulpit, surmounted by a sounding board. It was used by the parish until 1839, and was endeared to the parishioners by its sacred character and associations.

It has been noted that Mr. Moir left St. James's in 1747-48. After an interval of about seven years, he was succeeded by Rev. Mr. McDowell, who served the parish until 1763, the year of his death. In 1765 the Venerable Society sent Rev. Mr. Barnett to serve St. James's and St. Philip's. He was succeeded in 1766 by Rev. Mr. Wills. An extract from the contract made with Mr. Wills by the vestry throws a side-light on the times and the work of the parish. His stipend was 185 pounds proc. money, and he agreed to officiate at St. James's eighteen Sundays during the year, at Rocky Point six Sundays, at the sound six Sundays, at Long Creek six Sundays, at Black River six Sundays, and at Welsh Tract six Sundays—the remaining four Sundays to be at his disposal.

Another incident, noted in the records of the vestry, throws an interesting side-light and shows the temper of the times. Under the English law, the Crown had the right of presentation and induction of a rector in those cases where a church or chapel was built or endowed at the expense of the Crown. In 1770, four years after Mr. Wills's ministry began, Governor Tryon wrote the vestry that he proposed giving him letters of presentation and induction into the parish of St. James. The vestry replied courteously that they esteemed Mr. Wills, and were well satisfied to employ him, but they denied that the power of presentation and induction existed within the province, and would not agree thereto. Governor Tryon, thereupon, for the time withdrew the proposition. Mr. Wills served the parish, and had the respect and affection of the people, until 1775-76, when he resigned. He was the last rector under the colonial government.

The Revolution of 1776 put an end to the activities of the parish for fully twenty years. Clergymen of the Church of England, even those that remained neutral, were generally regarded as in sympathy with the Government of England, and were, rightfully or wrongfully, viewed with suspicion during the early Revolutionary period. During this long interval many persons formed affiliations with other denominations, but some held fast, awaiting the reëstablishment of their own church and parish. During the Revolution, in 1781, Wilmington became a British Army post in America, and the church building was seized and converted into a hospital.

There was no service in St. James's after Mr. Wills resigned until 1795, when the vestry reorganized, and called Dr. Halling, of New Bern, who served until 1809, when he retired and moved to Georgetown, S. C., where he died a few years later. Dr. Halling was also the first principal of the Wilmington Academy during his years of service in his parish.

In 1811 Rev. Adam Empie was made rector of St. James's and his work was most successful. He found twenty-one communicants when he arrived and left 102 when he resigned in 1814. He was succeeded by Dr. Judd, who served until 1816, when Dr. Empie returned to the parish, and guided its spiritual work until 1827, when he accepted the presidency of William and Mary College, in Virginia. The life of the parish was without special incident from 1827 until 1836. During those years it was served by Rev. Mr. Motte, Rev. Dr. Cairns, and Rev. Mr. Davis. In 1836 the Rev. R. B. Drane became rector. It was about this time that the old church was found to be in such bad repair that a new edifice was deemed necessary. It was therefore determined to destroy the old building, and to build a new one. The new church, which is the present one, was begun in 1839, and an interesting account of the laying of the cornerstone is found in the *Wilmington Advertiser* and the *Wilmington Weekly Chronicle,* of April 5, 1839. One of the records placed in the cornerstone recites that the old or original church stood about fifty yards east of the present church, near the corner of the graveyard. The lot on which the new church was erected was purchased from Dr. A. J. DeRosset for $1,000, of which sum the Ladies' Working Society and the Juvenile Working Society agreed to pay $600.

The building was designed by T. U. Walter, of Philadelphia, and executed under the supervision of John S. Norris, of New York. It was so far completed in twelve months as to be ready for consecration. Consecration was performed by Rt. Rev. Dr. Ives, bishop of the diocese, assisted by Dr. Drane. In January, 1843, Dr. Drane resigned as rector, to become president of Shelby College, Ky., and was succeeded by Rev. Richard H. Wilmer, later bishop of Alabama. Mr. Wilmer resigned on account of ill health, in 1844, and was succeeded by Dr. Drane, who was welcomed back by his old parishioners. The parish prospered under his administration and grew so that it was determined to build another church in the city. Accordingly, in 1853, through the efforts and principally through the subscriptions of St. James's parishioners, St. John's Church was built, on a lot given by Dr. DeRosset, and a new parish organized in 1860. Dr. Drane served St. James's parish lovingly and well until 1862, when he was stricken with yellow fever while serving the sick and needy during the fearful epidemic of that year. He died at his post, beloved of his congregation and the community.

After Dr. Drane's death, Bishop Atkinson, bishop of the diocese of North Carolina, who lived in Wilmington, served the parish as rector for a short time, and was succeeded by Dr. Alfred A. Watson, who was later to become bishop of East Carolina. Dr. Watson served during the War between the States. An interesting incident is mentioned in the parish records of this time. Anticipating the capture of the city by the Federal Army, Dr. Watson had obtained authority of his bishop to omit the prayer for the President of the Confederate States from the regular morning service of the Prayer-book. Upon the capture of the city, the Federal military authorities demanded that he should eliminate the prayer for the President of the Confederate States and substitute for it the prayer for the President of the United States. Feeling that he had no canonical authority to do so, and that he would thereby be a party to the infringement of religious liberty of the church, Dr. Watson declined to comply with the demand. Thereupon the church building was seized and converted into a hospital by the army authorities, the pews torn out and the building otherwise dismantled. There was no real need for an additional hospital, and it is reported in the records that the church building was never half filled with patients. The war ended shortly after this incident.

Dr. Watson made application to the Secretary of War for funds to restore the church, but was at first refused. Thereupon, the congregation raised the necessary funds, and by Advent, 1865, the building was repaired and again in commission for its sacred purposes. Since that time the Federal Government has paid the church claim, and the amount received has been expended on the church building.

Dr. Watson served the parish until he was made bishop of

39

East Carolina in 1883, when he was succeeded by Dr. Robert Strange, who also later became bishop of the diocese. The parish was blessed and prospered under Dr. Strange, and under his successor, Rev. R. W. Hogue, who was rector from 1903 until 1907. Mr. Hogue was succeeded in 1909 by Dr. William H. Milton, the present rector, under whose guidance the old parish is moving forward in its appointed sphere with renewed faith and vigor.

During the years since the war the parish has, for the second time, found it necessary to expand, and the mission established by it in the southern part of the city has prospered and has become itself the parish of the Good Shepherd.

Standing today at the corner of Market and Third Streets, the present church, with its earnest parishioners, constitutes a fitting monument to the efforts that have marked the growth of the parish through its trials and successes, its vicissitudes and accomplishments during the one hundred and eighty-five years of its life.

St. John's Episcopal Church.

In 1851 St. James's parish, then under the rectorship of the Rev. Robert Brent Drane, D.D., had outgrown the seating capacity of the church building, and it was decided to erect another church edifice rather than alter and enlarge the old historic St. James's.

The congregation, with the approval and encouragement of Dr. Drane, worked zealously to accomplish the undertaking. The ground at the corner of Third and Red Cross Streets was the gift of Dr. Armand J. DeRosset, senior warden and one of the pillars of St. James's Church.

Many of those who subscribed most liberally to the building of the new church still retained their connection with the old. The younger members of families joined the organization of the new parish, while their fathers worshiped in the old, and all worked heartily and harmoniously in the effort to erect a new building, no one being more zealous or more ready with counsel and assistance of every kind than the beloved rector of St. James's.

The plans of the new church building were accepted in December, 1852, and the cost of the finished structure was something over $16,000. On the 21st of November, 1853, the cornerstone was laid with appropriate religious ceremonies. The members of the church formed a procession at St. James's Church, and, led by Bishop Atkinson and Dr. Drane, walked to the site of the new building. As nearly as I can remember, the stone was placed at the angle of the wall just behind where the pulpit now stands. The ceremonies were imposing, but my childish recollection retains most clearly the figure of Bishop Atkinson, with his beautiful and benignant countenance and dignified carriage. His remarks were said to be "forcible, eloquent, and impressive."

Several years passed before the congregation was able to liquidate entirely the debt incurred in the erection of the building, but in the year 1860 this was done and the consecration took place and the church opened for divine service on April 1, 1860.

A small organ, given by the ladies of St. James's, was placed in the organ alcove. The chancel furnishing was temporary and unpretentious. The chancel window, of stained glass, and the windows in the body of the church, of plain ground glass with a narrow border of color, were the gift of the girls of St. James's.

The organization of St. John's parish was at a called meeting held in St. James's Church, February 16, 1860. The organization was effected by a declaration signed by eighty-seven adult members. A vestry of seven was elected: Nicholas N. Nixon, James A. Willard, S. L. Fremont, Samuel J. Person, John L. Holmes, William L. DeRosset, and Mauger London, the first two being appointed wardens. At the first meeting of the vestry the following delegates were appointed to the Diocesan Council held in Charlotte in May, 1860: S. L. Fremont, William L. DeRosset, James A. Willard, and Samuel J. Person, with Henry Nutt, Robert H. Cowan, J. J. Lippitt, and H. W. Burgwin as alternates.

On March 16, 1860, Rev. J. A. Wainwright took charge of the parish for one year, resigning and returning to his home in New York at the end of that time. Late in December, 1861, at the suggestion of Bishop Atkinson, Rev. R. E. Terry was called and accepted the rectorship. He carried on the work of the church with great zeal and was upheld by the whole congregation. The Sunday-school prospered, the membership increased, and a good voluntary choir added interest to the service. During the eight years of Mr. Terry's incumbency a fine organ and a beautiful font were purchased. Also, a handsome pulpit, given by a communicant of the church, and a memorial tablet to Dr. Drane, who had died during the epidemic of yellow fever, were placed in the chancel. In October, 1869, Mr. Terry resigned and Rev. George Patterson, at that time assistant at St. James's, was called to the rectorship and assumed his duties on Easter Monday, March 11, 1870. He continued with the church ten years and gained the love of his people and the good will of all the community. The inscription on the memorial window placed in the church by his friends, both in and out of the parish, testifies to the feeling entertained: "Chaplain Third North Carolina Regiment, Confederate States Army. Erstwhile rector of this church. Faithful soldier and servant unto his life's end."

Dr. Patterson was succeeded by Rev. Thomas D. Pitts, who served two years and resigned on account of ill health in his family, which necessitated their removal from Wilmington.

In 1883 Rev. James Carmichael accepted the rectorship of St. John's and served most acceptably for fourteen years.

In October, 1907, at the insistent call of the vestry and the earnest desire of the congregation, Rev. W. E. Cox became rector. The church has prospered greatly under his ministration and he has endeared himself to all by his earnestness of purpose and untiring zeal in his work, his hands being upheld by the faithful wardens, Mr. H. G. Smallbones,[1] who has held the office of warden for thirty-four years, and Mr. Washington Catlett, who has for a long time been warden and also superintendent of the Sunday-school.

Church of the Good Shepherd.

While the present site of the Church of the Good Shepherd is at Sixth and Queen Streets, where for more than twenty years a work of growing usefulness has been carried on, the parish really grew out of a previous work begun in 1870, during the rectorship at St. James's of Dr. Watson, the late revered bishop of East Carolina, in what was then known as St. James's Home, on the present St. James's Square.

This valuable property was the gift of Dr. Armand J. DeRosset, of honored memory in the church and community. In 1870 his daughter, Mrs. Kate DeRosset Meares, opened a

---

[1]Mr. Smallbones has since died.

Sunday-school and later a day-school, being assisted subsequently by Mrs. Rosa H. Ashe. Mrs. Meares gave herself to this service with a rare devotion, and it was by her untiring labors that the foundation of such a splendid work was laid.

In 1873, Mrs. Lawrence, afterwards Sister Cecilia, came to begin her labor of love. She left behind her a sainted memory and an influence that has been handed down from parents to children and is still strong in the community.

In 1892, while Dr. Strange, the late beloved bishop of East Carolina, was rector of St. James's, the chapel of the Good Shepherd was built on the present site of the church, and a vigorous work carried on under the leadership of Rev. J. B. Gibble, assisted by an efficient corps of women, who aided in the social and spiritual work of the mission.

Later, Miss Susie Price became resident parish worker. She has carried on a work that can not be easily overestimated in its beneficent influence, among the women and girls particularly, a large number of whom are now enrolled in various organizations, chiefly the Girls' Friendly Society, with its Junior Chapter of Candidates, the Parish Guild, and a very devoted branch of the Woman's Auxiliary.

A notable feature of this interesting work is the record of the late superintendent of the Sunday-school, Mr. J. Hal Boatwright, who served continuously for nearly forty years, acting also for a long time as lay reader. His was indeed a noble work of love performed with joy.

In 1906, Rev. Thomas P. Noe became rector, and under his direction and inspiration the congregation began earnest efforts to become independent and self-sustaining, and in May, 1907, the Church of the Good Shepherd became a regular parish and was admitted into full standing in the council of the diocese, having been aided in this achievement by an endowment fund, set apart for a term of years from the Armand J. DeRosset Memorial Fund by the vestry of St. James's parish.

Previous to this action, the hall of the Good Shepherd, a large, commodious, and well-appointed recreation hall and parish building, was erected in 1906, largely from this same fund. The Deaconess House, formerly occupied by Miss Price, has been remodeled and enlarged and a handsome rectory has been built on the church property, which now includes about one-quarter of a city block; and on All Saints' Day, 1911, with impressive ceremonies the cornerstone was laid for the present handsome brick veneer edifice, which was completed early in 1913. The following resolution was passed by the vestry: "That the cornerstone, or a suitable tablet in the new church bear the following or an equivalent inscription: 'Church of the Good Shepherd, erected to the glory of God and in grateful memory of Dr. Armand J. DeRosset.' "

The funds for this building were secured from offerings made by the members of the congregation, together with an Easter offering of $2,000 from St. James's parish and $5,000 from the Armand J. DeRosset Memorial Fund—a fund secured mainly from the sale of the original site of the home.

In 1914, Rev. Thomas P. Noe resigned to become archdeacon of the diocese, and was succeeded by his brother, Rev. W. R. Noe, under whose leadership the parish is continuing its work with enthusiasm and much success.

The church has grown in numbers and influence until it now has a communicant membership of about 300, with more than 400 baptized persons, and a Sunday-school that numbers over 300 pupils, with 30 officers and teachers. The large number of organizations for girls and boys and adults attests the wide range of usefulness that touches every phase of community life.

In 1912, the Good Shepherd established the Church of the Ascension, a very flourishing mission, at Third and Marsteller Streets, which now has a large Sunday-school and kindergarten and a growing congregation of adult communicants in a building of their own.

From its inception, the work of St. James's Home, and later the Church of the Good Shepherd received the faithful support of the mother parish of St. James, whose devotion can not be too highly praised.

First Presbyterian Church.

On the walls of the First Presbyterian Church in Wilmington there is hung a framed handbill, containing information with reference to the erection of a house of worship for the congregation of that church in 1818. It is circular in form, and around the outer edge there is the following:

Names of Trustees and Building Committee of the first Presbyterian house of worship erected in the town of Wilmington, in the State of North Carolina.

There is also an inner circle containing the following names of citizens of Wilmington: Thomas Loring, Simeon Baldwin, Richard Parish, Archibald Taylor, John Cowan, James Hughes Draughon, Thomas Cowan, George Cameron, Gabriel Holmes, jr., John Macauslan, Archibald Maclaine Hooper, John Walker, Murdock MacKay, Talcott Burr, William Harris, William Edward Jury.

Within the circle this information is given:

Builders: James Marshall and Benjamin Jacobs.

Forty-second year of American Independence. James Monroe, President of the United States.

Cornerstone laid: The 19th day of May, Anno Domini 1818.

Building Committee: John Maccoll, Thomas Clayton Reston, William MacKay, James Dickson, Jacob Hartman, Richard Lloyd, and Robert Murphy.

Printed at the office of the Cape Fear Recorder,
By William Hollinshead,
For Thomas Loring.

The congregation was formally organized the year previous, worshiping in the Episcopal Church.

The following memorandum furnished by Rev. J. K. Hall, stated clerk of Fayetteville Presbytery, refers to the organization.

"Under date of April 4, 1817, presbytery being in session at Euphronia Church, there is the following record:

" 'The stated clerk laid before presbytery a paper containing an authenticated copy of the deliberative proceedings of a large and respectable number of citizens of Wilmington, who convened for the purpose of forming themselves into a Presbyterian congregation. Those proceedings bore the signatures of Robert Cochran, chairman, and Alexander Anderson, secretary, and contained, in addition to the names of twenty-three trustees appointed for the management of their temporal concerns, a resolution expressive of their request that this presbytery would take the said congregation under their charge. Resolved, That the prayer of this petition be granted, and that presbytery promise these petitioners all the aid in their power, either in procuring a minister, or in promoting in other respects their spiritual interests. Ordered, That the Rev. Colin McIver be, and he hereby is appointed to preach to the Wilmington congregation, at least one Sabbath before the time of the next stated session of this presbytery. Ordered, That an authenticated copy of the above preamble, resolution, and order be transmitted to them by the stated clerk.'

"Rev. Artemus Boies was ordained and installed pastor of the Wilmington church May 12, 1819, at an adjourned meeting of presbytery in Wilmington. The church is reported vacant until this time."

For many years prior to that, Presbyterian ministers had visited Wilmington, where there had been more or less of a contingent of that denomination among the Scottish residents and others who had been reared in that faith. The first sermon preached in Wilmington by a regular Presbyterian minister was by Rev. Hugh McAden on February 15, 1756. He was followed by other missionaries who came from the North and from Scotland to work among the Presbyterian settlers in the Cape Fear section. Rev. George Whitefield, the Calvinistic-Methodist preacher and great evangelist of the eighteenth century, visited Wilmington and preached on December 29, 1739. He also preached in the town on March 29, 1765, and perhaps at other times.

The church built in 1818 was on Front Street between Dock and Orange. The cornerstone was laid with Masonic ceremonies. Its existence was of short duration, for it was destroyed by fire on November 3, 1819. Meantime, Rev. Artemus Boies had been installed the first regular pastor of the church on May 12, 1819.

A new building was erected, but it also suffered destruction by fire on April 13, 1859, when another site was chosen for the erection of a church for the congregation. This was on Third and Orange Streets. There was no insurance on the old church, and a subscription towards the new building was started on the spot at the time of the fire. On the evening of the same day a meeting was held in the office of James H. Dickson, M.D., and a committee was appointed to secure further subscriptions. At a later meeting, the sum of $14,000 was reported as having been raised. The new building was subsequently erected at a cost approximating $20,000, in addition to the cost of the lot, and was dedicated on April 28, 1861. It still stands, and is used by a congregation which has become noted throughout the South for its missionary and evangelistic influences. The present membership of the church (1915) numbers eight hundred and forty-nine; and, besides its large benefactions to other religious objects, it maintains a considerable foreign mission enterprise at Kiangyin, China, and numerous missions and chapels in its immediate section of North Carolina.

The ministers who have served the church are: Revs. Arte-
mus Boies, Leonard E. Lathrop, Noel Robertson, Thomas P.
Hunt, James A. McNeill, W. W. Eells, Thomas R. Owen, J. O.
Stedman, M. B. Grier, D.D., Horace L. Singleton, D.D., A. F.
Dickson, D.D., Joseph R. Wilson, D.D., LL.D., Peyton H.
Hoge, D.D., and John M. Wells, Ph.D., D.D. President Wood-
row Wilson was a youth when his father, the late Dr. Joseph R.
Wilson, served the church as its pastor.

As illustrating the missionary and enterprising spirit of the
church, it might be stated that on November 6, 1858, fourteen
persons were dismissed to form the Second Presbyterian Church,
which later became St. Andrew's Presbyterian Church; also,
that on March 1, 1859, a plan was formed to build a mission
schoolhouse in the southern part of the city, which later developed into Immanuel Presbyterian Church. This was before
the burning of the old church on Front Street. A lot for the
use of the mission was donated by John A. Taylor.

Seven ministers have gone out from the First Presbyterian
Church: Revs. Thomas R. Owen, Sidney G. Law, George W.
McMillan, William H. Groves, Alexander Sprunt, William E.
Hill, and Andrew J. Howell. It has also furnished the following foreign missionaries, who are at this time laboring in China:
George C. Worth, M.D., and his wife, Mrs. Emma Chadbourn
Worth, of Kiangyin, and Miss Jessie D. Hall, of Tsing-Kiang-
Pu, who is supported entirely by the Jane Dalziel Sprunt Missionary Society, composed of her immediate family and relatives. The foreign mission force entirely supported by the
church numbers thirteen, all of them in China, besides twenty-
five native helpers. In addition, there are several home missionaries and mission school teachers connected with the church.

The large addition to the church building, containing the
Anniversary Hall and the Chadbourn Memorial Hall, was completed in 1894 and bears an important part in the activities of
the congregation.

As a matter of general historic interest, which affected the
life of the Presbyterian Churches of the city, as well as those
of other denominations, mention should be made of the great
revival of 1858, and the special services conducted by noted
evangelists since as follows: Rev. R. G. Pearson, beginning
March 18, 1888; Rev. D. L. Moody, beginning March 18, 1893;
Rev. R. A. Torrey, D.D., beginning March 6, 1910; and Rev.
J. Wilbur Chapman, D.D., and Mr. Charles M. Alexander, be-

ginning April 9, 1916. The Chapman meetings were especially remarkable, enlisting the interest of practically the whole city, and awakening in our people generally a sense of the riches, beauties, and privileges of the Christian life. As many as 5,000 men attended one service, and at another all the fraternal societies of the city attended in a body. More than 1,000 members were added to the churches, and a vast number already communicants expressed renewed and deepened spiritual life.

The closing exercises were marked by a procession of 5,000 Sunday-school children, with banners flying, through the principal streets to the Tabernacle, headed by Dr. Chapman and his fellow-workers. It was an affecting and inspiring scene, and will live for many years in the minds and hearts of those who witnessed it.

St. Andrew's Presbyterian Church.

The Second Presbyterian Church, the name of which was later changed to St. Andrew's Presbyterian Church, was organized by the Presbytery of Fayetteville on November 21, 1858, with fourteen members from the First Presbyterian Church, who erected for the new church a building on Chestnut Street between Seventh and Eighth. This still stands, but was sold to the Presbyterian negroes of the city in 1867, for whom it has had a useful career as a place of worship.

The congregation of the Second Church worshiped in Brooklyn Hall, in the northern part of the city, until 1873, when a new house of worship was erected for its use on Campbell Street near Fourth. It was dedicated on May 4 of that year. This building served for the worship of the church for several years, until the increasing membership demanded a larger structure. Another building, therefore, on the corner of Fourth and Campbell Streets, was erected, and dedicated on June 9, 1889. It still stands, but additions have been made from time to time to meet the growing requirements of the congregation. The organization now numbers 589 members.

The original house of worship on Campbell Street has recently given place to the handsome memorial building which is attached to the church.

Rev. Martin McQueen was the first minister to supply the pulpit of the Second Church. He began his work in January, 1850, and continued until December, 1863. Thereafter for seven years the church had no regular minister; but, beginning in November, 1870, the pulpit was supplied for about three years by Rev. H. B. Burr. Then, after an intermission of several months, Rev. C. M. Payne, M.D., D.D., was called as the first regular pastor. He began his ministry on June 1, 1874, and continued as pastor of the church for about ten years. During his ministry the church had a large growth. Rev. J. W. Primrose was installed pastor on January 11, 1885, and served the church until December, 1890, when he was dismissed to become an evangelist of the Synod of Missouri. The church was without a pastor until July 1, 1891, when the Rev. Alexander D. McClure began his labors as pastor of the congregation. For twenty-four years he has been the wise and beloved leader of the religious life of his people, and has been closely identified with nearly every Christian and benevolent enterprise of the city. Reference is frequently made to Dr. McClure now not as pastor of St. Andrew's, but as "pastor of Wilmington."

The change of name from the Second Presbyterian Church to St. Andrew's was made on September 19, 1888, by vote of the congregation. This was just prior to the building of the more commodious structure.

The congregation of St. Andrew's enjoys a large share of religious leadership in Wilmington. They also maintain an important missionary interest in foreign lands and at home, supporting Rev. and Mrs. L. T. Newland, of Kwang-Ju, Korea, and Mrs. J. McC. Sieg, of Congo Belge, Africa.

From St. Andrew's Church grew the Pearsall Memorial Presbyterian Church, in East Wilmington, whose building was erected through the beneficence of Mr. Oscar Pearsall, then an elder of St. Andrew's, but now of the Pearsall Memorial Church.

A LAYMAN'S RECOLLECTIONS.

(Remarks of the author on the fiftieth anniversary of St. Andrew's Presbyterian Church, Wilmington, N. C., November 22, 1908.)

In response to Dr. McClure's kind request I have noted a few memories of the days of my youth connected with the origin of your church organization.

I shall refer briefly to the parent church, from which it sprang, and to its beloved minister, whose sermons often lulled me to sleep before I was old enough to understand the great truths which he expounded. I recall the soothing, soporific effect of his sonorous voice upon my drowsy spirit when he spoke in minor tones, and the painful excitement of his sudden high-pitched exclamations, which roused me with an abashed and startled countenance from fitful dreams. And I remember, while being nudged with expressive gestures by my parents to keep awake, how I longed to sink out of sight upon the floor of the pew and yield to the over-mastering desire for undisturbed repose.

How often in more recent years, when the cares of business made the burden of life almost insupportable, have I longed to hear one of those delightful sermons of my childhood, when the voice of the preacher, meaningless to me then, like the droning of a bee soothed the tired senses until they sank unconscious into the arms of Death's twin-brother, Sleep.

One of the great events in the church history of Wilmington, which I believe under the hand of God led to your original founding, was the wonderful revival of the Holy Spirit in the hearts of the Wilmington people in the year 1858. I was then eleven and a half years of age, and attended with my parents and brothers and sisters the First Presbyterian Church on Front Street, which I saw burned to the ground afterwards, and I also attended the morning session of the Sunday-school which was held in the lecture-room in the rear of the church building, and which still stands in the alley opposite our present Front Street market house. I can remember my first tottering steps when I was learning to walk, but I can not remember the first time I attended church: it must have antedated even that remote period.

Mr. Robert Gibbs was the superintendent, and a Mr. Sherwood, who was a merchant of Wilmington, was my teacher. The pastor of the church was the Rev. Matthew B. Grier, a scholar and a gentleman of the old school, who was perhaps more generally respected and honored in the town of Wilmington than any other minister of his time. He was a man of attractive and striking personality, of about six feet stature, remarkable intellectual attainments, most courteous and refined deportment, singular grace and ease of manner, and of extreme punctiliousness with reference to his immaculate clerical dress.

It was his custom to make regular visits, or visitations, upon the families of his congregation every month, and I have often recalled with great amusement some of the occasions when he visited my father's family and examined us with reference to that indispensable qualification of our faith, the Westminster Shorter Catechism.

I remember that his visits were timed for Saturdays, or after school hours on week days, so that no excuse would be valid with reference to other obligations. I recall also our brawny Scotch nurse, fresh from the Highlands, whose duty on the occasion of the minister's coming was to corral the youthful members of the family and prepare them by careful scrubbing and change of clothes for the ordeal of his examination.

About that time I had developed a remarkable fondness for the breeding of pigeons and possessed a flock of different varieties numbering forty or fifty, all told. These pigeons were known and recognized by familiar names, and to an especially fine pair of white fantails I had given the names of our pastor and his dignified wife. On one occasion the alarm was given to the boys at play that the minister was approaching and that we were to prepare for presentation. My two brothers and I immediately took refuge under a storehouse in the yard, from which we were ignominiously dragged by our heels by the Scotch nurse, and after a careful overhauling were sent into the house to be catechised. One of our number, however, escaped (I think it was our brother from Charleston). I may mention at this particular juncture that the female fan-tailed pigeon, already referred to by name, had been missing for several days. You can imagine the consternation of our good mother, while we were being examined on the question of "Effectual Calling," to hear from the back yard an excited and effectual call to us by the brother aforesaid, "Come out, come out, Mrs. Grier has alighted on the top of the stable!" The reassuring "Ha, ha," of our good pastor, however, relieved our embarrassment, and this incident, with his better acquaintance, established our hearts in mutual affection.

The personnel of the white members of the original organization of the church on Chestnut Street is doubtless well known to you, but I think that the excellent character of our colored members has not been sufficiently emphasized. I recall William Cutlar, Alfred Hargrave, Henry Taylor, and George Price, sr. They were all superior persons, skilled craftsmen, intelligent, courteous, self-supporting, and generally respected in this community, as their worthy sons are respected who are here tonight.

After they had bought and occupied the original building and engaged a talented colored pastor, named Rev. D. J. Sanders,

Alfred Hargrave was a ruling elder, and when the clergy of another denomination occupied the colored churches during their convention, or conference, here, a fervid preacher with great lung power conducted the Chestnut Street Church service. As his voice rose in a "powerful" prayer, so rose a feeling of great disgust and resentment in the mind of our dignified colored elder, who did not like such "doings," as he expressed it. When the voice of the preacher could be heard two blocks away, old Alfred Hargrave arose and with great dignity marched up to the pulpit, and, laying an accusing hand upon the shoulder of the astonished shouter, said loud enough for all the congregation to hear, "My brother, the Lord ain't deef," which had the desired effect.

I have referred to the great revival in Wilmington, which included all classes and denominations, in the year 1858. The daily morning prayer-meetings of our church on this occasion were held in the lecture-room, already described, immediately after an early breakfast, before the opening hour of the secular schools, and I remember that we carried our schoolbooks with us and sat in awed silence through the mysterious manifestation of God's holy presence. The building was crowded to the door, and the whole congregation was deeply moved by emotions which can not be described.

One morning a stranger in our assembly arose and made the most beautiful address I have ever heard. I think he said he had missed his railroad connection, and that while he was aimlessly walking on Front Street he was drawn to our meeting by the sound of the sacred music, and that he too had felt the power of that mysterious presence of the Spirit which was moving upon the hearts of us all. This stranger proved to be the Rev. Dr. J. L. Girardeau, of Charleston. He was subsequently entertained at my father's house, and then began a friendship with us all which lasted throughout his honored life.

When my father canvassed the means for a new church organization, to be known as the Second Presbyterian Church, but miscalled by some—very much to his annoyance—the Presbyterian Chapel, we lived on Princess between Eighth and Ninth Streets, and I remember that this street was in its primeval condition of deep sand without even a sidewalk, in a part of the town very sparsely settled.

When, after many deliberations and misgivings, a site for the Second Church had been selected on Chestnut Street be-

tween Seventh and Eighth Streets, we plodded through the deep
sand daily, watching the progress of the building, the total cost
of which was, I think, $2,500.

The church building was erected under contract with a Mr.
Moody, and the progress to completion was watched with anxious interest by the little band—a mere handful—which formed
its original membership. Conspicuous among these were my
father, Alexander Sprunt, John C. Latta, John R. Latta, John
Colville, and others, all of whom have gone to their reward.

It is a remarkable fact that the exterior of the original building on Chestnut Street has not been repainted in fifty years.
When it was painted after its erection, the first coat of color was
sanded by the usual process in imitation of brownstone. This
has withstood the exposure of half a century. I examined the
exterior a few days ago and found it in an excellent state of
preservation, with the exception of the pillars and front, where
the paint was visibly wearing away.

While I write these lines my eyes have fallen upon an item
in a newspaper entitled, "A Strong Church," which reads as
follows:

"Is it a strong church?" asked a man respecting a body of wor-
shipers.

"Yes," was the reply.

"How many members are there?"

"Seventeen."

"Are they so very wealthy?"

"No, they are poor."

"How, then, do you say that it is a strong church?"

"Because," said the gentleman, "they are earnest, devoted, at peace,
loving each other, and striving to do the Master's work. *Such* a congregation is *strong*, whether composed of *five* or *five hundred* members."

Such, I think, may be said of the little band of workers which
composed your original membership. The spirit of the work
entered into the heart of every one of our household and each
had something to do in connection with it. My mother solicited,
in person, contributions large and small for the purchase of a
bell, and although fifty years have passed since the first peal
resounded in my delighted ears, I never hear it now without
recalling my personal attachment for it.

There was an underlying principle involved in the origin of
this church to which I would ask your serious thought. The
blood of the martyrs is the seed of the church. The ancestors
of your founders sealed their devotion with the sacrifice of their

lives upon the bleak moors of Scotland. Your original members in turn gave liberally of their scanty substance with their lives of service. There was not one of them whose income for the support of a large family exceeded fifteen hundred dollars a year, and there was not then the full blessing of free schools, which you enjoy; and yet they rejoiced in pinching from their necessaries of life a liberal share for God's glory.

I could not tell you without emotion too deep for words, a memory too sacred for utterance, of the secret personal sacrifice of a saint of God, who, I believe in my heart, did more than all others for the upbuilding of this church, and in whose crown of rejoicing there shines with resplendent glory the gems of sacrifice and service.

Men and women of St. Andrew's, take it to your hearts, teach it to your children, that the foundation of your beloved church was Christ the Lord in the hearts of His people, who cemented it with willing service and personal sacrifice and who watered it with a woman's loving tears.

The first sexton of the Chestnut Street Church fifty years ago was Henry Price, who is present and who will now make his bow to the congregation.

Upon him devolved the duty on Saturday of opening the windows, sweeping and dusting the church, and making the fires in the two stoves in the rear of the building, and I was delegated by my father to assist him, particularly in the ringing of the bell on Sunday. Many a painful quarter of an hour have I spent in tugging at that bell-rope, when my strength was not equal to the task, but I recall this experience with feelings of gratefulness that I was permitted to make some sacrifice in the cause of a church which has been so blessed of God. My younger brother, John, had his duty to perform, and a most unpleasant task it was to him, because his was a retiring and modest disposition and the duty which my father imposed upon him made him conspicuous in the morning and evening service.

My father, true to the traditions of his Scotch training, regarded instrumental church music with disfavour and advocated congregational singing, which he led with the assistance of a tuning fork. None of our family thought much of my father's gift of singing, and when he broke down in leading the psalm or hymn by trying to adapt a long-metre verse to short-metre music, we boys slyly poked each other with unbecoming levity, for which we were afterwards duly punished.

After my father determined to adopt an old Scotch practice of exhibiting against the pulpit the name of the tune which the congregation was expected to sing, when the preacher gave out the psalm or hymn, my brother John was required to perform the duty of putting up the sign, which he thoroughly detested, and I would not like to say how many times he was corrected at home for insubordination.

In course of time the inevitable choir was formed and John was relieved of this unpleasant duty, but I think that box of gilt signs is still in the possession of the family.

In later years, when we were divided between the First Church and the Second, my youngest brother, William, chose the duty and the privilege of joining his parents in their devotions at the Second Church, to which they had given the service of their consecrated lives. For years he sat in the foot of the buggy and drove them from our home on Ninth Street to the little building which has since become your lecture-room, and in time he took up the work which was laid down by his father when he entered into rest some five and twenty years ago. How faithfully and how well he has served the Master and this congregation it is not becoming of me to speak. But I may be permitted to say, in all humility, that we are thankful to God and that we are proud of the record of our father and of his youngest son in this beloved church of their choice. It is also of much satisfaction to us that another brother has been in recent years added to its membership.

This secluded sanctuary has been in peace and in war, in pestilence and in famine, a refuge for God's people. Only four of its original members survive; the others have joined that "great multitude which no man can number" and "which came out of great tribulation and have washed their robes and made them white in the blood of the Lamb. They shall hunger no more, neither thirst any more; neither shall the sun light on them, nor any heat; and God has wiped away all tears from their eyes."

> "Ah, Christ, that it were best
> For one short hour to see
> The souls we loved,
> That they might tell us
> What and where they be."

40

IMMANUEL PRESBYTERIAN CHURCH.

Immanuel Presbyterian Church is an outgrowth of the missionary spirit of the First Presbyterian Church. For many years the latter had maintained a mission Sunday-school and industrial classes in the southern part of the city, making use of different locations for the purpose. The work had a very substantial growth, so that in May, 1890, it was decided to erect a new building on the site which had been used, near the corner of Front and Queen Streets, the building to be called Immanuel Chapel. Ground was broken on May 26, and the structure was completed before the end of 1890. A very material subscription towards the new building was obtained from a legacy left by Mrs. E. E. Burruss. The remainder of the cost was met by subscriptions from members of the First Presbyterian Church.

The first service was held in the new chapel on January 4, 1891, and on February 1, 1891, it was dedicated to the worship of God, Rev. Dr. Peyton H. Hoge preaching the sermon from texts illuminated on the walls of the building.

Mr. J. M. W. Elder, who later became an ordained minister, took charge of the work of the mission as a lay missionary on January 1, 1888. He was succeeded by Rev. William McC. Miller, of Virginia, in October of that year. Later, the pulpit of the chapel was supplied in turn by Revs. George H. Cornehlson, jr., B. E. Wallace, P. C. Morton, E. E. Lane, J. C. Story, and C. W. Trawick, until March 1, 1904. On May 16 of that year Rev. J. S. Crowley, who had served as a missionary in the Congo region of Africa, became stated supply, and continues to fill the pulpit at the present time.

Immanuel Church is now a separate organization, although its support and the personnel of its workers are to a large extent obtained from the First Presbyterian Church.

It has had a large and abiding influence in the moral and religious uplift of the people living in the southern part of Wilmington; and the long pastorate of Mr. Crowley has brought a large growth to the membership of the church, which now numbers two hundred and thirty-three.

In connection with Immanuel Church, Immanuel kindergarten is maintained, and has proved to be a great blessing to the children of that section of the city. Also, as an outgrowth of the work of the church, the Boys' Brigade came into existence.

Immanuel Building, standing on the corner of Front and Queen Streets, was erected a few years ago through the beneficence of Mr. James Sprunt, to be used for religious, educational, and social purposes in connection with Immanuel Church. Mr. Sprunt also gave the two residences adjoining for the use of the church.

OTHER PRESBYTERIAN CHURCHES IN NEW HANOVER COUNTY.

There are other Presbyterian Churches in New Hanover County, some established at a very early date.

Mention has been made of the Pearsall Memorial Church, in East Wilmington, in connection with the sketch of St. Andrew's Church.

The Winter Park Presbyterian Church is an outgrowth of the mission work conducted by the First Presbyterian Church in the Chadbourn Memorial Chapel at Winter Park Gardens. This chapel was built by Mr. James H. Chadbourn, jr., as a memorial to his children, George and Blanche. Services were first conducted there by Rev. J. M. Wells, D.D., and Rev. J. M. Plowden. Later, the work fell into the hands of Rev. Andrew J. Howell, laboring under the direction of the session of the First Presbyterian Church. There is a present membership of eighty-two, and the prospects are bright for a large growth in the near future. The congregation was duly organized as a separate church on December 14, 1913, with Mr. Howell as stated supply. With consent of the Chadbourn family, the Memorial Chapel has been moved to another location on the same lot, and a new church of brick, of colonial style of architecture, has just been completed and handsomely furnished. The modern arrangement and complete furnishings of this church building afford conveniences unsurpassed, and its great usefulness as a house of the Lord is clearly foreseen. Its grounds have been tastefully laid out and beautified, and the opinion expressed by many is that no more attractive and substantial church edifice and grounds are to be found in the Cape Fear section. The whole is the gift of Mr. James Sprunt, who erected the church as a memorial to his sister, Mrs. Margaret Tannahill Hall. Mrs. Hall was a devoted member of the First

Presbyterian Church of Wilmington. Over the main entrance is a marble tablet with the following appropriate inscription:

Winter Park Presbyterian Church,
Erected to the glory of God and as a
Perpetual memorial of
Margaret Tannahill Hall,
Beloved wife of B. F. Hall and
Daughter of
Alexander and Jane Dalziel Sprunt.
A. D. 1915.

The edifice was dedicated on March 5, 1916. The ceremonies were imposing and the attendance so large that the building could scarcely accommodate all. The sermon on this occasion was preached by Rev. Alexander Sprunt, D.D., of Charleston, S. C., a brother of Mr. James Sprunt and Mrs. Hall.

Bethany Presbyterian Church is a mission conducted by the First Presbyterian Church. The handsome little structure used by the congregation was built in 1912 as a gift of Mr. James Sprunt. It was dedicated on November 10, 1912. The work is in charge of Rev. Andrew J. Howell, and succeeded the religious services formerly conducted in a schoolhouse which was the property of Mr. and Mrs. William A. Lineker, English people who settled in that section of the county. The schoolhouse is now known as the "Lineker Memorial Hall."

The Delgado Presbyterian Church is also a mission supported by the First Presbyterian Church at Delgado Cotton Mills, which are now located within the corporate limits of the city. The work began as a Sunday-school on January 8, 1905, under the superintendency of Mr. Andrew J. Howell, then an elder of the First Presbyterian Church, who later became a minister and was placed in charge of the mission. In the meantime, the Rev. J. M. Plowden served the church as supply for several years.

The influence of the Delgado Church has been very great in the southeastern part of the city, and the employees of the Delgado Mills are indebted to it for many of the religious advantages which they have enjoyed.

In connection with the Delgado Church, Marion Mission is maintained by Mr. James Sprunt, who erected for it a handsome building in 1907. A kindergarten is conducted in the building during the school months, and a daily luncheon served to the children. The rooms are also used for Sunday-school and social purposes.

In addition to the above, a Sunday-school is conducted by the First Presbyterian Church, under the superintendency of Mr. G. C. Bordeaux, at Sunset Park; and Dr. McClure, of St. Andrew's, preaches regularly at Castle Haynes, with the end in view of establishing a Presbyterian mission at that place when interest develops sufficiently.

The First Presbyterian Church has a chapel on the corner of Twelfth and Queen Streets, in which it supports a Sunday-school for colored people; and St. Andrew's maintains a similar work on the corner of Eighth and Harnett Streets. Rev. W. M. Baker, who graduated from the Union Theological Seminary, took charge of this work for both churches on June 15, 1913, and still has it in hand.

GRACE METHODIST EPISCOPAL CHURCH.

Prior to 1886, the leading Methodist Church of Wilmington stood on the northeast corner of Front and Walnut Streets. It was the Front Street Methodist Episcopal Church. The existence of the church dated far back into the earlier life of the city, and it included many of its influential families. The first organization of Methodists in Wilmington was formed on December 24, 1797. This was the beginning of the Old Front Street Church.

The leading spirit of early Methodism in the city was William Meredith, who died in 1799, leaving a dwelling and a chapel to the church. He made provision, also, for the enlargement of both, and in a few years a congregation of 1,500, whites and blacks, was reported as worshiping in the enlarged church.

In 1800, Nathan Jarrett was appointed the first regular preacher of the church, which was at that time made a "station," according to Methodist custom.

In 1843, a fire which devastated a large part of the city destroyed the commodious structure which the congregation had used for many years as a place of worship. In it the fervid oratory of many Methodist divines of former years stirred the members to a deep religious life. In the gallery, there was always present a considerable number of negro slaves, joining in the worship of God with their masters, who sat in the main auditorium. This custom was general with the churches of the city, but was particularly noticeable in the Methodist Church.

After the fire of 1843 the church was rebuilt on the same site. This structure, which presented an imposing appearance, met a fate similar to that of its predecessor, for it was destroyed by the great conflagration of February 21, 1886. In it also were heard many prominent Methodist preachers. It was a favorite church with Bishops Whiteford Smith and William Capers, whose names are preserved in some of the older families of Wilmington.

Surrounding the church was the graveyard, with numerous vaults against the outer wall of the enclosure. After the fire of 1886, as many as practicable of the gravestones and bodies were removed to Oakdale Cemetery. The remains of William Meredith, which had been buried under the porch of the old church, were removed to the new Grace Church, where they now rest under the pulpit.

When the second church structure was burned, the Temple of Israel, or Jewish synagogue, located on the corner of Fourth and Market Streets, was tendered to the congregation for use, and for two years the Methodists worshiped there, thus proving the benevolent spirit of the Hebrew citizens of Wilmington.

The lot on the corner of Front and Walnut Streets was sold and a new location acquired on the corner of Fourth and Mulberry Streets, where the present Grace Methodist Episcopal Church was erected and its lecture-room occupied for the first time in the spring of 1888. The edifice stands as a handsome and worthy memorial to the faith and principles of Methodism. Its present membership is about 820. Through the influence of members of Grace Church, the name of Mulberry Street was changed to Grace Street.

As a matter of interest, it may be stated that in earlier years the Methodists of Wilmington were under the supervision of the Virginia Conference, and later were placed under the care of the South Carolina Conference; so that for some time there was a division among them between the conferences. Later, the church was under the sole control of the South Carolina Conference; and when it was proposed to have the North Carolina Conference take over the Wilmington church, there was a stubborn protest among several of the leading members, the effects of which were not overcome for many years.

Among the ministers who served the Front Street (now

Grace) Church may be mentioned Rev. Jonathan Dally, Rev. Charles F. Deems, D.D., Rev. R. S. Moran, D.D., Rev. James Mann, D.D., Rev. E. A. Yates, D.D., Rev. Frank Wood, Rev. W. S. Creasy, D.D., Rev. W. C. Norman, Rev. R. A. Willis, Rev. A. P. Tyer, Rev. John N. Cole, Rev. N. M. Watson, Rev. T. A. Smoot, D.D., Rev. J. C. Wooten, and Rev. J. D. Bundy.

FIFTH AVENUE METHODIST EPISCOPAL CHURCH.

The name of the Fifth Avenue Methodist Episcopal Church was changed in 1915 from the Fifth Street Methodist Episcopal Church, which name it had borne since its organization, about the year 1847.

Located in the southern part of the city, the Fifth Avenue church, throughout its long history of about sixty-eight years, has had a strong hold upon the Methodists in that section of Wilmington. Its membership now numbers about 750.

The old Fifth Street Church was originally a wooden structure, but this was torn down in the year 1889 to give place to the present handsome building of brick, which is an ornament to the neighborhood.

When the present building was erected, it was equipped with chimes, which are well remembered as pealing forth before every service some of the old tunes of the Christian church; but after a few years the chimes were given up.

Among the ministers who have served the Fifth Avenue Church may be named Rev. T. Page Ricaud, Rev. D. H. Tuttle, Rev. R. C. Beaman, Rev. L. L. Nash, D.D., Rev. W. L. Cunninggim, Rev. J. H. Hall, Rev. S. M. Shamburger, Rev. A. McCullen, Rev. K. D. Holmes, Rev. G. T. Adams, Rev. A. J. Parker.

BLADEN STREET METHODIST EPISCOPAL CHURCH.

The Bladen Street Methodist Episcopal Church came into existence in response to a need felt by many Methodists living in the northern part of the city for a place of worship of their own. It was organized about the year 1887, and has had a steady growth and a successful career, the present membership being about 235.

Among the ministers who have served the church are the Rev. Mr. Sawyer, Rev. Frank Butt, Rev. A. J. Parker, Rev. J. B.

Porter, Rev. B. B. Culbreth, Rev. G. B. Webster, Rev. W. L. Rexford, and Rev. T. C. Vickers.

The Bladen Street Church is located on the southeast corner of Bladen and Fifth Streets. Its present structure is a new and handsome building of wood, which takes the place of a smaller wooden building, removed in the year 1910.

TRINITY METHODIST EPISCOPAL CHURCH.

Trinity Methodist Episcopal Church occupies a site near the northeast corner of Market and Ninth Streets. The building is of brick. The erection of a larger connecting structure on the vacant lot on the corner is contemplated.

The church was organized in 1892 as the Market Street Methodist Episcopal Church, and originally occupied a site on the west side of Ninth Street, a little to the south of Market. Later, the new and better site was procured.

The church has done a good work in supplying the needs of the members of the denomination living in the eastern section of the city. Its present membership numbers about 200.

The ministers who have supplied the pulpit of Trinity Church are: Rev. E. C. Sell, Rev. T. H. Sutton, Rev. M. T. Plyler, Rev. A. S. Barnes, Rev. Marvin Culbreth, Rev. W. L. Rexford, Rev. E. R. Welch, Rev. C. T. Rogers, and the present pastor, Rev. W. V. McRae. Rev. J. W. Craig, an honored citizen and efficient life-long pilot on the Cape Fear River, who was also a local preacher of the Methodist Church, filled the pulpit for some time in its early history.

At the present time (1916), plans are being formed to consolidate the membership of Trinity Methodist Episcopal Church with the Methodists living in the eastern suburbs of the city in an effort to erect a Methodist Church farther out Market Street to take the place of the present organization and structure.

EARLY METHODISM IN WILMINGTON.

(Extracts from an address of Dr. Chreitzberg, delivered before the Methodist Conference at Durham, N. C., December 2, 1894.)

In the year 1813 there was stationed in Wilmington a young man who afterwards was long revered among us as Bishop William Capers. To him we are indebted for memorials of the time which none would willingly lose. Of Huguenot descent, with great beauty of person and a manner denoting the Christian gentleman, with an eloquence of speech that was charming, he was well calculated to captivate any with whom he associated. The parsonage to which he brought his bride of a few weeks was not palatial. It is best described in his own words:

"The parsonage, which I might call a two-story dwelling-house or a shanty, according to my humor, was a two-story house, actually erected in that form, and no mistake, with its first story eight feet high and the second between six and seven— quite high enough for a man to stand in with his hat off, as men ought always to stand when in a house. The stories, to be sure, were not excessive as to length and breadth, any more than height, each story constituting a room of some eighteen by twelve or fourteen feet, and the upper one having the benefit of a sort of step-ladder on the outside of the edifice, to render it accessible when it might not rain too hard, or with an umbrella when it did rain, if the wind did not blow too hard. And besides this, there was a room constructed like a shed at one side of the main building, which, as madam might not relish going out of doors and up a step-ladder on her way to bed, especially in rainy weather, was appropriated to her use as a bedchamber. But we were content. A palace might scarcely have been appreciated by us, who, by the grace of God, had in ourselves and in each other a sufficiency for happiness. This house, the church, and the lot they stood on (the church a coarse wooden structure sixty feet by forty), and several adjoining lots, rented to free negroes, had belonged to Mr. Meredith, and had been procured, for the most part, by means of penny collections among the negroes, who almost exclusively composed the congregation."

There you have fully the picture of your first church and parsonage in Wilmington. Mr. Capers speaks further of his flock. His remarks will not bear condensation:

"Of my flock, much the greater number were negroes. The whites were very poor or barely able to support themselves with decency. Here, too, none of the wise men after the flesh, nor mighty, nor noble were called. Indeed, of men of this class, I know not that there was one, and believe that if one, there was but one, who belonged to any church at all as a communicant. They were, very generally, at least, too much tinctured with the French deistical philosophy for that. Of churches in the town, claiming mine to be one, there was but one other, the Protestant Episcopal Church, of which the Rev. Adam Empie was rector.

Comparing numbers betweeen the churches as to white members communing in each, I had the advantage of Mr. (since Dr.) Empie, having some ten or a dozen males to his doubtful one, while the females may have been about equally divided as to numbers, giving him, however, and his church the prestige of worldly wealth and honor.

"At that time it was admitted that the Methodists on the whole were a good sort of enthusiasts, their religion well suited to the lower classes, especially the negroes, who needed to be kept in terror of hell fire. It was called the negro church long after the blacks had left the lower floor for the galleries. And by those of the historic episcopacy it was especially considered the proper cognomen. They, from the difficulty, as a plain countryman phrased it, of learning to 'rise and sot,' failed in capturing the masses. And though wanting the earth, this did not seem to trouble them. But as far as position, power, or the spoils of office go—ah, that was another matter. And that high claim is not abated yet in this year of grace, reminding one of the resolutions of the Puritan Conclave: 'Resolved (1st), The earth is the Lord's and the fulness thereof. Resolved (2nd), The Lord has given it to the saints. Resolved (3rd), We are the saints.'

"But what was the doctrine proclaimed from that plain pulpit? There had come down the ages from a master theologian the warning, 'Take heed unto thyself and unto the doctrine.' Was there anything of 'foolish questions, and genealogies, and contentions, and strivings about the law,' so vain and unprofitable? Anything of 'vain babblings and oppositions of science falsely so called'? Not a whit. But the grand doctrine of justification by faith, and its cognates of original depravity, regeneration, and the witnessing Spirit. These rang through those old walls and caught the understanding of the philosophic and the unlettered, and the white patrician and the negro plebeian were alike moved to repentance."

Mr. Travis, just two years before Mr. Capers, gives an instance: The Hon. Benjamin Smith, of Orton, governor of North Carolina, meeting him in the street at Wilmington, desired him to call and see his wife, supposed to be unbalanced in her mind, her head shaved and blistered, who, after all her seeking of physicians, grew worse. The preacher diagnosed the case at once and administered the proper remedy—instruction and prayer. In a few days a carriage drove up to that humble parsonage, and Mrs. Smith entered it exclaiming, "O sir, you have done me more good than all the doctors together. You directed me to Jesus. I went to Him in faith and humble prayer and confidence. He has healed my soul and body. I feel quite well and happy." Anything of hyperbole and eastern romance in this? Is it not entirely in accord with the doctrine?

William Capers gives another example: Mrs. G., of the first class of the upper sort, deeply interested in what she had heard, under cover of a call upon the preacher's wife, came to consult the preacher. The doubt on her mind was as to the possibility, since the Apostles' day, of common people knowing their sins forgiven. The preacher gave the scriptural proofs freely, received with the "How can these things be?" Mrs. G. was accompanied by her sister, Mrs. W., better established in the old creed. And Mrs. W., as a last resort, turning to Mrs. Capers, said: "Well, Mrs. Capers, it must be a very high state of grace, this which your husband talks about, and I dare say some very saintly persons may have experienced it, but as for us, it must be quite above our reach. I am sure you do not profess it, do you?" Mrs. Capers blushed deeply and replied in a soft tone of voice, "Yes, ma'am, I experienced it at Rembert's camp-meeting year before last, and by the grace of God I still have the witness of it." That was enough. This witness is true, and glory be to God, millions still testify to it on the earth.

THE FIRST BAPTIST CHURCH.

The First Baptist Church of Wilmington was organized April 13, 1833, with one hundred and twenty-seven charter members. Prior to this time, little is known of the history of the Baptist denomination in Wilmington. The first six years of the church's history is uncertain, owing to friction with the Primitive Baptists.

Through the changing years of the city's history, this church has gone forward steadily with varying degrees of success. The first pastor was Rev. A. Paul Repiton, who served the church for eight months, beginning April, 1839. For two years following this, the church was pastorless, during which time the pulpit was supplied by Rev. I. Innett. Rev. A. J. Battle became pastor February 6, 1842, and served until August, 1843. During this period, the spirit of evangelism began to spread through the membership, and quite a number were added to the church.

A second pastorate was begun by Rev. Mr. Repiton, October 26, 1843, and continued to October, 1844. This pastorate and the two succeeding were uneventful. Rev. James McDaniel served from October, 1844, to October, 1852. Rev. W. H. Jordan served from October, 1852, to September, 1855. With the coming of Rev. John L. Pritchard to the pastorate in January, 1856, the church took on new life. From the first the congregation had been worshiping in a frame building on Front Street, between Ann and Nun, overlooking the Cape Fear River. A lot was now purchased on Fifth and Market Streets, at a cost of $4,500, and an effort was made to raise money for a new building, $10,075 being realized. On February 16, 1857, a resolution was passed by the church, determining to erect a new building within two years, and the work was begun. Dr. Pritchard worked untiringly in behalf of the church and community. During the yellow fever scourge, he, the Rev. A. Paul Repiton, the Catholic priest, and the Episcopal rector, were the only ministers who did not become refugees. These all, except Mr. Repiton, died from this plague, and a monument was erected by the citizens of Wilmington in Oakdale Cemetery to the memory of Dr. Pritchard.

Rev. W. M. Young succeeded Dr. Pritchard in the pastorate. The building enterprise was hindered by the war. The house in which the congregation was worshiping was very unsatisfactory and the mayor of the city offered the City Hall for their use. This offer was accepted. It was at this time that the colored members of the church asked permission to hold regular worship to themselves, and to employ a minister at their own cost to preach to them, but to remain under the authority and government of the First Baptist Church. This request was granted. Rev. Mr. Young later resigned the pastorate, and in October, 1868, Rev. J. C. Heiden was called to become pastor. He continued with the church until April, 1875. The new church building was completed in April, 1870, and was dedicated, on the first Sunday in May of that year, Dr. E. T. Winklen, of Charleston, S. C., preaching the dedicatory sermon.

A small band desired to form another congregation, and April 3, 1871, a committee was appointed to secure a place in Brooklyn for holding services. They secured Brooklyn Hall, and began there a branch of the First Church. The present Calvary Baptist Church is the outcome of this enterprise.

Rev. James B. Taylor became pastor in December, 1875, and

continued to serve the church until 1883. It was during this pastorate that the church saw the culmination of their building enterprise. While the building had been in use for some years, there was a heavy debt on it of $11,000. By hard work, Dr. Taylor had the amount reduced to $6,000, and arrangements were made to wipe out the entire indebtedness. On the day set for raising the money, enthusiasm ran high, the people gave gladly and liberally, and by one o'clock, the entire amount had been raised, and the church was prepared to pay every cent it owed.

Rev. Thomas H. Pritchard succeeded Dr. Taylor in the pastorate in September, 1883, and remained the pastor until January, 1892. On April 4, 1887, the church passed a resolution to the effect that the imperative demands of the Sunday-school for more suitable accommodations were such that the church should not longer delay to erect a lecture-room, which, when done, would complete the original design of the church building. Work on this addition was begun in 1890. At the same time, a handsome pipe organ, valued at about $7,000, was installed. Rev. W. B. Oliver was pastor from March, 1893, to November, 1897. Rev. C. S. Blackwell became pastor of the First Church October, 1898, and remained in this office until March, 1903.

Rev. Fred D. Hale's pastorate extended from March, 1904, to June, 1909. The period of Dr. Hale's ministry was marked by many progressive steps. Many church improvements were made, including the building of several organized class-rooms for the Sunday-school. The membership of the church grew very rapidly. During the five and one-fourth years that Dr. Hale served as pastor, there were 719 additions, an average of 132 a year.

Rev. J. H. Foster became pastor in October, 1909, and continued with the church until June, 1915, when he resigned the work here to become president of the Bessie Tift College, of Forsyth, Ga. This pastorate was marked above other things by an expansive policy. Work was carried on at Castle Haynes, Farmers, Winter Park, and Delgado. At the last two named places, suitable and attractive church buildings were erected. Winter Park has now become an independent church. For a while, Miss Nettie King served as city missionary. Rev. M. C. Alexander was called as assistant pastor on January 1, 1911, and continued in this office until he resigned to resume his studies in the Southern Baptist Theological Seminary. Rev.

W. M. Craig assumed the duties as assistant pastor July 15, 1913, and is at this time the acting pastor of the church. Dr. Foster's pastorate, like that of Dr. Hale, was marked by an unusually large number of additions. During but little more than four years, 787 members were received into the church, an average of 186 a year. The present membership is 1,307.

CALVARY BAPTIST CHURCH.

The Baptists of Wilmington began mission work in the northern part of the city, April 3, 1871, when a committee was appointed by the First Baptist Church to secure a place to hold services. This committee secured the use of Brooklyn Hall, the second floor of what is now the J. H. Rehder & Co., department store. This work was begun as a branch of the First Baptist Church, and was carried on for a number of years with varying and doubtful degrees of success.

On April 4, 1886, the work was organized into an independent church, with just thirteen members. These charter members were: Daniel Yates, Mrs. Mary Yates, W. T. Walton, Mrs. W. T. Walton, Samuel L. Smith, J. W. Taylor, Mrs. J. W. Taylor, Z. E. Murrell, Nelson Jenkins, Mrs. Nelson Jenkins, Gaston M. Murrell, Mrs. Octavia Baskins, and Rev. G. M. Tolson. It was a small band, but they were of the stock that knew no failure. They continued to use the hall as a place of worship for some time, and were known as the "Brooklyn Hall Baptist Church."

About 1892, the church purchased a large building on Fourth and Brunswick Streets, known as "Minnie's Hall." The lower floor was occupied by two stores, and the upper portion was used for church purposes. During the time of the occupancy of this place and up to quite recently, the organization was known as the "Brooklyn Baptist Church." In August, 1914, the church, for satisfactory reasons, changed its name to Calvary Baptist Church.

On August 12, 1906, the present building was dedicated. The dedicatory sermon was preached by Rev. J. L. Vipperman, a former pastor. The membership at this writing is 450. The following have served the church during its career: Rev. G. M. Tolson, Rev. A. A. Scruggs, Rev. R. E. Peele, and Rev. J. T. Jenkins served to March 25, 1894; Rev. R. E. Peele (second pastorate), 1894; Rev. J. W. Kramer, 1895-1898; Rev. J. J. Payseur, 1899-1902; Rev. J. L. Vipperman, 1902-1904; Rev.

J. A. McKaughan, 1904-1907; Rev. C. F. Whitlock, 1907-1911; Rev. J. A. Sullivan became pastor December 5, 1911, and remains pastor at this time.

Southside Baptist Church.

Some time prior to 1870, the Baptists in the southern part of the city began work, and in the latter part of that year they applied to the First Baptist Church for assistance in the erection of a church building. The First Church responded generously by giving the lot and a large sum towards the building, which was soon erected and known as the Second Baptist Church. It was situated on Sixth Street, between Church and Castle. Rev. Joseph P. King was the pastor, but he shortly embraced the doctrines of the Second Adventists, which necessitated a severance of his connection with the Baptist denomination. The majority of the members of the new church went with the pastor and held the property; the remainder united with the First Baptist Church. They, however, continued the work begun in the southern part of the city, and established a Sunday-school at the present location of the Southside Church, Fifth and Wooster Streets. In 1894 letters were granted to thirty-five members of the First Church to form a new organization, and they established the Southside Church.

The first pastor was Rev. J. B. Harrell, who served only a short time, and was succeeded by Rev. F. H. Farrington. Then came Rev. R. H. Herring, Rev. C. H. Utley, Rev. W. H. Davis, Rev. G. A. Martin, and the present pastor, Rev. W. G. Hall, whose pastorate began April 1, 1911.

During these years the church has gone steadily forward, and the present membership is 517. Finding the old building too small for the congregation, in 1912 the church began preparations to erect a handsome brick structure, and in the spring of 1913 actual work was in progress. On the 26th of June of the same year the cornerstone of the new building was laid by Mr. J. S. Canady, one of the charter members. This new church edifice cost $20,000.

St. Paul's Lutheran Church.

The Lutheran denomination is represented in Wilmington by two flourishing churches, St. Paul's and St. Matthew's. The former was organized in the year 1858 and the latter in 1892.

Before 1858 Wilmington had developed a considerable German population, immigrants who had come from Germany in the course of a period of several years. They worshiped principally with the congregation of the First Presbyterian Church, and their children attended the Sunday-school of that church, but some of them joined in the worship of other churches of the city. In the year mentioned they decided that the time had come for the organization of a Lutheran church, such as they had been accustomed to in the Fatherland. Accordingly, Rev. J. A. Linn and Rev. G. D. Bernheim, of the Synod of North Carolina, were invited to aid in the necessary steps leading to the organization of the church.

The number who signified their desire to form a Lutheran Church was nearly three score persons; and they became enthusiastically interested in plans for providing a place of worship of their own. Meantime, at a congregational meeting, the Rev. John H. Mengert, D.D., who had labored with great success in the mission field of India and in the city of Baltimore, was called as first pastor of the church, and began his pastorate on December 23, 1858. He was a man of scholarly attainments and deep piety, and his devoted ministry made a lasting impression upon the Lutherans of the city.

The complete organization of the church, which was to be known as St. Paul's Evangelical Lutheran Church, was made on January 6, 1859, in the building of the First Presbyterian Church, which at that time was located on Front Street between Dock and Orange. At first the congregation worshiped in the Presbyterian Church, but later found it desirable to secure another place of worship, and the vestry house of St. James's Protestant Episcopal Church was rented and repaired for their use. The present location of St. Paul's Church was purchased in 1859, and the interest of the congregation was greatly stimulated thereby. At that time a constitution for the church was adopted, and bore the signature of seventy-two persons.

Dr. Mengert's pastorate continued for three years and a half. During its latter part the life of the church was greatly impaired by the war and also by the yellow fever epidemic in 1862. Meantime, however, a handsome church structure had been erected.

After the capture of Wilmington in 1865, the Federal military authorities occupied the church building. This necessitated considerable repairs.

After Dr. Mengert left, there was a vacancy in the pastorate for about six years, when the Rev. G. D. Bernheim, D.D., was invited to take charge of the church. He accepted the call, and for eleven years was an efficient and devoted pastor. The church greatly prospered under his ministry.

Rev. F. W. E. Peschau, D.D., was the third pastor, and served the church for several years. He was very successful in his religious work among the seamen visiting the port who spoke the German and Scandinavian languages. He was succeeded after an intermission of about eight months by the Rev. K. Boldt, D.D. Dr. Boldt introduced the common liturgical service in the church. His pastorate continued for four years.

The fifth pastor was Rev. A. G. Voigt, D.D., formerly professor of theology in the Lutheran College at Newberry, S. C. Under his ministry the resources of the congregation were largely developed.

After the resignation of Dr. Voigt, the Rev. W. A. Snyder, D.D., was called to be the sixth pastor. For eight years he served the church with great efficiency. He was succeeded by the present pastor, Rev. F. B. Clausen, under whose leadership the congregation of St. Paul's is in a most prosperous condition. The church now ranks among the leading congregations of the United Synod in the South in liberality and service.

St. Matthew's Lutheran Church.

St. Matthew's English Evangelical Lutheran Church, situated on North Fourth Street, was organized on March 14, 1892, by the Rev. F. W. E. Peschau, D.D., pastor of St. Paul's Church. Prior to that time a successful Sunday-school had been maintained by the members of St. Paul's and, in consequence of its work, the organization of St. Matthew's Church was easily effected. Its several pastors have been devoted ministers, and the church has been a great spiritual blessing to the people of its locality.

The following have served as pastors: Rev. G. D. Bernheim, D.D., Rev. C. R. Kegley, Rev. G. S. Bearden, Rev. H. E. Beatty, and the present pastor, Rev. G. W. McClanahan.

Under the present pastorate the church is enjoying a healthy growth and bright prospects for the future.

In the northern part of the city, the Synodical Conference of the Evangelical Lutheran Church has just begun an educational

41

and religious work for the colored people. The building used for this purpose is located on Nixon Street, and the work is in charge of Rev. Otto Richert.

The Lutheran Churches in Wilmington constitute the only congregations of that denomination within a radius of 150 miles.

ROMAN CATHOLIC CHURCH.

The Catholics of Wilmington are particularly fortunate in the building designated as St. Mary's Pro-Cathedral. A beautiful structure, of the Spanish Renaissance, located at Ann Street and Fifth Avenue, one of the most attractive spots in Wilmington, marks the successful growth of the mustard seed as far as this congregation is concerned.

The congregation of St. Mary's Pro-Cathedral was originally under the title of St. Thomas. Under this title Rev. Thomas Murphy was appointed pastor on January 1, 1845, by the Rt. Rev. Dr. Reynolds, bishop of Charleston, S. C. Father Murphy immediately entered upon his duties, with the zeal and energy characteristic of his race. He gathered about him the few of his members residing in Wilmington, and rented a small room to conduct their worship. An extract from the church records, in Father Murphy's handwriting, may be of interest:

"The number of Catholics, at the above date (January 1, 1845) did not exceed forty persons. A small room which was used as a chapel, was rented for $40 per annum. On the first of November, 1845, a suitable lot for the erection of a church was purchased for the sum of $797, by three individuals, viz.: Dr. William A. Berry, Bernard Baxter, and Miss Catherine McKoy. A subscription list was then opened, and the members subscribed liberally according to their means." The lot referred to is on Dock Street, between Second and Third Streets, now used as a church for colored Catholics.

It may be noted from Father Murphy's appointment, that the Catholics of North Carolina were under the jurisdiction of the bishop of Charleston, S. C. In 1868 the State was given separate spiritual jurisdiction, and James Gibbons (later, Cardinal Gibbons, of Baltimore) became the vicar apostolic. During his short administration, Bishop Gibbons saw with satisfaction the rapid growth of his congregation. He immediately set about securing other places in the city for the erection of schools. The property at Third and Dock was secured for additional church room. He next purchased the site bounded by Fourth, Fifth, and Ann Streets. In reference to this, we find the following in the church records:

"September 20, 1869. The Rt. Rev. Bishop Gibbons succeeded in founding in Wilmington city a convent of the Sisters of our Lady of Mercy. The establishment opened with only three sisters—Mother Augustine, Sister Charles, and Sister Mary Baptist. This is the first in North Carolina, and the latest foundation in the States, of the good sisters who came from the Charleston community as established by Dr. England."

Pioneer work of this character is always interesting. Like all the other religious bodies, the Catholic Church progressed with the growth of the population. In later years, when it became evident that Wilmington would grow towards the east and the south, the Catholic congregation became desirous of selecting a more suitable site for the erection of a cathedral church. Rt. Rev. Leo Haid, the present vicar apostolic, decided that Fifth and Ann Streets was the most attractive location. Ground was broken for the new structure May 20, 1908. The cornerstone was laid with great solemnity October 21, 1909. The solemn dedication occurred April 28, 1912. This was an important event for the city as well as for the Catholics. Their first vicar apostolic, Cardinal Gibbons, returned to Wilmington for this ceremony. Though raised to high dignity in his church, he has never forgotten Wilmington and has never lost interest in her welfare. His visit on that occasion was not only that of a bishop to his flock, but as a former citizen to view again the scene of his first labors. The day after the solemn dedication, a reception was tendered Cardinal Gibbons at the home of Maj. D. O'Connor. Thousands visited him on that occasion to renew their earlier acquaintance.

From the small beginning in 1845, we have now a building that is an adornment to the city; a beautiful structure of masonry work alone—no nails, no wood, but brick, cement, stone, and tile, all constructed under the supervision of Rev. Patrick Marion, of Asheville—a monument to his ability and genius.

TEMPLE OF ISRAEL.

The month of November, 1872, witnessed the organization of the first regular Jewish congregation in North Carolina, and at that time was inaugurated the movement which resulted in the erection in Wilmington of the first Jewish house of worship in the State.

That our Jewish fellow-citizens held religious services in the city prior to that time we are assured by the oldest inhabitants; but this was done occasionally only, although late in the sixties there was here a quasi-congregational organization under the spiritual leadership of the Rev. E. M. Myers. He conducted services, when a ritual quorum—ten adult males—attended, in an old building on South Front Street, formerly a Presbyterian Chapel. The earliest permanent organization, however, dates from November, 1872, and its birthplace was the hospitable home of the late Abraham Weill, at the northeast corner of Front and Mulberry (Grace) Streets.

On November 21, 1872, Dr. Marcus Jastrow, of Philadelphia, addressed a general meeting of Israelites in the city court room, and under the inspiration of his address and the chairmanship of Mr. Solomon Bear, an organization was effected, and committees were named to solicit members and subscriptions and to select a suitable location for a synagogue. As membership in Jewish congregations was confined to men, the women, anxious to aid in the good work, organized an auxiliary association under the name Ladies' Concordia Society, "to promote the cause of Judaism, and to aid by its funds the maintenance of a temple of worship in our midst." The wording of this resolution probably suggested to the men the name of the congregation, *Mishkan Yisrael*—Temple of Israel.

Together the men and women worked zealously with the desired end in view. Eventually they secured the lot on the southeast corner of Fourth and Market Streets, just across from St. James's Cemetery, which shelters the ashes of the builders of Wilmington and where also is the grave of the Samuel Adams of North Carolina, Cornelius Harnett, and contracted with the Abbotsburg Building Company, General Abbot, president, for the erection of a $20,000 church edifice, according to plans drawn in Philadelphia and altered and amended by our townsman, James Walker. Capt. R. S. Radcliffe was engaged to superintend the work. Ground was broken in March, 1875, and on the 15th day of June the cornerstone was laid. The Rev. Dr. Jastrow, whose exhortations had given the first impetus to the congregation, was present to bless the work; Hon. Alfred Moore Waddell, in a splendid oration, delivered the greetings of the city and of the Masonic Order, under whose auspices the cornerstone was laid, and with a beautiful benediction the rabbi closed the ceremonies, which were participated in by representatives of several churches.

In February, 1876, the congregation, looking forward to the early completion of the building, called Rabbi Samuel Mendelsohn to assume the rabbinate. The call was accepted, and Rabbi Mendelsohn came to Wilmington February 29, 1876, at once assuming the duties which he is still discharging. He organized Sabbath-school classes, inaugurated regular Sabbath (Saturday) services, both of which were domiciled in the basement of the building, and otherwise aided in arousing a spirit of congregational life among his parishioners.

On May 12, 1876, Rabbi Mendelsohn, once a pupil of Dr. Jastrow, solemnly dedicated the temple whose existence primarily owed so much to the eloquent addresses of this great teacher and famous scholar (1829-1903); and ever since the temple has been open and the rabbi at his post for divine services on the eve and morn of every Jewish Sabbath (Saturday) and of every Jewish festival, and on every occasion that calls for a solemn convocation.

The Ladies' Concordia Society still continues its activities and the Sabbath-school Aid Society, consisting of former and present pupils, is doing good work in providing for the needs of an institution of this kind.

Connected with the congregation is a Hebrew Relief Association, whose aim and object are to prevent an Israelite, resident or transient, from becoming a burden on the community or its charities; and we are assured that throughout the years of the existence of the Associated Charities only one Jewish applicant has received aid from that beneficent source.

But while the congregation is pursuing the even tenor of a Jewish institution and the Temple of Israel naturally resounds with the worship of the God of Israel, the Scriptural word employed by Dr. Mendelsohn in the course of his dedicatory sermon, "Mine house shall be called an house of prayer for all people," was practically exemplified during the spring of 1886 and thereafter. On the 21st day of February the beautiful and commodious edifice of the Front Street Methodist Episcopal Church went down in ashes in a conflagration that destroyed an appalling number of buildings, and the congregation became homeless. The morning of February 23, however, brought relief to that congregation in the form of a cordial invitation from the rabbi and directors of the temple, tendering to their grieving friends the use of that sacred edifice for any and all occasions that require a church, and, in general, to make the temple their religious home. The invitation was gratefully accepted, and for a little over two years the bereft Methodist Episcopal congregation regularly worshiped there, and the Young Men's Christian Association of that church met there. During that time there never was a conflict of the hours of service between the owners of the building and their guests. When either congregation needed the temple for special services, its minister informed the minister of the other congregation, and between them the hours were conveniently arranged. And not only did the ministers accommodate each other in the matter of time, but several times one took the place of the other when that other was out of town.

Officers, 1876: Solomon Bear, president; Abraham Weill, vice-president; Nathaniel Jacobi, treasurer; Jacob I. Macks, secretary. Directors: M. M. Katz, N. Greenwalde, F. Rheinstein, H. Marcus, H. Brunhied.

Officers, 1915: B. Solomon, president; M. W. Jacobi, vice-president; Albert Solomon, treasurer; J. N. Jacobi, secretary. Directors: Samuèl Bear, jr., L. Bluethenthal, Abe Schultz, Isadore Bear, G. Dannenbaum.

CHESTNUT STREET PRESBYTERIAN CHURCH.

The Holy Ghost, working when, where, and in whom He will, made it possible for negroes to receive religious instruction at a time when they could not provide intelligent and needful instruction for themselves. Master and slave, often at the same time, heard the same message of God's love, and together united in prayer and praise.

Slaves were usually inclined to the religious faith of their masters. Many were taught the catechism, and were acquainted with the Confession of Faith, the form of government, and the worship of the Presbyterian Church.

At the close of the War between the States, the negroes began to withdraw their membership from the white organizations, and form congregations of their own. The colored members of the First Presbyterian Church, thirty-four in number, were, on the 21st of April, 1867, organized as the First Colored Presbyterian Church. They purchased the house of worship on

Chestnut Street between Seventh and Eighth Streets, which was formerly used by the Second Presbyterian Church, known now as St. Andrew's Presbyterian Church, and the colored congregation has since been known as the Chestnut Street Presbyterian Church.

Splendid material was in the organization, and through the years the church has been proud of its membership. The distinguishing features of a Presbyterian Church have been maintained; an intelligent ministry, an orderly and dignified service, and a ceaseless effort to win souls.

Under the several pastors, some of whom were men of recognized ability, consecration, and piety, the church has had varying success, but has always exerted a healthful influence in the community. It is now enjoying a period of peace and progress, with one hundred and three members, a well organized Sabbath-school, a Young People's Society, and an active Woman's Missionary Society.

WILMINGTON SCHOOLS.

A rich and well-stored mind is the only true philosopher's stone, ex-
tracting pure gold from all the base material around. It can create its
own beauty, wealth, power, happiness. It has no dreary solitudes. The
past ages are its possession, and the long line of the illustrious dead are
all its friends. Whatever the world has seen of brave and noble, beautiful and good it can command. It mingles in all the grand and solemn
scenes of history, and is an actor in every great and stirring event. It
is by the side of Bayard as he stands alone upon the bridge and saves
the army; it weeps over the true heart of chivalry, the gallant Sidney,
as with dying hand he puts away the cup from his parched and fevered
lips. It leaps into the yawning gulf with Curtius; follows the white
plume of Navarre at Ivry; rides to Chalgrove field with Hampden;
mounts the scaffold with Russell, and catches the dying prayer of the
noble Sir Harry Vane. It fights for glory at the Granicus, for fame at
Agincourt, for empire at Waterloo, for power on the Ganges, for religion in Palestine, for country at Thermopylæ, and for freedom at
Bunker Hill. It marches with Alexander, reigns with Augustus, sings
with Homer, teaches with Plato, pleads with Demosthenes, loves with
Petrarch, is imprisoned with Paul, suffers with Stephen, and dies with
Christ. It feels no tyranny and knows no subjection. Misfortunes can
not subdue it, power can not crush it, unjust laws can not oppress it.
Ever steady, faithful, and true, shining by night as by day, it abides
with you always and everywhere.   George Davis.

In his admirable volume *Documentary History of North
Carolina Schools and Academies* 1790-1840, published by the
North Carolina Historical Commission, 1915, Professor Charles
L. Coon, superintendent of public schools, Wilson, N. C., prints
the following interesting matter on New Hanover County
schools:

Wilmington Academy, 1812.

An examination of the pupils of this establishment commenced on Thursday last and closed in the afternoon of the
ensuing day. A numerous assemblage witnessed this exhibition,
which throughout was highly gratifying. We congratulate our
town on the successful commencement of an institution, which,
though too long delayed in its operation, promises to produce
an abundant harvest of good to the rising generation. Praise
is due to all the Teachers; and were we to speak as we feel our
approbation of the Principal, his real merit might in the opinion of some be distinguished by the warmth of the eulogium
we should pronounce.

The Star, May 15, 1812.

Wilmington Academy.

A person of decent manners and unimpeached morals, capable of teaching the English Language grammatically, and the Latin Language in its earlier stages, also writing and arithmetic, is wanted in this Academy, to commence his duties on the first day of the ensuing November, and to continue until the first day of the subsequent August. July 15.

James W. Walker, Secretary.

Raleigh Register, July 23, 1813.

Halsley's School, 1836.

The subscriber will open a school at his plantation, on the sound, eight miles from Wilmington, formerly the property of Alexander Peden, deceased, on the 23rd May, ensuing, where scholars of either sex will be instructed in the different English branches. Eight or ten boarders can be accommodated at four dollars per month, each boarder will furnish his own bedding. Application can be made to the editor of this paper, previous to the above specified time, or to the subscriber.

Terms: Reading, Writing, and Arithmetic, $3.00 per quarter. English Grammar, History, and Geography, $4.00 per quarter. B. W. Halsley.

Wilmington Advertiser, May 6, 1836.

Corbin's School, 1836.

Mrs. Sarah Jane Corbin respectfully informs her friends and the public that she intends re-opening her school on the 1st. of November.

TERMS PER QUARTER.

Spelling, Reading, Writing, & Arithmetic.........................$4.00
The above with Grammar, including Parsing & Exercise.......... 5.00
The above, with Geography, History, Rhetorick, Philosophy & Mythology 6.00
For fuel 12½ cents per month.

Also Lessons in Practical Writing and Stenography will be given to Young Ladies between the hours of 12 A. M. and 2 P. M., having qualified herself for that purpose.

Wilmington, October 28, 1836.

Wilmington Advertiser, December 16, 1836.

RYCKMAN'S SCHOOL, 1836.

Miss Ryckman respectfully informs the inhabitants of Wilmington and its vicinity, that she intends opening a school on the 1st. of November next for Young Ladies. The pupils will be taught Orthography, Reading, Writing, Arithmetic (mental and practical), Grammar, Geography, History, the Elements of Natural Philosophy, Astronomy, Chemistry, and Botany, plain and ornamental Needle-work, together with the Spanish Language. Great attention will be given to the religious and moral advancement of the scholars.

Particulars with regards to Terms, etc., will be made known on application to Dr. Thomas H. Wright.

Wilmington, October 21, 1836.

Wilmington Advertiser, December 16, 1836.

STANLIFT'S WRITING SCHOOL, 1836.

A CARD.

Mr. J. W. Stanlift having completed his first course of lessons in writing, from the solicitations of many of the citizens of the town, has been induced to open his school for a second course.

His school room is in the second story of one of the buildings on Second Street, a few doors north of Mr. E. P. Hall's residence.

Lessons at private houses will be given if requested.

N. B.—He again states, that should he not succeed in giving entire satisfaction to such as will properly apply themselves, no remuneration will be asked.

Wilmington, December 9, 1836.

Wilmington Advertiser, December 16, 1836.

SPENCER'S ACADEMY, 1836, ACADEMICK SCHOOL.

This school will commence on Monday, the 28th inst. in the Wilmington Academy, under the care of Mr. E. M. S. Spencer.

Branches taught—English Grammar, Geography, Arithmetick, Reading and Writing, History, ancient and modern, Natural Philosophy, Astronomy, Rhetorick, Belles-Lettres, Declamation, Composition, and the Latin and Greek Languages.

Young Gentlemen wishing to prepare for College, or for any

business in life, can receive private lessons at the Clarendon House between the hours of 6 and 9 p. m.

Payment for Tuition in all cases in advance—First quarter to consist of 12 weeks. For Terms and Tickets of admission, apply to Mr. James Dickson.

Wilmington, November 25, 1836.

Wilmington Advertiser, December 16, 1836.

An Evening School will commence on Tuesday of next week, at the Academy, for those Young Gentlemen who may desire to attend; to be conducted under the care of Mr. E. M. S. Spencer. Schools every Tuesday, Thursday, and Friday evening, from 7 to 9 o'clock.

TERMS.

For English Branches $3.00
For languages 5.00

Wilmington, March 24th, 1837.

Wilmington Advertiser, April 14, 1837.

CROOK'S GRAMMAR SCHOOL, 1837.

The Rev. Mr. Crook intends opening a school in the Wilmington Academy during the first week in January next. Mr. Crook will thoroughly instruct in all the elementary branches of an English education, and he hopes by a conscientious discharge of the important duties of a teacher of youth, to afford satisfaction to patrons & pupils.

Wilmington Advertiser, December 22, 1837.

Mr. & Mrs. Cook will open a school at Smithville, between the 20th and last of June. In addition to all the branches of a correct English Education, Mr. Cook will teach the rudiments of the Greek & Latin tongues.

Wilmington Advertiser, June 8, 1838.

MULOCK'S ENGLISH SCHOOL, 1838.

Having removed his school to the house one door north of the store of Mr. J. M. Cazaux, in the town of Wilmington, [Mr. Mulock] will commence the first regular term on Monday, the 5th of November next. In this school, designed for males, will be taught the elementary and higher branches of English education, viz: Orthography, Reading, Writing, Geography, Grammar, Arithmetic, History, Philosophy, Chemistry, Rhetoric, Composition, Algebra, Geometry, Mensuration, Surveying & Astronomy.

Terms of tuition for the first seven branches in the above order, $6.50 per quarter or twelve weeks. An extra charge of $1 is made for each of the other higher branches.

As the number of pupils is limited, early application is desirable.

Wilmington Advertiser, October 26, 1838.

SIMPSON'S SCHOOL, 1839.

Miss Jessie B. Simpson respectfully informs the inhabitants of Wilmington and its vicinity that on Monday next she intends opening a school for Young Ladies, in which will be taught English in all its branches, French Language, Music, Drawing & Painting, Fancywork & Waxwork.

Wilmington Advertiser, January 4, 1839.

LLOYD AND BAILEY'S FEMALE SCHOOL, 1840.

Mrs. Lloyd & Miss Bailey propose to open a school for Young Ladies in Wilmington in October next. They will give a thorough course of instruction in the various branches of Literature & Science, usually taught in the Higher Schools, including the Higher Mathematics and the Natural Sciences; also the French & Latin Languages, Music on the Piano Forte and Guitar, accompanied by the voice. Further particulars will be given hereafter. They have had experience in teaching, and are permitted to refer to the Rev. Messrs. Drane & Eells, of Wilmington, Dr. S. B. Everett, of Smithville, and Rev. Messrs. Colton & Bailey, of Fayetteville.

Wilmington Weekly Chronicle, June 10, 1840.

REPITON'S SCHOOL, 1840.

The subscriber will open a school the 14th of September, for the instruction of the youth of this place, and the surrounding country. The branches of education which will be taught, and the prices charged per quarter, will be as follows, without any deduction except in cases of protracted illness.

Reading, Writing and Geography, $5.00; Arithmetic, English Grammar, History, Etc., $6.25; Latin & Greek, $8.00. Composition once in two weeks. Declamation once in two weeks.

Wilmington Weekly Chronicle, September 16, 1840.

Professor Coon also quotes on page 763 the rules of a school taught in Stokes County, as follows:

RULES OF SCHOOL.

No.		Lashes.
1.	Boys & Girls Playing Together	4
2.	Quareling	4
3.	Fighting	5
4.	Fighting at School	5
5.	Quareling at School	3
6.	Gambleing or Beting at School	4
7.	Playing at Cards at School	10
8.	Climbing for every foot Over three feet up a tree	1
9.	Telling Lyes	7
10.	Telling Tales Out of School	8
11.	Nick Naming Each Other	4
12.	Giving Each Other Ill Names	3
13.	Fighting Each Other in time of Books	2
14.	Swearing at School	8
15.	Blackgarding Each Other	6
16.	For Misbehaving to Girls	10
17.	For Leaving School without Leave of the Teacher	4
18.	Going Home with each other without Leave of the Teacher	4
19.	For Drinking Spirituous Liquors at School	8
20.	Making Swings & Swinging on Them	7
21.	For Misbehaving when a stranger is in the House	6
22.	For waring Long Finger Nailes	2
23.	For Not Making a bow when a Stranger Comes in or goes out	3
24.	Misbehaving to Persons on the Road	4
25.	For Not Making a Bow when you Meet a Person	4
26.	For Going to Girls Play Places	3
27.	Girls Going to Boys Play Places	2
28.	Coming to School with Dirty face and Hands	2
29.	For Caling Each Other Liars	4
30.	For Playing Bandy	10
31.	For Bloting Your Copy Book	2
32.	For Not Making a bow when you go home or when you come away	4
33.	Wrestling at School	4
34.	Scuffling at School	4
35.	For Not Making a Bow when going out to go home	2
36.	For Weting Each other Washing at Play time	2
37.	For Hollowing & Hooping Going Home	3

No.	Lashes.
38. For Delaying Time Going home or Coming to School	4
39. For Not Making a bow when you come in or go Out	2
40. For Throwing Any Thing harder than your trab ball	4
41. For Every Word you mis In your Hart Leson without Good Excuse	1
42. For Not Saying 'Yes Sir' & 'No Sir' or 'Yes Marm' or 'No Marm'	2
43. For Troubleing Each others Writing affares	2
44. For Not washing at playtime when going to Books	4
45. For Going & Playing about the Mill or Creek	6
46. For Going about the Barn or doing Any Mischief about the place	7

November 10th, 1848.   WM. A. CHAFFIN.

Professor Coon, in addition, copies the following interesting early advertisement for a private instructor:

A TUTOR WANTED:

A decent, sober, and discreet person, that can teach the Latin and Greek Languages, and the Mathematics, willing to engage in a private family to teach three or four Youths only, will meet with encouragement by applying to the Subscriber at Rocky Point, November 13.   SAMUEL ASHE.
Raleigh Register, January 21, 1808.

He also quotes the *Raleigh Star* of October 1, 1813:

There are Reading Rooms in Newbern, Wilmington, and Fayetteville, and they are the fashionable resort of all the respectable people of these places. It would be a reproach to the Metropolis to remain longer without such an establishment. The town wants a fashionable lounging place, where intelligent citizens and strangers can meet daily, and enjoy the pleasures of reading and conversation. A subscription paper will be sent round in a few days to obtain Signatures, when the conditions will be made known.
Raleigh Star, October 1, 1813.
and also the *Raleigh Register,* July 23, 1813.

OTHER CAPE FEAR PRIVATE SCHOOLS.

Antedating the period covered by Professor Coon, the Cape Fear was not without schools; indeed, that there were some

educational facilities on the river from the first settlement may
be gathered from the will of John Baptista Ashe, made in
1734, in which he directed that his sons should have a liberal
education. "And in their education I pray my executors to
observe this method: Let them be taught to read and write,
and be introduced into the practical part of arithmetic, not too
hastily hurrying them to Latin or grammar; but, after they are
pretty well versed in these, let them be taught Latin and Greek.
I propose that this may be done in Virginia, after which let
them learn French. Perhaps some Frenchman at Santee will
undertake this. When they are arrived at years of discretion,
let them study the mathematics. I will that my daughter be
taught to read and write and some feminine accomplishment
which may render her agreeable, and that she be not kept ignorant as to what appertains to a good housewife in the management of household affairs."

In 1745 there was a school taught in Brunswick, and in 1749
the Legislature appropriated £6,000 to establish a free school,
but during the Indian war the money was used for war purposes. In 1754 another appropriation was made, but the act
was not approved in England. In 1759, John Ashe, as chairman of a committee, brought in an address to the King, praying
that a part of a certain fund should be laid out in purchasing
glebes and in establishing free schools in each county, but that
money was to come from an issue of notes, and there was some
slight objection to the form of the notes which the Governor did
not communicate to the Assembly. Frequent application was
made, even up to 1765, but the objection not having been com-
municated to the Assembly, it was never removed.

In 1760, Rev. James Tate, a Presbyterian minister, opened
a classical school at Wilmington; and in 1785 Rev. William
Bingham began his famous school here. About 1800 the Innes
Academy was finished. The first teacher was Rev. Dr. Halling.

After a few years service Dr. Halling was succeeded by Mr.
Rogers. Mr. Rogers had been a midshipman in the navy. The
vessel on which he was employed was dismantled at Wilmington, and he sought employment as a teacher. After some years,
he moved to Hillsboro, where he married a daughter of Col.
William Shepperd, and had a famous school until he removed
to Tennessee. He was succeeded at the Innes Academy by Rev.
Adam Empie, rector of St. James's, at one time chaplain at
West Point, a man of fine culture, whose volume of published

sermons entitles him to fame. He married a daughter of Judge Wright, and was the father of Adam Empie, Esq.

Other teachers at the "Old Academy" were Rev. Mr. Lathrop, Captain Mitchell, who had been a sea captain, Messrs. Hartshorn, Lowry, Joy, Wilkes, and Burke.

A review of the educational facilities of Wilmington prior to the war of 1861 would be incomplete without reference to the admirable private school for boys conducted by Mr. Levin Meginney, a contemporary of Mr. G. W. Jewett, whose institute has been mentioned elsewhere in the *Chronicles*. These two school principals were widely divergent in their professional characteristics, but they worked in harmony, and Mr. Meginney extended to us (of the Jewett school) the courtesy of the use of his larger auditorium for our weekly declamations.

Mr. Meginney was a Marylander, who came to Wilmington during the forties. Buying the building that had been used for the Odd Fellows' School, he opened an institute that became the largest in Wilmington at the time. He was recognized as one of the foremost educators of his day, and his strong moral influence was a blessing to the community, the far-reaching effects of which are still felt in the men of character and purpose who, as youths, were trained in his school. Although unable, because of injury to one arm, to shoulder a musket, he did what he could, as a devoted Southerner, for the cause of the Confederacy during the War between the States, giving largely of his means, and in particular helping to fit out one of the first gunboats. Though giving his enthusiastic love and loyalty unreservedly to the Southern cause, both during the war and in the trying days following it, Mr. Meginney was just and generous to the teachers who came to Wilmington from other sections. He was the first to welcome Miss Amy Bradley, a Northern lady, who came after the war to open the Hemenway School. There are many yet living who remember his gracious, old-time courtesy to all, and the sweet and beneficent influence of his fine character. Some of the most prominent men in Wilmington were his pupils and remember him with gratitude and affection.

Shortly before the war, among other schools at Wilmington was Radcliffe's Military Academy; and for girls there were the high school kept by Rev. Mr. Backus and the fine school of the Misses Burr and James. After the war, the latter was reopened; and the wife of Gen. Robert Ransom had a finishing school, while General Colston for years kept a fine military academy.

Another excellent school was that of Miss Kate Kennedy and Miss Annie Hart, which was established shortly after the four years' war. It was thoroughly equipped with prominent and efficient instructors, notably Professors Mumford, Bunker, Meade, Graham, Baudry, Tallichet, Tamborrella, Joseph Denck, and Miss Mordecai. After Miss Kennedy's marriage to Dr. A. J. DeRosset, in 1877, the school passed under new management. It is now conducted by Miss Hart and Miss Brown, ably assisted by Miss Hobday, of Virginia. Mrs. A. M. Waddell and Mrs. Devereux Lippitt were for a time instructors in music and in painting. The reputation of this school in Wilmington is unexcelled.

One of the most useful teachers connected with private education in Wilmington was Mrs. Laura P. Rothwell, whose record as a teacher here extended over sixty-seven years. Her devoted Christian life was reflected in many homes blessed by her careful training and by her beautiful life of faithful service. Mrs. Rothwell died in 1899, at the age of eighty-three.

PUBLIC EDUCATION IN WILMINGTON.

In every community there are builders of character, and the building is based on the gold, silver, and precious stones of love and sacrifice. That great apostle of education, Lord Brougham, has said: "It is with unspeakable delight that I contemplate the rich gifts that have been bestowed, the honest zeal displayed, by private persons for the benefit of their fellow-creatures. How many persons do I myself know to whom it is only necessary to say there are men without employment, children uneducated, sufferers in prison, victims of disease, wretches pining in want, and straightway they will abandon all other pursuits, as if they themselves had not large families to provide for, and toil for days and for nights, stolen from their most necessary avocations, to feed the hungry, clothe the naked, and shed upon the children of the poor that inestimable blessing of education, which gave themselves the wish and the power to relieve their fellow-men."

Of Mr. James H. Chadbourn, sr., one of our citizens who presented his body a living sacrifice for others, it may be said

42

that his greatest and most effective work was that in the cause of education by public schools.

In his earnest, quiet, unobtrusive way, he became one of the pillars of this noble work of the State in Wilmington, and his chief characteristics—virtue, intelligence, decision, industry, perseverance, and economy—were brought to bear upon this great enterprise with such far-reaching results that eternity alone can reveal their extent. He honestly regarded public office as a public trust, and carefully fulfilled his obligations with unflagging zeal and painstaking economy. His business life and studious habits preserved his mind in vigorous and healthful action. He made a constant study of popular education, and mastered its problems in each successive stage.

Prof. John J. Blair, who has been for nearly fifteen years our capable superintendent of city schools, has kindly prepared for the *Chronicles* a narrative of the development of popular education in Wilmington.

PUBLIC SCHOOLS.

BY PROF. JOHN J. BLAIR.

The history of education in the Cape Fear section is, of course, similar to and in accordance with the State's educational policy, modified to a certain extent by local influences and needs, and the ideas of individuals.

In 1825, a "Literary Fund" was created, the author of the bill providing for this being Bartlett Yancey, but it was not until 1839 that the first bill providing for free schools in every county was passed.[1]

Between 1840 and 1850 a more elaborate system of schools was put in operation, but for lack of one responsible head and uniformity of administration, chaos and failure resulted.[2]

DECADE OF 1850 TO 1860.

The educational history of our State from 1850, extending over a period of the next sixteen years, centers around the character and deeds of one man, Dr. Calvin H. Wiley. He was

---

[1]Dr. Frederick Hill, of Orton, was a strong advocate of public education, was one of the authors of the legislation on the subject, and was called in Wilmington the "father of public schools."

[2]There was financial coöperation, the State furnishing a part and the people of the district a part of the fund. It was good for a beginning.

elected in December, 1852, and on January 1, 1853, at the age of thirty-four years, assumed the duties of this newly-made and responsible office, under the title of superintendent of common schools. He began at once many needed reforms, and made provision by which teachers could be prepared and secured for the work.

An extract from Dr. Joyner's address at the unveiling of a monument to Calvin H. Wiley in Winston in 1904 can not be too often repeated in connection with this notable administration. The speaker said: "Under his shaping hand, the system grew and improved, and the schools prospered until it could be truthfully said at the beginning of the War between the States that North Carolina had the best system of common schools in the South." Dr. Wiley continued to hold the office of superintendent until it was abolished in 1866.

THE UNION FREE SCHOOL.

In addition to the schools of the town of Wilmington, there were in the county New Hanover Academy, 1833; Rock Fish Academy, 1834; Black Creek Female Institution, 1846; and there were schools at Rocky Point constantly from 1846 at least to 1850; Topsail, 1851; Union (at Harrell's Store), 1854; Rocky Point, 1867.

The name "Union" was applied to any school in which private and public interests were united in accordance with an act of the General Assembly.

In a letter written to Silas N. Martin by John W. Barnes, a history of the Union Free School from 1856 to 1862 is given:

"A meeting of citizens was held in the summer of 1856 in the vicinity of 'The Oaks,' and it was decided to raise the necessary money and material for the purchase of a lot and the construction of a building. The deed was executed November 3, 1856, to James Green, John Barnes, and Thomas Freshwater, as trustees, and the same recorded December 31.

"In April, 1857, a meeting of the subscribers was held in the new building, in which it was decided to start the school the first of May, and to continue three months experimentally. Mr. Martin, Mr. VanBokkelen, and Mr. Fanning were appointed to employ a teacher and put the Union Free School in operation. The Board of Superintendents of Common Schools for New Hanover coöperated with the committee, whereby they received the benefit of all the funds appropriated, which arrangement existed until July 1, 1863, a period of six years. The schoolhouse originally seated one hundred pupils. In 1859 a room capable of holding forty scholars was added." The letter states further: "On account of the absence of Mr. Martin from the State in 1862, Mr. B. G. Worth was appointed his successor, and nobly sustained the school from his private means in connection with the amount received from the common school fund.

"The largest enrollment at one time was one hundred and forty-five, and the smallest about one hundred, this being the number for the summer months of June and July."

DECADE 1870-1880—THE WILMINGTON PUBLIC SCHOOL SYSTEM.

In the case of every great enterprise or achievement, interest in its first beginning increases with the passing of the years, while personal knowledge and first-hand information concerning the event diminishes proportionately with each generation. At this present time, when the city's rapid growth and increase in population made the expansion and enlargement of her school accommodations imperative, inquiry is frequently made concerning the origin of this most important and vital enterprise. So closely and intimately was the work of Miss Amy Morris Bradley interwoven with our early public school system, that her labors should always receive the public recognition which is justly due.

1. Her influence and suggestion are responsible for the name which the Hemenway and Union Schools bear.

2. There was never any conflict between her private interest and the community's public interest.

3. The trained and skillful teachers whom she gathered around her in turn trained others, who incorporated into the public schools the best and most modern methods of instruction.

4. Her schools were recognized by the State, for in the year 1870 she received from the State fund $1,266.71.

5. The Union School house, in which was taught the Tileston Normal School, composed from the Union Grammar School, passed into the hands of the county in October, 1871, when the new brick Tileston building was opened.

6. This building, in turn, by a deed of gift, became the property of the city of Wilmington in 1901, through the mediation of Mr. James H. Chadbourn, a personal friend of Mrs. Hemen-

way, and for many years chairman of the Joint School Committee of the city of Wilmington.

A large bronze tablet at the entrance bears the following inscription:

TILESTON MEMORIAL SCHOOL
Built by
MARY HEMENWAY, OF BOSTON,
Who established herein a school for the White People of this community in the year eighteen hundred and seventy-one and maintained the same at her own cost for twenty years under the devoted administration of
AMY MORRIS BRADLEY.
Given to
The City of Wilmington
In the Year Nineteen Hundred and One,
in the name of
MARY HEMENWAY.

Accordingly, on the 9th day of October, 1872, the old Union and Hemenway buildings were abandoned, turned over to the Free School Committee, and the schools were combined and established under the name of the Tileston Normal School in the new brick structure. The cornerstone had been laid with considerable ceremony, November 31, 1871, and the building was erected under the supervision of James Walker, builder, of Wilmington, at a cost of $30,000.

The school continued in popular favor until the summer of 1886. During all this period $5,000 a year was donated by Mrs. Hemenway for support and maintenance. This amount, together with a small tuition fee, afforded ample funds to carry on the work.

When the decade of 1870 to 1880 dawned upon the people of North Carolina, interference on the part of the United States Government with the affairs which rightfully belong to a State had begun to disappear. There was deep gratification at the improved condition of affairs, and the large gain made by friends of the South in Congress was also a source of encouragement. Energy and industry were fast removing the traces of war, and individuals bravely struggled to restore their shattered fortunes. During this decade a change of sentiment began to be felt in New Hanover County in regard to the attitude of the people toward free public education. Previous to this time "well-to-do people," and those who are usually spoken of as "socially prominent," entirely ignored and disregarded the free public schools.[1] The very name seemed to carry some reproach with it. In fact, until comparatively recent times, the boast of attending a "pay school" was thought to carry with it a mark of certain personal distinction.

For the year 1870-71 a reference to the free schools of the city is made in a letter to the commissioners of New Hanover County by James H. Chadbourn, William T. Carr, and William A. French. They say: "In the first communication you were informed that there were no schoolhouses within the limits of the township belonging to the State or county.

"The committee subsequently, with the approval of the board and the superintendent of public instruction, purchased the Hemenway schoolhouse of Miss Amy M. Bradley for $3,000, with the promise on her part that the money she received from it should be expended in continuing her two schools, then in successful operation.

"The cost of sustaining the Hemenway and Union Schools for the last two years has been $10,850.40—$1,266.70 from the State, $2,500 from the Peabody Fund, $3,000 from the sale of the Hemenway schoolhouse, and the balance, $4,083.70, from the friends of Miss Bradley and her work.

"It seems to the committee that the beneficial influence of these schools for the young of the city can not be overestimated."

The *Wilmington Post* of April 11, 1872, gives an account of a visit at that time of the State superintendent of public instruction, Alexander McIver, to the city of Wilmington. It says: "Mr. McIver comes to the work of educating the masses and the establishment of free schools throughout the State of North Carolina. His desire now is to interest the public in the work. He desires that united effort be made at once, so as to secure some complete system for the successful establishment of free schools in the city of Wilmington, by the city, as provided in its charter amended in 1868."

DECADE OF 1880-1890—ORIGIN AND DEVELOPMENT OF THE WILMINGTON
PUBLIC SCHOOL SYSTEM.

This sketch would not be complete without a reference to the campaign of enlightenment carried on under the direction of the Legislature by Dr. E. A. Alderman and C. D. McIver.

---

[1]While the public-school system was maintained during the War between the States, because of the results of the war the public schools were closed in 1865-66. In 1867 there was Reconstruction, and there were no public schools until 1872.

They met the teachers in every county in the State and taught them how to teach. They held public meetings and educational rallies. They made eloquent speeches. They urged the people to vote taxes to support schools. Since this notable campaign, educational progress in North Carolina has been easier.

Information with regard to the two free public schools, Union and Hemenway, between 1872 and 1882, is comparatively vague and indefinite. The year 1882, however, marked the beginning of an effective organization with an executive head, whose office was that of superintendent of city public schools, and the system then began to assume a different aspect as a factor in the educational life of the city.

The situation is described by the superintendent himself, Mr. M. C. S. Noble, who was elected to this responsible office in the summer of 1882. Previous to this the authority over the two white and colored districts was vested in the county superintendent. It does not take a vivid imagination to see the situation as it appeared to him at that time. In referring to his first visit to the schools, he says: "I pictured to myself large, imposing buildings, situated in well-kept grounds, when our buggy stopped in deep sand out in front of the old Union School on Sixth Street between Nun and Church, and just in the rear of Fifth Street Methodist Church. It contained three rooms, and had a seating capacity of one hundred and twenty-five pupils. There were three teachers, and the average attendance was one hundred. Lastly, we went to the Hemenway, then situated on the lot directly south of St. Andrew's Church, on Fourth Street. It was a little cottage-looking affair, with four rooms, a seating capacity of about one hundred and fifty pupils, and an average attendance of about one hundred and twenty-five."

The growth of the enterprise is noted by a comparison of this early report with that made by the superintendent of schools for the year 1886: "Number of children in school, white, 2,051; colored, 3,209: total, 5,260. Average monthly enrollment, white, 444; colored, 757: total, 1,201. Average daily attendance, white, 363; colored, 550: total, 913." This report also states that there were at this time 575 white children enrolled in the Tileston Normal School.

The school committees consisted of the following: District No. 1, Donald MacRae, chairman, William M. Parker, Joseph E. Sampson; District No. 2, James H. Chadbourn, chairman, Walker Meares, John G. Norwood.

In the paragraph on school buildings there appears this reference: "The Hemenway building for whites is well arranged and well supplied with comfortable seats. The Union building, in White District No. 2, is comfortable, but in every other respect it is entirely unfit for school purposes. After many years of waiting and vexatious delay, the committee hope to have a handsome building ready for occupancy next fall." This wish was realized, as the following extract shows: "In 1886, the pupils were moved from the old school into the handsome new Union building at the northwest corner of Sixth and Ann. It contained eight large schoolrooms and a beautiful hall."

In the spring of 1891 the fire alarm sounded "48," and it was the Union School building on fire. It caught from a defective flue and burned to the ground. The new structure was built upon the foundation of the old one, and on the first Monday of the following October the new building, as you see it today, was occupied. In 1889, a building like the Union was built upon a lot running through from Fifth to Sixth, between Chestnut and Walnut, which had been purchased through the earnest advice of Mr. Horace Bagg.

On Saturday night early in the summer vacation of 1897, some one set fire to the new Hemenway, and the next morning this beautiful building was a mass of smoking ruins. This school was at once rebuilt, and turned over ready for the opening on the first Monday in October in that year.

DECADE 1890-1900—GROWTH OF THE HIGH-SCHOOL IDEA.

The high school as an organic part of the public-school system had its origin at a very recent date. Previous to 1890 most of the graded-school reports show provision for primary and grammar grades only. The superintendent's report for Wilmington, 1886, shows a provision for six grades only. No reference is made in this report to a high school. It was evidently intended that the private schools which had flourished in the towns and cities for a long time should take care of advanced work, and in fact by many it seemed to be regarded as their rightful heritage and possession.

During this decade there was an aggressive opposition to the public high-school idea. In Raleigh, so determined was this opposition, in the interest of the existing academy, that some of its citizens had a law passed forbidding the teaching of high-school subjects in the public schools. Later, the Raleigh Academy gave way to the high school, its principal becoming the principal of the high school.

In Wilmington, the idea began to take shape in the mind of the superintendent soon after the schools were moved into the new Hemenway and Union School buildings, for he began gradually to add high-school subjects and thus to enrich the course of study.

The school committees, with prophetic vision, saw the necessity for it in order to close up the gap between the grammar school and the State University. As evidence of their faith in it, they bought at this time a lot at the corner of Third and Market Streets, where the Colonial Inn now stands, and moved the advanced classes from the lower schools into the little one-story schoolhouse just south of the courthouse, on Third Street. This remained Wilmington's high school until the year 1897, when the advanced classes from the Hemenway, Union, and Third Street Schools, numbering in all one hundred, with four teachers in charge, moved into the Tileston Normal building. The city came into control of this building by a lease obtained through the personal efforts of Mr. James H. Chadbourn, then chairman of the joint committee. The following May the first graduating exercises were held and certificates were given to three girl graduates. Each year there were gratifying increases. The class of 1914 numbered 30, bringing the total number of graduates up to 315. In 1910, nine more rooms were added and a faculty of fourteen teachers and a principal employed.

1900–1914.

On January 5, 1899, Mr. John J. Blair succeeded Mr. Noble as superintendent. A few leading events of this period are enumerated below:

In 1901, by deed of gift, the Tileston building and half of that city block became the property of the city of Wilmington.

In 1904 an addition of fourteen rooms was made to the Union School, and just previous to this, eight rooms were added to the Hemenway.

In 1909 a local tax of fifteen cents on the one-hundred-dollar valuation was voted by the entire county, and New Hanover was the first county to become a special tax district.

In 1910, under an enactment of Congress, eleven city blocks of land back of the Marine Hospital were secured by the Board of Education for park and school purposes.

In 1911 the gift by Mr. Sam Bear of a beautiful brick school building afforded a valuable and much-needed addition to the equipment of the system.

The schools have increased proportionately with the growth of the city, and the enrollment has reached the grand total of four thousand, nearly three thousand of whom are white children.

The faculty in charge now numbers nearly one hundred persons.

Fortunately, the management of the schools has been in the hands of capable and conservative business men, and to serve on the County Board of Education or on either one of the committees of the different districts, has been deemed a great honor. So, to the integrity and high character of those who fill these offices of trust and responsibility, rendering free of cost valuable service to the community, is largely due whatever of success may have been achieved.

LOYALTY OF THE CAPE FEAR PEOPLE TO THE STATE UNIVERSITY.

It is fitting to mention the devotion of the people of the Lower Cape Fear to the venerable University of North Carolina at Chapel Hill which has been manifest in the records of several generations. Reference has been made in the *Chronicles* to the larger gifts of Governor Benjamin Smith, of Orton, but the following list of donations from the Wilmington district as early as 1793-94, noted in Dr. Kemp P. Battle's admirable *History of the University of North Carolina,* will be read with interest by the descendants of the donors.

Alfred Moore	$200	Joshua Potts	$ 15
Edward Jones	30	Thomas Hill	40
Griffith John McRee	20	J. R. Gautier	60
Peter Mallett	80	James Moore, sr.	50
Nathaniel Hill	20	Thomas Ashe	50
Henry Toomer	60	Alexius M. Forster	12
John G. Wright	25	Henry d'Herbe	8
Robert Whitehurst Snead	40	James Kenan	50
William Wingate	15	Samuel Ashe (son of the general)	60
Samuel Houston	15		
Thomas Brown	30	Anthony Toomer	10
Hugh Waddell	30	John Brown	5

John Cathorda	$ 10	Thomas Moore	$ 60
Michael Sampson	20	William Hall (Sheriff of Bruns-	
James Read	20	wick)	20
William Montfort	10	Samuel Ashe, jr.	30
Nehemiah Harris	5	Samuel Hall	10
William Bingham	20	Samuel R. Jocelyn	20
Marshall Wilkings	10	John Fergus	25
William Davis	8	Duncan Stewart	25
John Allen	6	John Burgwin	100
John Blakeley	20	William Green	15
John Fulwood	10	Thomas Wright	15
John A. Campbell	30	Frederick Jones	30
John Lord	10	Henry Urquhart	10
Amariah Jocelyn	10	William Cutlar	10
William E. Lord	20	John James	20
James Walker	50	George Davis	20
John London	40	George McKenzie	60
William H. Hill	60	Spafford Drewry	10
John McKenzie	60	Daniel McNeil	25
Christopher Dudley	20	George Gibbs	8
James Moore (Clerk)	20	Hugh Campbell	10
Richard Quince, sr.	40	J. Scott Cray	20
Richard Quince, jr.	20	John Peter Martin	10
James Flowers	15	John Hall	15
John Hill	80	James Spiller	60
William Campbell	60	John Campbell	5

How well the genius of the University was described by President Venable a few years ago: "A shining light in the darkness, clearly and patiently directing the course of those who would travel the pathway to knowledge and the higher life; a center of gracious and helpful influence streaming out into the whole land; a strong foundation unmoved by frenzied passion, by the shifting sands of political change, by the bigotry of ignorance, or the selfish bias of wealth, a treasure which can not be bought or sold away from the people, by whom and for whom it was created; a loving mother of many noble sons, whom it is her pride to help and nourish and lead upwards to the light." And how well is his eloquent description of the true functions of the institution sustained by the succeeding administrations of that distinguished and devoted son of the Cape Fear, President Edward Kidder Graham, who writes thus in his annual report for the year 1914-15: "It is with a profound sense of happiness that I report the conviction, fortified in many substantial ways, that the alumni, the students, and the public at large are taking a more continuous and sympathetic interest in the serious work of the University. Loyalty to the institution is losing none of the enthusiasm that finds its occasional magnetic center in great athletic contests; but it is steadily receiving also a far deeper and richer interpretation. There have been, during the past year, many inspiring evidences that we are coming more and more to see that true loyalty to the University consists not merely in pride in the institution, nor merely in love for it as our Alma Mater; but also, and mainly, in our personal devotion to the high things for which the institution stands, and our practical service in making these things prevail. This devotion we share with all good men everywhere whose aims and ideals are kindred, and with every agency that seeks to make them effective in the life of the State. The essential character of the institution is coöperation in its fullest and deepest sense; it is the institution for expressing in intelligent and constructive terms all of those varied aspects of human effort that make complete and unified the life of the State. Adequate equipment, therefore, to do its work with freedom and vigor, it asks not in any selfish measure, but as the heart of the general good. If we view it in the lesser way of partisanship, whether friendly or unfriendly, we shall think too lightly of its mission, misconceive its true character and potential greatness, and so fail to give it the means to perform its functions with the strength, the vision, and the confident faith necessary to the leadership committed to its care."

THE ATLANTIC COAST LINE RAILROAD.

The equipment, rails, and rolling stock of the Wilmington and Weldon Railroad and its connections north and south were thoroughly worn out at the end of the war, so that when peace came there was need for entire rehabiliment. Mr. Walters, Mr. Newcomer, and Mr. Jenkins, of Baltimore, becoming interested in the property, so managed it that in a few years it became wonderfully productive, and under their control it was a nucleus of railway development. From it has arisen, Phœnix-like, the Atlantic Coast Line, in its equipment and management one of the finest examples of railroad development in modern times. It has been called the aorta of Wilmington's commercial and industrial life. Without it Wilmington could not have flourished. Many of our inhabitants of slender means depend upon its dividends for their daily bread—others of larger fortunes have always preferred to invest in its shares, not only on account of its admirable physical equipment and its stable financial policy, but also because Mr. Henry Walters, the chairman of the board, and his associates in its excellent management, command the respect, the confidence, and the admiration of its stockholders, large and small.

From this training school of the thousands who depend upon it for their occupation and support have arisen many young men, succeeding to vacant places of responsibility and honor, because the quality of their instruction has been of the best and their industrious application has resulted in deserved promotions.

In July, 1898, the connecting lines of the Wilmington and Weldon Railroad in South Carolina were consolidated under the name Atlantic Coast Line of South Carolina, and in November following the lines from Richmond to Garysburg were organized as the Atlantic Coast Line of Virginia. Two years later, the above companies were consolidated with the Wilmington and Weldon and its tributary lines in North Carolina under the name Atlantic Coast Line Railroad, and in 1902 the Plant system in Florida and Georgia was consolidated with the Atlantic Coast Line. Thus the present Atlantic Coast Line Railroad, having more than 4,600 miles of track, extends from Richmond and Norfolk on the north, to Tampa, St. Petersburg, and Fort Meyers on the south, and to Montgomery on the west, traversing the great coastal plain of the Atlantic seaboard, through the States of Virginia, North Carolina, South Carolina, Georgia, Florida, and Alabama. The country through which it passes is rich in agricultural development and possibilities, and the trucking industry on its lines has grown to enormous proportions. Near Wilmington is the greatest strawberry-producing belt in the world. These berries are shipped to the Northern markets from this section in great quantities each year, and are considered a most profitable crop.

Starting in Virginia, with its grain and other hardy crops, the line passes through the cotton and tobacco belt, thence through the wonderful garden-truck section of the Carolinas and Georgia into the semi-tropical sections of Florida, abounding in citrus fruits of unrivaled quality as well as early vegetables of every variety, which the fortunate introduction of the art of making ice, invented by Gorrie, and the use of refrigerator cars have enabled the carriers to transport in a fresh condition to the great markets of the North.

The remarkable diversity of soil and climate is steadily attracting the attention of settlers, and the Atlantic Coast Line Railroad Company, through its Industrial and Immigration Bureau, by cooperation with State agricultural colleges, and in other ways, has left no stone unturned to develop and advance an interest in agriculture. During the past year a car equipped with the agricultural products and resources of the States through which its line runs was exhibited at many fairs at the North and Northwest.

The products of the forest, including naval stores, form a most important part of the tonnage of the line, running as it does through the great pine and cypress belts of the South. Nor is this section dependent on the forest alone for its growth and prosperity, its manufactures, chiefly cotton goods, being important factors. The phosphate industry particularly is an important one, and the rails of the Atlantic Coast Line Railroad company reach the rich deposits of phosphate in Florida and South Carolina.

The Atlantic Coast Line has about 1,700 miles of its track in the State of Florida. New lines are now being built to open up further the rich phosphate beds and the citrus fruit belt of that wonderful section of our country.

This road took an important part in the War between the States, and, as already indicated, it had to be practically rebuilt at its close.

The general offices of the company have always been located in Wilmington. Starting with a few men in 1840, it now has employed at headquarters about one thousand men, and to meet the constantly increasing business there has been built in recent years one of the handsomest railroad office buildings in the South. This structure, six stories in height, is of concrete and steel construction, and cost, with train sheds and concourse, approximately $375,000.

Wilmington is one of the important points on the Atlantic Coast Line Railroad. Cotton is its principal export, although large quantities of naval stores, lumber, and other products are handled. It had at one time the distinction of being the largest naval-stores market in the world, but this industry has gradually moved southward, and now Savannah or Brunswick claims precedence. During the season of 1914 there was cleared from

Wilmington one of the largest single cargoes of cotton ever shipped from any Atlantic port.

It is a far cry from the passenger train of 1840, with its crude equipment, on which a passenger had to pay seven cents per mile or more to travel, to the magnificent trains of today, with their powerful locomotives and steel passenger equipment, on which one may ride for two cents a mile. The Atlantic Coast Line Railroad Company runs daily, during the winter months, four through passenger trains, with the most modern Pullman equipment, from New York and eastern cities to Jacksonville and other Florida points. It also runs daily five passenger trains, with modern Pullman equipment, from Chicago to Florida points, connecting with the Coast Line rails at Montgomery, Albany, and Tifton. From Key West and Tampa direct connection is made with modern passenger steamers for Havana and other points in Cuba.

At one time all of the through trains between the North and the South moved via Wilmington, but in 1892, in order to shorten the distance materially and thus to compete more effectively for the Florida travel, a line was completed from Contentnea to Pee Dee, a distance of 141 miles. This line opened up also a fine farming section.

The Atlantic Coast Line is generally known and advertised as "The Standard Railroad of the South." It is the constant aim of the management to maintain this standard and to merit this distinction.

THE SEABOARD AIR LINE RAILROAD.

The Wilmington, Charlotte, and Rutherford Railroad was chartered February 13, 1855, and by 1861 there were built 103 miles on the eastern division, and from Charlotte to Lincolnton on the western division. The road was sold April 10, 1873, and reorganized as the Carolina Central Railway Company, and was completed to Charlotte and Shelby in the latter part of 1874, comprising a total distance of 242 miles.

The Carolina Central Railway was sold May 31, 1880, and reorganized as the Carolina Central Railroad Company, July 14, 1880, when the late Capt. David R. Murchison was made president.

It traversed the counties of New Hanover, Brunswick, Columbus, Bladen, Robeson, Richmond, Anson, Union, Mecklenburg, Gaston, Lincoln, and Cleveland—a section highly productive of turpentine, cotton, and other articles of export, the class and grade of cotton grown in Anson and Union Counties being superior to that of any other section in the State.

Prior to the organization of the Seaboard Air Line Railway in 1900, the Seaboard had no lines south of its Carolina Central Railroad except its one line from Monroe to Atlanta. Before this consolidation in 1900, the old Seaboard Air Line system of roads had a total mileage of approximately 925 miles. Today its mileage is 3,074 miles, exclusive of its ownership of such lines as the Raleigh and Charleston, Marion and Southern, Tampa Northern, and other short lines of varying length.

The main track southwestward from the Carolina Central leads from Monroe through Atlanta to Birmingham, the center of the South's iron and steel manufacturing industry, connecting there for interchange of passenger and freight traffic with the direct lines to the Mississippi and Missouri River territory, and through New Orleans and Shreveport to the Southwest and Mexico.

The line southward from Hamlet leads to deep water at Savannah and to Jacksonville, where connection is made to the east coast of Florida, to Cuba, and to Nassau. Also, its line runs through the northern part of the State and along the Gulf of Mexico, and northward from Tampa. From Savannah it has lines to Montgomery and through southern Alabama.

The system is serving a very material portion of the South's progressive territory, and is entitled to its adopted trade-mark of "The Progressive Railway of the South," and on its list of directors and general officers there is shown a preponderance of Southern-born men in its management. Its headquarters are maintained at Baltimore, the chief Southern city on the Atlantic coast.

The original Carolina Central Railroad has performed for many years an obviously valuable duty to the people of North Carolina, connecting, as it does, some of the most attractive western and middle counties with the coastal section, and as the other parts of the system developed it added strength to this link, extending to the communities in proportion to their abilities. Thus Wilmington has felt a strong impetus from the extension of the Seaboard. Indeed, Wilmington's attractive shore front was found to be nearer to the populous communities of the interior, as far south as Atlanta, than any other Atlantic sea resort; and from all that section of Georgia and South Carolina, as well as from the sections of North Carolina served, many inhabitants of the inland areas seek the attractions of Wrightsville Beach during the summer months.

The original promoters of the Carolina Central Railroad had a vision that it would cross the mountain chain and afford ready connection with the States lying beyond, and in later years this has been realized by the construction of the fine Clinchfield property from Rutherford County across the mountains, through the States of Tennessee, Virginia, and West Virginia, to the most valuable coal deposit east of the Rocky Mountains; and thus has the dream of these original enthusiasts come true. Across the rugged mountain chain is an excellent carrier, offering easy and comfortable transportation to a territory which, in their day, was far from direct connection with the eastern section of North Carolina.

Agriculture, the backbone of all prosperity, widely extended in the States served by the Seaboard, has called for the amplification of fertilizer manufacturing and distributing facilities, and Wilmington has shared largely in the extension of this important industry. Favored with an excellent channel and capacity for docking ships, and a wide area of rail distribution therefrom, it serves the continued extension of territory with its accumulated fertilizer material.

At Wilmington, the Seaboard has terminal facilities of the value of one million dollars, comprising two thousand feet of water front on the Cape Fear River, with a twenty-six foot depth at mean low water, five large terminal warehouses, and three slips. There have recently been erected terminal mechanical facilities, including coal elevator, turntable, repair track, and additional yard facilities. Within the past seven or eight years the Seaboard has spent half a million dollars in improvement of its terminals at Wilmington. The storage capacity of its Wilmington warehouses is approximately one hundred thousand tons.

Mindful of the value to its territory of agricultural extension, the Seaboard has provided a department charged with this duty—to promote the best methods, better agricultural conditions, better marketing; the establishment of industries in its territory; the bringing in of good citizens from States of the Union less favored in climate and soil, and in every way to advance the welfare of the agricultural class.

William J. Harahan, president of the Seaboard Air Line Railway, whose office is in Norfolk, was born December 22, 1867, at Nashville, Tennessee. He entered the railway service in 1881. A messenger and clerk in the office of the superintendent of the Louisville and Nashville Railroad, New Orleans, in 1884, he has risen by gradations first to the vice presidency of the Erie Railroad, January, 1911, and then, September 26, 1912, to the presidency of the Seaboard Air Line Railway.

The evolution of a great enterprise illustrates the law of natural selection and the survival of the fittest.

Charles R. Capps, the vice president, was born in Norfolk, Va., March 4, 1871, and educated at Roanoke College, 1886-1888. He entered the railway service in 1888 as messenger of the Seaboard and Roanoke Railroad. Until July 12, 1895, he held various positions in the general freight office of the Seaboard Air Line, and from December 1, 1909, he has been vice president of the same system. Through many financial vicissitudes and changes of administration in the Seaboard Air Line, he has stood fast in his loyalty to his first love, declining attractive offers of more profitable employment elsewhere, and with his promotion step by step, he has fulfilled and exceeded the highest expectations of the Seaboard management, until today he is generally recognized as one of the most eminent traffic managers of the railroad world.

An important factor in the development of this great railroad system was that watchdog of the treasury, Capt. John H. Sharp, now of Atlanta.

When, in 1862, the Seaboard and the Raleigh and Gaston Railroad bought of Capt. D. R. Murchison the controlling interest in the Carolina Central Railroad stock, Capt. John H. Sharp, formerly of Norfolk, was employed by Mr. John M. Robinson, president, to take up his residence in Wilmington and proceed to open up a new set of books, in order to make the accounts of the Carolina Central correspond with those of the parent roads. On the retirement by reason of physical infirmities of Treasurer James Andrews, Captain Sharp, who had been the secretary of the company, was chosen treasurer to succeed him. On July 2, 1893, when the headquarters of the Seaboard System were moved to Portsmouth, Va., the treasury departments of all roads of the system were consolidated, and upon the recommendation of Mr. M. V. Chambliss, treasurer of the Seaboard, Captain Sharp was chosen treasurer of all roads of the system, which necessitated his leaving Wilmington. While a resident here he fraternized with our prominent citizens, and it was a matter of sincere regret upon the part of all that a separation took place. From that time until now he has felt an interest in Wilmington as great as when a resident here. This is manifested by his annual visits. When in January, 1904, Mr. T. F. Ryan obtained control of the Seaboard system, Captain Sharp and his colleagues were not reëlected to their respective positions. That Captain Sharp's services with the company were appreciated, however, is manifest by the fact that his name is still retained on the pay roll of the system.

HUGH MACRAE'S ACTIVITIES.

A remarkable family to whom Wilmington owes much is the MacRae family. In 1770 Roderick MacRae, called Ruari Doun (Brown Roderick), landed at Wilmington and went to Chatham County, where he married Catherine Burke. One of their sons, Colin, married Christian Black, of Cumberland County, and their eldest son, Alexander, in 1824, when about eighteen years of age settled in Wilmington, where for three generations the MacRaes have led in enterprises of importance to the community. The first of the name in Wilmington, Alexander, long known as Gen. Alexander MacRae, was a leader in the construction of the Wilmington and Weldon Railroad. To the intelligence and enterprise of one of his sons, Col. John MacRae, chairman of the building committee, was chiefly due the erection of our beautiful City Hall, one of the finest examples of classic architecture in the South. Another son, Donald MacRae, was for fifty years one of the foremost citizens of the town, ever promoting what was for its advantage, and his example has been followed by his two sons, Donald and Hugh.

Of Hugh MacRae it is to be said that of all the men of public spirit who have labored to advance the interest of the Cape Fear, he is entitled to preëminence. A philosopher has said that the man who plants a tree is a public benefactor. Of how much greater service to mankind is he who plants a colony of small farmers in a wilderness of waste land, and by the application of modern scientific methods makes that wilderness blossom and bear fruit and food products a hundredfold! This Hugh MacRae has accomplished, adding immensely to the debt of gratitude which the community owes to those whose name he so worthily bears for their public spirit and commendable enterprise.

For a number of years it was Mr. MacRae's wish to secure immigrants to be located in the vicinity of Wilmington, and eventually he was able to establish five colonies, with about three hundred people in each. He colonized Italians at St. Helena, Hungarians and Hollanders at Castle Haynes, Poles at Marathon, Germans at Newberlin, and Hollanders and Poles at Artesia. Americans and some of other nationalities also have been located at Castle Haynes and at Artesia. This enterprise has now passed beyond the experimental stage and is a pronounced success. It is a monument to the sagacity and perseverance of Mr. MacRae, and, in accomplishing what has been achieved, despite great obstacles, he has the satisfaction of realizing that he has been a benefactor to his community.

THE WATER POWER COMPANY.

Another of Mr. MacRae's enterprises has been of the utmost importance. No city can realize its greatest development without good public utilities, and it is a matter of record that Wilmington's period of greatest progress has been coincident with the organization and development of the Consolidated Railways Light and Power Company, and its successor, the Tide Water Power Company. The first public utility company of this city was the Wilmington Gas Light Company, organized in 1854, Edward Kidder, president, and John McIlhenny, superintendent. Mr. Richard J. Jones was elected treasurer on Friday, November 13, 1868, and today, after nearly half a century in the service of this corporation and its successors, he is the active treasurer of the Tide Water Power Company. During the early years, gas was made from lightwood, and at one time commanded a price of ten dollars per thousand. In 1888 the Wilmington Electric Light Company, which had operated a street lighting system with electric arc lights for a couple of years, developed such an amount of competitive activity as to bring about its purchase by the Wilmington Gas Light Company. Later, the gas company began to furnish incandescent lighting, but finally terminated its career in 1902, when it was absorbed by the Consolidated Railways Light and Power Company.

Among the other public utilities which subsequently formed

part of the Tide Water Power Company, was the Wilmington Street Railway Company, organized as a horse-car line in 1887, and purchased in 1892 by Northern capitalists, who changed the motive power from horses to electricity and built the dummy line which has since been a large factor in the growth of the city. This line for handling freight traverses the water front and affords a cheap and efficient delivery direct to the large jobbers and wholesalers. The entire property, after a series of financial troubles, finally failed in 1901, and was disposed of at a receiver's sale.

A third company, built in the period of activity which preceded the Baring Brothers' [London, Eng.] failure in 1893, was the Seacoast Railway. This road was designed to connect Wilmington and Wrightsville Sound. It began operations in 1888, with William Latimer as president. In 1902, through the efforts of Mr. Hugh MacRae, these three properties were brought together in an organization called the Consolidated Railways Light and Power Company, later known as the Tide Water Power Company, Hugh MacRae, president; A. B. Skelding, general manager; M. F. H. Gouverneur, W. B. Cooper, J. V. Grainger, H. C. McQueen, C. N. Evans, Oscar Pearsall, Jurgen Haar, J. G. L. Gieschen, Edouard Ahrens, C. E. Taylor, jr., Junius Davis, George R. French, G. Herbert Smith, and C. W. Worth, directors. Owned locally and managed by officials who have long been identified with home interests, this corporation enjoys a public confidence which in itself constitutes a valuable asset. From the wrecks of three unsuccessful enterprises has been built a property which, in efficiency and good service, ranks with the best in the country; and in addition it enjoys the distinction of being the only public service corporation in the South whose common stock is entirely held in its home town.

All the electric railway, electric light, electric power and gas systems not only in the city of Wilmington but in all New Hanover County are owned and operated by this company, and its success is due chiefly to the enterprise and excellent management of Hugh MacRae.

THE RIVER COUNTIES.

The sixteen counties from Onslow to Richmond constitute what has long been known as the Cape Fear country. From their first settlement the inhabitants of these counties have been allied in business and social interests, and their association has been so close that their history is largely inter-related.

The Upper Cape Fear having been settled principally by Highland Scotsmen, whose descendants still remain near where their forefathers found a home, the predominating strain in that region is Scotch. Lower down, the settlers were chiefly English and Scotch-Irish.

Since the Revolution there have been no considerable accessions from abroad, and the development has been through internal growth, which was very slow during those decades when so many North Carolinians were migrating to the new lands of the South and West. But on the cessation of that migration population began to thicken, and industries have been diversified to the great advantage of the entire region. Indeed, the development of all the counties of the Cape Fear country has been most gratifying, and, while every township has reason to rejoice in its social and material improvement, the uplift of the region has had a potent influence on the centres of trade. Especially has Wilmington felt the beneficial effects in the enlargement of its business and the strengthening of its financial resources, and in its increasing importance as an *entrepôt* of foreign and domestic commerce. While it is beyond the compass of this volume to describe the historical events of the entire region, whose history is so full of interest and such a source of pride to the inhabitants, yet the writer can not omit some slight mention of the river counties, Cumberland, Bladen, and Brunswick. New Hanover was laid off from Bath in 1729, and five years later Bladen was laid off, extending indefinitely to the west and reaching the Virginia line to the north. Bladen was named for one of the members of the Board of Trade, which had charge of the colonies, who was personally interested in North Carolina, as he owned lands in Albemarle and his son-in-law, Colonel Rice, had made his home on the Cape Fear. Bladen, so vast in extent, in time became the mother of counties. Its western and northern territory, clear to the Virginia line, was, in 1749, erected into a county called Anson. Then,

five years later, Cumberland County was likewise cut off from
Bladen. After the Revolution another part was taken off and
called Robeson, in honor of one of Bladen's heroes. Finally, in
1808, a slice of Bladen, added to a part of Brunswick, became
Columbus.

Cumberland was for many years a very large county, but in
1784 Moore County was cut off from it, and in 1855 Harnett;
and, more recently, Hoke was formed from parts of Cumberland and Robeson.

While Bladen and Cumberland were so extensive they played
a most important part in the stirring events that mark the history of the Cape Fear. During the Revolution the inhabitants
were much divided, many adhering to the government under
which they had lived and to which they felt that their allegiance
was due. But in both counties there were ardent Whigs, and
civil war at times raged, with deplorable consequences. No
Whigs were more determined than those of Bladen and Cumberland, and battles were fought in each county, some account being given elsewhere of the Battle of Elizabethtown.

After the Revolution, Fayetteville, being at the head of navigation, became the market for western products and the distributing point for imported goods, needed even beyond the
mountains. Its importance was so fully recognized that the
Legislature held sessions there, and it was regarded as the natural point for the State capital. Although improperly deprived
of this advantage, Fayetteville continued to flourish, becoming
in many respects the most important center in the State. There
was to be found one of the most elegant social circles in the
State, and her citizens were foremost in enterprises. In 1818
they started the steamer *Henrietta* to run on regular schedule
between Wilmington and Fayetteville, and they led in the erection of mills to make paper and cotton goods.

From the beginning Cumberland could boast of many fami-
lies of superior intelligence, virtue, and refinement, and the pas-
sage of time has only added to its high reputation in this regard.
The men of Cumberland were ever the equals of the best in the
State—the Hays, Rowans, Groves, Eccleses, Mallets, Donald-
sons, Winslows, McAllisters, McQueens, Campbells, Murchi-
sons, Smiths, McNeills, McCormicks, McDearmids, Bethunes,
Cochrans, Dobbins, Henrys, MacRaes, Camerons, Rays, Hales,
Steeles, Shepherds, Stranges, Shaws, McLaughlins, Robinsons,
Tillinghasts, Halls, Worths, Haighs, Huskes, Kyles, Cooks,

Curries, Stedmans, Williamses, Fullers, Hinsdales, Broadfoots, Starrs, Roses, Underwoods, and many others of equal importance.

Particular mention is to be made of Hon. James C. Dobbin, one of the most distinguished men of the Cape Fear, noted for his purity, gentleness, and wholly admirable character, as he was for his exceptional attainments and rare oratorical powers.

Mr. Dobbin was Secretary of the Navy from 1853 to 1857, and under his direction the naval service was brought to a high state of efficiency, and the navy was greatly improved by the introduction of more effective armaments and by the addition of some of the finest war vessels in the world. He ever had at heart the improvement of the Cape Fear River and the development of the resources and commerce of the Cape Fear section.

While the first settlements on the river were made on its western side and planters located well up into Bladen, it was not until 1764 that Brunswick County was cut off from New Hanover. Among those early planters were the Moores, Halls, Howes, Davises, Granges, Watterses,[1] Hasells, Ancrums, Campbells, Waddells, Hills, and others who were prosperous and fortunate in their surroundings. They constituted a large element in the social life of the Cape Fear and exerted a potent influence on political movements.

When the town of Old Brunswick dwindled away, there was no other town in the county. The county seat was at first established at Lockwood's Folly, but in 1805 the courthouse was removed to Smithville, where many of the old families, while retaining their plantations, built commodious and handsome residences.

In after years, other families likewise have been prominent— the Smiths, Leonards, Bakers, Laspeyres, Meareses, Browns, Russells, Everitts, Langdons, Bellamys, Frinks, Prioleaus, Taylors, Curtises, Galloways, and others who have maintained the high repute of their predecessors.

Of Dr. Walter Gilman Curtis some particular mention should be made. He was a native of New Hampshire, a graduate of Dartmouth, and received his medical diploma at Harvard. He

---

[1] In *Book E, New Hanover County Records,* is a deed from Schenking Moore to Richard Eagles (1763), in which it is recited that Landgrave Thomas Smith and his wife Mary conveyed to William Watters 700 acres of land opposite the junction of the two branches of the Cape Fear River, part of the grant of 48,000 acres made to Landgrave Smith in 1691.

settled at Smithville in 1847 and soon became the leading practitioner of that vicinity. During the War between the States he thoroughly sympathized with the South, and for a time acted as surgeon to the Confederate troops at Smithville. For thirty years he was the quarantine officer of the port, and he discharged his duties with rare intelligence and great acceptability. His official reports are very valuable. He was a man of unusual attainments, and his spotless character and admirable social characteristics endeared him to his friends. In 1900 he published a volume of *Reminiscences* of unusual merit, thus adding to the literature of the Lower Cape Fear and preserving memories that were fast passing into oblivion. Dr. Curtis won for himself an enviable place in the esteem of his contemporaries because of a life well spent, always devoted to the betterment of surroundings and the elevation of humanity.

The Galloways are a family that should also be particularly mentioned. Samuel Galloway, along with his brother, Cornelius, about the year 1750 emigrated from County Galloway, Scotland, and made his home on Lockwood's Folly River. The descendants of Samuel Galloway have always been men of ability and strong influence. Years ago several members of this family located at Smithville, but they have never ceased to hold their influence in the county, Mr. Rufus Galloway being one of the leading men of the county in this generation. When Major Swift was constructing Fort Caswell, Mr. John Wesley Galloway was employed under him, and a warm attachment arose from their intercourse. When the war came on, although over age for active service, Mr. John Galloway organized the Coast Guard Company and rendered valuable service. He died of yellow fever during the war. His son, Capt. Swift Galloway, named for Major Swift, was a splendid soldier and was greatly esteemed for his talents and high integrity in public life. He frequently represented Greene County in the Legislature. Maj. Andrew Jackson Galloway, of Goldsboro, was another scion of this family. He had the perfect respect and confidence of an extensive circle of friends and was an esteemed officer of the Wilmington and Weldon Railroad Company. All of the Galloways who were old enough to shoulder a musket served in the Confederate Army. Particular mention should, however, be made of John W. Galloway, who became a captain of artillery, and of Sam Galloway, a younger brother of Capt. Swift Galloway, and of Dr. W. C. Galloway, of Wilmington, who has attained merited prominence in his profession.

Another scion of this Brunswick family is Hon. Charles Mills Galloway, whose fine talents and high character led to his being selected by President Wilson as one of the three Civil Service Commissioners of the United States. He has added honors to the name he bears so worthily. He was born in Pender County, August 15, 1875, and attained prominence as a member of the South Carolina press. His father, James M. Galloway, was a member of the mercantile firm of Foyes & Galloway, in Wilmington, and clerk of Pender County. All through life he has been most highly esteemed.

Another descendant of Samuel Galloway—in the fourth generation—was Bishop Charles Betts Galloway, of Mississippi, who was more widely known than any other bishop of the Methodist Church of his time. He was one of the greatest orators of the South, and was a man of unsurpassed power and influence. Thousands flocked to hear him preach.

A review of prominent persons of Brunswick County who have served well their day and generation in public and private life would be incomplete without the mention of one of her fair daughters whose honored name, Kate Stuart, has been for many years a synonym for goodness and mercy and loving-kindness in the hearts and homes of the Cape Fear people. Of rare intellectual gifts and fine executive ability, her accurate knowledge of historical events and her wise counsel in local affairs have made her an authority on important local questions, and the charm of her conversation has added much to the enjoyment of those who are favored by her hospitality.

Bladen, unlike Cumberland, possessed no central settlement of overshadowing local importance, its principal inhabitants living on their plantations. William Bartram, Joseph Clark, Robert Howe, Hugh Waddell, William McRee, John Grange, John Gibbs, Thomas Robeson, William Salter, Thomas Owen, James Council, General Brown and Major Porterfield, in their generation, were among the first men in the province.

In after years the McRees, McNeills, McKays, Owens, Gillaspies, Browns, Wrights, McMillans, Gilmores, Melvins, Lyons, McDowells, Purdies, McCullochs, and Cromarties, proved themselves equal to the best, and some attained national reputations. General McKay and Governor Owen ranked high among the public men of their day.

While the development of these particular counties has been of great advantage to Wilmington, so also has the prosperity of each of the Cape Fear counties been of decided influence, and with pride we witness their substantial improvement and realize that in their continued prosperity Wilmington has a better hope of greater growth and importance in the years to come.

THE GROWTH OF WILMINGTON.

Coincident with the river improvement, there has been a gratifying increase in the business of the city of Wilmington. While one of the largest factors in this splendid growth has been the development of the trucking industry, yet much is to be attributed to the increased commerce of the port. To the trucking industry may be ascribed a considerable proportion of the large bank deposits, and the general diffusion of prosperity; but the remarkable increase in commerce speaks for itself and gives an assurance of the future importance of the city.

During the eighty years from 1829 to June, 30, 1909, there had been spent on the river below Wilmington $4,328,000, and the total annual commerce at the end of that period was 864,071 tons, of the value of $49,753,175. For the year ending June 30, 1910, there was expended for river improvement $400,000, and the value of the commerce rose to $52,214,254. At the end of the year, June 30, 1913, there had been a total expenditure of $5,368,000, and the tonnage had risen in 1912 to 1,072,205 tons, and the commerce for the year was $60,863,344. The exports were to eight foreign countries—Germany, France, England, Italy, Belgium, Spain, Haiti, and Chile, while there were imports from ten foreign countries. For the year ending June 30, 1914, the imports from foreign countries were $4,194,745, as against $3,460,419 in 1913; and the exports to foreign countries were $25,870,851, as against $19,510,926 in 1913, showing an improvement of about one-third in both exports and imports in one year. At the close of the year, June 30, 1915, a total expenditure of $5,974,868.48 had been made, and the results seem to justify it. The increased depth of water to twenty-six feet is having its expected effect on our commerce.

Since the opening of the Panama Canal, it is expected that a new impetus will be given to the commerce of the port because of the natural advantages of the situation, Wilmington being south of Hatteras, only 1,552 miles from Panama, and having superior railroad facilities, with connections uniting the great

marts of the interior States. Thus there is reason to hope, with
entire confidence, for even a larger development than that of the
last few years, gratifying as that has been.

In 1914 the total taxable city property, per assessment, was
$14,472,564. In 1915, it was $17,273,425, the increase exceeding 25 per cent. The estimated values show even a greater increase, being from $27,000,000 to $33,000,000. From 1910 to
1916 banking capital increased from $1,922,716 to $2,561,-
636.14; bank deposits rose from $9,292,088 to $11,688,675.57,
and banking resources aggregate $15,557,277.47.

It has only been in recent years that.the jobbing business has
had a fair chance for development; but, with the removal of
obstacles, the enterprise of the Wilmington merchants at once
brought results. In 1910 the jobbing trade had risen by leaps
to $50,000,000, and in 1913 it was estimated at $70,000,000.
With the new conditions and the rapid growth of interior markets, due to the wonderful prosperity of the country within the
reach of Wilmington, these figures are destined to be speedily
multiplied.

While manufactures are still in their infancy, yet they are
varied in nature, chiefly, however, cotton goods, lumber and
woodwork of many kinds, and fertilizers. In 1913, Wilmington
shipped 263,000 tons of fertilizers. In 1914, 17,100 carloads,
or 282,150 tons, were shipped. This was a record year for the
industry at this port. In 1915 the total shipment of fertilizer
was 11,587 cars, the decrease resulting from adverse conditions
caused by the European War, and is considered a good showing
under the circumstances.

It is interesting to note that just north of the Hilton Bridge,
on the Northeast, three large fertilizer factories are located, as
well as the Camp Manufacturing Sawmill. These have a water
traffic of 165,000 tons, valued at $2,271,849, and this in spite
of the existing disadvantage of a shallow stream. While vessels
drawing twenty-six feet of water can reach the bridge, north of
the bridge the river widens rapidly, so that within the distance
of half a mile the width of fifteen hundred feet is reached, and
then for a mile and a half it narrows to a normal width of six
hundred feet. In this wide stretch the channel is narrow and
only from twelve to fifteen feet deep—entirely insufficient for
the larger vessels bringing in raw material. It is now under
consideration to have the channel widened to one hundred and
fifty feet, with a depth of twenty-two feet, and when this is

accomplished that part of the river will become still more important.

But as important as are all the foregoing sources of prosperity, the development of the export trade has been the chief factor in the growth of the city. The increasing foreign commerce has led to the adoption of plans for a more pretentious custom house; and this branch of our trade will doubtless be much benefited if the proposition to increase the depth of water from the city over the bar to thirty-five feet is carried into effect, while the coast trade will receive a new impulse when the Coastal Canal is constructed.

LOOKING FORWARD.

The development of our resources since the War between the States probably surpasses that of any other country in any era since the world began.

Our Department of Agriculture at Washington estimated the production and value of fourteen of our largest farm crops in 1913 at nine billions of dollars. The estimate of our Southern cotton crop and its by-products was one billion dollars. The acreage of this vast wealth-producing area is one-seventh the size of Continental United States; and yet we are told by President Brown, an eminent authority, that consumption is overtaking production with alarming rapidity, and values have been rising by leaps and bounds; also, that gradually improved methods of agriculture will increase the yield per acre, but the supply may never again catch up with the demand.

Our population, now bordering upon one hundred millions, must continue to increase, while any large increase in the area of arable land is a matter of the past. Consumption of foodstuffs has increased in the past ten years almost three times as fast as acreage and almost twice as fast as production.

These startling developments accentuate the importance of conserving and utilizing the great waterways upon which the country depends for the movement of the larger proportion of our products. Already the railroads are congested, and water transportation becomes increasingly important.

The improvement of the Cape Fear River is, therefore, of momentous significance to our maritime community and to the State at large. Increased appropriations should be systematically sought through the aid of our representatives in Congress for the greater deepening and widening of the ship channel to the sea; for the building of stone jetties upon the shifting sands of the Western Bar; for the building of anchorage dolphins for waiting steamers, which can not swing to their anchors in our limited harbor basin; for continuous appropriations to sustain the important works already accomplished, which would deteriorate from erosion or other damage should the special appropriations fail for a term of Congress.

In the year 1851, the foreign exports of Wilmington were $431,095; in 1912 they were $28,705,448.

In 1851 our carrying trade employed small sailing vessels, eighty feet to two hundred feet long, of two hundred to four hundred tons net register. Now it requires steamers three hundred to four hundred feet long, of two thousand to three thousand tons register. In 1851, a vessel cleared from Wilmington was a large carrier if it could take one thousand bales of cotton. Recently the steamer *Holtie* sailed majestically down our river laden with 20,300 bales of cotton.

Bearing in mind these changes, consider the possibilities of our Cape Fear commerce fifty years hence!

Hundreds of great merchantmen will lie at our docks, taking in cargoes for coast trade and foreign commerce; the aeroplane, already useful to man, will have as a companion the hydroaeroplane, skimming the surface of the waters at fifty miles an hour, transporting passengers and mails to distant ports—a veritable handmaiden of commerce. Indeed, it is the opinion of many experts that the flying-boat will eventually become large enough for commercial purposes, the horsepower of its engines running into thousands; and that it will be used for pleasure, like the steam yacht and motor boat. Elsewhere I have said that the traffic of our blockade running during the War between the States would ever be unique in the history of the world, as the conditions that sustained it can never occur again. Hereafter it will be impossible to maintain an effective blockade because of the new instrumentalities of warfare. In the war in progress in Europe—the greatest war in human history—the practical value of the aeroplane and of the submarine have been thoroughly demonstrated; and within a decade the flying-boat will likewise become available both for commerce and war. Besides, because of the electric searchlight, the tremendous range and accuracy and destructive power of the modern projectile, and because of the submarine mines, the torpedo boats, and other destructive craft which have revolutionized warfare in the past fifty years, an effective blockade can not be maintained.

During our war with Great Britain in 1812, an attempt was made by a diving vessel of the Americans to destroy the *Ramillies,* a ship of seventy-four guns, commanded by Sir Thomas Hardy, which was blockading the port of New London. That attempt was termed "a most atrocious proceeding," and Sir Thomas adopted a very ingenious plan for preventing any further attack being made on his ship by this diving vessel. He ordered one hundred American prisoners of war to be brought on board his ship, and then notified their Government that in the event of the *Ramillies* being torpedoed those persons would share the fate of himself and his crew. The friends and relatives of the prisoners were so alarmed at the threats of Sir Thomas that public meetings were held, and petitions presented to the American Government to induce its Executive to prohibit the use of the diving vessel and its armament in future naval warfare.

When we recall this incident and compare conditions with those of today, we realize that there is no limit to the changes that time will bring. But we know that whatever comes—whatever progress is made—the enterprising people of the Cape Fear will utilize every new instrumentality to make sure their safety and to secure their prosperity and welfare.

Index

Owing to the length of the Cape Fear roster, the names are not all indexed individually elsewhere, but are covered by the entry Cape Fear Camp, U. C. V. Captains of Wilmington military companies will be found grouped on page 273, and Wilmington business and professional men of 1850 on pages 198-200. Both are entered in the index under Wilmington, and not all names in either group are entered individually.

Sketches of ministers, if any, will, in most cases, be found under Churches, of teachers under Schools, and of editors under Newspapers, but ministers, teachers, and editors are all indexed individually, and remarks on, if of sufficient length or importance, are mentioned under the individual entry.

Where the entries contain descriptive matter, if there are page numbers following the last semicolon and not separated from it by description, the word "mentioned" should be understood, as these numbers refer to pages on which the subject is merely mentioned, though often in interesting connection.

---

[1]This should be Agostini in the text.

---

[1] This should be Eugenie on page 395.

[2] This should be Burriss in the text.

Brown, Thomas W., commissioner of Wilmington, 174; 213.

Brown, Miss, teacher, 657.

Brownlow, J. P., 252.

Brunhild,[1] H., 646.

Brunswick, action of Committee of, 108; captured by Spaniards, 50; decay of, 45; desertion of, 114; founded by, 582; Governor Tryon writes from, 104; official records of destroyed, 142; Revolutionary patriots assemble at, 98-100; Safety Committee of, 8; settlement of, 38-40; trade of, 39; Tryon's palace at, 105, 106.

Brunswick County, cut off from New Hanover County, 40; prominent families of, 680-682.

Brunswick River, description of, 14; improvements of, 13.

Bryan, Anne, 126.

Bryan, William, 579.

Bryan, Hon. W. J., 583.

Bryant, Alfred, 219.

Bryant, historian, quoted, 30.

Bryce, Hon. James, quoted, 550, 551.

Buffaloe, Dr. W. H., 184.

"Buffaloes," 404.

Bullock, Capt. James D., Confederate naval agent, 459, 460.

Bundy, Rev. J. D., 631.

Bunker, Professor, 657.

Bunting, David, 357.

Bunting, Samuel R., military service of, 312, 313.

Bunting, Thomas O., sketch of, 312.

Burgoyne, Captain, 452, 469.

Burgwyn, George, 72.

Burgwyn, George (the younger), 72.

Burgwyn, Hill, 187.

Burgwyn, H. W., 252, 611.

Burgwyn, John, 72.

Burgwyn, Capt. John, death of, 72.

Burke, ———, teacher, 656.

Burns, Capt. Otway, of Snap Dragon fame, 138.

Burr, Aaron, duel of with Alexander Hamilton, 136.

Burr, C. E., editor, 558.

Burr, Rev. H. B., 619.

Burr, Col. J. G., quoted, 138; sketch by, 453-458; sketch of, 247; 159, 252, 313.

Burr, R., editor, 558.

Burr, Talcott, 615.

Burr, Talcott, jr., editor, 557; lawyer and journalist, 255; 187, 212, 252.

Burr, W. A., 252.

Burrington, Gov. George, description of, 63, 64; quoted, 25; residence of, 57; sketch and administration of, 81-83; 68.

Burruss, Mrs. E. E., 626.

Butler, Gen. B. F., commanding in Federal attack on Ft. Fisher, 469, 490, 493.

Butler's "powder ship," 493, 574.

Butt, Capt. Archibald B., 541.

Butt, Rev. Frank, 631.

Cairns, Rev. Dr., 608.

Calder, Miss Mary, 572.

Calder, Lieut. Robert E., sketch of, 313; 278, 279.

Calder, Lieut. William, sketch of, 313, 314; 278, 532.

Calhorda, J. P., 189.

Calhoun, Hon. John C., reception of the remains of, 223-227; visits Wilmington, 210.

Calvin, John, member New Hanover County Committee of Safety, 111.

Cameron, George, 615.

Cameron, William, 252.

Campbell, Farquhar, member N. C. Sons of Liberty, 106.

Campbell, Marsden, residence of, 57.

Campbell, William, member N. C. Sons of Liberty, 106; 77.

Campbell, W. B., 566.

Canady, J. S., 639.

Cane Creek, Battle of, 115.

Cantwell, Edward, 226, 252.

Cantwell, John, 240.

Cantwell, Col. John L., narrative by, 276-280; sketch of, 300-302.

---

[1]This should be Brunhild in the text.

Coon, Prof. Charles L., quotations from his history of N. C. schools, 648-654.

Cooper, Sir Anthony Ashley, 4. See *Shaftesbury.*

Cooper, W. B., director Tide Water Power Co., 677.

Coosa, Wat, explorers buy Cape Fear River from, 29.

Corbett, M. J., president W., B., and S. R. R., 546; 561.

Corbin, Mrs. Sarah Jane, teacher, 649.

Cornehlson, Capt. C., 280, 303.

Cornelson,[1] Rev. George H., jr., 626.

Cornwallis, Lord, comes to Wilmington, 114; headquarters in McRary house, 592; surrender of, 115.

Coastal Canal, 548, 549.

Costin, Miles, 212, 219.

Council, James, 682.

Courtenay, Hon. William A., 538.

Cowan, David S., 186.

Cowan, James H., editor, 564.

Cowan, Capt. John, sketch of, 250, 314-316; 121, 226, 249, 252, 257, 273, 300, 325.

Cowan, Col. Robert H., director W. and W. R. R., 150, 151; memorial address on Governor Dudley quoted, 229, 300; residence of, 160; sketch of, 299, 300; 210, 212, 226, 251, 252, 269, 296, 360, 611.

Cowan, Col. Thomas, 141, 250, 615.

Cowan, W. D., 252.

Cox, Gen. Jacob D., diary of quoted, 495-499.

Cox, Quartermaster John W., 360.

Cox, Rev. W. E., 612.

Coxetter, Captain, 417, 419.

Coxetter, Mrs. Easter, teacher, 164, 170.

Craig, Maj. James H., gave no quarter, 209; goes to New Bern, 115; McRary house headquarters of, 592; marches into Duplin, 115;

Craig, Maj. James H., *continued.* takes possession of Wilmington, 114; tyrannical conduct of, 137.

Craig's "bull-pen," 65, 114.

Craig, James N., 398.

Craig, James William, narrative by, 396-406; 632.

Craig, Rev. W. M., 638.

Craighill, Col. Wm. P., 10.

Crane Island, scene of treaty with Indian chief Wat Coosa, 29, 584.

Crane Neck heron colony, 61-63.

Crapon, Capt. G. M., 301.

Cray, William, member N. C. Sons of Liberty, 106.

Creasy, Rev. Dr. W. S., 631.

Crenshaw, Col. James, 433.

Cronly, Mike, 176, 191.

Crook, Rev. Mr., teacher, 651.

Cross Creek, x; Flora Macdonald arrives at, 39, 125; in possession of the Tories, 118; Scotch settlers of Loyalists, 126; 69.

Crossan, Capt. Thomas N., assists in purchasing steamer Advance (Lord Clyde) for the State, 454; commander of the Advance, 455.

Crowley, Rev. J. S., 626.

Cruizer, H. B. M.'s sloop of war, 45.

Cuban man-of-war incident, 514, 515.

Culbreth, Rev. B. B., 632.

Culbreth, Rev. Marvin, 632.

Cumberland County, prominent families of, 679, 680.

Cumming,[2] Capt. James D., sketch of, 316; 193, 312.

Cumming, Sergt. Preston, sketch of, 316.

Cumming, William A., sketch of, 316.

Cunninggim, Rev. W. L., 631.

Curtis, Federal leader in second attack on Ft. Fisher, 389.

Curtis, Dr. M. A. (botanist), quoted, 15, 132.

Curtis, Dr. Walter Gilman, quoted, 202, 282; sketch of, 680, 681.

[1]This should be Cornelson in the text.

[2]On page 193 this should be J. D. Cumming.

---

[1]This should be Greenwald in the text.

1This should be Hiden in the text.

Holmes, H. L., 228.

Holmes, James D., 356.

Holmes, John L., eminent member Wilmington Bar, 187, 566; 212, 226, 232, 611.

Holmes, Dr. Joseph A., quoted, 203; report of on Indian mounds, 19-24; 16.

Holmes, Rev. K. D., 631.

Holmes, Lucian, eminent member Wilmington Bar, 187, 566.

Holmes, Owen, death of, 187; eminent member Wilmington Bar, 566.

Holt, Obadiah, 78.

Holtie (modern steamer), comparison of with vessels in the carrying trade of an earlier time, 501, 686.

Hood, Gen. John Bell, 365.

Hooper, Anne, witness to Harnett's will, 122.

Hooper, Archibald Maclaine, editor, 177; sketch of, 258, 556; 615.

Hooper, Johnson, author, 556, 557; sketch of, 258, 259.

Hooper, William, eminent member Wilmington Bar, 565; member Wilmington Committee of Safety, 110, 111; procures call of first Revolutionary Convention, 110; signer of the Declaration of Independence, 556; sketch of, 76.

Horne, Robert, publishes description and map of North Carolina, 2, 5.

"Horse Pond," description of, 160, 161, 164.

Horsey, Captain, 421, 422.

Hort, Dr. William P., promoter W. and W. R. R., 147, 148.

Hoskins, Mrs., 141.

Hoskins, Rev. B. L., promoter Odd Fellows' School, 171.

Houston, Samuel, 103.

Houston, Capt. William J., 103.

Houston, Dr. William, appointed stamp master, 91; patriotic service of later, 103; resignation of, 93; sketch of, 100-103.

Howard, Emily, 191.

Howe, Gen. Robert, distinguished in French and Indian War and in the Revolution, 50, 120; in command of Fort Johnston, 54; leader in resistance to Stamp Act, 92, 98; promotes Revolutionary Convention, 110; residence of, 57, 60; sketch of, 76.

Howell, Rev. Andrew J., 617, 627, 628.

Howey, Thomas H., 170.

Howquah, blockader, attacks blockade runner Lynx, 450, 451; 481.

Huggins, Lieut. George W., sketch of, 325.

Huggins, James B., military service of, 325.

Hughes, ———, assists in purchase for the State of the blockade runner Advance, 454; officer of the Advance, 455.

Hunt, Rev. Thomas P., 617.

Huntsville, Federal ship, chase by, 429.

Hyrne, Colonel, residence of, 71.

Immortality (poem), 264, 265.

Indians.

Account of tribes of:
Algonquin, 17; Burghaw, 25; Catawbas, 25; Congarees, 25; Iroquois, 17; Keyawees, 25; Old Cheraws, 25; Sapona, 14, 25; Saxapahaw, 16, 25; Siouan, 16, 17; Toteras, 25; Waccamaws, 43; Warrennuncock, 16; Waxhaw, 25; Woccon, 16; Yamassees, 24, 25; black drink of, 15; disappearance of, 25; last settlement of on the peninsula, 18; massacre in Albemarle, 38; mounds of, 19-24; occupancy of, 16-18; pirates supposed to have amalgamated with, 37; pottery of, 17; trade with, 30; Tuscarora War, 38.

Innes, Capt. James, commands Cape Fear troops at Cartagena, 49, 52, 119; commands Virginia forces

[1]This should be Lebby in the text.

---

[1] McDiarmid (not indexed), page 679, should be McDiarmid in the text, and not McDearmid.

Price, Capt. Richard W., sketch of,
    358.
Price, Susie, 613.
Price, Dr. William J., editor, 178;
    252.
Primrose, Rev. J. W., 619.
Primrose, W. S., 24.
Pritchard, Rev. John L., 287, 636.
Prometheus, first steamboat on the
    Cape Fear, account of arrival of,
    138, 139.
Public buildings, account of, 591-603.
Purdie, Col. Thomas J., 303.
Purviance, Samuel, fortifies Wil-
    mington against approach of
    British, 113; Revolutionary of-
    ficer, 120.
Purviance, Judge William, 78, 92, 186.

Quince, John, member New Hanover
    County Committee of Safety,
    111.
Quince, Mrs., 208.
Quince, Parker, colonial merchant,
    73, 74; goes to relief of Boston,
    110.
Quince, Richard, sr., lived at Orton,
    57; member N. C. Sons of Lib-
    erty, 106.
Quince, Richard, jr., member N. C.
    Sons of Liberty, 106, 109.
Quince, Lieut. W. H., 310, 344.
Quincy, Josiah, 53, 579.

Radcliffe, Col. James Dillard, sketch
    of, 307; 343, 363.
Radcliffe, Capt. R. S., 644.
Radcliffe, W. C., 141.
Railroads.
    Declaration of State policy, 148;
    first American built locomotive,
    149; first railroad project, 149;
    history of different lines: At-
    lantic Coast Line, history and
    present condition of, 668-671;
    Cape Fear and Yadkin Valley,
    projection and failure of, 147;
    Carolina Central, history of,

Railroads, *continued.*
    671-673; Wilmington subscribes
    to, 196, 197; Seaboard Air Line,
    history and present condition
    of, 671-674; Wilmington, Bruns-
    wick and Southport, account of,
    546; Wilmington, Charlotte, and
    Rutherford, anticipated value of
    in cotton transportation, 513;
    becomes Carolina Central, 671;
    Wilmington and Manchester,
    small loss sustained by in fire
    of 1864, 535; Wilmington sub-
    scribes to, 196, 197; Wilmington
    and Weldon (Wilmington and
    Raleigh), chartered, 149; con-
    necting lines consolidated, 669;
    equipment of worn out at end
    of war, 668, 670; history of, 150-
    156; 194-196; longest railroad in
    the world (1840), 153; Internal
    Improvement Convention of
    1833, 148; origin of railroad
    project, 149, 507.
Rake's Delight, early trading
    schooner, 39.
Raleigh, Confederate ironclad ram,
    attacks blockading squadron,
    480-483; 401, 487.
Raleigh Sentinel, service of to
    North Carolina, 564.
Raleigh, Sir Walter, spelling of
    name of, 2.
Raleigh, U. S. S., two services of
    silver presented to by North
    Carolina, 532.
Ramousin, Augustus, 252.
Ramsey, Capt. John A., 359.
Rankin, Capt. John T., fire engine
    named for, 537; sketch of, 359;
    242, 243.
Rankin, Laura (Mrs. Rothwell),
    teacher, 164, 170, 191.
Rankin, N. B., 243.
Rankin, Robert, 141.
Rankin, Capt. Robert G., chairman
    Citizen's Committee of Safety
    (1861), 277; sketch of, 358, 359;
    193, 214, 249, 269, 304.

---

[1]Since printing the text, it has been found that Captain Usina did not belong to Charleston. He was born in St. Augustine, Florida, and was a resident of Savannah prior to the war and afterwards.

Printed in the United States
64497LVS00001B/1-24